CAMBRIDGE WORLD ARCHAEOLO

M000251226

THE ARCHAEOLOGY OF MAINLAND SOUTHEAST ASIA

FROM 10,000 B.C. TO THE FALL OF ANGKOR

CAMBRIDGE WORLD ARCHAEOLOGY

BRIDGET AND RAYMOND ALLCHIN The Rise of Civilization in India and Pakistan
DAVID W. PHILLIPSON African Archaeology
CLIVE GAMBLE The Palaeolithic Settlement of Europe
ALASDAIR WHITTLE Neolithic Europe: a Survey
CHARLES HIGHAM The Archaeology of Mainland Southeast Asia

Burial 15 from Khok Phanom Di. This 35–40 year-old woman was interred about 3500 years ago with a spectacular array of rich grave goods. Her burial illustrates particularly well the main theme of this book: that much social change in early Southeast Asia concerned the status and role of individuals within their wider community.

CAMBRIDGE WORLD ARCHAEOLOGY

THE ARCHAEOLOGY OF MAINLAND SOUTHEAST ASIA

FROM 10,000 B.C. TO THE FALL OF ANGKOR

CHARLES HIGHAM
University of Otago

The right of the University of Cambridge to print and sell all manner of books was granted by Henry VIII in 1534. The University has printed and published continuously since 1584.

CAMBRIDGE UNIVERSITY PRESS

CAMBRIDGE
NEW YORK PORT CHESTER MELBOURNE SYDNEY

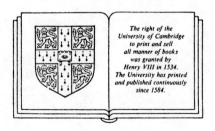

Published by the Press Syndicate of the University of Cambridge
The Pitt Building, Trumpington Street, Cambridge CB2 1RP
40 West 20th Street, New York, NY 10011-4211, USA
10 Stamford Road, Oakleigh, Melbourne 3166, Australia

© Cambridge University Press 1989

First published 1989
Reprinted 1991

British Library cataloguing in publication data
Higham, Charles, 1939–
The archaeology of mainland Southeast
Asia: from 10,000 B.C. to the fall of Angkor. –
(Cambridge world archaeology).
1. South-east Asia civilization; 1499
I. title
959'.01

Library of Congress cataloguing-in-publication data
Higham, Charles.
The archaeology of mainland Southeast Asia:
from 10,000 B.C. to the fall of Angkor / Charles Higham.
p. cm. – (Cambridge world archaeology)
Bibliography.
Includes index.
ISBN 0 521 25523 6. ISBN 0 521 27525 3 (pbk)
1. Asia, Southeastern–Antiquities.
2. Man, Prehistoric–Asia. Southeastern.
I. Title. II. Series.
DS523.H54 1988
959'.01–dc19 88–20303

ISBN 0 521 25523 6 hardback
ISBN 0 521 27525 3 paperback

Transferred to digital printing 1999

CONTENTS

ILLUSTRATIONS

ACKNOWLEDGEMENTS

This book has been written because of my growing enthusiasm for the prehistory of Southeast Asia which began, with the initial stimulus from Chester Gorman and Bill Solheim, in December 1969. Ever since, I have been afforded nothing but the kindest and most helpful cooperation from the Thai Fine Arts Department. Without the friendship and encouragement of Pisit Charoenwongsa and the assistance in the field and laboratory of Amphan Kijngam, Warrachai Wiriyaromp, Rachanie Bannanurag, Metha Wichakana, Anat Bamrungwongse, Payom Chantaratiyakan, Praphid Choosiri and Pirapon Pisnupong, I could not have developed my interest in any practical way.

I began the book with the intention of confining it to Thai prehistory, but following encouragement from the Cambridge University Press and, in particular, Robin Derricourt, I extended its scope to include the valleys of the Red and Mekong rivers. At various stages in its development, parts or all the text have been read and criticised by Raymond Allchin, Donn Bayard, Peter Bellwood, David Chandler, Ian Glover, Jack Goody, Chui Mei Ho, Elizabeth Lyons, Elizabeth Moore, Michael Pietrusewsky, Vincent Pigott, Bill Solheim, Per Sørensen, Michael Vickery, William Watson, Paul Wheatley, Joyce White, Richard Wilen, Peter Wilson and Douglas Yen. Leonard Andaya also helped most kindly with the provision of unpublished papers from his collection. I am most grateful to all these friends and colleagues for making time to help and advise. A particular mention must be made of Peter Wilson's suggestions on the importance of domesticity and display, which are contained in an unfinished manuscript made available to me, and the considerable time devoted to criticism and helpful suggestions by Donn Bayard. Michael Vickery also most kindly gave me access to important unpublished material which greatly assisted me in writing chapters 5 and 6.

Most of the illustrations in this book were drawn in the Anthropology Department of the University of Otago, and I acknowledge a deep debt of gratitude to Martin Fisher, Richard Newell and Leslie O'Neill for their unfailing professionalism and good humour. Most of the photographs are taken from my own collection, but I offer my thanks to Elizabeth Moore, Per Sørensen, Donn Bayard, Chui Mei Ho and William Watson for supplying copies of illustrations.

Wherever appropriate, radiocarbon dates have been corrected for the secular effect according to Klein *et al.* (1981) and are expressed as years B.C. or A.D. A few dates, however, are beyond the present scope of such correction techniques and are expressed as years b.c.

I wish to acknowledge a debt to my teachers Grahame Clark, Sheppard Frere and Eric Higgs for their friendship and stimulus. My final, and most profoundly felt indebtedness, is to my wife Polly. Over almost twenty years of raising a family of four children, she has been steadfast in her support of my research even when it involved long periods apart. I wish to dedicate this book to her, coupled with the words of John Donne

> Thy firmness makes my circle just,
> And makes me end, where I begunne.

CHRONOLOGICAL TABLE

DATE	PERIOD	PRINCIPAL EVENTS AND SITES
A.D. 1500 A.D. 200	GENERAL PERIOD D	The rise of states or *maṇḍalas* in the lower Mekong valley, coastal Viet Nam, Northeast Thailand and Chao Phraya valley. Increased centralisation in court centres, Indian inspired religion, statecraft and the Sanskrit language. Angkorian *Maṇḍala* founded in A.D. 802 and attracted widespread loyalty. Han Chinese set up commanderies in Bac Bo. *Key sites: Oc Eo, Īśānapura, U Thong, Mi Son, Muang Fa Daet, Angkor.* See Chapters 5-6.
500 B.C.	GENERAL PERIOD C	Iron-working, centralisation and formation of chiefdoms. Initial contact with Indian traders and Han Chinese armies and increased exchange, social ranking and agriculture. Specialist bronze-workers produced ceremonial drinking vessels, decorative body plaques, bowls and great decorated drums. Chiefly burials in boat coffins. *Key sites: Non Chai, Ongbah, Ban Don Ta Phet, Ban Chiang Hian, Ban Tha Kae, Co Loa, Viet Khe, Chau Can, Dong Son, Sa Huynh.* See Chapter 4.
2000–500 B.C.	GENERAL PERIOD B	Bronze-working spread among autonomous lowland communities. Ores mined in hills, ingots traded and implements cast in lowlands. Increase in ranking within small communities. Some family groups had high rank signified by jewellery and bronze implements. Subsistence wide-ranging and included rice which was probably cultivated. *Key sites: Ban Chiang, Non Nok Tha, Ban Na Di, Khok Charoen, Ban Kao, Samrong Sen, Doc Chua, Phung Nguyen, Dong Dau, Go Mun.* See Chapter 3.

3000 B.C.	GENERAL PERIOD A	Settlement expansion into the tributary streams of the Khorat plateau, middle country of Bac Bo, the Tonle Sap plains, margins of the Mekong delta and Chao Phraya valley. Settlements small, and social organisation weakly ranked. Stone implements and shell were exchanged between communities which probably cultivated rice in swamp margins. *Key sites: Samrong Sen, Non Nok Tha, Ban Chiang, Non Kao Noi, Phung Nguyen*. See Chapter 3.
5000-1500 B.C.	COASTAL SETTLEMENT	Sea level rose sharply from about 7000–4000 B.C.; probably drowned coastal settlements. At 4000 B.C., sea level stabilised at a higher level than today. Evidence for rich sedentary coastal settlement involving ranking, exchange and elaborate mortuary ritual at Khok Phanom Di. Pollen evidence for settlement by 4700 B.C. Marine resources important, rice consumed. Latter may have been harvested from natural stands in freshwater swampland. *Key site: Khok Phanom Di*. See Chapter 2.
10,000 B.C.	EARLY HUNTER-GATHERERS	Sea level began much lower than today, rose to about 3 m higher than at present. Former coastal settlements now drowned under sea. Main surviving sites in inland rock shelters. Limited range of stone tools, wooden implements for hunting and gathering probably important. Small, mobile groups collected wild plants and shellfish. Evidence for hunting, fishing and trapping. *Key sites: Spirit Cave, Laang Spean, Sai Yok, Khao Talu, Con Moong*. See Chapter 2.

CHAPTER I

INTRODUCTION

Aspects of diversity

Previous studies in this series have treated the prehistory of Africa, India and Europe. Each has readily defined boundaries. This is not so for Southeast Asia, a situation which permits flexibility in placing borders. The mainland area covered, which could in principle extend from the Irrawady to the Yangzi, has been rigorously circumscribed to comprise the valleys of three major rivers and the intervening terrain. These rivers are the Red, Mekong and the Chao Phraya (Fig.1.1). While it is tempting to expand the area considered below to include the islands of Southeast Asia and the lands to the north and west, the temptation has been resisted largely because the uneven nature of the evidence available would have greatly lengthened this study without modifying its basic conclusion.

At first sight, it is difficult to identify a unity for this area. Whatever the variable, the picture is one of diversity. In terms of climate, it could be argued that we are dealing with a subtropical monsoon area, and at a very general level, this is true. But the impact of the monsoon is tempered by numerous local factors. Proximity to the sea, altitude and relationship to the uplands, affect the amount of rainfall, the duration of the dry season and, for some regions, even the existence of one. From a political point of view, there has never been uniformity. The closest approaches to overall control of the three rivers came with the Khmer Empire between *c* 1000–1300 A.D., and French colonial rule (from the 1890s until 1954). The former, however, never ruled the Red River valley, and the latter's control excluded Thailand. Today, each valley has its own political apparatus. The valley of the Chao Phraya has been Thai for at least seven centuries. The lower Mekong is Khmer, and has been for at least two millennia, and the Red River is the heartland of the Vietnamese. Each is distinct linguistically, and it is in the field of languages that we encounter diversity at its most apparent.

The earliest European contact with Southeast Asia revealed a considerable diversity of languages. Indeed, Simon de la Loubère (1693) suggested that the presence of Thai and Pāli at the Thai capital city of Ayutthaya was due to the complex origins of the present inhabitants of Thailand. The visitor to a market place in the uplands of Northern Thailand today could, within minutes, hear at least three separate languages being spoken. For the prehistorian, present language distributions are both a lead and a pitfall for an understanding of the

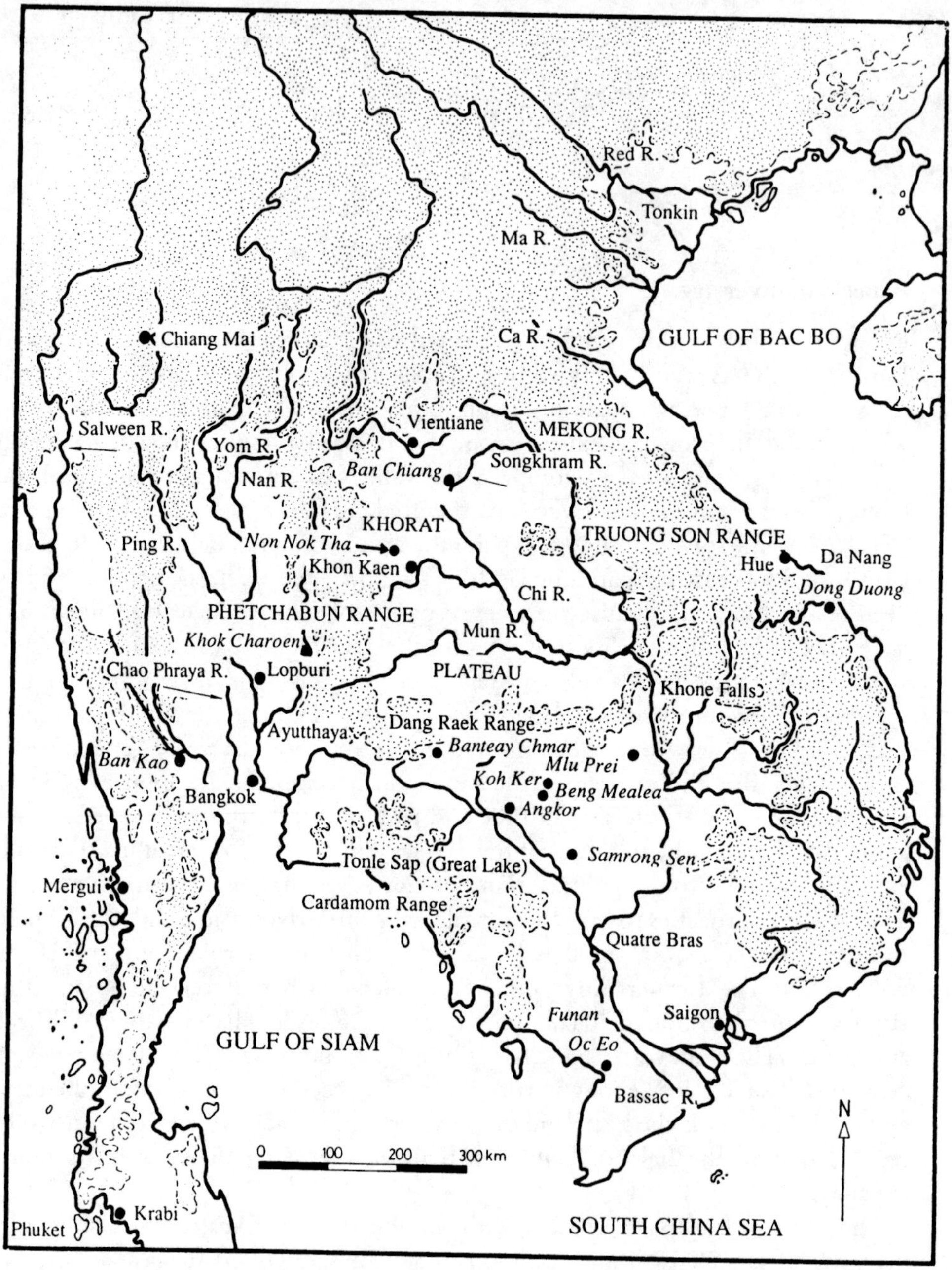

1.1 Map of mainland Southeast Asia showing the location of places and sites mentioned in chapter 1. (Italics: prehistoric and historic sites, stippled area: land above 182m.)

prehistoric period. This situation results from the possibility of a stable population being influenced by exposure to an alien language to the point of adopting it, as well as the possibility of the replacement of a language as a result of expansion and friction by a dominant group. Thus, the replacement of Cham by Vietnamese reflects military pressure and expansion by the latter (Shorto 1979, Bayard 1979). For some parts of Southeast Asia there are inscriptions which indicate that, with the development of early states, three of the major languages of the area were present. In the Chao Phraya valley, some of the early inscriptions were written in Mōn, a language closely related to the Khmer which is employed in the inscriptions of the Tonle Sap plains and the Mekong valley. Along the coasts of Central Viet Nam, inscriptions were written in Cham, and, north of the Ca River, albeit without supporting inscriptions, the language spoken in later prehistory was probably Vietnamese.

Lebar *et al.* (1964) recognise four major language groups in Southeast Asia today (Fig. 1.2). The Sino-Tibetan need not detain us for long as the upland speakers of this group such as Lahu, Lisu, Akha and Yao are small immigrant groups which have entered the area during the last few centuries. The older groups are Thai, Austroasiatic and Austronesian. The Thai language probably has a time depth in the Mekong and Chao Phraya valleys of less than a millennium, and represents movement into the area from Southern China. Bayard (1979) has suggested that this might have taken the form of small groups of warrior nobles and their retainers moving into the Chao Phraya valley, an area which had for at least a millennium previously been occupied by Mōn speakers. Mōn is an Austroasiatic language whose affinities lie with Khmer and Vietnamese. The Cham language is quite distinct, being Austronesian. Its closest affinities lie with the languages spoken in Sumatra, and its time depth on the mainland before *c* 400 A.D. is unknown. It is likely to have a much more recent history on the mainland than the widely distributed languages of the Austroasiatic group. Khmer, Cham and Vietnamese are spoken in the uplands, where there is some evidence that Austroasiatic languages preceded Thai. Thus the Khmu, an upland people in Central Laos, are referred to by the Lao (Thai group) as their "older brothers" in the area. The Yumbri, a surviving group of hunter-gatherers in upland Northern Thailand, are also probably Austroasiatic in terms of language, although the duration of their presence there is not yet defined. Most languages spoken by the inhabitants of the Truong Son cordillera are of Khmer affinities, though upland Cham groups are found in the southeastern area.

While parts of Southeast Asia have been subjected to colonial rule, there has never been overall colonisation. The Han Chinese occupied the Red River valley in the 1st century A.D., and stayed for nearly a millennium. They stopped their southward expansion, however, at the Truong Son cordillera. The French occupied the same area during the 19th century, and added Cambodia, Laos and Cochin China, but their presence was for a far shorter period. Both these episodes of colonisation excluded Thailand.

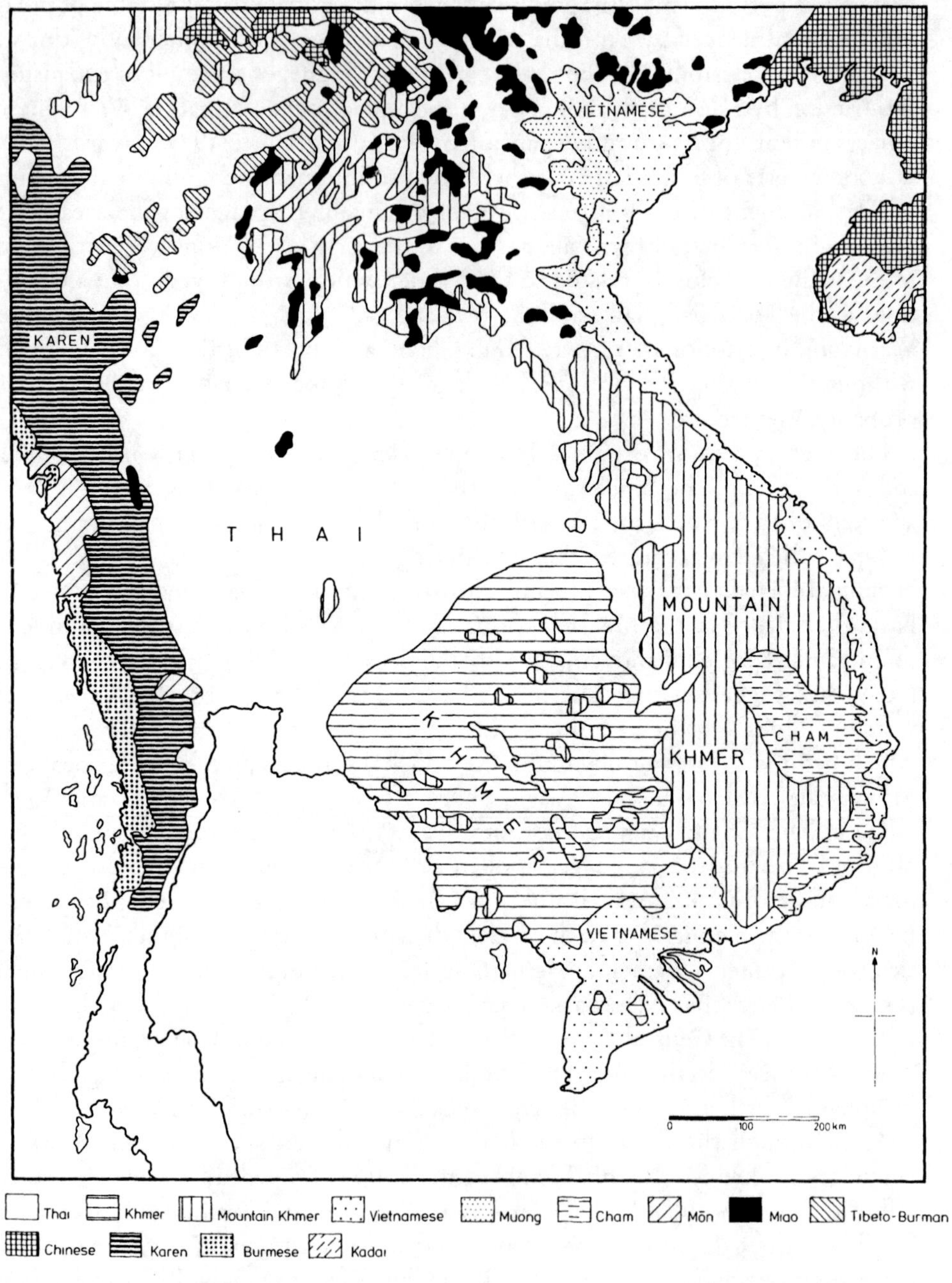

1.2 Map of the current distribution of the main languages spoken in Southeast Asia.

If the environment, political organisations and languages are so diverse, then what is the value in isolating this part of Southeast Asia as a specific region at all? This is, in essence, the point of this study, for it will be argued that it is in the prehistoric period that we can detect a coherence in human adaptation to three of the great river systems and their intervening uplands. Until about 3000 B.C., there appears to have been a similar adaptation to the evergreen uplands by groups of mobile foragers whose lifestyle contrasts, wherever the evidence has survived, with more sedentary coastal societies. Again, we can perceive uniformity in the expansion of village settlements along the inland river valleys and their tributaries, a process which was probably underway by about 3000 B.C. and which laid the foundations for the later development of centralised chiefdoms. It is becoming increasingly clear that the rivers were arteries of communication during that period. One of the most elegant demonstrations of this is the distribution of the whole apparatus of bronze metallurgy in the Mekong and Red River catchments. Here, there were no political boundaries, but rather the unimpeded flow of new ideas between networks of autonomous village communities.

From about 400 B.C., these riverine and apparently successful groups began to display a trend towards centralisation, that is, deference to a paramount in their territory. It was at this time – when first a knowledge of iron-working and then exposure to the forces of Indian and Chinese expansion manifested themselves – that we find the development of the first political forms called *maṇḍalas* which underlie, in a remote ancestral manner, the modern nation states of Southeast Asia. But, again, there was an element of uniqueness in our Southeast Asian context, for if we exclude the Red River valley, which was overtaken by Chinese arms, we find that early state-like societies had in common the adoption of Indian forms of religion, language and aspects of government. Given the particular structure of state societies in Southeast Asia, we shall employ the Sanskrit term *maṇḍala* to describe the early civilizations which developed from local chiefdoms in the valleys of the Mekong and Chao Phraya rivers and along the littoral of Viet Nam. In this context, the *maṇḍalas* each had their vernacular languages, Mōn, Khmer and Cham but, as with Latin in Medieval Europe, were linked at aristocratic and administrative levels by the common use of Sanskrit.

The consideration of mainland Southeast Asia as a coherent cultural entity during prehistory can, however, only be prosecuted in the context of the environment. To this variable we will now turn.

The personality of Southeast Asia

The Southeast Asian landscape has undergone a series of profound changes over the years covered by this book, which prehistorians ignore at their peril. The seas which now separate the mainland from the islands of Sumatra, Java and Borneo are uniformly shallow, rarely exceeding 36 m in depth. The sea bottom bears soil sediments and the channels of drowned rivers. Geomorphological studies undertaken in the Straits of Malacca and the South China sea (Tjia 1980) have revealed a pattern of rapidly rising sea levels. According to Geyh, Kudrass and Streif (1979), 10,000 years ago the sea level was between 40–60 m below its present level. This would have exposed an immense area of low-lying terrain traversed by the extensions of the Chao Phraya and Mekong rivers (Fig. 1.3). Between 8000–6000 years ago, the sea level rose from −12.8 to +1.2 m relative to the present coast, and subsequent raised beaches dating between 5000–4000 years ago reveal a sea level between 2.5 and 5.8 m higher than at present. The reduction in sea level to the current situation occurred from 4000 to as recently as 1000 years ago, and was accompanied by numerous minor oscillations. During the period of elevated levels between *c* 7000–1000 B.P., areas which now comprise the Chao Phraya, Mekong and Red River lowlands were shallow extensions of the sea. Takaya (1969) has shown that, during this period, clay laid down under brackish water attained a depth of up to 14 m in the vicinity of Bangkok. Even greater depths of marine clays have been reported from Northern Viet Nam, where Nguyen Duc Tam (1969) has traced the major rise in the post-Pleistocene sea level to a point when, at its maximum extent, the coast was located well to the west of Ha Noi (Jamieson 1981).

These drastic changes clearly altered the personality of Southeast Asia. Ten thousand years ago it comprised extensive mountain chains and a vast region of low-lying marshy land across which snaked several major rivers and numerous tributaries. Five millennia later, the latter had all but disappeared, and with it an entire chapter of Southeast Asian prehistory. We can pick up the thread of coastal settlement only when the sea level stabilised and then began to fall, revealing once again a low-lying riverine landscape but, by now, covered by a mantle of marine clay.

The three major river valleys we can recognise today as the core areas of modern population density are truncated versions of their ancestral channels, but each has built up a substantial delta in the recent past. Indeed, the Mekong is now adding to the length of its delta at the rate of about 80 m per annum as recent deforestation has led to increased soil erosion. Dobby (1967) has recognised a series of regions determined on the basis of their landscape (Fig. 1.4). These fall into two major groupings: river systems and their associated flat, flood-prone valleys, and the intervening uplands. The former group incorporates Middle Thailand and the Chao Phraya delta, the valleys and deltas of the Red, Ma and Ca rivers, and the lower Mekong and Tonle Sap plains. To these, one should add the floodplains of the Mun and Chi rivers on the Khorat plateau, both tributaries of the Mekong. All three valleys share a marked seasonality in water flows. This reflects the seasonal nature of the rainfall in their respective catchments and, in the case of the Mekong, the coincidence between the onset of the rainy season and the spring melt of snow in the Himalayas. The rivers regularly break their banks and flood huge areas before branching into their respective deltas. Such

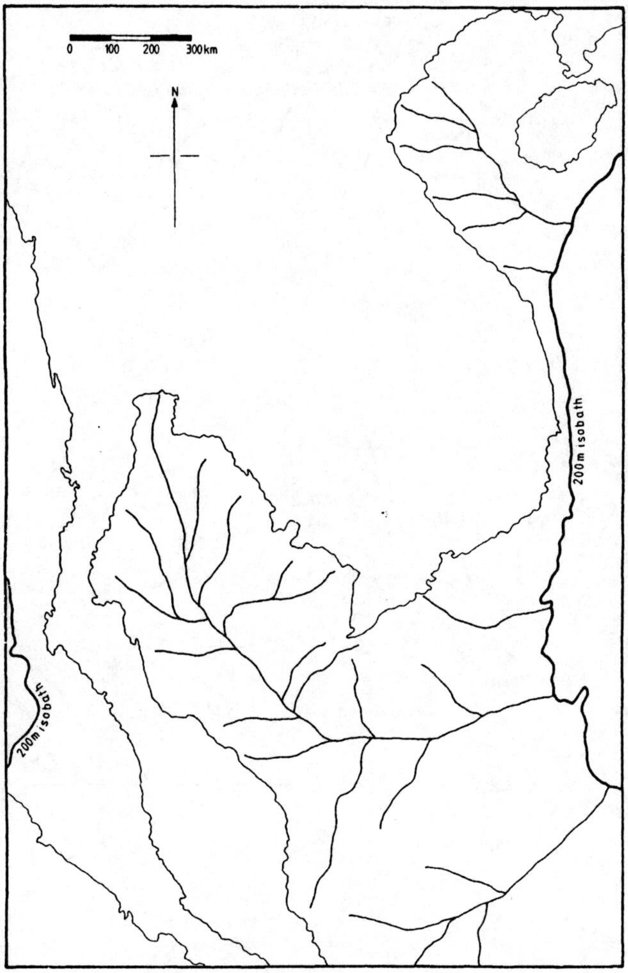

1.3 The assumed coastline of Southeast Asia approximately 10,000 years ago.

floods deposit silt over a broad area and, where not too deep, permit the growth of "floating" rice, a variety with a long stalk and very rapid growth rate. The floods also create natural levées behind which there is commonly a swamp forest where floodwaters rest. The Mekong has its minimum flow in February. In 1949, this was just 1700 m^3/second (cumecs). The maximum flow seven months later was 34,000 cumecs, carrying 10,200 kg of silt per second. Such is the spate that the Mun catchment acts as a safety valve, with water being unable to enter the Mekong. Under natural conditions before the recent provision of flood controls, the Mun floodplain was a lengthy and broad swampland. This situation was exacerbated by the bottleneck to the passage of river water at the Khone falls. At the Quatre Bras, where the Mekong, Tonle Sap River, Bassac and lower section

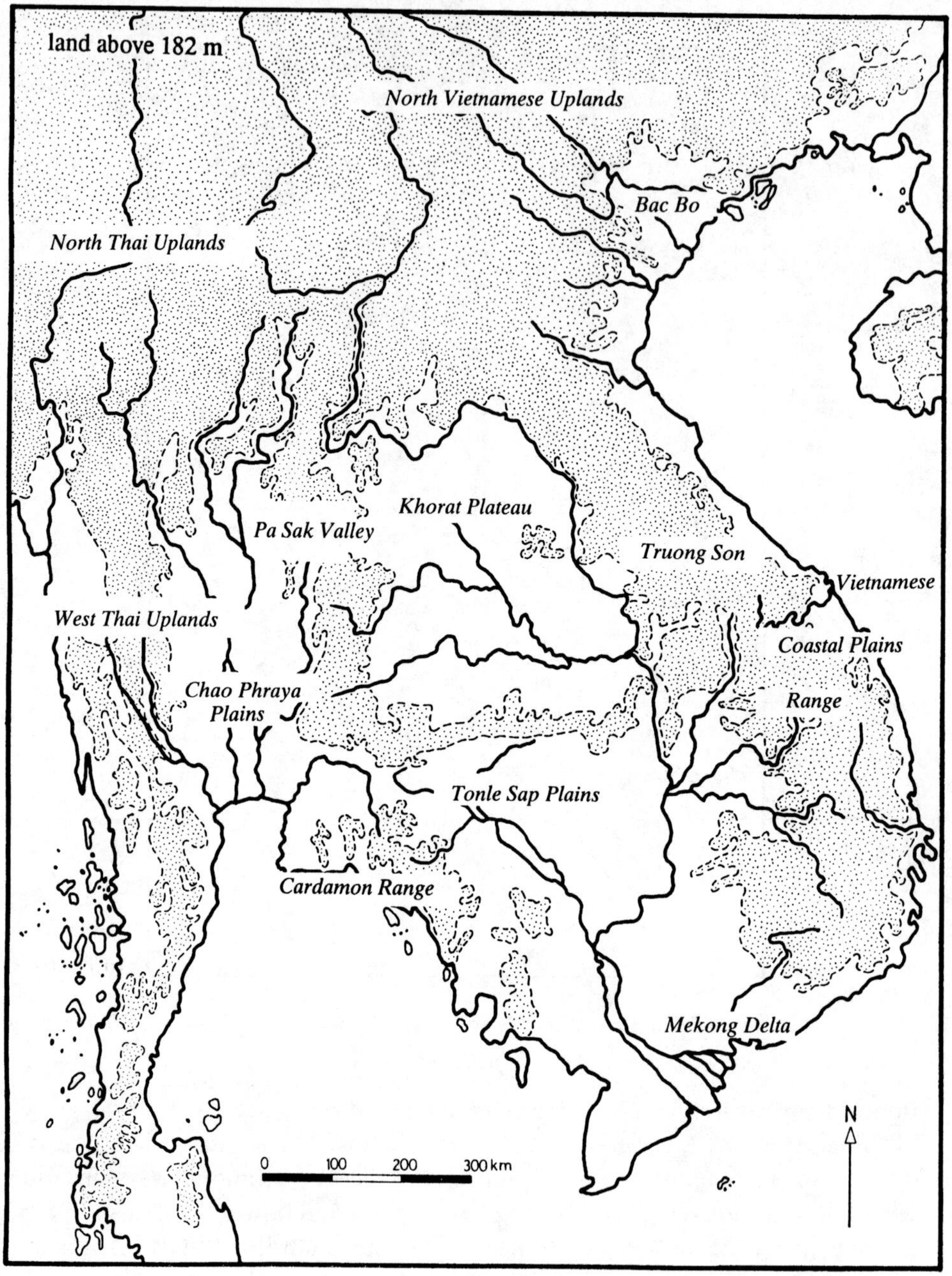

1.4 The principal regions of Southeast Asia employed in this book.

of the Mekong come together, the spate is so great that the Tonle Sap River reverses direction and flows into the Tonle Sap Lake. The lake then quadruples its dry-season area of 2700 km^2. This lessens the suddenness and extent of flooding in the delta country below the Quatre Bras, and makes the cultivation of floating rice a viable proposition.

In the absence of such unique safety valves, the Red and Chao Phraya rivers formerly experienced more extreme and rapid flooding. In the latter area, this problem has been offset by the construction of dams in the tributaries and of canals and pumping stations. The Red River also flows in part through canals, and is constrained by the construction of linear embankments along its margins.

These three river valleys, the foci of cultural complexity for millennia, are bounded by uplands. The Red River delta is ringed on all but its eastern margin by rugged sandstone and limestone hills. A similar mountain spine lies between the coast and the Mekong River, and it historically served as the frontier between the Khmer and the Chams. The lower Mekong and Tonle Sap plains are hemmed in by this, the Truong Son cordillera, to the east. To the north lie the Dang Raek mountains and, to the west, the Cardamom range. These uplands are not without passes, which usually follow river valleys. There is, however, a broad corridor between the Dang Raek and Cardamom ranges which provides ready access from the Tonle Sap plains to the Chao Phraya valley. The latter is again ringed by hills. To the west lies a further old granite and limestone karstic mountain chain which today separates the Thai and the Burmese. The northern mountains comprise a very old and much folded and eroded system of shales, schists and limestone. On the eastern margins lies the Phetchabun range which forms a natural barrier between the Chao Phraya plains and the Khorat plateau.

It is often said that the plains and mountains provide the basic contrast between two distinct modes of human adaptation. It should also be noted that the relief itself is a determinant in the patterns of rainfall and vegetation. The whole area is subject in varying degrees to the sharply seasonal wind patterns which underlie the monsoonal regime. Between October and April the wind flows from the northeast, but in May this reverses to bring air from the southwest. The impact of the changing wind patterns varies with location and altitude (Figs. 1.5 and 1.6). The Cardamom, Phetchabun and Western ranges of Thailand receive much rainfall with the southwest monsoon, whereas the Chao Phraya and Tonle Sap plains and the Khorat plateau lie in rain shadows. Again, the Truong Son cordillera attracts more rain than the coastal plains of Viet Nam and the Red River delta lying to the east. Indeed, the monsoon rains which bring moisture to the Truong Son range become the hot and dry "Lao" wind when they enter the rain shadow which lies to the east. Paradoxically, therefore, though these areas produce much rice, there is often insufficient rainfall and the farmers rely on river floods and their annual discharge of silt. This problem is exacerbated by the unpredictability of the rainfall and uncertain timing for the commencement of the monsoon rains (Fig. 1.7). Between 1914–25, the wet

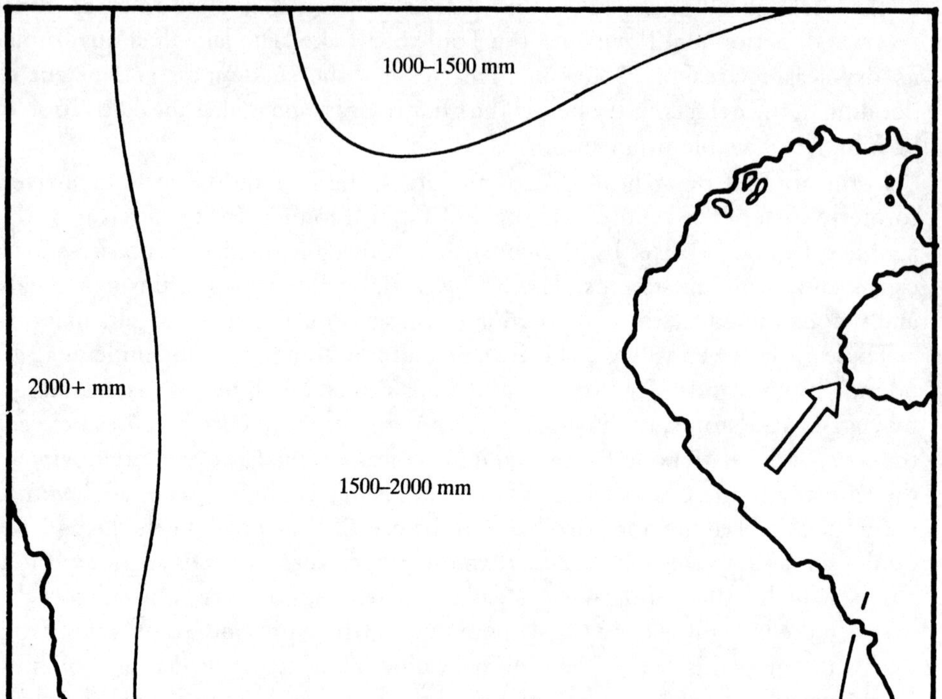

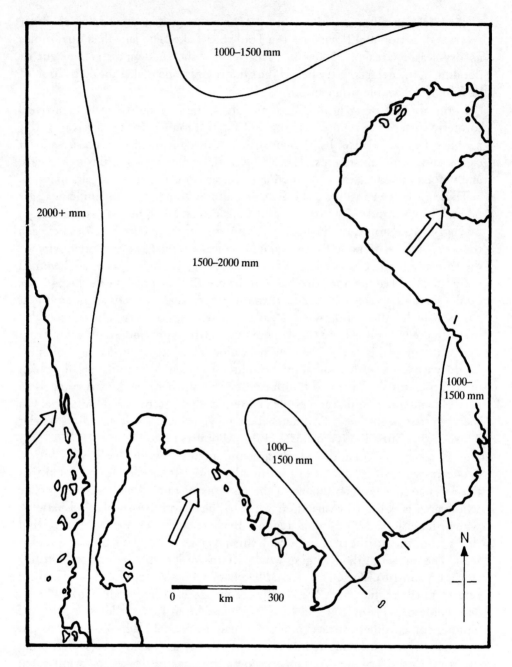

1.5 In May, the prevailing wind moves to the southwest, bringing humid moist wind to the coasts of the Gulf of Siam. The lower Mekong valley and coastal Viet Nam suffer from the rain shadow effect imposed by the Cardamom and Truong Son ranges.

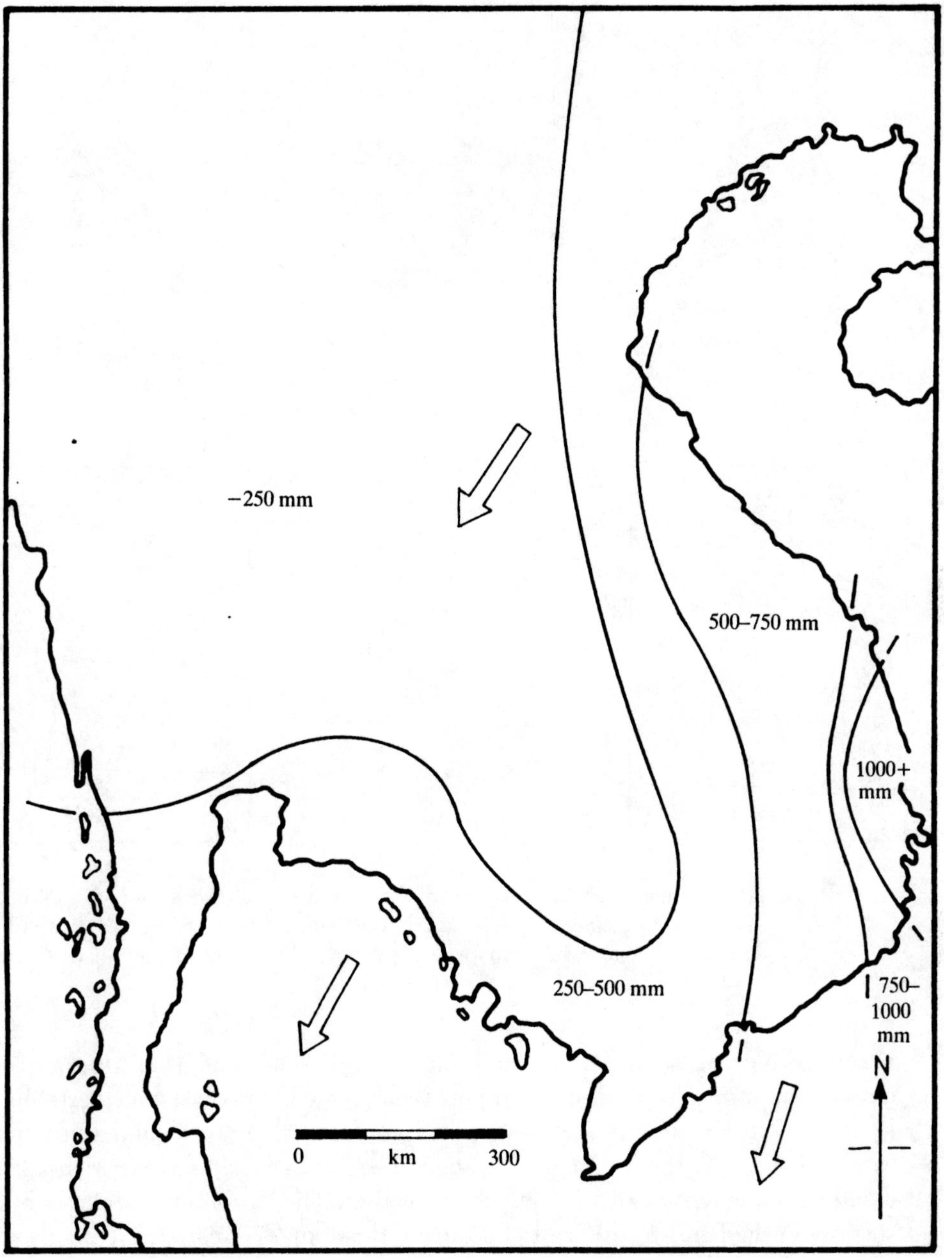

1.6 The distribution of rainfall during the dry season is controlled by the flow of dry air from Eastern Asia. While relatively damp on the coast of Central Viet Nam, it is dry for months on end in the interior.

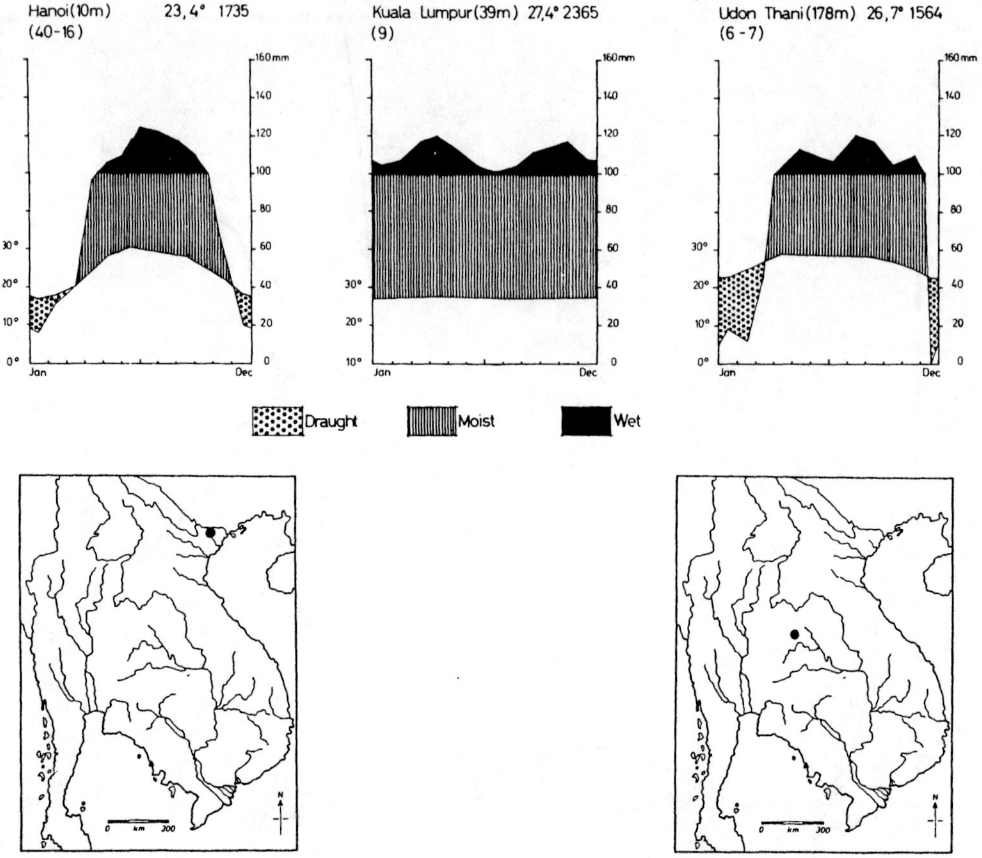

1.7 The principal characteristics of the climate at Udon Thani, Ha Noi and Kuala Lumpur (see Fig. 1.1). Kuala Lumpur, located 3.5 degrees north of the equator, is chosen to illustrate a tropical climate with rainfall distributed uniformly throughout the year.

season in Northeast Thailand lasted a minimum of 174 and a maximum of 236 days per annum. The predominantly northeastern wind pattern which establishes itself in October and November brings cooler temperatures and rain to the eastern fringes of the Truong Son range. The Red River delta experiences low cloud cover, extensive drizzle and cool weather. The Truong Son induces a rain shadow in the lands to the west and during this long dry season, the plains west of the Mekong experience hardly any precipitation, no cloud cover, and a combination of cool nights and hot days. The uplands, however, are less affected, and experience an abbreviated dry season.

Holdridge (1967) has employed relief, altitude and drainage as variables in his analysis of the natural vegetation of the area. Subsidiary variables include exposure to the wind and the ground-water regime. In his terminology, distinct

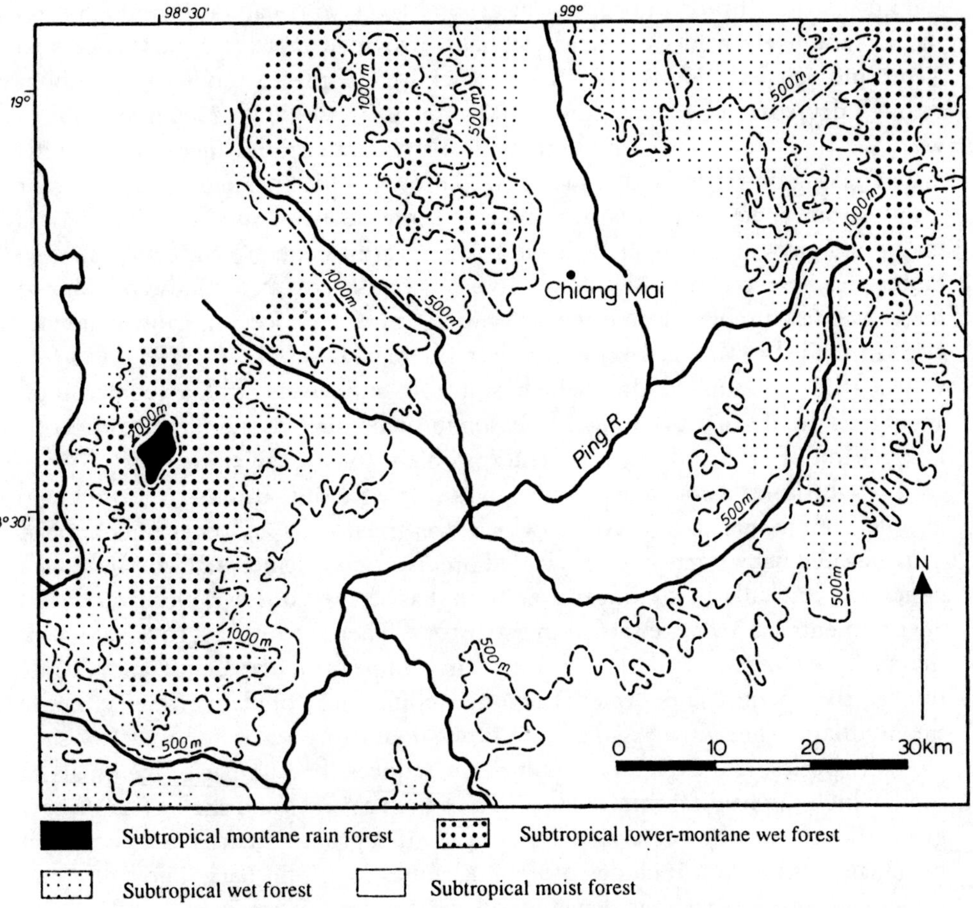

1.8 The life zones in the Chiang Mai study area as proposed by Holdridge (1967). Note the close relationship between altitude and vegetation.

associations of plant and animal communities are known as "life zones". Several such associations are of particular relevance in the patterns of human adaptation to the environments of Southeast Asia. In one of his study areas, located in the vicinity of Khon Kaen in Northeast Thailand, he found that under *c* 400 m, dry, deciduous, forest-cover predominated, merging, over that altitude, with a subtropical, wet, evergreen forest. The conversion from one to the other was also identified in the Lopburi and Chiang Mai areas (Fig. 1.8). The distribution of the deciduous forest is linked with a sharply seasonal availability of water, and hence a capacity to withstand drought. The dipterocarp trees are particularly adapted to this habitat, and one aspect of the adaptation process is the shedding of leaves and a period of dormancy during the dry season. As a result, there is no permanent canopy of evergreen trees to screen the ground from the direct impact of rain, and grasses and shrubs can survive at ground level. This habitat favours grazers such as the deer, wild cattle and elephant, provided there is regular access to water and salt licks. It is also much easier for people to modify this habitat through dry-season burning. Above 400 m, in areas with over 2000 mm of rain a year, we find a new configuration, with plant communities merging and ultimately taking on the form of a canopied rainforest which presents quite different features. Since the ground is permanently screened from sun and rain there is little grass growth and, apart from in forest clearings and stream margins, large herbivores are rare, and only the omnivorous pig thrives at ground level. Where there are favourable cleared enclaves one finds rhinoceros, gaur, banteng, elephant and the sambar deer. Elsewhere, the regular supply of leaves sustains a varied arboreal fauna within which squirrels and civets find a regular food supply. In the absence of a long dry season in such upland terrain, the rigours of a long period of aridity do not present a problem for human settlement.

This subtropical, wet forest in turn gives way, at about 1000 m, to a subtropical, lower-montane, wet forest, in which evergreen oaks and chestnuts appear. This elevated habitat has not yet yielded prehistoric settlements. Two further life zones are particularly significant, and emphasise the considerable diversity of environments which were settled in prehistory. There is the mangrove habitat of the sheltered coasts, and the swampy environment of the deltas and deeply flooded river plains. The former is a pioneer community of plants which colonise the mudflats exposed to regular tidal flows. Plants are restricted to a few salt-tolerant species, and exposure to salt water reduces the number of mammals to those which can feed off intertidal resources such as crabs and shellfish at or near ground level, and the nectar and fruits of the mangroves themselves. The list of mammals is short but includes otters, macaques, pigs and bats. The deltas and floodplains are too wet for dense woodland to form. They include large open areas of reeds and swampy grasses well adapted to the rhinoceros, water-buffalo, and three varieties of swamp-deer.

Such broad divisions into life zones leaves only the most generalised impression of the complex mosaic of plant and animal communities within which human societies operated. By employing such information, and that regarding the nature of the terrain and climate, Dobby has subdivided the area into 13 constituent regions (Dobby 1967). Upland areas under largely evergreen varieties of forest are to be found in Western Thailand, the Northern highlands of Thailand comprising the valleys of the Ping, Nan and Yom rivers, the Cardamom mountains, the highlands north and west of the Red River delta, and the Truong Son range. Lowlands with variable swamp or deciduous forest, or mangrove associations include Central Thailand, that is, the Chao Phraya plains and the Pa Sak River valley, the Chao Phraya delta, the Khorat plateau, the deltas of the Red and Mekong rivers, the Tonle Sap plains and the coastal plains of central Viet Nam. There is considerable scope for local variety and, not least, for human influence on the habitat.

The history of archaeology in Southeast Asia

The replacement of speculation on the past by scientific enquiry took place in Europe during the 19th century. In Southeast Asia, there was no such development and, in due course, the foundations of archaeological investigations were laid by European workers. The initial continuous contact between the indigenous kingdoms of Southeast Asia and Europeans, in contrast to visits by Roman entertainers and explorers like Marco Polo, followed the Bull promulgated by Pope Alexander VI which divided the world between Spain and Portugal: Spain to take most of the Americas and Portugal the lands beyond Africa. Portuguese policy was to take strong points as foci for trade, with Macao and Goa as centres for Chinese and Indian trade. For Southeast Asia, they chose Malacca. This involved forcible seizure from the Sultan by d'Albuquerque in 1511. As it happened, the Sultan of Malacca was then a vassal to the king of Siam, so wisely d'Albuquerque sent an emissary, Duarte Fernandez, to the Court of Ayutthaya to report on the event. Thereby, in 1511, diplomatic contact was established between the Portuguese and the Kingdom of Siam. The Portuguese rapidly established themselves as a force. A commercial treaty was concluded in 1516, and two decades later, 170 Portuguese were employed as royal bodyguards. In 1538, 300 Portuguese were settled at Pattani and, by the end of the century, a Jesuit priest had his own ministry in Ayutthaya. The Portuguese intermarried with the Siamese such that by the 17th century when the Dutch, Japanese, French and English vied for commercial favours at the court of Ayutthaya, the local Portuguese had largely been incorporated into the local populace (Hutchinson 1940).

The early 17th century was a period of intense commercial rivalry. By 1605–1610, King Ekathot Sarot employed Japanese bodyguards. In 1609, 16 Siamese were sent as envoys to the court at The Hague and, a few years later, Geritt Van Wuystoff travelled up the Mekong on an exploratory trading mission. His interests were in hides, pepper and gold, in exchange for which he supplied cotton cloth (Garnier 1871). On 17 September 1612, Lucan Antheuniss presented the King with a letter from James I of England, and the English were granted a cantonment at Ayutthaya between the Dutch and the Japanese. Antheuniss then set in train inland exploration by despatching Samuel Driver to Chiang Mai. The same century saw the French interest quicken, not just in commercial terms, but also in military activity. In 1664, a Catholic mission was established at Ayutthaya, and priests were active in the provinces.

One early French embassy included Simon de la Loubère. The 1687 treaty he helped conclude with King Narai was principally for commercial purposes. The French obtained a trading monopoly over the tin of Phuket and the cession of an island trading base at Mergui. De la Loubère wrote a detailed account of his visit and it contains, in effect, the impressions of a cultivated European mind on a variety of issues (Fig. 1.10). Indeed, they may be the earliest speculations on the

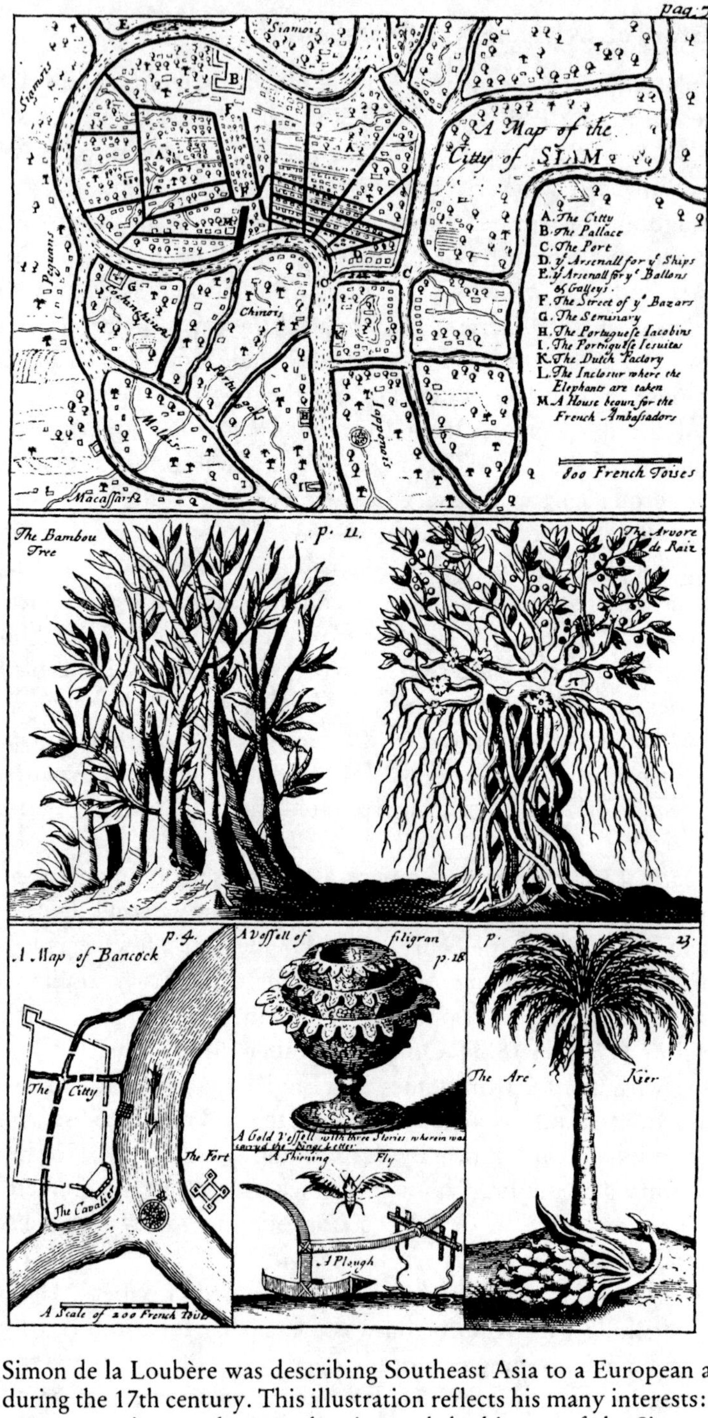

1.9 Simon de la Loubère was describing Southeast Asia to a European audience during the 17th century. This illustration reflects his many interests: agriculture, vegetation, settlement planning and the history of the Siamese.

geomorphology of the area and the origins of the inhabitants. His speculations on origins were based on linguistic evidence, for he observed the presence of two languages, the vernacular Thai and the court language of Pāli. He wrote:

As for what concerns the origine of the Siameses, it would be difficult to judge whether they are a single people, directly descended from the first men that inhabited the countrey of Siam, or whether in the process of time some other nation has not also settled there, notwithstanding the first inhabitants. The principal reason of this doubt proceeds from the Siameses understanding of two languages viz. the vulgar, which is a simple tongue consisting almost wholly of monosyllables, without conjugation or declension, and another language, which I have already spoken of, which to them is a dead tongue known only by the learned, which is called the Balie tongue, and which is enricht with the inflexions of words, like the languages we have in Europe." (De la Loubère 1693:10.)

He also recorded perhaps the earliest purely archaeological and cultural-historical observation when he wrote:

They do likewise daily discover pits anciently dug; and the remains of a great many furnaces which are thought to be abandoned during the ancient wars of Pegu. (De la Loubère 1693:14.)

He noted too, the nature of the soil. With considerable accuracy, he commented that:

(the soils) are not stony; it being difficult to find a flint, and this makes me believe of the country of Siam, that some have reported of Egypt, that it has been gradually formed of the clayish earth which the rain waters have carried down from the mountains....it is therefore this mud descending from the mountains, that is the real cause of the fertility of Siam, wherever the inundation extends itself. (De la Loubère 1693:15.)

The same commercial and missionary interest which brought Europeans to Ayutthaya likewise brought them to the Annamese Court at Hue. It must be recalled that the ancient kingdom of the Chams had been overwhelmed by the Vietnamese expansion from the Red River delta (see chapter 6). By the 19th century, the Vietnamese had also seized the Mekong delta, and were pressing hard against the southeastern flank of Cambodia. The Emperor in Hue held sway, therefore, over a tract largely equivalent to modern Viet Nam. In contrast to the situation in Thailand, the French resolved to take parts of Viet Nam by force. The initial pretext for conflict was official disapproval of missionary activity in Viet Nam. This led to a punitive French expedition against Tourane (Da Nang) in 1847 and, on 31 August 1858, a concerted attack was mounted by four vessels and 2500 men under the command of Admiral Rigault de Genouilly. Having seized the port and its environs, the French occupied Saigon and proceeded with the colonisation of Cochin China. Four years later, after much bloodshed and resistance, three provinces and trading rights were ceded to France by Emperor Tu Duc. In 1866, an expedition under Captain Doudart de Lagrée retraced the voyage of the Dutchman Van Wuystoff up the Mekong to explore the possibility of opening trade links with Western China (Doudart de

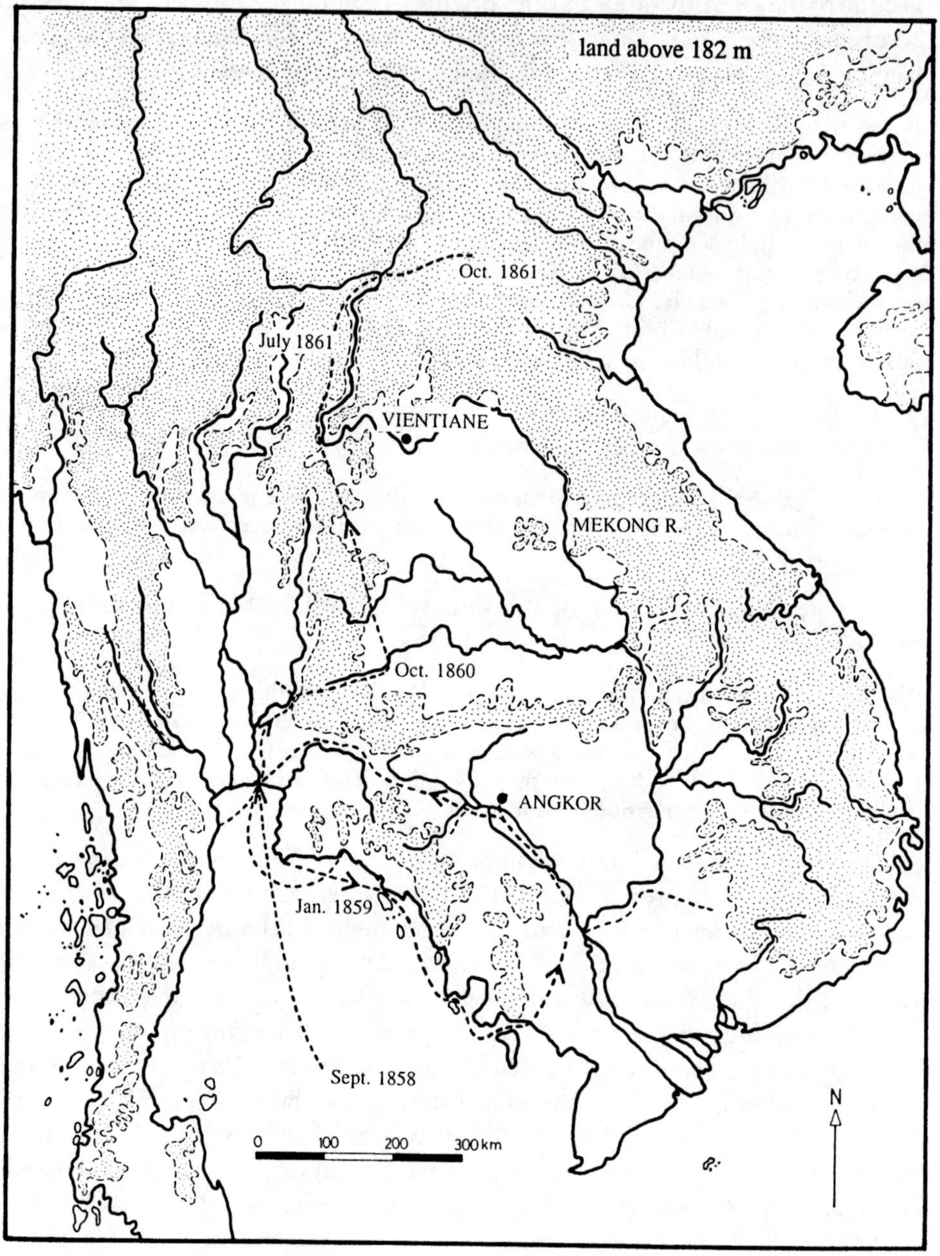

1.10 The routes taken by Henri Mouhot on his pioneer explorations of inland Southeast Asia.

Lagrée 1883). When it became apparent that such contacts were better served by using the Red River, the French turned their attention to Tonkin. The French flag was raised in Ha Noi for the first time in 1873. This did not pass without the most spirited and enduring resistance until the turn of the century. The establishment of a protectorate was accomplished at a heavy price involving brutal repression but, by 1900, they had established control over Viet Nam and imposed a fully fledged, extractive colonial regime. This was combined with their domination over Cambodia, which had been in effect since 1884, and the Kingdom of Laos, which had been taken over in 1893.

It was during this progressive annexation of their various colonies that the French scholar, Henri Mouhot, following in the footsteps of Catholic missionaries such as Père Charles-Emile Bouillevaux who rediscovered Angkor in 1850, undertook the first purely scientific European exploration of Southeast Asia. He embarked from London in April 1858, and died in Laos in November 1861. Although principally concerned with plant, animal and invertebrate species, his observations extended to the customs of the indigenous inhabitants and their origins. The routes of his expeditions are seen in Fig. 1.10. Although he died with his work incomplete, his journals have survived. They permit us to appreciate the intensity of his research and depth of his insight. Like his compatriot de la Loubère, Mouhot was a keen observer of the terrain through which he travelled. Of the plain flanking the Chao Phraya River he wrote:

> At the first glance, one distinguishes what was formerly the bed of the sea, this great plain having taken the place of an ancient gulf; proof of which is afforded by numerous marine shells, many of which I collected in a perfect state of preservation. (Mouhot 1864 vol.1:128.)

His journeys took him to the Great Lake (Tonle Sap) of Cambodia, and thence to the great monuments of Angkor. He spent several weeks there, recording both the dimensions of each major structure and noting the folklore concerning its origins (Fig. 1.11). Very wisely, he resisted the temptation to interpret the monuments which confronted him. His comments were reserved:

> Until some learned archaeologist shall devote himself to this subject, it is not probable that ought but contradictory speculations will be promulgated. (Mouhot 1864 vol.2:20.)

Mouhot's journal, when published in 1864, attracted much interest. It was clear that the new colonies had an immensely interesting archaeological heritage and many new discoveries followed in his wake. Two years later a major expedition, which was mounted under the direction of Captain Doudart de Lagrée, left Saigon to follow the course of the Mekong River into Southern China. While its principal objective was commercial – to discover a trade route into China from the new colony – the expedition also showed much interest in ancient monuments and undertook a survey of Angkor which included making the first copies of the inscriptions there (Fig. 1.12, Garnier 1873, Malleret 1969,

Osborne 1975). This initial exposure to the monuments of the ancient Khmer led to further field studies under the direction of a member of the Mekong expedition, Louis Delaporte. These resulted in the discovery of other great centres including Koh Ker, Beng Mealea and Banteay Chmar (Delaporte 1880). Etienne Aymonier then undertook a detailed reconaissance for Khmer sites in Cambodia, province by province, which added again to the growing number of inscriptions available for study (Aymonier 1900-1903). He was also able to expand his fieldwork into Southern Viet Nam where he identified, for the first time, numerous sites belonging to a different civilization, called after the Chams.

The inscriptions were written in Sanskrit and the local language. In Cambodia, it was archaic Khmer and, in coastal Viet Nam, Cham. When translated, a task in which Français Barth and Abel Bergaigne were the pioneers, they were found to contain king lists, records of military exploits, and lists of donations to temple foundations (Barth 1885, Bergaigne 1893). By degrees, dynastic histories of these early civilizations gave substance to the historic and cultural background of the great cities which were being found deep in the jungles of Cambodia and Viet Nam.

While the clearly visible monuments of the Khmer and Chams attracted most interest, prehistoric sites were not overlooked. The first record of a prehistoric site was made by a Dr Corre in 1879 (Corre 1879, Saurin 1969), when he

1.11 Henri Mouhot drafted his impressions of the places he visited, including this view of Angkor Wat.

described a large mound covered in potsherds and shells known as Samrong Sen. He described polished stone tools from the site, and rare objects of bronze. This site attracted numerous subsequent visitors and was, in 1902, the scene of the earliest excavation with any pretensions to scientific enquiry. It was directed by Henri Mansuy, who descibed an archaeological sequence to a depth of 4.5 m (Mansuy 1902). He recovered much pottery, freshwater shellfish, stone adzes, and shell and stone jewellery. The few bronze artefacts were not found in any stratified context, but came from the general area of the site. According to Noulet's analyses, these objects comprised a 5% tin bronze, and established the existence of a Bronze Age in Southeast Asia (Noulet 1879).

It was a realisation of this rich cultural heritage which encouraged the new colonial administration to support the foundation of the École Française d'Extrême Orient. Under the inspiration of Paul Doumer and members of the Académie d'Inscriptions et Bêlle Lèttres in Paris, the school was promulgated, in 1898, on the model of the existing French schools in Athens, Rome and Cairo. The founding regulations, set out and published on 15 December 1898, specified a permanent archaeological mission to explore the archaeology and philology of the Indochinese peninsula. Stress was given to the history of monuments and

1.12 The members of Doudart de Lagrée's Mekong River expedition who visited Angkor between 23 June and 1 July 1866. They made the first detailed description of the monuments. This group photograph, taken on the steps of one of the temple-mausolea, shows from left to right: Garnier, Delaporte, Joubert, Thorel, de Carné, and the leader, Doudart de Lagrée.

1.13 The present National Museum of Viet Nam is located on the southern bank of the Red River. Formerly the Musée Louis Finot, it now houses the world's finest collection of Southeast Asian bronzes.

idioms, and for contributing to the scholarly study of neighbouring regions, not least, India and China. The foundation director, Louis Finot, was charged with the establishment of a museum (Fig. 1.13) and a library, and through the efforts of research appointees, to further archaeological and philological knowledge.

Finôt was fortunate in his choice of early appointees and his team rapidly entered what we can, in retrospect, recognise as the Golden Age of archaeological research in Southeast Asia. Paul Pelliot was a foundation pensioner, appointed in 1899. A brilliant student of Chinese, and aged only 26 when he joined the school, he worked on the historical geography of the area through the analysis of Chinese texts. His contributions were seminal, and remain the principal source in a Western language for the early institutions of Southeast Asia. Henri Parmentier was appointed in July 1900 and, more than any other, laid the foundations for our appreciation of the historic monuments of Indo-China (Fig. 1.14). His paper, in volume 2 of the *Bulletin de L'École* on excavation procedures, remains a model of common sense and was in many ways ahead of its time, even in European contexts. He noted, for example, that an excavation is not an amusement, as is generally considered, but a scientific pursuit, very delicate because if badly executed, it means the destruction of an historic document.

Parmentier put theory into practice. He was responsible for recording all the known monuments of the Chams, as well as the early and later Khmer. His reports were accompanied by his own drawings, photographs and maps showing the location of all the sites. A third early appointee was Capt. E. Lunet de Lajonquière. Seconded from the army, he was charged with the mission of locating and describing all the monuments, inscriptions and statues, in addition to reporting on their condition and need for conservation. His task was undertaken before Parmentier commenced his own fieldwork, and his report was published in 1902. It comprises one of the first scholarly analyses of historic sites in Southeast Asia, for he included part of Thailand in his survey area.

In addition to this widespread and intensive archaeological research, Finot himself was continuing the long and important French tradition of Sanskrit studies by translating the inscriptions which were being found in increasing numbers. In 1902, for example, he reported on two new inscriptions of the Cham King Bhadravarman. Together with his predecessors, M.A. Barth and A. Bergaigne, and his successor Georges Coedès, Finot was instrumental in establishing the dynastic sequences of early Cambodia and Champa. The wide range of interests which made up these early studies is revealed in the École's third bulletin, which was issued on a quarterly basis during 1903. It included a further analysis of an inscription, this time a stela raised under Jayavarman VII in Vientiane, which revealed the wide extent of the Khmer Empire in the 13th century A.D. Henri Parmentier reported on his excavation at the great Cham centre of Dong Duong. There was also a report on the modern Chams, and a consideration of a visit to Tonkin, in 1626, by the Portuguese. The first reproduction of the bas-reliefs of Angkor Thom by Dufour and Carpeaux was

1.14 (Left to right), Victor Goloubew, Louis Finot, an un-named Khmer and Henri Parmentier at Ta Prohm, Angkor. Goloubew was well-known for his work on the irrigation system of Angkor, Finot was the first director of the École Française and Henri Parmentier was one of the first research appointees at the École. (Reproduced from *Asian Perspectives* 12 courtesy Wilhelm Solheim.)

reported in the same volume, soon to be followed by their definitive report (Dufour and Carpeaux 1910). The representations of battle scenes involving ballistae mounted on elephants reached a wide audience, and stressed the deep fund of information present in this medium. Perhaps the most significant contribution to this issue, however, was Pelliot's work on the ancient state of Funan, assembled on the basis of Chinese documentary references. This tour-de-force of historic scholarship laid the foundations for all later attempts to establish the location and nature of the earliest state in Southeast Asia (Pelliot 1903). Nor did the École Française have a monopoly over archaeological research, for the Geological Service of the Indochinese Union had on its staff two gifted fieldworkers, Madeleine Colani and Henri Mansuy. Their respective contributions laid the foundations for understanding the early hunter-gatherers of the region then known as Tonkin, but now called Bac Bo (Colani 1927, Mansuy 1924).

At a more practical level, the museum building was completed and the galleries filling, while the library acquisitions were already being catalogued. A congress of orientalists was held, and it attracted 128 scholars.

The 1904 bulletin contains a significant reference to the foundation of a scholarly society in Thailand. On 26 February, a meeting, held at the Oriental Hotel in Bangkok and attended by 39 interested people, resolved to found a society "for the investigation and encouragement of arts, sciences and literature in relation to Siam and neighbouring countries". It also aimed to publish scholarly papers, form a library and maintain an ethnographic museum. The Siam Society, as it was named, has always been enthusiastically patronised by the royal family, and the first paper, on the foundation of Ayutthaya, was presented by Prince Damrong. Its interests have been broad, but archaeology has been among its concerns since the society's foundation. Indeed, at the first annual general meeting held on the 7 April 1904, Colonel Gerini stressed the importance of archaeology and inscriptions, and encouraged those living outside Bangkok to send details of new discoveries to the society. This precept was followed, for the third meeting heard a paper on the antiquities of the Mun valley. By the end of the first year, the membership list had increased fourfold over those attending the inaugural discussions. The interest in archaeology is further shown by W.W. Bourke's communication, in 1905, which described archaeological remains from peninsular Thailand. He referred to the number of beads of Indian origin found at Krabi, and suggested an Indian origin for the mine shafts for extracting the tin ore identified on Phuket Island (Bourke 1905).

Although the Siam Society brought together scholars interested in a wide range of disciplines, it lacked state funding, and never employed its own archaeological research staff. The Thai Government, however, founded the Archaeological Service of Siam in 1924, and this organisation devoted itself largely to the care and conservation of the great historic sites such as Lopburi and Ayutthaya. Two years later, the National Museum of Siam was founded and charged with the conservation of sites and relics.

The École Française has always been supported financially by the French taxpayer, and during the 56 years of its direction of affairs within the Indochinese Union, it was able to mount and maintain major research programmes. Its director also controlled access to research opportunities by non-French western archaeologists. This had two effects. Firstly, archaeology in the French Colonies bounded ahead compared with that in Thailand. Secondly, most research was undertaken by French archaeologists. One searches in vain for any training of, or professional participation by, Vietnamese, Khmer or Laotians. The history of archaeological enquiry reached a fulcrum with the defeat of French forces in Viet Nam and subsequent involvement of Cambodia in armed conflict. Until the mid 1950s, the school, with its headquarters in Ha Noi, maintained a steady stream of fundamentally important reports. The foundations were laid for a proper appreciation of the Khmer and Cham civilizations. The late Bronze Age and Chinese occupation of the Red River delta were explored through archaeological remains, while in the surrounding uplands, Colani (1927) and Mansuy (1924) were excavating caves yielding the remains known collectively as "Hoabinhian" and "Bacsonian". Mansuy (1923) at Samrong Sen, and Lévy (1943) in the Mlu Prei area examined open prehistoric occupation sites and anticipated by up to 80 years the discovery of similar sites at Non Nok Tha and Ban Chiang in Northeast Thailand. Along the raised shorelines of Viet Nam, Patte (1924, 1925) identified coastal occupation sites, commonly referred to as kitchen middens. Even before the second world war, Paris (1929, 1931) was describing the canals visible from the air along marshy lowlands of the Mekong delta. Research continued unabated during the Japanese occupation, and it was during the second world war that Malleret (1959-63) excavated at the great port city of Oc Eo, and was able to show that the site was once part of an early complex society called Funan by the Chinese.

Perhaps the outstanding contribution to knowledge of this mature era in the history of the École Française was the compilation by its director, Georges Coedés, of all the Sanskrit inscriptions known from mainland Southeast Asia. Each inscription was set out first in its original language, and then translated into French, before being set in its historic and cultural perspective (Coedès 1937-1954). It will always remain a crucial source of information on the early civilisations of the area.

The situation changed dramatically with the withdrawal of the French. The new regime under Ho Chi Minh placed much emphasis on archaeological research and turned to the Soviet Union for the necessary training of archaeologists. The Musée Louis Finot in Ha Noi became the National Museum, and the Vietnamese Institute of Archaeology took over the central organising role of the École Française. Despite the absence of facilities, the research undertaken has greatly expanded our knowledge of the prehistoric period in Viet Nam. Even during the height of the American bombing, excavations continued unabated and, with the assistance of the radiocarbon-dating laboratories in China, East

Germany and New Zealand, a chronology for the later prehistoric cultures is slowly emerging. The picture now is one of immense vigour, largely devoted to the identification of the prehistoric origins and development of the Vietnamese people.

The development of prehistoric archaeology in Thailand has taken a different course. The Thais themselves have been to the fore in the analysis of art history and monuments of early Thai civilisations, but the prehistoric period was silent until the first few foreign fieldwork programmes. Two early contributions were stimulated by the second world war. Van Heekeren, a Dutch archaeologist, was despatched as a prisoner of war to labour on the railway line in Kanchanaburi Province. He identified some prehistoric stone implements there and, after the war, he returned for further investigations under less demanding constraints (van Heekeren and Knuth 1967). Williams-Hunt served with the Royal Air Force, and became interested, through aerial photography, in the circular moated sites of Northeast Thailand. These concentrate in the valley of the Mun River, and were the subject of an exploratory paper (Williams-Hunt 1950). A third early figure was Quaritch-Wales, whose interests were mainly art-historical. He examined many of the large early historic town sites and excavated several before and after the second world war (Quaritch-Wales 1957).

During the 1960s, prehistoric research in Thailand was stimulated by several major excavation programmes. These involved the recovery of inhumation cemeteries in association with a range of complete artefacts. Sørenson at the Bang site near Ban Kao pioneered these discoveries when he excavated a cemetery with human inhumation burials associated with complete pottery vessels and stone axes (Sørensen and Hatting 1967). Watson (1979) and Loofs-Wissowa identified a second important cemetery at Khok Charoen (Watson and Loofs-Wissowa 1967) which yielded inhumation burials with whole pots, shell jewellery and stone axes. Bayard's excavations at Non Nok Tha began in 1966 and continued in 1968. These were conceived as a joint programme between the University of Hawaii and the Thai Fine Arts Department by Wilhelm Solheim, and his foresight and overall direction of the fieldwork established a landmark not only of the significance of the finds, but also because it was a pioneer teaching programme for 30 young Thai students of archaeology. This site, in addition to the finds of whole pots, shell and stone artefacts in association with human burials, also added bronze to the repertoire of finds, and posed the possibility of a far earlier start to metallurgy in Thailand than had hitherto been imagined (Bayard 1972, Solheim 1968).

The excavations of Ban Chiang in 1974-5, under the direction of Gorman and Charoenwongsa (1976), added a further landmark, because it was conceived as a joint programme between the University of Pennsylvania and the Thai Fine Arts Department, with further emphasis being given to the training of young Thai archaeologists. This, and subsequent training programmes, have led to the establishment of Thai archaeologists in institutional bases, not least the Fine Arts

Department and the University and Museum systems. Their contribution in terms of fieldwork and analysis now exceeds by far that of visiting foreign workers.

Clearly, however, problems remain. Archaeology in Cambodia, always a focal area, has been dormant for over a decade. The young archaeologists working there before 1975 are either dead or in exile. The political divisions between Viet Nam and Thailand mean that communication is at a premium and joint research impracticable.To these formidable obstacles, one must add the problems of synthesis in a region where, quite rightly, much basic information is now available only in local languages. Nevertheless, great strides have been and continue to be made.

Themes and approaches

Human adaptation to Southeast Asia remains little known. It is true that various aspects have been scrutinised, and usually interpreted, within the framework of ideas on prehistory brought from Europe or America. State formation is one instance, while there is a clear temptation to name the cultural sequence according to the three-age system of Neolithic, Bronze and Iron Ages. This temptation should be resisted if only because we deal with a little-known area in prehistory and there are no grounds for assuming that these sub-divisions have any affinities with those proposed elsewhere. The view adopted here is that we now know enough of the pre- and proto-historic material to identify at least six themes, each relating to a particular adaptive pattern. By deploying available data in conjunction with appropriate models, it might be possible to approach an understanding of how such configurations came about.

While obtaining data through excavation is straightforward, if arduous, interpreting it is a different matter. It is exacerbated by the very diverse theoretical approaches made by archaeologists over the past century and, at present, between the Western orientation in vogue in Thailand and the more conservative interpretative schemes employed by many Vietnamese colleagues. This is particularly evident in considering the Vietnamese coastal "Neolithic". The approach adopted in this book places emphasis on identifying both cultural and environmental variables and examining their interplay. Cultural change is rarely the result of one particular causal factor such as climatic adjustments, overpopulation or sudden exposure to a new technology. Rather, we should recognise the possibility of dividing a particular cultural configuration, as well as the environment in which it operates, into its component parts such as the social, economic, technological, religious and psychological aspects of behaviour. The environment may, for convenience, be disarticulated into the faunal, floral, climatic and geographic variables, as well as the impact of alien groups. Understanding how change occurs is never easy, and is often speculative. We can, however, edge a little closer to appreciating at least the complexities of the situation if we try to identify how change in one area of behaviour, for example the economy, may be coupled with adjustments in, say, the social organisation or technological innovation. A good example would be the effect of the introduction of the plough in place of the hoe. The former requires a large domestic animal such as the buffalo or horse to pull it. It is helped by the adoption of a metal share, thus fostering further technological innovation. Again, with a plough, a man can bring under cultivation more land, even beyond that required for his immediate commitments. The production of a surplus made technically possible through ploughing may then be used to sustain a non-food-producing elite which could devote itself to religious specialisation. Naturally, the expansion of agriculture both turns on the nature of the environment, and has an impact upon it.

This approach is a general one, which may be applied to any given prehistoric situation. It can, however, lead to a construction of specific interpretative frameworks, often termed "models". The first theme is the nature of hunter-gatherer societies, their distribution and propensity for stability or change. Hunter-gatherer, in this context, is a shorthand notation for those groups which derived energy by assembling and consuming food which was naturally available. This may well have incorporated trapping, fishing, collecting and netting as well as hunting. At present, it seems probable that while the mighty temple-mausoleum of Angkor Wat was under construction during the 11th century A.D., there were still groups of hunter-gatherers in upland areas under evergreen, canopied forest. There was no uniform progression towards complexity in Southeast Asia. It is not unreasonable to seek shifts in emphasis among the subsistence activities of some such groups – such as increasing consumption of rice. Given the remarkable variation and abundance of wild plants which could have been exploited for food, it is not regarded as possible, or even likely, that emphasis on rice underwrote a neolithic revolution of the sort noted in the Near East. We shall consider the evidence for the intensification of plant utilisation, including cultivation techniques, and attempt to illuminate the place of rice in the broader patterns of subsistence.

One of the main points about Southeast Asia, however, is the relative ease of obtaining food, particularly in the rich coastal-estuarine areas, but also in the inland marshy river valleys. It is true that the impact of the long dry season in the latter area places a premium on systems of food preservation and storage, but rice is tailor-made for storage and fish, when salted, may be preserved for months on end. It will be argued, in the context of domestication, that sedentary occupation of a particular place, involving the construction of houses and maintenance of long-term cemeteries for the ancestors, is more significant than modifying the behaviour of plants and animals. In this view, it is the domestication of human beings which is the really significant modification because, in its turn, domestication encouraged larger aggregations of people, opened up the possibility of accumulation of material possessions, of attaining status and rank, and acquiring the sumptuary goods used as insiginia of such rank.

There is evidence for a major expansion in the number and distribution of domestic settlements which were foci of sedentary communities, an expansion which was probably underway by 3000 B.C. We need to ascertain the nature of this process, and attempt to understand why it took place. Probably between 2000–1500 B.C., the Mekong catchment, Red River delta and coastal Viet Nam witnessed the adoption of bronze-working. This has been the subject of much speculative comment over the past two decades, particularly concerning the issues of dating and origins. The increasing body of data now permits a judicious view to be presented. It is argued that, during the period 500–1 B.C., there was a move, in some lowland riverine locales, from village autonomy towards centralised chiefdoms. This move occurred at approximately the same time as when the knowledge of iron-working was being established in Southeast Asia, and slightly earlier than initial contact with Indian and Chinese expansion. Quite rapidly, we find the establishment of small states, or to give them their Sanskrit name, *maṇḍalas*. Given our expanding knowledge of later prehistory, it is considered opportune to re-examine such centralisation, including better-defined local cultural variables, in addition to the long-established documentation of an Indian presence.

The approach adopted below is to examine these successive themes which exhibit major adaptive patterns and shifts in behaviour within a subtropical monsoonal habitat. It may be that some of the variables invoked will be enlarged upon or replaced as the discipline advances. Thus, the roles of sedentism, exchange of exotic goods, capacity to attract followers and control of the means of destruction, are all given advocacy. They have replaced earlier and rather simpler models involving diffusion of ideas and migration of peoples which have been well aired in the past, and will not be given further attention (Heine-Geldern 1932, 1951).

These themes and approaches are necessary prerequisites and, indeed, underlie the principal point of this study. It has been stressed above that mainland Southeast Asia is a diverse area with little apparent coherence. It will be argued, however, that it has a critical unity, which is provided by the pattern of human adaptation during prehistoric and early historic times. It is for the reader to judge on the basis of the chapters which follow, whether or not this unity is illusory.

CHAPTER 2

HUNTER-GATHERER COMMUNITIES AND EARLY DOMESTICATION

Hunting and gathering in Southeast Asia is not an extinct lifestyle. Even among the most specialised rice-farming communities, there remains a vigorous tradition of collecting wild food resources. Fish, for example, are an essential ingredient in the diet. Shellfish are collected and, although drastically reduced in numbers during the last century, wild animals are still hunted and trapped. The remoter forests of North Thailand sustain mobile groups which rely entirely upon food collection. They practice neither agriculture nor stock-raising.

A detailed appreciation of the hunter-gatherer societies which occupied Southeast Asia during the past 10–12,000 years or so is not possible. This is due to the probable destruction or loss of sites as a result of sea-level fluctuations and the consequent changes in the landscape. The known rise in sea level submerged all possible hunter-gatherer sites of a lowland orientation throughout the drowned Sunda shelf. The layer of marine clay now covering the drowned landscape under the Bangkok plain makes location of the submerged settlements virtually impossible. To this problem we may add the likely destruction or, at best, covering of lowland sites by a mantle of alluvial silt laid down by floodwaters. This process would have been greatly accelerated by the major land clearance, and resultant exposure of soils to intense rains, which increases silt loads markedly and thereby the pace of sedimentation.

The recovery of upland settlement sites is far simpler, particularly those under rock shelters. The major river systems of Southeast Asia, as we have seen, are separated by uplands which include a limestone-karst terrain. It is in such areas, where elevation protected sites from natural processes of erosion and sedimentation, that the first indications of a widespread occupation by hunter-gatherers were obtained (Fig. 2.1).

Given the wide range of environments in question and the lengthy timespan involved, it is reasonable to expect local variations in the characteristics of hunter-gatherer societies. This might involve regional distinctions in terms of the pattern and form of material artefacts, as well as in subsistence activities and preferred burial practices. Not least, it is quite possible that where some local groups were conservative, others were innovative. It is, for example, within local hunter-gatherer societies that one might legitimately seek the initial moves towards domestication. This is here defined as the sedentary occupation of a given settlement. It often involves the construction of permanent houses and accumulation of artefacts. When compared with a more mobile lifestyle, this is a

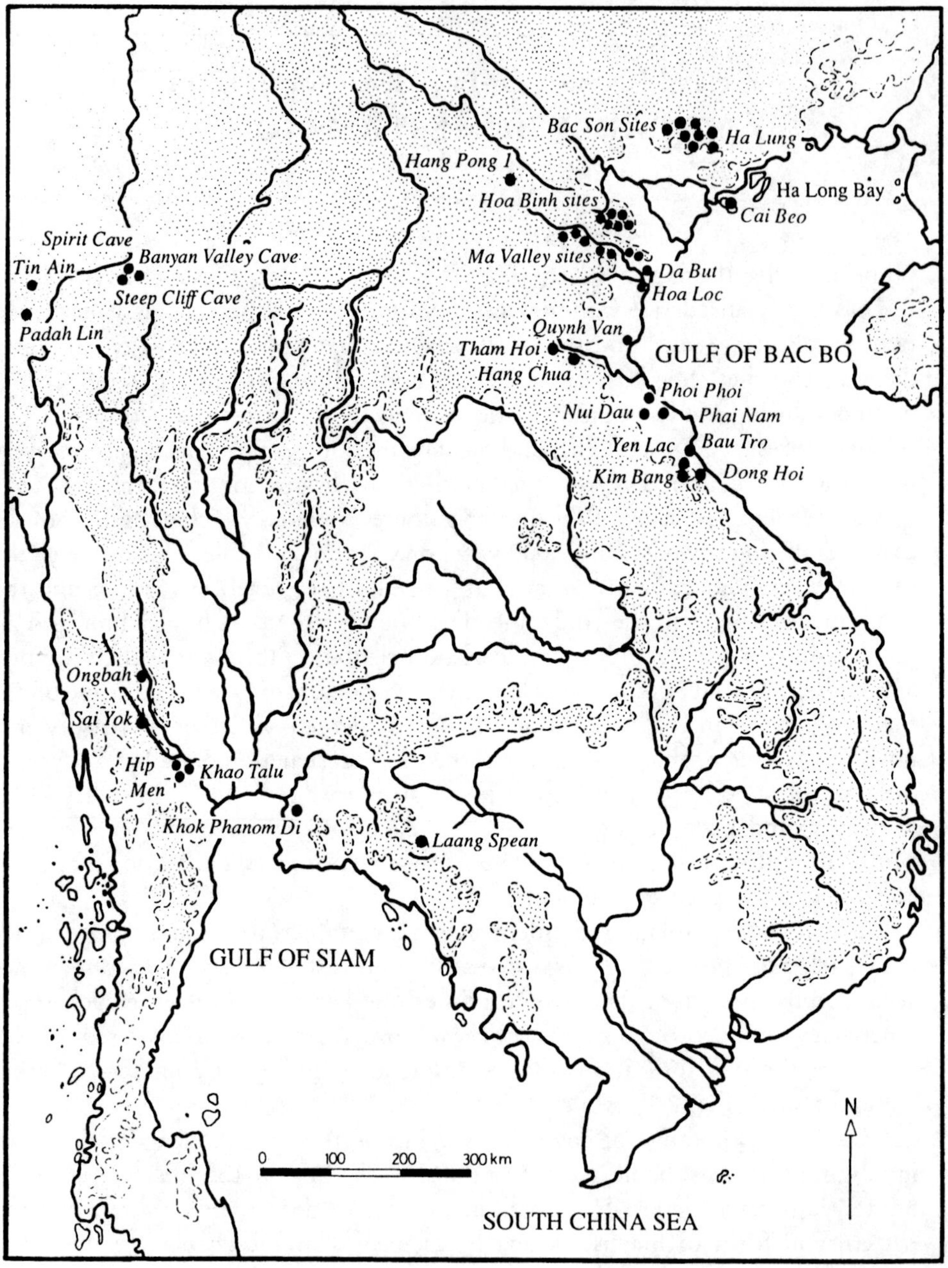

2.1 The distribution of the principal hunter-gatherer sites mentioned in chapter 2. The location given for Ha Lung is approximate. For a more detailed map of the sites in Bac Bo, see Fig. 2.5. Stippled area: land above 182m.

major change in human behaviour, because domestication often involves subsequent modifications to the surrounding plant and animal communities, as well as the development of more varied and complex human social relationships.

In considering the available data, particular emphasis will be accorded to four distinct regions because they are the best documented. The first comprises Bac Bo, the land surrounding the Red River and associated coast. The second comprises the inland and elevated terrain in the karst uplands of Northern Thailand and, as the third region, we will consider the hills flanking the Chao Phraya plains. Finally, we will turn to the recently excavated evidence for the occupation of the coast of the Gulf of Siam.

The coast and hills of Bac Bo

Bac Bo is the name given to the Red River delta and its surrounding uplands and coast. It was in 1906, just six years after the foundation of the École Française, that the first site revealing evidence for a prehistoric hunter-gatherer group was excavated at Tham Khoach. Subsequently, the foundations were laid for a more detailed knowledge of the earlier prehistory of the area by energetic site location and excavation by Madeleine Colani and Henri Mansuy (Colani 1927, Mansuy 1924). Before considering the sites and the evidence now available for this important stage in the sequence of events, it is necessary to outline some of the principal features of the environment. Today, the area centres on the intensely settled and farmed Bac Bo plain (Fig. 2.2). During much of the period under review, the Red River would have had some distance to travel before reaching the Gulf of Bac Bo due to a lower sea level, and it may well have been the case that the marshy floodplain of the river was settled by groups of hunter-gatherers. If so, there is no surviving evidence available, because the sites would lie under alluvial deposits which have steadily accumulated with regular inundations. Where the terrain is elevated, and, in particular, where human habitation occurred under the protection of rock shelters, evidence is abundant. The survival of much undisturbed vegetation on the upland hills of Cuc Phuong give some idea of the habitat present during the early prehistoric period under review. The moist and cool winds which flow across the Bac Bo plains from November until March–April rule out an extended dry season even at low levels. Consequently, there is a dense and canopied rainforest, with the upper canopy reaching up to 45 m above ground surface. Further sub-canopies occur at 30 and 20 m. The area is well-watered, and there are numerous short streams which flow into the Ma River (Gourou 1955).

The continuous advance of the Red River delta, allied with sedimentation following flooding, has meant that no relevant sites have been found along the delta coastline itself. Both to the north and the south of the delta, however, prehistoric coastal settlements have been identified. These are usually located on raised beaches which represent the shoreline from about 5000–4000 B.C. to 1500

2.2 The Red River delta of Bac Bo gives way quite suddenly to precipitous limestone uplands. Madeleine Colani used to cross the delta from Ha Noi on her way to examine prehistoric sites in Hoa Binh Province.

B.C. There are also sites on some of the islands which stud Ha Long Bay. Over the past 80 years, the prehistoric sites in this diverse area have been successively subdivided into regional groups defined largely on the basis of similarities or differences in material culture. Radiocarbon dating has made it possible to order these groups into the semblance of a chronological framework. Although the situation is by no means finalised, we shall recognise three inland groups and three coastal ones. The inland groups with their associated chronologies are called Son Vi (*c* 18,000–9000 B.C.), Hoabinhian (*c* 9000 B.C. –, and Bacsonian (*c* 8000 B.C. –). The terminal dates for the Bacsonian and Hoabinhian are not yet known, but probably lie in the period 3000–2000 B.C., depending on the region in question. The stratigraphic and chronological relationships between these three is best demonstrated at the site of Con Moong (Fig. 2.5), located within the Cuc Phuong upland (Pham Huy Thong 1980). The lowest of the three levels at Con Moong contains stone tools of Son Vi type. These comprise pebbles, usually made of quartz, which were flaked along one surface to create a working edge. This meant that much of the original surface of the pebble remained in place. Ha Van Tan (1976) has distinguished four main types of artefact, in addition to the flakes, which result from the manufacture of stone tools. One is a large quartzite cobble with a transverse cutting edge which he feels was used as a chopper and/or scraper. The second type has a cutting edge on the longitudinal edge of the tool. These side choppers, or scrapers, normally make up the majority of implements found in Son Vi sites. There are also a few implements with flaking on two working surfaces and, lastly, pebbles with flaking along only one edge, termed "round-edged pebbles".

There are few caves, such as Con Moong, which reveal the Son Vi industry underlying the next stage, that called Hoabinhian. The majority of the 60 or so known Son Vi sites are found on elevated terrain above the Bac Bo plains in Vinh Phu Province. Under such circumstances, the survival of organic remains representing food debris, or charcoal suited to radiocarbon dating, is rarer than in the protected environment of rock shelters. This situation only stresses the importance of the finds from Con Moong and from the cave of Hang Pong 1, located near the headwaters of the Ma River (Ha Van Tan 1976). At this second site, the stone industry characteristic of Son Vi has been found mixed with characteristic early Hoabinhian material. This suggests that the Hoabinhian originated in an earlier Son Vi context. The two available radiocarbon dates from Hang Pong 1, as well as those from Son Vi (Fig. 2.3), suggest that this transition was underway about 11,000–12,000 years ago. According to Nguyen Duc Tung and Pham Van Hai (1979), the pollen record for the Bac Bo plains witnessed a transition at that juncture from a hot-and-dry to a hot-and-moist climate, a change which may have been associated with the rapid rise in the post-Pleistocene sea level. This change also heralded a more complex stone industry known as the Hoabinhian following the pioneer research of Colani and Mansuy. Their recognition of a presumed late hunter-gatherer tradition in Southeast Asia results from excava-

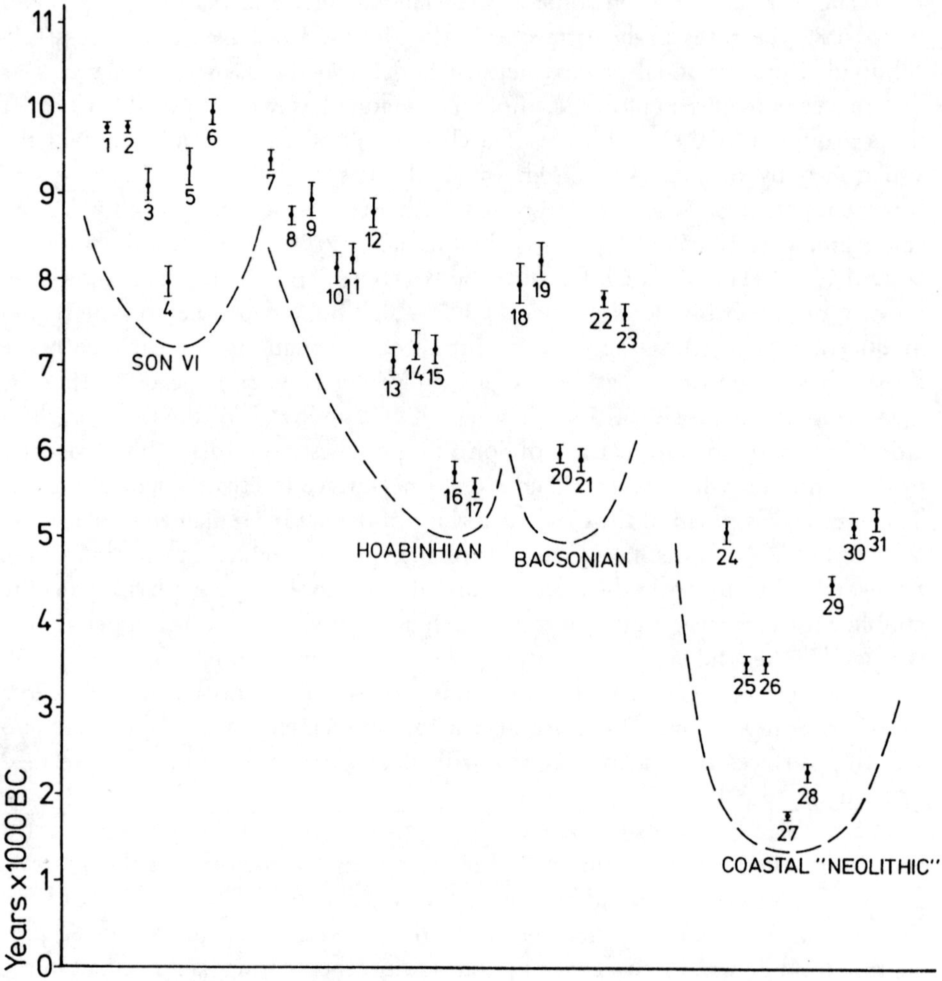

2.3 The available radiocarbon dates for the inland and coastal hunter-gatherer groups in Bac Bo. 1-4: Con Moong, 5-6: Hang Pong 1, 7-8: Sung Sam, 9-12: Tham Hoi, 13-15: Hang Chua, 16-17: Hang Dang, 18-19: Bo Lum, 20-21: Bo Nam, 22-23: Tham Hai, 24: Da But, 25-26: Quynh Van, 27-29: Cai Beo, 30-31: Ha Lung. 1-23 are dates b.c., 24-31 are expressed B.C. at 2σ ranges. (For further details, see Bayard 1984c. For the the location of the sites, see Figs. 2.1 and 2.5.)

tions by Colani (1927) in the eastern margins of the Truong Son cordillera. Her excavations in about 20 rock shelters concentrated in the province of Hoa Binh, hence the adoption of the term "Hoabinhian" to describe them. Colani noted that these sites had in common a hunting- and food-gathering economy, flaked stone tools made from river cobbles, and an associated fauna comprising extant

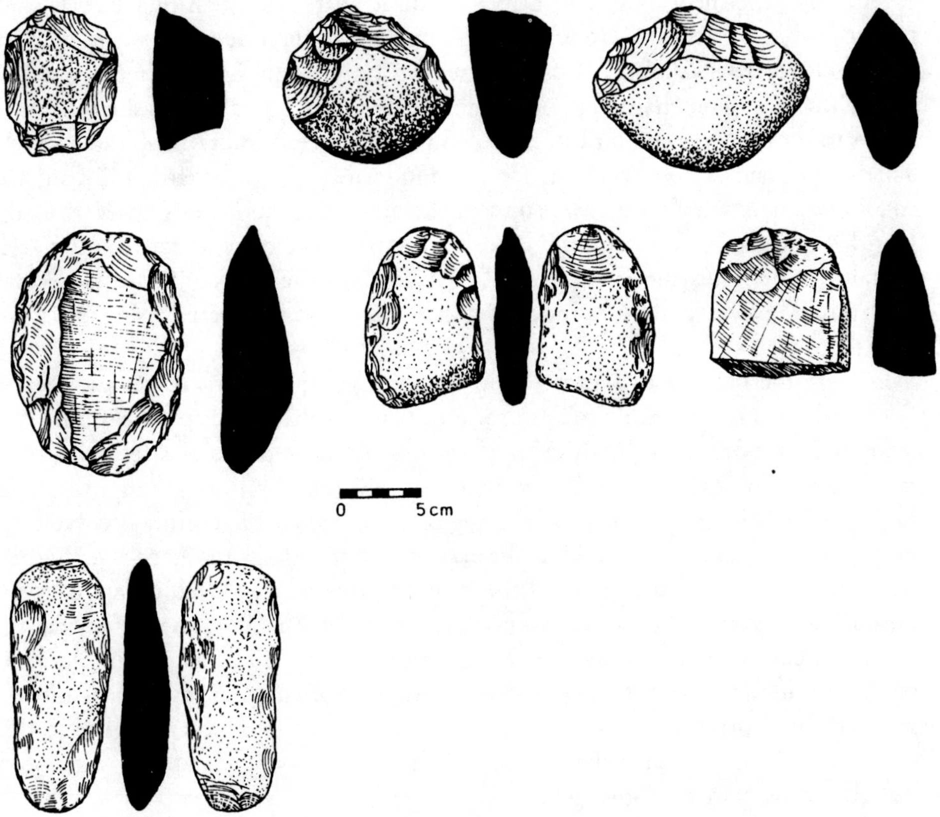

2.4 Stone implements from hunter-gatherer contexts in Bac Bo. Top row: flaked Son Vi implements; Middle row: Sumatralith or unifacial discoid, axe and short axe; Lowest row: a partially polished Bacsonian axe.

species. She concluded that the assemblages were relatively recent, and certainly after the end of the Pleistocene period.

The stone implements centre on a tool known as the sumatralith, or unifacial discoid (Fig. 2.4). This was made by removing flakes from one side of a river cobble. Modification of such river pebbles by flaking forms the basis of the Hoabinhian stone-working tradition. The range of tools was limited. Apart from the sumatralith, there is the simple removal of a row of flakes along one edge of a pebble to form a cutting edge. More common are the "short axes" – an artefact modified to form a convex cutting edge at one end. Since the recovery of flakes which were probably removed when sharpening a dull-edged implement is not uncommon, it is considered likely that such short axes reflect either a continuous process of sharpening, or the accidental breaking of a sumatralith. It is also apparent from the bruised surfaces of some pebbles that they were used for crushing or pounding without any prior modification.

Although the most abundant artefacts found in Hoabinhian phase rock shelters are made of stone, there was also a vigorous bone industry, as evidenced at the Da Phuc rock shelter. Most of the 105 bone tools found there comprise points or awls. The characteristic Hoabinhian site is a small rock shelter where access to both the rugged limestone uplands and the resources of tributary stream valleys is possible. Food remains include modern types of shellfish and fish, and small mammals which are still found in the area. Vu The Long's analysis of the Con Moong fauna, for example, revealed the presence of wild cattle and water-buffalo, rhinoceros, forest birds and both water turtle and land tortoise. Many freshwater bivalve and gastropod shellfish were also recovered (Vu The Long 1977).

Despite the passage of half a century since Colani undertook her pioneering fieldwork, it is still possible to sift useful information from her publications. Not least, it is important to analyse the location of the individual sites relative to major geographical features such as rivers, minor tributaries and hills. Her original work in the vicinity of the regional centre of Hoa Binh involved the excavation of several sites. Her reports were, for their time, of the highest quality. She observed the depth of the stratigraphy and the development of stone technology through the successive layers (Colani 1927). Thus, she noted that the basal contexts at such sites as Sao Dong contained large flaked stone implements while the first, and very rare, polished stone tools made their appearance in the intermediate horizon. The stone itself was exotic to the region, suggesting that early polished implements were obtained through exchange. Pottery, she noted, was found only in the latest layers.

The same approach was adopted in her work on the sites in the Ma River basin (Fig. 2.5). She described eight caves or rock shelters, all of which, on excavation, yielded a Hoabinhian material culture (Colani 1930). The characteristic location of these shelters was in the margins of the tributary streams, on high ground above flood level. Such a situation is an ecotone, whereby the occupants had access to the resources of both the stream margin and the stratified vegetational and animal communities of the hillside. Lang Bon is one such site, only 40 m above sea level, but still safely above the Ma floodplain (Figs. 2.6 and 2.7).

Colani also reported the presence of shellfish, crabs and water turtles. The present river is only 200 m from the cave. Again, the bones and teeth of rhinoceros, carnivores and deer were found. The same general points can be made of the more southerly group of sites, about 80 km north of Dong Hoi, in the valley of the Nan River. Two rock shelters, Yen Lac and Kim Bang, lie on opposite sides of the river, at the junction of the floodplain and the limestone massif. Yen Lac is characteristically small, measuring only 25 by 6 m. Deer, gastropod and bivalve shellfish were excavated, but no stratigraphy was noted there.

The Hoabinhian rock shelters rarely yield human remains. A major and important exception is Lang Cao, where Colani (1927) found no fewer than 200 skulls within an area of only 25 m^2. They were propped up by stones, with few associated limb bones. No grave goods were identified. It is evident from the layout of this mortuary area that the bodies were buried some time after death within a confined space. If the social group responsible was mobile for at least some of the year, then this cave may represent a central focus for the burial of the dead whose partial remains were returned there at some interval after death. This particular rite differs from that represented at Hang Dang and Moc Long caves, where the dead were buried in a crouched position, covered in red ochre and associated with stone tools (Ha Van Tan 1976).

Fig. 2.3 provides the radiocarbon chronology for some Hoabinhian contexts in the Bac Bo area. It is evident that these rock shelters were occupied from about 10,000 B.C. During the ensuing four or five millennia, we can discern two major changes in material culture: the advent of grinding and polishing the working surfaces of stone tools, and the manufacture of fired pottery vessels. It is important to recognise that, when the initial trends towards polishing stone tools and making pottery occurred, the coast was some distance from the present shore, and any prehistoric settlement there has been lost through subsequent

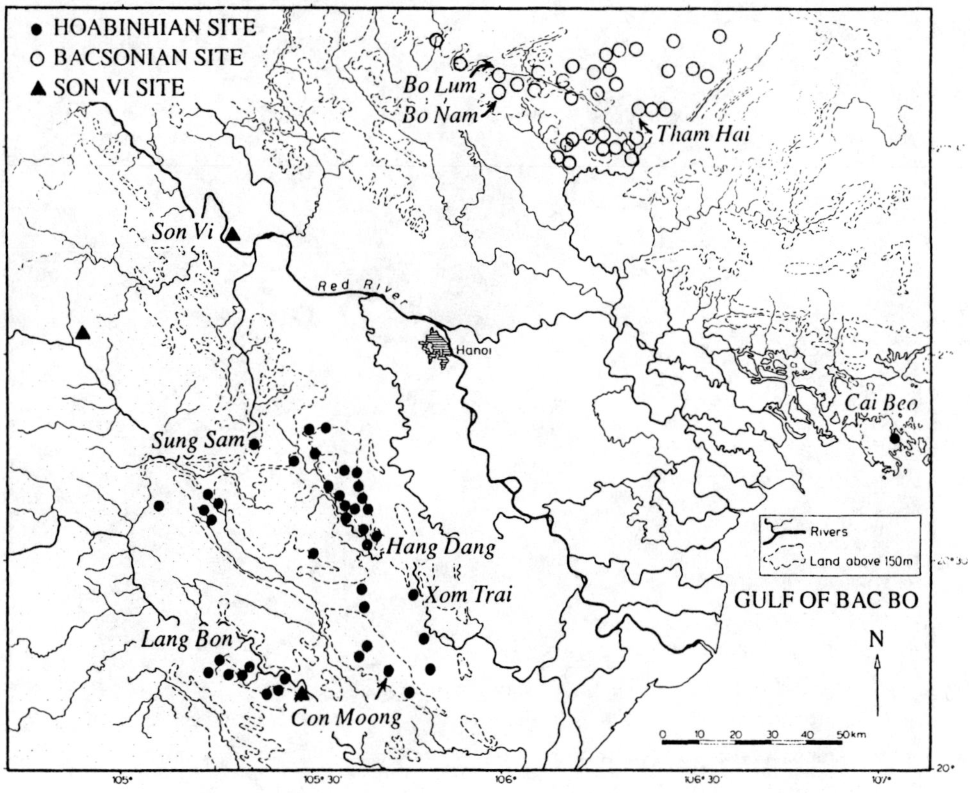

2.5 The distribution of hunter-gatherer sites in the Bac Bo region.

2.6 The site of Lang Bon before Colani commenced her excavations there.

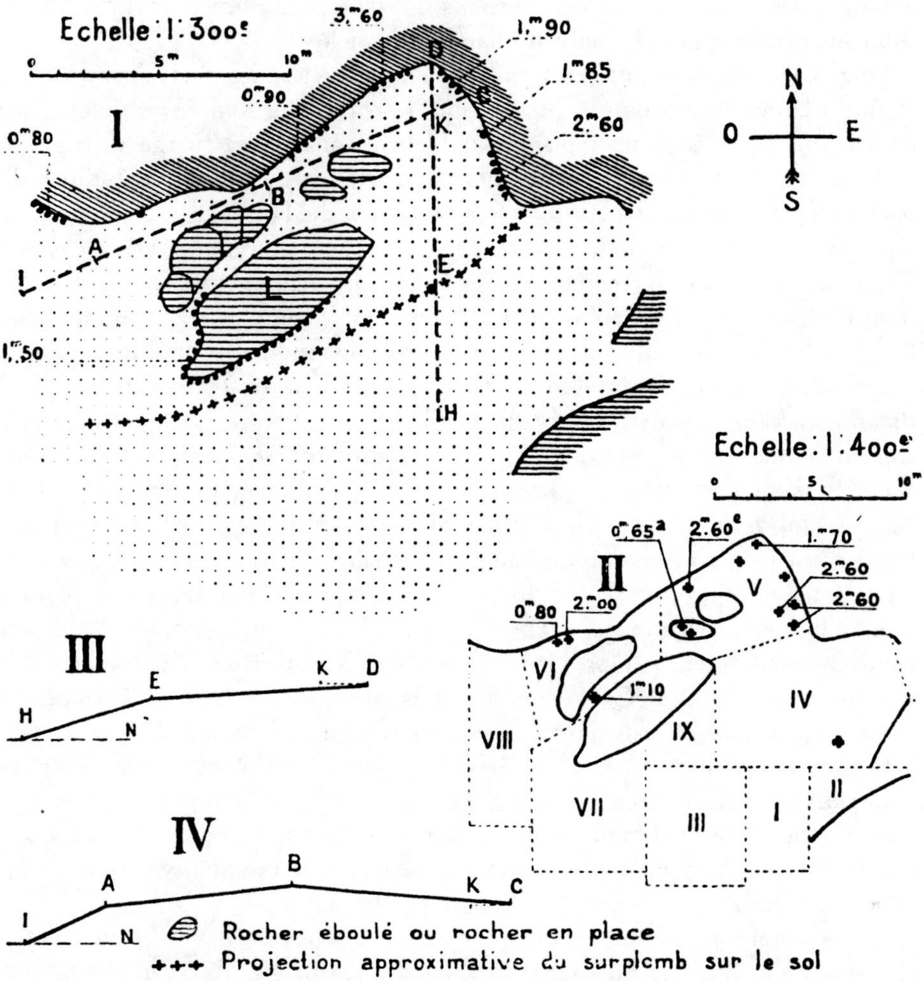

Pour le reste de la légende, voir la fig. 12.

Fig. 24. — Abri sous roche de Lang Bon. I, Plan. II, Plan des fouilles. Les nombres indiquent les profondeurs auxquelles gisaient les crânes. a, actuel, e, entier. 1re section fouillée jusqu'à 3 m. 70 ; IIe jusqu'à 3 m. 15 ; IIIe jusqu'à 2 m. 25 ; IVe jusqu'à 3 m. 25 ; Ve jusqu'à 3 m. 70 ; VIe jusqu'à 3 m. ; VIIe jusqu'à 3 m. 65 ; VIIIe jusqu'à 1 m. 90 ; b. IXe fouillée incomplètement. III & IV, Principales dénivellations selon les lignes déterminées dans le plan I. III, de E en H, dénivellation 1 m. 05 ; de E en D, 1 m. IV, de B en A, dénivellation 70 cm. ; de A en I, 1 m. 40 ; de B en C, 70 cm. C K, D, K, petite plate-forme ; pour simplifier, nous n'en avons pas tenu compte.

2.7 The plans of Lang Bon, as published by Colani in 1930. The policy of making all her findings available facilitates a re-evaluation of her work.

inundation. Contact with coastal groups did take place, however, as is evident from the presence of sea shells in inland rock shelters.

One of the initial foci of research into early hunter and gatherer communities in this area was the province of Bac Son, north of the Red River delta. Early excavations by Madeleine Colani and Henri Mansuy led to the recovery of ground and polished stone implements (Mansuy 1924). These have traditionally been set apart from the flaked stone implements of the Hoabinhian, and given the separate name of Bacsonian, after the province where they were first discovered. There is no general agreement among Vietnamese prehistorians on the relationship between the Hoabinhian and Bacsonian groupings. On the one hand, Luu Tran Tieu thinks that the Bacsonian had Hoabinhian roots but developed independently north of the Red River.[1] Chu Van Tan, on the other hand, feels that the Bacsonian evolved out of the Hoabinhian and represents a technological shift in favour of edge-grinding. This does not, of course, mean that the change occurred simultaneously in all regions with Hoabinhian occupation. Hoang Xuan Chinh feels that the Hoabinhian and Bacsonian were originally separate foci which, with contact and exchange, increasingly merged in terms of a common material culture until they had virtually the same artefact types. Nguyen Van Hao argues that the two were different cultures which developed independently of each other. The problem is that there is insufficient dated material to test these possibilities. Consequently, it is perhaps best not to become too involved with these historic tags, and to recognise that within the hunter-gatherer groups of inland Bac Bo, first edge-grinding of stone cutting tools and then pottery making were adopted. It is also stressed that, during this later context, the sea level started rising, so that from about 7000 years ago we might expect some maritime sites to have survived on the raised fossil beaches left stranded when the sea later fell to its present level.

There is some technological evidence for the succession from flaking to early edge-grinding. Both at Bo Lum and Bo Nam caves, Ha Van Tan (1976) confirmed earlier findings by Mansuy that polishing was applied to the cutting edges of what are, for all intents and purposes, flaked Hoabinhian sumatraliths. Neither site, however, yielded any pottery, suggesting that the technique of polishing was under way there before a ceramic industry. A shell from Bo Nam has been radiocarbon dated to about 6000 b.c., but a specimen from Bo Lum has yielded a radiocarbon date 2000 years earlier (Ha Van Tan 1980). The latter seems extremely early and needs confirmation from further determinations. The same problem applies to dates from a level at Tham Hai Cave containing evidence for edge-grinding. This again has been dated in the vicinity of 7500 b.c. Of course, there is no reason why edge-polishing should not belong to this early horizon. Nor is there any interdict on an earlier trend to polishing in one region over another. In

[1] The opinions expressed in this paragraph were made during a discussion with the author in Ha Noi during May, 1983. To avoid numerous citations involving personal communications, unreferenced referrals to the opinions of Vietnamese scholars in this section involve discussions which took place in Ha Noi.

terms of stratigraphic succession in a given region, however, we can again turn to Con Moong, where polished implements are found in level 3, above the layers containing characteristic Hoabinhian flaked tools.

Hoang Xuan Chinh (1984) has argued very much in favour of the development of edge-ground implements within a Hoabinhian context and has pointed out the importance of this technological development. Not least, he has suggested that it involves the conversion of a hand-held flaked stone tool into a hafted polished axe. The latter is considerably more efficient, particularly in forest clearance and the working of wood. He has also pointed out the existence, in such sites as Xom Trai, of large hoe-like implements which, under microscopic examination, reveal scars suggestive of use in working soil.

One of the principal recent advances in our appreciation of the Hoabinhian has been the light thrown on the environment and economy on the basis of pollen and plant remains. Four sites have yielded pollen spectra spanning the late Pleistocene to the Hoabinhian occupation, and the results reveal that, in the latter, a complex of plants including chenopods, legumes, palms and plants of the Rubiaceae made their appearance. The last named includes about 400 genera and 7000 species, comprising, in the main, herbs, shrubs and climbers. It has been argued that these plants could indicate not only forest clearance, but also the favouring of food plants. The evidence is insufficient to confirm this interesting possibility. It is nevertheless the case that, to this day, the vegetation in the area incorporating Hoabinhian sites includes beans, yams and taro. Excavations at the late Hoabinhian site of Xom Trai have also yielded, for the first time in a Hoabinhian context, the remains of rice. Dao The Tuan (1982) has discerned a distinction between the slender variety in the lower levels, and the presence of both a slender and a rounded grain in the upper ones. He has tentatively proposed that the distinction reflects the process of increased cultivation of this plant. However, caution should be applied because, according to Hoang Xuan Chinh (1984), the site has, like so many others, suffered disturbance in its upper levels.

Nguyen Van Hao (1979) has recently considered the later occupation deposits of the Bacsonian phase, dating to the sixth millennium B.C. (Ha Lung Cave: 5275±60 and 5443±60 B.C.). Cord-marked pottery was common by this period, which now overlaps that when the sea level reached its post-Pleistocene maximum, and it becomes possible to consider coastal as well as inland settlement sites.

Coastal groups in Viet Nam

There is a long tradition of coastal archaeology in Viet Nam and currently Ha Van Tan (1980) recognises three principal early groupings of sites which he calls "cultures". They are termed the Bau Tro, Hoa Loc and Ha Long cultures. Nguyen Van Hao (1979) has added the Cai Beo culture. Although only one site is involved in this last group, it is convenient to begin with it. Cai Beo is situated on the island of Cat Ba, 40 km from the present shore of the Gulf of Bac Bo. The particular importance of this site is that the sequence starts with a stone tool assemblage with strong Hoabinhian affinities. The layer in question also contains pottery bearing basketry impressions. The second layer includes a shouldered axe of a type found occasionally by Colani in Hoabinhian contexts, as well as incised and cord-marked pottery. The early parts of this assemblage have provided a radiocarbon date of 4545±60 B.C. The final assemblage includes shouldered, polished axes and adzes of a type paralleled in the sites of the Ha Long culture. The importance of Cai Beo then, is its documented development, including polished stone axes, of a Hoabinhian-inspired stone technology, to one which the Vietnamese prehistorians describe as Neolithic. A report on the associated biological material should be most revealing.

The individuality of the various groupings of coastal sites in Viet Nam is based on regional distribution and the typology of pottery and stone artefacts. All have in common a marine orientation to the economy, with archaeological layers incorporating the remains of coastal species. Most contain burials interred in a flexed position and associated with some artefacts. It is usually the abundance of pottery and polished stone axes, adzes and "hoes" which have convinced the Vietnamese that they are dealing with an agriculturally orientated society. The remains of plants and animals are rarely mentioned.

Perhaps the best documented such grouping is the Bau Tro culture, called after a site first examined by the French archaeologist, Etienne Patte (Patte 1924). It is a small site set among sand dunes. Within a 3 m stratigraphic sequence, there are three lenses of shell-midden interspersed with sand. One of the middens is notably thicker than the other two and *Placuna*, an oyster-like marine bivalve, is the dominant species. Other food remains include cockles, fish and turtle. There was much evidence for a stone industry based on the manufacture and local sharpening of polished stone adzes. The shouldered variety dominates, but there are also rectangular examples. The rejuvenation of adzes is evidenced by the recovery of stone flakes bearing a polished surface. The pottery is, in the main, decorated with cord-marked impressions, although some have incised decoration and lines of circular indentations. The evidence from Bau Tro indicates a marine adaptation by a people who probably occupied the area for three successive, but fairly brief, periods. They were well familiar with the use of ceramic containers and polished stone cutting implements.

The best insight into the cultural development of this group, however, comes from the recently excavated sites of Phoi Phoi and Phai Nam (Ha Van Tan 1977). The main changes are seen in the increasing predominance of polished, shouldered adzes and the appearance of polished "hoes" attaining at least 30 cm in length. At Phai Nam, however, despite the clear parallels in pottery with that from Phoi Phoi, more of the shouldered adzes were polished. Whereas Ha Van Tan (1980) considers that this reflects a difference in chronology, it could equally be the result of Phai Nam being a site wherein stone adzes were roughed out before being exchanged or completed elsewhere. Adze roughouts were found at Nui Dau, which indicates that such specialisation in the manufacturing process did occur (Ha Van Tan 1976). A similar absence of polishing characterised the stone assemblage of Quynh Van. Two radiocarbon dates from the uppermost horizon suggest that later occupation there is dated to the mid fourth millennium B.C. Since the site is *c* 6 m thick, initial occupation may have been considerably earlier. Thirty-one flexed inhumation burials have been recovered from Quynh Van. Agriculture has been mooted there, but the evidence is based on the presence of pottery rather than any diagnostic plant or animal remains (Ha Van Tan 1980).

The situation is a little clearer for the ensuing periods. Analogous sites are known from the north in Thanh Hoa Province. During the 1930s, Patte (1932) excavated the shell-midden of Da But and recovered polished-edged stone adzes markedly similar to those of the inland Bacsonian sites, much pottery and 12 burials inhumed in a flexed position. Recent Vietnamese excavations have obtained a radiocarbon determination of 5085±60 B.C. from a layer 70 cm from the site's surface (Bayard 1984c). Similar ceramics were recovered in 1977, during excavations at Go Trung. The axes there are distinct from those of the Bau Tro culture. They are polished, and have an ellipsoid cross-section. Shouldered forms are notable for their absence.

It must be clear that this early coastal Vietnamese "Neolithic" is an enigmatic entity. In the absence of detailed appraisals of settlement patterns, biological data and palaeo-environments, we are left with the unsatisfactory situation of documenting the presence of agriculture on the basis of pottery and polished stone axes, rather than on biological materials which reflect subsistence activities.

In due course, the recovery of biological material, and the establishment of a chronological framework, will assist greatly in the formulation of models which bring the coastal and inland settlements together in a coherent relationship. It is predicted that trends towards the establishment of food production will be identified among the growing number of sedentary coastal groups. Such groups may well have initiated the settlement of the Middle Country, the name given to the lowlands immediately above the confluence of the Red and Black rivers. These sites are ascribed to the Phung Nguyen culture (see pp. 175-80). The obstacle to testing this possibility is the rarity of well-provenanced biological remains and the consideration of inter-site relations through the exchange of goods. As we shall see below, a model for a similar situation is available for the Chao Phraya valley.

A hunting and gathering tradition in the North Thai uplands

During the mid 1960s, Chester Gorman initiated a research programme in the uplands of Northern Thailand, his objective being to find out more about local prehistoric hunter-gatherers and ascertain whether they became involved in plant cultivation. He chose the rugged karst terrain of Mae Hongson Province as his specific area, where the limestone crags and valleys are cut by swift-flowing streams (Fig. 2.8). Unlike the other two areas considered, it is far from the coast. Kiernan *et al.* (1987) have recently re-examined the distribution of rock shelters in this area and have identified numerous sites which reveal either prehistoric or more recent wooden boat burials. If it is confirmed that these caves, the distribution of which is seen in Fig. 2.9, were all occupied by hunter-gatherers, then their distribution with its close relationship to streams would match that documented in Viet Nam.

Gorman's first excavation took place at Spirit Cave, located on a hillside overlooking the Khong stream (Fig. 2.10). This perennial stream flows into the Pai River, a tributary of the Salween. The cave commands a fine view over the valley and surrounding hills which, even during the dry season, are covered by a canopied, evergreen forest. Kuchler and Sawyer (1967) described the valley floor vegetation in this region as a dense cover of tall canopy trees, with *Dipterocarpus obtusifolius* and *Tectona grandis* (teak) predominating, a sub-canopy of medium trees, and a floor-cover which includes vines, grasses and bamboo. Ascending from the valley floor to the cave, we encounter, at *c* 450 m above sea level, a transition to a forest with two distinct canopies. *Dipterocarpus costatus* and *Mosinda angustifolia* are important in each layer, but there is much more open ground-cover. This vegetation pattern surrounds the cave, located *c* 650 m above sea level, and so on up to the ridge tops at 750 m. Within reach of the cave, however, there are ridges and summits over 900 m where we encounter a forest of pine and oak with a dense, grassy ground-cover. Assuming a generally similar pattern in prehistory, the site would have been located within Holdridge's subtropical, wet forest. Recently deposited alluvium covers the narrow Khong stream valley, while the hill slopes comprise either limestone outcrops or pockets of red, limestone-derived soils. None of these is currently cropped in the vicinity of Spirit Cave, but they are favoured for horticulture where they occur within easy reach of modern Shan villages. The distribution of animal species today integrates with these three vegetational resource-zones. The river and its margins sustain the otter and fishing cat, and a wide range of shellfish and fish. The canopied forest harbours the main arboreal animals which include the langur, macaque and gibbon, a range of civets and small cats, the clouded leopard and a considerable range of squirrels. Terrestrial species are thinly distributed but comprise deer, pig, wild cattle, serow, goral and their predators, the leopard and tiger. Formerly, rhinoceros and elephant were present.

The complex of caverns which comprises Spirit Cave is quite similar in size to the Hoabinhian shelters in Bac Bo (Fig. 2.11). All three shelters revealed prehistoric occupation, but the middle one had the deepest stratigraphical sequence, and it was there that excavation began during May 1966 (Gorman 1972, 1977). The cave was divided by Gorman into metre squares, and excavation followed

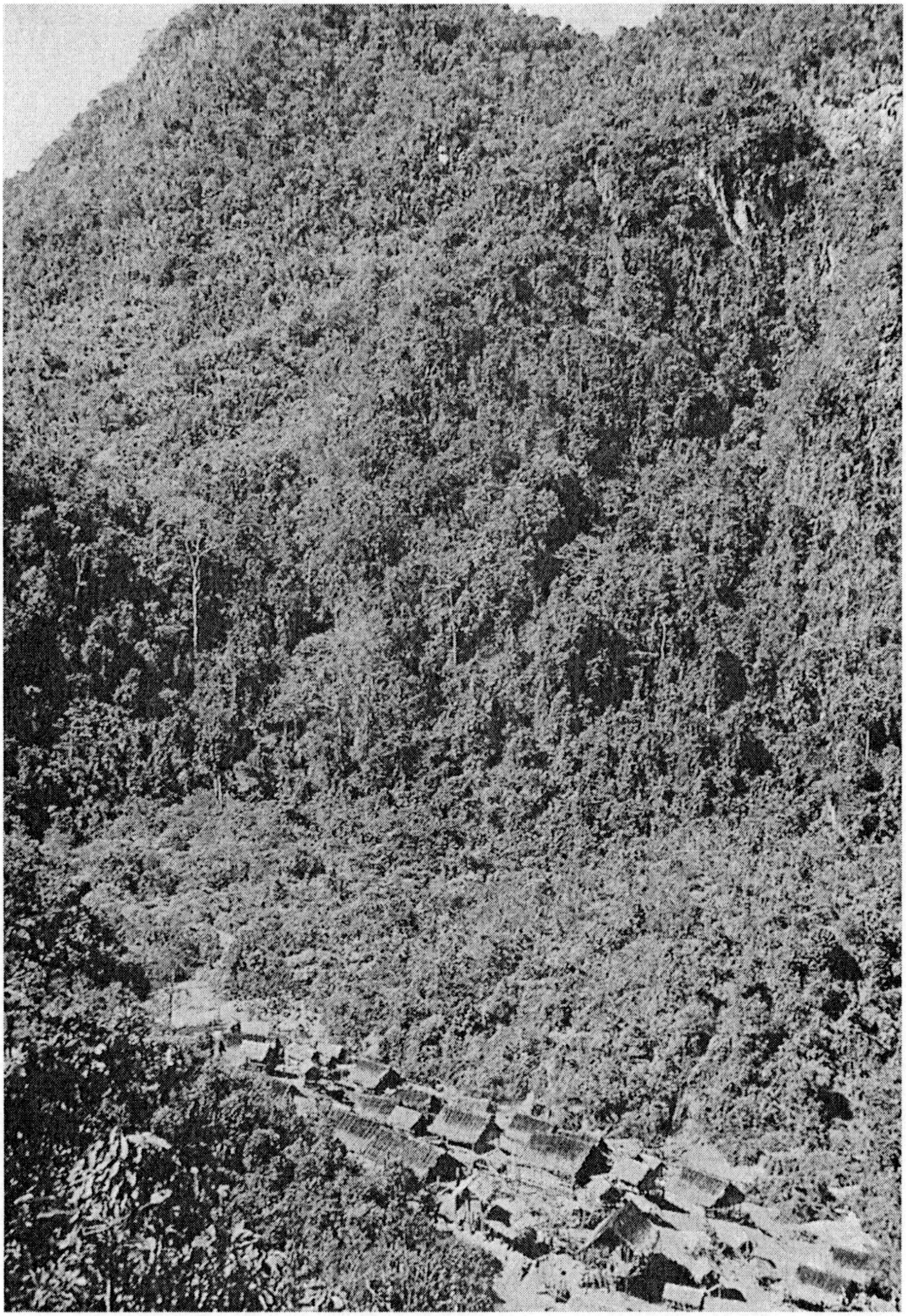

2.8 The karst uplands of Thailand are very rugged and are currently occupied by the so-called "hill tribes". A Lahu village is seen here, near the prehistoric site of Banyan Valley Cave.

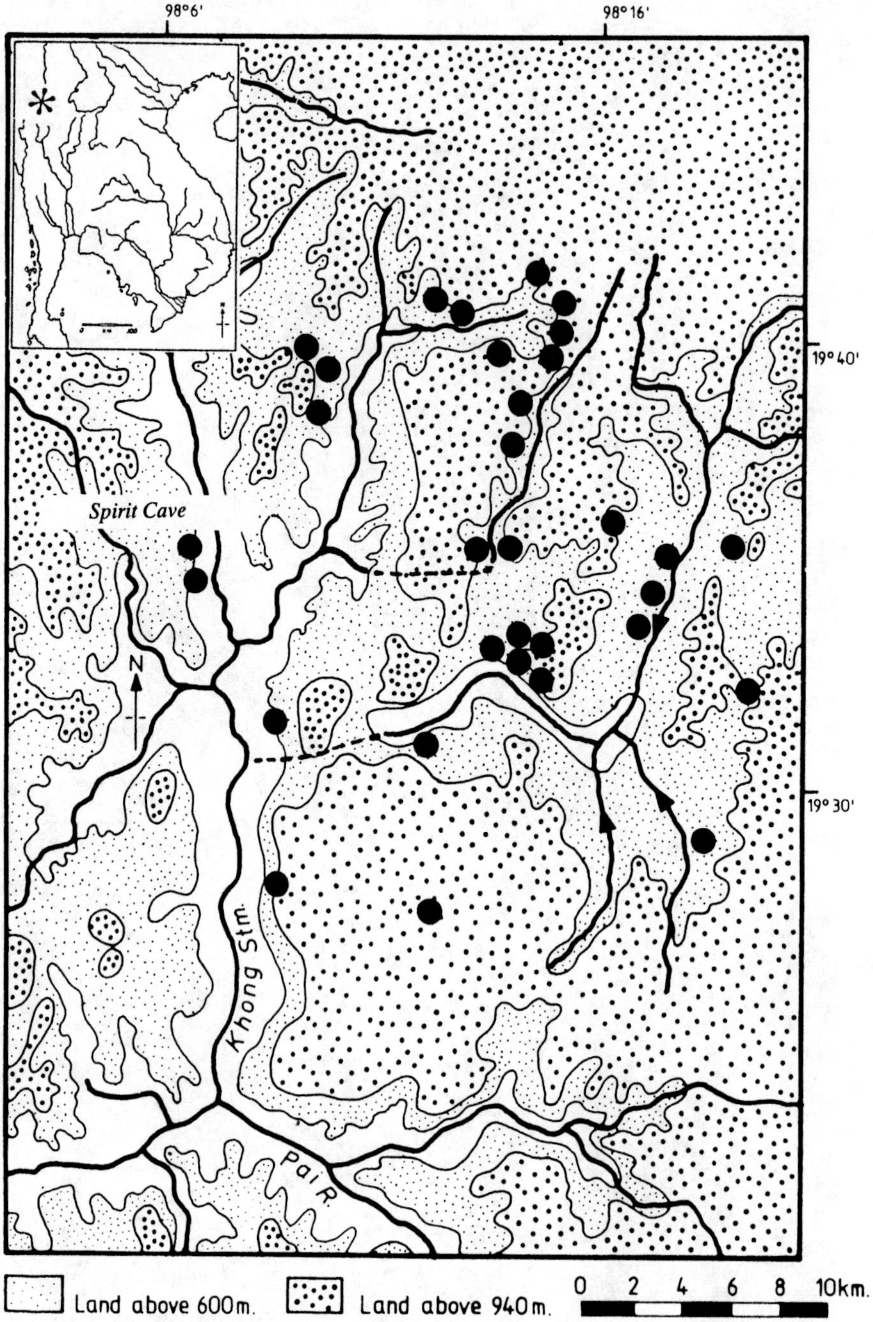

2.9 The distribution of rock shelter sites in the North Thai study area. It is not yet established that all were occupied by hunter-gatherers during prehistory, but the discovery of surface finds makes it highly likely. (Courtesy, Kevin Kiernan.)

the cultural stratigraphy. Progress was slow, because all material excavated was passed through screens in order to recover microscopic plant remains. Although pits and hollows reflecting animal disturbances were encountered, it was possible to recognise a very clearly stratified series of different soils, some with superimposed ashy lenses representing hearths.

When the site was first occupied, it was a small, dry rock shelter. Its occupants scooped out shallow depressions, laid sticks in a radial manner like the spokes of a wheel and lit their fires. This activity was followed by a build-up of soil containing cultural material: stone artefacts, food remains and further ashy lenses. This bottom layer was homogeneous, spreading across the excavated area, and may well represent intermittent occupation over a lengthy period. The next layer in the sequence included hearths overlying patches of scorched soil. The greatest depth of build-up took place in the middle part of the shelter, which contrasts with the superceding layer 2. The latter was thickest towards the cave mouth and again comprised a maze of hearths, charcoal lenses and pits dug into layer 3. The surface of layer 2 was so compacted by subsequent occupation that the distinction between it and layer 1 was particularly clear. Moreover, several sherds were found on the trampled surface. One hearth on the surface of layer 2 was associated with a small quadrangular adze and part of another. Several small slate knives were also found. The uppermost and latest cultural layer, number 1, was relatively thin, but is found across the whole excavated area.

2.10 The Khong stream flows along the valley floor below Spirit Cave. Although it is a sharp half-hour climb up the surrounding hillside, prehistoric people took shellfish up to the cave to eat.

When the excavation was complete, Gorman turned to the question of dating, and removed charcoal samples from the baulks between squares to ensure that their relationships to the excavation layers were known. It was possible to identify most of the charcoal fragments as derived from bamboo, a plant which decays rapidly under tropical conditions. This is particularly advantageous, because it rules out the possibility of old wood fragments producing spuriously early dates. It seems that the concentration of pottery sherds and the quadrangular adze from the surface of layer 2 date to about 6000 B.C. The transition from layer 4 to 3 occurred about 7500 B.C. and layer 4 has dates in the region of 9000 – 10,000 B.C. The occupation of Spirit Cave thus took place intermittently from at least 9500 and perhaps as early as 11,000 B.C. and ended about 5500 B.C. (Fig. 2.12). All the stone artefacts found in layers 2–4 correspond with the several forms found in Bac Bo. We find unifacial discoids, grinding-stones and flakes which bear signs of edge damage. The surfaces of all the grinding-stones bear traces of crushed red ochre or iron oxide, fragments of which are found at the site. Of particular interest was the finding that about a third of the flakes had clearly been used, for microscopic examination revealed thin striations running both along the worked surfaces and vertical to them. White and Gorman's (1979) analysis suggests that they result from sharpening the tool by removing flakes from the working edge. A group of small calcite blades also have abrasions and striations. Their function is hard to document, but the possibility that they were

2.11 Spirit Cave during the course of the excavations. It is a small rock shelter, remote from a source of water, but well placed for hunting and foraging.

used, at least in part, to fashion wooden implements, must be seriously considered. The large unifacial discoids bear many small stepped flake scars along their edges suggesting use in battering or crushing.

The break between layer 2 and those preceding it saw the advent of pottery, quadrangular stone adzes and small, slate knives. Characteristic flaked stone tools continued in use, however, and some were even found lying on the surface of the rock shelter when it was first visited by Gorman. An important point about Spirit Cave is that pottery is associated with artefacts of long local ancestry. When we turn to the ceramics themselves, it is possible to recognise several styles of finish. The great majority (331 out of 426 fragments) were shaped by using the paddle and anvil technique. This involves using a paddle, commonly made of wood, to beat the exterior surface of the clay, while an anvil is held against the interior to facilitate shaping. Those who made the Spirit Cave pottery also wrapped cordage round the paddle, hence the surface of the vessels contains a negative imprint of the cordage used. By taking an impression, it is possible to define the characteristics of the twine. There are many ways of plaiting and a wide variety of plant materials which can be used in this manner. One can twist the fibre clockwise or anticlockwise, and subsequently join together the strands so created into thicker cordage. In so doing, the strands can be tightly or loosely coiled, a variable which affects the so-called "helix" angle. This fine division is relevant for the prehistorian, because it admits a detailed grouping of an otherwise amorphous category of "cord-marked" ware. Most of the ceramics from Spirit Cave have both the clockwise and anticlockwise twist, and a relatively loose (10–20°) helix angle suggesting a coarse parent fibre such as rafia. There are,

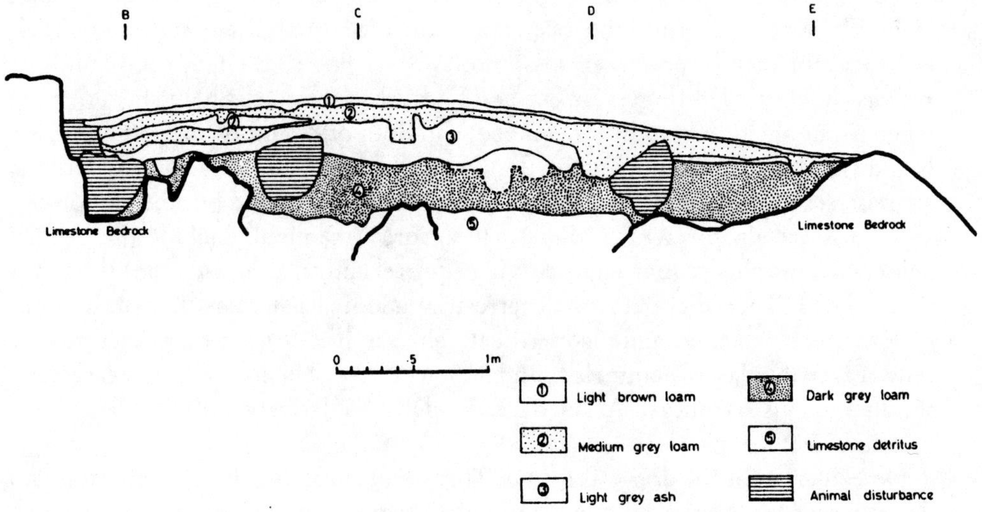

2.12 The stratigraphic section of Spirit Cave reveals a fairly shallow build-up of occupation material, largely dominated by ashy hearths.

however, a few distinct sherds with a very tight twist and fine fibre, while another restricted group was impressed with a fine net, then coated with an organic resinous substance. Cordage is a basic component of bamboo traps, but we are left to speculate on the availability of the latter.

The unmarked vessels had burnished interiors. This technique involves turning a pebble or alternative hard implement across the clay when leather hard, and makes the fired vessels better suited to retain water. The netted ceramics, however, had a continuation of the resinous coat on the interior surfaces. The potters also crushed local calcite as a tempering agent, and mixed it with the clay before shaping the vessel. The exterior colour of individual pots varied, the principal range being from dark grey to dark brown. The balance of the sample was characterised by all-over exterior burnishing with occasional incised lines. Both the tempering material and form of the sherds suggest that the manufacturing technique was similar to that of the cord-marked vessels.

The screening undertaken at Spirit Cave led to the collection of a microfauna which complements the larger animal bones found and described at most other hunter-gatherer sites where such a procedure was not undertaken. Moreover, the retention of all fragments of bone made it possible to outline aspects of behaviour such as cooking techniques and animal processing. The assemblages from each level are extremely fragmentary, and many of the large limb-bone fragments bear the traces of battering. The close conjunction of unifacial discoids with such comminuted bone fragments at the related site of Steep Cliff Cave hints strongly that they were used, among other tasks, in food preparation. Intense charring on broken bone surfaces further suggests that the meat adhered to the bone during cooking or drying over an open fire.

Many species were brought to Spirit Cave. Although a sharp half-hour climb from the Khong stream, the occupants included the valley bottom in their territory, for each layer contains fish bones belonging to the Cyprinid family as well as the discarded fingers or chelae of a freshwater crab. Shellfish, too, were taken to the shelter from the stream bed, and both otter and fishing cat bones are found there. Arboreal animals predominate. All local primates apart from man are represented, the langur and macaque being most common, but the gibbon and slow loris are also present. Other small arboreal mammals include the banded palm civet, the elusive marten, the flying squirrel and small squirrels of the genus *Callosciurus*. Then there are small terrestrial mammals such as the bamboo rat, badger, porcupine and agile leopard cat. The sambar deer and pig deer are the only reasonably large mammals found at Spirit Cave. The former is the largest of the indigenous Southeast Asian deer, while the relatively rare pig deer is of medium size.

No evidence for the dog was found. This is not surprising because there are no native wolves in Southeast Asia from which dogs could have been domesticated. Dogs are particularly useful in hunting the large ground-dwelling animals such as the wild cattle, rhinoceros, pig and deer. While it is not contested that all those species can be obtained by other means, such as spear-traps, it is possible that their rarity reflects the hunting techniques employed. Indeed, anyone who has lived in the canopied jungle of upland Northern Thailand cannot fail to be impressed by the number of animals adapted to the upper tree-cover. Obtaining squirrels, langurs and the marten would have been greatly facilitated by a system of traps or light, accurate, projectile points. Traps, too, could have been effective in securing the smaller ground-dwelling mammals such as the rat, badger and porcupine.

One of the most important aspects of the excavations at Spirit Cave was the recovery of plant remains. Yen (1977) has recognised about 22 genera and has suggested their possible uses. Quite the most numerous were seed fragments of the genus *Canarium*. All were smashed, probably to obtain the edible kernels. Three samples of betel nut calyces were found in layers 1 and 2 which suggest that this widespread stimulant was in use at least towards the end of the occupation period. The kernels of *Madhuca* (butternut) and fruit of the *Euphorbiaceae* are particularly interesting because they are a source of poison. Poison-tipped projectile points would help account for the presence of the bones of elusive arboreal mammals. Seven fragments of bamboo stem indicate interest in this valuable plant. Yen has noted that Canarium and *Madhuca* are exploited by the local Shan for their resins and gums, substances valuable in hafting composite implements and coating pottery vessels to improve their water retention. The genera *Prunus* (almond), *Terminalia* and *Castanopsis* were all represented by seed shells or kernels in layer 3, and probably evidence food collection in the surrounding forests.

Thus far, the plants described grow in the present forest in Northern Thailand. We can now turn to a group of plants currently cultivated in the area, fragments of which were found at Spirit Cave. Layers 2 and 3 yielded the remains of *Lagenaria* (bottle gourd) fruit shell. This plant may be eaten or, when mature, used as a container. It is difficult to be sure of some of the identifications which must, like those for the mammalian species, remain tentative. Among this group are nine specimens which look like peas. The problem is that their condition of preservation makes it difficult to rule out the possibility that they are, in fact, palm kernels. Two bean-like seeds were found in layers 2 and 4 respectively, but precise identification is again not possible.

The great value of this assemblage was to demonstrate beyond doubt that the occupants of the cave exploited a range of local plants with a variety of potential uses. Some today are used solely for food, others as condiments and stimulants. Then there are sources of poison, gum and resin. Indeed, any survey of hunter-gatherer occupation of the evergreen forest habitat following the research at Spirit Cave must acknowledge the broad spectrum of resources, and the intimate aquaintance of the occupants with the plant and animal world around them. The Spirit Cave assemblage, however, added to the questions surrounding such societies by raising new issues.

2.13 Banyan Valley Cave is larger than Spirit Cave, and is located adjacent to a rushing stream just as it disappears into a sinkhole in the limestone bluff. Excavations there in 1972-3 led to the discovery of wild rice remains.

Among these was the possibility that the leguminous plants and nuts came from cultivated plants. Were this the case, then the occupants of this site would rank among the earliest plant cultivators known. There is also the association between the flaked stone tool industry and novel artefacts including pottery and ground stone adzes in the uppermost layer. While pottery vessels *per se* do not indicate agriculture, their common occurrence in agricultural contexts does raise the possibility that major economic change was underway in the orbit of Spirit Cave. In prehistoric research, one site imparts only limited information. Hence the concern for locating a number of sites in order to reconstruct a settlement pattern. It is possible that Spirit Cave represents but one facet of a given group's activities. Gorman therefore returned to Mae Hongson in 1972 to seek further sites and, by excavation, resolve some of the problems posed above. In the event, two further caves were excavated.

Banyan Valley Cave is located about 30 km east of Spirit Cave. Unlike the latter, it is situated beside a permanent stream just as it cascades into a cleft in the limestone bluff (Fig. 2.13). It is hemmed in by precipitous slopes, and by the canopied, evergreen forest. The hillside has a series of caverns. The one yielding prehistoric remains is considerably broader and deeper than Spirit Cave. A test square excavated there during April 1972 revealed stratified occupation layers

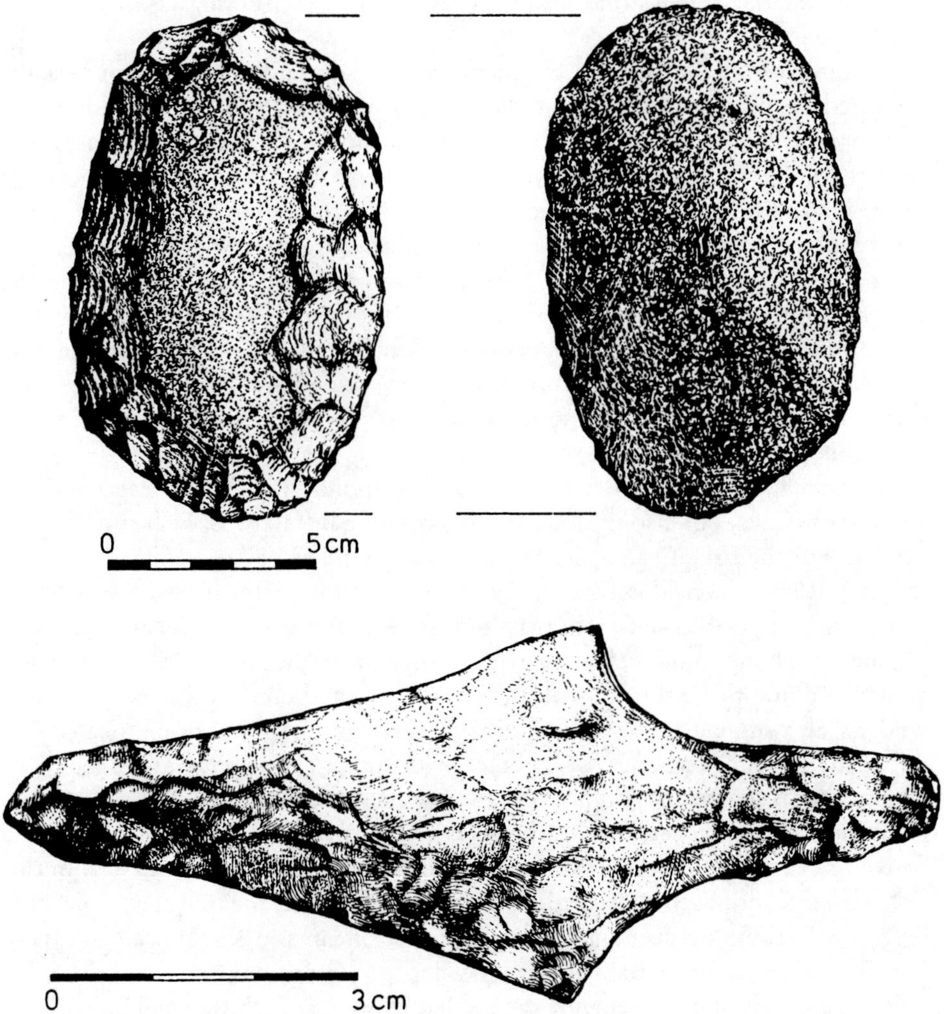

2.14 A sumatralith or unifacial discoid from Banyan Valley Cave, together with a unique tanged stone projectile point found there in 1972.

with hearths, just like those at Spirit Cave, and the uppermost contained cord-marked pottery. Gorman, however, also recognised several husk fragments unmistakably derived from rice. A larger excavation was underway by December of the same year. The impression gained during excavation was that the sequence and contents of the layers were similar to those at Spirit Cave. Screening yielded numerous small animal bones and fragments of plants. The same range of stone tools was present (Fig. 2.14). Again, the upper layers provided a sample of pottery sherds, even the same little bifacially-worked slate knives and quad-rangular edge-ground adzes. More rice husks were present in the upper layer and a sophisticated, tanged stone projectile point, unlike anything else found in a similar context, was found.

Examination of the pottery fragments in the laboratory has shown that the preferred decorative technique at Banyan Valley Cave was cord-marking, but there was a greater variation of styles than at Spirit Cave. In some cases, the cord-marking was restricted to bands with narrow undecorated strips between them. In another, irregular striations were cut at right-angles across a sherd otherwise completely cord-marked. As vertical cord-marking approached the rim on a third specimen, it gave way to a band of burnishing. Apart from the presence of the burnished wares similar to those from Spirit Cave, there were a few examples with meandering incised lines set in pairs, enclosing a row of dots impressed with a pointed implement. While showing parallels with Spirit Cave, the Banyan Valley assemblage seemed more variable, and possibly represented a later timespan.

The animal bones from Banyan Valley correspond, in most respects, to those from Spirit Cave, but also indicate some intriguing differences. Fish and crab are present, but the fish are smaller. The stream at Banyan Valley, while adjacent to the cave itself, is considerably smaller than the Khong stream near Spirit Cave. The same range of small arboreal and terrestrial mammals recurs, but one fragmentary bone could well come from a dog. Given the absence of wolves from which to domesticate this animal, the specimen could conceivably come from a wild jackal, a cuon, a domesticated form of jackal, or possibly a domesticated dog obtained through exchange or contact with an intrusive, but alien group of people. At present one cannot be sure which of these alternatives is most plausible. It is, however, interesting to note that nearly all the large herbivores native to Northern Thailand were recognised among the bone sample from this site. This includes both species of rhinoceros, wild cattle, the muntjak or barking deer, pig deer, mouse deer and serow. The only one missing is the water-buffalo, but the environment of Banyan Valley Cave would not have attracted it.

Yen's analysis of plant remains shows that many match those from Spirit Cave (Yen 1977). Canarium seeds, bamboo, cucumber and gourd fragments, together with the same possible legume seeds, point to an interest in plant communities in the cave's vicinity. The discovery of 110 rice husks, however, added a new dimension, and these have been analysed by Yen to ascertain whether they come from a wild or cultivated form, or from one documenting early trends towards a domesticated variety. In order to clarify this issue, Yen collected 128 samples of modern wild and cultivated rice grains from tribal subsistence contexts. A characteristic of most domesticated varieties is the presence of an awn at the tip of the grain sheath. None of the Banyan Valley specimens displayed any such development. The surface structure of the husks is also a clue to domestication. Again, the Banyan Valley specimens had the ragged character of the wild form. At present, it seems that the sample is more likely to come from a wild stand of rice than a cultivated source. Only husks were found at the site, many of which were fractured. By experimenting with tools similar to the grinding-stones found there, Yen was able to replicate, on modern rice, the breakage pattern of the prehistoric husks while removing the grain.

At the time of excavation, it was anticipated that the site was occupied during approximately the same timespan as Spirit Cave. The pottery and stone adzes looked of similar style and tradition, and the unifacial discoids were virtually identical. Both displayed a broad-ranging food quest in the forested, riverine habitat characteristic of the area. The dates, however, indicated that the site was occupied much later than expected. The lower levels yielded dates of about 3500 B.C., but the uppermost was as late as *c* A.D. 900. The site assumes, therefore, a particular interest because it demonstrates the long currency of hunting and gathering in the uplands of Northern Thailand by essentially small, mobile groups.

Steep Cliff Cave was the last of the three rock shelters to be excavated (Fig. 2.15). A narrow shelter on a precipitous slope, it added a further dimension to our knowledge by providing a bone sample in which, while large animals predominated, the small arboreal mammals were still present. Beginning with the latter, we find small numbers of squirrels and civets. One species not found at Banyan Valley and Spirit Caves is the Himalayan striped squirrel, a tiny animal

2.15 Steep Cliff Cave, excavated in 1973, revealed a thick, ashy bone-midden which may reflect the local smoking of meat obtained from wild cattle, deer and water-buffalo.

weighing under 50 gm which lives in the middle and upper tree-canopy. Macaques and langurs are again present, as well as the giant red flying squirrel, which nests in tall trees or in clefts on cliff faces. The slow loris is mainly nocturnal and arboreal.

The excavation provided almost a thousand fragments of turtle or tortoise carapace and plastron fragments, some of which came from a ground tortoise adapted to a woodland habitat. Fish bones are absent, however, and only one fragment of crab claw was found. This site is a long walk from the nearest permanent water. Given this situation, it is remarkable that the larger species include a sample of five water-buffalo. Indeed, the thick bone-midden which represents one of the cultural layers includes the bones of at least three wild cattle, two water-buffalo, seven sambar deer, four muntjak, two pig deer, two pigs and 600 fragments of turtle or tortoise carapace. It may be significant that the two fragments of dog bone from the site were also found in this midden. It is possible that, by this juncture, the domestic dog had been introduced into Southeast Asia. The tiger, leopard and clouded leopard are rarely represented.

All the major bones of the large bovids (cattle and buffalo) and of the sambar deer were found at Steep Cliff Cave. Skull fragments, teeth, vertebrae and even hoof-bones were no rarer than the more favoured bones, if meat alone was the objective of butchery. This situation is the more remarkable because access to the site from any direction is precipitous. It is far removed from the favoured environment for at least the water-buffalo, if not for wild cattle and deer as well. Moreover, most bones were smashed and charred. Even compact and robust bones bore the marks of heavy and persistant battering.

There are a number of reasons which may explain this situation. One is that the animals were tame and killed *in situ*. This seems unlikely given the distance from the site to water, a daily requirement for all the animals in question. The cattle bones are also as large as the modern wild animals in the area today, so to suggest that all six large species in question were tamed would be highly implausible. Nevertheless, some of the animals may have died locally after being driven over the edge of the precipice above the site. A third possibility is that the whole carcass was jointed and carried to the rock shelter for processing. In an area where competition with large scavangers is present, this would have been a logical procedure. The Lahu living in this region today often gut and dismember game in this manner. They then slowly smoke the meat, and the ash lenses from their fires were strikingly similar to those being excavated in the prehistoric layers encountered by Gorman. An interpretation which sees dismembered limbs manhandled to Steep Cliff Cave, further butchered and the meat dried, accords best with the available data.

At the same time, the people involved obtained canarium seeds and seeds resembling the pea or the palm, both of which are found in the thick bone-midden. Pepper-vine seeds, almond shells, bamboo and bean-like remains occur in other levels of the site which are not dominated by concentrations of bone.

The Northern Thai uplands: summary

Radiocarbon dates for Steep Cliff Cave fall within the range 5500–3500 B.C. The three caves thus form a sequence of occupation, beginning at *c* 9000 B.C. at Spirit Cave and ending about a thousand years ago at Banyan Valley. This sequential aspect in the dating is bound to affect any interpretation of this hunting-gathering group in Northern Thailand, because it is necessary to seek differences between the sites which might reflect the course of cultural change. It would, for example, be feasible to propose that, following a period of concentration on small game animals and forest foraging, the occupants of the Northern Thai uplands increased their hunting repertoire to include the larger herbivores, and finally augmented their subsistance base with the collection of wild rice. We are, however, dealing with a large area and only three excavated sites. We have no information to illuminate activities away from rock shelters, if only because such dry shelters protect cultural remains from decay and erosion. A reasonable objective under such circumstances, is to define common factors in each site as consistent aspects of the North Thai hunter-gatherer complex, particularly given local environmental features. At the same time, it is felt desirable to explain changes which occurred with time in order to define any apparent historical trends.

All sites reflect a generalised subsistance economy in which plants, reptiles, fish, crabs, shellfish, land snails and small forest mammals were sought. While all sites differ in their physical setting, at least Spirit and Banyan Valley caves were still within wet, evergreen, canopied forest with access, albeit at times distant, to water resources. They also reveal an interest in bamboo, and yield a common range of unifacial discoids probably used to process animal remains. They used stone tools to fashion implements of wood. At least by 6000 B.C., and probably much earlier still, they employed twine, poison and resinous gum which, together with bamboo, remain to this day the constituents of composite trapping, snaring and hunting implements.

From *c* 6000 B.C., however, a series of changes occurred. These include novel forms of artefact, and their implications are profound. Those who occupied Spirit Cave after the accumulation of level 2 used pottery vessels, hafted polished stone adzes, and found a use for small slate knives. Yet they also adhered to the traditional forms of stone implements. The occupants of Steep Cliff and Banyan Valley caves left behind dog bones. We cannot be sure that these do not come from the native wild jackal, but we do know that, by at least 2000 B.C., people with dogs domesticated from wolves were already living in the Khorat plateau to the east. Moreover, the presence of the dog bones coincided with those of large wild cattle, water-buffalo and a variety of deer. Towards the end of this long sequence, wild rice was exploited.

The discovery of leguminous plant remains at Spirit Cave prompted a suggestion that they were from a cultivated species (Solheim 1970). This notion formed the basis of claims that Northern Thailand was an area in which cultivation of plants occurred at a very early date. It is now felt that the early plant remains from that site are so few, and so tentatively identified, that a more cautious interpretation is necessary. Certainly, broad-spectrum foraging was the mainstay of subsistence at the three sites. It is not inconceivable that certain forest plants were favoured by the removal of their competitors, but this is a widespread phenomenon among plant gatherers, and does not constitute the same potential basis for major cultural changes as does sedentism or the cultivation of rice.

There remains the problem of explaining the appearance of novel artefact types in layer 1 at Spirit Cave. Let us first consider what function these artefacts may have performed. Pottery vessels can fulfil a wide variety of roles. The visitor to a modern Thai–Lao village will find them used for steaming rice, storing water, rice and a host of other foodstuffs, for protecting young silkworms from red ants, or in use as flower pots and drums (Calder 1972). Ceramics are often made by specialists and traded widely, depending on the form of transport available. No complete vessel shapes are known for these three sites, but some attention was clearly given, through organic coating and burnishing, to the question of permeability. It is possible that the local people themselves experimented with firing clay vessels in response to a perceived need. It must be recalled, that there may have been a hiatus of many generations between the abandonment of Spirit Cave at the close of layer 2, and its subsequent re-occupation by people bringing ceramics with them, or, alternatively, the occupants may have traded with full-time pottery-making specialists.

Although there are rare exceptions, pottery has a strong relationship with sedentary societies. This is not fortuitous. After all, pottery is useful for storing foodstuffs, but its fragility is an encumbrance to people accustomed to mobility. Pottery, once it appeared at Spirit Cave, was not found consistently in Northern Thailand. It is absent from basal layers at Banyan Valley. This intermittent presence does suggests that exchange with another, possibly sedentary, group is a more likely explanation than its local development and manufacture. There is at least one further possibility. During the dry season in Thailand, when the harvest is in and agricultural tasks are minimal, farmers may take to the hills to hunt. We have no evidence documenting activity away from upland rock shelters. Under these circumstances it is possible that, from *c* 6000 B.C., prehistoric people divided their time between cultivating in the lowland valleys and moving into the forested uplands for dry-season hunting and trapping.

Whichever interpretation is borne out by future findings, the three excavated caves do permit clear insight into a local adaptation by broad-spectrum hunter-gatherers. For many millennia, they opted for elevated rock shelters for part, if not all, of their activities. If modern hill tribes' opinions are any guide, this pattern of settlement would have lessened the impact of spirits, particularly those appearing under the guise of the lowland malarial mosquito.

The lengthy occupation in the uplands manifested by transient use of rock shelters poses the possibility that these foragers attained a position of equilibrium with their environment. Much recent research has shown that, far from being concerned over food supplies, hunter-gatherer societies, even those surviving under harsh marginal conditions, spend relatively little time engaged in the food quest. Sahlins (1972) has described hunter-gatherers as "the original affluent society". While such groups may be poor in material goods, their ideological and spiritual lives are often more complex than the modern city dwellers'. Archaeological research has shown that some hunter-gatherer peoples have successfully survived and maintained their way of life over very long periods of time. The Australian Aborigine has an ancestry stretching back over 50,000 years. During that time, there have been periods of adjustment to cope with fluctuations in climate and to accommodate new peoples and ideas. When the first European explorers described the way of life of the Inuit, the buffalo hunters of the Great Plains and even the inhabitants of Tierra del Fuego, they were witnessing the product of many millennia of successful adaptation by hunter-gatherer societies. The question posed is not so much how hunter-gatherers survived for so long, but rather why some of them adopted agriculture and stock-raising at all.

When we consider the characteristics of the hunter-gatherers in Northern Thailand, we find a long-term adaptation to the subtropical, wet, evergreen forest. One characteristic of this forest type is the insulating effect of the upper tree-canopy. Humidity and the temperature range at ground level are far more stable than under deciduous cover, or following forest clearance. Of course, in monsoonal conditions, there is a dry season, but its impact is dulled and its duration decreased in the higher altitude, wet, monsoon forest. Operating in such an environment was facilitated by a succession of available foods. While the hardest time of the year was undoubtedly the end of the dry season, there were still the stream resources and game animals to exploit. Indeed, Gorman (1971) has shown that the shellfish at Spirit Cave were collected in both the wet and dry seasons. Such a changing mosaic of food sources, an economy without specialisation or reliance on any given plant or animal, and even any specific technique of food procurement, is held to favour long-term stability. This is further supported if, as data from the three caves suggest, hunter-gatherer groups were, at least seasonally, small and accustomed to regular movement within their territory. It is a tenable proposition that their broad-spectrum subsistence in this remote place continued until at least A.D. 900 and possibly longer still.

The hunter-gatherer occupation of the Chao Phraya plains

In many respects the environment of the Chao Phraya valley and the surrounding uplands matches that of Bac Bo. Until about 7000 B.C., the sea level was considerably lower, which meant that the Chao Phraya's passage to the sea was longer, and there were more extensive tracts of lowland. With the rise in sea level, the river valley was truncated, and a window opened on prehistoric coastal settlement through the analysis of sites located on raised beaches. The river valleys are likewise surrounded by uplands, within which there are rock shelters containing the remains of hunter-gatherer occupation. Such sites have been identified in the valleys of the Khwae Yai and Khwae Noi rivers in Kanchanaburi Province, Thailand. The first research was undertaken at the caves of Sai Yok and Tham Ongbah by a Danish expedition (van Heekeren and Knuth 1967). It is not possible to consider the results in detail because, in the absence of appropriate methods of screening the deposits, no microfauna has survived for analysis. Only a handful of large animal species is represented, and these almost certainly provide a distorted picture of subsistence activity. The stone artefacts, however, reveal marked similarities to those found in the Hoabinhian caves of Bac Bo. Such is the degree of similarity that the term Hoabinhian has become a general one to encompass sites across the face of Southeast Asia and beyond. The justification for this is the similarity of stone tools and occurrence of them, together with biological remains documenting broad-spectrum foraging and collecting. This usage of the term is not a happy one, particularly since it tends to lend a possibly spurious affinity between sites and regions where we should rather seek individuality and differences. Consequently, in the pages which follow, the sites are referred to as components of regional sequences, with the term Hoabinhian reserved for sites in the eponymous area.

Our knowledge of hunter-gatherer adaptation to the Chao Phraya valley and its surrounding uplands has been greatly enlarged by Pookajorn's excavations at four rock shelters (Pookajorn 1981). All are located on the slopes of low limestone hills which command the terraces of the Khwae Noi River and were probably located in an area of deciduous woodland. The research undertaken has greatly expanded our knowledge of hunter-gatherer groups.

The richest material and best evidence for chronology came from Khao Talu, a cave with several distinct chambers, one of which had been used as a burial area in later prehistory. Many stone beads, polished adzes and broken potsherds, as well as fragments of human bone were found, but unfortunately the whole area had been looted. Under this layer, and within a 3 m section of the adjacent chamber, at least three earlier living floors were found intact. The excavators found sumatraliths as well as flaked points, picks, scrapers and hammer stones. The associated faunal material was rare in the lowest occupation layer, and much bone was so fragmented that identification to species was ruled out. Among the larger species, the sambar deer, pig deer, cattle, pig and muntjac were present. There were also a few tiger bones and the remains of freshwater shellfish, turtle and frog. By screening all excavated soils, Pookajorn recovered fragments of gourd and nut palm. The earliest hunter-gatherer occupation has been dated, on the basis of two radiocarbon dates, to the tenth millennium B.P. There is a date of 5580±850 B.C. for the middle period of occupation, and two dates of 1470±380 and 2265±95 B.C. have been obtained for the latest period of occupation at Khao Thalu. By that period, cord-marked and incised pottery were found in association with the stone implements which, in all levels, reveal marked similarities with the flaked stone industries of the Bac Bo Hoabinhian.

Men Cave is only 30 m from Khao Thalu. A 1.6 m thick horizon of prehistoric occupation material was found there. The stone artefacts included scrapers, side choppers and sumatraliths, and these were associated with a rich assemblage of animal, shell and plant remains. In addition to the species represented at Khao Thalu, there were remains of crocodile, birds, dog and the goral. Excavations at Hip Cave revealed a very similar sequence to that from Khao Thalu. There were four successive living floors, all associated with a characteristic stone industry and assemblage of animal species. Only in the uppermost were pieces of pottery recovered. No radiocarbon dates are available yet, but the chronology is expected to match that from Khao Thalu. Nearby Phet Kuha Cave contained one living floor, but no pottery was encountered. The excavations at these four sites reinforces the idea that hunter-gatherer societies in the western Thai uplands practiced broad-spectrum hunting, gathering and foraging over a period spanning at least nine millennia.

Further research into hunter-gatherer occupation of this area has been undertaken at the cave of Laang Spean, or "bridge cave" (Fig. 2.16). It is located 150 m above sea level on a limestone hill in the valley of the Stung Sangker. The site was excavated by Roland and Cecile Mourer (1970) and, in their principal excavated area, they encountered five successive cultural levels, all of which provided evidence for the material culture, subsistence activities and environment of the hunter-gatherers who lived there. The cave is located about 400 km east of the sites just described in the Khwae Noi valley, and 150 km northeast of the present shore of the Gulf of Siam.

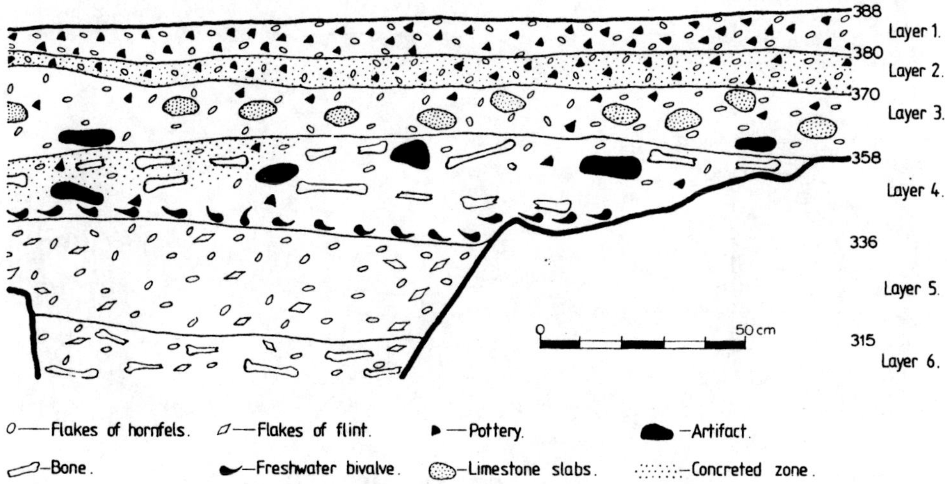

2.16 The stratigraphic section obtained at the site of Laang Spean, an important hunter-gatherer site in Western Cambodia.

The excavators took a series of pollen samples from the archaeological deposits, which revealed that the environs of the cave were probably under forest. It was also noted that fern spores and grass pollen were found, and it is is likely that they were blown to the cave from the surrounding lowlands.

Radiocarbon dates from the successive layers indicate that the initial settlement took place about 7000 B.C., and that the successive occupation events took place 4000, 2000 and 500 B.C and A.D. 900. The lowest layer contained a few flakes of stone, and is not as rich as that laid down during the second occupation, when short axes, scrapers and sumatraliths were encountered. This same level also revealed increasing quantities of cord-marked and paddle-impressed potsherds. The pottery in the succeeding cultural level was also associated with stone flakes and core tools, but was much more complex in terms of shape and decoration. Some pots had ring-footed bases and bands infilled with shell impressions (Fig. 2.17). Cultural levels 4 and 5 have provided some stone flakes and pottery, but the details are not yet available. It can, however, be asserted that most of the stone found is in the form of flakes removed in the manufacture of core tools, indicating local manufacture. Moreover, unlike the situation in Bac Bo, no evidence for edge-grinding or hafting polished axes was found.

The evidence for subsistence is abundant, particularly in the form of animal bones. There is clear evidence for the exploitation of water resources, in the form of turtle remains, crab claws and shellfish. There are many bones from birds,

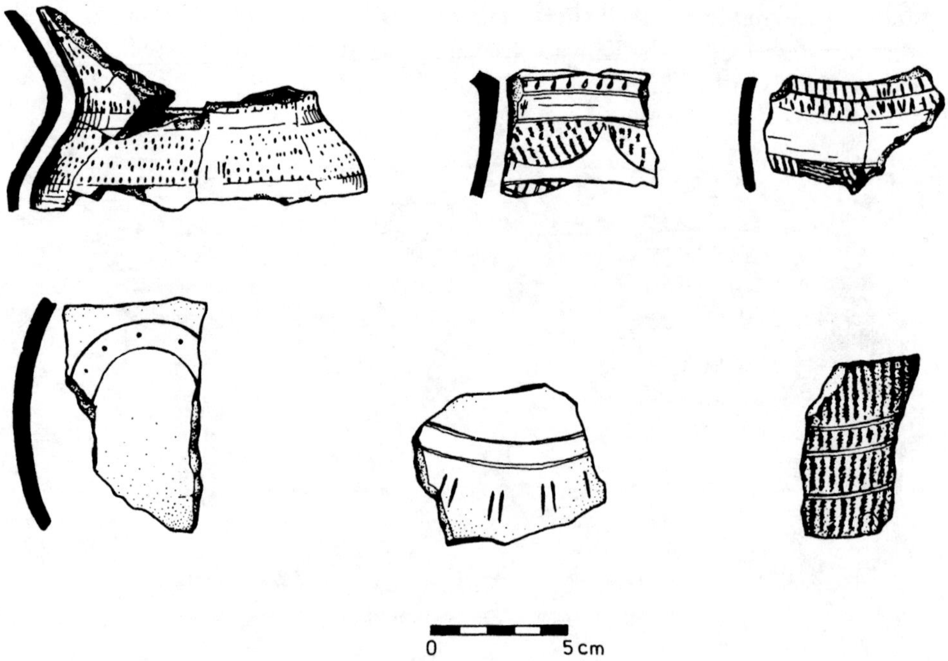

2.17 The pottery from Laang Spean reveals a wide range of decorative styles.

snakes, reptiles and fish. Among the large species, there are the remains of rhinoceros, deer, cattle and monkey. It has often been noted that such hunter-gatherer groups exploited a wide spectrum of available food resources. Mourer (1977), however, is adamant that there is no biological evidence at Laang Spean for agriculture.

Coastal settlement round the Gulf of Siam

As is seen in Fig. 1.3, the terrain underlying the present Gulf of Siam is covered by a shallow sea. This means that any rise or fall in the mean sea level was translated into either extensive inundation, or the exposure of marine sediments. Such adjustments make it imperative to follow the environmental changes associated with the establishment of human settlements. When we turn to this coastal tract, we encounter an entirely new dimension to human settlement, one involving the establishment of sedentism and domestication. This dimension has opened up following the excavation, during seven months in 1985, of Khok Phanom Di, a large (*c* 5 ha) site now situated about 22 km from the present shore of the Gulf of Siam (Figs. 2.18 and 2.19). Much emphasis was given in the field to the issue of the palaeoenvironment. While the excavations were in progress (Fig. 2.20), Maloney was taking cores for the analysis of sediment and pollen remains from the vicinity of the site (Maloney 1987). He has confirmed that the soils of the Bangkok plain comprise, in essence, older marine clays, younger marine clays and the present tidal flats. The first two have not yet been dated in detail, and doubtless there were numerous local changes reflecting isostatic adjustments and sedimentation regimes as well as sea level changes. Maloney's preliminary review of a core taken 200 m southwest of Khok Phanom Di has revealed marine clay to a depth of 2 to 3.5 m below the present ground surface. He has tentatively equated this with the older series of acid sulphate soils of the Bangkok plain. This underlies clays containing pollen from the plants of a brackish-water lagoon. The transition to the brackish-water clays probably equates with the initial occupation of the site nearby. Subsequently, there was a brief episode of higher sea level, indicated by a thin (2.5 cm) band of marine clay. At this point, Khok Phanom Di may have been situated on an island or offshore river-mouth bar. This brief episode was followed by the deposition of further acid sulphate soils laid down under alternating brackish and fresh water conditions. Maloney has also identified possible riverine deposits, which suggest that the course of the ancestral Bang Pakong River may have been close at hand. Hylleberg and Anuwat have added to the preliminary assessment of the palaeoenvironment by identifying some of the microscopic gastropods to freshwater species. Access to permanent freshwater ponds throughout the occupation of the site is also shown by Kijngam's identification of fish species.[2] Thompson oversaw the sampling of exca-

[2] The laboratory analysis of biological remains from the site is in progress and no reports are yet available.

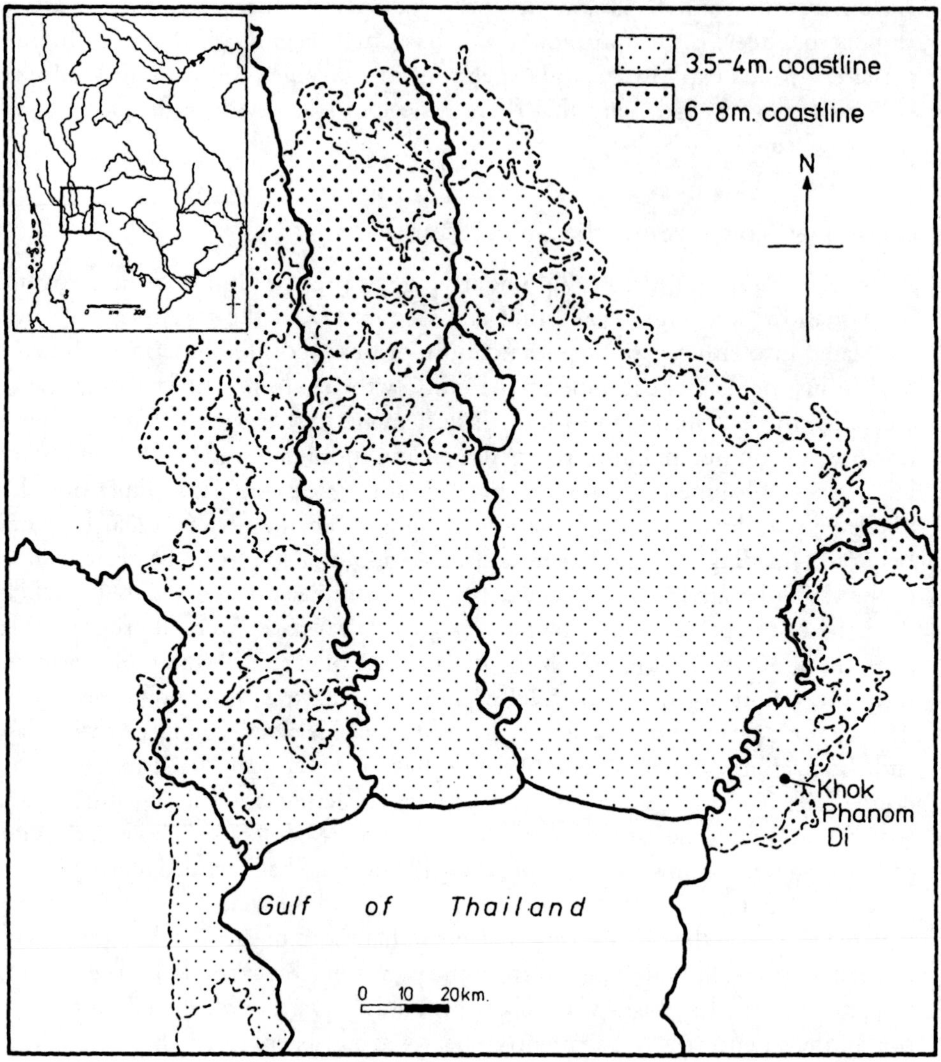

2.18 The location of Khok Phanom Di relative to the raised shorelines of the lower Chao Phraya valley. (Source for sea levels: Supajanya and Vanasin 1979.)

vated material for microscopic plant remains, and is currently analysing the sample, which includes much rice.

When we combine the results of the analysis of the pollen cores and the cultural deposits of the site itself, we are confronted by a sequence lasting about 3300 years. To judge from the 8 radiocarbon dates which have so far been obtained from the pollen cores, the earliest acceptable evidence for human settlement along the shoreline occurred between about 4710-3960 B.C. This is

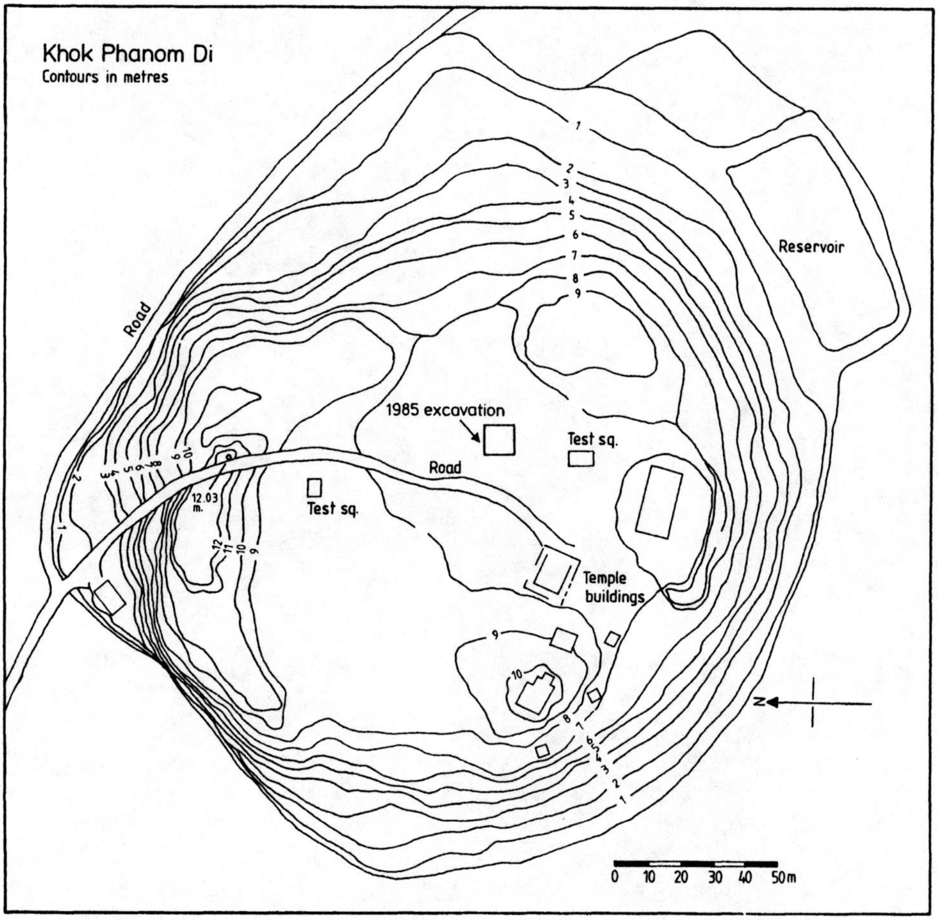

2.19 The site of Khok Phanom Di, showing the areas excavated.

manifested in one of the pollen spectra by a sharp increase in charcoal fragments associated with a simultaneous rise in grass pollen and of plants which flourish today as rice-field weeds. This evidence hints strongly that there was a settlement in the vicinity. Khok Phanom Di itself was occupied, according to the 18 available radiocarbon dates, between about 2000 and 1400 B.C. Thus, while the main body of our evidence comes from this site, there are strong grounds for suspecting that there are earlier, ancestral coastal settlements in the vicinity which are now, presumably, covered by a mantle of marine clay deposits.

It is highly likely that Khok Phanom Di was situated on a coastal barrier giving access to a mangrove-fringed shore, an estuary, and freshwater ponds. Fluctuations in this habitat will become clear with the course of further research (Fig. 2.21). It is important to stress some characteristics of such a coastal-estuarine ecosystem. The Bangkok plain is heavily influenced by the southwest monsoon.

2.20 The excavation of Khok Phanom Di in 1985 involved one 10 by 10 m square. This allowed patterns of burials and structures to be identified.

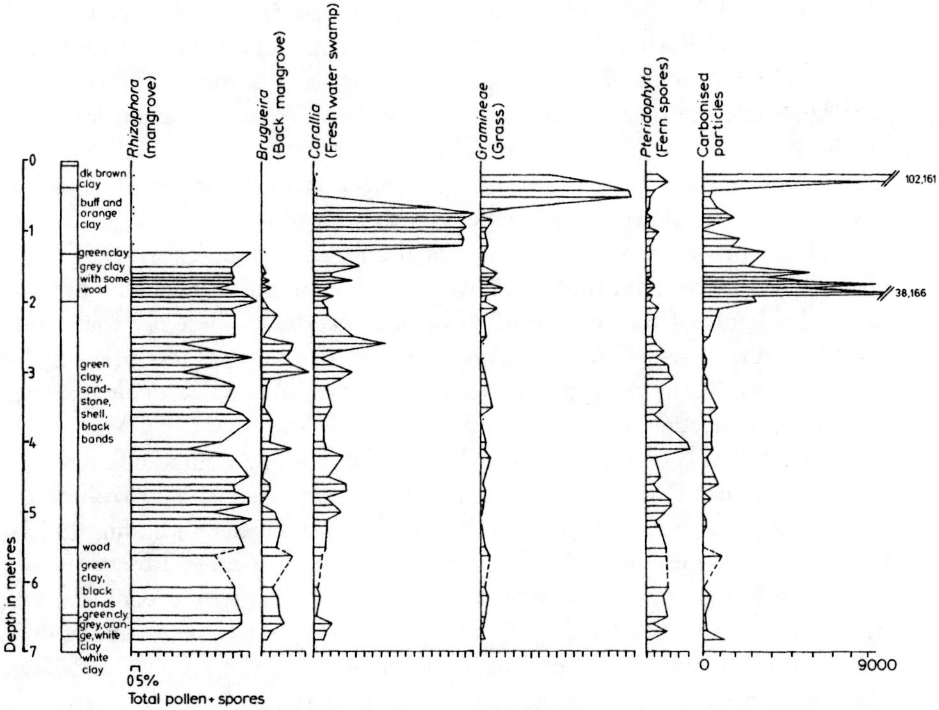

2.21 The partial pollen diagram from Khok Phanom Di site BMR2. It is dominated for most of the sedimentary build-up by *Rhizophora* pollen, which indicates that the settlement was located near coastal mangrove swamps. High peaks of carbonised particles probably reflect clearance of the natural vegetation. These appear to be contemporary with slight rises in grass pollen, which might be due to the propagation of rice. (Courtesy, Bernard Maloney.)

This brings rain between May and November. The rest of the year is characterised by dry conditions as the wind pattern shifts and brings dry, cool air from Eastern Asia, although temperatures rise sharply in March to April as a prelude to the rains. The present reaction to this sharp seasonality places a premium on food storage. Rice is readily stored in granaries, and fish are converted into a fermented meal and stored in pottery jars. This process requires salt, and explains its continuing importance. The abundant wet-season feed for cattle is stored, in a sense, by killing animals for consumption as the dry season progresses. Although fish and shellfish are less readily available during the dry season, many species can be obtained through increased effort. Freshwater gastropods such as *Pila*, for example, can be collected from lake margins or rice-fields during the rainy season, but one has to dig for them in the dry months because they aestivate, that is, become physiologically inactive, underground.

The effects of the monsoon are considerably offset by proximity to the sea.

The extensive intertidal zone, which reflects the flat terrain characteristic of the Gulf of Siam, yields harvests of sedentary shellfish and crustacea, irrespective of season. The resources of the mangrove swamp are likewise unaffected by seasonality, while the presence of a major river nearby has important implications for the supply of fresh, potable water as well as transport facilities and food. A subtropical coastal habitat is not, however, necessarily an optimal habitat, and it is important to look at the general characteristics of the shoreline ecosystem in more detail before reviewing what was found during the excavation of Khok Phanom Di. Essentially, there are three different situations to which the prehistoric inhabitants of the site would have been exposed. These are the standstill, regression and transgression. It is recalled that Maloney has identified evidence, in a core only 200 m from the site, that the sea level fluctuated during the period of prehistoric occupation.

Chappell and Thom (1977) have described the likely course of events under such conditions. During the standstill, they envisage a mangrove-dominated fringe giving way to a raised beach backed by tidal creeks and a high tidal-flat. During a regression, the high tidal-flat would be transformed into an area under temporary freshwater ponds, while the exposed terrain would comprise evaporite basins interspersed by dunes, giving way to the mangrove belt at the high-tide mark. Most food resources would be found along the active beach fringe. A transgression would involve the formation of a beach ridge behind which there would be a shallow lagoon favouring the growth of mangroves. The extent to which one of these idealised portraits is the case for Khok Phanom Di will be determined by pollen and sediment studies now under way (Maloney 1987). It is relevant to note that under regressive conditions, former tidal creeks and flats would be converted into seasonal freshwater ponds likely to sustain such annual wild grasses as rice. Again, the lack of predictable fresh water in the absence of a river, would impose severe limitations on human settlement along such a coast. It has to be noted, therefore, that the coastal habitat probably incorporated a few rich estuarine oases, interspersed by long stretches of inhospitable dunes or mangrove swamps.

Let us now turn to the excavation of Khok Phanom Di. It is currently situated *c* 22 km from the shore, the surrounding sediments comprising marine clays. It covers *c* 5 ha and rises 12 m above the surrounding plain. It is an extremely large settlement given its assumed age, and no comparable sites in terms of size and location have yet been identified round the shores of the Gulf. The excavators resolved to depart from the traditional long and narrow excavation format, which had been dictated at earlier excavations by the maximum span of a bamboo roof. In the event, they opened a 10 by 10 m square under a steel roof in the hope that it would allow the recovery of complete burials, their spatial distribution, and the recognition of structures and activity areas (Higham *et al.* 1987). After seven months of excavation, natural soil was reached at a depth of 6.8 m and, for the present purposes, it is possible to recognise three major stratigraphic zones which are named zones A, B and C. Zone A, the earliest, comprises a complicated series of lenses. In the main, they are made up of ash, occupation material including pottery and biological remains, discrete shell-middens and small lenses of red soil. There are numerous small hearths filled with ash and charcoal, as well as postholes, some of which retain the very wood of the prehistoric structures. Zone A was about 3 m thick and, within it, there were 104 inhumation burials. The earliest six were found isolated from one another and, with the exception of one shell bead, were devoid of grave goods. The remaining 98 burials were set out in rows or superimposed, the distribution revealing several nucleated clusters separated by areas with no burials (Fig. 2.22).

Zone B offers a sharp contrast. The burial of men, women and infants in what appear to have been ancestral groups came to an end and, in their place, there were four outstandingly rich graves containing the remains of a woman and three infants. This interval was followed by the interment of two women with moderately rich grave offerings over which a rectangular structure was built (Fig. 2.23). It was raised half a metre high on a series of levelled layers surmounted by clay wall foundations. A further burial was subsequently interred by cutting through the floor of this building. In front of the platform mound, and lying along the same orientation as its walls, there was a row of burials ringed by a set of postholes which indicate an above-ground mortuary structure. These burials were accompanied by more modest grave goods

Zone C, which occupies the uppermost metre of deposit, is a much darker soil than zone B. Where zone B comprises a sandy matrix interspersed with a few shell-middens and ash lenses, zone C is rich in pottery, animal bone and the implements used in the manufacture of pottery. It contained no burials.

Zones A and B yielded much faunal material. With the exception of a few pig, dog, macaque and deer bones, there is scarcely any evidence of the exploitation of

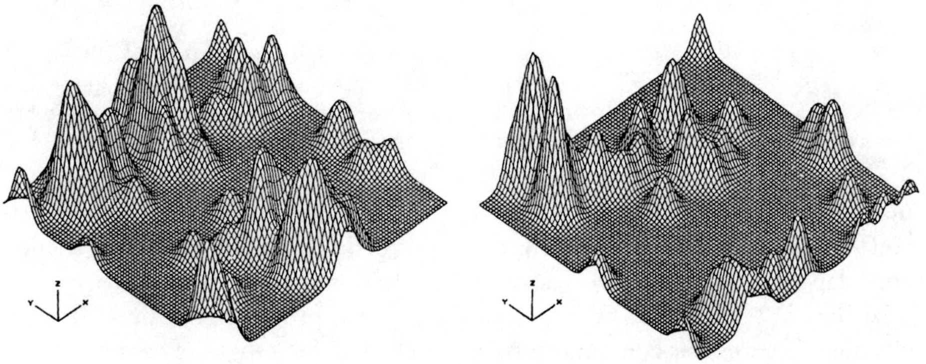

2.22 The clustering of burials at Khok Phanom Di is clearly seen in this computer-generated diagram, wherein peaks reflect concentrations of inhumations. The diagrams for zones A and B suggest long-term continuity in preferred, possibly family, burial areas. (Courtesy Glen Standring.)

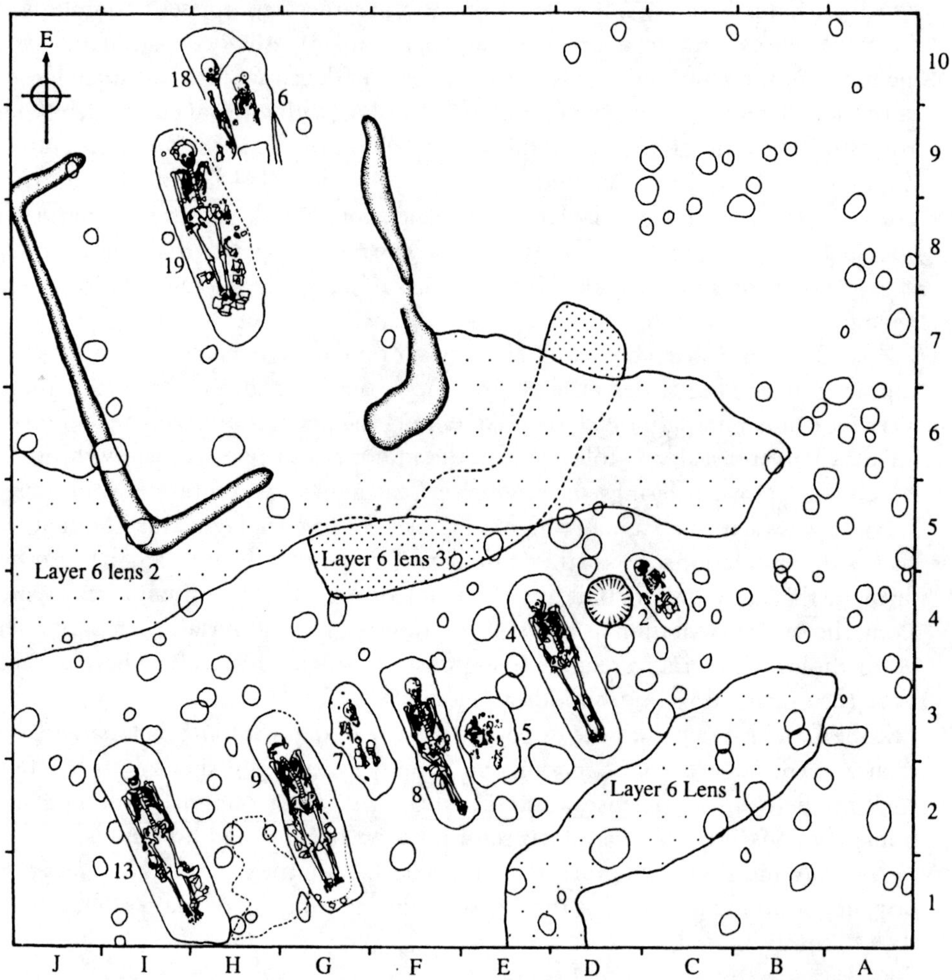

Fig 2.23 The mortuary structure found in a zone B context at Khok Phanom Di was raised over burials 18 and 19, with burial 6 being placed in the same area later. In front of the structure, there is a row of graves which probably belong members of the same family.

mammals, either domestic or wild. The overwhelming majority of remains are aquatic, particularly fish, shellfish, crab and turtle. The main species of shellfish are adapted to a mangrove habitat, though some, too, are found on sandy tidal-flats. A sample of all archaeological layers was processed through a flotation chamber. The residue contains numerous small fish bones whose habitats include the open sea, river estuaries and freshwater ponds. In zone C, the presence of marine species suddenly halted, giving way to mammalian remains associated with a swamp-woodland, including pig, monkey and a large, probably wild, water-buffalo.

Khok Phanom Di yielded a large sample of rice. Husk fragments were found in the occupation layers. It was also represented by chaff impressions on the clay adhering to the exterior surfaces of broken potsherds and, in the case of at least zones A and B, rice chaff was used as a tempering agent when preparing clay for pottery manufacture. The first two sources reflect the local availability of rice, the last may be due to the local use or the importation of pots from an area where rice was preferred as a tempering agent. At present, it is not known whether the rice comes from a wild or domestic plant, or perhaps from both.

On two occasions, human remains were found with the partially digested remains of the stomach contents still in place (Fig. 2.24). Small fish bones and fish scales protrude from this material and the complete analysis should be most interesting. Faecal remains were also relatively common. It is considered likely that these have a human origin, since the remains of dog, the principal other candidate, are very rare. They contain fish bone and, occasionally, rice chaff. During the build-up of zones A and B then, subsistence activities were concerned with fishing, shellfish collecting, and obtaining turtle, crab and other marine resources. The harvesting of rice is represented, but we must defer the question of whether it was harvested as a wild plant or deliberately propagated until the remains have been considered in more detail. Such rich resources, of which rice and some of the estuarine fish were seasonal and could be easily stored, must have underwritten either a fully sedentary life or at least a system where food was obtained from a fixed base. There are very few estuaries with gently shelving beaches round the Gulf of Siam, and it is reasonable to assume that the position of Khok Phanom Di was desirable. Certainly, the absence of estuarine conditions would have presented a problem with fresh water, particularly during the dry season.

When we turn to material culture, we find that the site was located so as to command at least two major sources of raw materials: clay and marine shell. While the area was deficient in high-quality stone, its estuarine situation conferred considerable advantages as a nodal point in exchange. From the initial occupation to the final abandonment, the occupants made pottery vessels. Numerous clay anvils for shaping pots, as well as burnishing stones with worn facets, have been recovered. Clay cylinders representing the formative stages in shaping individual vessels have been found from the basal to the latest levels. Numerous superimposed ash spreads, interpreted as the remains of the bonfire method of firing vessels, also indicate a vigorous local pottery-making tradition (Vincent 1987). Again, some inhumation burials included anvils, burnishing pebbles and pots. In contrast to the preponderance of cord-marked sherds in the zone A occupation layers, most of the grave wares were a lustrous black, burnished style with incised decoration. There is no hint of developmental stages in the pottery-making tradition. Pottery was fully operational from the moment the site was first occupied (Fig. 2.25).

The same situation applies to fishing technology. Clay net weights, harpoons

2.24 The remains from burial 56 at Khok Phanom Di included the residue of the person's last meal. This can clearly be seen in the pelvic area in the photograph below. It included many small fish bones and fish scales.

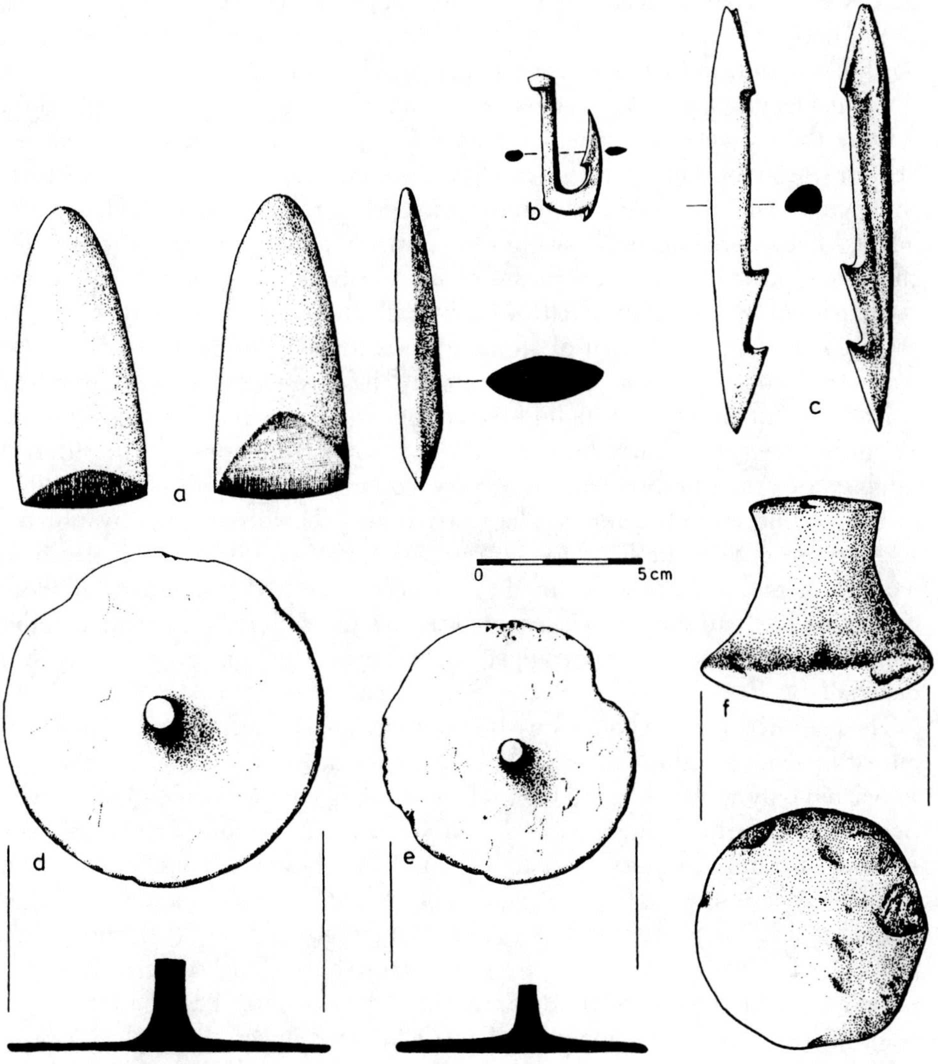

2.25 Some of the material items recovered during the 1985 season at Khok Phanom Di. The ceramic anvil was used in shaping pottery vessels, and the circular objects are decorative shell discs, probably indicating high status.

and fish hooks were present from the earliest contexts. Access to marine shell was also important: local manufacture of shell jewellery is attested by the discovery of shell from which tabs have been drilled in order to shape disc beads, and shell jewellery is a component of the grave goods in both zones A and B.

Participation in a regional exchange network is also evidenced by the presence of stone adzes. These are present from the earliest occupation. A cache of 10 was found in the earliest level and they are present, albeit rarely, in burials. Many adzes were sharpened to such an extent that they were worn down to a very small size. There is a variety of stone, implying multiple sources. The number of postholes found, and volume of ash and charcoal in hearths and firing areas, hints at a considerable use of such adzes in the modification of the local vegetation.

Only the most general statements can be made about the mortuary remains, because the important task of sexing and ageing the skeletons has yet to be completed. The six lowest skeletons comprise three adults, a child and two infants. They were interred in shallow graves with heads pointing to the east. The child was buried in a flexed position on the back. One of the adults was accompanied by a solitary shell bead, but all the others were buried without grave goods. Grave 151, that of an infant, was found with the body covered in red ochre and wrapped in white, unwoven fabric, resembling bark cloth. This "tapa" covering became common in later zone A burials. There is a gap of about 40 cm between these early burials and the balance from zone A. The latter set exhibits a marked preponderance of very young infants, there being 52 infant burials, 5 children and 30 adults. The mortuary ritual involved the excavation of a shallow grave with the head to the east. At least two bodies were placed on wooden biers, a practice which might have been recovered more often had wood been more likely to survive. The corpse was covered with red ochre and, together with any grave goods, was wrapped in binding sheets made of an unwoven material.

The presence of grave goods varied with individuals. Twenty-one infants were buried in scoops with none of the ritual activity described above. Twelve were associated only with ochre and tapa. The remaining complete infant burials were richer in terms of offerings. All had ochre over the bones and, in addition, two were accompanied by pots, three by pots and shell beads, two by bracelets, two by shell beads and bracelets, one by pots, beads and bracelets. These richer infant burials tended to be late within zone A. Grave goods associated with adults include red ochre, pottery vessels, shell beads, burnishing stones, a polished stone adze and clay cylinders of prepared clay. In contrast to the infants, no adults were interred with bone bracelets. Ochre was universally applied to adult bodies. Of the 30 complete examples, seven were associated with pebbles bearing burnishing facets used to decorate pottery vessels. None of the interments stands out, as do the few infant burials mentioned above, on the basis of grave wealth or ritual of burial, though further analysis is necessary, particularly of the pottery fabric, before this can be demonstrated beyond reasonable doubt. The two richest adult graves from this assemblage are numbers 72 and 91. The former contains three pots, three burnishing stones and some shell beads placed between the knees. There is a concentration of fish bones over the left shoulder, and the body was covered in red ochre. The latter contained pots, as well as two burnishing stones and a string of shell beads over the chest. Eight adults were interred with either one or two pots, and eight others with pots and shell beads.

There was a major stratigraphic break between zones A and B, as well as a

40–50 cm hiatus in the presence of burials. The later zone revealed a more homogeneous build-up without the intense differential lensing found between 4–6.8 m. Moreover, the northeast corner of the excavation square contained the building which has already been described. The proportion of infant burials fell from 55% in zone A to 30% in zone B. There was a wider range of grave goods in zone B. In addition to those described for zone A, we also encounter clay anvils, large shell bracelets, shell discs, shell ear ornaments, a fish hook and shaped "breastplates" made from sections of turtle carapace. The shell beads and pots reveal typological changes from the preceding forms, but the basic rite remained the same with the head orientated to the east.

During the period of zone B, a dislocation in the mortuary ritual occurred when the long-term burial areas were abandoned, to be succeeded by one very rich adult burial and three opulent child graves. The adult interment, burial 15, was the richest. The body of a woman in her late thirties was found in a grave which stood out on account of its size: it was 3 m in length, 1 m wide and 80 cm deep. Her body was covered by a pyramid of shaped clay cylinders representing an early stage of pottery manufacture. Three pots had been balanced on top of this pyramid, reaching almost to the surface of the grave. Four or five further pots of considerable quality were placed over the woman's legs, and a particular feature of the burial was the richness of the shell jewellery (Fig. 2.26 and frontispiece). About 120,000 shell-disc beads were encountered, disposed as strands both above and under the chest. She also wore several necklaces made of large I-shaped beads linked by the smaller disc variety. Two horned shell discs covered each shoulder. She wore a shell bracelet and shell-disc ear ornaments. At her feet was a clay potter's anvil and two burnishing pebbles in a shell container. Her body was covered in red ochre. An adjacent grave of the same date contained an infant buried in an identical manner, and accompanied by nearly as rich an array of grave goods. Again, the ochre-covered body lay under a pile of clay cylinders. A bracelet had been placed over the left wrist, and the burnished pots over the legs lay beside a miniature potter's anvil. The upper part of the body was covered in the same types of shell bead as were found with burial 15. The grave was also far larger than necessary to contain the body.

Another rich infant burial was found to be roughly contemporary with, and in the same row, as the two rich interments just described. This one, however, was found in a circular grave. The body was contained within two pots, one of which stood out on account of its size, superb decoration and almost eggshell-thin fabric (Fig. 2.27). Two smaller pots were found inside the large vessels and beside the infant's feet, and a quantity of shell beads were present over the chest area. The third child burial was rather earlier than the other two. The child was accompanied by three or four pots and a considerable number of I- and disc-shaped shell beads.

After this interval of rich individual graves, there was a further modification to the burial rite. Two adult females were buried with moderately rich grave goods,

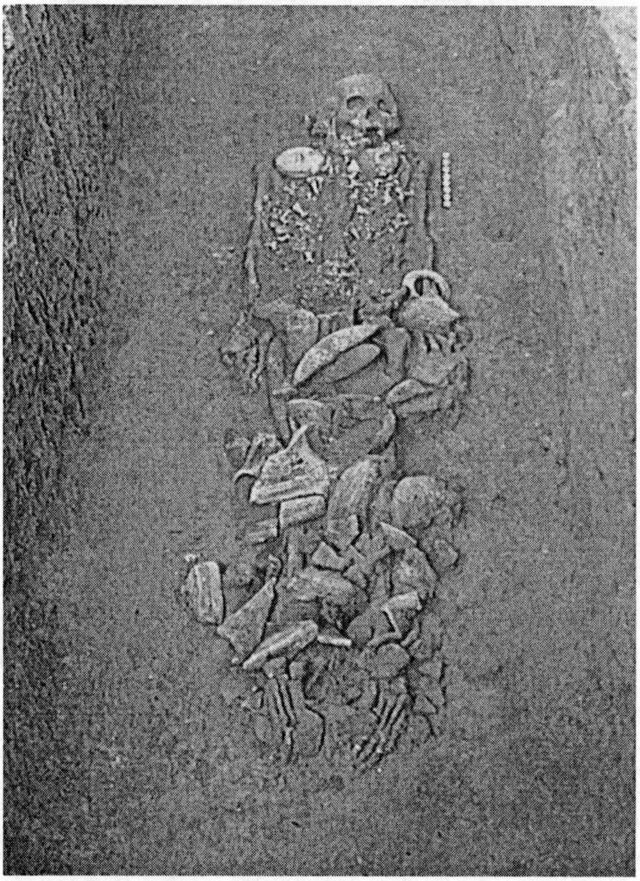

2.26 The remains from burial 15 at Khok Phanom Di came from a woman aged about 36 years old at death. She was interred with outstandingly rich grave goods including about 120,000 shell beads, shell ear pendants and shell horned discs over each shoulder. The pottery vessels in the grave have been classed as masterpieces.

but over them, was raised a square mortuary structure with a plastered floor. In front, there was a rather later row of burials distinguished from the other zone B graves by the presence of postholes set round individual graves and, indeed, possibly round the entire grave cluster as well. This finding suggests the presence of mortuary structures. Indeed, the lack of any intercutting graves surely indicates a planned cemetery in which the location of earlier graves was known. Within this area, there were several discrete shell-middens and spreads of ash and charcoal which lap up to the top of individual graves as if reflecting that feasting was part of the burial ritual (Fig. 2.23).

Although the analysis of mortuary behaviour has hardly begun, it is possible to

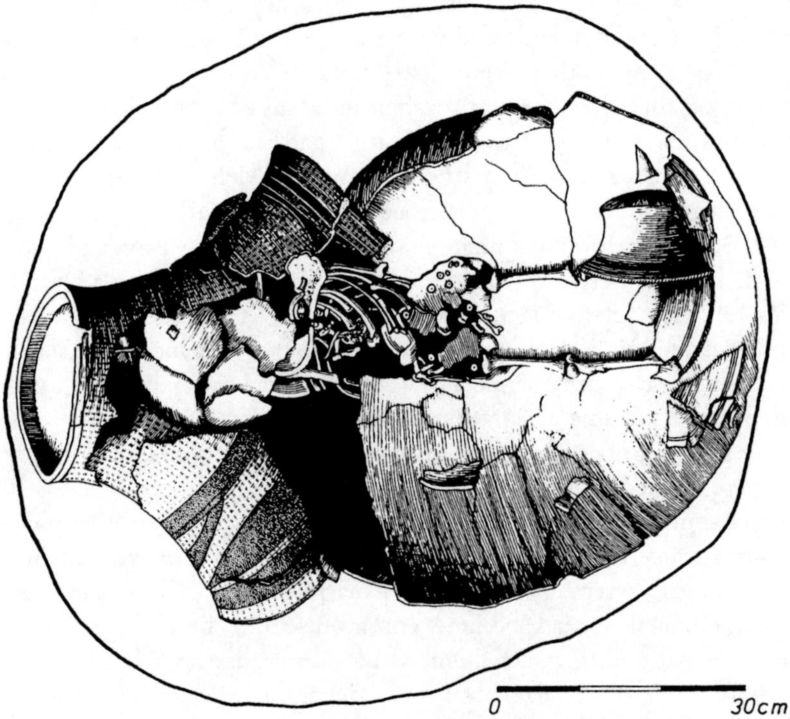

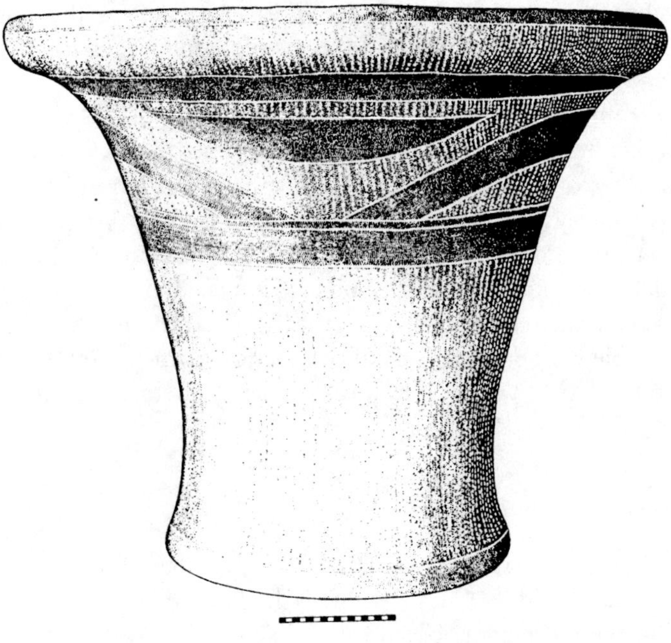

2.27 This burial of an infant from Khok Phanom Di was particularly rich in grave goods. It included a pot ranked as a masterpiece (below).

offer one or two tentative conclusions. The earliest six zone A graves were not grouped. Nor were they endowed with a range of grave goods. Like those found in the rest of zone A, they were distributed in an occupation-industrial area. Some were cut through or set within shell-middens or occupation layers. There is variation in the number of grave goods for zone A as a whole, but no individual or group of graves stands out as being unusually rich. This situation contrasts with the establishment of a specific cemetery in zone B. Much attention was given to the construction and maintenance of a raised structure, and graves show a sharp dichotomy between considerable wealth associated with a few adults and children, and the relative lack of wealth with the balance. Some women were accorded particularly rich and elaborate burials, but only men were accompanied by turtle-shell breast ornaments. The essential burial ritual, however, was similar in both zones. The same orientation to the east was employed, ochre was used to cover the corpse, pots and shell beads were commonly placed with the dead, and graves were located in clusters.

The last burial was cut from just below the distinct stratigraphic change involving a transition from sand to a dark occupation layer rich in material culture and organic remains. No further marine shells or crabs were found, and mammalian faunal species became common. Stone bracelets were favoured, pottery was made *in situ*, as evidenced by numerous clay cylinders and anvils. There were many stone adzes, but no evidence for prehistoric metallurgy. This change is correlated with a lowering of the sea level and a considerable adjustment in subsistence and exchange activities. Analysis of the pottery should inform us on the issue of continuity in terms of people occupying Khok Phanom Di in late zone B and in zone C.

The data from the Gulf of Siam area are, in an important way, distinct from those from Bac Bo. The coastal occupation as seen at Khok Phanom Di reveals a rich, sedentary group which specialised in the manufacture of pottery and shell jewellery, and engaged in elaborate rituals in disposing of the dead (Fig 2.28). The biological remains indicate exploitation of mangrove swamps, the open sea, river estuary, tidal flats and freshwater ponds. Rice was one of the plants consumed. The inland rock shelters identified in the Khwae Noi and Sangker valleys are more compatible with brief periods of occupation by groups given to mobility, at least from time to time who, while at those rock shelters, engaged in broad-range foraging.

Domestication

Recent excavations in Northeast Thailand, the Chao Phraya valley, Central Cambodia and the Middle Country above the Red River delta are unanimous in disclosing village settlements based on a mixed economy of hunting, gathering, stock-raising and the cultivation of rice. As far as we can judge on present evidence, such expansionary settlement was under way by the third and possibly

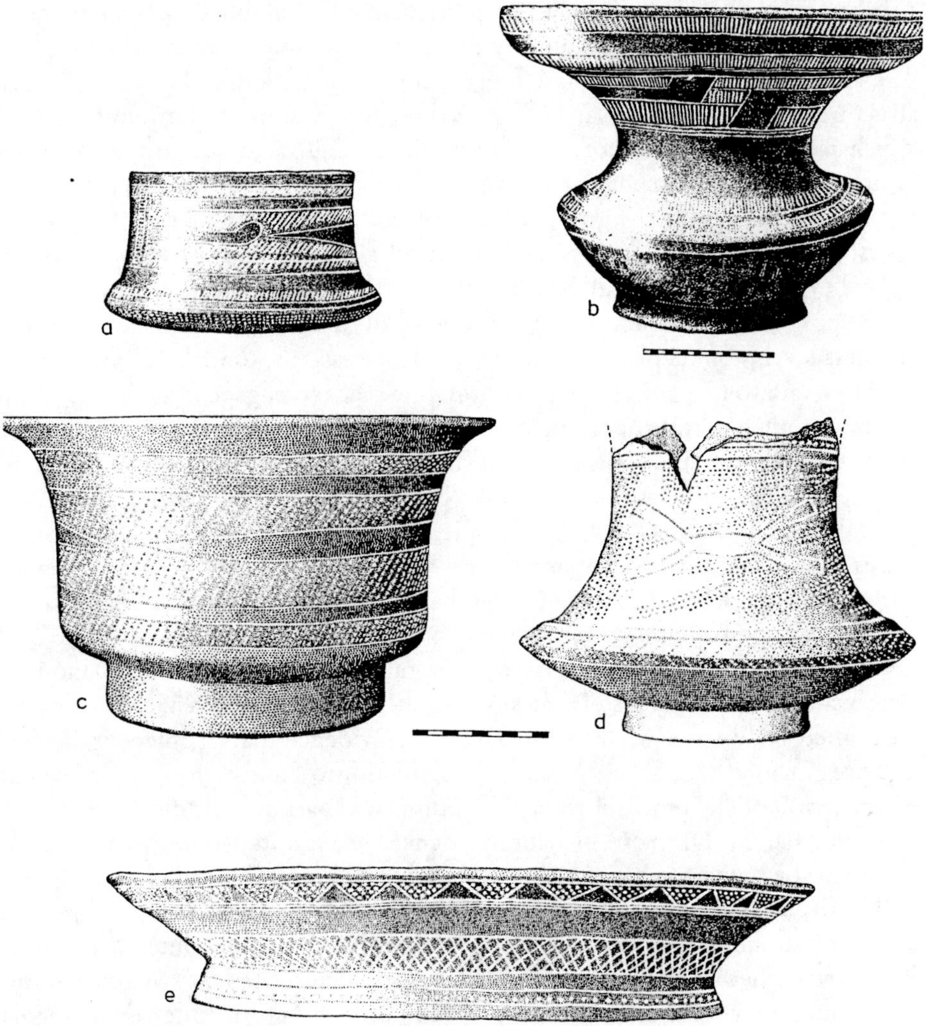

2.28 These vessels from Khok Phanom Di mortuary contexts reveal complete mastery of the potter's art.

the fourth millenium B.C. The most logical source for such settlement lies in local hunter-gatherer groups. We have detected the possibility of long-term adaptation by mobile hunter-gatherers in the elevated, evergreen, canopied forest. At present, it seems more likely that trends to population growth and expansionary settlement occurred among the complex sedentary coastal communities, of which the best-documented is Khok Phanom Di, rather than immigration from outside Southeast Asia. Settlement at Khok Phanom Di was located within a mangrove-estuarine habitat where marine resources were overwhelmingly dominant.

It has been argued above that this particularly favourable habitat encouraged and indeed permitted the community there to live permanently in the same place. The architectural features found suggest the construction of houses and ritual structures. Continuity for at least five centuries is seen in the human burials which follow the same mortuary tradition through 5 m of cultural deposits. Living together permanently in the same place, occupying houses, regarding the settlement environs as the group's preserve and sharing the living place with the ancestors, are all new variables, and represent a radical contrast with the mobile upland groups described for Bac Bo and Northern Thailand.

The contrast can be summarised in the word, domestication. Sedentism at its simplest level permits people to accumulate possessions, to make a new range of artefacts, and to be predictably present in one place to engage in exchange. But it is far more than that. It opens up a new conception of the place of the individual in the community and, indeed, in the very ordering of it. Where food resources are predictable, sufficient and storable, burgeoning sedentary communities can expand their horizons, develop complex ranking behaviour, and accumulate status and obligations. New demands are made on the creation of goods to signal such status. At Khok Phanom Di, we have turtle-shell breastplates (Figs. 2.29 and 2.30), superb pottery vessels and a woman buried with over 100,000 shell beads. Again, ranking invokes ritual. The raised building at Khok Phanom Di remains unique, but then so is the site. No other such large coastal sites have yet been intensively studied. We now have clear evidence that people were buried, and presumably lived, in a community divided into family groups and that the construction of elaborate mortuary structures was part of their display of status.

Khok Phanom Di, then, provides evidence through its structures and burials for domestication, not necessarily of plants or animals, but rather of people. It will be argued that the sedentary nature of the settlement also fostered population growth and fissioning into new communities. In this context, it is quite immaterial whether the plants found there were cultivated, or whether animal behaviour was yet modified by man to the point of herd maintenance. Regular harvesting of rice will, in any case, modify it away from the local wild variant for, as Oka and Morishima (1971) have shown, harvesting wild rice results in modifications to the seeding rate and the number of spikelets per panicle even over five generations. Clearly, much detailed research on the pollen cores and actual remains of rice from the site is necessary before a clear picture of the status of the rice in the successive layers is known. Nor should it be forgotten that, in historic times, the inhabitants of the margins of the Tonle Sap have harvested wild floating rice by tapping the seed heads into their boats (Delvert 1961). For the purposes of the present discussion, we will regard the earlier occupation contexts as reflecting an essentially coastal-gathering orientation, wherein a very high proportion of the food was obtained by fishing, collecting marine and estuarine resources such as turtle, crabs and shellfish, harvesting nuts and rice, and either hunting or maintaining domestic pigs. As such, it is felt legitimate to consider

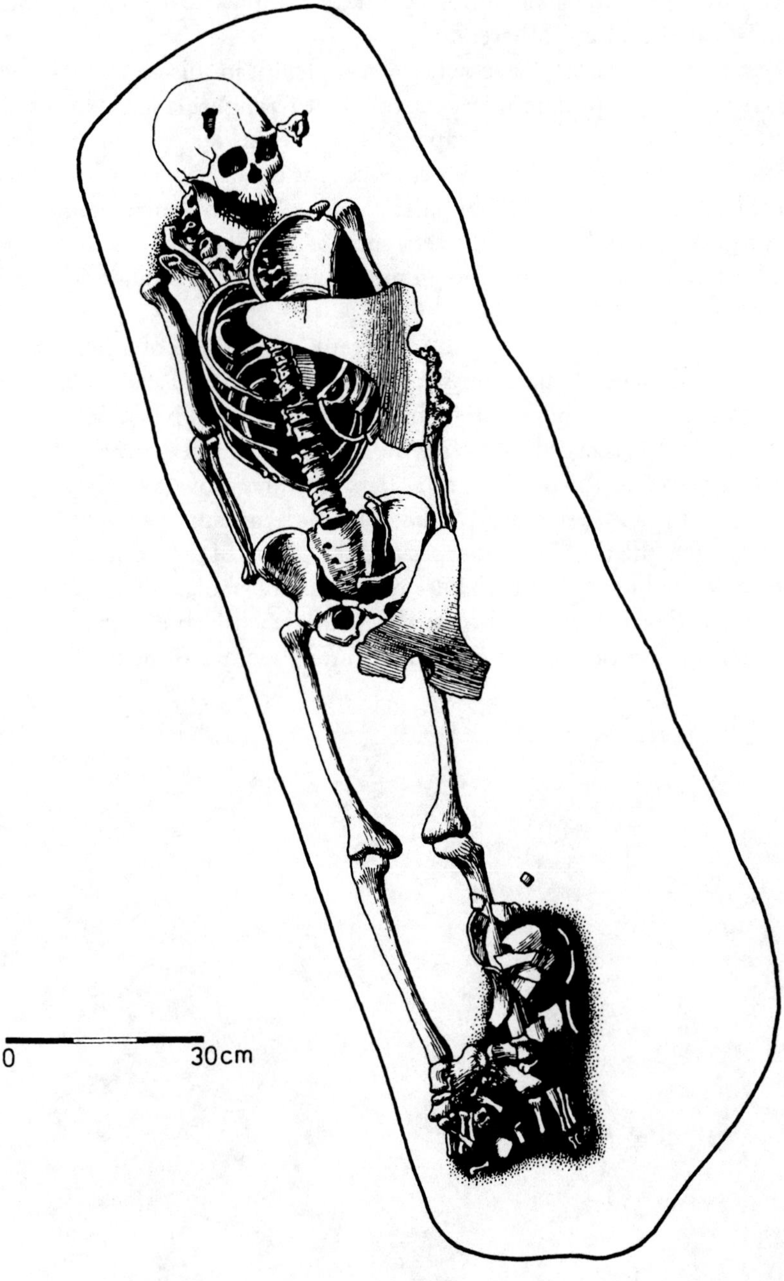

2.29 Burial 24 at Khok Phanom Di was one of a group which included a turtle-shell breast ornament. This man died in his early twenties.

their culture within the general framework of complex sedentary and increasingly domesticated hunter-gatherers.

Price and Brown (1985) have defined complexity in this context as involving a dense co-residing population, large settlement size, permanent houses, evidence for differential wealth, energy expended in the burial rite and pattern in the location of interment, and permanent occupation of the same settlement. The preferred approach to explaining the development of such complex hunter-gatherer groups avoids prime movers such as population pressure on available food resources. Rather, it stresses interactions between a range of cultural and environmental variables.

In terms of the environment, our present knowledge of prehistoric coastal Thailand recalls several characteristics noted by Yesner (1980) as being relevant for maritime hunter-gatherers as a whole. These begin with a high biomass. It has already been emphasised that there would have been access to the sedentary and productive resources of the intertidal flats and mangrove swamps. These shellfish, fish, turtle and crabs are predictable, and can survive high culling rates. There were also the riverine resources and the plants of the backswamps. Among the latter, we include wild rice. These resources are stable and predictable given a consistent sea level. It must also be noted that such rich estuarine enclaves are rare. Indeed, only four major rivers flow into the Gulf of Siam.

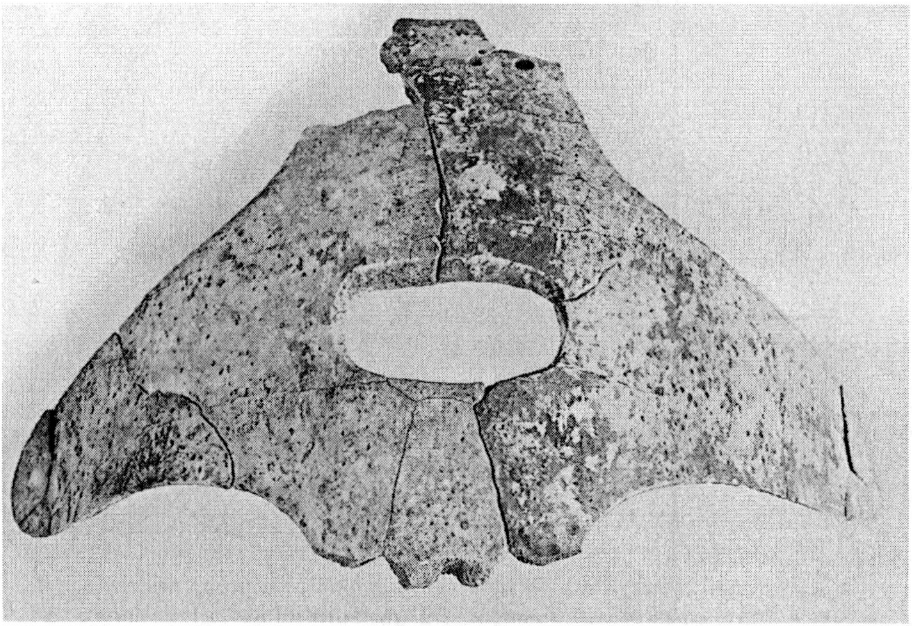

2.30 This photograph shows the reconstructed turtle-shell breast ornament from burial 24 at Khok Phanom Di. It has holes for suspension and a large cut hole in the centre. It measures 38 cm at its widest.

Yesner also notes a number of common cultural variables among those who occupy these optimal enclaves. One is that their rarity fosters a high degree of territoriality on the part of the favoured occupants. Another is that young and old can contribute to the diet by collecting shellfish, thereby reducing constraints on population growth felt by mobile forager groups. A third is the development of a high population density within a circumscribed area. Again, since a marine diet based on shellfish, fish and crabs is low in vitamins and calories, inclusion of vegetables and plant supplements in the diet is important.

With reference to monsoonal subtropical Southeast Asia, it is relevant to add the reduced impact of seasonality in the maritime tract when compared with the more stressful conditions in low-lying parts of the interior, where the full impact of a long dry season is felt. If the contrast between coast and interior resources encourages exchange, then those dominating both the coast and river valleys, with access to boats, are well placed to occupy nodal positions in any emerging exchange network. Consummation of these theoretical statements about Khok Phanom Di is seen in its outstanding size. There is no known site in Southeast Asia of similar antiquity which approaches the 12 m depth and 5 ha area of this mound. The actual occupation followed soon after the land was exposed by a falling sea. There probably remain earlier sites which followed the coastline as it receded and before it stabilised at Khok Phanom Di, for the initial occupants were already conversant with pottery-making, had access to numerous polished stone adzes and had a developed fishing technology.

The lower levels of the site suggest a sedentary population in that there are no clear lenses revealing site abandonment and the build-up of layers is patterned: most hearths were found, often superimposed, in one area; pottery firing in another; and, shortly after initial settlement, specific areas were used over time for burying the dead. The adzes were made of exotic stone, hinting at an early inception of exchange networks which, in itself, probably involved locally specialised craft production, particularly in the manufacture of pottery vessels and shell jewellery.

Sedentary communities set in rich habitats, as at Khok Phanom Di, permit population growth though, given the high incidence of infant mortality in zone A, this may have taken some time to manifest itself. High co-residential populations invoke the problems recently addressed by Johnson (1982) and which he described as scalar stress. This involves a series of population thresholds which, when approached, invite new responses. One option is fission, whereby a segment of the community moves elsewhere. This is straightforward in the absence of social circumscription and was doubtless commonly taken. When alternative coastal enclaves are already taken up, however, and the more marginal hinterland also suffers a packing of communities, options are narrowed, and may invoke conflict or new forms of social organisation such as ranking and the increased use of ritual behaviour to restrain conflict. Ranking is a means of reducing stress through vesting leadership and status in one or a few individuals.

It hardly needs emphasis that it is also a convenient mechanism for the ordering of exchange relationships, and storage and distribution of foodstuffs. In turn, it accentuates a demand for prestige goods which act as emblems of the highly ranked.

The question of food storage brings us to rice, a plant which was harvested at Khok Phanom Di and, to judge from the context of the rice remains, was locally husked. Processing rice is not arduous as it is usually cooked as whole grains. Once the husks are removed, rice can be stored and consumed without further processing. Indeed, brown rice is more nutritious than the white polished grain. Rice was present from the basal 40 cm as an inclusion in potting clay, and then became more abundant as chaff found in occupation layers.

Data from zone A are interpreted as reflecting a sedentary population which, as it grew in numbers, expanded its resource base and encountered scalar stress. Let us assume that initially, at least, the last problem was resolved by fission. Similar coastal enclaves would soon be taken up if they weren't already. The next best option for settlement was probably along the river valleys and particularly the tributary streams which provided routes, water, aquatic resources and suffered minimal flood risk. In Northeast Thailand, it is just these positions which witnessed early occupation at, for example, Ban Chiang, Non Kao Noi and Non Nok Tha. The earliest biological remains from Ban Chiang reveal a broadly based gathering, fishing and collecting pattern, allied with the maintenance of domestic cattle, pig and dog, and the harvesting of rice. This form of adaptation appears to have been successful biologically as there are numerous such sites and their inhabitants were robust, well-fed and healthy. They are held to represent a successful adaptation to the inland stream valleys by sedentary, partially agricultural, village communities. Being removed from the coast meant that such inland areas were more affected by the long dry season, and, in this respect, they can be termed "marginal".

This habitat, however, is marginal only in relation to the concentrated biomass characteristic of the coastal estuarine enclaves where the impact of the long dry season was lessened by proximity to the sea. It is not hard to imagine that the tracts just behind the optimal coastal zone filled fairly rapidly, since the sedentary coastal settlements are seen as the original donors. The point is that for sites like Khok Phanom Di, fission is an option only until social circumscription takes effect. The converse is continuing population growth and the possibility that more intense social-ranking systems and attendant ritual developed to cope with scalar stress.

Evidence for this proposition could take the form of (a), growing disparity in the wealth of grave goods among individuals buried at about the same time, (b), differential energy expended in burying the higher-ranked individuals, (c), evidence for population growth, (d), more restricted distribution of valuables, and perhaps, (e), modification of the environment to encourage certain food resources. Such intensification, for example, could take the form of expanding through clearance of the natural freshwater swamp vegetation, the area within which rice flourished. The local intensification of rice production could have involved no conceptual break with the preceding system of harvesting, but rather increased interference with competitors to enlarge suitable habitats. Such improvement of the natural habitat for rice, however, could have increased territoriality.

The above model sees sedentism, population growth and fissioning to more marginal habitats, followed by crowding in the optimal zone and increased social ranking, as factors involved in trends towards intensified exploitation of rice. How do the data from Khok Phanom Di fit the model, and how might it be tested in the future? Initial permanent settlement is seen as reflecting the pull of predictable and concentrated marine food resources. The group secured food through exploiting optimum resources, a strategy greatly assisted by marine transport. As settlement developed through zone B, population grew and the co-residing group underwent a process of fissioning whereby certain emigrant groups occupied more marginal inland locations, including tributary stream valleys. Marsh clearance there expanded or opened up areas suitable for the proliferation of rice but this plant was one, possibly minor, component in a very flexible and wide-ranging subsistence strategy. Domestic cattle, which were not suited to the coastal swamps, and domestic pigs, were maintained in the interior valley sites. The relatively large co-residential group at Khok Phanom Di encouraged ranking behaviour, as did participation in exchange networks to supply interior communities with desirable marine products, particularly shell jewellery and ceramics.

The accumulation of beautiful and rare possessions would not have been an end in itself. The purpose is more to demonstrate status, respect and standing. The rarer the goods, the greater their beauty, the longer it takes to make them, the higher the status of the owner. In the burial ritual of Khok Phanom Di this is clearly shown in burial 15, where a pottery masterpiece was smashed over the corpse, which wore an outstanding array of ornaments. In other burials, turtle carapaces were carved to elegant shapes and pots were embellished with attractive designs. The labour employed in their manufacture was thus converted into prestige. Less tangible, but just as important, is the evidence for feasting at the funeral. This feasting, it is argued, was not to satisfy hunger, but to advertise the status of the deceased and his or her relatives.

Different status may well be reflected in the disparity in individual wealth among the zone A burials of adults and children. By the sharp change seen with the start of zone B, increased circumscription and the developing exchange networks, as well as the growing population, entailed investing more energy in ritual and ascriptive ranking. Burials display an increased dichotomy between rich and poor, and there is some evidence that women skilled in primary production of quality ceramics were among the most highly ranked echelon. Indeed, a child too young to have been skilled in pottery-making was buried with

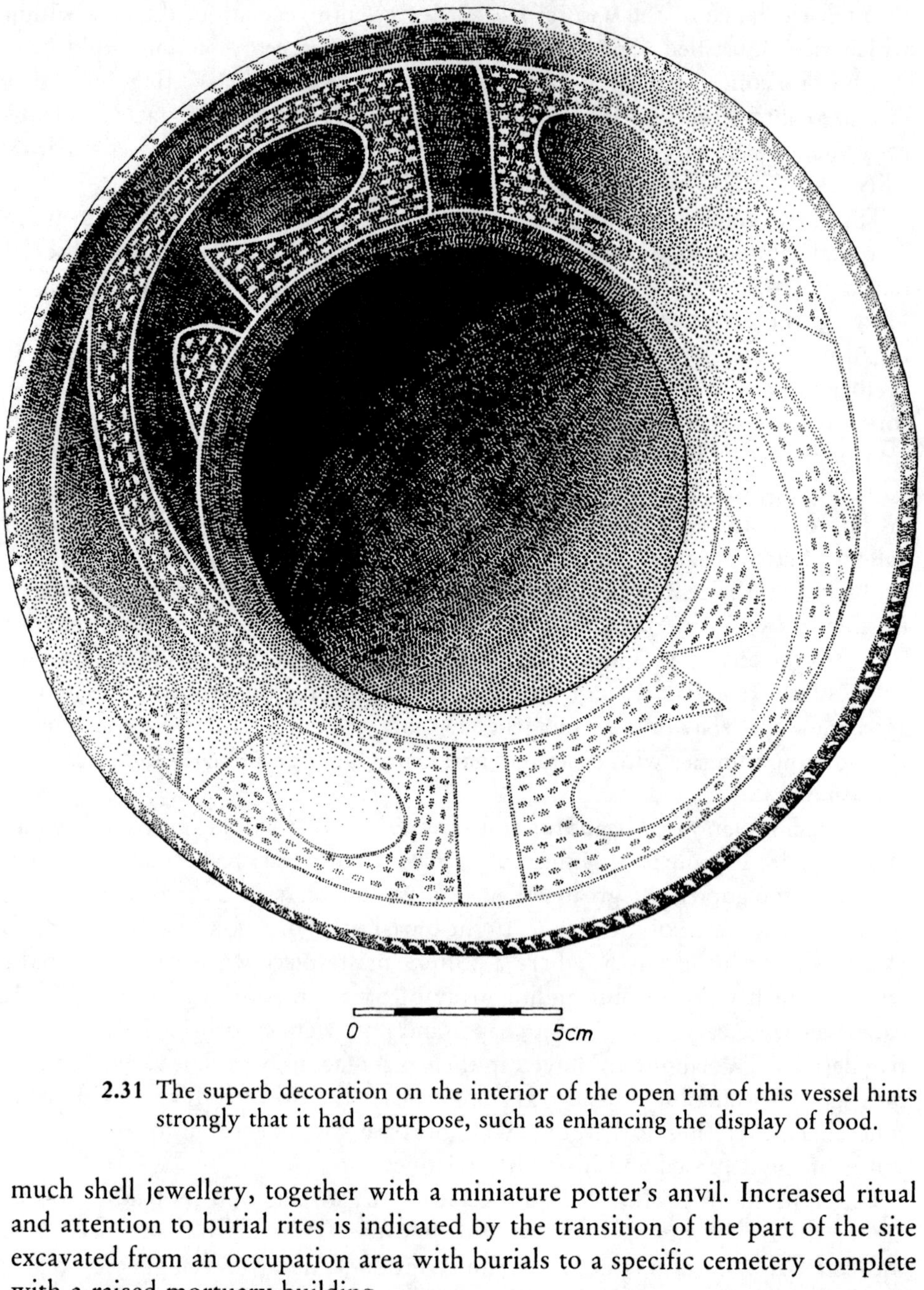

2.31 The superb decoration on the interior of the open rim of this vessel hints strongly that it had a purpose, such as enhancing the display of food.

much shell jewellery, together with a miniature potter's anvil. Increased ritual and attention to burial rites is indicated by the transition of the part of the site excavated from an occupation area with burials to a specific cemetery complete with a raised mortuary building.

In the particular case of Khok Phanom Di, it is clear also that much attention was devoted to achieving excellence in pottery-making. Vincent (1987) has described some of the funerary vessels recovered there as masterpieces. One, in particular, stands out for the attention given to the visible decoration on a broadly flaring rim (Fig. 2.31). This vessel, if used in feasting, would have been a vehicle for enhancing the presentation of food and the prestige of the owner. The raised mortuary structure suggests a long-term commitment to mortuary ritual, while some of the burials themselves contained most impressive assemblages of grave goods.

The preferred model visualises rice harvesting in both the marginal and optimal zones as a component part of a flexible subsistence strategy. During the period under review, rice was significant more for its potential for intensification than the realisation of more extensive or productive cultivation. Indeed, the first major intensification in agricultural methods probably came with the formation of centralised chiefdoms between 500–1 B.C. The crucial issue is not the cultivation of rice, nor any other food resource, but rather the increasing domestication of human beings through the conditions of sedentism, territoriality and reworking of their personal relations. It was this change, now perceived through the excavation of Khok Phanom Di, which stimulated the rich cultural expression of social ranking and leadership expressed in the material panoply of status. It is also argued that domestication set in train the great expansion of human settlement which we shall now explore.

CHAPTER 3

THE EXPANSION OF DOMESTIC COMMUNITIES

We have seen that the known hunter-gatherer sites concentrate in the upland limestone rock shelters and along raised former shorelines. There is little doubt that the protection afforded by caves, and the relative ease with which they were discovered, has biased our sample in their favour. Doubtless, there were also numerous open sites now obscured by soil deposition or destroyed by subsequent erosion. The rising and falling of the sea which drowned extensive low-lying terrain in the post-Pleistocene period must also have destroyed much evidence for the adaptation of hunter-gatherers to the coastal mangrove habitat. The wealth of this latter environment, however, is clearly demonstrated at Khok Phanom Di.

When we turn to the extensive river or lacustrine floodplains of inland Southeast Asia, there is an almost complete absence of evidence for hunter-gatherer communities. It is true that Bayard (1980) has found what may be a hunter-gatherer site on the southern bank of the Mekong River, and the occasional stray find has been reported on the Khorat plateau, yet the recognition of a widespread hunter-gatherer occupation of such areas has yet to occur. There is no obvious reason to account for this lacuna. We are concerned with areas which today sustain the greatest concentrations of population: the broad valleys of the Mekong, Red and Chao Phraya rivers, and their numerous tributaries. If our understanding of the environment of these valleys in prehistory approaches reality, they would have been well suited to settlement by hunter-gatherers.

These low-level river valleys may genuinely have been avoided for environmental constraints of which we remain unaware. The Lamet, for example, avoid valleys because of the malign spirits which reside there (Izikowitz 1951). Such malignancy might, of course, reflect the presence at low levels of malarial mosquitoes. A rather more plausible factor is the series of geomorphological changes which have occurred over the past five millennia both naturally and as a result of human modification of the environment. The incidence of flooding during the latter stages of the rainy season involves much sedimentation and erosion, a process which is greatly magnified by forest clearance (Fig. 3.1). Once the monsoon rains have direct access to cleared land, the erosive power of water comes into play, and the sediment loads carried by rivers and streams markedly increases. These forces could both remove and bury the remains of hunter-gatherer sites as, indeed, could the remodelling of the landscape which has attended the adoption of wet rice farming in levelled fields. It is also possible that

3.1 Forest clearance can still be observed. This scene shows two stages in the preparation of rice-fields in an area near Ban Na Di. The workers find many species of animal and shell which recur in basal midden contexts of prehistoric sites.

archaeologists engaged in site surveys have not looked in the right places, nor asked the right questions of local informants. It is much easier to identify a raised mound covered in broken potsherds than it is to track down the more fugitive scatter of stone flakes which might indicate a transitory hunter-gatherer site.

Whichever the case may be, there is very little evidence for hunter-gatherer occupation of the main river valleys and their tributary systems. This contrasts with the abundance of sites which indicate the arrival there of domestic communities, a finding which encourages the conclusion that groups including agriculture and stock-raising among their subsistence activities were increasing in numbers and expanding territorially (Fig. 3.2). So far, it is possible to detect such settlement in the Chao Phraya plains, the Khorat plateau, Tonle Sap plains and the margins of the Mekong delta, Bac Bo and central coastal Viet Nam. The preliminary results of the excavation of Khok Phanom Di suggest that the origins of such domestic communities may lie in the rich, sedentary coastal contexts.

The Khorat plateau

While hunter-gatherer sites in the inland river valleys are virtually unknown, domestic sites are legion. It appears that the number of people, and the areas settled, increased greatly from a period beginning in the fourth or early third millennium B.C. This expansionary process is probably best documented on the Khorat plateau of Northeast Thailand. Indeed, the northern part of the plateau has been more intensively studied than any other in Southeast Asia, and numerous occupation sites are now known there ranging from relatively small (0.8 to 5.0 ha) low mounds to defended settlements covering up to 117 ha. Since the earliest period of archaeological enquiry there during the 19th century, clear evidence for the Khmer civilization was recognized (Mouhot 1864), while Williams-Hunt (1950) pioneered the application of aerial photography by compiling a map of moated sites clustering in the Mun valley. Any observer descending from the surrounding uplands onto the plateau, which is only about 150 m higher than the Chao Phraya plain, is struck by its aridity during the dry season. Indeed, we encounter two distinct environments. The wet season, when the more favoured low river terraces are under rice, and the dry season, when the soil is baked to the consistency of concrete. It will be shown below that there is some evidence for similar seasonality during the prehistoric period.

The plateau is bounded to the north and east by the Mekong River, beyond which the terrain becomes considerably more elevated. To the west and south there are the Phetchabun and Dang Raek ranges respectively. There are two major drainage basins, the smaller Songkhram to the north, and the Mun–Chi system in the south. Moorman *et al.* (1964) have noted five principal land forms (Fig. 3.3). There are the floodplains, low, middle and high river terraces, and some igneous outcrops in the southern sector. The present river floodplain begins with the incised channel and extends through river levées and oxbow lakes

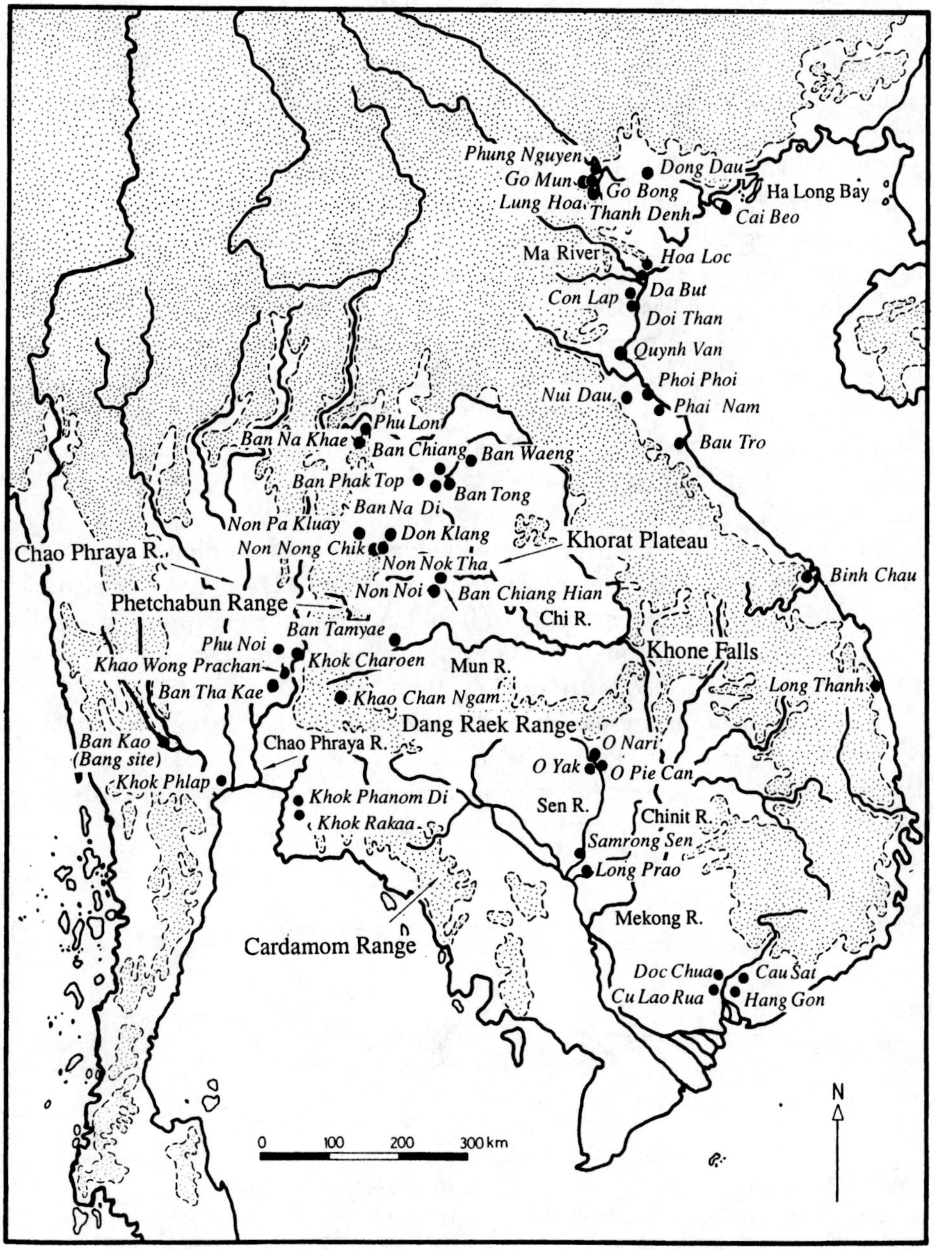

3.2 The location of sites mentioned in chapter 3. Stippled area: land above 182m.

to the backswamp. Under natural conditions, the low parts of the floodplain bear permanent lakes and swamps. All this landscape, however, is prone to severe seasonal flooding. Smaller tributary streams commonly have narrower floodplains and lack the levées and oxbow lakes. An important feature of the main rivers is the presence of floodplains between lengths of the river where the bed is deeply incised. This situation fosters intense flooding.

The low terrace takes the form of slightly undulating terrain, normally fringing the present floodplains. It is broadest near the confluence of the Mun and Chi rivers, and is more restricted in smaller tributary regions. The low terrace is probably of upper Pleistocene date, and its soils are river-transported alluvia. The surviving middle-terrace areas have an uneven distribution due to local forces of erosion and re-deposition. They comprise sandy surface soils overlying lateritic concretions and an increasingly clayey substrate. The high terrace has been subjected to considerable erosion and often survives only as elevated "islands" of high ground. These sandy soils probably date to the early Pleistocene period.

The soils of the three terraces and the floodplain vary according to their degree of permeability, salinity, slope, texture and fertility. Their qualities also vary with micro-relief and susceptibility to flooding. From the viewpoint of growing rice, the soils have been subdivided into five major groups (Robinson and Steel 1972). The low-terrace soils are the best suited to rice cultivation.

Five millennia of human modification make it difficult to assess the vegetation of the Khorat plateau in detail. The monsoonal climate with a long dry season favours a subtropical moist forest. This comprises variably open or fairly dense stands, with a canopy height of *c* 15 m in drier areas, and 25 m where moister

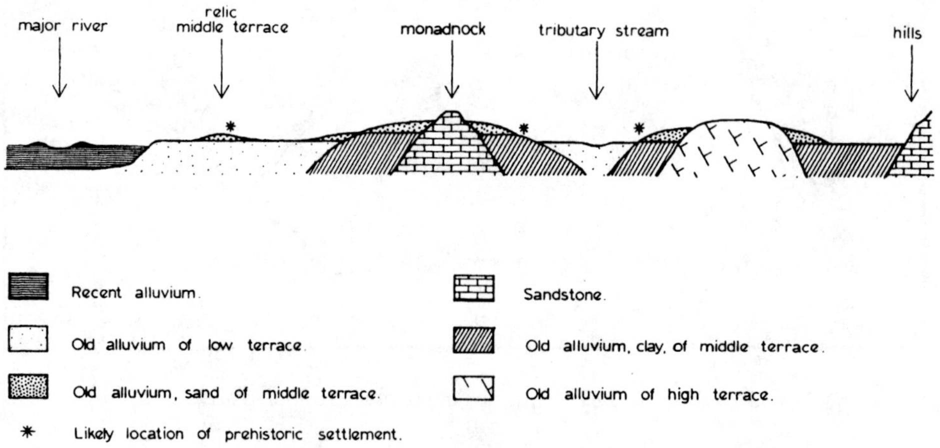

3.3 A schematic cross-section showing the principal landforms of the Khorat plateau. They had a considerable impact on the pattern of prehistoric settlement.

conditions prevail. Many species are deciduous. The transition to a subtropical wet forest with only a few deciduous trees takes place at 400 m and so hardly concerns the study of prehistoric settlement patterns. Dipterocarp species are adapted to strong variations between dry and wet conditions, and predominate in the deciduous moist forest. This tree cover was probably present on the low to higher terraces during prehistory. The nature of the floodplain vegetation is more problematical. If the historic vegetation of the Chao Phraya floodplain is a guide, however, it was probably dominated by swamp grasses, with tree growth being scattered and stunted, (Boonsong and McNeely 1977), but the narrower river valleys may have sustained a moist, evergreen forest.

Soils and vegetation also affect associated animal communities. Boonsong and McNeely (1977) note that the grasslands of the river floodplains attract elephant, rhinoceros, water-buffalo, pig deer and Schomburgk's deer. Alternatively, the moist monsoon forest favours wild cattle, pig, the sambar deer, muntjak and large carnivores such as the tiger.

Given the survival of wild rice on the plateau in the margins of permanent lakes, and the mosaic distribution of different soils veined with small streams, the preferred location of prehistoric settlements is likely to be particularly informative. Archaeological research in this region has a long history, stretching back to the pioneering work of Aymonier (1900–1903), Lunet de Lajonquière (1907) and Seidenfaden (1922). The specific quest for prehistoric rather than historic sites began in 1963–4, when a proposal to dam the Nam Phong River led Solheim to instigate a site survey in the area threatened by inundation. Gorman, a participant in the fieldwork, located a series of small, low mounds, one of which, known as Non Nok Tha, was subsequently excavated (Solheim and Gorman 1966). In 1969, Higham surveyed in Roi Et Province and inside Phu Wiang, a large sandstone monadnock (residual hill surrounded by a plain) enclosing an extensive area of good agricultural land. Four of the sites located there were test excavated, perhaps the best known of these being Non Nong Chik (Higham and Parker 1970, Buchan 1973, Bayard 1977). As part of the Ban Chiang research programme in 1974–5, Schauffler (1976) undertook a third survey and test excavated three sites, Don Klang, Ban Phak Top and Ban Tong (Fig. 3.4). Five years later, Kijngam and Higham sought prehistoric settlements in the area surrounding Lake Kumphawapi (Wichakana 1984). This area was chosen because of the presence of all major plateau landforms within a circumscribed area. The study area encompassed the watershed between the Songkhram River system flowing north and the Pao flowing south.

The margins of Lake Kumphawapi are flanked by seasonally flooded marshes. The terrain is very flat, and swollen streams during July and August greatly extend the lake area. The soils which border the seasonal marsh belong to the Phimai group. These are well suited to rice cultivation, with the proviso that they are susceptible to flash floods. To the west and east of the Phimai tract there is an extensive area of low-terrace Roi Et soil, dotted with islands of slightly elevated

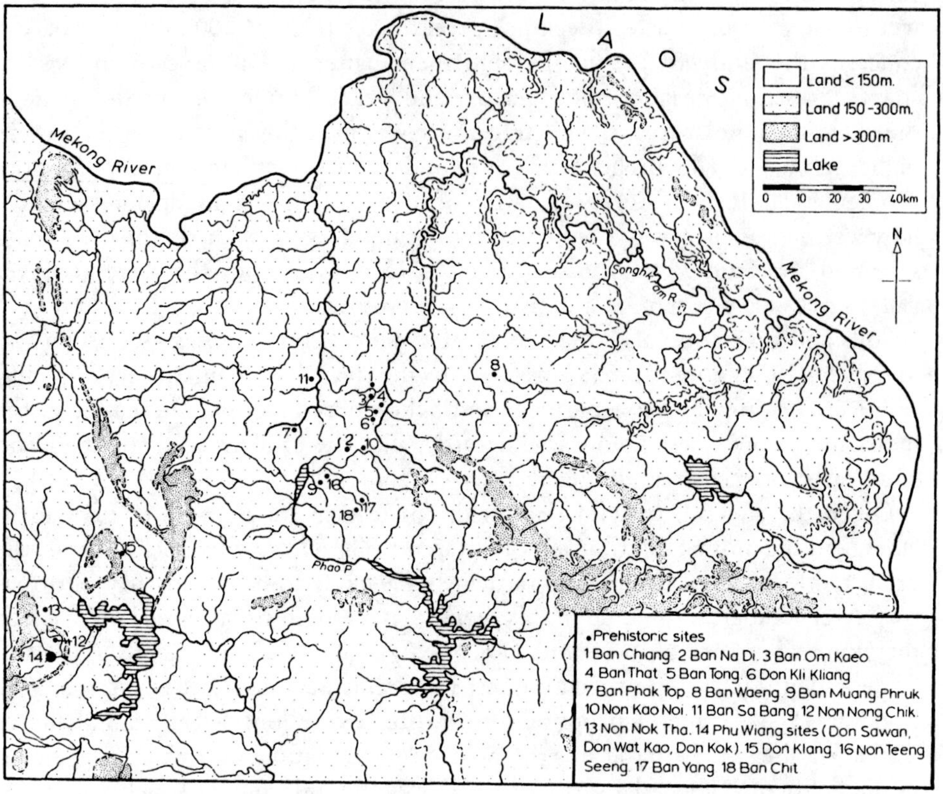

3.4 The distribution of the principal prehistoric sites in the northern part of the Khorat plateau.

middle-terrace soil. The low terrace is crossed by numerous small streams which originate in the surrounding high terraces.

Numerous prehistoric sites were located in this area, recognised on the basis of the pottery found eroding from the margins of low mounds, or villagers' reports of inhumation graves under existing settlements. A detailed statistical analysis of the distribution of these prehistoric sites has shown that close proximity to both small streams and low-terrace soils were the principal factors determining where people lived (Wichakana 1984, see also Fig. 3.28).

Higham and Kijngam then undertook a site survey on the southern margin of the Chi River which has been reported by Chantaratiyakan (1984). This revealed a similar pattern to that identified in the vicinity of Lake Kumphawapi (Fig. 3.5). The heavy clay soils of the Chi floodplain did not attract prehistoric settlement, whereas many sites were found along the edge of the floodplain and in the margins of the small tributary streams giving immediate access to low-level rice-land. White (1982a), basing her conclusions on fieldwork undertaken in the

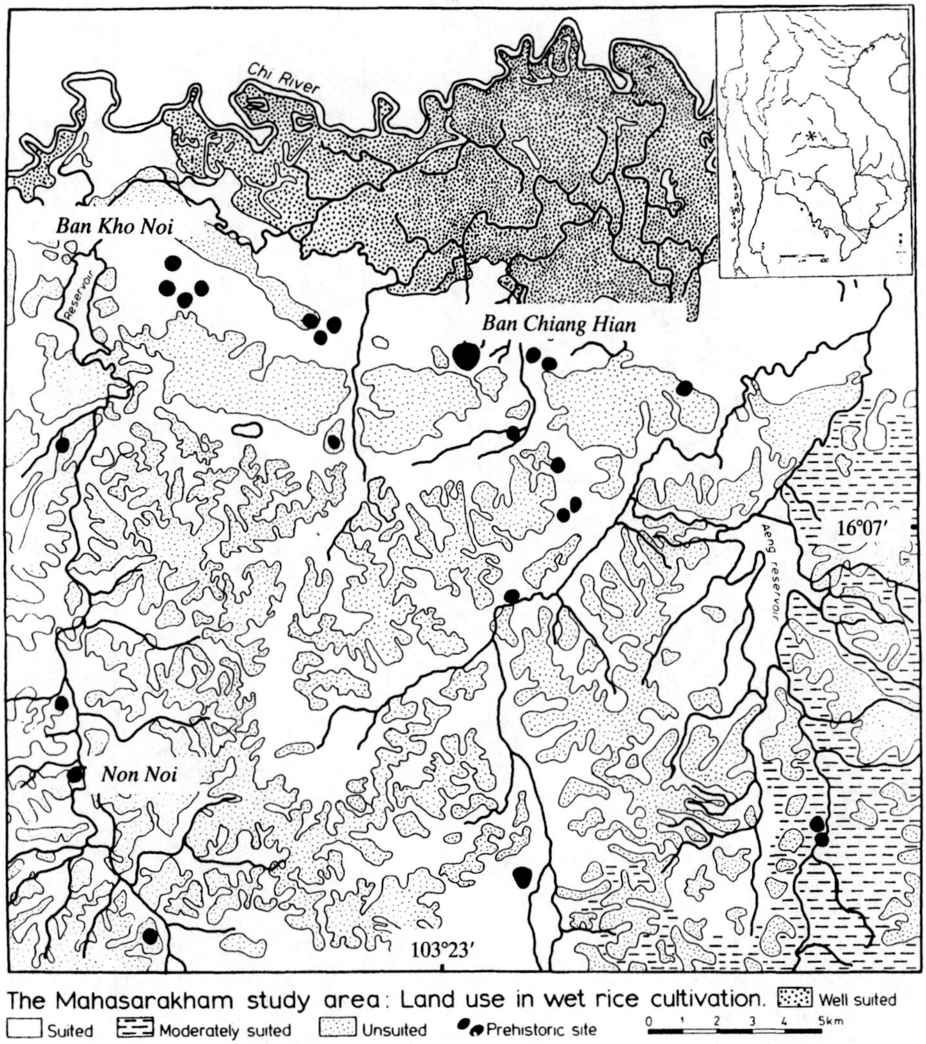

3.5 An intensive site survey in the middle Chi valley undertaken in 1981 revealed prehistoric sites clustered along the margins of the river's floodplain and in convenient locations along tributary streams. Ban Chiang Hian is a site first occupied during General Period B, but it was subsequently ringed by moats and a rampart (see page 121).

Sakon Nakhon basin, suggested that the latter location would have avoided the dangers posed to rice cultivation by wet-season flooding.

To the southeast of the Chi valley, Higham has undertaken a site survey in the valley of the Lam Siao Yai, a tributary of the Mun River (Higham and Parker 1970, Higham 1977). He found a concentration of settlements adjacent to an extensive exposure of salt, and excavations revealed that the exploitation of salt

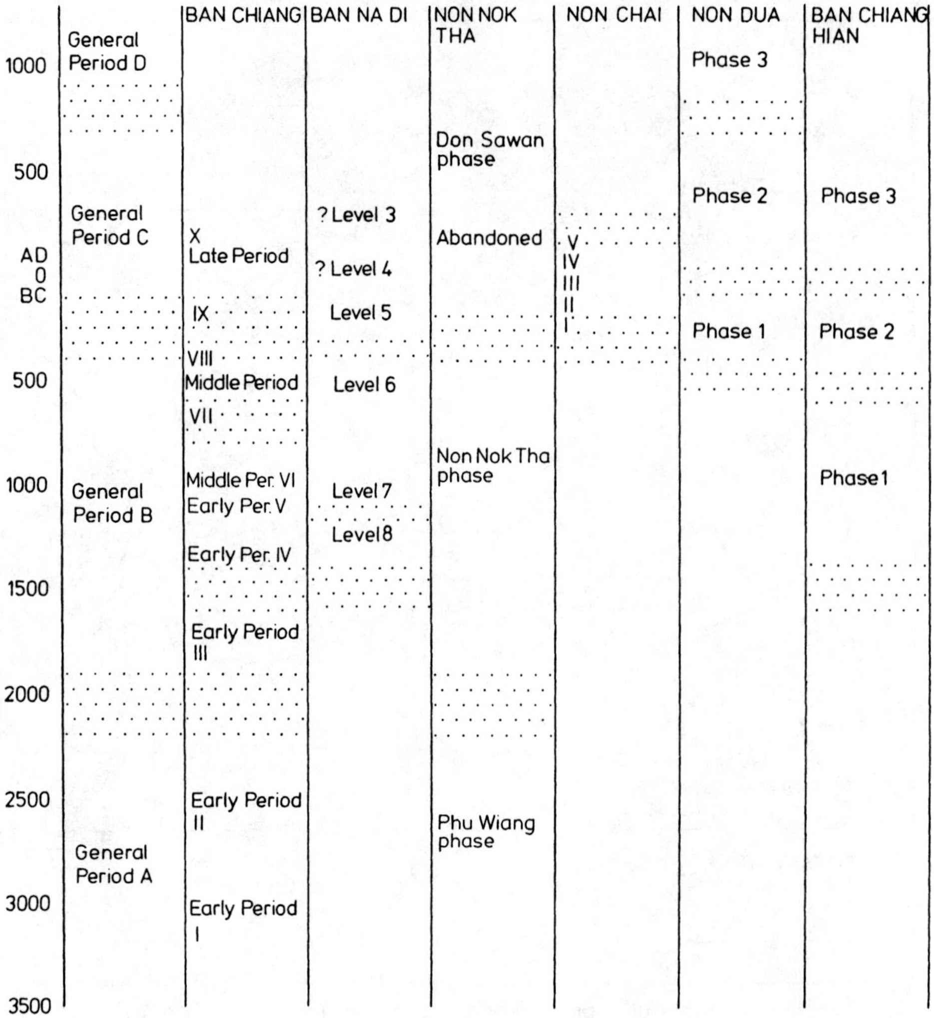

3.6 The relationships between sites in Northeast Thailand set against the General Periods employed.

began during the prehistoric period. The Chi and Mun are the two principal rivers of the Khorat plateau, and a site survey has recently been undertaken in the valley of the Mun River, in the vicinity of Phimai. Phimai was a focus of Khmer civilisation settlement and Welch (1984) has been able to identify a number of prehistoric settlements there. On a broader scale, Vallibhotama (1982, 1984) has identified and examined numerous moated sites in the area of the lower Mun. In 1984-5, Wilen (1987) undertook a major site survey in the area to the west of Non Nok Tha, identifying a number of prehistoric sites, and excavating at Non Pa Kluay. This has added important new information to our understanding of the western piedmont of the Khorat plateau during the prehistoric period. Finally, although more concerned with the western piedmont rather than the plateau proper, Penny has site surveyed and excavated a series of sites which add considerably to our knowledge of the expansion of human settlement during the first millennium B.C. (Penny 1982, 1984).

A general cultural framework

There have been four major prehistoric excavations in the Khorat plateau, and several sites have been examined by small test squares of limited scope. It is on the basis of these recent excavations that Bayard (1984b) has proposed a fourfold cultural framework (Fig. 3.6). This will now be summarised, and then the sequences at the best-documented sites will be correlated with it. General Period A refers to the initial settlement phase, and is described by Bayard as one involving noticeable but fairly weak social ranking, an agricultural base and absence of metallurgy. General Period B saw an increase in the degree of ranking and the advent of bronze-working. The ensuing Period C involved the development of centralised societies and iron-working. Many have recognised a major cultural change with the transition from General Period B to C. Ho (1984) refers to the latter as the "High Metal Age". Higham (1983) has called it Mode 2 and Welch refers to General Period B as the "Formative" and General Period C as the "Classic Phimai" phase. For the sake of overall simplicity, however, we will retain Bayard's framework. General Period D equates with the presence of regional states. This chapter is concerned only with General Periods A and B. The former was probably under way between *c* 3600–3000 B.C. and lasted until *c* 2000-1500 B.C., and the latter from 2000-1500 B.C. until about 500–300 B.C. It is stressed that the dates are by no means finalised and future research may well modify them. Most of our information for General Periods A and B comes from three sites where major excavations have taken place. These are Non Nok Tha, Ban Chiang and Ban Na Di.

Non Nok Tha

Non Nok Tha lies in the vicinity of the confluence of two small streams set within an extensive tract of low-terrace sandy-loam soil (Fig. 3.7). About 2.5 km to the southwest, the land rises abruptly to the sandstone ridge which comprises part of the monadnock known as Phu Wiang. The rise in altitude incorporates the transition from a moist, deciduous forest to a wetter, evergreen forest makes the resources of two distinct environments available to the site's occupants. A further advantage, to the modern rice farmer at least, is the concentration of water which runs off the hillside during the rainy season.

Test excavations undertaken in 1965 revealed the presence of inhumation burials associated with whole pottery vessels and fragments of bronze. The

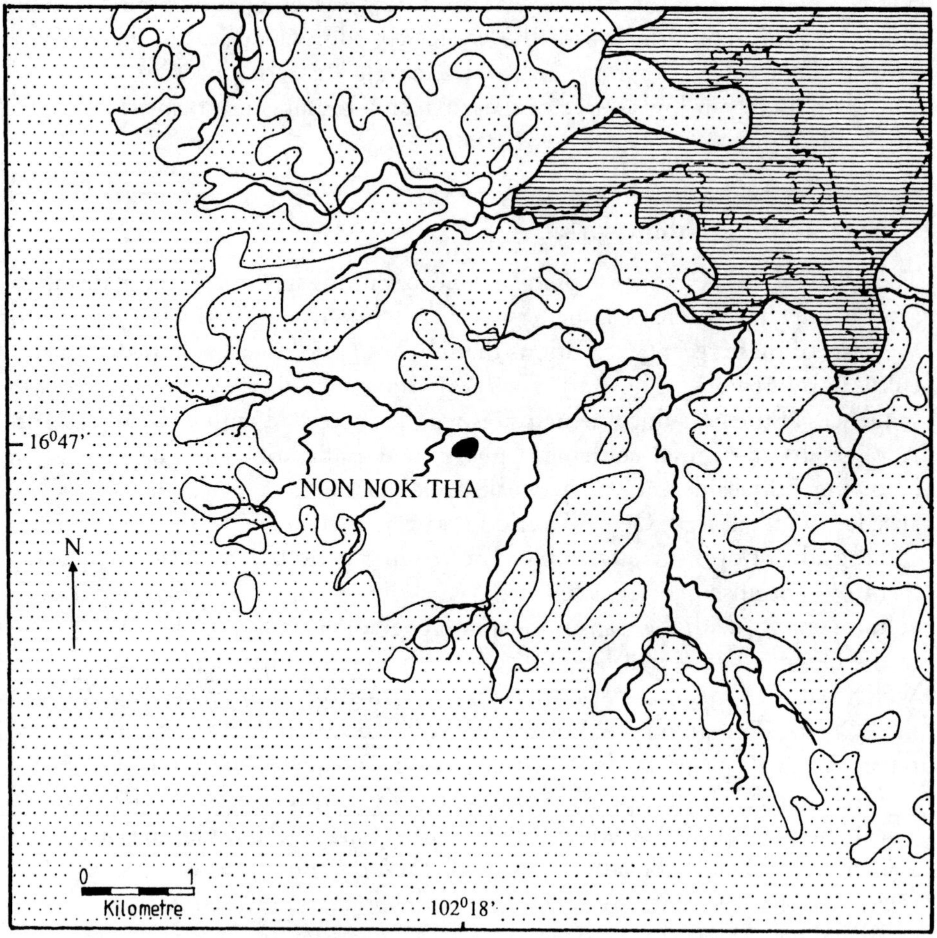

3.7 The location of Non Nok Tha relative to soil capability for rice. The white areas are those best suited to rice, and shaded areas are generally unsuitable.

presence of bronze was held to be surprising, given the then widespread view that metallurgy was introduced late in prehistory, with China the ultimate source of the necessary skills. It is the case, however, that bronze artefacts and moulds had long since been documented in prehistoric contexts at O Pie Can and Samrong Sen in Cambodia. The unknown factors were their chronological context and whether they represent an introduced or indigenous metallurgical tradition. This test excavation made it possible to investigate these two alternatives in conjunction with proper stratigraphic control over the data.

Full-scale excavations were planned for 1966 as part of the University of Hawaii Fine Arts Department's major research programme in Northeast Thailand. Working under Solheim's overall direction, Bayard was assisted by Parker

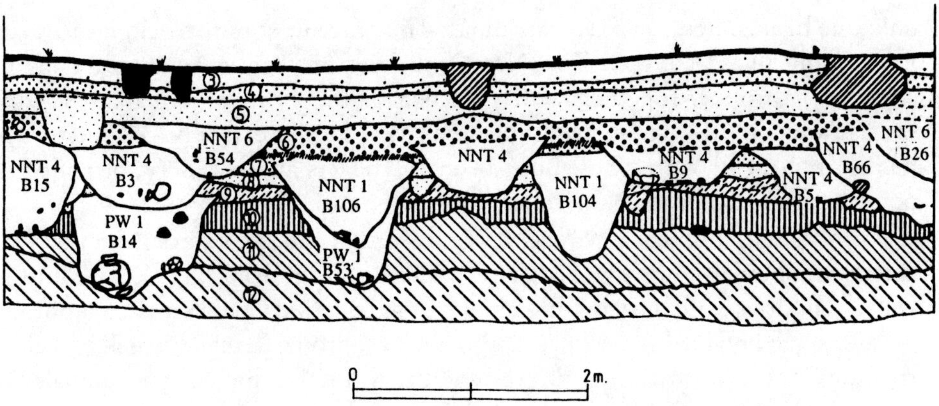

3.8 An example of the stratigraphy recovered at Non Nok Tha.

in the first season but returned on his own in 1968. These excavations opened 340m^2 of a site covering 1.1 ha. Although only a small fraction of the site was revealed, it was, and remains, the largest area excavation to be undertaken in Northeast Thailand. This is important because areal excavations provide the opportunity to recover the spacial distribution of prehistoric activity. Proper dating of the bronzes was one of the principal objectives, although the recovery of a large sample of human skeletons, intact pottery vessels and biological remains, would clearly lay the foundations for understanding the area's prehistory. These excavations confirmed that the site had served as a cemetery, but some posthole patterns also suggested the layout of prehistoric houses. The prehistoric deposits were not deep, the average depth being 1.4 m, but the intercutting and superposition of burials made it possible to obtain a sequential series. Wherever possible, excavations followed the actual cultural layers rather than arbitrary levels of consistent thickness determined by the excavator. This allowed Bayard (1971) to subdivide the occupation into successive soils and occasional periods of erosion (Fig. 3.8). No less important was the determination of layers from which graves were cut. This allowed the establishment of successive phases within the mortuary tradition.

An examination of the changing artefact typology, the orientation of individual graves, and the succession worked out from intercutting grave pits, are the bases for a subdivision of the sequence into three periods, each with constituent phases. In earlier publications, Bayard named these the early, middle and late periods. The early period had three, the middle period, eight, and the late period, six phases. Subsequently, Bayard has renamed these three periods calling them in chronological order the Phu Wiang, Non Nok Tha and Don Sawan phases (Bayard 1984a). Basically, the three are technologically distinct and only the first two concern us. The first was derived from the results of the 1968 excavations. Pottery was distinctive and there was a marked rarity of bronze objects. Indeed, only one bronze item, an axe, was found. The grave in question belongs to a late Phu Wiang phase context. The Non Nok Tha phase saw an increase in the amount of bronze, together with evidence in the form of crucibles, casting spillage and moulds, that metal implements were locally cast. The conjunction of human interments with whole pots, bronze artefacts and jewellery, provided an opportunity to consider numerous issues.

From its initial use as a cemetery, we learn that the site's burial rite involved extended inhumation in a grave between 40 and 90 cm deep (Fig. 3.9). Adults as well as children were buried with a range of grave goods which included pottery vessels, small polished stone quadrangular adzes, bronze artefacts, shell bracelets, shell-disc beads disposed in strings round the waist and the bones of animals. As was later found at Ban Chiang and Ban Na Di, the number of graves which contained artefacts exotic to the region was not great. Of 87 well-provenanced and relatively complete burials encountered, a figure which remains the largest sample by far from Northeast Thailand, only five were accompanied by shell beads, and there were two burials with shell bracelets. Bronze artefacts were uncommon, there being one axe in a late Phu Wiang phase context and three in the Non Nok Tha phase interments. Five burials in the latter phase incorporated bronze bracelets, and 10 included small stone axes which were probably obtained by exchange from the Phetchabun range to the the west. The most abundant grave offering comprised whole pottery vessels. As is the case for nearly all Southeast Asian sites, we will not know how many, if any, of these were locally made or were exotic to the area until a petrographic analysis of the fabric has been undertaken.

Ritual practices associated with burials are represented throughout the Phu Wiang and Non Nok Tha phases. Burial 8 belongs to the Phu Wiang phase 1. The child was interred with three whole pottery vessels. The rear limbs and jaw of a young pig were placed on the child's chest, and beyond the feet lay the remains of an adult dog. Burial 14 also came from the earliest mortuary context at the site. It contained the bones of a child. Four complete cord-marked vessels were placed in the grave, and the body was also covered with a sheet of broken sherds which, it seems, were deliberately smashed over the body. Two rows of shell-disc beads lay round the child's pelvis, a further two beads were found on the skull, and a bone spatula over the left thigh. After the interment, the burial ritual included the placing of an entire pig and the fore-limb of a cow round the child's head. The fore and rear limb-bones of a pig were found on the child's shoulders and ankles. These particular bones are often left on a pigskin when it is cured. It is quite likely that they are all that remains of a pigskin shroud which covered the body before funerary urns were smashed and the grave filled in.
Another complete pig's skeleton was found in burial 16, with three funerary urns and a concentration of beads in the area of the pelvis (Fig. 3.10).

While animal bones were common in Phu Wiang 1 graves, they were not always found. Thus, an adult was interred with a stone adze and six vessels, but

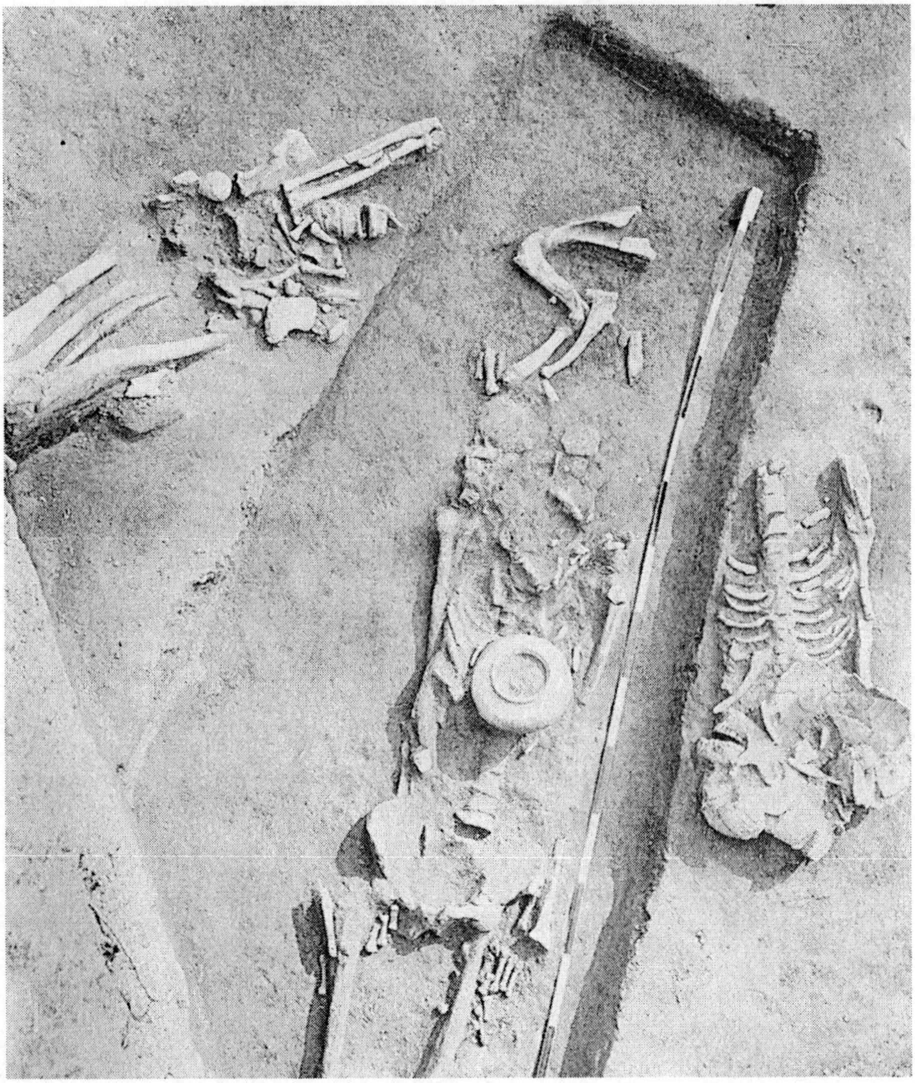

3.9 Burials 21, 22 and 26 from Non Nok Tha. Note how later graves were cut through earlier ones, thereby disturbing them.

no animal remains. Some burials were covered by mounds. In one case, the mound itself contained the remains of three limbs from a cow, the bones still being in articulation.

Apart from slight changes in the typology of pottery vessels, Phu Wiang 1 and 2 presented similar features. Graves tended to be shallower, with one part of the excavation area containing only child burials and another, with one exception, adult interments. Burial 112 contained a child's skeleton with four complete

3.10 Non Nok Tha burial 14. The child was buried with a rich array of grave goods and may have been covered by a pigskin shroud. (Courtesy Donn Bayard.)

vessels, three stone adzes and a shell under the right knee. The tusk of a young pig had been placed on the chest. In burial 90 of Phu Wiang 3, the first bronze implement was recovered in position over the chest of an adult male. This socketed axe was made of a 17% tin bronze. Round-based, cord-marked pots were found, one immediately next to the skull and three over the ankles. A pig's foot had been placed adjacent to the human thigh. Phu Wiang 3 graves were almost all of adults and no mounds were raised over them. Although the sample is not large – there are 11 substantially complete burials from the Phu Wiang phase – there were fewer burial goods when compared with earlier interments.

Differential wealth in burial goods in a given cemetery, whereby a few interments attracted rich offerings, is often used by prehistorians to distinguish social ranking. Bayard (1984a) noted evidence for ranking during the Phu Wiang phase, and it became more pronounced with the early part of the succeeding Non Nok Tha phase. The six burials concentrated in the northwest quadrant of the excavated area were buried deeply, and the mounds over them contained offerings of pottery and animal limb-bones. A second group occupied shallow graves in which the bones had been disarticulated before burial. They were arranged in approximate anatomical order, but two of the six burials also contained an extra human skull. Animal bone and pottery vessels were found in these graves. There are, in addition, four graves without mounds and with few burial goods. Finally, six mounds containing animal bones and broken vessels, but no human burials, were encountered.

Metal finds became more common during the Non Nok Tha phase, not only in the form of finished socketed axes, but also the stone moulds in which they had been cast. Ceramic styles changed too, the potter adding such novel features as raised pedestalled bases and sharply carinated shoulders. Moreover, 56 of the 100 complete mortuary vessels examined were found to contain fish bones, suggesting that they were designed to carry food for the dead.

As the Non Nok Tha phase proceeded, so the preferred styles of pottery continued to change, but always following the same basic traditions of manufacture. Animal bones continued to be interred, and some burial urns, smashed. Non Nok Tha 4 yielded more burials than any other. Most are orientated to the southwest, and have a standard assemblage of about four footed vessels placed beyond the head, associated with several bivalve shellfish. Burial 32 had five such shells near the skull and three pierced animal canine teeth in the vicinity of the neck, indicating the presence of a pendant at the time of burial. The fragmentary remains of an ox skull were found in the vicinity of his right arm, and a chicken had been placed over the chest area. Burial 85 included a bronze socketed axe and abundant remains of a large bovid. Although no mounds were located in Non Nok Tha 4 contexts, two crucibles containing fragments of casting spillage attest to local metallurgy. Non Nok Tha 5 revealed a configuration of postholes which Bayard has reconstructed as a structure measuring 12 x 6 m. The 12 burials belonging to this phase were orientated in a north, or northwesterly, direction. By this juncture, orientating burials to the southwest returned. Ceramic styles changed, however, and red-slipped vessels with flat bases became popular. A bronze halberd-like implement and a bracelet demonstrate the continuing availability of bronze. No burials belonging to Non Nok Tha 7–8 were found during the 1968 excavation season. Thirteen inhumations belonging to this period were recovered during 1966. None contained animal bone.

3.11 This aerial view of Ban Chiang shows the preferred location of many of the early settlements on the Khorat plateau, near the confluence of two or more streams.

As is seen in Fig. 3.6, the Phu Wiang phase at Non Nok Tha belongs to General Period A, and the Non Nok Tha phase to General Period B.

Ban Chiang

Ban Chiang is located near the junction of three small streams which are slightly incised into the low-terrace soils currently under rice cultivation (Figs. 3.11 and 3.12). Unlike Non Nok Tha, it is set in rolling lowlands without access to the resources of the surrounding hills. During the 1960s, several visitors to the village reported finding partial or complete red-on-buff painted pots of great beauty (Fig. 3.13). These reports led to a small test excavation in 1967, directed by Vidya Intakosai (You-di 1975). He uncovered a complete, inhumed skeleton with bronze and iron artefacts, painted pottery vessels and glass beads. This encouraged further research. In 1972, Pote Gueagoon excavated within the grounds of the Wat (temple) Pho Si Nai which lies on the flank of the present mound. He uncovered two layers of burials: the uppermost containing red-slipped, the lower, painted ceramics together with bronze and iron axes, and animal bone. The same year saw Nikhom Suthiragsa excavate a 65m^2 area, in which he recognised five layers containing cultural material (Suthiragsa 1979). He noted

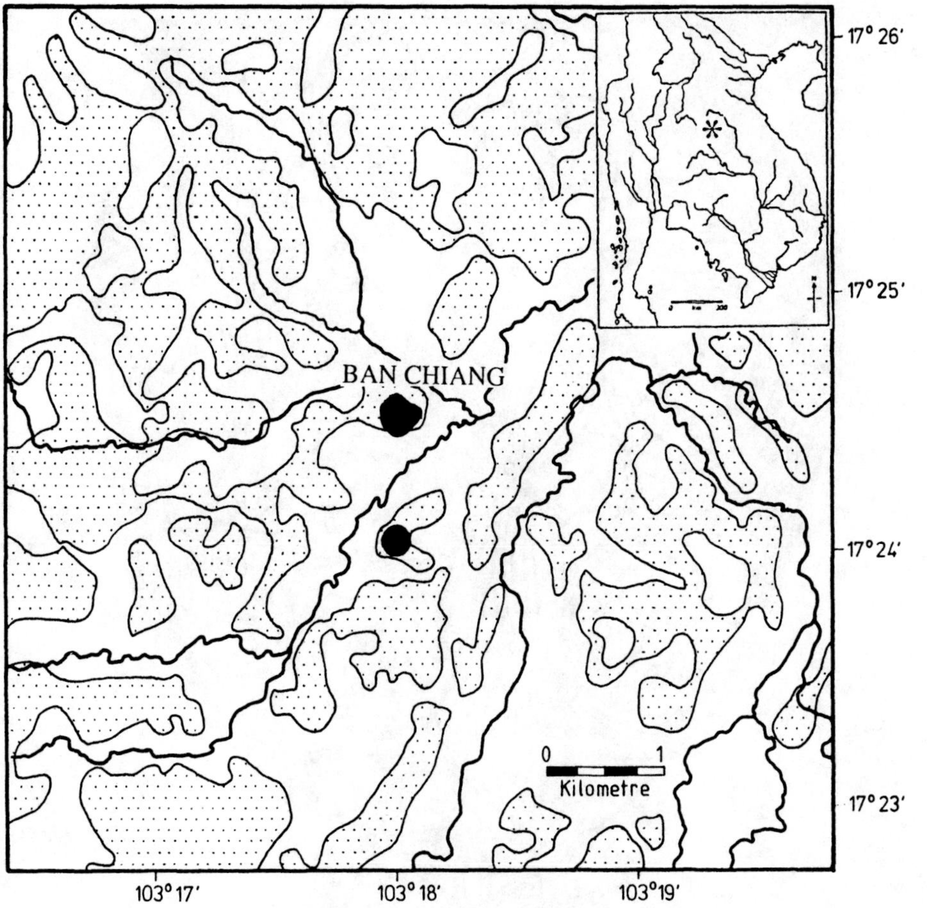

3.12 The location of Ban Chiang relative to rice soils. The white areas are those best suited to rice and the shaded areas are generally unsuitable.

that cord-marked pottery predominated in the lowest layers and that painted styles became increasingly dominant from layer 3. In the uppermost layer, he found iron spear-blades, glass beads and cylindrical objects of clay bearing carved designs. Suthiragsa then excavated two further squares. One revealed a very deep burial containing a novel dark-brown or black burial pottery bearing incised decoration. The burial in question also contained a deer skull and clusters of shellfish. The second square, which he excavated in 1973, had the deepest stratigraphy of all with a depth of about 4 m. The same black incised pottery was found at the bottom and the skeletons had eight metal, presumably bronze, bracelets. He also refers to impressions of cloth, ash lenses and rice remains from the basal horizon. Above these remains there was a new style of pottery characte-

3.13 An example of a Ban Chiang Late Period red-on-buff mortuary vessel. It stands about 45 cm high.

rised by incised patterns infilled with red paint. In one grave he noted the remains of a silk shroud. Bronze bracelets and anklets were also found. Given the fact that the recording of excavation layers was through arbitrary units 10 cm thick, the presence of iron down to a depth of 2.20 m may or may not have chronological significance. There followed a further change in the style of burial pottery: the higher layers were characterised by the red-on-buff painted wares for which the site is best known. Again, bronze bracelets were found in several graves together with some axes and glass beads.

By 1973, 30 squares had been excavated at Ban Chiang, and these revealed that the prehistoric mound covered an area of at least 3.5 ha. There was clear evidence of bronze and iron metallurgy and of a long period of occupation. The inhumation burials contained animal bone and complete vessels, clay animal figurines and glass beads. The site was clearly of immense importance. It presented many parallels, and some differences, with Non Nok Tha. Both had similar burial rites and evidence for metallurgy, but Ban Chiang had distinct pottery styles and a more varied range of artefacts. Consequently, the Thai Fine Arts Department combined with the University Museum, University of Pennsylvania, Philadelphia, in a major research programme under the direction of Pisit Charoenwongsa and Chester Gorman (Gorman and Charoenwongsa 1976).

Several factors distinguish the Ban Chiang excavations of 1974–5 from preceeding research undertaken at this and related sites. Specialists in soils, pollen analysis, zoology, dating techniques and physical anthropology participated in the actual fieldwork. This allowed a much more detailed and better informed analysis of resultant finds. Also, all excavated soils were screened to ensure that small remains were retained. Soil conditions at Non Nok Tha had ruled out the use of screens. Like everyone else in Northeast Thailand, archaeologists defer to the monsoon. The hot dry-season sun bakes the soil and turns slight colour differences to a uniform grey colour within minutes of exposure, and seasonal deluges fill excavation squares with serious implications for stratigraphic control. At Ban Chiang, both problems were obviated by constructing a thatched shelter over the squares. This allowed excavations to proceed uninterrupted for nine months in 1974, and again in 1975 (Fig. 3.14).

There remained a major problem. Looting was so intensive that it was doubtful if any prehistoric deposits remained intact. In 1974, five squares covering 75.5 m^2 were laid out in the garden of a family which maintained that no looting had occurred there. After the top metre of heavily disturbed garden soil was removed, this prediction proved correct. In May 1974, the first intact skeletons were uncovered, and soon they were found across the excavated area. These were accompanied by complete pottery vessels, the predominant form being a red-slipped and footed jar with constricted neck and broad burnished rim.

These uppermost burials contained iron fragments as well as knives, axes and spears, demonstrating full competence in iron metallurgy. Glass beads were relatively common, as were the curious clay rollers with deeply carved, curvilinear and rectangular designs. Underlying these, were further graves with an equally distinctive pottery style. Pots with everted rims and incised, painted designs on the shoulder were found. In one grave, a bronze socketed axe head and bracelets were found.

At this juncture, a major problem became apparent. Accustomed to the reports from Non Nok Tha that the burials not only frequently intercut each other but were placed in graves of ascertainable depth, those working at Ban Chiang expected to find evidence for grave cuts defined by differences in soil colour. The first evidence for an impending burial at Ban Chiang, however, was not the definition of a grave, but its uppermost contents. Once the appearance of complete pots was noted, the excavation procedure was to excavate away from them to locate the grave edge. This was nearly always fruitless. There was no visually apparent change in soil colour or structure.

There are several possible reasons for this. The dead may have been buried on the former ground surface and a mound subsequently raised over them. Certainly, mounds had been observed at Non Nok Tha and normal stratigraphic excavation should allow them, if they existed, to be recognised. Is it possible that shallow graves were dug into a soil so homogeneous and the same soil returned in such a way that distinction between grave-fill and the surrounding matrix was ruled out? That graves had indeed been excavated was demonstrated beyond doubt by burials covered with broken pottery sherds. These formed a discrete heap, and some sherds still stood vertically at the former grave edge. The nature of the soils finally suggested the explanation, for they were mottled in colour and lacked distinctive, overall consistency. The upper 2 m of soil had been redeposited by a species of burrowing beetle so thoroughly that the burials seemed to be floating in marbled, reddish soil. Ascription of burial to layer was ruled out, and seriation had to be undertaken on the basis of the style of burial goods and the orientation of the skeleton. Equally difficult was the rarity of charcoal in clearly

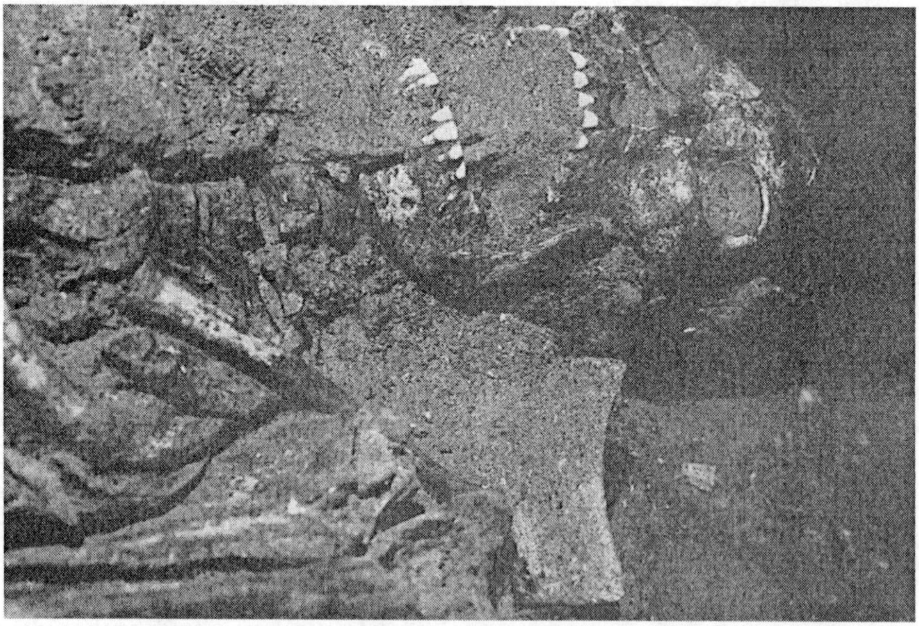

3.14 In Early Period III at Ban Chiang a few burials contained bronze grave goods. This example includes a bronze axe. (For a description of the cultural sequence at Ban Chiang, see below, p.113.)

undisturbed contexts. Considerable rigour needs to accompany the collection of samples. Charcoal found within whole funerary vessels or as part of a large and intact concentration, as in a hearth, are considered more reliable than pieces which may have been relocated in antiquity.

A further problem also confronted the 1974 excavations as they proceeded. No characteristic "Ban Chiang" painted pottery was found. There were, however, burials associated with a distinctive incised and painted ware. One was particularly interesting. The adult male held a tanged bone projectile point or spearhead in his left hand. The handle was broken, and the detached portion was placed in the vicinity of his right hand. Immediately above the spearhead was a complete muntjak antler with a hole bored through its base. The dead man had been buried wearing a double tiger-tooth pendant round his neck. His skull lay on a bone pin which may have been part of his head dress. This ritual assemblage of grave goods suggested to the excavators that the dead were buried with their own particular possessions.

Below this context, with its distinctive incised and painted wares, was a horizon in which the ceramics were cord-marked and incised with curvilinear designs. Some pots had ring feet, others were globular with rounded bases. Some such vessels contained the remains of infants, others were associated with adult burials.

The lowest layer revealed another pottery style, still associated with extended and inhumed burials. Vessels were divided into zones of distinct decoration. The pedestals at the base were polished and incised with parallel lines. The lower body was often cord-marked below a cordon, and burnished and incised with curvilinear decoration above it. The lowest graves were found cut into the yellow natural soil which had been the surface of a low mound when Ban Chiang was first occupied.

While of considerable interest, the 1974 excavations left several unanswered questions. Inspection of the still open square excavated the previous year by Suthiragsa revealed a layer containing red-on-buff painted vessels which was not paralleled in the 1974 sounding. The basal burials of the same square yielded some bronze bracelets. These, again, were not recovered from the base of the latest excavations. Expectations of a clear relationship in terms of the ceramic sequence with Non Nok Tha were not sustained. Certainly, the curvilinear incised style resembles vessels from the Phu Wiang phase, but it was felt that much closer parallels should exist given the distance of only 180 km between the two sites. Yet the bronze axes and bracelets, fragments of sandstone moulds and crucibles, were very similar.

Further excavations in 1975, therefore, were located only 10 m from Suthiragsa's 1973 square, and in the same narrow lane. The layout of squares, which covered 55.75 m^2, was thus linear, and constrained by the flanking houses. There was little doubt that their gardens had already been looted, and the possibility that galleries had mined the area under the lane itself was a probability. The

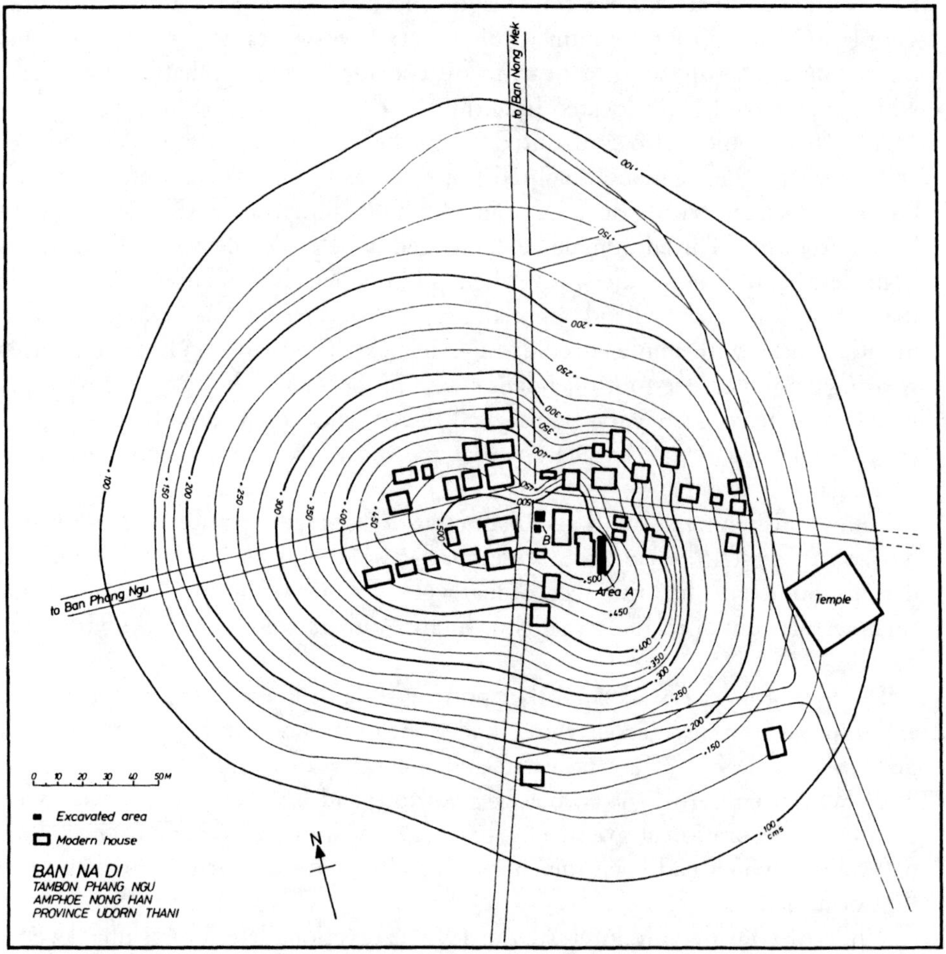

3.15 Ban Na Di is a modern village, and excavations took place between houses. The size of the excavation squares illustrates clearly how little of the prehistoric site was sampled, even in a campaign lasting six months.

sequence of cultural events uncovered during the ensuing nine months was long and detailed. Four ceramic phases matched those found in 1974. In addition, it was possible to clarify the position of the phase containing the curvilinear red-on-buff painted ware as being relatively late in the prehistoric sequence.

Tragically, Gorman died in 1981, when the analysis of finds was in full swing. Joyce White, who had assisted in the laboratory research for several years, and had already undertaken extensive ecological studies in the Ban Chiang region, continued his work, with the first objective of establishing a cultural and chronological framework for the site. Having identified 17 provisional types of pottery vessel, and established their chronological relationships on the basis of burial

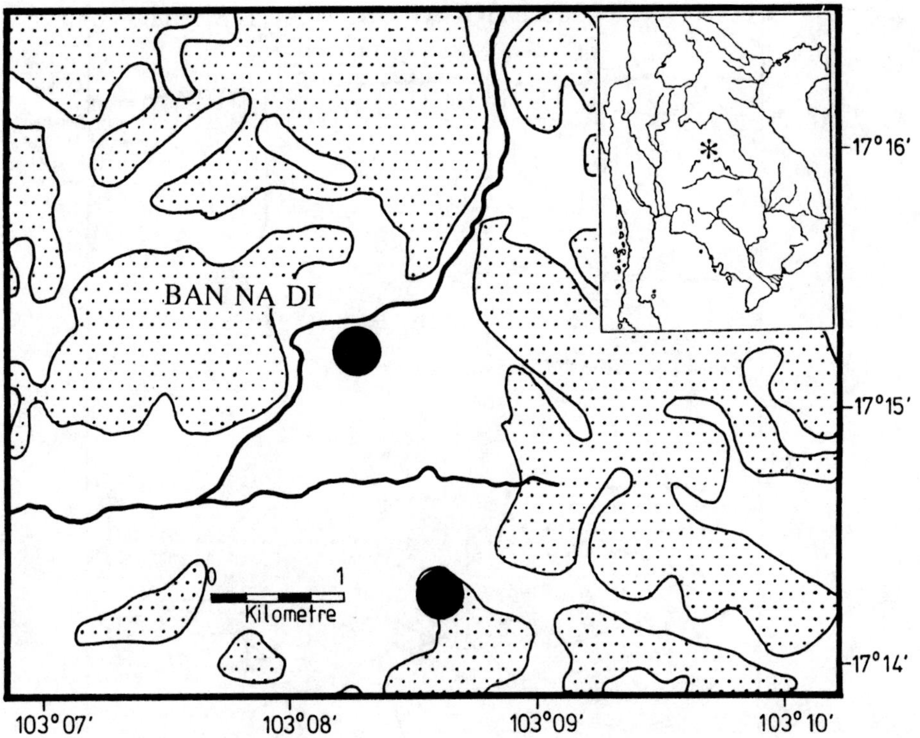

3.16 The location of Ban Na Di. It lies near good rice-land near the confluence of two streams. The white areas are those best suited to rice and shaded areas are generally unsuitable.

stratigraphy, she subdivided the sequence into Early, Middle and Late Periods. The first comprises five phases (EP I–V), the second three (MP VI–VIII), and the last, two (LP IX–X). This sequence is set against those from other Khorat plateau sites in Fig. 3.6. It will be seen that the earliest bronze from a burial belongs to EP III, and that iron made its appearance by MP VII. Thus, this most recent assessment of the Ban Chiang cultural sequence sees EP I–II as corresponding to General Period A, and EP III to MP VI as belonging to General Period B.

Ban Na Di

Ban Na Di is located only 23 km southwest of Ban Chiang (Fig. 3.15). It was one of the sites identified during the 1980 site survey in the vicinity of Lake Kumphawapi, and excavations began in November 1980 (Higham and Kijngam 1984). As with Ban Chiang, it is located near the confluence of small tributary streams which command a tract of low-terrace soils particularly valued today for wet rice cultivation (Fig. 3.16). White (1982a) has suggested that such a position would

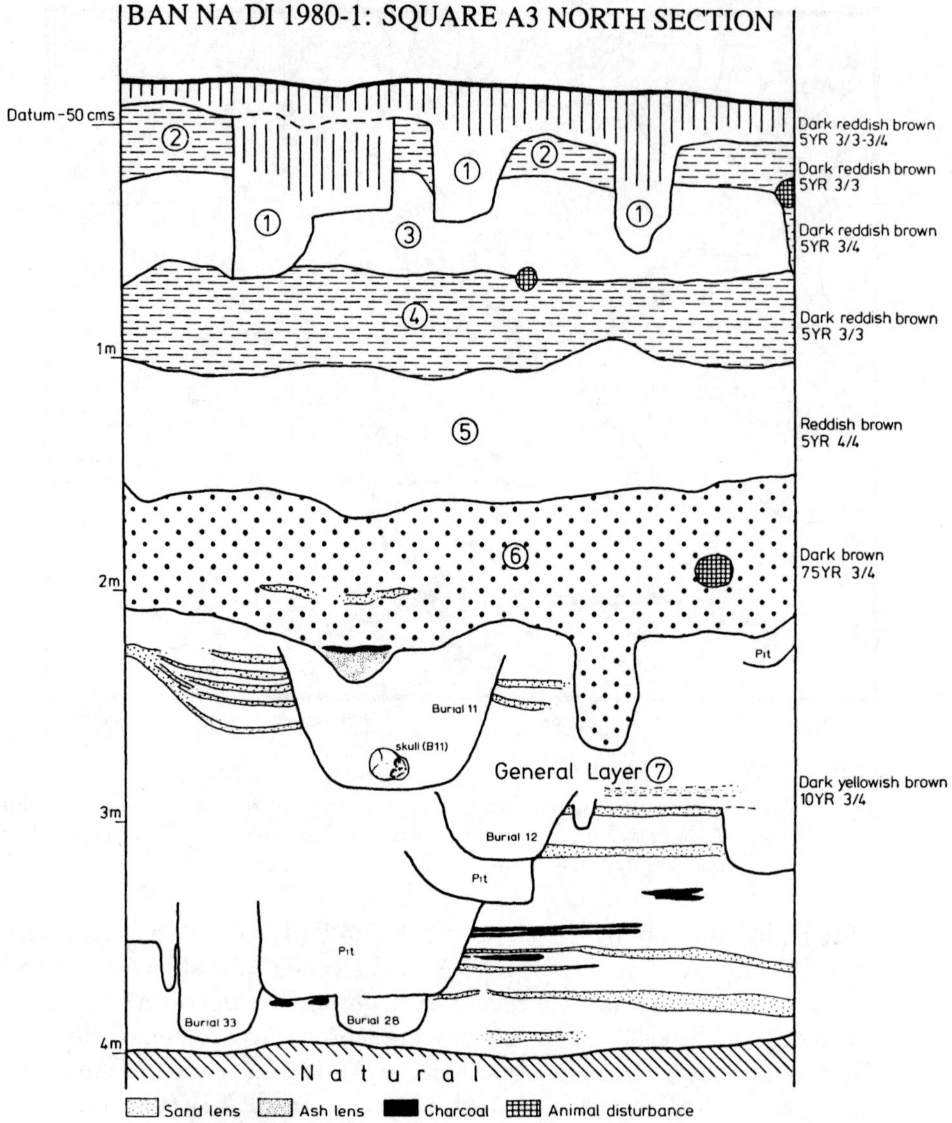

3.17 Ban Na Di revealed a clear stratigraphic sequence and charcoal samples for dating were collected from well-provenanced locations, such as within bronze-working furnaces. The results have helped to resolve the thorny issue of the chronological context of metallurgy.

have favoured prehistoric settlement because of the relatively gentle flood regime associated with the middle courses of tributary streams. Flooding, however, did occur during the early occupation of Ban Na Di, as is indicated by the numerous sand lenses found there which had been deposited by floodwater.

The site revealed a stratigraphic sequence including five prehistoric levels to a depth of 4 m below the present ground surface (Fig. 3.17). The basal level, designated level 8, comprised occupation material which included the remains of freshwater molluscs and a wide range of mammal and fish bones. Some of the bones came from domestic cattle, dog and pig. An innovation at Ban Na Di was the screening of a sample of all excavated soils through a 1mm mesh. This mesh size was much smaller than that employed at Ban Chiang, and its use resulted in a greater recovery of the remains of small species. The analysis of this microfauna, for example, made it clear how much emphasis was placed on fishing (Fig. 3.18).

This lowest level yielded much pottery, pits containing occupation refuse and hearths. There were several broken fragments of crucible to which metal scoria still adhered, fragments of bronze and bronze artefacts.

The next levels, numbers 7 and 6, were associated with a change in the use to which at least part of the excavated area was put. Two areas covering 70 m^2 were excavated, the intervening distance being *c* 30 m. Both yielded burials laid out in rows and superimposed over a depth of almost 2 m. The mortuary rite matches that at Ban Chiang and Non Nok Tha, except for local variations. Thus, the food remains found comprise the left fore-limbs of pigs and cattle. The orientation is invariably on a north-south axis, and bodies were interred with a variable assemblage of artefacts which included whole pottery vessels, clay figurines and of personal jewellery made from shell, stone, bronze and, in the latest graves, of iron. Grave goods were associated with the remains of children, adolescents and adults of both sexes, but not with very young infants. The pottery vessels were often found to be complete, and they contained food remains such as fish bone and, in one case, the fore-limb of a pig. In terms of form, the vessels are similar to those found in Early Period IV–V and the Middle Period at nearby Ban Chiang.

The excavation showed that, during the build-up of levels 7 and 6, the area was not solely used as a cemetery. There were also pits and hearths outside the burial area and, as in level 8, crucibles and bronze were found. One particularly interesting feature comprised the remains of a clay-lined furnace ringed by bronze detritus and the remains of crucibles. It had been used to raise copper and tin to melting-point prior to casting (Fig. 3.19). That this occurred on the spot is further documented by the recovery of stone mould fragments.

The last interments in this mortuary phase included a few iron objects, though these are found in only two graves cut from lower level 6. There is an iron spear-blade, a knife and a ring, used perhaps as a bracelet or armlet. The cemetery, or at least that part revealed by excavations, then seems to have fallen into abeyance. Level 5 involved a new and distinct tradition of pottery-making and a new range of artefact types. The old cemetery area was now used for bronze-working. It was dotted with clay-lined furnaces, each of which was ringed with bronze-casting spillage and broken crucibles. The crucibles were associated, too, with fragments of clay moulds designed to cast bells and bracelets. Level 5 also included the first find of iron slag, indicating that iron ore

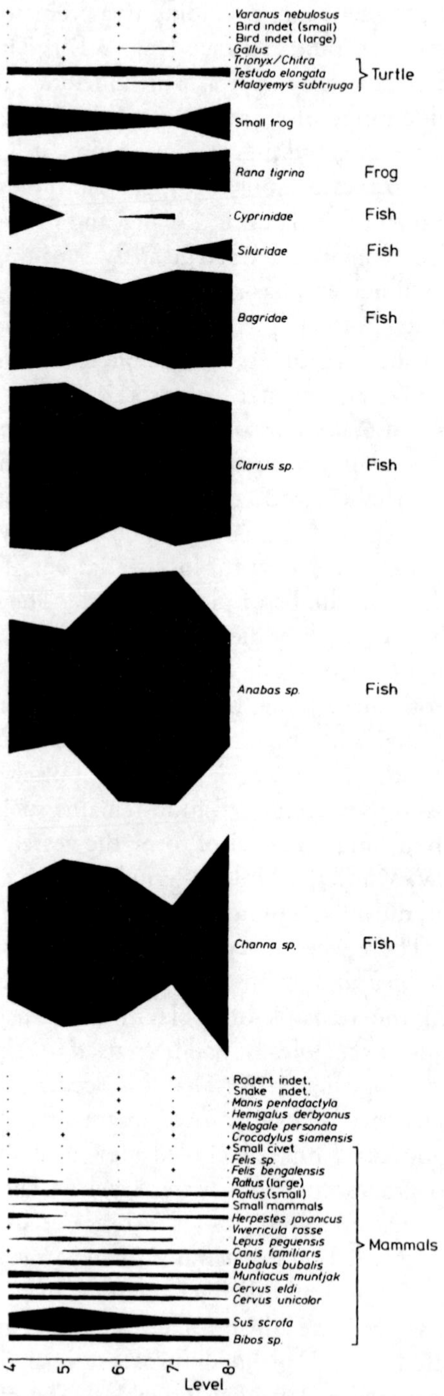

3.18 The faunal spectrum from Ban Na Di. The great dominance of fish species reflects the use at the site of a very fine screen to recover biological remains.

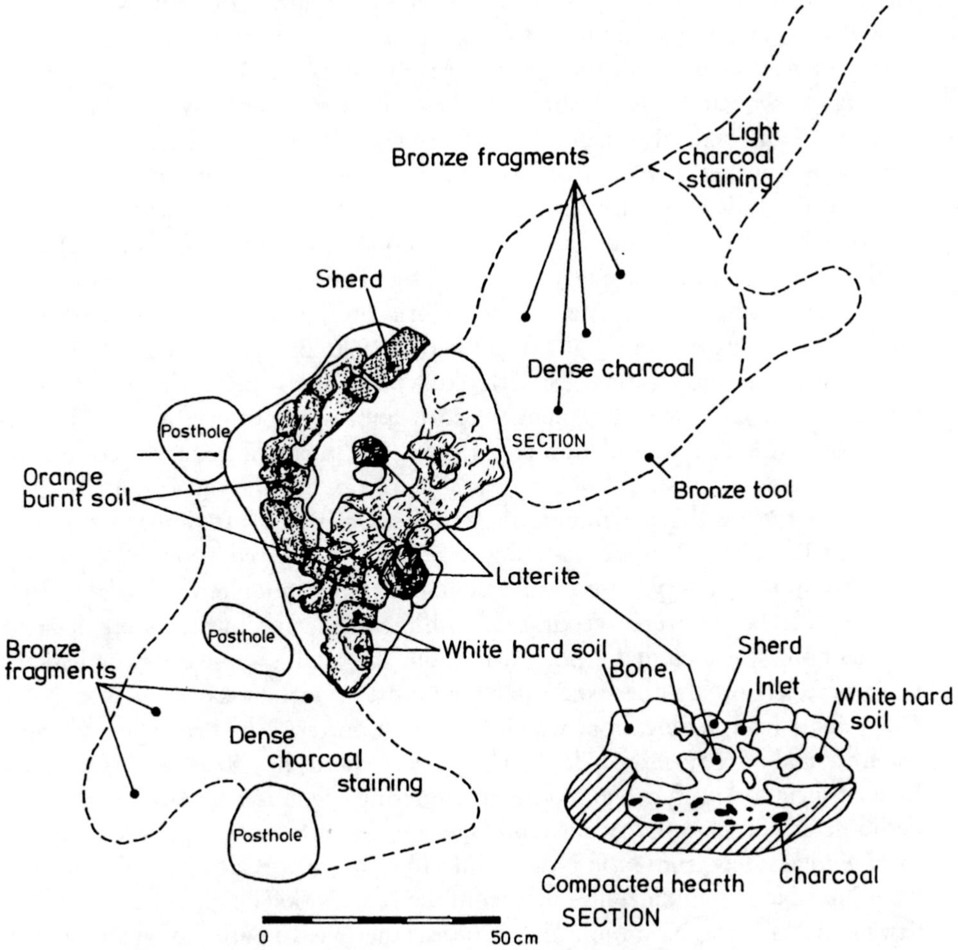

3.19 The bronze-casting furnace from level 7 at Ban Na Di. Copper and tin ingots were brought to the site, melted in small crucibles, and locally cast in stone and clay moulds.

was now being worked locally. No burials were found, but five jar burials containing the remains of infants were recovered, each cut down from the overlying level 4. Some of these infants were buried with bronze and iron artefacts, and one was found together with five blue-glass beads. These levels, however, equate with the Late Period at Ban Chiang and Bayard's General Period C, so we will return to them later (p.129).

Other excavated sites in the northern Khorat plateau

Test excavations at other sites on the Khorat plateau have provided further useful information. In the year following the completion of excavations at Non Nok

Tha, a site survey was undertaken within the confines of Phu Wiang. This monadnock looks like a huge volcanic crater. Easy access is possible only through a narrow defile in the mountain wall cut by a river. Within the ring of mountains, flat land covers about 14 km^2. It is now densely settled by rice cultivators who take advantage of the encircling hills, with their forest cover, for dry-season hunting. The interior has the advantage of receiving water which runs off from the hills, and there are perennial streams which link with a series of permanent swamps and ultimately flow into one major river. Non Nok Tha lies on the northeastern outer edge of Phu Wiang. The survey in the interior discovered a series of prehistoric and early historic sites, and small test squares were excavated in four of them (Higham and Parker 1970, Buchan 1973, Bayard 1977). One, known as Non Nong Chik, looked particularly promising, because its surface was covered with fragments of cord-impressed pottery, resembling that from Non Nok Tha. Its isolation is intriguing and, again, it lies at the confluence of two streams in an enclave of soils suitable for rice cultivation (Fig. 3.20). Only 150 m to the north, the mountain wall rises sharply, providing a series of horizontally stratified resource-zones. Excavations covered 12 m^2 and encountered complete pottery vessels in association with inhumation burials. Eight stratigraphic layers were recognised within which five burials were located. Animal bone was included in the burials, but the small sample did not yield any stone bracelets or shell beads. Perhaps the most important aspect of Non Nong Chik, apart from its location, was its funerary pottery, the presence of bronze and iron, and its radiocarbon dates. The pottery sherds have been analysed on the basis of their surface finish and type of tempering agent used. It would have been desirable to compare the two assemblages on the basis of complete vessels, but there were too few from Non Nong Chik. In terms of surface finish, the material from Non Nong Chik matches that from the Non Nok Tha phases 5–6 and Don Sawan phases 2–3 at Non Nok Tha. Whereas there was a period of abandonment after the Non Nok Tha phase at Non Nok Tha, Non Nong Chik was used as a cemetery throughout. Thus, it fills in a gap and shows how plain and cord-marked wares were evolving locally during the interval between the Non Nok Tha and Don Sawan phases.

During 1984–5, Wilen (1987) expanded our knowledge of the prehistory of the Upper Nam Phong valley area by undertaking a site survey and excavation programme in the area to the west of Non Nok Tha. He identified 25 probably prehistoric village and cemetery sites most of which, as in the Ban Chiang region, were located so as to have easy access to the type of soils which are suited to modern rice cultivation. At Non Pa Kluay, he excavated an area of 15m^2 down to a depth of 2 m and, in the lower of two cultural horizons, he recovered material belonging to General Period B. He found a close similarity, in terms of pottery forms and decoration, with the material beginning with the Non Nok Tha or even the late Phu Wiang phase at Non Nok Tha itself. Again, bivalve sandstone

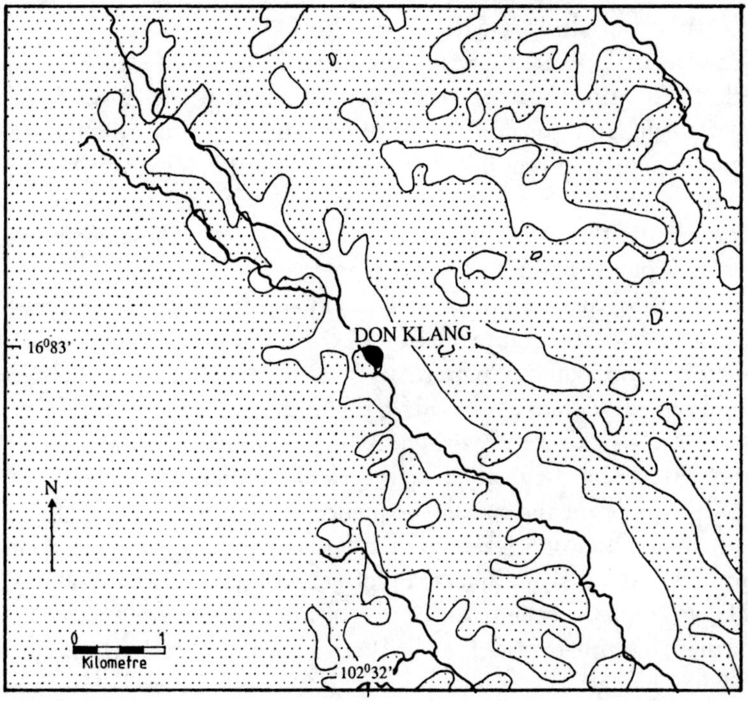

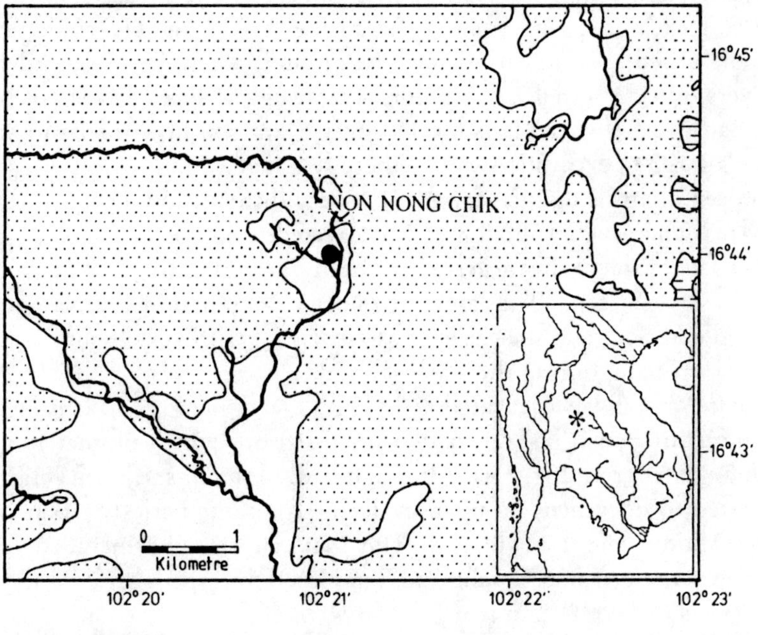

3.20 The location of Don Klang and Non Nong Chik. The white areas are those best suited to rice, and the shaded areas are, in general, unsuitable.

axe moulds were recovered. His three radiocarbon determinations suggest that the earliest burials post-date about 1700 B.C.

The site of Don Klang lies in the eastern margin of Phu Kao, another monadnock 30 km northeast of Non Nok Tha (Shauffler 1976). It lies about 3 km downstream from the confluence of two small streams which have their headwaters in the surrounding hill (Fig. 3.20). Schauffler's excavations revealed a series of burials and some occupation layers. The material culture was very similar to that from the Phu Wiang phase at Non Nok Tha. These layers were cut into by later pits, one containing 10 water-buffalo skulls.

Excavations at sites nearer to Ban Chiang and Ban Na Di have added little in terms of our detailed appreciation of the Ban Chiang sequence and chronology, but have illuminated a pattern of settlement, and upheld observations which would remain tentative if based on the findings from one site, however prolific in data and painstakingly excavated. All related sites mentioned above have a similar burial rite, and most have yielded ceramics which recall some of the wares used by White to define the cultural sequence she has proposed for Ban Chiang (White 1986). Thus, Ban Om Kaeo was particularly rich in wares which characterise the Middle Period at Ban Chiang (Preecha and Pukajorn 1976). Ban Phak Top (Fig. 3.21) was looted to the point of practically complete destruction during 1974–5. The many complete pots for sale there correspond to Early Period I–II ceramics at Ban Chiang. The looted area was liberally littered with complete human crania, partial ivory bracelets, and numerous sherds and figurines. Schauffler (1976) excavated one square, measuring 3 × 3 m. He could only locate an undisturbed area on the edge of the mound, where he recovered 11 occupation layers, but no burials. These thin layers suggest brief periods of occupation.

Ban Tong (Fig. 3.21) is located only 5 km southeast of Ban Chiang. Schauffler's 3 × 3 m excavation square there revealed a stratigraphical sequence about 3 m deep comprising nine layers. It is very difficult to be sure of the sequence of events when such a small area is excavated. There is little doubt, however, that this part of the prehistoric site had been intermittently used for both occupation and as a cemetery. The latest of the two inhumation burials equates with the Middle Period, and the earlier was associated with vessels similar to some found at Ban Chiang during the Early Period.

Ban Waeng was excavated in 1980 by Daeng-iet (1980). It is located about 40 km east of Ban Chiang near two small streams which ultimately join the Songkhram River (see Fig. 3.4). Although badly looted, sufficient intact burials were located to document occupation during the same period as Ban Chiang during the Middle and Late phases. The material remains included clay "rollers", characteristic of Ban Chiang and Ban Na Di during General Period C, and many artefacts of bronze and iron.

During the site survey in the Kumphawapi area in 1980, a particularly interesting and small (*c* 0.5 ha) site situated at the confluence of two streams was identified. Its name Non Kao Noi means, literally, "small old mound". A test square measuring 3 by 3 m excavated towards the edge of the mound revealed a cultural stratigraphy only 1.5 m deep, the square containing the remains of five inhumation burials. They were accompanied by pottery vessels and, apart from three stone beads, no other grave goods were encountered (Higham and Kijngam 1984). The pottery vessels (Fig. 3.22) are similar in form and decorative style to those from early Ban Chiang and Ban Phak Top, a situation suggesting that this is a complete settlement occupied only during General Period A. This is a very rare occurrence. No bronze was found during the excavation nor, unfortunately, any *in situ* charcoal. Consequently, no estimate of the site's age is available.

The southern Khorat plateau: Ban Chiang Hian and related sites

Ban Chiang Hian is a large (*c* 38 ha) moated site located on the southern edge of the Chi floodplain. A small test square was excavated there in 1981, and prehistoric deposits were encountered to a depth of 6 m. The characteristics of its pottery came as a surprise. In the Sakon Nakhon basin sites of Ban Chiang and Ban Na Di, red-on-buff painted pottery characterises the General Period C, and dates from *c* 300 B.C. At Ban Chiang Hian, red-on-buff pottery decoration was found in the basal layers associated, as we shall see, with dates in the second millenium B.C. Naturally, there is no reason to link the two painted pottery traditions. They may well have been independent. Given the distinct differences between the ceramics of Ban Chiang and Non Nok Tha during General Periods A and B, the presence of a third distinct style of decoration suggests regionality, rather than widespread homogeneity, in ceramic traditions. The Ban Chiang

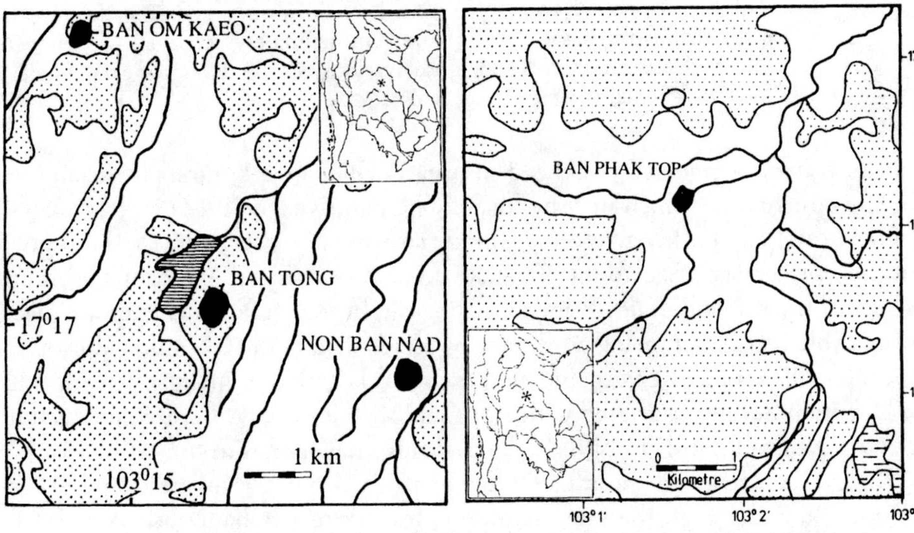

3.21 The location of Ban Tong and Ban Phak Top. The white areas are those best suited to rice and the shaded areas are generally unsuitable.

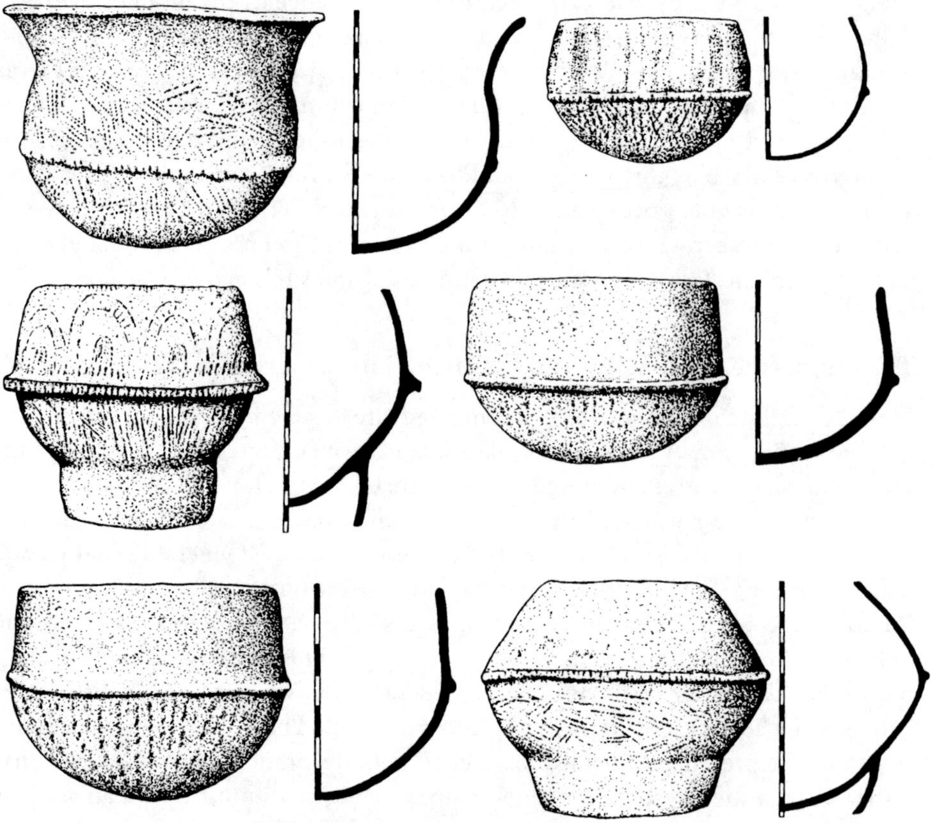

3.22 The burial pottery from Non Kao Noi shows many similarities in style with that from basal Ban Chiang. Unfortunately, no well-provenenced charcoal was recovered during excavations, so the dating of early General Period A remains hazy. Scale in cm.

Hian excavation involved one 3 × 3 m square which greatly limits the usefulness of any conclusions which may be made. Chantaratiyakan (1984), in her analysis of the pottery and other artefacts from the site has, however, noted a sharp break in the pottery styles at about 300–500 B.C. associated with the first iron and bones of the water-buffalo. Prior to that break, bronze fragments and rare pieces of crucible reveal that metal-working was established in the Chi valley during the second millennium B.C. Again, the lower levels at Ban Chiang Hian included inhumation burials associated with stone and shell jewellery. Limited excavations at Non Noi and Ban Kho Noi (Fig. 3.5), both smaller sites in the vicinity of Ban Chiang Hian, revealed the same styles of painted pottery in the deepest levels and, at Ban Kho Noi, the same chronological context (Chantaratiyakan 1984).

Hitherto, all the sites described for General Periods A and B were lowland villages revealing occupation material, cemeteries and, during General Period B, evidence for bronze-working. Yet many of the imported exotic goods had their sources in the surrounding hills. Clearly, there must have been an exchange network in operation bringing tin, copper, stone and shell into the lowlands of the Khorat plateau. Fieldwork in the uplands which ring the plateau has led to the discovery of two most important categories of site. The first incorporates caves or rock faces bearing prehistoric art. The second involves the copper mines and processing areas which supplied the lowland communities with metal.

When we turn to the rock-art sites, it must be stressed that there is currently no evidence for dating. It is quite possible that the pictures do not belong to General Periods A and B. Scenes incorporate people and animals. A particularly spirited example from Khao Chan Ngam reveals males and females, a domestic dog and a man firing a bow and arrow (Fig. 3.23). Cattle are the commonest animal represented, but elephants and fish are also frequent. In one case, a person is depicted wearing large earrings. It is hoped that further research, particularly applied to the question of chronology, will place these important and attractive paintings in their correct cultural and chronological perspective (Charoenwongsa *et al.* 1985).

The dating issue is less of a problem for the important recent discovery of a copper mining and processing area in the Phetchabun mountains (Pigott 1984). At Phu Lon, a hill located near the Mekong River, Pigott and Natapintu examined a series of mine-shafts dug to extract malachite ore. The nearby flats are covered with crushed ore-bearing rock to a depth of 10 m. Clearly, this was a scene of intensive activity over a lengthy period. An excavation in a flat area rich in pottery revealed, in association with the cord-marked sherds, the stone hammers and anvils which had been used to dress the ore prior to smelting. The same area yielded stone mould fragments which attest to on-site casting as well as smelting, and a rejected, incomplete, shale bracelet. The latter hints at an origin in the Phetchabun area for the exotic and, presumably, highly valued stone bracelets found at Non Nok Tha and Ban Na Di. Pigott has recently obtained three radiocarbon dates for this activity. It seems that exploitation of copper was underway some time after *c* 1600 B.C. Two dates indicate continuity of exploitation between about 1000 and 250 B.C. (Pigott 1984). Rutnin has greatly enlarged our appreciation of the provision of stone to the lowland sites by her excavation of a substantial stone quarry and adze manufacturing site at Ban Na Khae. A source of andesitic tuff was exploited there probably during the first millennium B.C. Doubtless many more such sites will be discovered in due course, and the prospect of mapping exchange networks which link different regions on the basis of distinct stone sources is a real one.

Dating General Periods A and B

Before turning to a more detailed examination of the technology, economy and social organisation of the sites under review, it is necessary to consider the

3.23 The recovery of prehistoric cave art in Thailand has been a major achievement of the last decade. Many sites are now known but the dating and cultural affiliations are unclear. The example above is from Khao Chan Ngam (Charoenwongsa *et al.* 1985), and that below is from Khao Pla Ra (Thongmitr and Karakovida 1979). Scale in cm.

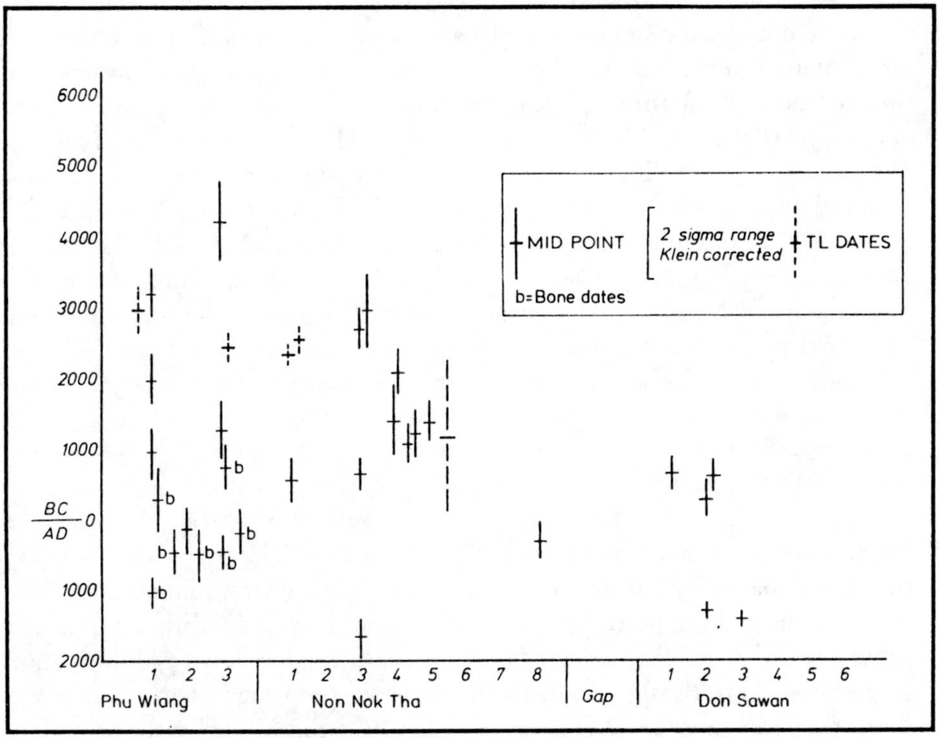

3.24 The radiocarbon dates from Non Nok Tha have been the centre of debate over the past two decades, but the issue is now becoming clearer as new excavations are undertaken and more dates become available.

question of chronology. The establishment of a chronological framework for these sites has not been straightforward, largely because of their stratigraphic complexity. In situations where people lived in houses raised on posts above ground level, the recovery of building levels is virtually ruled out. Again, nearly all excavated sites have yielded inhumation burials, some of which have disturbed earlier interments and, in turn, been cut into themselves. Insect and animal disturbance has blurred if not removed the stratigraphic build-up of recognisable layers, and monsoon downpours re-deposit soil and, with it, material remains. All these factors result in a situation where well-provenanced charcoal is rare, if not absent, and radiocarbon dates are liable to be contradictory or confusing.

Essentially, the chronology of the Khorat basin sites during General Periods A and B has been based on radiocarbon dates derived from Non Nok Tha, Ban Chiang, Ban Chiang Hian, Ban Na Di, Non Pa Kluay, Ban Phak Top, Ban Tong and Ban Kho Noi. The first results came from Non Nok Tha. Fig. 3.24 shows these dates set against their stratigraphic origin. This figure should be considered against a background of the problems encountered in the field by the excavators. It was very much a pioneer project. There was no roof to protect the excavation from sun and rain, so stratigraphic breaks involving soil colour change rapidly disappeared under the sun's glare. The site's layers were not deep, and there was much intercutting of graves and disturbance by later activities. Under such trying circumstances, it is hardly surprising that the resulting dates have proved difficult to interpret (Bayard 1972a, 1972b, Smith 1979a, Higham 1983). When Non Nok Tha was alone in revealing the presence of bronze-working in the Khorat plateau, attempts were made to estimate the chronology in question (Solheim 1968, Bayard 1972a). It is to be hoped, however, that technical advances in the dating of human bone may one day make it possible to re-open the question of dating the Phu Wiang and Non Nok Tha phases at Non Nok Tha on the basis of material from well-provenanced graves. At present, determinations obtained from excavations at related sites, and the reasonable step of eliminating the clearly erroneous dates from Non Nok Tha, make it possible to reach a reasonable consensus. Thus, the bronze-bearing levels probably fall within the timespan 2000-1000 B.C., though greater precision is still not possible.

Similar problems have beset the dating of Ban Chiang. While the prehistoric layers there were four times the depth of Non Nok Tha, they have been, and continue to be, badly affected by the activities of ground-dwelling beetles. These creatures make their nests by fashioning soil into spheres with a diameter of about 8 cm. This activity, repeated over the centuries, has destroyed the integrity of prehistoric stratigraphy and, in the process, re-located charcoal fragments from their original source. This problem has been magnified by the activities of the prehistoric inhabitants. The act of digging a grave, interring a body, and covering it with soil, clearly has the effect of relocating charcoal. Consequently, any charcoal found in the proximity of a skeleton need not, and probably does not, date its interment. Indeed, if the grave cut through earlier deposits, and charcoal was replaced near the skeleton, that sample could antedate the act of burial by a considerable time.

White (1986) has recently looked again at this problem of dating charcoal derived from graves, and has pointed out an ethnographic instance among the Mnong Gar of deliberately placing charcoal firebrands in the grave as part of the mortuary rite (Condominas 1977). It is not possible to be sure whether this practice occurred at Ban Chiang in prehistory, but the scattered nature of the grave charcoal there makes it seem rather unlikely. In any event, the problem of dating the interments remains, and is illustrated in Fig. 3.25. In her detailed review of the data, White has suggested that EP I–II (General Period A) belongs *c* 3600–1900 B.C. Bronze, and with it General Period B material, was found from 2100 B.C., and the initial use of iron falls within the timespan 800–400 B.C.

Ban Phak Top has been very badly looted, but its pottery is clearly related to the black incised ware found in early contexts at Ban Chiang. Schauffler has submitted a large radiocarbon sample interpreted as pre-dating the first occupation. The resulting date is about 2500 B.C. The lowest cultural level has a date of 2000 B.C., and level 8 has three dates of between 1000 and 1500 B.C. Until we know a lot more about the material recovered from Ban Tong, the dates are of little value. The small square excavated at Don Klang yielded the remains of at least 16 burials, some of which were accompanied by iron artefacts. The radiocarbon samples are consistent with a date for the uppermost contexts in the region of 200 B.C and A.D. 200.

The excavators of Ban Na Di had the good fortune to encounter charcoal in clearly undisturbed contexts. Thus, the deposition of thin but discrete sand lenses made it possible to conclude that material beneath them was not disturbed by later activity such as grave digging. The charcoal samples come from several different contexts. Some derive from hearths, and four samples were removed from stratified layers comprising the fill of a pit. The neck of this pit was sealed by a layer of sand laid down by floodwater. Another sample was taken from a thick layer of charcoal which sealed a second pit, while some further determinations were based on the charcoal found within clay-lined bronze-working furnaces. Finally, a large piece of charcoal from the base of a posthole was dated on the assumption that it was a surviving piece of the original post. Fig. 3.26 sets out the resulting dates and corresponding stratigraphic contexts. These form a more acceptable pattern than those from Non Nok Tha or Ban Chiang, but there does remain one problem. This is the finding that the four dates from the sealed level 7 pit are all rather later than expected. Although the material culture from Ban Na Di and Ban Chiang, sites only 23 km apart, presents more differences than

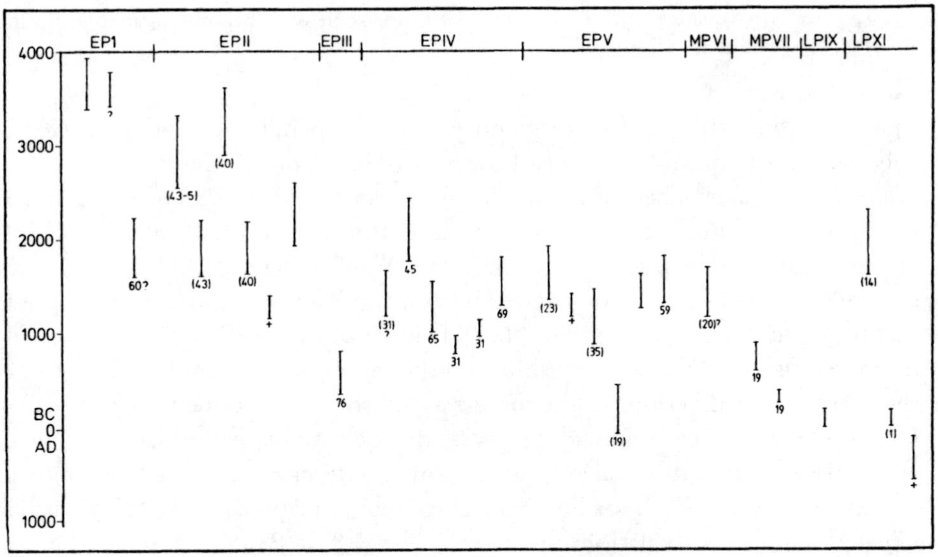

3.25 The radiocarbon dates from Ban Chiang are set out at 1 σ ranges against their context. Figures refer to burial numbers, those bracketed being found in the 1974 season. +: the assigned phase or later, ?: a tentative phase ascription.

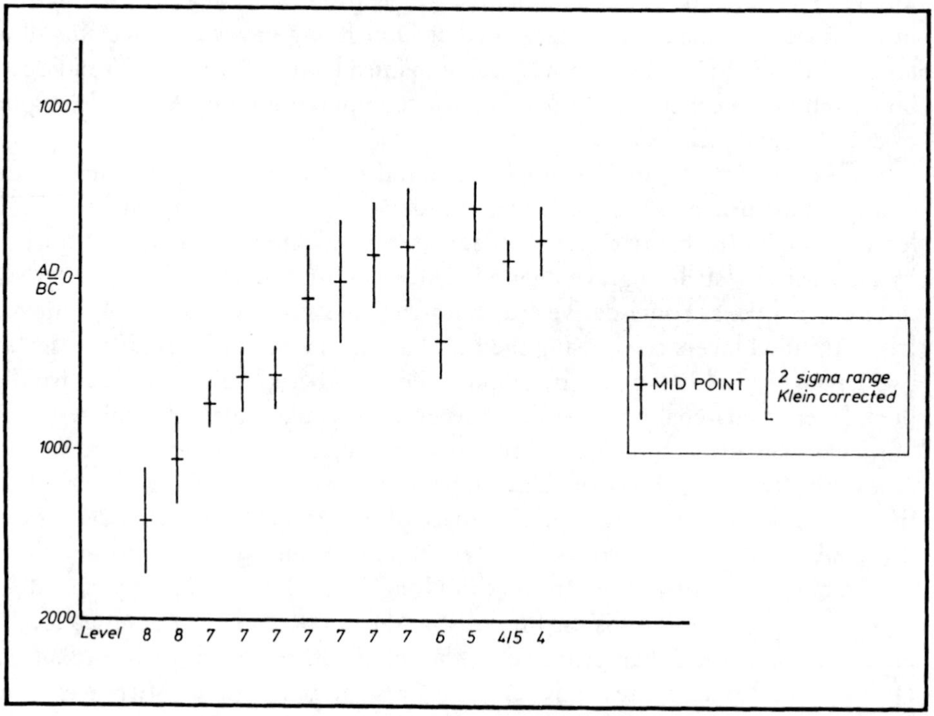

3.26 The radiocarbon dates from Ban Na Di come from charcoal of sure provenance within the site. As more such data become available, dating problems diminish.

similarities, it is still possible to identify sufficient parallels to derive an acceptably integrated chronology. This, however, only applies to the later part of the prehistoric sequence, because Ban Chiang was occupied over a far longer timespan. One very similar vessel, in terms of decoration and form, is found in MP VII at Ban Chiang and in levels 6–7 at Ban Na Di. While White (1986) has suggested a span of 800–400 B.C. for this phase, Higham and Kijngam (1984) have proposed that the equivalent context at Ban Na Di belongs to the period 700–300 B.C. The data from Ban Na Di are compatible with the earliest iron technology later rather than earlier in that period. White prefers a slightly earlier context for iron at Ban Chiang. Despite these minor differences, the clear similarity in dating evidence and other aspects of material culture support an interpretation which sees mortuary phase 1a at Ban Na Di as being the chronological equivalent of MP VI at Ban Chiang. The precise relationship between level 8 at Ban Na Di and the Ban Chiang sequence is less clear, but a correspondence with EP V, dated 1600–900 B.C., seems the most likely.

Ban Na Di and its dates are no help in attempting to date the assemblages which characterise Ban Chiang EP I–IV. However, White's proposal that Early

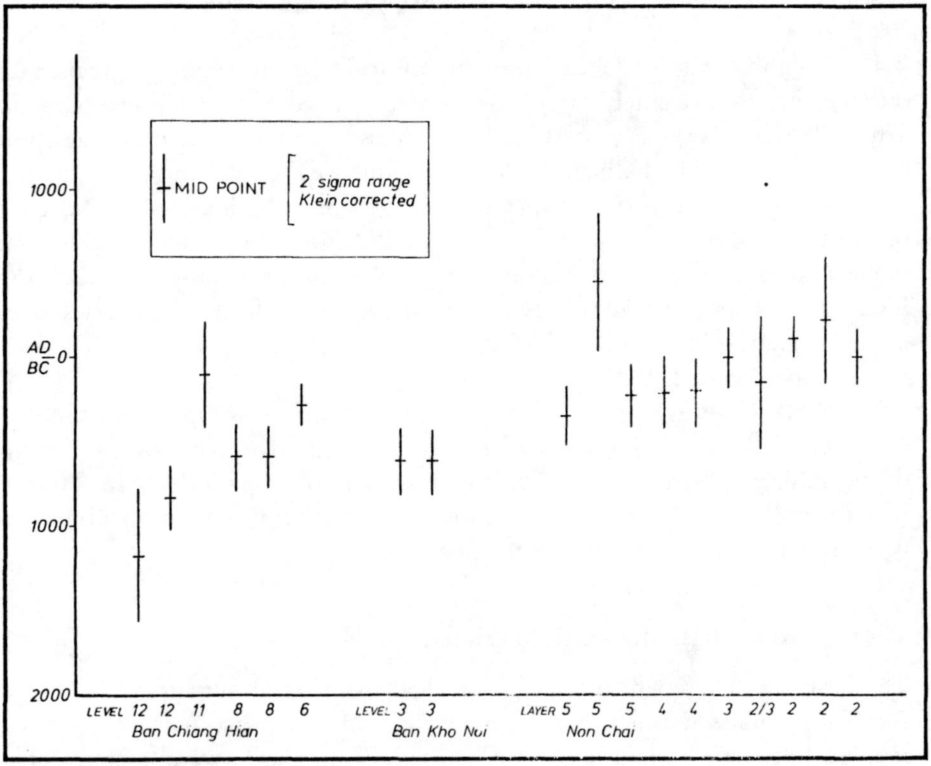

3.27 The radiocarbon dates from Ban Chiang Hian, Ban Kho Noi and Non Chai. Once again, a pattern emerges as a result of careful selection of well-provenanced charcoal for dating.

Period III dates to between 2000–1700 B.C. is clearly in harmony with the Ban Na Di determinations. This chronological framework dates the initial use of bronze, that is, Ban Chiang EP III, to within the period approximately 2000 to 1500 B.C., and the earliest evidence for iron to the middle to late first millennium B.C. These dates harmonise with those recently obtained from three sites in the Chi valley.

Ban Chiang Hian revealed a clear stratigraphic build-up of cultural layers and, with one exception, all dated charcoal samples come from *in situ* contexts. Fig. 3.27 shows the relevant dates set against the cultural layers. The pattern, when the unprovenanced sample is set aside, is clear. The site was initially occupied about the same time as Ban Na Di, and the first evidence for the use of iron was found in contexts dated to about 500 B.C. Equivalent cultural contexts from the nearby site of Ban Kho Noi have been dated to the same approximate period (Chantaratiyakan 1983, 1984). Finally, the dates obtained from excavations at Non Chai in the upper reaches of the Chi River form a tight and coherent set, all of which were found in association with iron-working, to the period 400 B.C. – 200 A.D.

The accumulating evidence from the Khorat plateau requires a revision of earlier claims for extremely early bronze- and iron-working traditions. Now that White (1982b, 1986) has placed the beaker vessels and associated bronze spear-head in burial 76 at Ban Chiang later in the sequence than was initially suggested, we may date initial bronze between *c* 2000-1500 B.C., with a pre-metal occupation in the third or possibly the late fourth millennium B.C. This would likewise suggest that Phu Wiang 3 at Non Nok Tha ended in the vicinity of *c* 2000-1500 B.C. There is some artefactual evidence for this in the form of pottery bearing incised roulette-filled motifs found at Non Nok Tha during Non Nok Tha 1 and Ban Chiang during EP III.

Non Nok Tha was probably abandoned before iron was locally available, but at Ban Chiang, Ban Na Di, Ban Chiang Hian and Ban Kho Noi, iron, and with it the beginning of General Period C, appeared within the period 800 to 400 B.C., with the preference of the present author being towards the end of that timespan. Being more precise is not at present possible.

The subsistence basis of General Periods A and B

The subsistence base which underwrote the expansion of human settlement into the Khorat plateau and other inland valleys of Southeast Asia remains little known, but some conclusions may be made. There are several sources of information. These begin with the location of settlements relative to available resources. The resources themselves are documented on the basis of food remains from excavated sites, though it is stressed that some survive more readily than others, and we must guard against bias due to differential preservation. The same reservation applies to the recovery of artefacts associated with subsistence activities.

Having reconstructed aspects of the diet, we may take our appreciation of subsistence a stage further by considering the size of settlements, their likely population and the capacity of the territory in the vicinity of the site to provide for the number of people. The acid test for the success of subsistence is, of course, the health of the people. This can be considered on the basis of their skeletal remains.

A review of settlement location for individual sites occupied during General Periods A and B is straightforward. We usually find them on slightly elevated ground, adjacent to tracts of low-terrace soil in the middle courses of tributary streams. There are as yet no signs of settlement on the more elevated high terraces, nor on the floodplains of the major rivers or lakes. This is such a consistent situation that there is surely a close relationship between subsistence and this particular habitat. White (1982a) may have identified one major element when she stressed that such a location may have been optimal for regular, but not deep, flooding. Wild rice still grows along the margins of such small streams, and its growth during the wet season is dependent on the regular, but not excessive, presence of surface water. It is, therefore, possible that the expansion of natural swampland by judicious clearance of natural vegetation expanded the habitat suited to the rice plant. Proximity to water is equally important for people as well as domestic stock, while flooded terrain is a rich source of aquatic species including fish, shellfish, amphibians and reptiles.

The siting of individual settlements can be readily considered, but it is far more difficult and, at present, nearly impossible, to reconstruct and assess the changing pattern of settlements across the landscape. All attempts at identifying prehistoric sites within a circumscribed area on the Khorat plateau face the same problem. The recognition of a surviving prehistoric site is not difficult. What is next to impossible, short of excavation, is knowing at what periods in the past the site was occupied on the basis of surface features. Thus, at Ban Chiang Hian, the prehistoric deposits attained a depth of over 6 m and none of the early pottery styles discovered at that depth through excavation was represented on the site's surface. How, then, are we to know if other sites in the area have early occupation horizons? Fig. 3.28 shows the distribution of prehistoric sites identified in the Kumphawapi survey area. At first sight, it appears to be a light network of settlement over the low-lying terrain with the uplands being ignored, but this would be a false conclusion. Excavation at Ban Muang Phruk, which is located close to the shore of Lake Kumphawapi, has shown that settlement there commenced only in General Period C (i.e., from between 500–300 B.C.). Indeed, the sites known to have been occupied during Early Periods A–B are few, as is seen in Fig. 3.28. All such known early sites are set back from the zone of maximum flooding, and it seems a reasonable supposition that this reflects conditions compatible with rice harvesting and the exploitation of both forest fringe and aquatic fauna.

Biological remains from all the sites under review are abundant and well preserved. This allows insight into subsistence during General Periods A and B, as well as aspects of burial ritual exemplified by the placement of animal bone in human graves. However, it is necessary to stress that while soils at Non Nok Tha were so hard that screening was not undertaken, at Ban Chiang all soils were passed through a 10 mm screen and, at Ban Na Di, 20% were further screened through a mesh size of 1 mm. These procedures resulted in the recovery of many small animal and fish bones.

Few species were represented in human graves at Non Nok Tha. Pig and cattle bones predominate, with a total of 45 and 36 individuals, respectively, from graves of all periods. Others lag far behind. There are only two dogs and one water-buffalo specimen. Fish are found rarely, and are confined to the contents of 56 funerary vessels. There are also the remains of two chickens, three deer and three fragments of turtle. The prehistoric occupants of Non Nok Tha placed pig remains, sometimes complete animals, in human graves. This has led to the

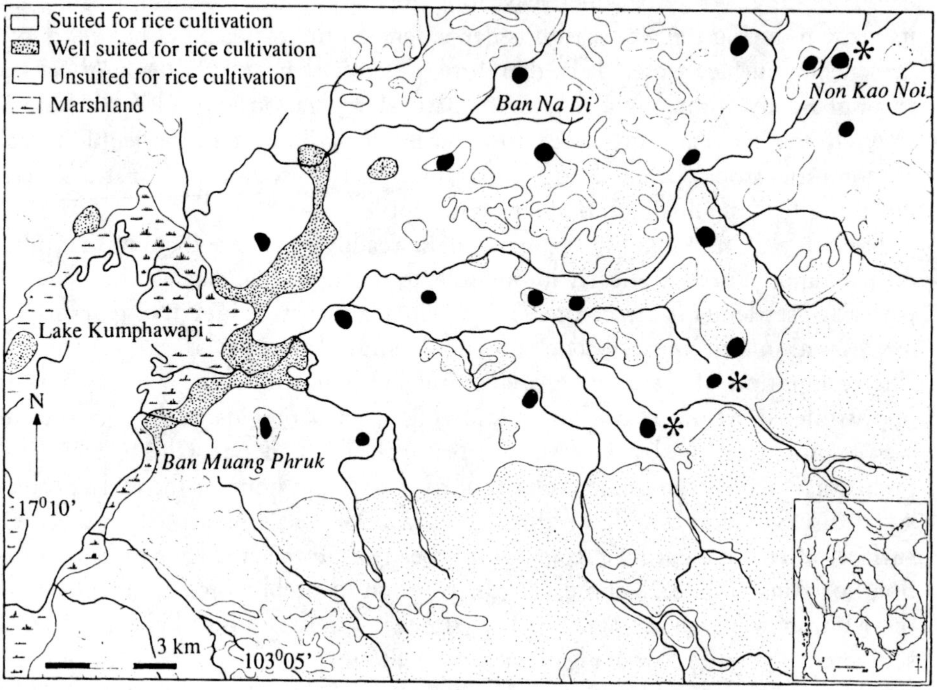

3.28 The intensive site survey in the vicinity of Lake Kumphawapi revealed numerous prehistoric sites which indicate a preference for settlement near small stream confluences giving access to low-terrace soils. The sites marked with an asterisk have documented occupation during General Period A.

survival of relatively complete skulls. Adult wild pigs have long and narrow crania. The three intact adult skulls from the Non Nok Tha burials are short and relatively broad. This strongly suggests that they came from a domesticated breed. The cattle bones from burial contexts at Non Nok Tha were significantly smaller than known modern wild ones, suggesting that cattle, too, were domesticated.

One of the surprising features of the animal bones is the rarity of the water-buffalo. This animal is of critical importance to the modern inhabitants because its strength allows it to plough rice-fields. There is a single water-buffalo metatarsal from Phu Wiang 1, a second from Non Nok Tha 8, and a collection of charred bones was located in a Don Sawan phase pit. The earliest, which corresponds in size to the modern domestic animal, was not found in a clear grave association, and more finds are necessary before any firm conclusions on its early appearance can be drawn. Dog bones are relatively rare, but there is no doubting the presence of a domestic breed from the earliest occupation because a complete skeleton was recovered from a Phu Wiang phase 1 burial. Both cattle and pig are common in the non-burial contexts. Other animals present are the sambar deer, pig deer, muntjak and tiger (Higham 1975a, 1975b). A small number of fish and turtle bones were found, suggesting the exploitation of water resources. Some of the cattle, pig, water-buffalo and chicken, and all the dog remains, were from domestic animals. Cattle, pigs and dogs were used in the ritual of burial and, judging from butchering marks and charring on non-funerary specimens, for consumption as well. The inhabitants of Non Nok Tha also hunted, though the wide range of small species found at the upland caves is absent. There appears to have been a concentration on the larger game, particularly the deer.

Given that the site lies adjacent to modern rice-fields and that the inhabitants not only maintained domestic stock but were familiar with bronze, the investigators were interested in the possibility that rice was cultivated there. During the late 1960s hardly anything was known of the prehistoric environment, but the presence there of fish and water-turtle bones did suggest exploitation of aquatic resources, and wild rice still grows in low-lying swampy habitats on the Khorat plateau. In the absence of any rice grains, Solheim turned to an analysis of the material used to temper clay when making pottery. Bayard's subsequent detailed analysis showed that, although an admixture of sand was the predominant technique used during Phu Wiang 1, about 1.5% of the 680 sherds examined were tempered with sand and a vegetable material identified as rice chaff. This proportion rose to 5.7% in Phu Wiang 1-2 (n=334) and 13.51% (n=1197, Bayard 1977). The contents of Non Nok Tha phase funerary vessels contained small fragments of rice chaff. Botanists are divided on the status of the rice remains. Chang (1976) has suggested that it lies between a wild and a weed rice. Vishnu-Mittre (1975) has concluded that it is not possible to be sure whether it was cultivated or wild. Yen (1982) has likewise been unable to be sure whether the rice chaff used to temper the clay used at Ban Chiang comes from a wild or domestic species. At Ban Na Di, however, flotation was employed to recover rice grains, and Chang and Loresto (1984) have suggested that they were cultivated.

The Non Nok Tha faunal sample revealed the husbanding of cattle and pigs, hunting the local mammalian fauna, fishing and shellfish collecting. The faunal spectrum of Ban Chiang has enlarged our perspective. The range of species belonging to General Periods A and B contexts found at Ban Chiang was greater than at any of the upland hunter-gatherer sites so far studied, and four were domestic: pig, cattle, dog and chicken (Higham and Kijngam 1979). Furthermore, the faunal material from Ban Na Di includes a very high proportion of fish and other aquatic species.

The importance of the non-human bone lies, not only in its illumination of the subsistance patterns, but also on the insight it gives into the former environment. A favourite location for settlement was at or near the confluence of small streams, with access to low-terrace soil. Even if the occupants were engaged solely in hunting, which they were not, this position would have been sensible given the need for drinking water in the dry season and safety from floods in the wet. For anyone raising cattle and possibly cultivating rice, proximity to low-lying, well-watered land would have been critical. It could, of course, be argued that the climatic regime differed 5000 years ago, and that monsoons were more predictable and brought more water. One feature of the Ban Chiang area today is that rainfall is less variable than in any other part of the Khorat plateau (Schauffler 1978).

Some information on the nature of the environment at Ban Chiang following the initial settlement may be gained from an analysis of the shellfish collected at the time. Perhaps one of the more surprising aspects of the faunal samples is the presence of rich shell-middens in the lower levels. Since individual shell species have different habitat requirements, their presence in prehistoric levels permits a realistic appraisal of the palaeoenvironment. When the detailed review of the shells began, some specimens were identified as landsnails. These, too, have habitat preferences. Indeed, during a survey undertaken in 1978 to assess the relationship between landsnails and specific habitats, it was found that some species only survive today in the enclaves of woodland which surround rural temples. Elsewhere, forest clearance has led to their local extinction (Fig. 3.1). One surviving species is *Hemiplecta*. This large landsnail lives in shaded leaf-litter and is mainly found today in regenerating woodland. A group of men clearing trees to create rice-fields were observed collecting this snail. Its presence in the Ban Chiang shell-middens indicates the existence of shaded woodland in prehistory. The freshwater gastropods are equally informative. *Pila polita* requires the permanent water found in lakes and swamps for survival and is not found naturally near the village today simply because these habitats are not available. At Ban Tung Fon, 10 km to the north, they are abundant in the large, permanent lake. *Pila polita* is found in early contexts at Ban Chiang, providing strong *prima facie* evidence that the terrain included marshland and lakes during initial occupation.

This species is closely related to *Pila ampullacea*, a gastropod which has the capacity to aestivate, or go into extended hibernation, during the dry season. The present villagers collect these shellfish from soft banks between paddy fields during the dry season, where they have burrowed about 75 mm into the soil to aestivate. This species is particularly well adapted to survival in small ponds in the margins of lakes which dry out for part of the year. By aestivating, they survive until the next monsoon. Specimens were found during the end of the 1978 dry season in paddy banks, in dried out seasonal ponds, and on the margin of the same large lake which harbours *Pila polita*. This species was found regularly at Ban Chiang during the excavations. It would, of course, be expedient to conclude that monsoonal conditions existed during the third and possibly the fourth millennia B.C. This point is more than academic: an extended dry season, if demonstrated, would allow the conclusion that a dry, deciduous, dipterocarp forest predominated. It would also permit us to infer that indigenous annual grasses grew along lake margins.

The reality, however, is that *Pila ampullacea* can survive in permanent lakes, and aestivates only when necessary. The collection of provenanced modern specimens has allowed the investigation to proceed a stage further. When the opercula (the small, protective plates which seal the soft part of the anatomy) are cross-sectioned, they reveal a series of growth bands. Microscopic examination shows that major bands comprise a series of about 28 extremely small rings. These are interpreted as a monthly growth pattern. When the animal goes into dry-season aestivation, growth ceases. It only recommences with the rains during the following wet season. Such physiological inactivity can be recognised between the series of monthly bands. When the growth patterns of prehistoric pilids were examined, it was found that sharp seasonal banding was present. While this study is only a beginning, it is noted that there is some evidence for a sharp dichotomy between wet and dry seasons during the early phases of Ban Chiang (Higham and Kijngam 1982).

Filter-feeding bivalve shellfish, such as *Corbicula*, prefer clear water. Turbidity is detrimental to their survival. Again, the small gastropod *Filopaludina* is thought to develop a high whorl if it lives in slow-moving water, but a squat one in rapid streams. A consideration of these two species from early Ban Chiang shell-middens suggests that the site lay within reach of slow-moving, clear streams. The shellfish and landsnails thus allow us to reconstruct a wooded habitat which was probably deciduous away from the edges of water courses. Some bodies of water were permanent, but shrank during the dry season. Permanent, clear streams flowed past the site and were prone to flood with the monsoon rains. These conditions were favourable in many respects. The water sustained fish and aquatic mammals, turtles and crocodile. Cattle, deer and elephant require regular access to water. The lake margins would have sustained edible aquatic plants. There would also have been hazards. The swamps would have favoured swarms of malarial mosquitoes, and the shellfish, so common in the early layer, are hosts to often lethal organisms, such as bilharzia, which afflict people if the shellfish are eaten raw.

The earliest settlers exploited the water resources intensively. We have seen that shellfish were abundant, but the middens also contain the bones of three species of fish. One of these, *Channa striatus*, has a suprabranchial cavity, which allows it to settle in soft mud and survive the dry season without access to water. It is not unusual to see women in the area today probing the mud in dried-out lake-beds to obtain such fish. The three species identified are, in fact, those with robust skeletons likely to survive in archaeological contexts. Many of the smaller, more delicate fish consumed to this day may have been eaten whole. Frog bones were relatively common, too. There are many species of frog in Thailand, some adapted to evergreen forest, others to the deciduous form. Most frogs represented in Ban Chiang are known as *Rana tigrina*, a species which is adapted to life in riverine floodplains, but which has found seasonally flooded rice-fields a congenial habitat. They are collected and eaten at Ban Chiang.

Fragments of turtle and tortoise carapace and plastron were found in the early Ban Chiang samples. They may come from a wide variety of species, each with its own habitat preferences. Examination of the diagnostic sections of carapace indicates the presence of the water turtle, *Malayemys subtrijuga*, and the land tortoise *Testudo elongata*. The former occupies small streams and lakes. The latter prefers deciduous forest, and is particularly well known for its ability to withstand forest fires. Given the abundance of aquatic species, it is not surprising to find some of their predators in the faunal assemblage. Otter bones are present, but never common. The bony scutes of the crocodile evidence permanent bodies of water, and the elusive fishing cat was represented. The former presence of water, and the exploitation of its resources, is clearly demonstrated.

Although the relationship is not always as clear cut as for shellfish and fish, native mammals in Thailand do exhibit preferences for particular habitats. Most squirrels prefer evergreen forest, with a succession of fruits or leaves to eat. Monkeys too, prefer the shelter and food resources of evergreen, rather than deciduous, forest. The porcupine and pangolin are adapted to forest, but wild cattle proliferate where there is a plentiful grassy undergrowth found in deciduous forest or in forest clearings. The mammalian bones from Ban Chiang may be expected, therefore, to illuminate subsistence activities and aspects of the prehistoric environment. The details of the faunal spectrum are most revealing. Species adapted to evergreen forest are practically absent. There is a handful of squirrel bones, but no non-human primates at all. This is in complete contrast to upland, hunter-gatherer faunal spectra. Alternatively, the bones of hare, small Indian civet and mongoose are present in fair numbers given their fragility. All three species prefer an open habitat, such as a forest clearing or woodland in its early stages of regeneration. The mongoose definitely prefers life on the ground rather than in trees, and the hare is a terrestrial grass eater.

Larger wild species were numerically dominated by the muntjak and brow-antlered deer (*Cervus eldi*). These were hunted throughout the occupation of the site, and were still obtained within living memory. Firearms, however, have rendered them locally extinct. Like wild cattle, deer enjoy shade, access to water, and plentiful grassy or herbacious ground cover. It is not easy to distinguish between wild and domestic cattle or pigs on the basis of fragmented or juvenile bones. Some of the many cattle, and pig specimens probably came from hunted animals. Older men at Ban Chiang recall hunting wild cattle and wild pigs are still, very occasionally, encountered. Rhinoceros and tiger are represented in prehistoric contexts, but two large species are notable for their absence: the elephant, which is represented on Late Period pots, and the water-buffalo, which was absent from Early Period contexts. The former is indigenous to the area, and ivory bracelets are present in some Ban Chiang burials.

The early absence of the water-buffalo is unexpected, but it is stressed that this animal requires daily access to water as well as open, grassy terrain. Its ideal habitat is the margins of broad river floodplains where a constantly high water-table stunts or rules out tree growth. It is possible that a gallery forest along the relatively narrow floodplains would have been unattractive to wild water-buffalo. With one exception, all water-buffalo bones found in and after Middle Period layers were smaller than wild animals and correspond in size to those raised in Thailand at present.

The recovery of two partial dog skulls, and a sample of 15 mandibles, has allowed a detailed statistical analysis to be undertaken, the purpose of which was to define their relationships with possible wild progenitors. Thailand has a wild jackal (*Canis aureus*) and the cuon, or wild dog (*Cuon alpinus*). It would be interesting if either had been domesticated. There are, however, no indigenous wolves in Southeast Asia. If the Ban Chiang dogs had close morphological affinities with the wolf, it would be particularly interesting. Thus, the wolf may have been domesticated where it is found wild, and the resultant breed taken elsewhere by man. The nearest areas which sustain the wolf are India and Central to Northern China. Initially, the analysis sought to locate consistent differences in the crania and teeth of wolves, jackals and the cuon. The cuon has a distinct dental formula, and was immediately ruled out as a possible source for the Ban Chiang dogs. Apart from size, jackals differ from wolves on the basis of the shape of certain cranial bones and the cusp pattern of their teeth. The Ban Chiang specimens were clearly affiliated with the wolf. A multivariate statistical test to compare the shape of the skulls and jaws with wolves and jackals and modern Ban Chiang dogs, also related them with the wolf, but the closest size and shape affinities are with the modern village dog. Indeed, the earliest jaw bones are practically indistinguishable from those of dogs living in Ban Chiang today (Higham, Kijngam and Manly 1980).

These dog jaws, as well as the numerous limb bones found in successive phases, bear marks of butchery and charring. Only the specimens from human graves were complete and unburnt. The pattern of butchering occurs in nearly all bones found in non-burial contexts at Ban Chiang which indicates that domestic stock, as well as game animals, were locally processed for consumption.

The use of a 1mm mesh screen at Ban Na Di resulted in the recovery of minute bones, nearly all of which came from fish and many frogs. The result of estimating the percentage of individual animals per species is seen in Fig. 3.18. It is known, on the basis of the stratigraphy at Ban Na Di, that the site was subjected to floods. The high incidence of fish bones may reflect proximity to flooded terrain. There can be no doubt that net or trap fishing was important at Ban Na Di, just as it is today. With the onset of the monsoon, water fills the enclosed rice-fields, and these are a ready source of fish. The rarity of fish during the long dry season is compensated for by the preparation of a salted fish paste which can be stored for later consumption. Apart from the many small fish bones, the faunal spectrum for General Periods A and B at Ban Na Di is very similar to that from Ban Chiang. There are the same domestic species, and deer are well represented. Again, shellfish are abundant in the lower layers and include the same species as at Ban Chiang.

The evidence available indicates that subsistence activities included harvesting rice, maintaining domestic stock, hunting, trapping, fishing and collecting shellfish. There is little doubt, too, that this represents only a partial picture. Even today, when the casual observer would conclude that subsistence is dominated by rice and fish, much gathering and foraging is undertaken. Women will return to the village with a basket containing dung beetles, bamboo shoots, wild yams, mushrooms and frogs. Many vegetables are grown and wild plants collected. Termites and ants are considered delicacies. It is unfortunate that so many possible sources of food leave no trace in the archaeological record. Nor would hunting or trapping implements made of wood. Indeed, bamboo remains, to this day, the medium for a wide range of fish and animal traps.

It was in order to illuminate this problem of differential survival that White (1982c) undertook extensive fieldwork in the vicinity of Ban Chiang, being particularly concerned with the present pattern of exploiting wild plants in order to provide some insight into the potential of the area in prehistory. Despite the apparent concern today with the cultivation of rice, virtually to the exclusion of other crops, she found that the remaining areas of woodland, normally confined to the slightly elevated middle terraces, are a rich source of collected plants. Wild yams, for example, are available, and small plots cleared by fire can be put down to a variety of vegetables. Bamboo shoots, as well, are collected. Uncultivated rice – wild would be a misnomer because of the probable interbreeding with cultivated forms – is available in naturally swampy areas, though White doubts if there would have been large amounts available in prehistory without human modification to encourage its proliferation.

The principal tools which would have been useful in such modification of an essentially forested habitat is the stone axe or adze. We shall review below the material culture and local raw materials available. The polished stone axes found are relatively small, due no doubt to the local rarity of finely grained stone and prolonged sharpening. They could, however, have been critical in clearing natural vegetation, creating conditions suited to feeding cattle and encouraging rice. The initial settlers lived in a monsoon environment which incorporated lakes, clear perennial streams and deciduous woodland. They selected slightly elevated terrain, and cleared the vegetation in low-lying wetlands to encourage the proliferation of rice. It is highly likely that this rice was of a domesticated strain. They also maintained domestic cattle and pig, and introduced domestic chickens and dogs. The local wild fauna was hunted or trapped, and both fishing and the collection of shellfish were prominent activities. This subsistence base was multifaceted. No reliance was placed on any single activity. At the same time, the investment in permanent facilities such as wooden houses, and the maintenance of cemeteries over many centuries, suggests a commitment to permanent, sedentary occupation. The implications of this situation will be explored below (p. 185).

The human remains

One measure of the success of a prehistoric subsistence strategy is the health of the people concerned. The level of health may, of course, be affected by factors other than food supply: endemic disease may so debilitate a community as to affect the viability of subsistence activities. However, we are fortunate in having access to three samples of human remains, sufficient to provide some insight into health and nutrition during General Periods A and B.

The excavation of Non Nok Tha provided a sample of 188 complete or partial human skeletons. The analysis of this particularly large and important sample has provided much valuable information. Pietrusewsky (1974), who analysed the remains from the 1966 season and has partial results from the later season, has considered evidence for disease, age at death, pathological conditions and the affinities of the crania, with other relevant samples.

Having subdivided the sample into two groups representing the Phu Wiang phase and Non Nok Tha 1, and the balance to Non Nok Tha phase 2–7, Pietrusewsky compared life expectancy and age at death to discern any major trends with time. The age at which an individual died can be determined, albeit approximately, by the appearance of centres of ossification and epiphysial fusion, dental eruption and calcification of teeth, pubic symphyses, tooth wear and cranial suture closure. On the basis of such information, six main age stages were proposed: infant (0–1); early childhood (2–6); late childhood (7–11); adolescent (12–16); young adult (17–31); middle-aged (32–46); and old (over 47). The earlier sample revealed a high mortality among the two- to six-year-olds and again among the young adults, and the middle-aged. No individual survived into old adulthood; the average age at death was in the early twenties.

The later sample revealed interesting differences. There were fewer young children and a relatively greater life expectancy. We are unsure what the causes of fatality were. Bayard (1971) has suggested that there was some inter-group hostility, perhaps even head hunting. Pietrusewsky (1974) failed to note any bone damage reflecting combat. Just over half the adults, however, exhibited a condition known as porotic hyperostosis. This describes a thickening of the skull vault due to lesions, and can result from several possible causes, including nutritional deficiency or iron deficiency. There is also a relationship between this condition and a disorder in the haemoglobins such as sickle cell anaemia and thalassemia. This last pathology is strongly correlated with homozygous individuals among populations suffering from malaria. Malarial mosquitoes rely upon stagnant water for breeding. Being a relatively flat plain with a considerable number of permanent ponds and lakes, malaria remains a health hazard to this day.

The Non Nok Tha men stood between 1.62 and 1.78 m, and the women from 1.42 to 1.57 m. In terms of a multivariate analysis of skull measurements and non-measurable attributes, such as bone shape, the Non Nok Tha specimens have a close relationship with prehistoric so-called "Neolithic" specimens collected by Mansuy and Colani in Viet Nam (Pietrusewsky 1984). When non-metrical variables alone are considered, the Non Nok Tha and Ban Chiang crania are very similar. There are further similarities between the people of Ban Chiang and those of Non Nok Tha (Pietrusewsky 1982). The average life expectancy at Ban Chiang was 31 years, and earlier occupants of the site suffered higher infant mortality. The male height at Ban Chiang varied from 1.62–1.72 m, and the women, from 1.48–1.55 m. Blood-related disorders such as anaemia are indicated by porotic hyperostosis, and some evidence of arthritis is present. The teeth reveal a rough diet, there being much wear and staining which possibly reflects the chewing of betel nut. Pietrusewsky has also identified evidence for physically robust individuals in the sample of 127 people, and a preference for adopting a squatting posture when at rest.

The skeletal remains from the level 6–7 Ban Na Di cemetery have been analysed by Houghton and Wiriyaromp (1984). They found a similarly high frequency of death among infants and young children, and low mortality for adolescents (Fig. 3.29). Adult males tended to die at an earlier age than females. The maximum age was in the vicinity of 40–45 years, and the life expectancy at birth was 22.8 years. This figure might appear low, but it must be stressed that only in the last century have medical advances greatly extended the human lifespan. Such an apparently low life expectancy by no means implies poor nutrition or health, but, rather, the susceptability of all people to infections prior to recent major advances in medical science. Among the most intriguing aspects of the analysis of the Ban Na Di remains is the absence there of evidence for squatting facets. As we shall see, the General Period B material culture from Ban Na Di and Ban Chiang is remarkably different for two sites little more than 20 km apart, and there is a real possibility that the people occupying them were different, not only in their styles of pottery, but also their habits and even origins. One way of approaching the question of prehistoric diet is to measure the cortical thickness of bone. Nordin's score, which treats the second metacarpal, is an index of the plane of nutrition, and its values for Ban Na Di and comparative samples reveal that the prehistoric occupants of Ban Na Di were as robust as Finnish farmers and modern inhabitants of the State of Ohio. Harris lines reflect retarded bone-growth due to checks in health such as illness or malnutrition. Houghton and Wiryaromp have found few such lines, a situation which is expected, given the high values for Nordin's score. The examination of areas for muscle-attachment in the bone likewise reveals physically active and robust people. Indeed, one female aged about 17 at death had already borne a

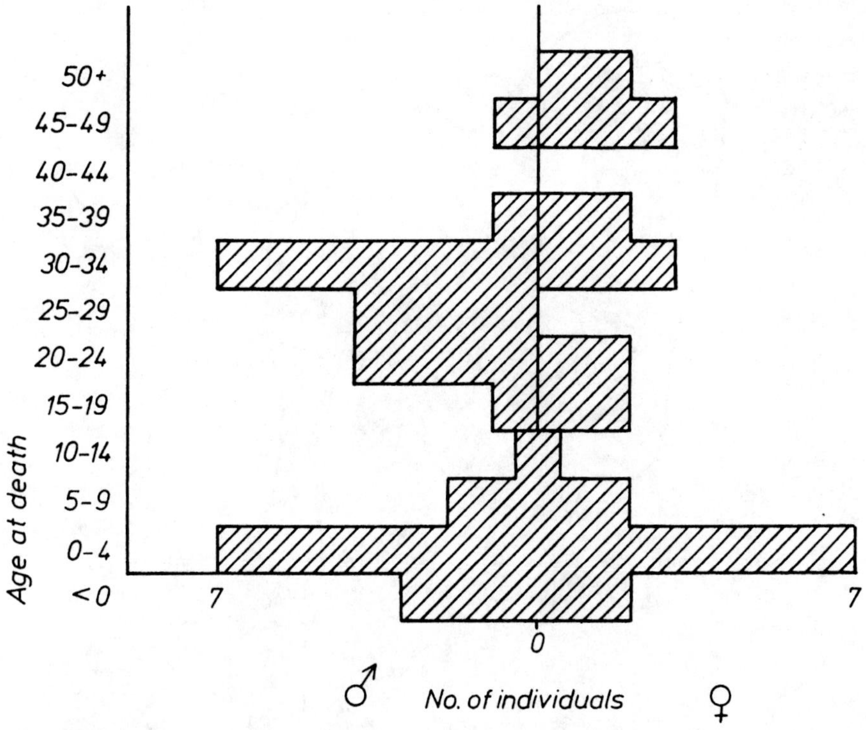

3.29 High infant mortality and a maximum age in the vicinity of 50 years are indicated by the pattern of death at Ban Na Di.

child. This indicates an onset of menarche at age of about 15 (Fig. 3.30). Since menarche is affected by diet, it is a reasonable conclusion that the young woman in question enjoyed good nutrition. The human remains considered in conjunction with the evidence for subsistence reveal active, robust and well-fed communities. The time is opportune to turn to their industrial activities and then to the way they ordered their social relationships.

The material culture of General Periods A and B

Raw materials for making utilitarian or prestige goods are distributed unevenly on the Khorat plateau, and some sources for desirable materials were located considerable distances away. Clay, for example, occurs in restricted locations, and is of varying quality. Being a sedimentary area, the plateau has only a few good sources of stone for the manufacture of cutting tools. As is seen in Fig. 3.31, copper and tin ores are found in the surrounding hills, while some shell used in the manufacture of jewellery was of marine origin. One of the many tasks facing the archaeology of the area is the identification of sources for the many artefacts

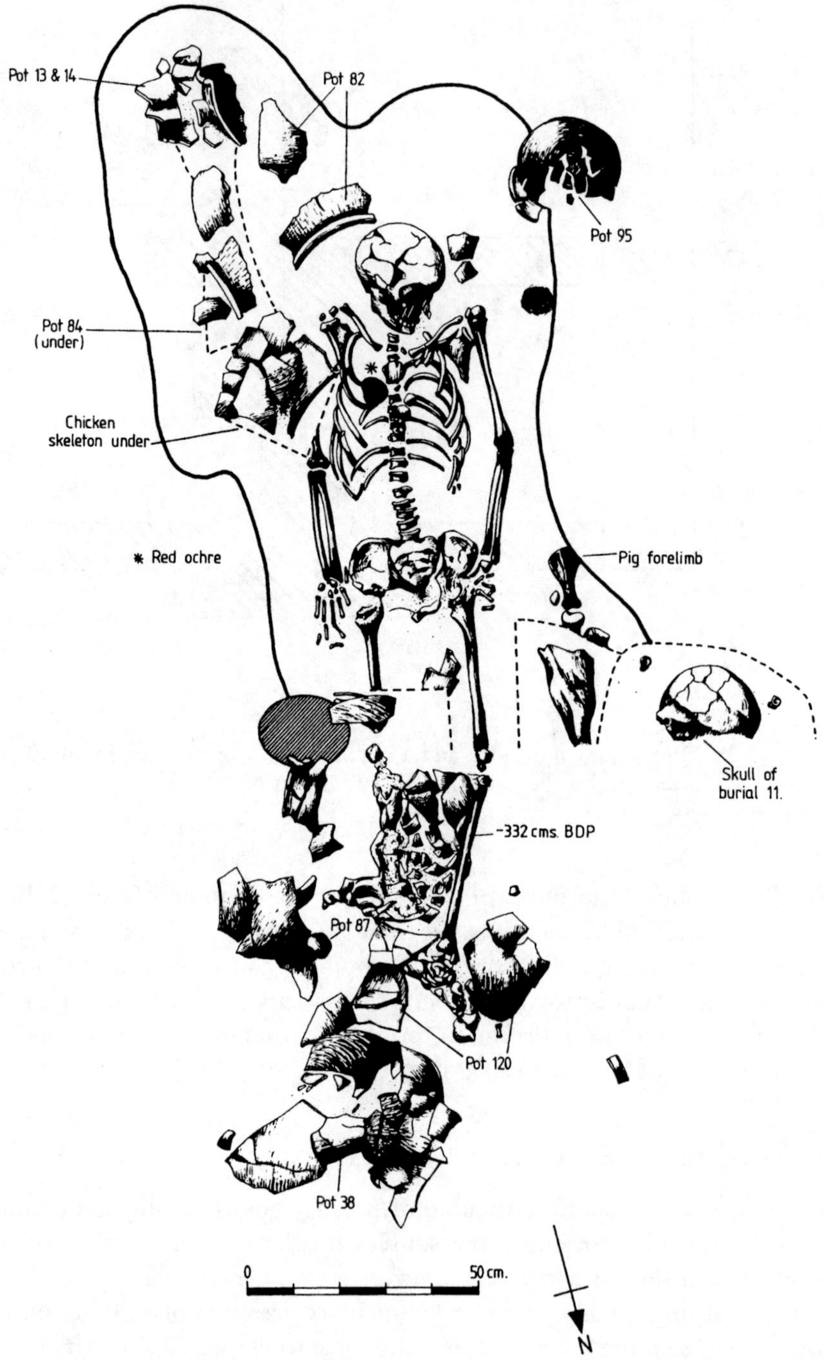

3.30 Burial 12 from Ban Na Di was of a girl in her late teens. She had already borne a child, which indicates an early onset of menarche and, therefore, a good diet.

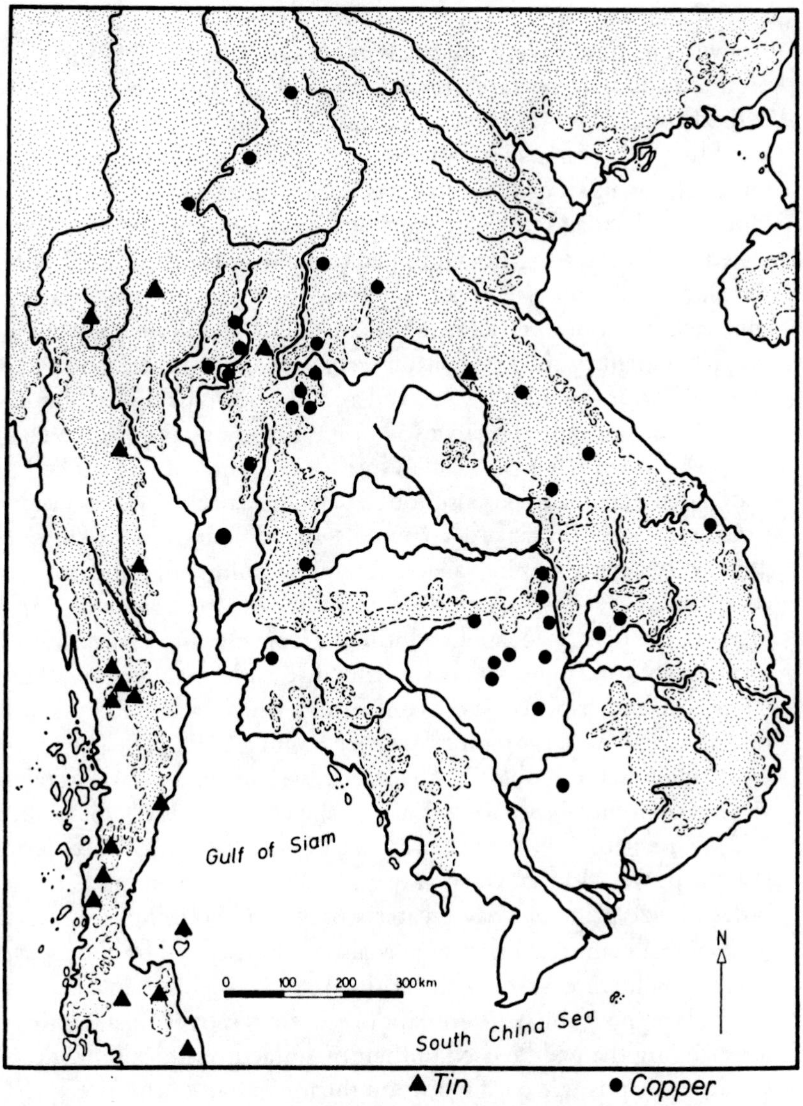

3.31 The ores of copper (circles) and tin (triangles) are found at some distance from General Period A and B settlements on the Khorat plateau. Exchange systems involving such rare and prestigious goods were probably widespread. Stippled area: land above 182m.

encountered. So far, we have very little published information, though a start has been made for Ban Na Di.

Several materials were used at Ban Na Di, either as the source for locally made products, or as imports. Artefacts made of clay predominate, and we will begin with them. Clay is a most important substance because its plasticity permits moulding to an almost infinite variety of shapes and firing maintains its desired form. The analysis of fired clay has been largely undertaken by archaeologists in Northeast Thailand who are capable of recognising the style and form of completed artefacts but are not equipped to make judgements on the characteristics of the clay itself. For the latter, one must turn to the specialist ceramicist. This approach is important, because the ceramicist is equipped to source the clay to its origin, to identify the non-plastic inclusions or "temper" and the way the clay is prepared prior to moulding, as well as to ascertain firing techniques and temperatures. Such specialised analysis is in its infancy in Northeast Thailand (Vincent 1984, McGovern, Vernon and White 1985). Vincent has studied the Ban Na Di material in detail, and has also looked at some specimens from Non Chai and Ban Chiang Hian. This approach entails the preparation of thin sections of the pottery for petrographic analysis, and sampling of modern clay sources for comparative purposes. Vincent found that the occupants of Ban Na Di used a local source of clay located about 6 km from the site. This clay was not entirely satisfactory for firing, so they blended it with an imported clay and mixed in temper. This permitted successful firing, which was undertaken probably on a raft of wood up to a temperature of about 950°C. The range of locally made wares included a "goblet", that is, a vessel set in a tall pedestal support, and a variety of round-based pots with in-curving shoulders and everted rims (Fig. 3.32). These come in three distinct sizes, and were probably designed for different purposes. Modern vessels are quite similar in shape, and are used in declining order of size principally for water storage and cooking rice, meat and fish.

The local manufacture of pots is also demonstrated by the presence of the clay anvils which were used to shape them. Some of the Ban Na Di vessels and, in particular, the goblets, were smoothed to remove most of the cord imprints imparted by the paddle used in their manufacture. Locally made vessels, however, also bore positive cord marks on the lower half of the interior. This reflects an initial stage in the forming process when the clay was beaten over a mould. With the removal of the mould, the upper half was joined to the basal half, and then the rim was added. These Ban Na Di vessels were decorated further by painting, burnishing or the incision of designs.

Clay at Ban Na Di was fashioned into several artefacts other than vessels and anvils. The local clay source was also used to hand mould figurines. Indeed, some of the large cattle figurines from burials still bear their makers' fingerprints. These cattle, deer and elephant figurines have considerable artistic merit with their stylised bodies and feet, but lifelike curved horns (Fig. 3.33). A series of much smaller cattle figurines comes from the occupation contexts. Clay was also

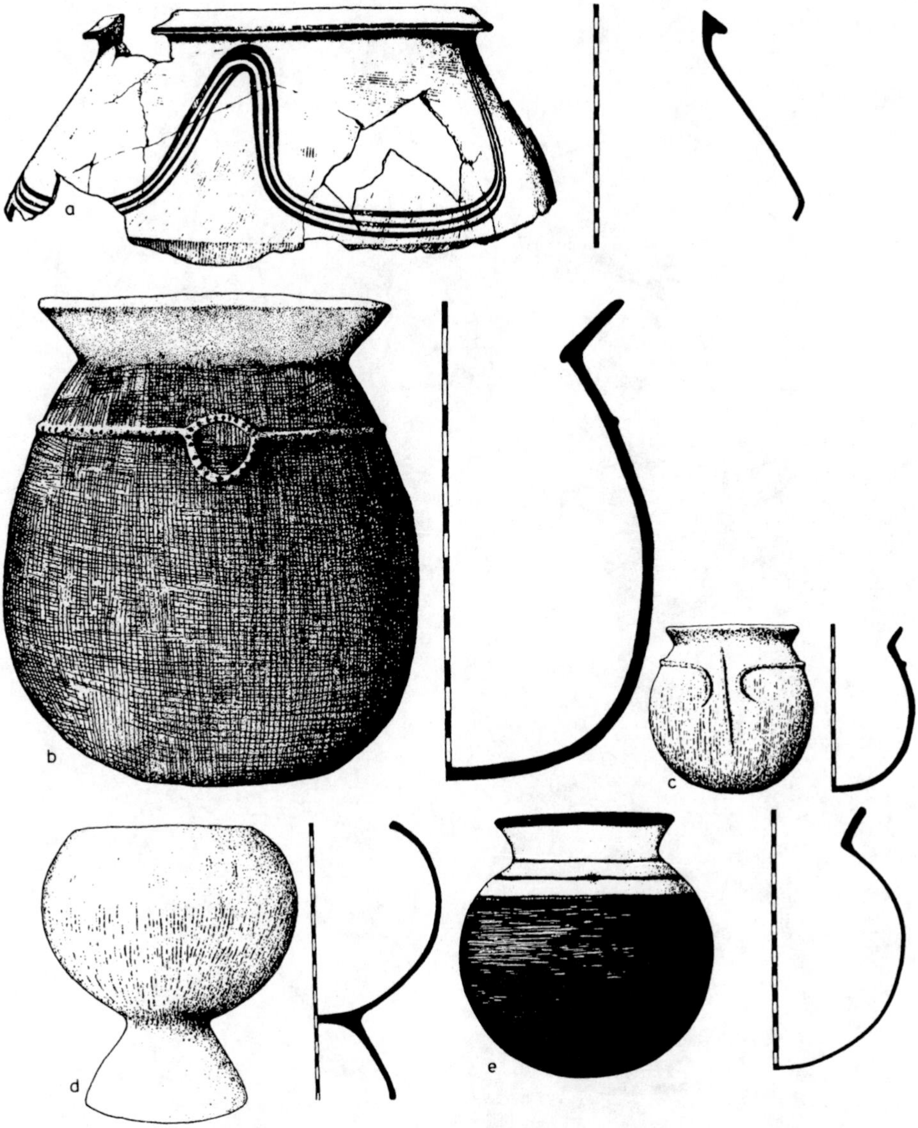

3.32 Pottery vessels at Ban Na Di were often interred complete in human burials. Most were locally made but some were exotic to the area. Many locally made vessels were formed over a mould. Some contained food: the fore-limb of a pig, fragments of fish bone or the remains of rice. The uppermost vessel in this picture is a rare example of a form closely paralleled at Ban Chiang during Middle Period VII.

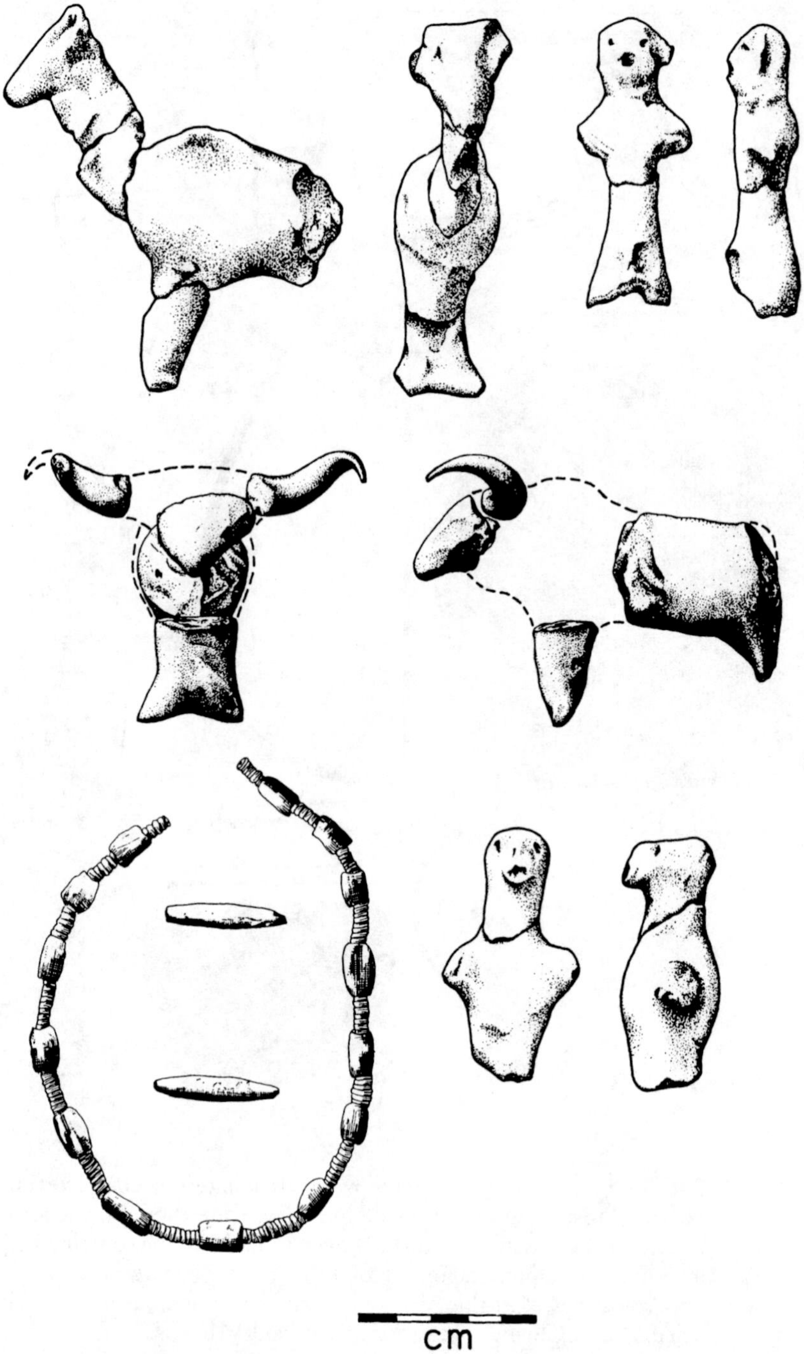

3.33 The people of Ban Na Di made figurines of cattle, elephant and people. They also cast bronze locally into ornaments, projectile points, fish hooks and axes.

used in the manufacture of the small, spouted crucibles used to bring tin and copper to melting-point. These were tempered with grog, a term used to describe fragments of fired clay. The most enduring artefact form at Ban Na Di is the rounded clay pellet. These have been used within living memory with a special wooden bow to hunt small birds, and they are very common throughout the occupation layers at the site.

The analysis of pottery from the many other sites on the Khorat plateau has revealed a marked regionality in pot forms and preferred methods of decoration. The longest sequence comes from Ban Chiang and, as White (1986) has shown, there is a notable lack of similarity even with a site 23 km away. There are also marked differences in the way the pots were fashioned. The most important task awaiting ceramicists in this region is first determining clay sources and manufacturing centres, then analysing clays and tempers to find out whether pottery vessels were locally made or imported from specialised communities of potters (Vincent 1984).

Until the excavation of the Khorat plateau sites, it was generally held that both bronze and iron were introduced into Southeast Asia during the first millennium B.C. The nature of the metal technology must, therefore, be considered, and its cultural implications assessed. The properties of bronze, when compared with stone, allow for greater productivity in transforming the environment and creating conditions favourable to agriculture. The axe is a recurrent feature of bronze-using societies there. There is also the fact that sources of copper, tin and lead do not often coincide with each other or with centres of population. As a consequence, exchange and trade routes multiplied, and affected the accumulation of wealth and gaining of prestige. The addition of bronze to the repertoire did not involve the substitution of one material by a superior one. Bronze, initially at least, was inevitably a rare commodity, valued industrially as well as for personal adornment. Our appreciation of Southeast Asian metallurgy has been greatly augmented by the documentation of ore sources and processing areas, and the recovery of casting facilities within settlements which participated in overlapping exchange networks.

Any review of bronze metallurgy must take into account the relationship of the sites in question to sources of copper and tin ores. The nearest source of copper ore to Non Nok Tha is situated on the western edge of the plateau, about 50 km to the northwest of the site, where chalcopyrite, galena and chalcolite ores are known. Shallow pits near the city of Loei reveal past exploitation, though they are not dated. There are small items of chalcolite, with some malachite and azurite, 150 km to the south in the vicinity of Phetchabun. Across the Mekong, malachite and azurite are known in Champassac Province of Laos, and to the east in Khammouane Province. Indeed, copper sources practically ring the Khorat plateau in all directions but the southeast and we are now informed on extraction processes following the excavations of a mine at Phu Lon (Pigott 1984). Tin ores are found in the Nam Pa Then valley in Khammouane Province, Laos. There is a

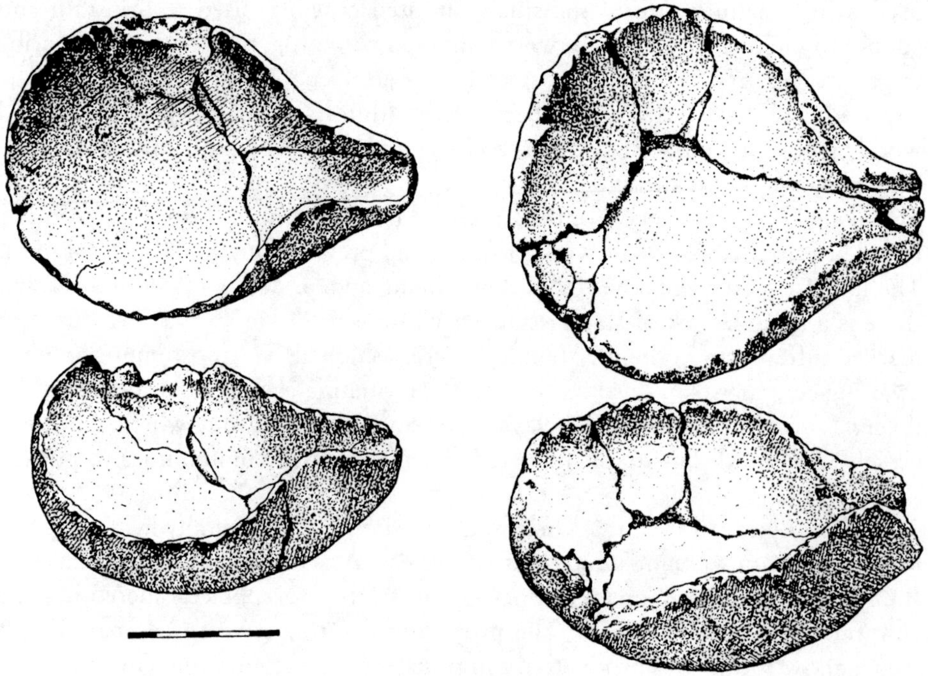

3.34 Crucibles at Ban Na Di and related sites were small and could only have cast a few objects at a time. Scale in cm.

further source in the Nan valley, almost 200 km northwest of Non Nok Tha, and several further ore bodies are known in the western hills of Thailand (United Nations 1968).

Having established the mining and processing of ores within a reasonable distance of the Khorat plateau sites, there follows the need to establish whether the artefacts were locally made. Here, again, we are on sure ground, because the crucibles represent but one stage in the local manufacture of bronzes. Bronze-casting was undertaken from the initial occupation of Ban Na Di, and practically all stages in the process are in evidence. Maddin and Weng (1984) have examined the bronze scoria which still adheres to the crucibles, and have concluded that they were used to bring copper and tin to a liquid state prior to pouring. These two metals were imported to Ban Na Di probably in ingot form. At least, there is no evidence for local smelting, and it seems most unlikely that the ore itself was exchanged. The smith first constructed a small clay-lined furnace measuring no more than 50 cm in diameter within which he placed charcoal (Fig. 3.19). He probably then employed tuyeres attached to bellows to fire the furnace, to attain the temperature necessary to melt copper and tin. The molten material was then transfered in small crucibles to the awaiting mould (Fig. 3.34).

There is evidence for two types of mould. One was a double mould, ground from sandstone, with a pouring spout and conduits leading to the object to be cast. Ban Na Di has furnished two broken pieces of such moulds, one for casting an axe, and the other for two arrowheads. Since the thermal shock of contact with molten metal may have cracked such stone moulds, it is possible that they were used initially for casting a template in lead. Lead has a much lower melting-point than copper, and the complete lead axe could have been encased in clay, then melted out prior to the pouring of bronze into the vacated space. A casting funnel or "sprue" made of a lead-tin alloy was found at Ban Na Di, but in a later cultural context (Rajpitak and Seeley 1984). There is, as yet, no other supporting evidence that this intermediate lead-casting stage was employed. Another technique may have been to pre-heat the stone mould gradually and thereby lessen the risk of fracture. In the absence of clay mould fragments for axe or arrowhead casting, the latter technique seems the more plausible. The second mould type was made of clay and involved the lost wax process. This was used in casting bracelets, and began with the manufacture of a clay core. Wax was then placed over the clay and moulded to shape. The wax, being malleable, could be a vehicle for complicated designs. When the wax was shaped, a very fine clay lining was built up over it, perhaps by dipping it into a container filled with a thick suspension of clay in water. Finally, the clay was encased in a covering of coarser clay. It was then necessary to melt out the wax, and pour in molten bronze to replace it. In her analysis of the Ban Na Di bronze jewellery, Pilditch (1984) recovered the remains of insect wax from the space between the metal and the clay core of a bracelet found associated with a burial. It is most improbable that this wax could have survived the casting process, because the application of molten bronze to wax would cause an explosion. It is more likely that the surviving fragments of wax were used to polish the bracelet after casting was complete.

Nearly all metal artefacts made during General Period B at Ban Na Di were cast from copper and tin in which tin comprises about 10% of the alloy. The ornaments received no treatment after casting other than trimming away casting imperfections. The arrowheads, however, appear to have been annealed. This process involves heating and hammering, and it hardens the metal. Repairs were also undertaken to broken, but highly valued, stone bracelets, by boring a hole against each fractured edge, and building up a clay mould over each hole such that the metal took the form of wire. This wire then kept the broken halves together. One bracelet was repaired in this manner twice, and a broken chip was replaced using the same technique (Maddin and Weng 1984).

There is no doubting the expertise of the Ban Na Di bronze-worker, and we can gain some insight into his role in the community by considering what he made. Tools, weapons and ornaments were cast. Among tools and weapons, only arrowheads survive (Fig. 3.35), although we know from moulds and from the artefacts recovered at Ban Chiang and Non Nok Tha, that the repertoire included spearheads and axes. Bracelets were the commonest bronze artefact form from

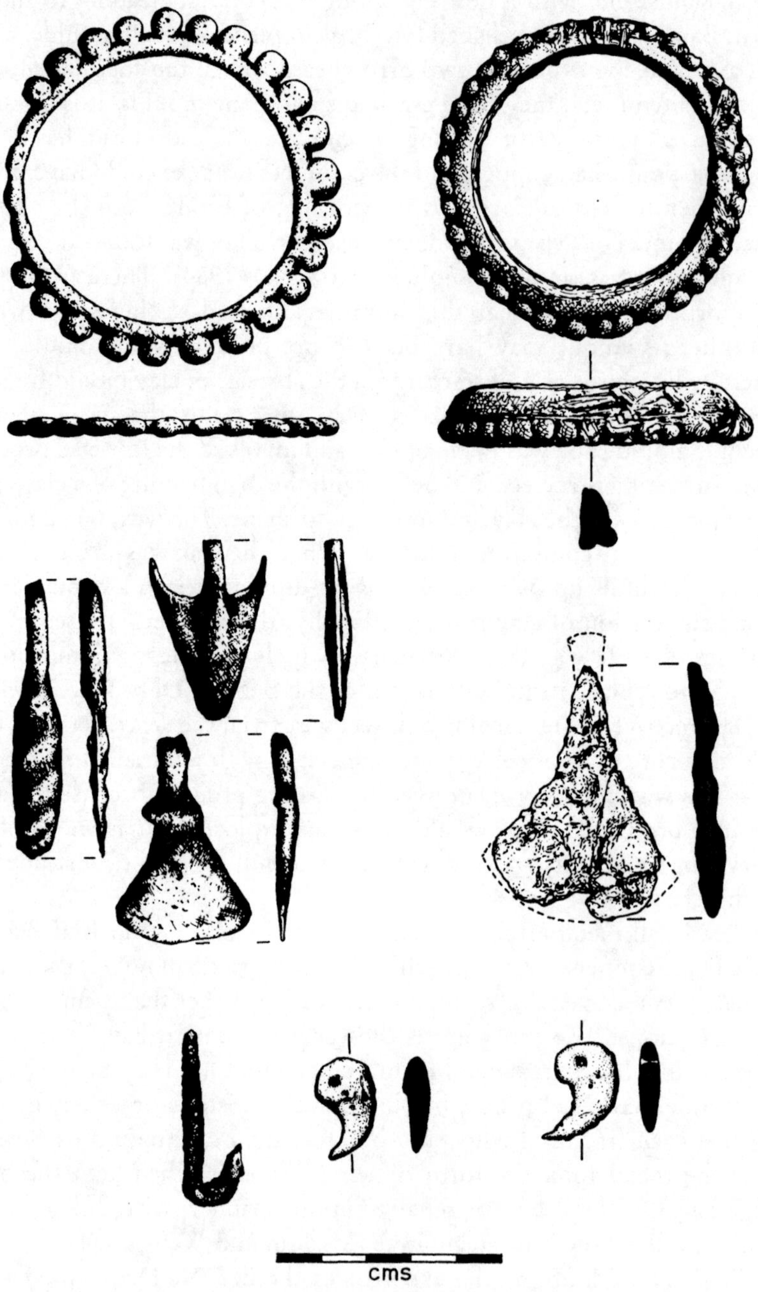

3.35 Bronze artefacts from Ban Na Di, General Period B. Top row, bracelets; middle row, arrowheads; bottom row, beads and fish hook.

Ban Na Di (Fig. 3.35). These follow a variety of shapes, some small and plain, others, larger and decorated. One child was buried wearing a pair of solid anklets. As at Non Nok Tha and Ban Chiang, however, bronze was uncommon in mortuary contexts. Only one in ten of the people buried were accompanied by bronzes.

In some cases, bronze bracelets led to the corrosion or the replacement of cloth fabric by copper oxide, and this has allowed Pilditch (1984) to identify both the raw materials used and the weaving patterns. Burial 36, for example, was buried with either a shroud or a garment made of silk. Other fabrics include a coarsely woven matting material which may have been used to wrap the body prior to interment.

Bronze artefacts were made within the same tradition at Non Nok Tha and Ban Chiang. At the former, six sets of double moulds for casting axes are known, together with six complete and several fragmentary crucibles. Fragments of bronze interpreted as casting spillage and, in one case, the recovery of an axe in association with its mould, provide compelling evidence for local casting, if not for smelting. As is the case in all sites of the Southeast Asian bronze tradition, the inventory of actual artefact-types is short. There are 28 bracelets and nine socketed axe heads. The axe heads were cast within the double sandstone moulds, and later shaped by annealing and hammering when cold. Bayard has subdivided them into four types, though all have in common raised ribs round the socket, which he interprets as a device to assist in hafting. Stech and Maddin, in their review of nine of the Non Nok Tha bronzes, have shown that decorated bracelets were cast in one piece, probably shaped by the lost wax technique and clay moulds (Stech and Maddin 1976). Axe moulds, however, were made from local sandstone, and several fragments from unfinished specimens attest to local manufacture. The clay used for crucibles was heavily tempered with rice chaff, a device which would disperse the forces generated by the heating process. Smith (1973) has concluded that these crucibles were heated by building the fuel over them until the alloy melted. The evidence shows conclusively that bronze-casting took place Non Nok Tha.

In addition to the nine bronzes from Non Nok Tha, Stech and Maddin (1976) have also undertaken an important analysis of bronze artefacts from Ban Chiang (Stech and Maddin 1986). Their study of six artefacts from the Early Period shows that all were cast from an alloy of copper and between 5.5 and 12.4% tin. The socketed axe seen in Fig. 3.14 has a tin content of 18.4%, but the analytical technique involved, when applied to a badly corroded specimen, can result in a spuriously high estimate, and it is most unlikely that this is the true percentage. Most interest was generated by the spearhead illustrated in Fig. 3.36. In the original published analysis, the tin content was found to be as low as 1.3%, but Stech and Maddin (1976) warned that this figure was probably far too low. Further analyses now reveal a higher tin content (9.17%), which places this bronze squarely within the early tradition of metal-working found at Ban

Chiang and Ban Na Di. This particular implement has also been subjected to microscopic investigation to reveal whether it was simply cast, or whether further working to modify its shape or improve its cutting properties followed. Microanalysis demonstrated that the spearhead had been cold hammered and annealed after casting. The process known as annealing involves reheating to remove the stress weakness which results from cold hammering. The excavations at Ban Chiang also yielded remains of crucibles with scoria matching those from Ban Na Di, a casting area with the remains of a clay furnace, and fragments of sandstone moulds. The analysis of the Middle Period bronze bracelets and anklets from Ban Chiang disclosed that they were normally left as cast, with no subsequent working. An innovation in half of the sample of 10 was the deliberate addition of lead. This would have made it easier to cast objects with complex designs.

Our knowledge of personal ornaments at Ban Na Di is derived almost entirely from burials. While the metal ingots for casting were imported, at least some of the finished artefacts were made at the site. Other ornaments were made of shell and stone, and these were probably obtained in a finished state since we have no evidence for local manufacture. Take, for example, the stone bracelets. These were rare at Ban Na Di, and made from exotic stone such as slate and marble. The armlets found with burial 32 were cut from trochus shell, a marine species which is not found within 600 km of the site today. There were also thousands of small shell-disc beads for which a marine origin is likely. The jewellery from Ban Chiang and Non Nok Tha has not yet been published in detail, but White (1982b) has described stone bracelets from Ban Chiang which look very similar to those from Ban Na Di, while small shell-disc beads and shell bracelets figure in Bayard's references to grave goods from Non Nok Tha (Bayard 1984a).

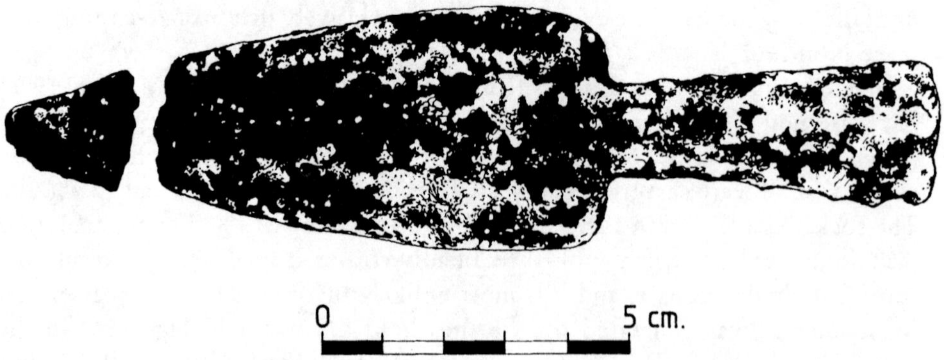

3.36 The bronze spearhead from burial 76 at Ban Chiang. It is the earliest evidence for bronze in a burial context there, and it has been assigned to Early Period III.

The social organisation

It is relatively straightforward to describe aspects of the prehistoric subsistence and technology, but the way in which a given group or groups of people ordered social relationships is less easily assessed. There are several variables which need to be approached, and only partial conclusions or tentative statements may be made on the basis of the available evidence. For the individual, the person's status and role in the community are important. In the case of the community as a whole, there is a basic distinction between local autonomy and deference to an elite based in a controlling centre.

The status of a person within the community relates to a number of factors and these vary between societies. On the one hand, unusual skills or charisma may confer prestige upon a given individual. This type of prestige is particular to the individual and is not bequeathed to anyone else at death. On the other hand, high rank may be inherited by a person of little personal worth. Many groups, be they agriculturalists or hunter-gatherers, structure their social relationships and individual place in society on the question of hereditary rank – whereby community leadership is vested in the senior male closest in linear descent from the ancestors. The role of the senior ranking person – let us call him a community leader – is often economic, religious and social, though these three concepts can be so embedded within each other as to be virtually indistinguishable. The leader may arbitrate in disputes, mediate with ancestral spirits, and oversee the receipt and distribution of valuables such as exotic stone, leather or shell ornaments. Where intercommunity relationships include exchange of people, such as brides, it is often found that prestigious goods circulate in the opposite direction. The amount and quality of such goods is a measure of the leader's status and prestige (Friedman and Rowlands 1977).

The leader of a community may well exercise influence in, but not beyond, its precincts. Decisions affecting the village are taken within its confines. The converse to this situation represents a change of fundamental importance: when a community becomes part of a network where one community exercises domination over the rest. This domination is often reflected by an upward movement of tribute goods to the settlement which houses the principal residence of the chief. Some surpluses may be redistributed down the chain, and others may be accumulated to sustain the chief's followers, be they artisans or warriors.

Let us consider the Khorat plateau sites during General Periods A and B to assess whether we are dealing with an autonomous or centralised society and, if the former, whether there is evidence for ranking. Identifying ranking on the basis of archaeological data is not easy. If it is possible to reconstruct house plans, the presence of one residence set apart from others on the basis of size, method of construction or contents, could reflect the presence of a highly ranked individual. Such data, however, are rare, and not yet available for mainland Southeast Asia during General Periods A and B. Archaeologists often seek evidence for ranking in cemeteries on the premise that the treatment of a dead individual should reflect, in part at least, that person's status when alive (Binford 1971, Saxe 1971, Tainter 1978). The criteria employed have included the dead person's accompanying grave goods, presence of structures over the grave, the relationship between age, and the abundance of grave goods and the relative location of burials within a cemetery as a whole. Many of these variables relate to the amount of energy expended in the disposal of the corpse. The construction of Angkor Wat is an extreme example, but even such factors as the depth of a grave or the heaping up of a mound over it are indices of energy expenditure. Where spatial variation can be assessed, it is possible that the higher-ranked individuals are buried together in a particular part of the cemetery or even quite separately in a distinct place. The recovery of infants or children buried with unusually rich grave goods has often been used as evidence for hereditary ranking on the assumption that children could not, in their own brief lifespan, have accumulated the necessary status to warrant such treatment. Binford (1971) has further suggested that special artefacts used, for example, as symbols of office or rank, may be found in mortuary contexts.

Peebles and Kus (1977) have suggested several variables which may allow the recognition of centralised chiefdoms on the basis of archaeological data. One follows on from the preceding discussion of burial practices and suggests that the identification of one elite set of rich burials in the central settlement is an index of a centralised chiefdom. To this they add the recognition of a hierarchy of settlements within which the dominant centre may be distinguished by high-energy facilities such as a temple, walls or moats. The central place could also be recognised as a focus for redistribution on the basis of its accumulation of a wider range of goods than at any other site. Peebles and Kus have further noted the relevance to this issue of regionally based facilities to buffer environmental problems such as a reservoir for water storage and distribution.

What, then, can be said of social organisation during General Periods A and B? Let us begin with three prehistoric settlement patterns. The Kumphawapi survey area (Fig. 3.28) incorporates many prehistoric sites, most of which are interpreted as settlements. Of those excavated, none stands out as being unusually large, nor has any yielded evidence which Peebles and Kus have seen as being indicative of a superordinate centre. The two sites which might qualify are both interpreted as late, and irrelevant to the question at issue. The Middle Chi survey area (Fig. 3.5) has revealed one large centre, Ban Chiang Hian, ringed by moats, a reservoir and, possibly, ramparts. There are numerous similarly moated settlements elsewhere on the Khorat plateau (Moore 1986) as well as the Chao Phraya valley. In the latter area, Bronson has suggested construction in the period A.D. 500–1000. Chantaratiyakan (1984) has proposed that the moats at Ban Chiang Hian are later than General Periods A and B. If excavations sustain the suggestion that the site reached its present size during General Period C, then the settlement size distributions in both the Middle Chi area and the vicinity of Lake

Kumphawapi lack any site defined as a central place on account of its size, moats or defences. Welch (1984) has suggested, on the basis of his fieldwork in the upper Mun valley (Fig. 3.37), that during the Tamyae or early part of his Formative Phase (General Period B), which lasted until about 600 B.C., there is no evidence for a settlement hierarchy.

There are two cemeteries which have been considered from the point of view of social organisation. One is Ban Na Di, the other is Non Nok Tha. The assemblage of burials from Ban Chiang is still under analysis. Excavations at Ban Na Di involved two areas separated by about 30 m. It is necessary to stress that the area excavated covered a smaller area than Non Nok Tha (70m^2 against 340m^2), although the deposits were up to 4.2 m deep, against 1.4 m, at Non Nok Tha. The sample of burials is also smaller than at Non Nok Tha, there being 60 burials or partial interments available. In both areas, these were laid out in rows and, with time, were superimposed one on another. According to the site's stratigraphy, the bodies in each area were interred throughout the same timespan. The basic ritual was identical in that the body was laid out on its back on a north-south axis within an excavated grave. The ritual usually involved the placement of the fore-limb of a pig or cow, and a range of pottery vessels, some still containing the remains of food, with the body. The dead person sometimes wore items of jewellery, such as necklaces, bracelets, armlets and anklets. Some

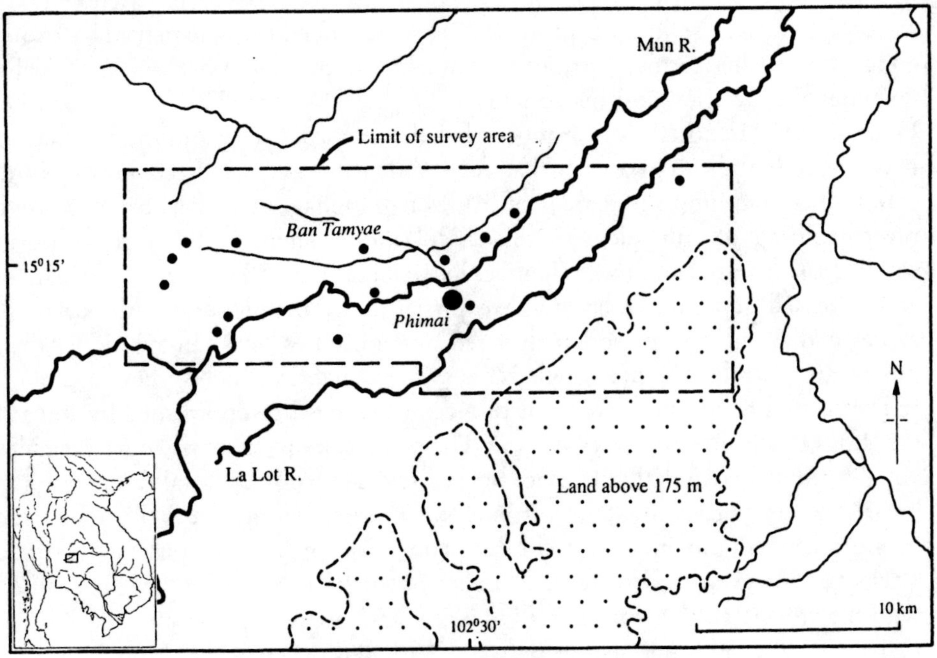

3.37 The distribution of prehistoric settlements in the upper Mun valley (after Welch 1985).

bracelets were worn, some were placed on the body. Other artefacts found in mortuary contexts are two cowrie shells, clay figurines, fragments of cloth and, in the two latest graves, an iron spear-blade, knife and bangle.

The remains of infants, children and adults were present in both excavated areas which are called Areas A and B. When we compare the distribution of "exotic" goods between each area, however, there are several intriguing differences. The vast majority of shell beads (97%) were found in Area B graves, although about two-thirds of the total came from one grave. The five stone bracelets were restricted to four Area B burials, and the clay figurines and trochus shell armlets were all found in Area B. One child in Area B was interred under a crocodile skin shroud, and a woman nearby was found with a large pierced object made of crocodile skull. These graves in Area B yielded 25 bronze artefacts, far more than area A ($n=5$), and only Area B graves contained iron weapons and jewellery. There is, therefore, some evidence to support the possibility that one excavated area yielded graves which attracted more exotic grave goods. The disparity in relative wealth found throughout the use of the cemetery invites explanation.

There is no possibility that the differences reflect an early (Area A) and late use of the cemetery: the site's stratigraphy and parallel typological changes in burial pottery rule this out. It is possible that excavations between Areas A and B would reveal a gradation in relative wealth which would lessen the sharp distinction now apparent. But this would still not explain why one area reveals richer graves so consistently for so long. Dalton (1977) has described the role played by exotic goods or, in his terms, "primitive valuables", in a number of historically documented societies, and his conclusion may throw some light on the Ban Na Di cemetery. He noted, for example, that the reciprocal circulation of valuables between communities plays a critical role in the maintenance of relationships and community standing. Movement of brides from village A to B is balanced by a reverse gifting of valuables. In this circulatory system, inability to conform entails loss of status and even alliance. Participation aids the forging of alliances and increased standing. One possible explanation for the higher wealth of Area B graves is that one group, perhaps related by family ties, was ranked higher than others, and thereby had preferred access to the valuables which symbolised rank.

The second major social analysis of a cemetery has been published by Bayard (1984a). He considered the Non Nok Tha cemetery on the basis of 54 variables and 87 complete or relatively intact burials selected from the total sample of 217 burials or mortuary contexts. As at Ban Na Di, exotic stone and shell goods were by no means abundant, and a similar proportion of burials contained bronze artefacts. However, the greater time depth of the Non Nok Tha cemetery, allied with the advantage of a considerably greater area excavated, has allowed Bayard to recognise a most interesting pattern. With the onset of the Non Nok Tha phase, he found that two similar yet distinct forms of footed jar were rarely found in the same grave. This distribution cross-cut age and sex differences, and there is some slight indication that the groups occupied distinct parts of the cemetery area. One of the two groups of graves containing these vessels was distinguished by a greater number of grave offerings, although there is an area of overlap. In addition, there are graves which contain neither form of jar, and these are invariably poor burials in respect of other grave offerings. Bayard has suggested that the cemetery area was used by at least two distinct affiliative groups, one being more highly ranked than the other. The poor set may have comprised junior kin groups, or people of low achievement or status, and, therefore, not accorded the same ritual as people in the richer graves accompanied by the footed jars. This finding underwrites his conclusion that, during the Non Nok Tha phase, the cemetery area was used by two contemporary social groups with one ranked rather higher than the other. Absent, however, were any graves which were clearly set apart on the basis of high energy expenditure in burial ritual. Thus, both the Non Nok Tha and Ban Na Di data support the conclusion that, in this part of Southeast Asia at least, domestic communities contained differently ranked affiliative groups but not yet with dominant regional centres.

The lower Chao Phraya valley

The theme of this chapter is the expansion of domestic communities which practiced a wide range of subsistence pursuits including agriculture. This phenomenon is best documented, at present, on the basis of the sites on the Khorat plateau, but it is clear that other major lowland areas likewise participated in this expansionary phase of settlement. We will now turn to the prehistory of the three major valleys, and that of the coast of Central Viet Nam. The area described under the heading of the Chao Phraya valley encompasses several other smaller rivers which also flow into the upper Gulf of Siam (Figs. 3.2 and 3.38). One of the major problems besetting the student of this area lies in establishing the pattern of sea-level changes during the last five millennia, and the positions of sites relative to the coast. This is significant, not just from the point of view of subsistence, but also of transport and exchange. Behind the shoreline itself, with its fringe of mangrove and nipa swamps in sheltered areas, there probably lay a series of different environments. In historic times, for example, the lower floodplain of the Chao Phraya River was too waterlogged to sustain woodland, and bore a dense growth of grasses. In the better-drained margins, this gave way to subtropical, moist forest, while the surrounding uplands above 500 m or thereabouts were covered by a canopied, evergreen forest. These uplands west of the Chao Phraya are known for their deposits of copper, iron and lead, while the valleys of the Khwae Yai and Khwae Noi rivers comprise the eastern end of the Three Pagodas pass. Any traveller wishing to reach the Chao Phraya valley from the west would find that this pass provides ready access. It is probable that similar conditions prevailed during General Periods A and B.

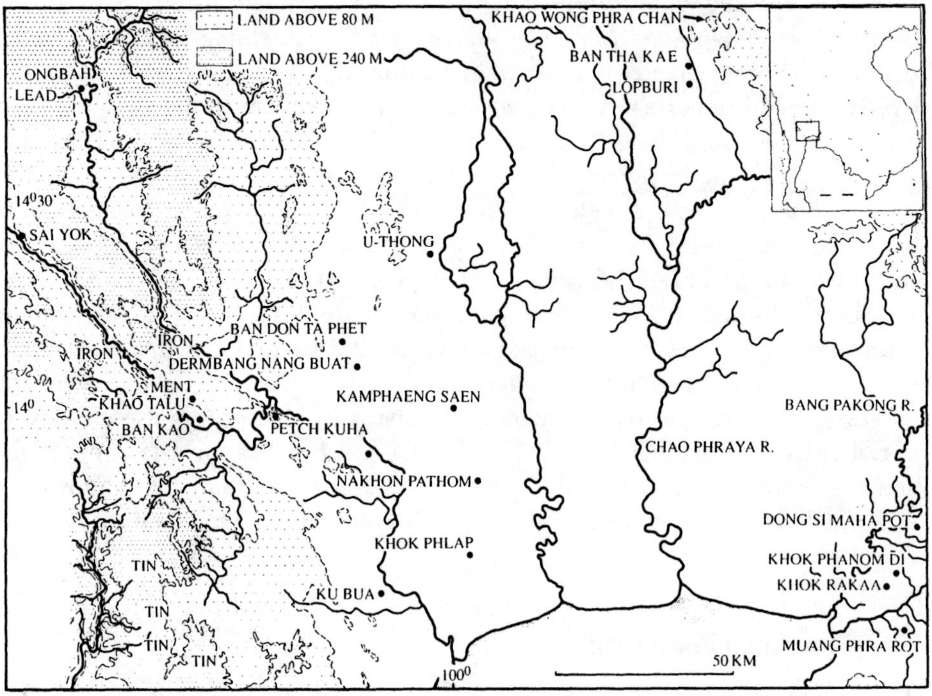

3.38 The distribution of archaeological sites and important mineral resources in the Chao Phraya valley and its environs.

Several sites have been excavated, and a pattern is emerging which reveals some parallels with General Periods A and B described for Northeast Thailand. The practice of inhuming the dead with a range of grave goods has been documented for a series of sites in this region. During the early 1960s, Sørensen excavated the Bang and Lue sites near the village of Ban Kao which lies next to a small tributary of the Khwae Noi River. Without doubt, this was the single most significant step in our understanding of later prehistory in the area, because it brought to the attention of prehistorians the presence of sites containing burials and artefacts reflecting agriculturally based, sedentary communities. When Sørensen began his research he was working with virtually no prior information or comparative material to refer to. The Bang site comprises an occupation level into which graves had been excavated for inhuming the dead (Fig. 3.39). The corpses had been buried in an extended position, and were accompanied by grave goods which included pottery vessels, animal bone and stone adzes. During the course of 1961–2, Sørensen uncovered almost 400 m^2 of the Bang site, finding 44 burials in the process (Fig. 3.40). This step into the unknown has attracted several reviews, each attempting to re-interpret Sørensen's findings (Parker 1968, Solheim 1969, Bayard and Parker 1976, Macdonald 1978). One of the problems faced was the lack of any clear stratigraphy. Subsequently, the level from which graves were cut could not be ascertained, and ordering the relative sequence of burials was ruled out. Nevertheless, he concluded that there were three phases in the prehistoric occupation. The earliest was characterised by burials associated with round-based pottery vessels equipped with hollow, tripod legs, ring feet or pedestals. This was followed by a phase in which shallow, unfooted, carinated bowls with a red or black burnished finish were preferred (Fig. 3.41). Finally, two graves were found associated with iron axes, and these represented the terminal mortuary phase.

With meticulous attention to detail, Sørensen recovered almost a million fragments of pottery as well as material culture which included polished stone adze heads, bone arrowheads and bone points. Pottery vessels were found in groups placed beyond the head and feet, and adzes on the chest or by the head. Eight radiocarbon dates have been published (Sørensen and Hatting 1967, Sørensen 1973). Three of these bracket the early group of burials, and suggest that they fall somewhere within the period between 2500 and 1500 B.C. A further four determinations reveal that the second burial phase followed without any major interruption, terminating by about 1800 B.C. at the earliest, and 1350 B.C. at the latest. The assumed dating of iron indicates a subsequent period of mortuary activity about a millennium after the terminal dates for the second burial phase. Since no trace of bronze was discovered in graves of the first two phases, Sørensen labelled them early and late Neolithic, respectively. On the basis of the early pottery styles, Sørensen also stressed the parallels with the Malaysian Neolithic sites such as Gua Cha. Similarities with General Period A in the Khorat plateau are also seen in the burial rite – the presence of stone adzes and the absence of bronze artefacts. While the absence of bronze from the 42 pre-iron graves suggests that some communities in the Chao Phraya area were unfamiliar with bronze-working at a time when it was already established in the Mekong catchment, the non-burial contexts at the site did yield a number of bronze and iron artefacts. Bronzes include bracelet fragments and a bell (Sørensen 1973), and their stratigraphic context is actually below some of the later, second phase graves. One of the problems with this site is the lack of clear stratigraphy and, as Sørensen rightly stresses, artefacts can be relocated in prehistory, and their actual depth below a modern datum is not necessarily an indication of relative age. At least the possibility exists, however, that during the second mortuary phase at the Bang site, the occupants were familiar with bronze, but chose not to include any in their burials.

Parker (1968) and Bayard and Parker (1976) have suggested that the burials are considerably later than the excavator believes. In their view, the graves all belong to the same general timespan as the two with iron implements, the burials being interred in graves cut into an earlier General Period B, and perhaps even A, occupation site. Macdonald (1978) has examined in some detail the distribution of the graves from a social stance, to see if there is any clear evidence in favour of

3.39 Per Sørensen's pioneer work at the Bang site near Ban Kao represents the most significant step taken towards an understanding of domestic societies in the Chao Phraya area. (Courtesy P. Sørensen.)

differential location of subsets distinguished by wealth or time. He found neither, but did suggest the possibility that the part of the Bang site excavated may have covered the boundary between the graves of two different affiliated groups. Perhaps the final word on this historic site and excavation programme must be deferred until Sørensen has published the final report on the non-mortuary data.

At the same time that Non Nok Tha was being excavated research was being undertaken at Khok Charoen, a mound located in the Pa Sak valley which enters the Chao Phraya plains from the east (Figs. 3.42 and 3.43, Watson and Loofs-Wissowa 1967, Loofs-Wissowa 1970, Watson 1979, Ho 1984). This site is located at the junction of two small streams and on an ecotone between the Phetchabun range and the Pa Sak floodplain, a position broadly comparable to the situation of the General Period A to C sites on the Khorat plateau.

Trial excavations, in 1966, revealed five inhumation burials accompanied by pottery vessels and polished stone adzes, so the following year almost 400 m^2

3.40 The burials at the Bang site near Ban Kao were associated with complete pots, jewellery and stone adzes. (Courtesy P. Sørensen.)

were excavated and 44 burials uncovered. Natural soil was encountered at a depth of just over a metre. The burials follow a widespread pattern of being extended inhumations with an array of grave goods. Ho (1984) has concluded that there is a considerable differential in wealth between graves, the richest being accompanied by 19 pottery vessels, stone beads, 10 shell and 9 stone bracelets, and many small shell-disc beads of the type found at Khok Phanom Di and Ban Na Di. Other burials were less well endowed, though shell-disc beads were found in the pelvic areas of some skeletons and small, trapezoid, polished stone adzes were common. Much of the shell used to make ornaments had a marine origin, trochus being used for bracelets, ear ornaments and, possibly, finger rings, and conus for small rings, which Ho feels could have been worn on the fingers (Fig. 3.44). There are two thermoluminescence dates from burials 1 and 10. They are 1180±300 and 1080±300 B.C., respectively. Watson (1979) has stressed that no metal remains were located there. This is puzzling, since the

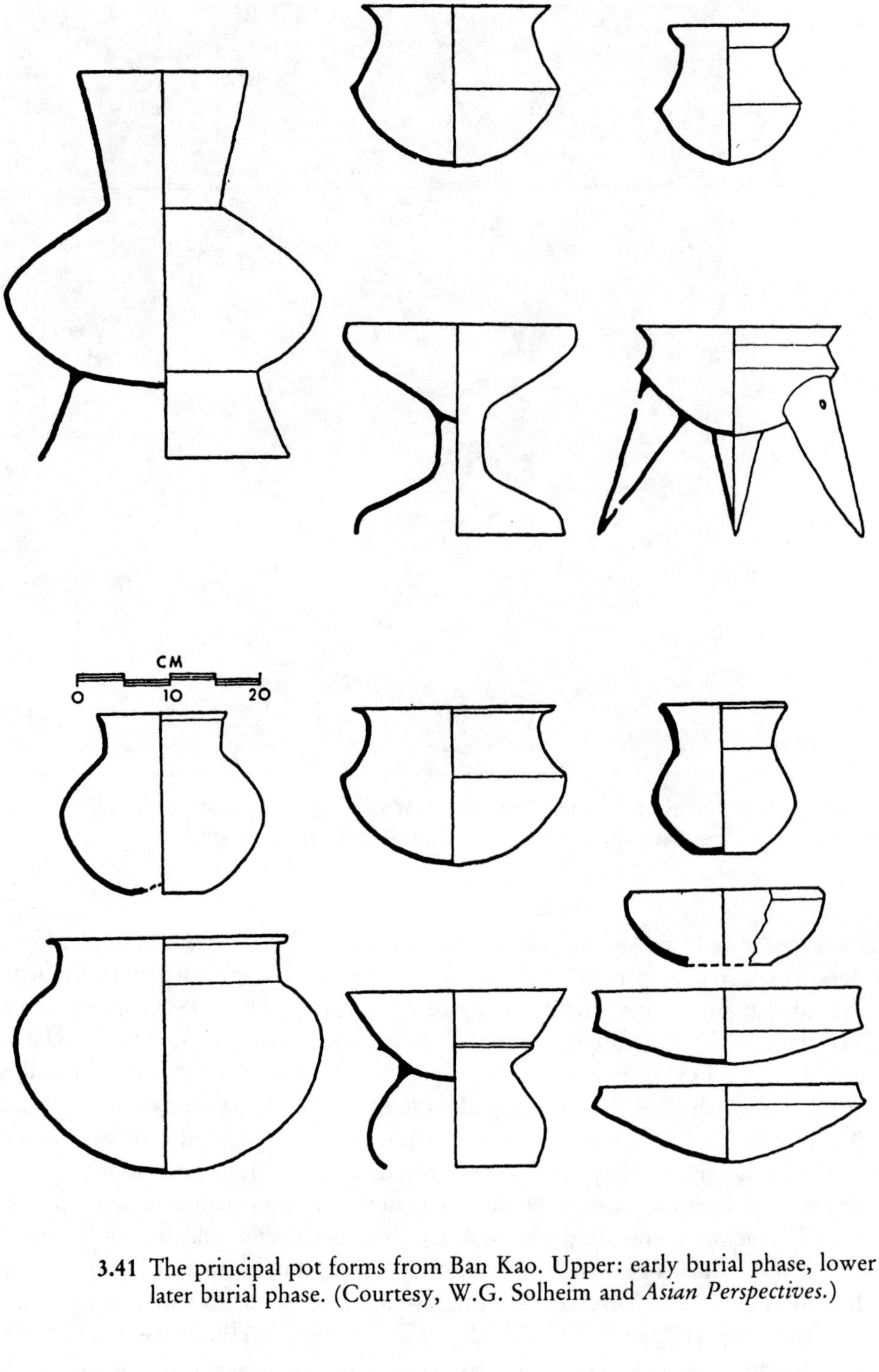

3.41 The principal pot forms from Ban Kao. Upper: early burial phase, lower: later burial phase. (Courtesy, W.G. Solheim and *Asian Perspectives*.)

3.42 The excavation of Khok Charoen was, along with that of Ban Kao and Non Nok Tha, one of the pioneer programmes in Thailand. (Courtesy William Watson.)

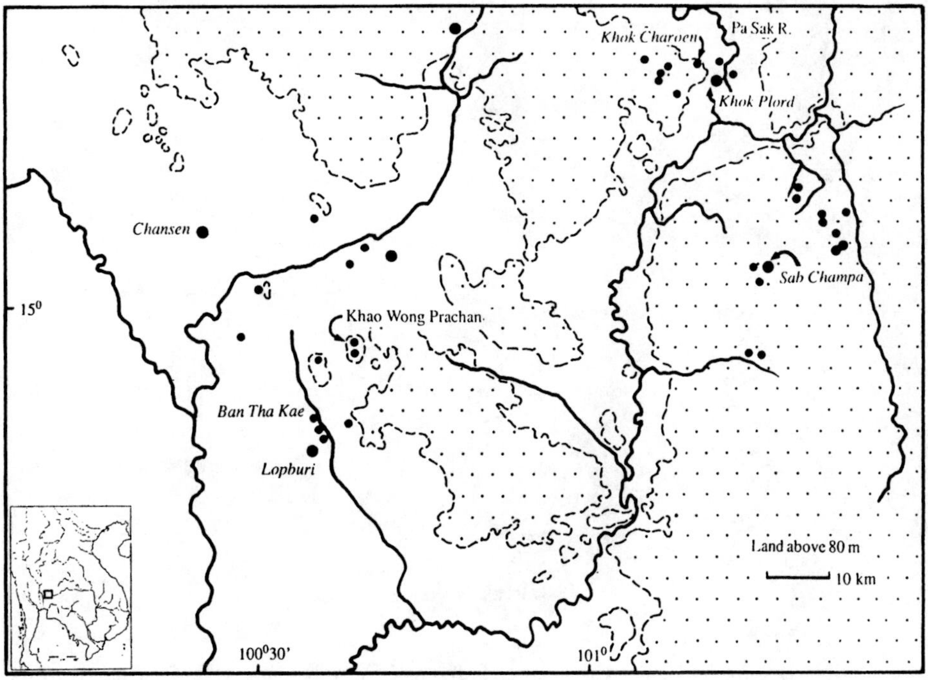

3.43 The distribution of prehistoric sites in the Pa Sak valley and eastern margins of the Chao Phraya plain.

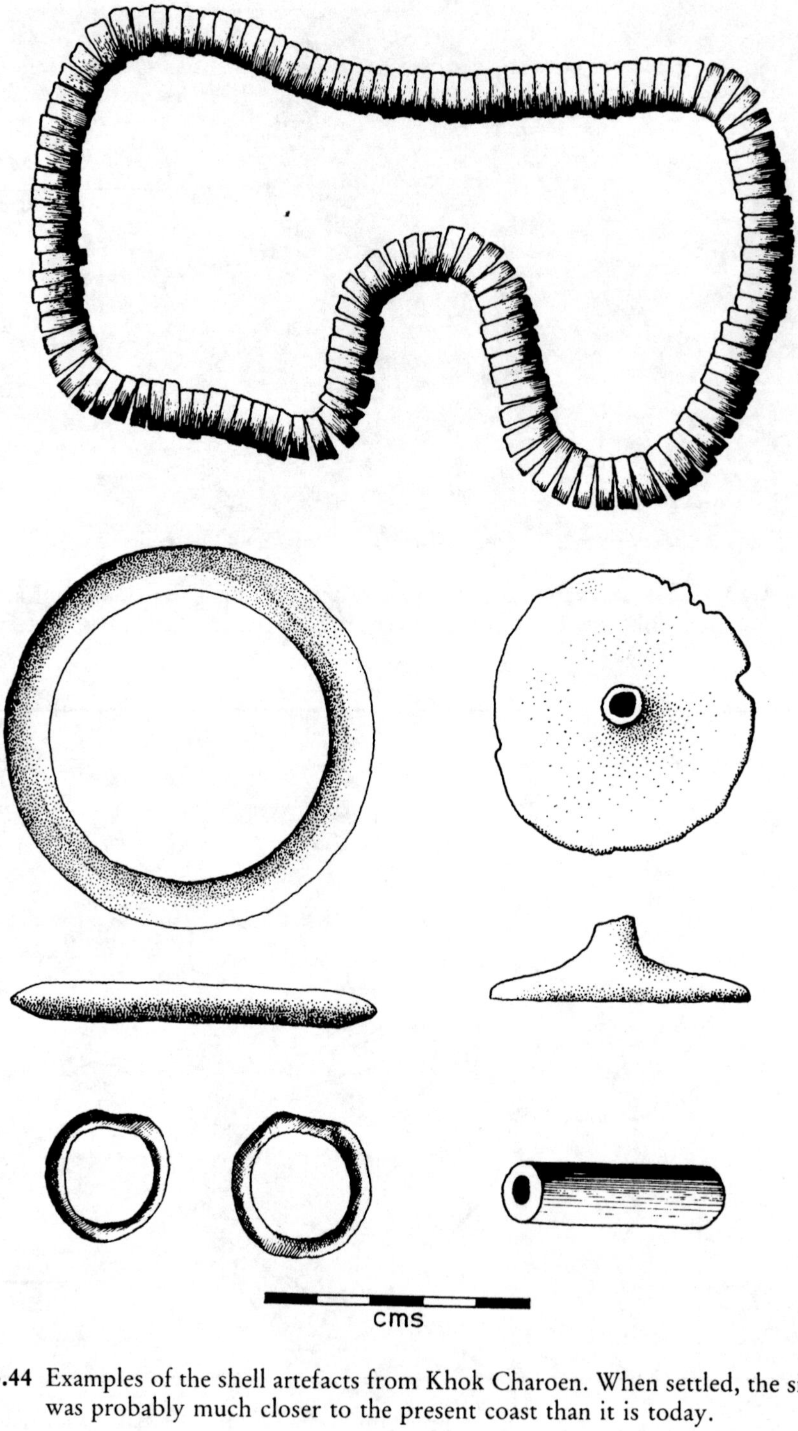

3.44 Examples of the shell artefacts from Khok Charoen. When settled, the site was probably much closer to the present coast than it is today.

characteristic vessels from Khok Charoen find their main typological parallels in the funerary wares from contexts at Non Nok Tha, during the Non Nok Tha phase, which do reveal evidence for metallurgy. Again, there are hints here that bronze came later to the Chao Phraya than the Mekong valley.

We have already discussed the development of the Khok Phanom Di cemetery. The latest phase at this site represents a period of occupation after the local retreat of the sea. Faunal remains from this context represent a complete change from the exploitation of a marine habitat to one in which riverine and woodland species predominate. No mortuary remains have been found, but the excavation disclosed the local manufacture of pottery. In addition to the clay anvils used in fashioning pots, the excavators found clay cylinders, interpreted as the first stage in the conversion of clay into a vessel, and a mound of raw clay presumably collected with a view to fashioning the cylinders. The periphery of the mound comprises lenses of ash associated with dumps of potsherds which look very like the remains of firing vessels in an open bonfire.

If Khok Phanom Di was a specialist potting centre, as the excavators have suggested, what was being exchanged for finished vessels? Khok Phanom Di gave access to good potting clay and riverine-coastal transport, but the immediate area lacks a source of high-quality stone. As at Ban Kao and Khok Charoen, there is no evidence for bronze, but axes and bracelets of exotic stone are common. Indeed, Khok Phanom Di in its latest phase saw adaptation to an inland, riverine habitat based on rice, domestic cattle and pigs, as well as hunting and fishing. No evidence for the use of any kind of metal was found. Specialisation in pottery manufacture, which already had a long local tradition, permitted participation in an exchange network embracing the transport of stone adzes and bracelets and doubtless less-durable items.

Until recently, evidence for a bronze industry, comparable with that described for the earlier phase in Northeast Thailand, has been absent from the Chao Phraya basin. This situation has now been redressed by the excavations at Khok Phlap (Daeng-iet 1978), Ban Khok Rakaa (Bannanurag 1984) and Ban Tha Kae (Natapintu 1984, Siripanith 1985). Khok Phlap is a low mound covering an area of about 1.5 ha. No radiocarbon dates have yet been published, but the parallels with the General Period B sites in Northeast Thailand are clear. Several burials were accompanied by whole pottery vessels containing sea shells. Ornaments included bracelets made of turtle carapace, stone, shell and bone, as well as of bronze (Fig. 3.45). One grave contained three anvils used in making pots, in addition to four complete vessels. The inhabitants of the site showed a predilection for coloured stone beads and ear pendants, while their interest in bronze extended to barbed metal tips for their arrows.

There is no report of iron at Khok Phlap but, at a second relevant site, Ban Tha Kae, there is a clear succession from the use of bronze in limited amounts to a context including considerably increased bronze and local iron-working (Natapintu 1984). Ban Tha Kae is a few km north of Lopburi, and comprises a mound

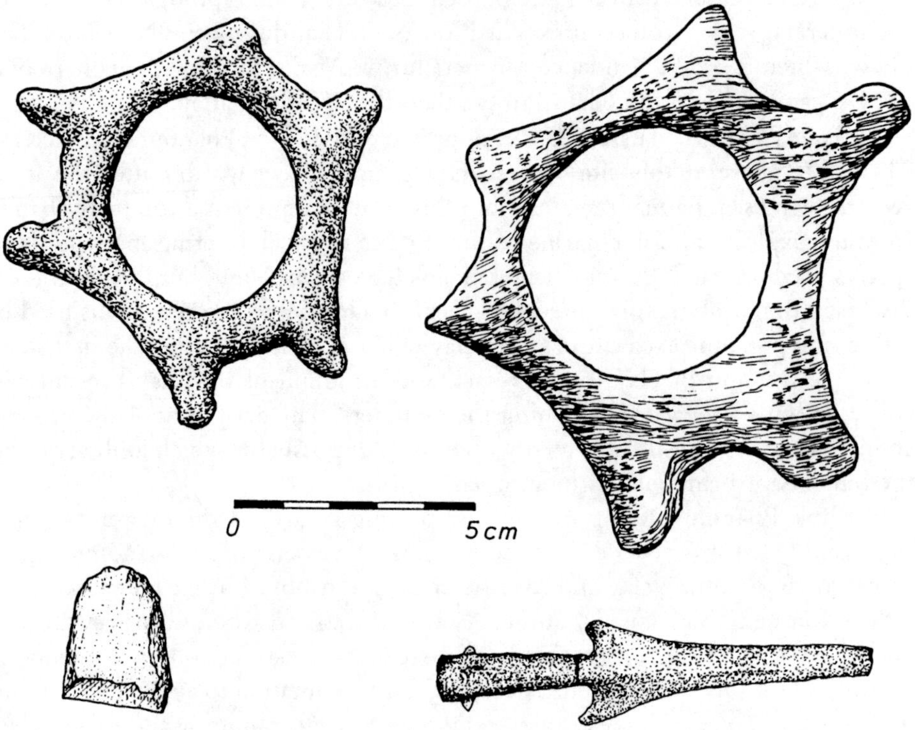

3.45 Khok Phlap, like Ban Tha Kae, has provided evidence for a local General Period B bronze tradition in the Chao Phraya area. The bangle at the upper left is of bronze, the other is of turtle shell. There is also a stone axe or adze and a bronze spearhead.

measuring about 1200 by 800 m. Excavations by the Thai Fine Arts Department, in 1983, uncovered a sequence of considerable interest. The 2.5 m deep stratigraphic build-up was subdivided into three phases. The lowest contained burials associated with bronze artefacts in the form of bracelets (Fig. 3.46). Other offerings included shell beads and earrings, as well as stone bracelets with a T-shaped cross-section recalling those repaired with bronze from Ban Na Di. This same context revealed compelling evidence for the manufacture of shell bracelets. Using the marine tridacna shell as the source material, circular tabs were removed from the centre of the blanks before final grinding to the desired shape. Stone axes were found in this early context, together with a pottery style incorporating the impression of curvilinear designs. Puthorn Pumaton, the excavator, found that the succeeding middle period witnessed the first use of iron, and included blue and orange glass beads. The radiocarbon dating of the site, or of similar exposures elsewhere, has great priority. The same remarks apply to Ban Khok Rakaa, where Bannanurag's test excavation, in 1983, revealed

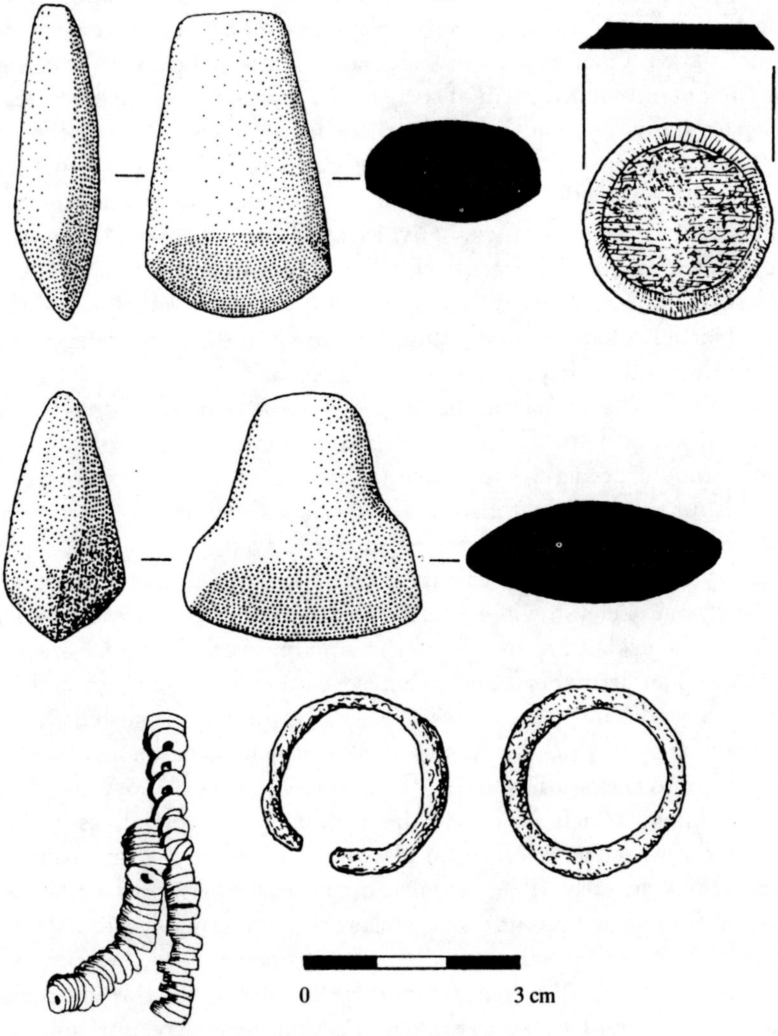

3.46 Ban Tha Kae is now recognised as one of the key prehistoric sites in the Chao Phraya plains. It has a long sequence, is located near the copper sources of Khao Wong Prachan, and has yielded bronze bracelets, shell beads, and polished stone axes ascribed to General Period B. Top right is the central core taken from a shell bracelet during manufacture at the site.

skeletons accompanied by bronze bowls in a site with a stratigraphic sequence extending to 6 m (Bannanurag 1984).

The Lopburi area is clearly one of considerable relevance, and the Central Thailand Research Program is in the process of transforming our knowledge about it. Under the leadership of Surapon Natapintu, 105 prehistoric sites have been identified in two field seasons, and several have been sounded by excavations. Natapintu (1985) has excavated a small (3 by 5 m) exposure at the site of Ban Phu Noi. Within it he recovered an assemblage of no fewer than 32 burials associated with marine shell bracelets and shell-disc beads. Bronze was present at the site but only in the form of stray finds. Bracelets were made of sea shell, turtle carapace and ivory. These, and the shell-disc beads, so reminiscent of those made at Khok Phanom Di, provide strong evidence for exchange networks linking interior sites with the coast. Another major contribution has been made in the Khao Wong Prachan valley, only 15 km from Lopburi. There, the Fine Arts Department has collaborated with the University of Pennsylvania, and Pigott and Natapintu have excavated three sites: Non Pa Wai, Non Ma Kla and Nil Kam Haeng. All are located within easy reach of the copper deposits of Phu Kao where three mines have been identified.

Non Pa Wai is a 5 ha mound comprising the remains of smelting activity to a depth of about 3 m. There are the fragmentary remains of thousands of clay bivalve moulds, crucibles for smelting, tuyeres, fragments of copper ore and cup moulds for the casting of ingots. The moulds are very fragmentary, but it is now known that arrowheads, bracelets, spears and axes were locally cast. Under the thick layer of smelting and casting debris, Pigott and Natapintu found a cemetery in which one skeleton was associated with a pair of ceramic axe moulds. At Non Ma Kla, the excavation of a 4 by 4 m square revealed a metre deep stratigraphy containing an arrowhead and axe head of unalloyed copper, and fragments of clay furnace lining and tuyeres. The excavator has suggested that this area of intensive copper-working was contemporary with basal Ban Tha Kae, located only 5 km to the south. Among the surface finds at Khao Wong Prachan was a copper ingot, which indicated the production of metal, as well as finished artefacts, for exchange. Nil Kam Haeng is located only 2 km from Non Pa Wai. Excavations, in early 1986, revealed many lenses of copper ore which had been crushed using stone pounders, as well as slag and crucibles, to a depth of 5.25 m. At that point, the excavation ceased without reaching the bottom of the cultural deposit (Pigott 1986). When the radiocarbon dating for this industrial activity is available, it would be surprising if the timespan were not within the period 1500–250 B.C.

In her summary of the evidence for metal-working in this area, Bennett (1986) has stressed that all stages in the process of mining, ore dressing, smelting and casting are represented in contexts which argue against centralised control of the operation. The copper ingots which resulted from this procedure doubtless entered the exchange circuits to be converted, in sites such as Ban Na Di and Ban Chiang, into bronze ornaments and weapons.

During the course of the initial site survey of the Bang Pakong valley, many prehistoric sites were identified which will surely be found to relate to General Period B. Surface finds revealed bronze-working and imported glass and agate beads. One such site, Ban Khok Rakaa, has been subjected to trial excavations, and several burials were recovered in association with bronze artefacts. It is becoming increasingly evident that the adoption of bronze-working in the Chao Phraya valley antedated the first use of iron, and that it involved the same range of artefacts as have been recovered in similar contexts in Northeast Thailand.

The lower Mekong and its hinterland

Although the excavation of prehistoric sites in the lower Mekong area has a history of over a century, only during the last five years has the cultural sequence of the area assumed a structure of its own. In 1963, Malleret could only describe the known prehistoric settlements in the most general terms. Cu Lao Rua, formerly known as the Isle de la Tortue, was the best documented, having been described as early as 1888 by Cartailhac (Cartailhac 1890, and Fig. 3.47) Excavations ensued in 1902 and 1937, and a local businessman assembled a collection of artefacts from the site. These included shouldered and quadrangular adzes, much pottery, and stone bracelets, pendants and polishers. In 1937, a local villager showed Malleret a bronze axe which, he claimed, was found at this site. Rach Nui falls into the same category: it covers 120 by 50 m, and four occupation layers were noted. These contained much pottery and quadrangular stone adzes, but local informants again claimed that a bronze axe had been found there (Ha Van Tan 1980).

Bronze metallurgy in this region was definitely attested at Hang Gon (Saurin 1963), although the site has never been systematically excavated. Indeed, the material collected by Saurin was revealed by a bulldozer when clearing woodland. Hang Gon is one of many prehistoric sites in the Dong Nai valley. Surface sherds there cover an area of 350 by 150 m, and the site lies on a ridge which commands the junction of two streams. Its particular interest is the discovery of three sandstone moulds, two for casting axes and the third for casting three ring-headed pins. Saurin stressed the typological similarities between the shape of the axes and specimens known from the Red River valley, Luang Prabang in Northern Laos, and from the Mlu Prei region in North Central Cambodia. The site had a cultural stratigraphy of only 0.5–1.0 m, and neither iron nor glass beads were found among the material turned up by the bulldozer. A radiocarbon date falling within the third millennium B.C. has been obtained from an organic crust adhering to a potsherd. Little if any value attaches to such a sample. The cultural sequence in this area, and, in particular, the date of metallurgy there has, however, been clarified by recent Vietnamese investigations. Pham Quang Son (1978) has advanced a fourfold subdivision of later prehistory in the Dong Nai valley.

The sequence begins with the site of Cau Sat, which is characterised by shouldered adzes and stone armrings with a rectangular or trapezoid cross-section. The pottery from this site includes pedestalled bowls and tall jars with a flat base (Hoang Xuan Chinh and Nguyen Khac Su 1977). The second phase incorporates sites described by Fontaine (1972), of which Ben Do is the best

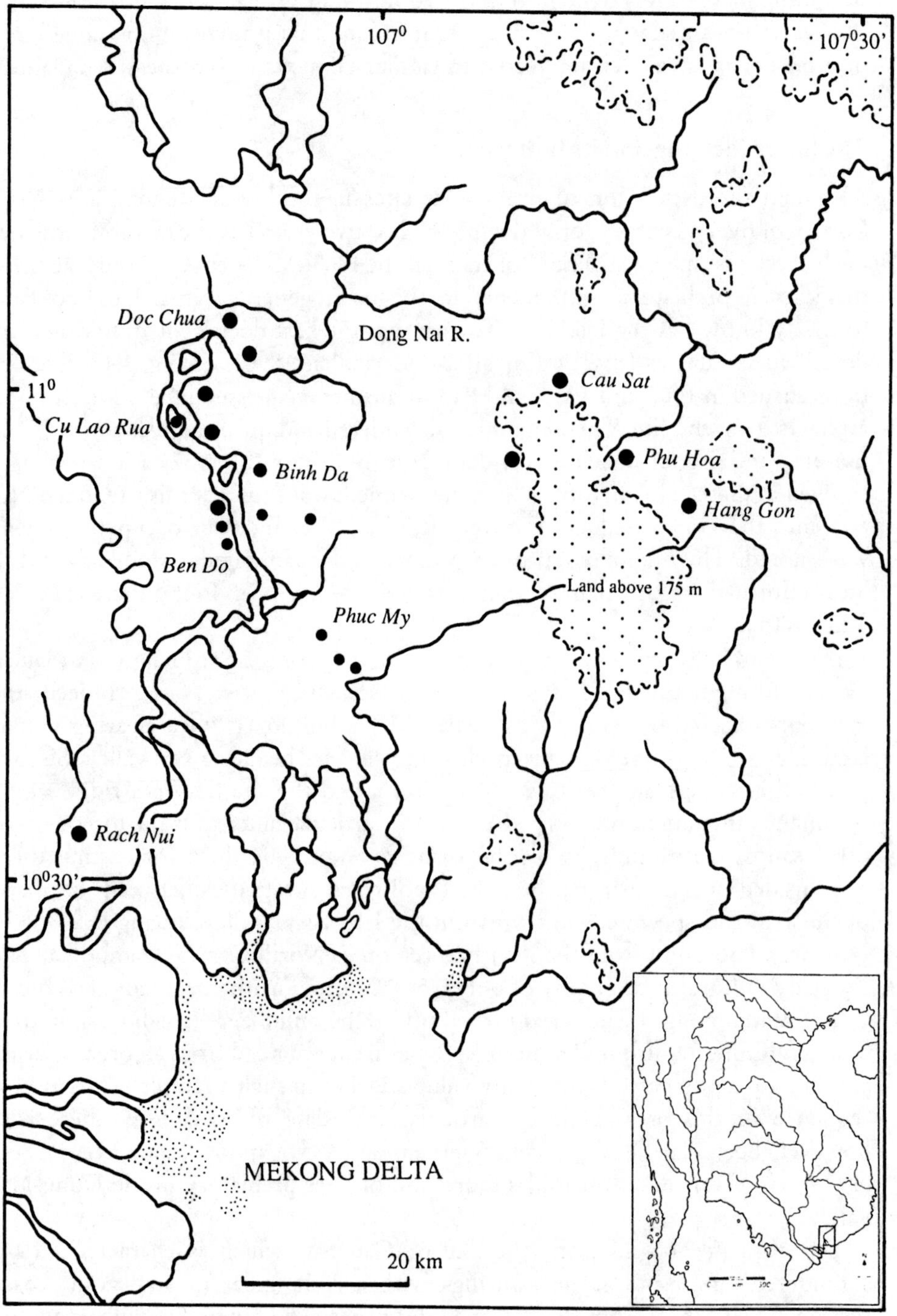

3.47 The distribution of prehistoric sites in the Dong Nai valley.

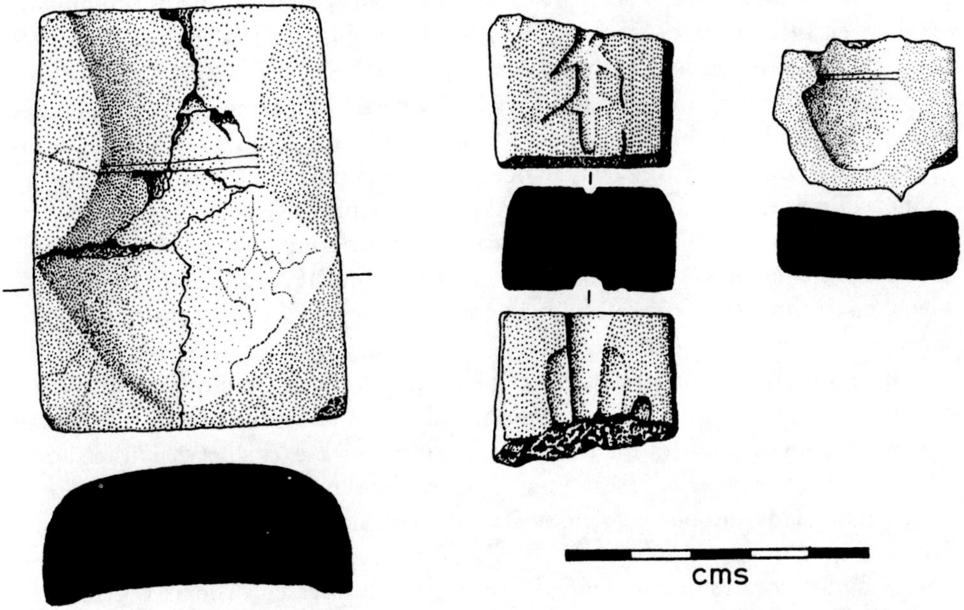

3.48 The sandstone moulds from Doc Chua show striking similarities to those from Northeast Thailand and extend the area of this Southeast Asian metallurgical tradition to the Mekong delta.

known. Pham Van Kinh (1977) has described the many large shouldered adzes from this site. The shouldered form is much more abundant than adzes with a quadrangular cross-section and no shoulder. The third phase incorporates Cu Lao Rua. We have seen that there is a possiblity of bronze being in use there. Certainly, the large forms of shouldered stone adze fell away in popularity during this phase. It is likely that the sandstone moulds of Hang Gon belong to this part of the Dong Nai sequence.

By phase four, bronze was abundant and locally cast. In 1976, the important site of Doc Chua on the bank of the Be River was discovered, and excavations ensued then and during the following year. The finds documented a mature tradition of casting bronze. No fewer than 50 mould fragments of clay or sandstone were found, and implements locally cast included tanged arrowheads, axes, small bells, socketed spearheads, harpoons and chisels (Fig. 3.48). Examination of the sandstone moulds revealed several which were incomplete before being discarded due to imperfections. The process of cutting and polishing the interior surfaces of the sandstone was clearly most demanding. The shape of the axes, chisels, arrowheads and spearheads, is remarkably similar to the examples from the General Period B contexts in Northeast Thailand (Le Xuan Diem 1977). There are also general resemblances in some stone artefacts such as the bracelets and adzes. There are few shouldered adzes at Doc Chua. The radiocarbon dates of 1420±130 and 608±50 B.C. are quite consistent with the bronzes and moulds and suggest that bronze-working was already established at a period equivalent to General Period B in Northeast Thailand.

Indeed, there are hints that there was a network of bronze-using communities from the mouths of the Mekong up to the Ban Chiang area. A major link in this proposed chain is Samrong Sen, an occupation and burial site with a stratigraphy almost 6 m deep, situated on the banks of the Chinit River. The site was first investigated by Noulet (1877), but excavations adopting any semblance of stratigraphical control were only undertaken in 1902 and 1923. Mansuy (1902, 1923) recognised three layers, one of which attained a depth of 4.5 m, and was said to incorporate numerous shell lenses.

Given the almost complete absence of concern for stratigraphy in a site clearly having a lengthy period of occupation, only the most general conclusions are possible. Among these is the clear relationship which exists between the shouldered and rectangular adzes of Samrong Sen and those from the lower Mekong sites. Armbands and beads of stone also link this site with others in the Mekong catchment. Pottery is less easily paralleled at other sites. Much of the ware is plain, and decoration is, in general, confined to impressed or incised geometric motifs. The complete vessels probably come from inhumation graves, though flooding is said to have redeposited the human bone in antiquity. A characteristic form has a broad pedestalled base supporting an open bowl. Some were decorated all over, others left plain and painting is absent. While there are no precise parallels between these vessels and those from Northeast Thai sites, Loofs-Wissowa (pers. comm.) has pointed out a remarkable similarity between two complete vessels from Samrong Sen and the earliest style recovered at Ban Chiang.

Mansuy recovered a fragment of bronze mould from Samrong Sen, while unprovenanced bronze artefacts fall within the range of types documented in the lower Mekong, Northeast Thailand and coastal Viet Nam. The stratigraphical associations of the tanged arrowheads, socketed axe heads, bells, armrings, fish hooks and chisels are unknown (Worman 1949). During a visit to the site just before the second world war, Janse collected various artefacts, and these have recently been examined by Murowchik (1986). They include a crucible still containing scoria, erroneously described by Janse as a spoon (Janse 1951), and several bronzes, including bracelets, socketed spearheads, axes and a bell. The analyses of the alloy composition of five of these artefacts have revealed that three specimens have a high (11.74 to 26.47%) lead content, which suggests that they were cast during General Period C. Murowchik's examination of these bronzes further indicates a technological tradition of casting and annealing which matches that represented in the other sites of the Mekong catchment. Indeed, this tradition extends up into the upper reaches of the Mekong, where a bivalve axe mould has been recovered recently (Wang Dadao, pers. comm.). There was a rich faunal assemblage at Samrong Sen which, from the vague and generalised reports available, matches the findings at related sites in Northeast Thailand. In addition to domestic cattle, pig and dog bones, there was a clear orientation towards water resources documented by fish hooks, net weights, the bones of crocodile and water turtle, as well as numerous shellfish. Shellfish from two locations have been combined to provide one radiocarbon sample, which yielded a date of 1650±120 B.C. (Carbonnel and Delibrias 1968). The material dated comes from 1.0 m and 1.5 m below the surface, so at best dates only the later part of the cultural sequence. However, a date in the late second millennium B.C. would fit the typology of the bronze artefacts.

Samrong Sen must surely represent many similar sites in Central Cambodia. Indeed, Mansuy was aware of a very similar site, to judge from surface finds, at nearby Long Prao. It has never been excavated, but Lévy (1943) has examined three prehistoric sites, located near the headwaters of the Sen and Chinit rivers, where finds attest to both General Periods B and C occupation. Surface remains from one of these sites, O Pie Can (Fig. 3.2), covered an area of about 1 ha. The site is located at the confluence of two streams, and the culture layer is 40 cm in depth. Lévy has reported finding pieces of sandstone moulds on the surface, as well as crucible fragments containing bronze, and pieces of iron slag. The excavations revealed sandstone moulds for casting a sickle and an axe (Fig. 3.49). The shape of the sickle is very similar to those from Go Mun contexts in Viet Nam. The site also yielded many fragments of stone and clay bangles, and clay stamps bearing deeply incised curvilinear designs. Reports of looting at nearby O Yak referred to human inhumation burials incorporating bronze bracelets, animal bone offerings and brown-red glass beads. Burials were also noted in eroded material at O Pie Can. The surface finds from the third mound, O Nari, included much pottery, as well as fragments of polished stone adzes and some bronze. As at Samrong Sen, the adzes were both shouldered and rectangular in shape. Stone beads and bracelets, as well as round clay pellet-bow pellets, were also recovered there.

The coastal plains of Central Viet Nam

The coastal plain which abuts the Truong Son cordillera between the Ca and Dong Nai valleys is generally narrow. Only where the Thu Bon, Con and Ba rivers reach the sea are there enclaves of good agricultural soils. Archaeological research in these areas is in its infancy, but already it is clear that the Thu Bon valley was occupied in prehistory by a society proficient in metallurgy. The evidence for this finding comes from Binh Chau, where Ngo Si Hong (1980) has recently investigated occupation and burial remains. Three mounds have been excavated, the areas covering between 0.5 and 1.0 ha. Today, all command tracts of flat rice-fields. Preliminary findings have revealed that the occupants inhumed the dead in association with several pottery vessels, some with red, black and white painted designs. The widespread form of split earring was rendered in fired

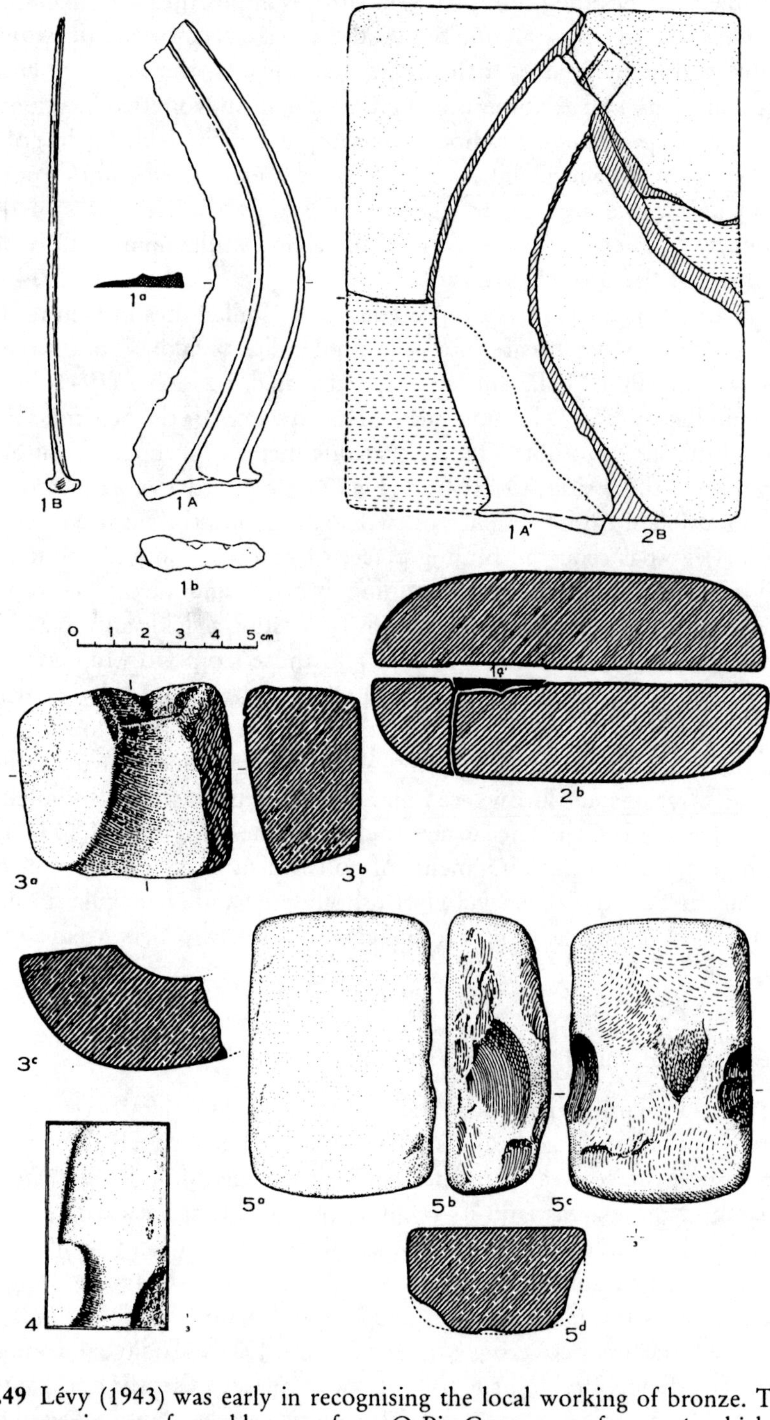

3.49 Lévy (1943) was early in recognising the local working of bronze. These specimens of moulds come from O Pie Can, except for no. 4, which was found even earlier, at Samrong Sen.

clay at Binh Chau. Of particular note were the fragments of crucibles and moulds found in addition to bronze socketed axes and tanged arrowheads. The excavator has suggested that the material is equivalent to the Dong Dau–Go Mun assemblages to the north, and Doc Chua to the south. Slightly further north, but still in the coastal tract, is the important site of Long Thanh, where Ngo Si Hong (1985) has described a 2 m thick habitation yielding fish hooks, grinding-stones, stone axes and hoes. It is not clear whether there were any remains of metal. The two radiocarbon dates (1718±40 and 1065±60 B.C.), come from 1.6 and 0.6 m deep, respectively. Long Thanh may well provide the antecedents for the material recognised at Binh Chau.

The Bac Bo region

The coasts and hills of Bac Bo sustained maritime and inland settlements, but the status of subsistence activities during the currency of the inland "Hoabinhian" and coastal Da But and Cai Beo groups is in doubt. While there is no question that hunting, gathering and fishing were mainstays, the degree of commitment to plant cultivation and animal husbandry is not yet established. The situation is much clearer for the third millennium B.C., and one of the principal tasks for the future lies in documenting the articulation between the late hunter-gatherer groups and those in which rice cultivation and animal husbandry was undeniably established. During General Periods A and B there are two aspects to the settlement in this region, one inland and the other coastal. The inland focus centres on the Middle Country, an area of rolling lowlands dissected by minor tributaries of the Red River (Fig. 3.50). It is studded with archaeological sites, and much research has been devoted to them (Fig. 3.51). The cultural sequence now emerging reveals close parallels with that 500 km to the southwest on the Khorat plateau, and there is simplicity in employing the same general cultural framework.

Three successive phases belong to General Periods A and B. In chronological order, they are called Phung Nguyen, Dong Dau and Go Mun. The Phung Nguyen phase has been subdivided, on the basis of pottery typology, into three successive groupings. Of the 52 sites excavated, only 11 have yielded bronze. Metal is recovered from the latest contexts of the Phung Nguyen phase and takes the form of corroded fragments and slag. As yet, no bronze artefacts have been recovered. Consequently, in terms of metallurgy at least, most Phung Nguyen phase sites appear to equate with General Period A in Northeast Thailand. There are relatively few radiocarbon dates for this sequence. The Phung Nguyen phase appears to have developed into early Dong Dau by about 1500 B.C. The date of the earliest Phung Nguyen contexts is not yet known but they probably belong to the third millennium B.C. (for a checklist of the available Vietnamese dates up to the end of 1983, see Bayard 1984c). As may be seen in Fig. 3.50, the distribution of Phung Nguyen, Dong Dau and Go Mun sites lies in the same

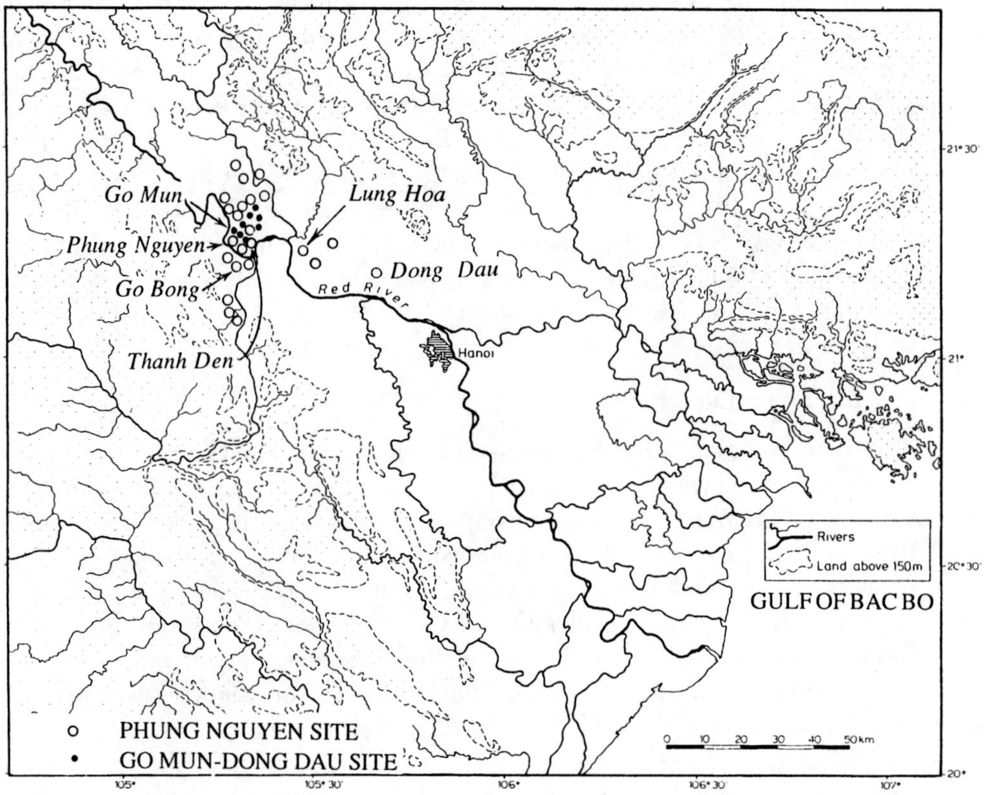

3.50 The distribution of General Period A–B sites in Bac Bo.

region, most being found above the confluence of the Red and Black rivers. They cover between 1.0 – 3.0 ha, and are found on slightly elevated terrain near small stream confluences. The principal excavated site is at Phung Nguyen itself (Hoang Xuan Chinh and Nguyen Ngoc Bich 1978). It covers 3 ha, of which 3960 m^2 have been excavated. The stratigraphy is shallow, as in most Phung Nguyen sites, and barely exceeds a metre. Excavations began in 1959, and were followed by two further campaigns. The earliest excavations were relatively restricted, two squares measuring 3 by 9 m and 2 by 7 m were opened, with six others covering 4.5 by 4.5 m. The 1961 campaign was massive: seventeen 10 by 10 m squares, and five measuring 20 by 20 m. The final campaign, in 1968, added a further small area excavation. Opening up such an immense area was possible because the cultural stratigraphy was only 0.5 m deep.

All this activity provided a large sample of most interesting material culture (Nguyen Ba Khoach 1980). No trace of bronze was recovered, but there was a substantial sample of pottery and stone artefacts. The stone adzes take a variety of forms (Fig. 3.52), but the rarest was the shouldered variety, of which only four were found. This compares with 777 examples of quadrangular form, some of

3.51 The Phung Nguyen site of Doi Giam in the Middle Country. Phung Nguyen sites favour high ground overlooking small tributary streams. Doi Giam is the mound in the immediate foreground.

which had been sharpened so consistently that they are broader than they are long. When one adds stone adze fragments for which the shape is indeterminate, 1138 adzes or adze fragments were recovered. There are also 59 small stone chisels, some with cutting edges only 10 mm wide, and almost 200 grinding-stones were found bearing grooves which result from sharpening the stone adzes and chisels. Stone projectile points were rarer. Three reach the dimensions of a spear-point, but the remainder are more likely to be tanged arrowheads.

The inhabitants of Phung Nguyen also fashioned stone rings, mostly in nephrite. The total sample of 540 specimens has been subdivided into eight types, based on the shape of the cross-section. Most are rectangular, but some are much more complex having a range of ribs and flanges. While some are large enough to rank as adult bracelets, others have small diameters, and were either designed for children or perhaps for display as earrings. Stone beads, mostly tubular and measuring up to 1.3 cm in length, were also made (Fig. 3.53).

There was a vigorous tradition of working clay. Clay pellet-bow pellets matching those found so often in the General Periods A and B sites in Thailand were found, as were clay net weights, but most attention was accorded the manufacture of clay vessels. It is on the basis of changing decorative styles that the Vietnamese archaeologists have advanced their threefold subdivision of the

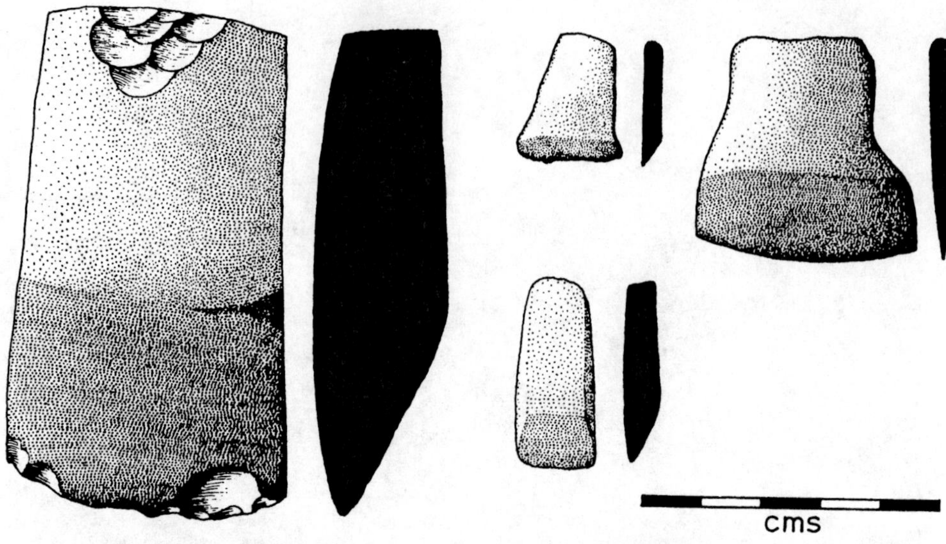

3.52 The stone adzes from Phung Nguyen were abundant and quite variable in size and shape.

Phung Nguyen sites. The earliest, called after the site of Go Bong, is characterised by incised parallel bands infilled with rows of impressions made with a pointed implement. The favoured motif is in the shape of an "S" meander. The second sub-phase incorporates a range of designs based on "geometric asymmetry" (Ha Van Tan 1980). Again, incised bands infilled with dentate impressions alternate with bands to form a series of attractive design fields. Extraordinarily, this technique of decoration, and the same asymmetry of motifs, is matched at Khok Phanom Di and Northeast Thai sites at approximately the same period. Watson (1983) has also drawn attention to the very widespread distribution of this design technique (Fig. 3.53).

One site, Lung Hoa, has yielded a sample of 12 burials in an excavated area of 365 m^2. The excavators felt that there was some evidence for differential wealth despite the small sample. There were, for example, two burials associated with stone bracelets, beads and earrings, as well as pottery and polished adzes. The other burials were accompanied only by pots and adzes. Clearly, larger samples are necessary before this possibility can be tested.

Dong Dau is a most important site not least because of the unusually deep stratigraphic record (Ha Van Phung 1979). It is located to the east of most Phung Nguyen sites, within sight of the Red River (Fig. 3.50). It was recognised in 1961, and excavations undertaken in 1965 and 1967–8 uncovered 550m^2 to a depth of between 5 and 6 m. The mound itself covers about 3 ha, and its basal cultural material has been ascribed to the final Phung Nguyen sub-phase. It contains a sample of rice grains which attest to rice cultivation as one of the subsistence

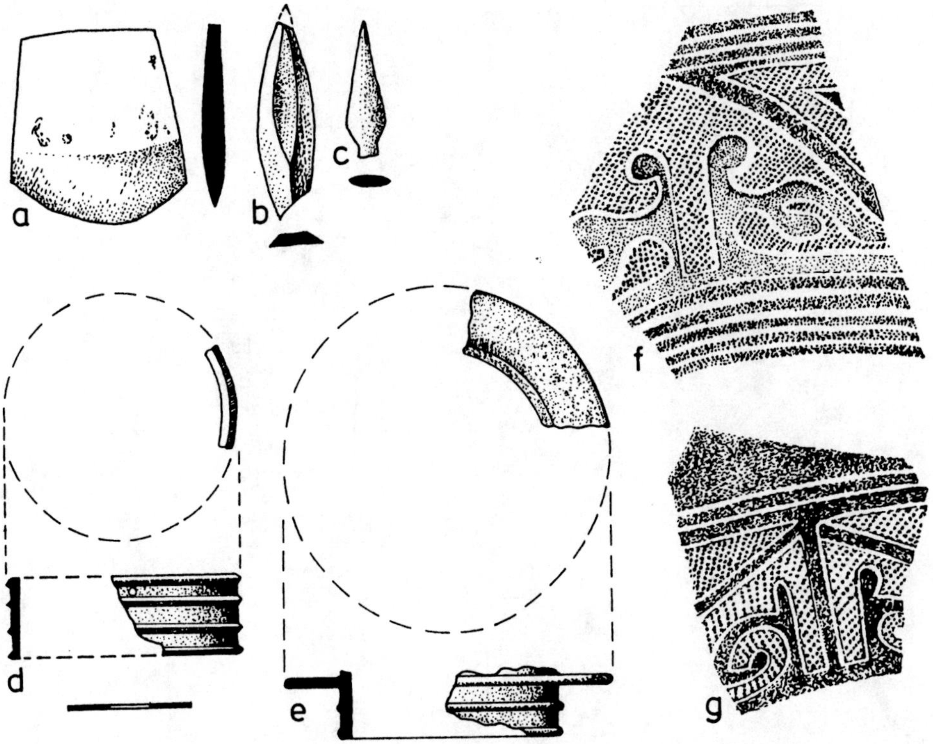

3.53 Material culture from Phung Nguyen includes many stone artefacts such as axes, bracelets and arrowheads, subsequently rendered in bronze during the Dong Dau phase. a; stone axe, b–c; stone projectile points, d–e; stone bracelets, f–g; decorated pottery incorporating curvilinear designs. Scale in cm.

activities of the Phung Nguyen phase (Nguyen Xuan Hien 1980). While the pottery of the Dong Dau site reveals Phung Nguyen origins at least in style and mode of decoration, we also find compelling evidence for a local and vigorous bronze industry. Trinh Sinh (1977) has stressed that many of the Phung Nguyen phase stone artefacts were replaced in bronze. The bivalve moulds recovered by Ha Van Tan from a small ($50m^2$) excavation in a Dong Dau context at Thanh Denh are virtually identical with those from General Period B contexts on the Khorat plateau (Fig. 3.54). The 30 or so fragments of stone and clay moulds were designed for casting axes and fish hooks. The site has a cultural stratigraphy of only a metre, and the three radiocarbon dates closely match the dates obtained for General Period B in Northeast Thailand (1580±100, 1440±70 and 700±130 B.C.). Bronze was also employed to make socketed spearheads, arrowheads and chisels. The Dong Dau axe began to take on the initial pediform shape so diagnostic of later decorated examples from the Dong Son phase.

Towards the end of the second millennium B.C., the Dong Dau developed into

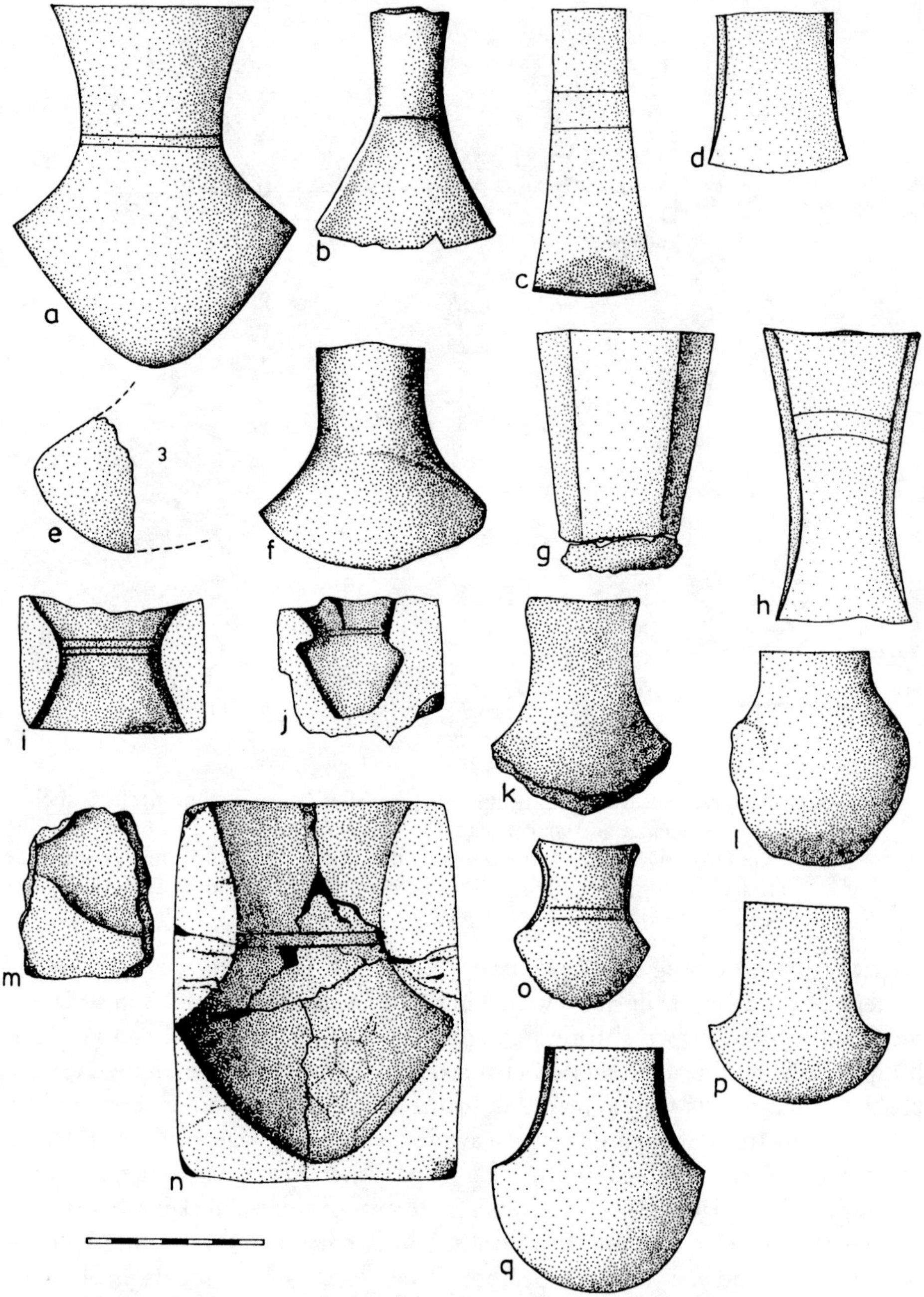

3.54 Bronze axes are widespread within the General Period B metallurgical tradition. a: Doc Chua, b: Ban Chiang, c: Dong Dau, d: Go Mun, e: Ban Na Di (from a mould), f: Go Mun, g: Non Nok Tha, h: O Pie Can, i–k: Doc Chua, l: Samrong Sen, m: Ban Na Di (mould), n–o: Doc Chua, p: Go Mun, q: Dong Dau. Scale in cm.

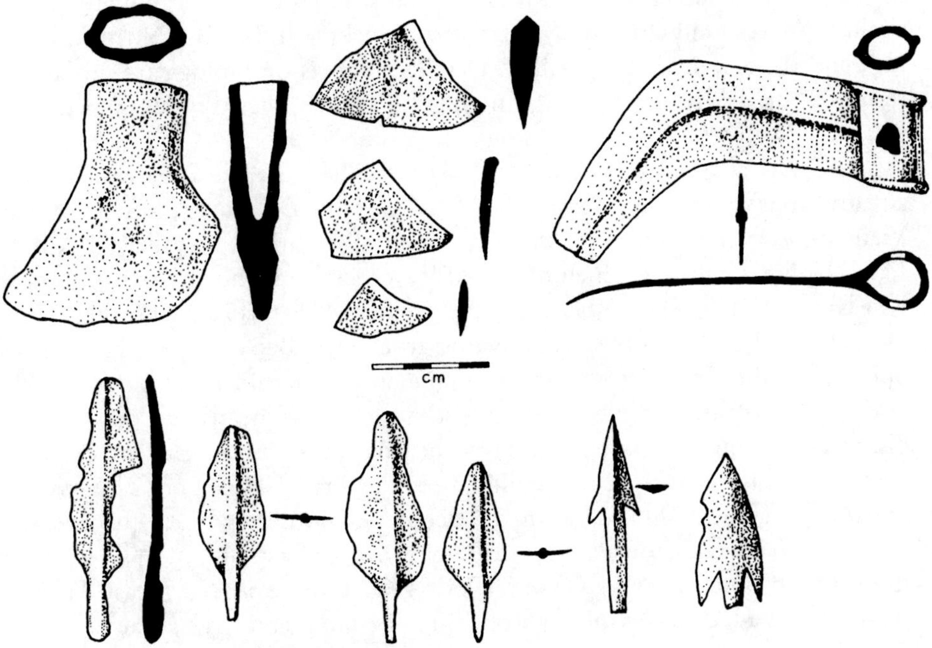

3.55 Bronze implements from Go Mun include the earliest evidence for a sickle in the Bac Bo sequence.

the Go Mun phase, named after the site of Go Mun. This site is located only 3 km northeast of Phung Nguyen, and indeed the 25 or so known Go Mun sites are located within the same general area as those of Phung Nguyen and Dong Dau. There have been four campaigns of excavations at Go Mun, starting in 1961 and finishing a decade later (Ha Van Phung and Nguyen Duy Ty 1982). In all, 1500 m^2 have been excavated, the cultural stratigraphy being only 1 m deep. As at Phung Nguyen, stone adzes were, in the main, quadrangular. Of the 87 recovered, 80 were quadrangular, and only one was shouldered. Similar stone chisels to those from Phung Nguyen were also encountered. The inventory of bronze artefacts reveals that many forms in stone were copied in metal. Thirteen axes have been found, and seven chisels. The spearheads, arrowheads and bracelets were, likewise, rendered in bronze. Fish hooks were the most abundant bronze artefact, followed by narrow projectile points. One sickle was recovered and a figure of a seated individual, which was presumably cast by means of the lost wax technique (Fig. 3.55). The Dong Dau pottery bears curvilinear and rectangular patterns which look like developed Phung Nguyen motifs, and it is in these that Ha Van Tan (1980) sees models for the decoration later found on the well-known Dong Son drums. It is apparent from the excavation carried out at Go Mun and related sites that bronze-working was increasing in intensity and range of artifacts cast. This phase, which lasted until about the 7th century B.C., brings us to the end of General Period B in the Bac Bo area. It has been intriguing to note the similar progress and chronology of bronze-working in Bac Bo, Northeast Thailand and the lower Mekong valley. Detailed reports on biological finds and the rarity of burials, however, render the Bac Bo sequence less revealing than hoped for.

There was also a coastal aspect to settlement in the Bac Bo area. We have already considered the site of Cai Beo and the Da But grouping of sites. Vietnamese archaeologists see these as ancestral to various so-called Middle and Late Neolithic cultures which occupied the coastal tract north and south of the Red River delta. Thus, the Ha Long culture of the islands in the northern sector of the Gulf of Bac Bo is seen as derivative from a Cai Beo context. They base this opinion on the similarities in the rectangular and shouldered adzes recovered. Sites of this group also yield polished stone bracelets, beads and pendants, not dissimilar to Phung Nguyen examples. Moving south of the delta, we encounter sites of another coastal group, called after the site of Hoa Loc. This group is known for a most unusual form of decorated pottery with a quadrangular-shaped rim. They also used clay seals with deeply excised patterns resembling those found much later in General Period C contexts in Northeast Thailand. Again, stone adzes and grinding-stones are common, and large stone hoes recur. The faunal associations from Hoa Loc are dominated by marine species, but Vu The Long (pers. comm.) noted the remains of domesticated dog, pig and probably cattle. Le Van Thieu (1979) indicated that some of the pigs' teeth display a bimodal size distribution, probably reflecting the presence of wild and domesticated animals. Hoa Loc itself is located on a raised sandbar now about 4 km behind the shoreline. It is evident that, as the sea level fell back from its post-Pleistocene high, so coastal settlement followed it. A few pieces of bronze were found at Hoa Loc when it was excavated in 1976. It seems to equate, in terms of its metallurgy, with the latest Phung Nguyen sub-phase in the inland area.

South of the Ma River, the raised beaches are rich in prehistoric sites (Fig. 3.56), some of which comprise shell-middens up to 15 m deep. One such group is called after the site of Quynh Van. Con Lap is a characteristic site and it comprises dense layers of shellfish, principally a brackish-water species called *Placuna placenta*. The shellfish remains predominate almost to the point of suggesting that these middens were built up naturally of dead valves. Occasionally, however, one encounters fragments of pottery and flaked or polished stone adzes. These Quynh Van sites are further inland than those of Hoa Loc, and are probably earlier. The Vietnamese refer to them as Middle Neolithic, although the biological remains point overwhelmingly to coastal gathering. Closer to the present shore in this same area are sites ascribed to the Thac Lac culture. Doi Than is one such site (Fig. 3.57). It covers only about 0.5 ha and during a six-week excavation there in 1983, Cao Xuan Pho (pers. comm.) recovered an enormous sample of pottery decorated with asymmetric infilled bands similar in

3.56 The site of Con Lap is one of many indicating an adaptation to a marine habitat.

3.57 Excavations at Doi Than revealed the successive dumping of food remains, most of which reflect a maritime adaptation.

general style to the Phung Nguyen material. This decorative form extends to the inside of the rim, and is a hallmark of the 12 or so other Thac Lac sites in this area. The stratigraphy of the site differs from the compacted masses of *Placuna* shells found in the Quynh Van sites, since the shell lenses are set in clear midden lenses interspersed with more general cultural fill (Fig. 3.57). The Thac Lac material culture, apart from its pottery, includes shouldered adzes and associated grinding-stones, and arrowheads and bracelets of stone. It appears, according to Vietnamese archaeologists, to be contemporary with the Ha Long sites dated to between *c* 3000 to 2000 B.C. No metal has yet been found in a Thac Lac site, although their distribution is very close to Hoa Loc where a few pieces of bronze have been recovered.

It is an opportune moment to reflect on this mass of new data from Bac Bo. There is a major contrast between inland and coastal settlement from the point when the marine transgression reached its climax and sites in the latter area assume archaeological visibility. On the one hand, there is the inland Hoabinhian complex and, on the other, the basal material from Cai Beo and Da But. These display similar stone artefacts with pottery and polished stone implements present in each. There is evidence for exchange between the inland habitat and occupation on the coast. This view, however, overlooks the issue of coastal settlements inundated under the sea off Bac Bo. The early coastal settlements of Cai Beo and Da But probably developed with time into new cultural groups: Cai Beo into Ha Long, and Da But into Quynh Van. Further, but later, derivative groups are known as Hoa Loc, Thac Lac and Bau Tro. Some biological data, as well as the evidence of stone hoes, are seen as evidence for increasing attention to cultivation and stock-raising. These last assemblages have been ascribed to the period 3000 to 2000 B.C. By the end of that timespan, a few objects of bronze were detected at Hoa Loc. At this same juncture, that is, perhaps, 2000 B.C., we find a rash of settlements in the Middle Country above the Red River delta. It should be remembered that the sea would have been in the region of 3 m higher then than now. These sites are called after Phung Nguyen where, despite the extensive area opened, not a single piece of bronze was recovered. The Phung Nguyen assemblage had, in common with the coastal groups, the polished stone adze assemblage, stone jewellery and band-decorated pottery with a range of asymmetric motifs. It is held prudent, at this early stage of enquiry, to follow Ha Van Tan in his general, rather than specific, attribution of a coastal origin to the Phung Nguyen settlement (Ha Van Tan 1980). This expansion is, within its broader context, a further example of the spread of human settlement into the major lowland tracts of Southeast Asia. It represents the inland riverine settlement by societies which included rice cultivation among their subsistence pursuits, and recognised their fellows' status in their mortuary rituals. The stage is now set for a consideration of variables which might assist in appreciating why this expansive settlement occurred.

The expansion of domestic communities and the adoption of bronze-working

We have identified numerous settlements in the size range from 0.5 to 5.0 ha, located, as a rule, in low-lying interior stream valleys where gentle flooding favoured rice cultivation. At the end of the last chapter it was proposed that this expansionary settlement had its origins in domestic coastal communities which included rice harvesting in their subsistence activities. Expansion up river courses provided for the settlement of the Mekong and its tributaries, as well as the middle course of the Red River and the major tributaries of the Chao Phraya. Two General Periods have been proposed, the later distinguished by the adoption of bronze-working. It is now necessary to consider the significance of this widespread metallurgical tradition.

Emphasis has been given above to the issue of site size. As a very general yardstick, it is assumed that there is some relationship between the size of a site and the number of people occupying it. Thus the modern village of Ban Na Di in Khon Kaen Province, Northeast Thailand, has a population of 800–1000 people in 23 ha of settled area. For Ban Chiang today, the figures are 4500 people in 75 ha. During their site survey and analysis of the Central Valley of Mexico, Sanders *et al.* (1979) cited four different levels of population density. The lightest had 5–10 people per ha, rising to a high density at 50–100 people per ha. Applying these ranges to prehistoric settlements, a risky but interesting exercise, would indicate a maximum of up to 500 people in a settlement covering 5 ha. The real figure may have been far less. One variable in our model for the settlement expansion into the inland terrain of Southeast Asia, therefore, is that during General Periods A and B, settlements did not exceed a population of 500 people. During General Period A, they may have been much smaller.

We have already concluded that the coastal communities represented by Khok Phanom Di occupied an optimal zone. By contrast, those expanding into the inland valleys entered what we call a marginal zone (Binford 1968). This contrast reflects the increasingly long and difficult dry season, and the unpredictable nature of the rainfall as one leaves the coast. Prior to the settlement expansion there was a vigorous, perhaps predominantly coastal, exchange, but this ramified with increasing penetration of the interior.

This expansion saw a marked preference for settling near marshland. From the point of view of subsistence, this made sense, in that rice grows wild in such areas and can be encouraged through the removal of its competitors or actively cultivated. One of the great advantages of rice is the ease with which it can be preserved for consumption during the dry season. Domestic animals represent a way of converting wet-season feed into dry-season meat and, by fermenting with salt, fish can be consumed even in the most difficult time of the year. Initially, at least, the early settlement phase saw little exchange in exotic substances. The excavation of Non Kao Noi revealed a handful of burials with no goods which could be described as rare or unusual. The larger sample of 12 Phu Wiang phase interments from Non Nok Tha contained three burials with shell-disc beads, four with stone adzes and one with a bone tool. Further consideration of the evidence for social organisation, however, stresses the importance of obtaining rare goods to fulfil rituals involved in rites of passage and to display status. One such substance seems to have been marine shell jewellery. Perhaps stone adzes were also important in ritual and economic activities. It is suggested that exchange for such goods was an adaptive mechanism to ensure that the social and technological necessities in settlement expansion were available.

Let us take a closer look at the ritual and social factor. For this, we are reliant on the evidence for mortuary behaviour. Take, for example, the burials from Ban Na Di. It has been suggested that there were two groups of burials, and exotic or unusual artefacts have been shown to concentrate in one of them (Higham and Kijngam 1984). These objects include imported stone bracelets which were repaired, when necessary, with bronze wire. It is notable that the internal diameter of these bracelets is so small that they could only have been actually placed over the wrist when the owner was young. There are also marine shell bracelets and beads, cattle figurines, and, in two late graves, eight objects of iron. Several graves also included the remains of silken garments, a finding which suggests that the metal, stone and shell objects were probably just the durable subset of goods exchanged during the currency of the first phase of burials at the site.

The circulation of such exotic goods has attracted considerable interest in the archaeological literature. Dalton (1977) emphasised their critical role in cementing the foundation and maintenance of alliances between autonomous communities. In the ethnographic cases he cited, he noted that the acquisition of such goods usually resides with lineage leaders, who then dispose of them as part of the exchange system, thereby forming war alliances and fostering the process of peace-making. Display of valuables is a statement of an individual's social ascendancy. Their absence has the contrary effect. External relations in autonomous societies are horizontal and occur between settlements. Relative ascendancy turns on alliance structures, population numbers and the disposal of valuables. Accordingly, marriage and alliance are intimately connected with transactions of food and treasures. Dalton views the economy, alliance networks and social organisation, as embedded within each other.

The archaeological context of exotic goods at Ban Na Di is interesting. They concentrate in one of the two concentrations of burials found. The origin of the shell beads and shell and stone bracelets is not known with precision, but it must have been remote. Clay figurines and exotic pots, perhaps with their perishable contents, may also have been perceived as valuables. There is little doubt that the upper Songkhram area, at least, was linked with other contemporary communities through a widespread system of exchange reaching out ultimately to the sea and the surrounding ore-bearing hills. This same situation has been documented east of the Truong Son cordillera among the stone and bronze-using communities of the Middle Country of Bac Bo. In the Chao Phraya, the middle Mekong and the lower Mekong area, there was again a system incorporating the exchange of exotic goods. This situation presents a very different connotation to that advanced by Wolters (1982). He suggested a prehistoric pattern of scattered and isolated settlements at the beginning of the Christian era. This indicates little prospect of inter-site or area contact. Naturally, the alternative picture presented above influences our appreciation of the processes invoked below.

The juxtaposition of lowlands with upland massifs presents interesting parallels with the situation described for the Maya lowlands by Voorhies (1973). She stressed the archaeological visibility of certain items from the uplands, such as obsidian, when compared with that for lowland products. A similar situation obtains for the Southeast Asian theatre where the importation of copper, tin and lead clearly illustrates lowland-upland exchange. Again, the presence of marine shell reflects even wider contacts. There were doubtless many rarities or surpluses which originated within lowland and coastal contexts. Specialised ceramic vessels are one such product. Salt has a restricted distribution, and was probably a crucial commodity then as now. We may also add silk as an archaeologically documented, but perishable, commodity. Certainly, cloth is a strong candidate as a prestige item in exchange. The point at issue is that there was inequality of access to prestige goods. Under such conditions, strategic location was advantageous in obtaining and maintaining prominence.

Within such an integrative exchange system, information, as well as goods, was open to transmission, with the lines of least resistance following river courses or coastal routes. It is suggested that the knowledge and practice of bronze-working from copper and tin could spread rapidly, with finished bronzes taking their place alongside stone and shell as objects signifying the status of the owner. The production and distribution of copper and tin surely added a further dimension to the existing exchange links. There were new routes to open and opportunities to grasp. Bronze goods were rare in mortuary contexts, and many of the products were clearly for display. This introduces a further point: the attainment of status was flexible rather than fixed. Thus, where a community and its leader commanded a strategic resource or distribution point, it could increase its prominence within the system. A breakdown in the source of supply, or the opening of a new route, would diminish its wealth and status. Likewise, group ownership of a rich tract of cultivable land would confer, at least, the possibility of realising higher status if soil potential were realised. It is important to appreciate that the relative position of each autonomous settlement was given to fluctuation and, therefore, instability.

Let us, for the moment at least, accept that settlements during periods A and B were autonomous, and harboured two or more unequally ranked social groups. What bearing does this situation have on the process of settlement expansion? This issue takes, as its departure, the finding that sites did not exceed 5 ha. When

Table 3.1 *Settlement size and social organisation among Southeast Asian rice cultivators.*

Group	Settlement size	Social organisation
Nosu	max. 250-300	Nothing permanent above clan level
Lisu	av. 450	Hereditary chiefs over several villages
Lahu	120-160	Village chief, settlement autonomy
Akha	av. 300	Village chief, settlement autonomy
Naga	av. 438	Subdivided into wards
Lamet	av. 56	Village autonomy
Lawa	av. 210	Village autonomy
Palaung	2-50 houses	Petty court after Shan model
T'in	av. 150	Village headman
Wa	up to 200-300 houses	Confederation of villages under chief
Loven	7-12 houses	Village autonomy

Source: Lebar, Hickey and Musgrave 1964.

we turn to the available human remains, two important points are evident. The first is that the prehistoric people enjoyed a high level of nutrition and were, to judge from their bone size and development, healthy individuals. Second, the life tables tend to suggest reduced infant mortality and longevity in later phases, a finding compatible with a rising population (Wiriyaromp 1983).

In the absence of regulatory mechanisms sites could, in theory, have grown considerably larger than 5 ha. During General Period C, they did. Even if General Period B sites did attain 5 ha in size, and that remains to be proven, then, at even the most generous estimate, populations could not have exceeded 500 people. It would be straightforward, but quite possibly erroneous, to cite problems of food supply as a limiting factor on population and, therefore, site size. The literature abounds with examples of intensification to counter this particular constraint. Forge (1972) has outlined a more sophisticated set of variables which operate in the context of New Guinean cultivators and these, it is held, may be incorporated as part of the flexible status model just outlined.

Basically, Forge's analysis relates to autonomous villages lacking a formal hierarchy or ascribed status. On the surface, this egalitarian social organisation contrasts with the ranking perceived in General Period B contexts but, as will be argued, this is not necessarily so. In his ethnographic examples Forge found that the size of the village population, consistent with the maintenance of social order, varies between 70 and 300 people. When the settlement can field over 35 adult fighting men, then sub-groups form, and these emerging groups are a focus for ritual, exchange and concentration of prestige. Basically, major settlements dispose of between 35 and 80 adult men, and 150 to 350 people. With population growth, expansion of settlements significantly beyond 350 people generates internal friction and promotes village fission. It is the alternative to fission which is arresting: to expand beyond the threshold figure of 350 people requires classification by occupation, ascriptive rank or both.

It could be argued that Forge's data are irrelevant when considering communities reliant upon rice cultivation rather than root crop horticulture, as in New Guinea. Some relevant information from Southeast Asian societies which do incorporate rice in their subsistence system has therefore been assembled. Several interesting points are evident (Table 3:1). Most groups listed occupy autonomous villages and have populations under Forge's threshold. Those with larger communities include the Wa, where sites are fortified, large, and linked into confederations under a supreme chief. The Naga, by contrast, subdivide large settlements into wards or *khels*. This latter situation, indeed, stresses that Forge's specific finding cannot be applied generally without an awareness of alternative options to cope with settlement growth. Johnson (1982) has undertaken a detailed review of the resolution of friction with population growth and has shown that an expansion of ritual activity is one means of resolving potential conflict. There is no doubting the need for new measures to maintain order and cohesion where numbers of individuals in constant occupation of a settlement increase beyond a threshold in the general area of 300–500. It is possible that the social organisation incorporating affiliated groups, as suggested for Non Nok Tha, or lineage leaders at Ban Na Di, integrated best with populations under about 300 to 500 people, and that any significant increase beyond that point encouraged either (a), settlement fission and, therefore, territorial expansion or (b), the development of new forms of social control and intensification of agricultural production. Naturally, many more studies of mortuary assemblages and settlement patterns will be necessary before we can ascertain whether the proposed social organisation in Northeast Thailand was matched elsewhere. At present, however, it is considered possible that population growth stimulated settlement fission, and that this process operated until the supply of easily settled land was taken up. In this manner, domesticity proved immensely adaptable and expansive, but it ultimately encountered a fresh set of constraints, the implications of which we shall explore in the next chapter.

CHAPTER 4

THE END OF AUTONOMY AND EMERGENCE OF CHIEFDOMS

When turning to the transition from autonomy to centralisation, we encounter a most intractable period of Southeast Asian prehistory wherein answers to specific questions are not yet available. It was a period during which iron was increasingly adopted, and personal ornaments made in India such as beads of glass, agate and carnelian, entered exchange circuits. The basic question at issue is whether the iron-using chiefdoms were developing before the first Indian and Chinese contact, or whether the initial impact of such contact was a contributory variable in their emergence (Fig. 4.1). The kernel of the problem, is that we simply do not have satisfactory dating evidence for the initial use of iron, for the commencement of Indian contact, or the establishment of large centrally placed settlements. This dilemma cannot be resolved on present evidence, but its importance should not be underestimated (Bronson 1986). Iron ore is much more widespread than the ores of copper and tin in Southeast Asia, and, once steeled, iron has a greater efficiency when used in agriculture and in conflict (Pigott and Marder 1984). We know that the Chinese were becoming increasingly proficient in iron-working from *c* 600 B.C., and that iron-working was established in India by the same date. The interesting unanswered question is whether the knowledge of smelting iron ore was introduced along existing lines of contact, or whether it had an earlier local origin. Pigott and Marder (1984) have contributed to the resolution of this issue by describing how bronze-workers in the area could have encountered iron if they used copper ores such as chalcopyrite which contain iron oxide, or, again, if they used a flux containing haematite when smelting their copper ore.

This chapter will adopt the hypothesis that the knowledge of iron was gained by local bronze-workers at some time between 600–400 B.C. It must also be recognised that further excavations may show that early iron-working reflects Indian contact at an earlier date than has been envisaged hitherto, contact with the Chinese iron tradition or a combination of the two in different regions. Forging was the technique used in early Indian contexts, but in China there was an early development of iron-casting (Li Chung 1986). The distinction is important. Forging usually follows the smelting of iron ore in a small bloomery furnace. Casting involves control of great heat to raise the metal to a molten form. The Chinese had developed a large and highly sophisticated iron-casting industry by the 3rd century B.C., to a level not matched in the West until the Middle Ages. Pham Minh Huyen (1984) has referred to evidence for iron-casting

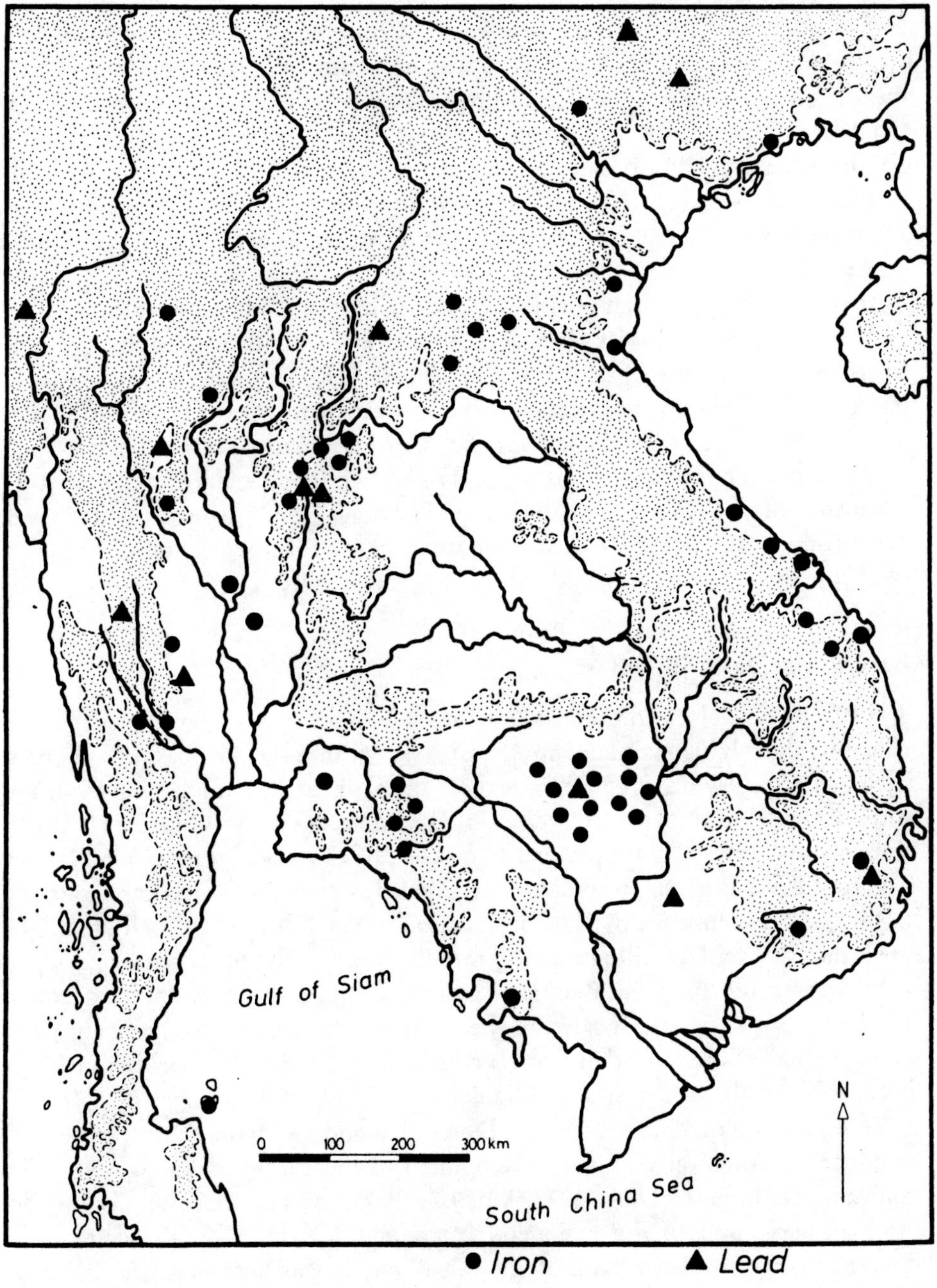

4.1 Iron and lead sources are more widespread than are copper and tin. Surface remains of laterite are particularly abundant in Northeast Thailand. Stippled area: land above 182 m.

in Bac Bo in late Dong Son contexts, and the source of this knowledge is most logically ascribed to the expansion of the Chinese under the early Han. Iron-working in the rest of Southeast Asia was, according to available evidence, based on the small bloomery furnace to produce the iron, followed by forging. This hypothesis does not rule out the possibility that iron-working had origins within Southeast Asia, but at present the evidence is fugitive. Whichever the case, by 400 to 200 B.C., iron-smelting and forging were very widespread in Southeast Asia. Evidence for casting is restricted to later contexts in areas which came under direct Chinese control.

Most workers agree that during the latter half of the first millennium B.C., and perhaps for a century or two earlier, there were profound cultural changes in the riverine and lacustrine floodplains of Southeast Asia. These areas, now the foci of modern states and concentrations of population, witnessed the transition from autonomous to centralised societies and, with it, a marked intensification in the fields of production, agriculture and ceremonial. The area was exposed to the expansion of the Chinese and Indian civilisations which brought in their wake new products and novel ideas. We will now examine the principal manifestations of change before trying to understand possible causes.

Bac Bo: the Dong Son phase

The Red River delta and the valleys of the Ma and Ca rivers have a less extreme climate of low-lying mainland Southeast Asia because the dry season is tempered by moist winds which move across the Gulf of Bac Bo. On reaching land, they form a low cloud cover often associated with drizzle. As Gourou (1955) has shown, this moist climate permits two crops of rice a year on favourable soils. The Red River is given to sudden rises in level, a characteristic compensated for in the last few centuries by the construction of earth banks. Its load of silt is so great that the delta is still advancing rapidly. During the prehistoric period, the delta area would have been subjected to widespread flooding and, indeed, the Phung Nguyen sites are located in the more elevated middle country above the delta proper. Thereafter, there was a continuing process of expansion involving occupation of the upper and middle delta itself (Fig. 4.2).

The sequence of Phung Nguyen, Dong Dau and Go Mun phases witnessed a major transformation with the development of the culture of Dong Son (Trinh Sinh and Na Nguyen Diem 1977, Fig. 4.2). Paradoxically, the site of Dong Son itself is peripheral to the main concentration of activity on the delta, being located on the southern bank of the Ma River. It was here that first Pajot and then Janse undertook excavations which revealed a rich prehistoric cemetery containing objects of bronze, iron, pottery and semi-precious stones in addition to objects of Chinese origin (Janse 1958). This was the first exposure to Europeans of a rich bronze-using society on mainland Southeast Asia, and its origins were sought in the context of prehistoric societies in Eastern Europe which

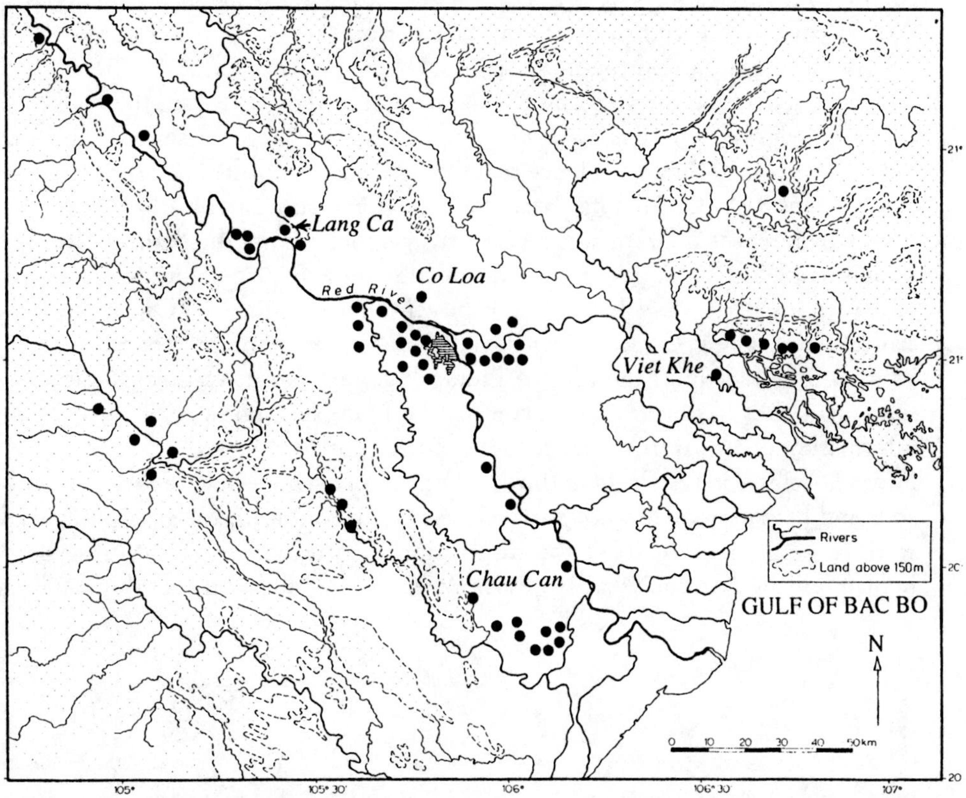

4.2 The distribution of Dong Son sites in Bac Bo shows a considerable expansion of settlement over the flat lands of the delta as the shoreline advanced over the former sea bed.

exhibited similar proficiency in working metals. More recently, Vietnamese scholars have sought less exotic origins in stressing the continuity in terms of the similar motifs used to decorate Phung Nguyen pottery and the Dong Son bronzes. This has encouraged them to stress cultural continuity throughout the prehistoric occupation of the Red River valley.

The period covered by the Dong Son phase saw an increasing exposure to Chinese expansion to the south which culminated in the arrival of Chinese armies. This chapter treats Bac Bo until the major intensification of Chinese influence. In the next chapter, we will cover the development of the Dong Son phase after Chinese dominance was established. Our appreciation of the Dong Son people is, indeed, coloured by literary allusions to the area which have survived in Chinese documents. Viewed from the Han capital, the Dong Son people were the most distant of several groups known as the southern barbarians, and there is no doubt that the Chinese encountered a society controlled through paramount chiefs of high status. Although most of our information on Dong Son comes from burial sites, Co Loa is one major settlement which probably dates, at least in part, to the end of the Dong Son period (Fig. 4.3). It is located 15 km northwest of Ha Noi on the floodplain of the Red River. There are three sets of ramparts at Co Loa, the two outer being moated and oval in plan, the innermost being rectangular. There is no doubt that it was added to over several centuries, but there is some literary evidence that Co Loa was established as a centre during the 3rd century B.C. This has been confirmed by recent archaeological excavations which revealed Dong Son-style pottery under the middle rampart. In 1982, a complete Dong Son-style bronze drum containing over one hundred socketed bronze ploughshares was located near the central part of the site. One of the most critical points about Co Loa is its size. The outermost ramparts cover about 600 ha, two hundred times the area of Phung Nguyen. No concentrated survey of settlement sites has been undertaken for the Dong Son phase, and most of our information is drawn from cemeteries and the contents of graves. This source of information is also restricted in the sense that many cemeteries are found in acidic soils and human bone has not survived. At Dong Son itself, for example, burials were recognised more from the disposition of artefacts than the presence of human remains. At Lang Ca, 314 burials were found but hardly any human bone

4.3 The centre of Co Loa probably had a long and chequered history. Its beginnings certainly go back to the 3rd century B.C., and to judge from nearby Phung Nguyen remains, probably much further. Recent excavations have revealed a superb Dong Son drum and a huge cache of arrowheads.

(Fig. 4.4). Even so, the excavators noted that a small group of graves were differentially rich and contained axes, daggers, situlae and spearheads. Further evidence for rich burials has been found at Viet Khe and Chau Can (Luu Tran Tieu 1977). Both have yielded opulent boat burials (Fig. 4.5). The richest at Viet Khe was interred in a hollowed tree trunk about 4.5 m in length, and contained over 100 artefacts. No human remains were found, but there is little doubt that the bronze weapons, receptacles and utensils were grave goods. This particular coffin also contained bronze bells, relatively small bronze drums and even a painted wooden box. Some of the metal goods in the coffin are said to be of Chinese derivation (Pham Minh Huyen, pers. comm.). Interment in such impressive boat-coffins surely signalled the burial of a particularly important person. The three samples taken from the coffin wood have 2σ ranges of 790–275, 810–395 and 760–170 B.C.

Wooden artefacts, as well as the human remains, were found inside some of the eight boat burials found at Chau Can. These are smaller than the Viet Khe example and contain fewer grave goods: bronze axes and spearheads with their wooden hafts in place, earrings made of a tin-lead alloy and a bamboo ladle. There are two radiocarbon dates taken from coffin wood, the 2σ ranges being 1195–895 and 595–205 B.C. The latter range fits better the received opinion on the dating of the Dong Son phase.

The suggested local origin of the Dong Son bronze industry has been supported by recent research at Dong Son itself. The first use of the cemetery involved burials accompanied by pottery vessels but only a few bronze axes, spearheads and knives. These are said to equate with the Go Mun phase in the Red River valley dating to 1000 to 500 B.C. (Ha Van Tan 1980). The second phase saw a proliferation of bronze artefacts and extension of types to include daggers, swords, situlae (large bucket-shaped vessels) and drums. It is dated to the period 500 to 1 B.C. The third and last prehistoric phase comprises burials containing objects of Chinese origin such as seals, coins, mirrors and halberds. Ha Van Tan (1980) has suggested a date within the 1st century A.D. for these burials. Indeed, the site was later used for interments in the Han style following the incorporation of the delta region into the Han Empire during the 1st century A.D.

We can learn much about the people of Dong Son from these surviving bronzes. As has been demonstrated at the Dong Son cemetery, both the quantity and range of bronze artefacts increased greatly from *c* 500 B.C. This intensification of production can be illustrated in two ways. The Co Loa bronze drum, for example, weighs 72 kg, and would have entailed the smelting of between 1–7 tonnes of copper ore (Nguyen Duy Hinh 1983). One burial from the Lang Ca cemetery contained the remains of a crucible and four clay moulds for casting an axe, spearhead, dagger handle and a bell. The mould for the bronze dagger handle suggests that it may have been intended as a bimetallic weapon, with the blade itself being made of iron. Bimetallic spears are known from both Dong Son and

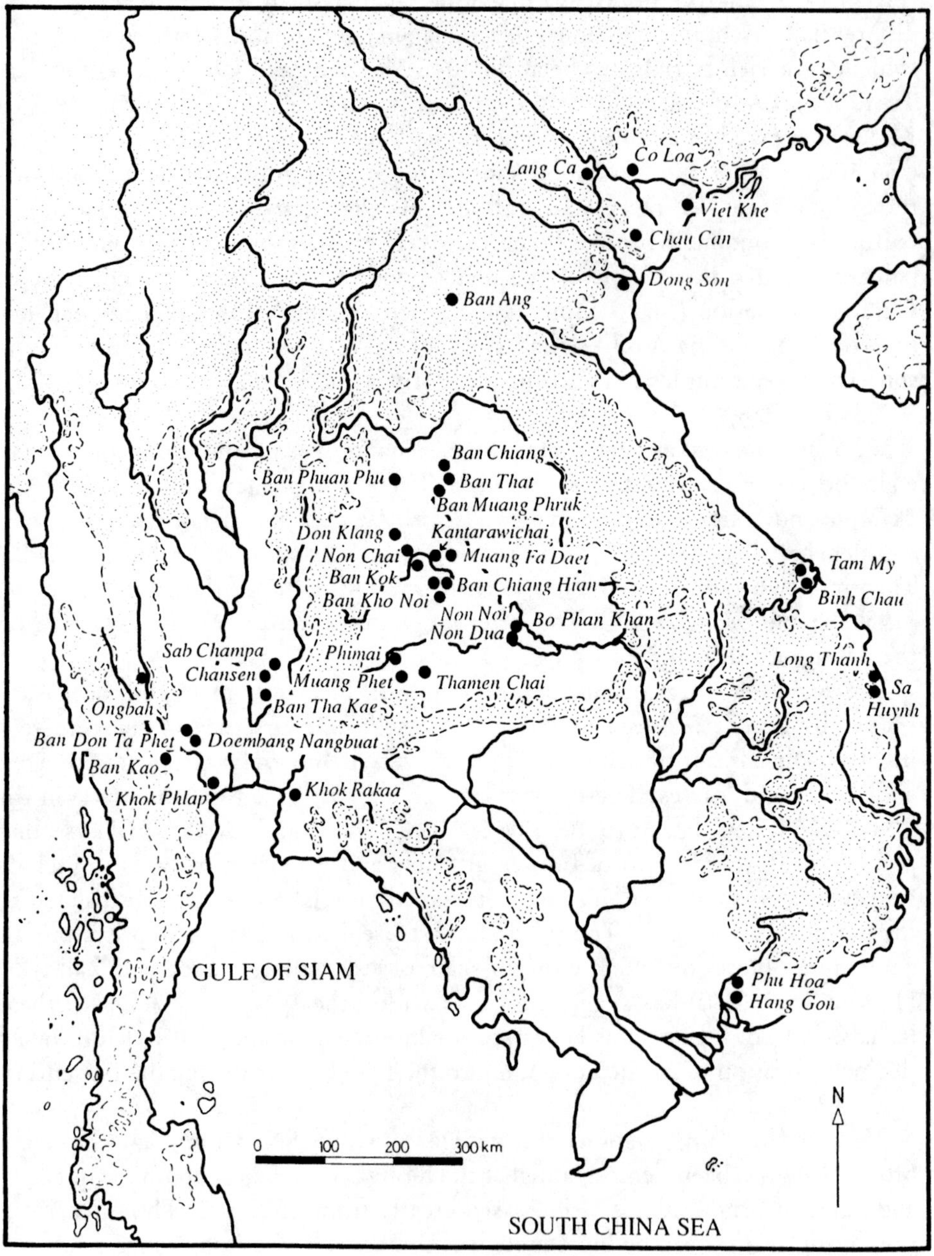

4.4 The location of sites mentioned in chapter 4. Sippled area: land above 182 m.

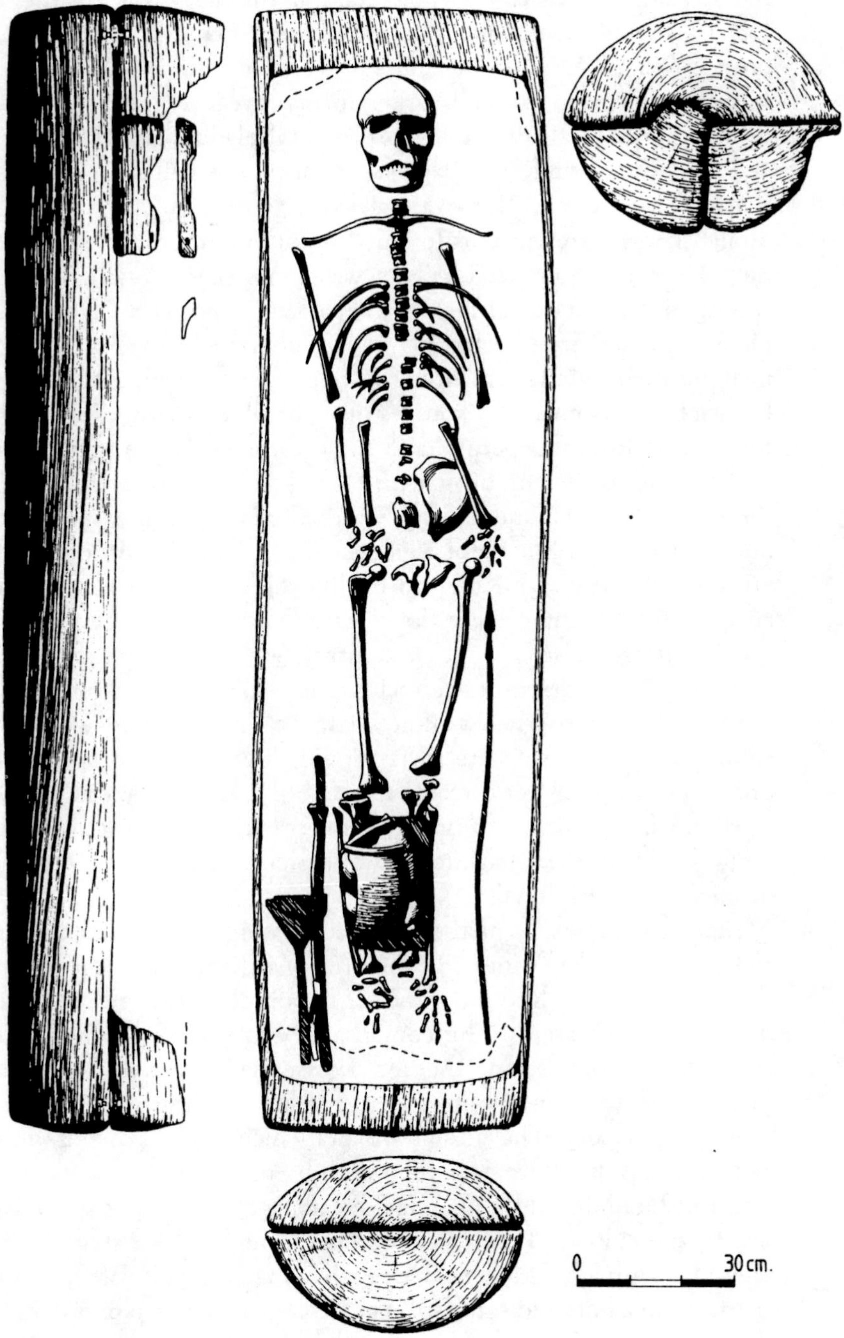

4.5 The boat burials of Chau Can, while not as large or rich as the longest Viet Khe specimen, do provide compelling evidence for an upper echelon in Dong Son society.

Ban Chiang. The crucible, while retaining the shape of the earlier ones found in Dong Dau contexts, is much larger. Indeed, it could have held 12 kg of molten bronze (Vu Thi Ngoc Thu and Nguyen Duy Ty 1978). Many novel artefact forms were developed, and earlier forms reveal an interest in decoration. The drums, situlae, and rectangular ornamental plaques suggest an interest in ritual and ceremony, while the daggers, swords and halberds reflect concern with personal weaponry. Nor was agriculture overlooked: the socketed bronze ploughshares represent a profoundly important innovation in the field of agriculture. The Dong Son metal-worker was a master in the difficult field of bronze-casting, but the status of local iron-working is not clear. During the Dong Son phase, Chinese iron technology reached a high level of proficiency. Their methods involved the demanding system of iron-casting rather than forging. It is known from documentary sources that iron objects were exported from China to the south during this period, and the presence of some bimetallic spears, comprising iron blades with bronze hilts that had been cast on in Dong Son contexts shows that iron, if by now locally worked, remained rare. It is also instructive to note that the rich burials of Viet Khe and Chau Can do not contain any iron grave goods. The status of iron during the Dong Son phase requires detailed analyses to determine the ratio of cast to forged artefacts. Evidence for local iron-smelting is also basic to an appreciation of iron and its importance to the local people. At present, the direct Chinese contact with Dong Son people is the most likely means whereby knowledge of iron-casting reached Bac Bo. The specialised bronze-workers there would doubtless have been interested in its properties. Iron did not threaten the central role of bronze in agriculture, war or ceremonial. The casting of bronze ploughshares is a direct application of metallurgical skills to the intensification of agriculture, and the social implications of this need to be explored.

There are numerous methods for cultivating rice, some being more efficient and productive than others. In the previous chapter it was concluded that early rice cultivation involved the clearance of competitors to rice in naturally flooded river or stream margins. This could have been effected during the dry season by means of fire, the axe and the hoe. It essentially involves interference with the natural vegetation in favour of rice, a plant which grows wild in such marshy habitats to this day. The amount of land which can be brought under cultivation by this means, however, is limited both by natural factors such as soil slope and extent of flooding, and human factors such as the amount of land which can be cleared and cultivated with axe and hoe. Ploughing represents a radical change. Equipped with a buffalo-drawn plough, a man can cultivate far more soil than if restricted to a hoe, and can also, therefore, produce surpluses over and above his own subsistence requirements. Ploughing itself aerates the soil, and turns over and kills weeds before the rice is planted. Under the anaerobic conditions of the water-logged rice-field, such weeds actually encourage rice by decomposing and releasing nutrients into the water. The rice plant is further sustained by oxygen in the water, and nitrogen fixed by blue-green algae. Indeed, rice can be grown year in, year out, even on the poorest soils if there is a sufficient supply of gently percolating water. The dominant form of lowland rice farming in Southeast Asia today involves the creation of nearly level rice-fields demarcated, where necessary, by low soil banks (Fig. 4.6). Where the terrain is flat, fields are large. Where there is more slope, they tend to be terraced and smaller in size. The bunds retain rainwater, which is allowed to flow slowly through the fields to the natural stream or lake shore. Water is not introduced to the fields but its out-flow is controlled. With the onset of the monsoon, the farmer ploughs and harrows his fields with an iron ploughshare drawn by a solitary water-buffalo. He then transplants rice manually from a seed bed into the awaiting paddy field. Weeding and tending is much easier when the rice is planted in rows rather than broadcast, and returns are predictably higher than under broadcasting (Hanks 1972). This system entails several periods of high labour input. Initially, there is the creation of fields (Fig. 4.7). During the early part of the rainy season it is necessary to prepare the soil and transplant seedlings, and at the end of the wet season there is harvesting, threshing and the transport of the crop to storage. The surpluses generated by this system have underwritten the modern states of Southeast Asia. A major issue, then, is the antiquity of this intensive plough-based agricultural system.

There are two sources which help resolve this issue, one archaeological and the

4.6 The creation of bunded rice-fields represents a major intensification of agriculture, particularly when linked with ploughing.

other literary. The Chinese, under the Han Dynasty, interred the dead and, depending on their status, buried with them objects used or required by the living. Where such items were too large for inclusion in a grave, they rendered clay models. Among these models are agricultural scenes (Bray 1984). It is stressed that these are Chinese, but they are contemporary with later Dong Son and, indeed, the Han impact was direct with the incorporation of Bac Bo into their empire in the 1st century A.D. One such model clearly depicts the agricultural system described above. Moreover, the bronze ploughshares which are so common in Dong Son contexts, are very similar to those found in China at the same date.

The second source of information is literary. Wheatley has reviewed the relevant Chinese sources and has stressed that in the later part of the 2nd century B.C. the area was designated a Chinese protectorate which decreed that "the Lac chieftains, in whose persons were institutionalised customary rights to land, be confirmed in their traditional authority" (Wheatley 1983:368).

Nguyen Viet (1983) has built on these two sources of information by considering the botanical and technological evidence for rice farming. He has concluded that the first millennium B.C. witnessed the adoption of plough agriculture requiring water-control and double cropping of rice on favourable terrain.

Large bronze drums are one of the outstanding artefacts of the Dong Son

4.7 The creation of level paddy fields by forest clearance and the construction of bunds is most labour intensive. This photograph was taken near Ban Chiang in 1978.

workshops. The bronze drums themselves are not confined to Bac Bo, but have a widespread distribution in Southern China (Barnard 1986, Wu Kunyi *et al.* 1986). The ownership of drums is still a hallmark of high status among the ethnic minorities of Southern China, and their abundance in Dong Son contexts indicates a society given to ritual and display. It is fortunate that the Dong Son bronze-smiths decorated their drums with scenes drawn from the world around them: these allow a glimpse into the activities of the very lords described in Chinese documents. We can, for example, recognise the importance attached to elegant boats equipped with cabins and fighting platforms. They were crewed by paddlers, and carried plumed warriors (Fig. 4.8). The spears, halberds and arrows found in aristocratic graves are seen in action, either being fired or, in one case, chastising a captive. The Dong Son drums themselves are represented mounted in sets of two or four, with the drummers on a raised platform. Houses were raised above ground level on piles, gable ends being supported by posts and decorated with bird-head carvings identical to those seen on the canoe prows (Fig. 4.9). These, and other scenes of musical instruments being played, bring home to us the importance of music in ritual activities at the Dong Son aristocratic centres (Fig. 4.10).

The new excavations at Dong Son confirm a rapid change from the Go Mun to the Dong Son phase proper, with a major intensification in the quantity and range of bronze artefacts. These include swords and daggers as well as objects of ritual and ceremonial importance such as drums, situlae and decorative body

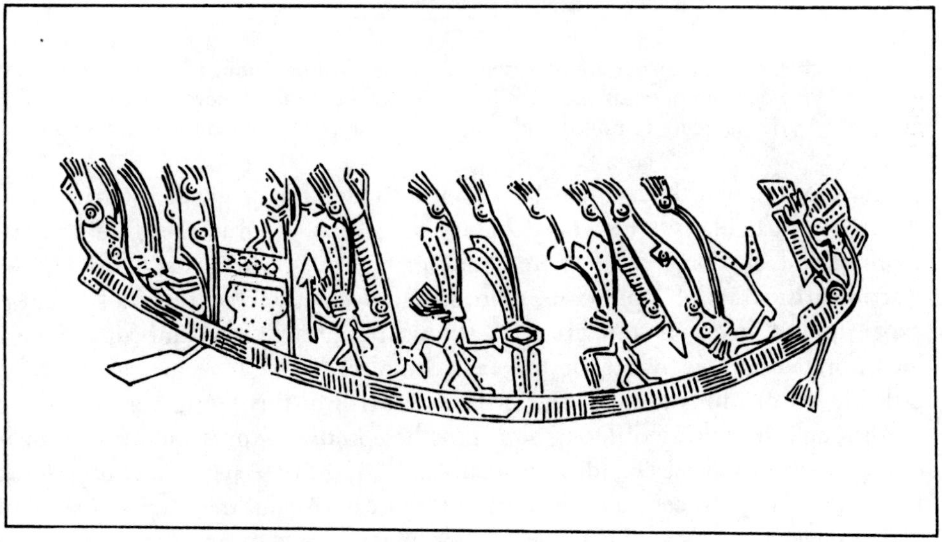

4.8 The Dong Son boats represented on the Ngoc Lu drum reveal a war captive and well-armed warriors. Note the cabin containing a drum and the archer on the fighting platform above.

4.9 Domestic scenes are represented on the Co Loa drum. Here we see a raised house on piles (above), while below there is a raised storehouse from which rice is being removed and ground in a mortar by a man and a woman.

plaques for the first time. Intensification is also identifiable in subsistence and in exchange, particularly with Han China. This is again seen in the third and last brief period at Dong Son when Chinese imports peaked. In A.D. 43, the warrior-aristocrats of Dong Son, who had survived three centuries of Chinese expansionism, invasion and periods of subjugation, finally succumbed, and were incorporated as a province of the Han Empire. We will return to consider possible reasons for the rapid and brilliant growth of this Dong Son society.

Although the culture of Dong Son is the best-known expression of the transition to the centralised chiefdom in mainland Southeast Asia, it was not alone. Indeed, the trend to centralisation was widespread. Again, the foremost symbol of the new aristocracy, the Dong Son drum, is by no means confined to the valleys of the Red and Ma rivers: the distribution of such drums covers much of southern China where rich chiefdoms contemporaneous with the Dong Son phase are well-known.

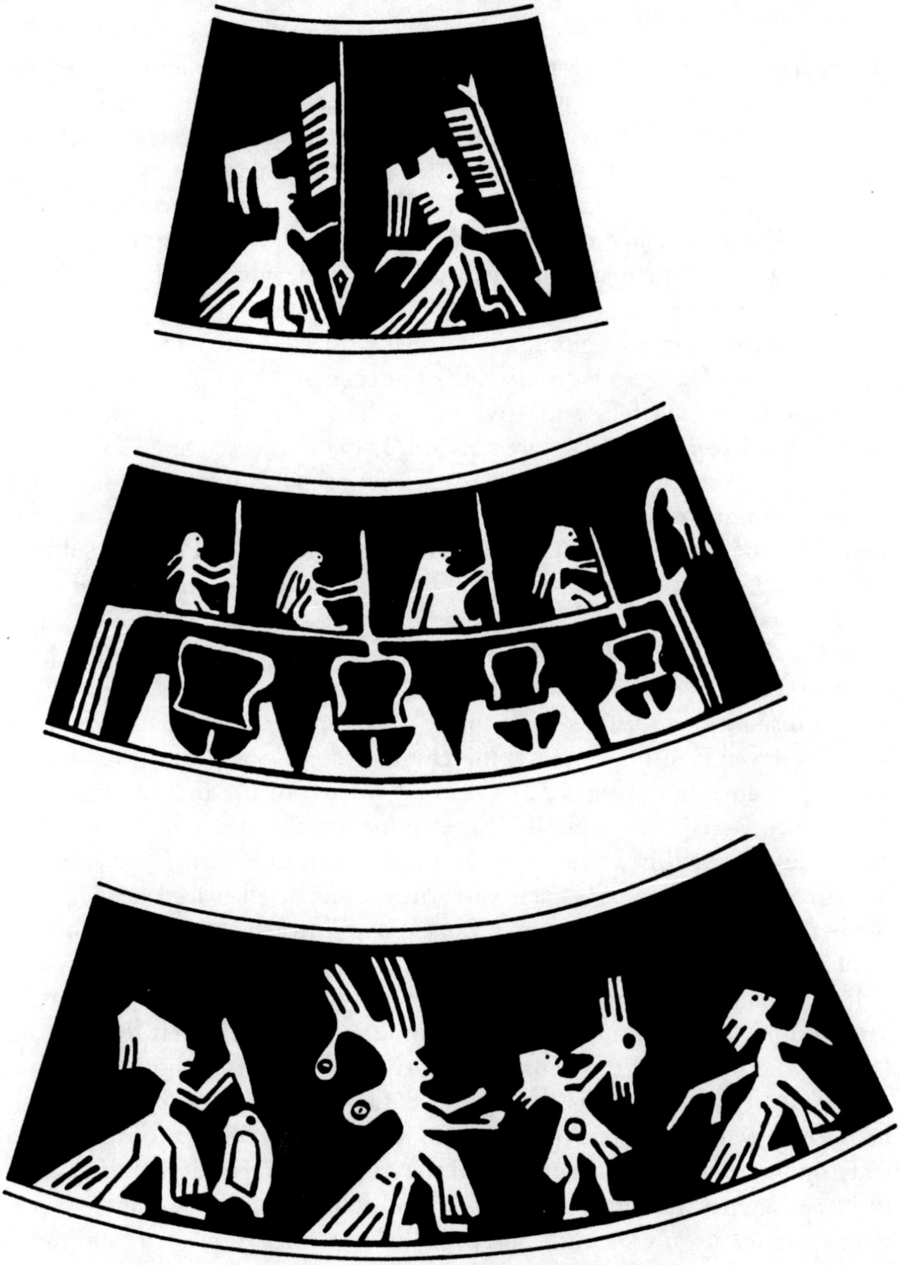

4.10 Scenes drawn from the decoration on Dong Son drums are a rich source of information. These examples, from the recently discovered Co Loa drum, show from top to bottom, two armed warriors, four drums being played by people seated above them on a platform and a musical ensemble. All these and many other examples point to the ritual and display which characterised Dong Son aristocratic centres.

The Chao Phraya plains

There has been far less research done in the Chao Phraya plains than in Bac Bo, but the few investigations undertaken reveal both similarities and differences. The former area was never subjected to the immediacy of foreign expansion, but it does command the eastern edge of the Three Pagodas pass which was one of the routes providing Indian contact. The Gulf of Siam also permitted movement of people and exchange of goods by sea, which allowed the occupants of the coastal tracts to participate in the expansion of trade which took place during the period under review.

One of the most intriguing sites, Ongbah, has yielded the remains of five drums of clear Dong Son affinities, the presence of which hints at direct contact with Bac Bo. Ongbah is a massive cavern located in the upper reaches of the Khwae Yai River (Fig. 4.4). Sørensen (1973, 1979) has recovered some information from the site following its near destruction by looters. He found that the burial technique comprised extended inhumation in wooden boat-shaped coffins. A radiocarbon determination of one such coffin gave an estimate of between 400 to 1 B.C. There were also several intact burials within the cave, of which 10 were excavated. These lacked the wooden boat-coffins, but both groups contained a similar assemblage of iron implements (Fig. 4.11). Sørensen has suggested inferior social status, rather than chronological change, to account for such a disparity in relative wealth. The 10 poorer burials have yielded several well-preserved iron implements, thereby affording insight into the uses of this metal, presumably during the last century or two of the first millennium B.C. (Fig. 4.12). Burial 5 incorporated an iron hoe on the chest. Burial 6 included a tanged knife, possibly a spearhead, and five beads. Other burials yielded chisels and arrowheads. One contained seven iron objects, all placed near the ankles. Similar arrowheads, socketed axes, chisels and knives were found in burial and occupation contexts at Ban Kao (Sørensen 1973).

It is particularly unfortunate that we are unable to present a clear list of associations between funerary artefacts and the boat-coffins left by the teams of looters who destroyed the remains from Ongbah. Sørensen, however, has recovered fragments of artefacts which hint at the wealth they once contained, and has interviewed the looters' labourers to establish certain relationships between stray finds and the original contents of the coffins. On the basis of this admittedly unsatisfactory but necessary procedure, it is possible to point out several interesting features: the coffin burials included strings of beads round the waist and neck, they also formerly included bronze and iron artefacts including earrings, bracelets, and at least one bronze vessel made of a very high tin-bronze, an alloy increasingly seen as a major innovation of General Period C. As has been mentioned, a set of drums was found near, and probably associated with, the coffins. These elaborate objects were decorated with zones of different motifs, including flying birds, human beings and geometric designs.

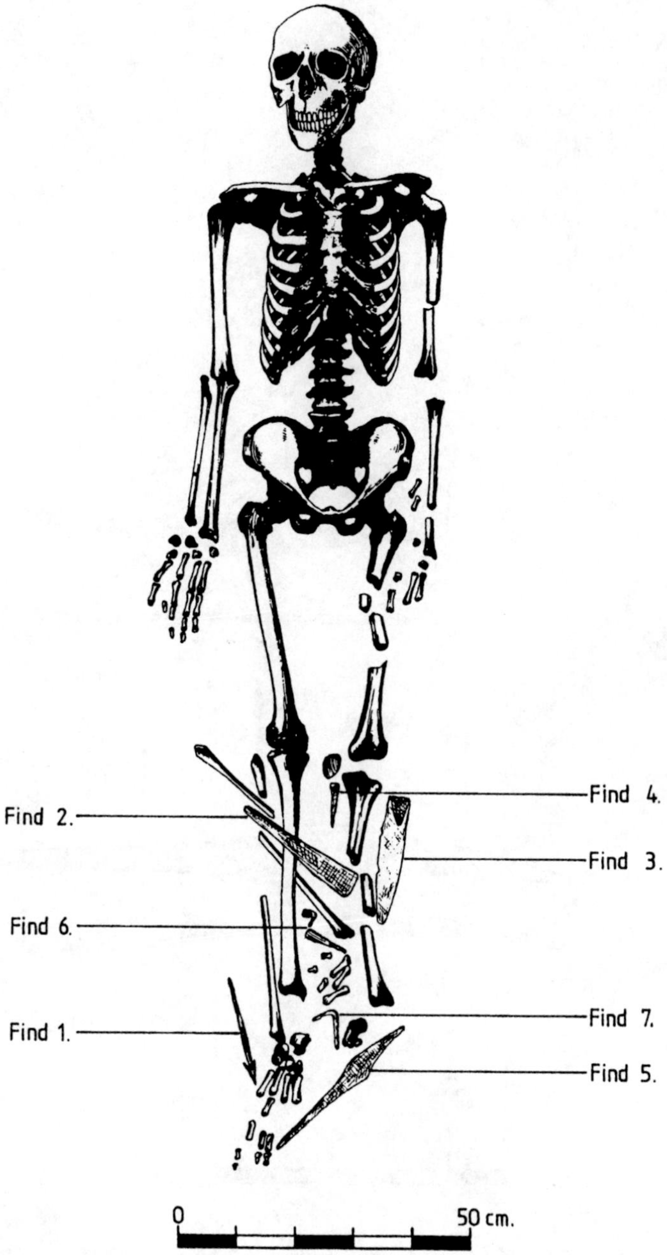

4.11 Burial 8 from Ongbah shows the prevalence at the site of iron implements with human interments.

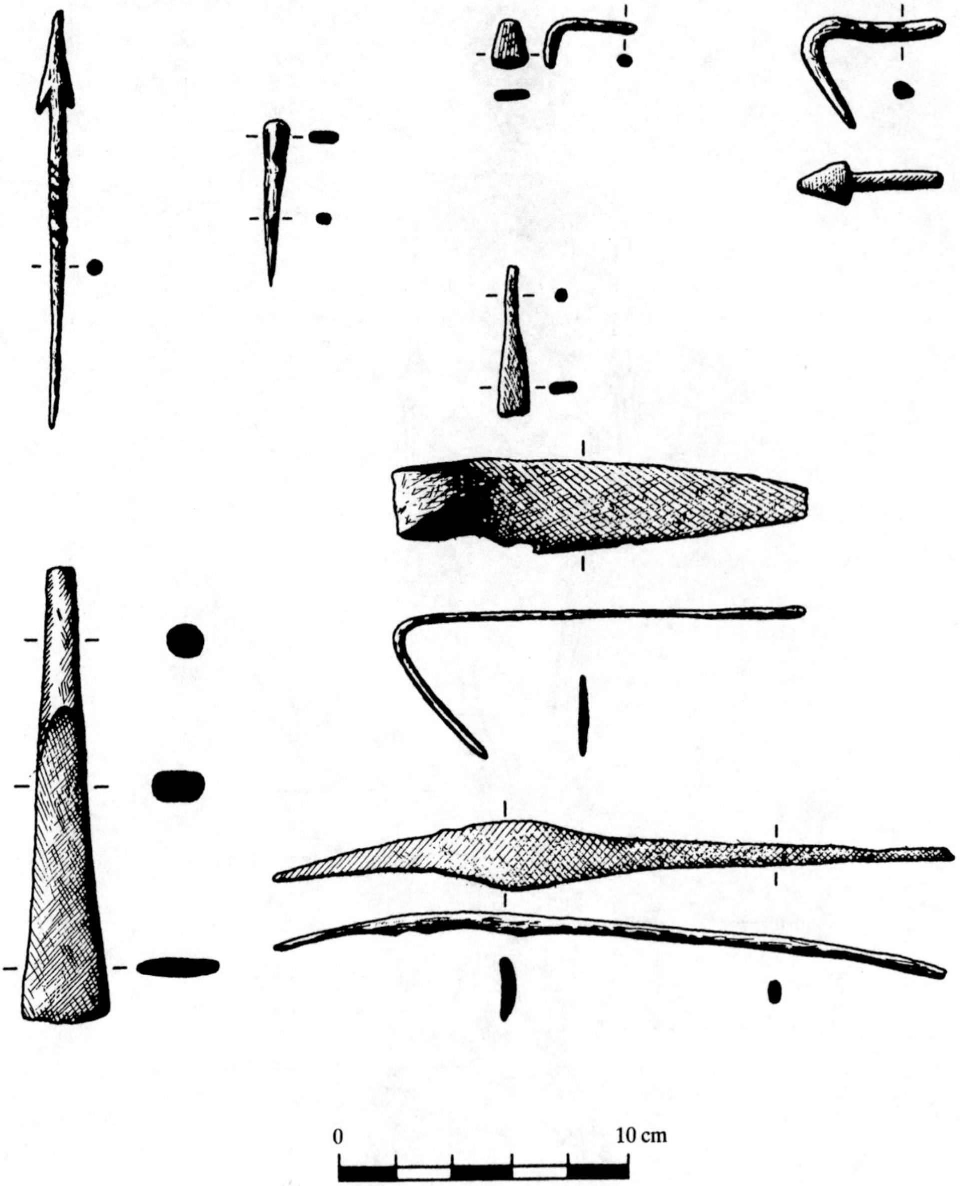

4.12 Iron implements from Ongbah burial 8 include projectile points, an axe and hooks.

Contact of one sort or another between the occupants of the Chao Phraya and the Red River valleys is also indicated by a more recent find at Doembang Nangbuat. Suchitta (1985) has reported a series of artefacts of clear Dong Son affinities, the remains of ornamented drums and bowls. Whether this find reflects exchange or an actual movement of people from Bac Bo remains to be seen.

Ban Don Ta Phet is located on the western margins of the Chao Phraya lowlands. Its position on a terrace commanding low-lying terrain matches the placement of the prehistoric settlements on the Khorat plateau. This cemetery site has been the object of several excavation seasons since its discovery in 1975 (You-di 1978, Glover 1980, 1983, Glover *et al.* 1984) and it already plays a central role in our understanding of the late prehistoric period in Central Thailand.

Unfortunately, bone does not survive in the acidic soils there, but excavation has, as at Dong Son, revealed dispositions of artefacts, with the occasional scrap of bone, which are clearly the remains of human interments. When compared with General Period B burials, the grave goods are considerably more abundant and the range of materials is greater. Thus, Glover (1983) has described four burials from the 1980–1 season. The number of complete or fragmentary pots averaged 20 per burial, a far higher figure than in the General Period B burial assemblages. The burials were also associated with tools and weapons made of iron, ornaments and bowls made from bronze, and both stone and glass beads. The blades of socketed iron spearheads were often bent back to break, or ritually kill them, prior to burial. One iron implement looks very like the modern sickle blade, while the application of iron technology is revealed by the socketed tips for either digging sticks or hoes, harpoons and knives. Bennett's (1982) analysis of the 13 iron artefacts has shown that they were forged probably from the local limonite ores, and then edge-hardened by hammering to produce what Bennett describes as a "fairly homogeneous low-carbon steel". This would have allowed the iron to retain a tough and easily sharpened cutting edge.

The beads were manufactured from agate, carnelian and glass. These are all exotic, and recall specimens dated to the 2nd and 3rd centuries B.C. in India. There is a very strong probability that the beads are Indian exports.

The burials at Ban Don Ta Phet have also furnished a series of thin-walled bronze bowls which exhibit interesting features (Rajpitak and Seeley 1979). They are decorated with incised motifs and, occasionally, representations of people. The alloy employed is a high (19-21%) tin-bronze which is very brittle and hard to work, yet imparts a gold-like colour to the finished article. The number of such bowls at the site, and the long tradition of established bronze-working, point alike to local and, indeed, specialised manufacture. A few similar bowls have been found in India. Two come from the Bhir Mound at Taxila dating to the late first millennium B.C. (Marshall 1951). The inferences are clear: exchange linked Indian and Southeast Asian societies towards the end of the first millennium B.C., and some individuals at Ban Don Ta Phet were interred with imported beads made of glass and semi-precious stone. It is unfortunate that the acidic soils at the site have ruled out the preservation of large enough samples of charcoal for radiocarbon dating, but one determination made on the basis of the organic content of pottery indicated use of the site at least during the 2nd and 3rd centuries A.D. (Glover *et al.* 1984).

The presence of moated settlements in the Chao Phraya valley has long been known and some were clearly major centres of the Dvāravatī civilization. Excavations at two of these sites, Sab Champa and Chansen, have provided evidence for initial occupation during the late prehistoric period. At Chansen, Bronson found a basal cultural layer containing an inhumation burial associated with a socketed iron implement, interpreted as a hoe or ploughshare (Bronson and Dales 1973, Bronson 1979). This same context has yielded the remains of water-buffalo bones. Veerapan (1979) has discovered inhumation graves at the moated site of Sab Champa, associated on this occasion, with pottery vessels and moulds used in bronze-casting.

In many ways, our knowledge of General Period C in the Chao Phraya lowlands remains sketchy and unsatisfactory. Excavations have not been undertaken in the context of regional settlement pattern studies, so little information on relative site sizes and the possible presence of regional centres is available. Glover has stressed that we are not yet able to say whether the Ban Don Ta Phet cemetery was unusually rich or typical of other sites in the area as a whole. At Ban Tha Kae, however, there is some indication that the site ultimately covered a considerable area, probably in excess of 20 ha. The site itself has been destroyed, but early aerial photographs reveal a large mound. The question is, how much of the mound was occupied during General Period C. There is now no way of being sure on this point.

An important step towards a more complete understanding of this period has recently been taken by Ho (1984). Within the context of her analysis of the material from the excavations of Khok Charoen, she undertook a series of site surveys. These suggested strongly that, after an initial occupation during what she calls "the early metal age" (equivalent to our General Period B), there was a move toward centralisation wherein one site grew differentially large and, it is assumed, exercised political dominance over others in its area. Indeed, Ho was able to identify three distinct areas each dominated by its large, and eventually moated, site. The centres are about 30 km apart from each other (Fig. 3.43). She has ascribed these sites to a "high metal age", which saw a marked increase in bronze-working and the initial use of iron. This equates culturally and chronologically with General Period C. It is important to note how her results from the Chao Phraya valley match those proposed by Welch (1985) and Moore (1986) in the Mun valley, and Higham and Kijngam (1984) in the Chi valley.

There are, then, some grounds for suggesting that there was a trend towards centralisation during the mid to late first millennium B.C. The chronological relationship between this trend and direct or indirect contact with Indian coastal traders remains to be determined. Evidence for the exchange of goods between coastal communities in Southeast Asia itself are apparent in the Dong Son-style drums from Ongbah, the few bronzes in the Dong Son tradition and a two-headed ear ornament characteristic of the Sa Huynh culture at Ban Don Ta Phet (Suchitta 1985).

The Khorat plateau

It has been suggested that, towards the end of General Period B, the occupants of the Khorat plateau lived in autonomous villages and followed a system of ranking between different affiliated groups. The expansion of settlement resulted from the fissioning of communities as they reached critical population thresholds thought to be in the region of about 300 to 500 people. This process of expansion was not constrained so long as there was sufficient land with the necessary properties for (a), the cultivation of rice along stream or river margins where flooding was not severe, and (b), the fishing, trapping and stock maintenance which characterised subsistence activities. Suitable terrain was not, however, limitless. The Khorat plateau includes substantial elevated terraces and hilly areas quite unsuited to the cultivation of rice.

General Period B settlements are known in the favourable valleys which feed the Mun, Chi and Songkhram rivers. While pottery styles suggest individuality even at the village level, the sourcing of exotic materials will lead to the linking of settlements into exchange circuits. We already know that the exchange in valuables reached out from the Khorat plateau into the surrounding hills for copper, tin and stone, and to the coast for trochus and cowrie shell ornaments.

It is now nearly forty years since Williams-Hunt (1950) published the results of his analysis of aerial photographs covering the Khorat plateau. These disclosed a considerable number of large mounds, enclosed by moats and ramparted defences, clustered in the Mun-Chi drainage basin. Most sites are oval in plan and some look as if they have been added to with time. Thus Muang Fa Daet comprises three moated enclosures with a fourth feature, thought to have been a reservoir, nearby. Williams-Hunt also concluded that three sites were considerably larger than the rest, indicating a hierarchy of sites according to size. Similar oval moated sites are now known on the margins of the Bangkok plain, and in Northeastern Cambodia. These sites are intriguing not only for their distribution pattern, size and date, but also for their origins. It is this last point which we will consider first.

Quaritch-Wales (1957) was attracted to these sites in the Mun valley, excavating small squares at Thamen Chai and Muang Phet (see Fig. 4.20). The sites yielded cultural stratigraphies about 3 m and 2 m thick, respectively. The excavator noted the presence of iron down to the basal layers of Muang Phet and concluded, on the basis of ceramic typology, that the first settlement reflects at least influence from, if not occupation by, people from the Chao Phraya valley.

Quaritch-Wales regarded the presence of iron as a result of contact with India, and suggested that the sites were first occupied during the first millennium A.D. Moreover, Muang Phet has yielded a radiocarbon date of A.D. 150±150 from a depth of 1 metre from the surface.

A series of more recent settlement pattern studies and excavations favour a greater antiquity for some sites, and innovation reflecting internal changes rather than incursions. The best-documented settlement pattern analysis incorporating a moated site took place on the southern margins of the Chi River (Fig. 4.13). The chosen study area incorporates the Chi floodplain, which reaches a maximum breadth of 7 km. Three tributary streams flow north across the floodplain and into the main river. They have smaller floodplains surrounded by low-terrace terrain of varying width, which gives way to the slightly more elevated land of the middle terrace.

The prehistoric sites concentrate near the low terraces of the tributary streams and fringe the extensive tract comprising the Chi floodplain. One site in this area, Ban Chiang Hian, incorporates a double set of moats, a reservoir, and possibly the remains of ramparts (Figs. 4.14 and 4.15). Three sites have been excavated including Ban Chiang Hian itself. All three yield a distinctive red-on-buff painted ware in the lowest occupation layers. Non Noi had only an horizon of early red-on-buff painted pottery, but at Ban Kho Noi and Ban Chiang Hian, this was superceded, in the mid first millennium B.C., by a plainer ware. At that juncture, the excavators found the first evidence for iron and the water-buffalo. The moated area of Ban Chiang Hian covers about 38 ha. It significantly exceeds the size of all other prehistoric sites in the surveyed area and was clearly a special central site. As with all other moated sites in the Khorat plateau, we cannot yet answer the question of their construction date. This is a critical issue, because the existence of so large a site with such extensive earthworks is precisely the sort of evidence which is held to reflect the existence of centralised chiefdoms. There is, however, some evidence which suggests that such social groupings were present in at least the Mun and Chi valleys during the period 400 B.C. to A.D. 300.

Let us begin by considering the site of Non Chai, which was excavated, in 1978, by Pisit Charoenwongsa (Bayard, Charoenwongsa and Rutnin 1986). This most important site is located in the upper reaches of the Chi catchment (Fig. 4.16). It is found on a small surviving tract of the old middle terrace, but in such a location as to command low-lying alluvial soils which are today classified as moderately suited to rice cultivation. The size of the site cannot be stated with precision because it has been removed for road-fill. According to plans made after removal had commenced, it covered at least 18 ha, and the excavators estimated an area during its prehistoric ocupation of 38.5 ha. It was, therefore, considerably larger than any known General Period B site. Proximity to flooded areas is reflected in the aquatic resources identified by Kijngam (1979). He described a considerable number of shellfish, fish, crabs, frogs and water turtle from the middens there. At the same time, the early settlers brought with them

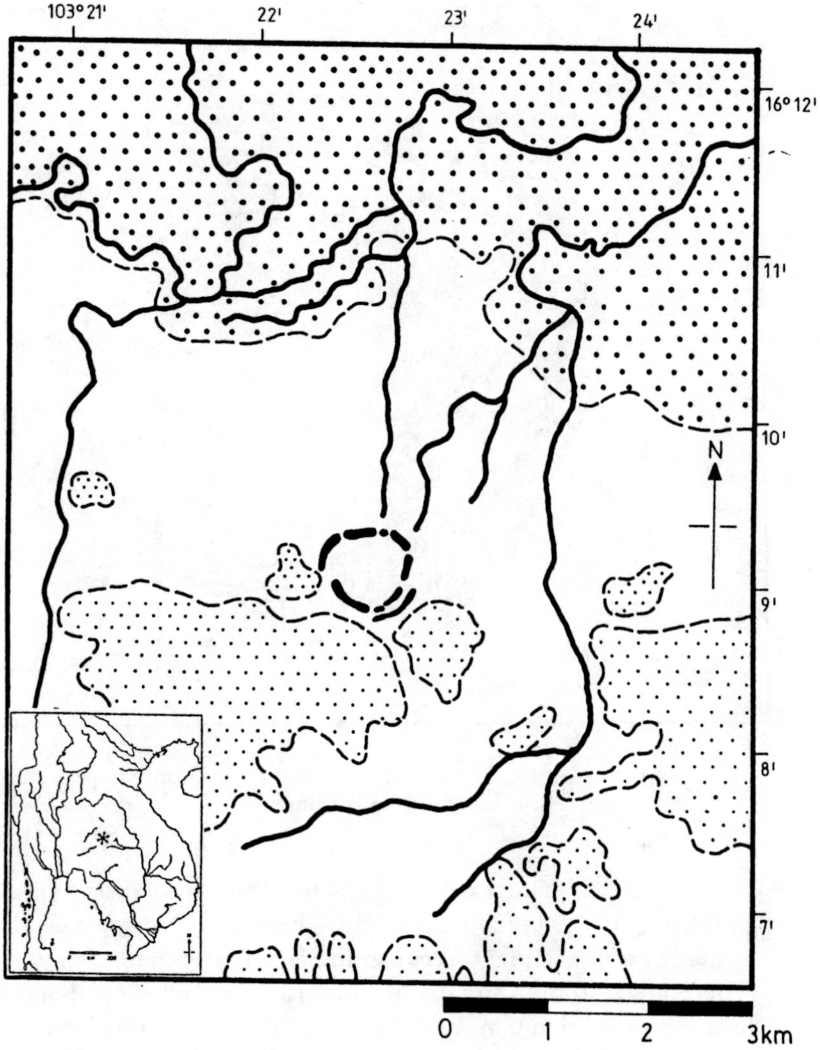

4.13 The location of Ban Chiang Hian shows a preference for access to the good low-terrace soils for rice cultivation. The white areas on the map are good for rice cultivation, the stippled areas are, for a number of reasons, not so well suited.

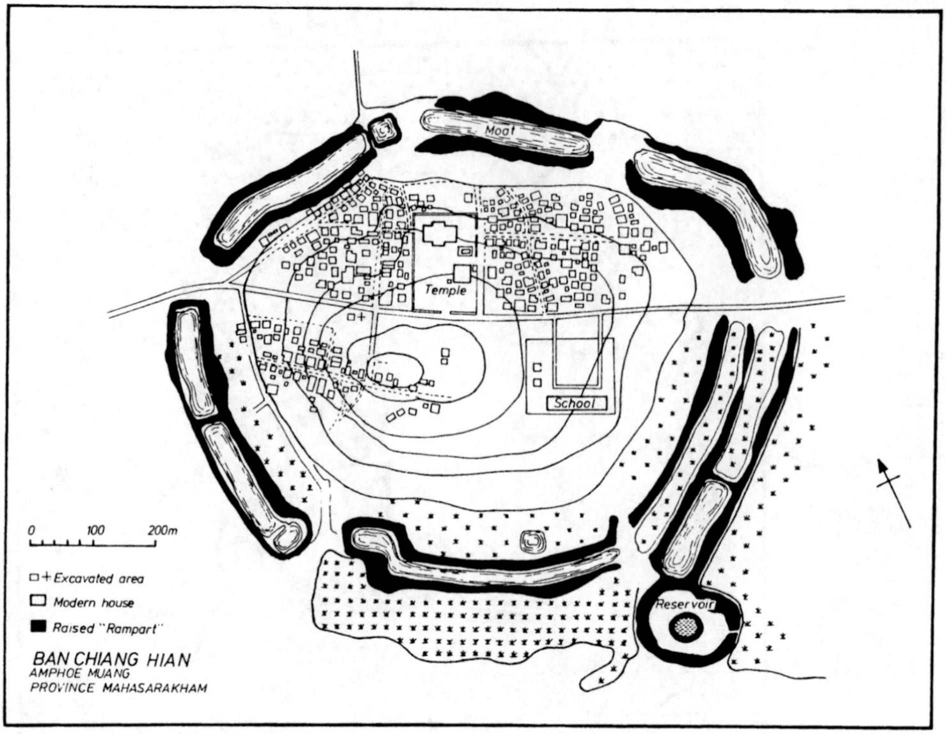

4.14 Ban Chiang Hian lies behind moats, possibly ramparts, and a small reservoir. The excavated area is centre left.

domestic water-buffalo, cattle, dog and pig. Like the occupants of Ban Na Di and Ban Chiang, they hunted extensively. The bones of deer, crocodile, rhinoceros and many small mammals, recur in the faunal spectrum (Kijngam 1979).

The pottery from Non Chai is dominated by red-slipped and painted wares which echo later Ban Chiang styles (Rutnin 1979). In this context, the radiocarbon dates confirm a relatively late prehistoric settlement and a rapid build-up of cultural material. Apart from one date of 1810±240 B.C. for the lowest layer, the rest vary little throughout the cultural layers. While the excavator has yet to comment on the context and status of the earliest date, an eroded section near the excavated area clearly revealed a thin band of occupation followed by a sterile soil build-up, and then evidence for the continual occupation of the site. Thus, some occupation may have occurred during the second millennium B.C., but the weight of evidence points to continuous occupation from towards the end of the first millennium B.C. The excavators have suggested that phase I dates from about 400 B.C., phases II and III between 300 to 200 B.C., phase IV to 200 to 1 B.C. and phase V into the 2nd century A.D. The material culture from Non Chai includes small amounts of iron slag, but only in abundance from phase IV. There

4.15 The Ban Chiang Hian moats and ramparts represent a considerable concentration of effort, and lend support to the idea that this and other moated sites were centres of small chiefdoms.

are also four glass beads from contexts earlier than phase III at the site, and over 200 belong to phases IV and V. The surge in the number of beads probably dates to about 200–1 B.C. Clay moulds for casting bronze bracelets and bells are likewise found in phase III to V contexts, though fragments of bronze and crucible fragments were identified in layers attributed to phases II to V.

The critical point about this well-dated site is that it covered at least 18 ha at some point during the period from 400 B.C. until about A.D. 250, when it seems to have been abandoned. At present, we do not know during which part of the sequence, if any, the site actually attained that area under continuous occupation. If it did, and a population figure of 50 people per ha is adopted, then the site at its maximum extent would have harboured about 1000 people. Further, if estimates of nearly 40 ha for the site's area are adopted, then the population could have been twice that figure. The pottery is very distinctive in form, surface finish and fabric. There are sharp differences between it and the contemporary wares at Ban Chiang Hian, though a few exotic sherds from the latter were found and probably represent imports (Chantaratiyakan 1983).

Non Chai is by no means the only General Period C site in this part of the Chi drainage system. Kijngam's excavations at Ban Kok, located only 6 km from Non

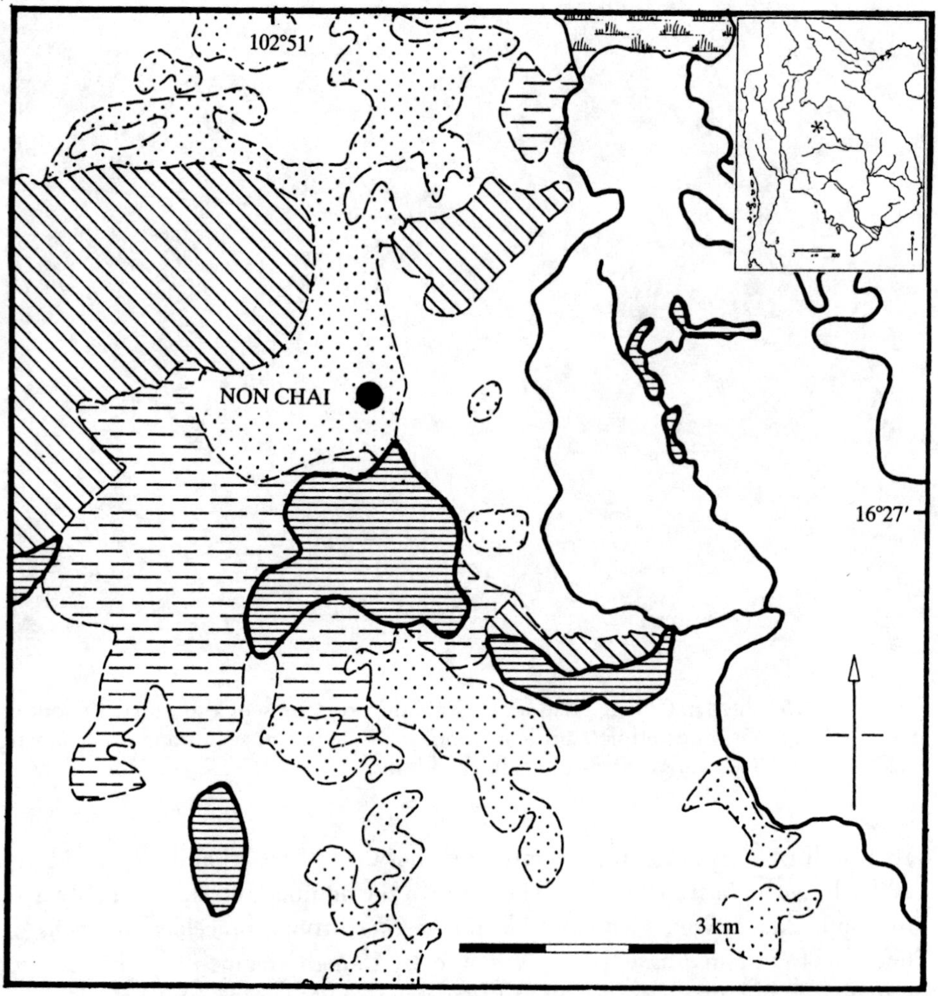

4.16 The location of Non Chai, a site occupying a nodal position for exchange in the upper valley of the Chi River. The white areas are well suited to rice cultivation, and the stippled areas are less well suited for a variety of reasons.

Chai, also revealed red-slipped and painted pottery in association with iron (Kijngam 1981). His 3 m by 3 m test square reached natural soil at a depth of 4 m. He found much iron in the middle part of the sequence over a radiocarbon date of about 900 B.C. If an intensive site survey were undertaken in the region round Non Chai, it would be possible to determine whether this site stood out, on account of its size, over smaller villages. Such a pattern would match those documented in the middle Chi valley and the Phimai region.

The valley of the Lam Siao Yai is found about 60 km southeast of Ban Chiang

Hian (Fig. 4.4). Here again, we encounter a large moated site. Non Dua is located so as to command an extensive deposit of rock salt as well as low-terrace soils suited to rice cultivation (Fig. 4.17). The salt exposure, known as Bo Phan Khan, is surrounded by evidence of industrial activity in the form of mounds and quantities of thick-walled pottery. At present, the salt is obtained by removing the salty soil and passing water through it. The brine is then boiled in flat metal trays. Excavations in one of the mounds around the deposit exposed evidence for salt extraction to a depth of about 6 m and starting, according to the radiocarbon date, in the 1st–2nd century A.D. Some examples of the crudely fashioned industrial wares were found during excavations within the moated site itself, which suggests that its occupants were concerned with the extraction of the salt. The extent of the activity, measured in terms of the huge mounds which have accumulated all around Bo Phan Khan, points to the production on a scale far greater than would have been necessary to satisfy local demand alone. Non Dua, the moated site, also yielded a deep stratigraphic sequence, and the initial phase of occupation has been assigned to the period 500–1 B.C. Some of the distinctively decorated rims and body sherds have been noted in phase 2 at Ban Chiang Hian, but otherwise the pottery there was not matched in the Middle Chi valley.

Further information on the Khorat plateau settlement during General Phase C has been obtained by Welch (1985) and Moore (1986). Welch chose, as his study area, the region surrounding the great Khmer site of Phimai (Fig. 3.37). His site surveys, undertaken to document and explain the beginnings of centralisation in the area, revealed 15 prehistoric sites. He found a concentration of them on recent terraces elevated above the floodplain. Excavations at two sites, the most productive of which was Ban Tamyae, allowed him to establish a chronological and cultural framework for the upper Mun valley. The five test pits excavated at Ban Tamyae covered an area of $24m^2$, and revealed a cultural stratigraphy about 2.5 m deep and comprising 8 successive levels. Bronze was found in the lowest, with iron appearing for the first time in level 7. Among the well-preserved faunal material, Welch found the remains of domestic pigs and cattle, with the first positively identified water-buffalo bone coming from a level 4 context. It seems that the excavations encountered occupation areas, so the advantage of considering the evidence of burial ritual was not available. On the basis of the very large sample of pottery, Welch subdivided his Formative Period (600 B.C. – A.D. 600) into four phases, dated principally on the basis of seven radiocarbon dates from Ban Tamyae (Fig. 4.18). The sequence began with the Tamyae phase, which corresponds best, it seems, with our General Period B. There followed the Prasat phase (600 – 200 B.C.), Classic Phimai phase (200 B.C. – A.D. 300) and the Late Phimai phase (A.D. 300 – 600). It was during the Prasat phase that local iron-working, represented by iron slag in level 3 at Ban Tamyae, and water-buffalo made their appearance. Welch was able to observe a marked trend towards centralisation during the Prasat and Classic Phimai phases as some settlements, such as Phimai itself, grew larger. We shall return to his stimulating

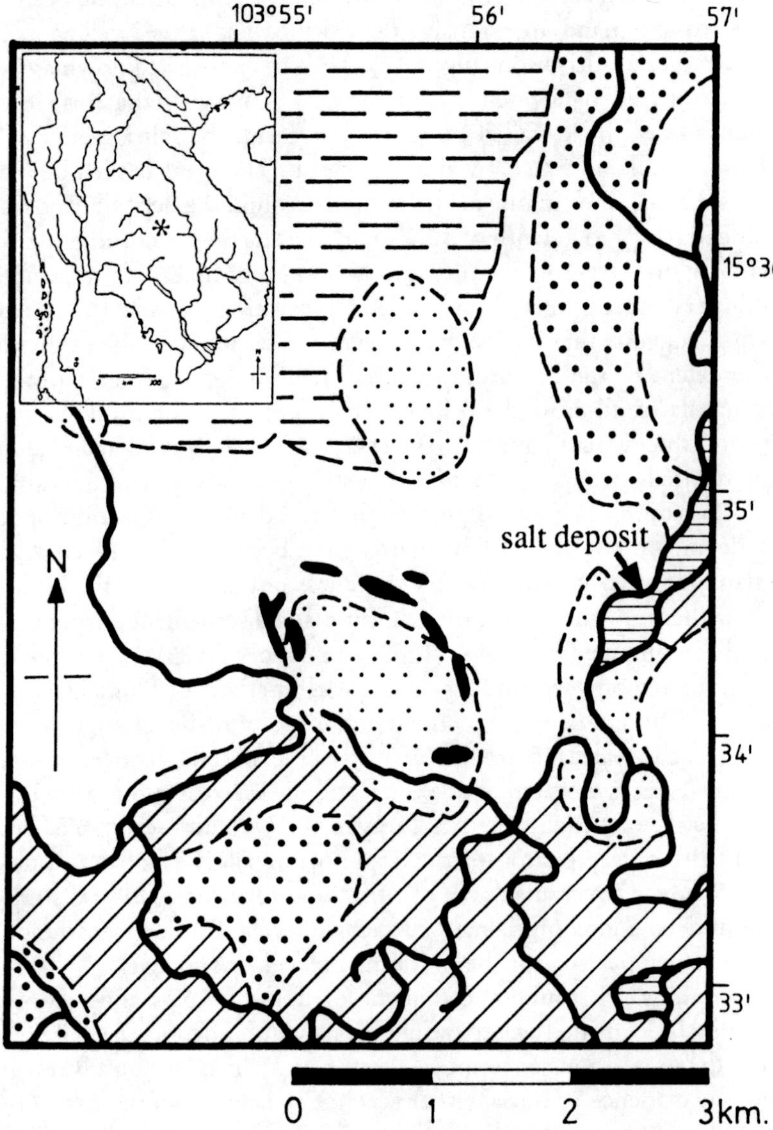

4.17 The location of Non Dua confers control over a strategic salt deposit, which is worked to this day, and good rice-land which is shown in the above map as white, rather than shaded, areas.

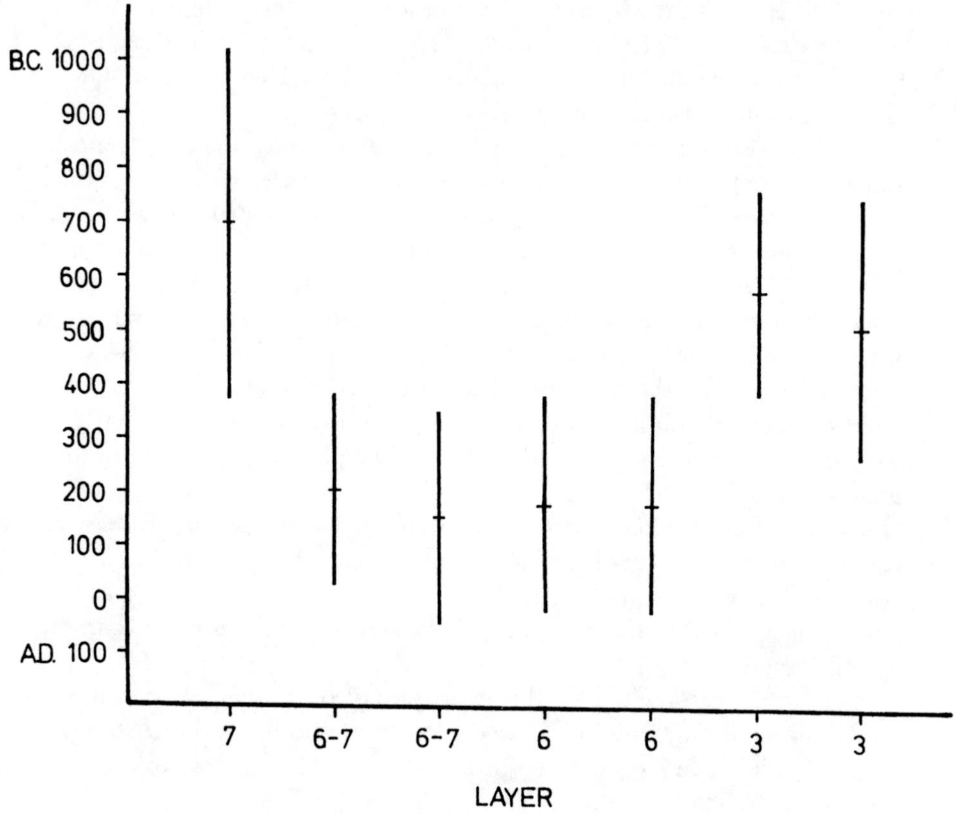

4.18 The radiocarbon dates from Ban Tamyae assist in the dating of the prehistoric sequence in the upper Mun valley. They are given as 2σ ranges (Welch 1985).

interpretation of this situation when reviewing possible reasons for the widespread trend towards centralisation during General Period C.

Moore (1986) has recently completed an innovative and important study of a sample of the Mun valley moated sites identified on the basis of the World War II photographic archive, the Williams-Hunt collection. She has analysed 91 of these sites on the basis of their size, architecture and distribution. Unlike the Chi valley survey described above, Moore examined the moated settlements as a technological group, rather than as a constituent of an overall settlement pattern which includes both the larger moated, and smaller, unmoated, sites. The Mun valley moated sites are distinctive in their circular layout and common occurrence of multiple moats and banks (Fig. 4.19). Moore has calculated the area of each. The resulting data are not directly comparable with the areas of Ban Chiang Hian and Non Chai because she included the area of the moats and ramparts in her figures, whereas the area of 38.5 ha for Ban Chiang Hian was taken within the earthworks. Nevertheless, the figures are of considerable interest. In her small group, the area varies up to 20 ha. Sites of the intermediate group have areas of between 21 and 40 ha, while the large sites extend up to 68 ha. These areas are far greater than those estimated for General Period B villages.

The distribution of these large enclosed sites includes the floodplain of the Mun River, the lower terrace, middle terrace and, on three occasions, actually on the high terrace. Out of 91 recorded sites, 78 were located on the floodplain (n=15), low terrace (n=50) or low to middle terrace (n=13). Again, compared with the General Period B villages, there seems to have been a significant expansion of settlement to include the middle and high terraces. When Moore turned to the architecture and degree to which moats and reservoirs encircled sites, she found that the elevated settlements incorporated more water-control systems and commonly exhibited more stages in their expansion. This is hardly surprising where water supply was likely to be a particular problem in the drier middle- and high-terrace areas.

In terms of chronology, Moore has suggested that the initial phase in the provision of water-control measures took place during General Period B, perhaps during the first half of the first millennium B.C. The major expansion, however, is ascribed to the period 500 B.C. – A.D. 500, that is, the currency of General Period C.

One possible reason cited for this expansion of settlement away from slightly elevated terrain on the floodplains to the knolls of middle- and high-terrace land commanding tributary stream margins, is the pull of such resources as timber,

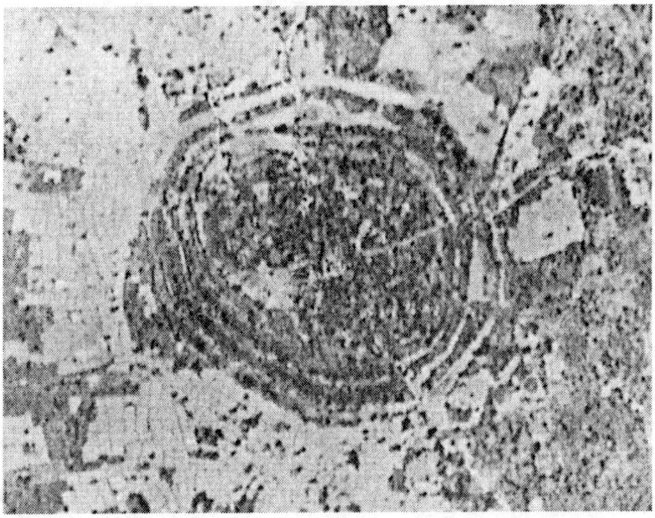

4.19 The moated Mun valley site of Ban Muang Fang is one of many in the Mun catchment studied by Elizabeth Moore. (Courtesy Elizabeth Moore.)

salt and lateritic iron ore. Certainly, a high proportion of these sites, even on the basis of their modern names, indicate local iron-smelting (Figs. 4.20 and 4.21).

The large moated sites in Northeast Thailand are very much a feature of the Mun and Chi valleys. They are significantly larger than any other site in their surrounding territory. Non Chai, Phimai, Ban Chiang Hian and Non Dua have produced distinctive local styles of pottery, and there is some suggestion that vessels were exchanged between centres or, at least, regions. Iron-working and bronze-casting were undertaken, and glass beads are included among imported items. In no case has a Dong Son import been found in a stratigraphic context in one of the moated sites, but then, excavations have been minimal. Objects of Dong Son origin, however, are known in Northeast Thailand from surface or looted sites, and two axe halberds were found in a burial context at the site of Ban That (Kethutat 1976). Given the contemporaneity of these sites with Dong Son, it is noted with interest that no bronze ploughshares have yet been found in the Khorat plateau.

If we accept a figure of 50 people per ha as a reasonable population estimate for these prehistoric sites, then Non Chai would have accomodated at least 1000 people, and Ban Chiang Hian, twice that number. The earthworks at Ban Chiang Hian are substantial, and would have entailed much energy in their construction. Even if the moats and reservoir were a mere metre deep, 100,000m^2 of soil would have been moved in their excavation. It has been estimated that it would have taken 500 well-fed adults a year to complete the task (Chantaratiyakan 1984). Again, the very presence of a reservoir argues for the need to supply water to a large number of people during the dry season. The point is clear: the moated sites represent a signal departure from the earlier system of village autonomy, and involved a far higher investment in buildings.

The excavations at Ban Chiang and Ban Na Di have revealed that a major cultural dislocation occurred about 300 B.C. It will be recalled that in the level 6 and 7 cemetery at Ban Na Di, the latest two burials were accompanied by iron artefacts: a spearhead, circlets and a knife. Level 5 represented a radical change in activity. It yielded the remains of a bronze-working area complete with crucibles, furnaces and clay moulds for casting bells and bracelets. The crucibles, while similar in shape and size to those in preceding layers, were now tempered with rice chaff rather than grog. The bronze alloys from levels 6 to 8 inclusive comprised a 10–12% tin bronze. Level 5 alloys were much more variable (Fig. 4.22). Lead became a common additive, and a few pieces were made from the very high (over 20%) tin bronze which was used in the manufacture of the Ban Don Ta Phet bowls. The bronze industry during levels 4 and 5 was concerned with the production of bracelets, bells and bowls. There is no evidence that axes and spears, which characterised the General Period B repertoire, were cast in bronze. It is considered highly likely that the metal work during the period, as at Non Chai during phase IV, represents an increased degree of specialisation.

During the build-up of level 4, part of the excavated area at Ban Na Di was

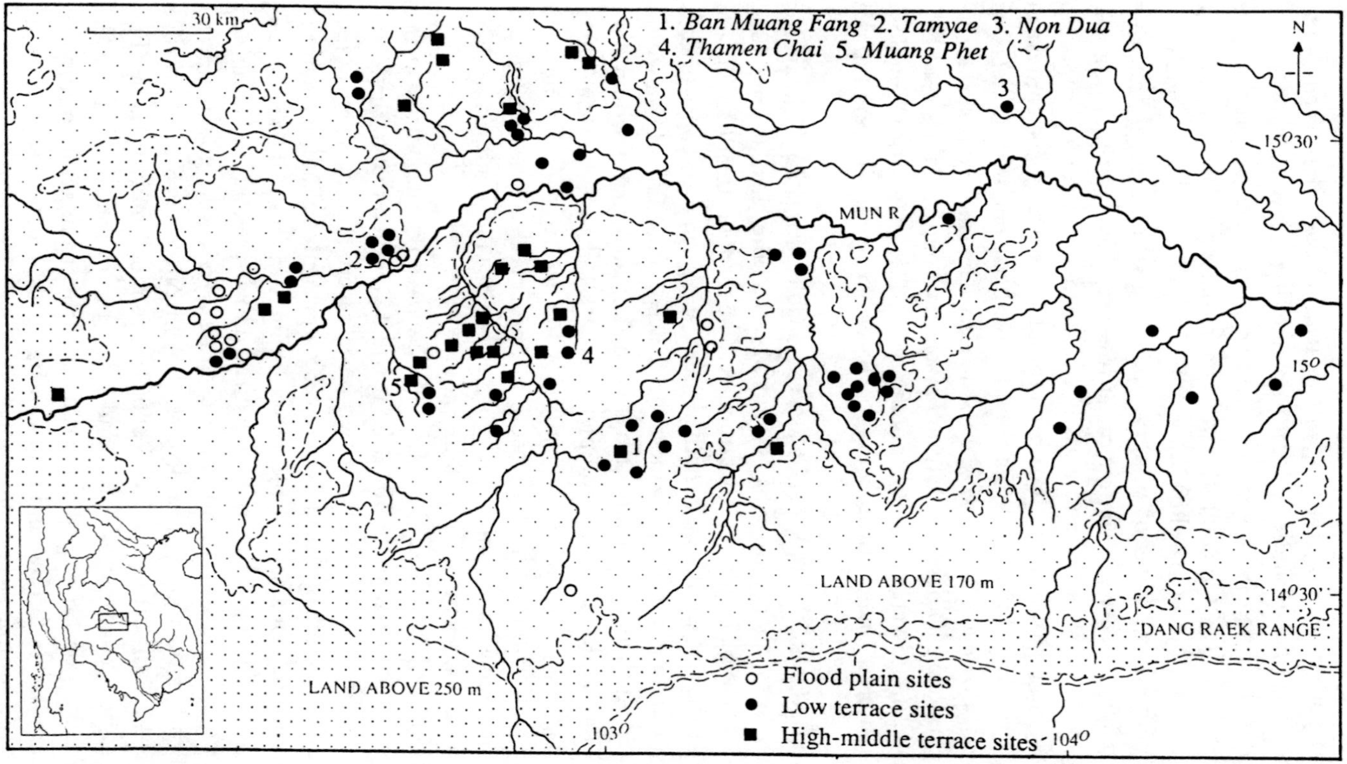

4.20 The location of the moated sites in the Mun valley on the basis of the major environmental variables.

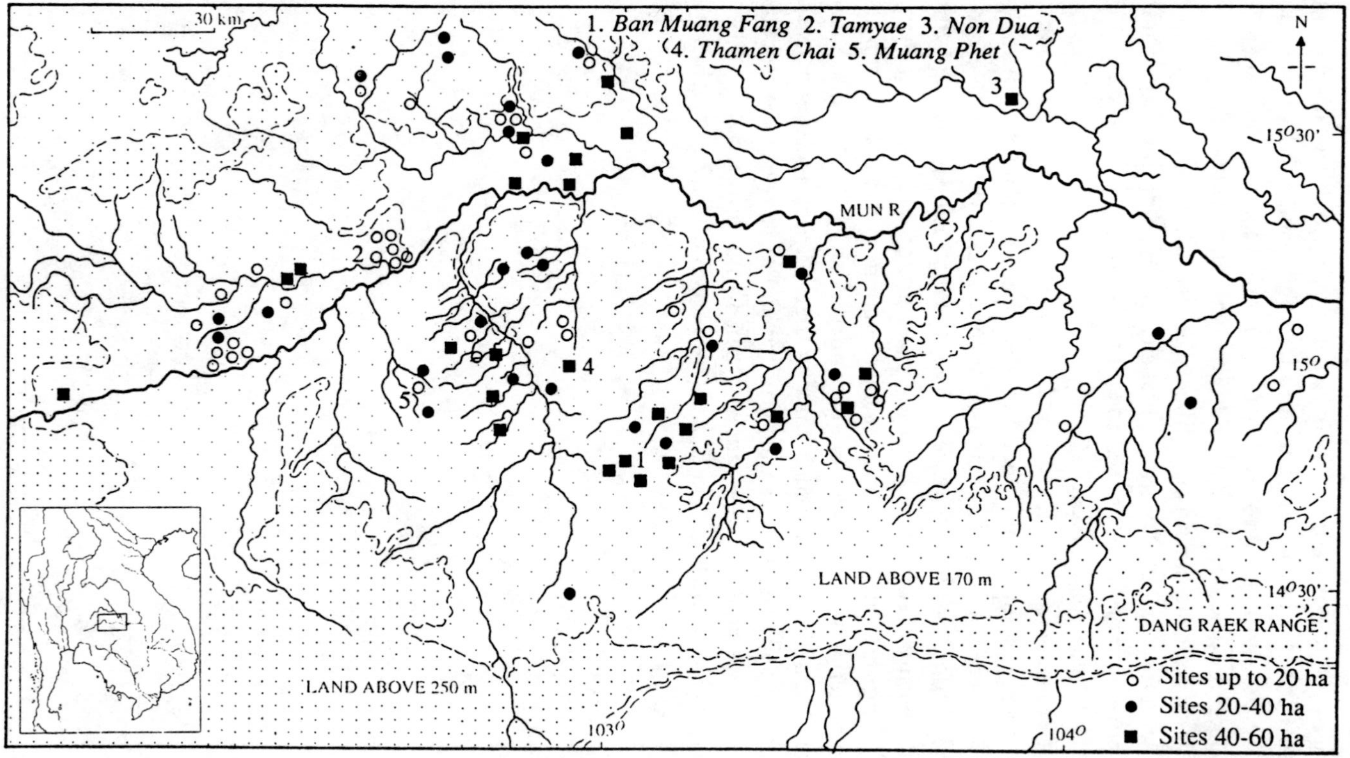

4.21 The location of the moated sites in the Mun valley on the basis of size.

used as a burial ground for infants. Their remains were found in lidded urns, associated with artefacts of bronze and iron and, in one case, with five blue-glass beads. There are also miniature bronze bracelets and iron knives, and a socketed iron tip for a digging stick very similar to those found at Ban Don Ta Phet. The iron implements were coated with the remains of rice which survived through impregnation with iron oxide. The grave ritual clearly distinguished between the area used for burying infants as opposed to adults, a distinct departure from the earlier level 6 and 7 cemetery phase.

The range of artefacts found in levels 4 and 5 also differs. There were no more clay figurines. Shell-disc beads and shell bracelets were no longer evident, and most of the beads were now made of orange or blue glass. Although a few iron artefacts were found in two level 6 graves, levels 4 and 5 yielded iron slag which indicates local smelting of iron ore. One of the most impressive indices of change is Vincent's finding that the pottery was made from a new clay source, and that the tempering material was quite different from the earlier tradition (Vincent 1984). This new temper was prepared by mixing together rice and clay balls and lightly firing them. The material was then crushed and mixed with the raw clay. Wichakana (1984) has analysed the range of rim forms in all layers and has identified a major change with the transition from levels 6 and 7 to 5. The body

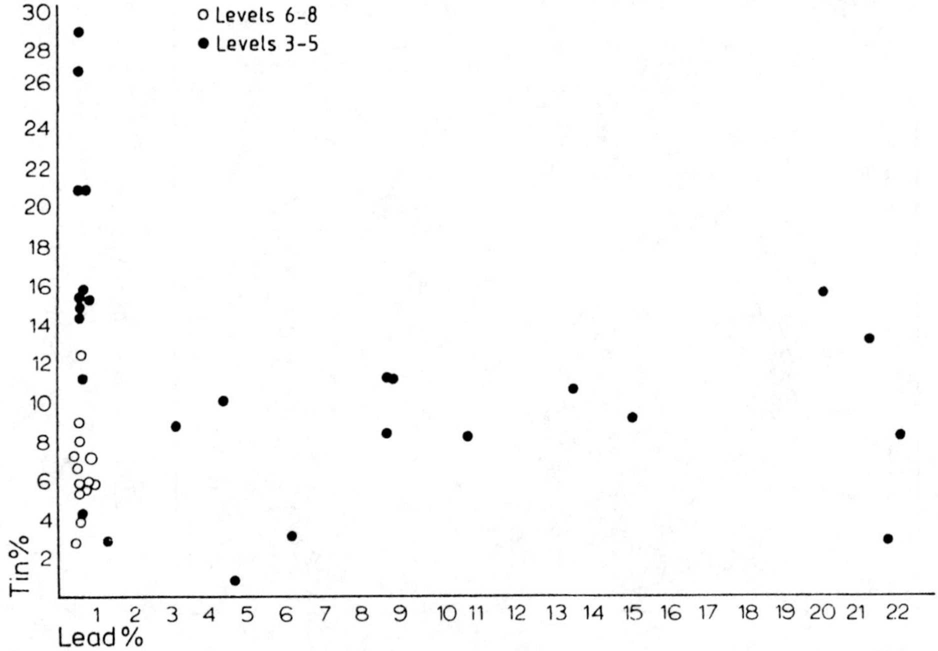

4.22 Scatter plot of the lead-tin ratio from Ban Na Di bronzes. With General Period C, the variation in the chosen alloys became far greater than during General Period B.

decoration also changed from a preference for plain or cord-marked wares to red-slipped or red-on-buff painted designs.

The replacement of a cemetery by a bronze-working atelier, and the clarity of associated changes in material culture, poses the question of whether we are dealing with the replacement of one group of people by another. Before considering this issue, it is necessary to enquire whether a similar change occurred at other sites in the area. Three sites have provided some useful information. One is Ban Muang Phruk, which is located 10 km southwest of Ban Na Di, and only 2.5 km from the present dry-season bank of Lake Kumphawapi. A small excavation there, in 1980, revealed stratigraphy to a depth of 3.6 m. The basal cultural layer contained pottery – the rims, temper and surface decoration of which closely match that from levels 4 and 5 at Ban Na Di (Wichakana 1984). There is no hint there of any pottery reminiscent of the level 6 and 7 assemblage from Ban Na Di. Only 1 km east of Ban Muang Phruk, there is a cluster of small mounds. One has been investigated and was found to have built up as a result of salt extraction. The basal layer contains some red-slipped pottery and has been dated to the first couple of centuries A.D. This suggests that salt-working, using the same techniques as at Bo Phan Khan in the lower Chi, was underway at about the same period. Finally, we can return to Ban Chiang. The first mortuary evidence for the knowledge of iron has been dated to the course of MP VII (800 to 400 B.C.). There followed a major dislocation in both burial ritual and many aspects of material culture (White 1986), changes recognised by the transition from the Middle to the Late Period. The earliest iron artefacts there (MP VII) comprise two bimetallic spears, the hafts in bronze and the blades in iron (Fig. 4.23). Very similar artefacts have been found in Dong Son contexts. Stech and Maddin (1986) have shown that the iron blades were forged and the bronze sockets later cast on. One iron specimen from Ban Chiang has a relatively high carbon content along the edge which hints that it was deliberately hardened. Iron became more abundant in graves assigned to the Late Period. This period was also defined on the basis of major changes in pottery styles, the new ware being both red-slipped and painted with red designs on a buff background. This much publicised "Ban Chiang Painted Pottery", which has now been dated between 300 – 1 B.C., bears

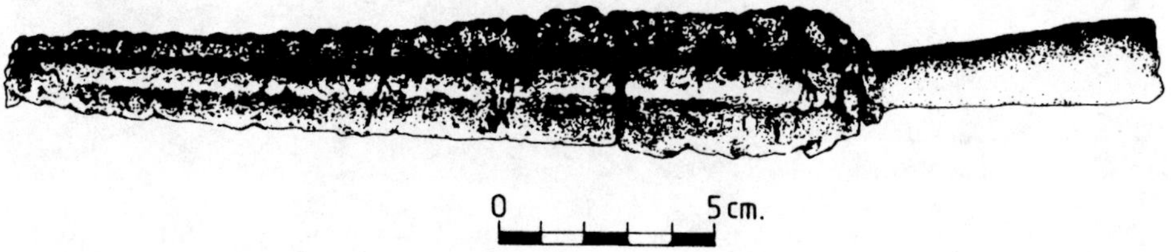

4.23 The two bimetallic spearheads from Ban Chiang Middle Period VII are of uncertain status. Do they evidence a local and indigenous iron-working tradition or were they prestige imports from Bac Bo?

decorative patterns of great beauty. Motifs include curvilinear and spiral designs, and representations of humans, animals and insects (Figs. 4.24 and 4.25). There are clusters of burials at Ban Chiang, in particular in squares excavated by Suthiragsa and Gueagoon, in which numerous red-on-buff pots were found associated with clusters of burials. In the 1974–5 campaigns, however, they were very rare. It is possible that these pots were employed in display and ceremonial activities. Certainly, some of the vessel forms, allied with their elaborate decoration, are compatible with this interpretation. No detailed petrographic analyses have yet been undertaken on a reasonable sample of Ban Chiang Late Period pottery, although two pots have been looked at in detail (McGovern, Vernon and White 1985). The surface collections of this red-on-buff pottery made during the Kumphawapi survey in 1980–1, however, certainly belong to the same ceramic tradition as the material recovered from levels 4–5 at Ban Na Di.

The Late Period graves are associated with a range of goods which find close parallels with the level 4–5 finds at Ban Na Di. We find, for example, the same clay rollers or seals (Fig. 4.26). These have a hole running down the centre, and the exterior surfaces have been excised to form coupled geometric and curvilinear designs. The wear pattern noted in the holes, as well as the survival of fragments

4.24 The Late Period painted pottery from Ban Chiang represents one of the outstanding achievements of the prehistoric Southeast Asian craftsman. It is seen as an example of the interest in conspicuous display which characterises General Period C societies. This specimen, recovered during the 1975 excavations, stands about 30 cm high.

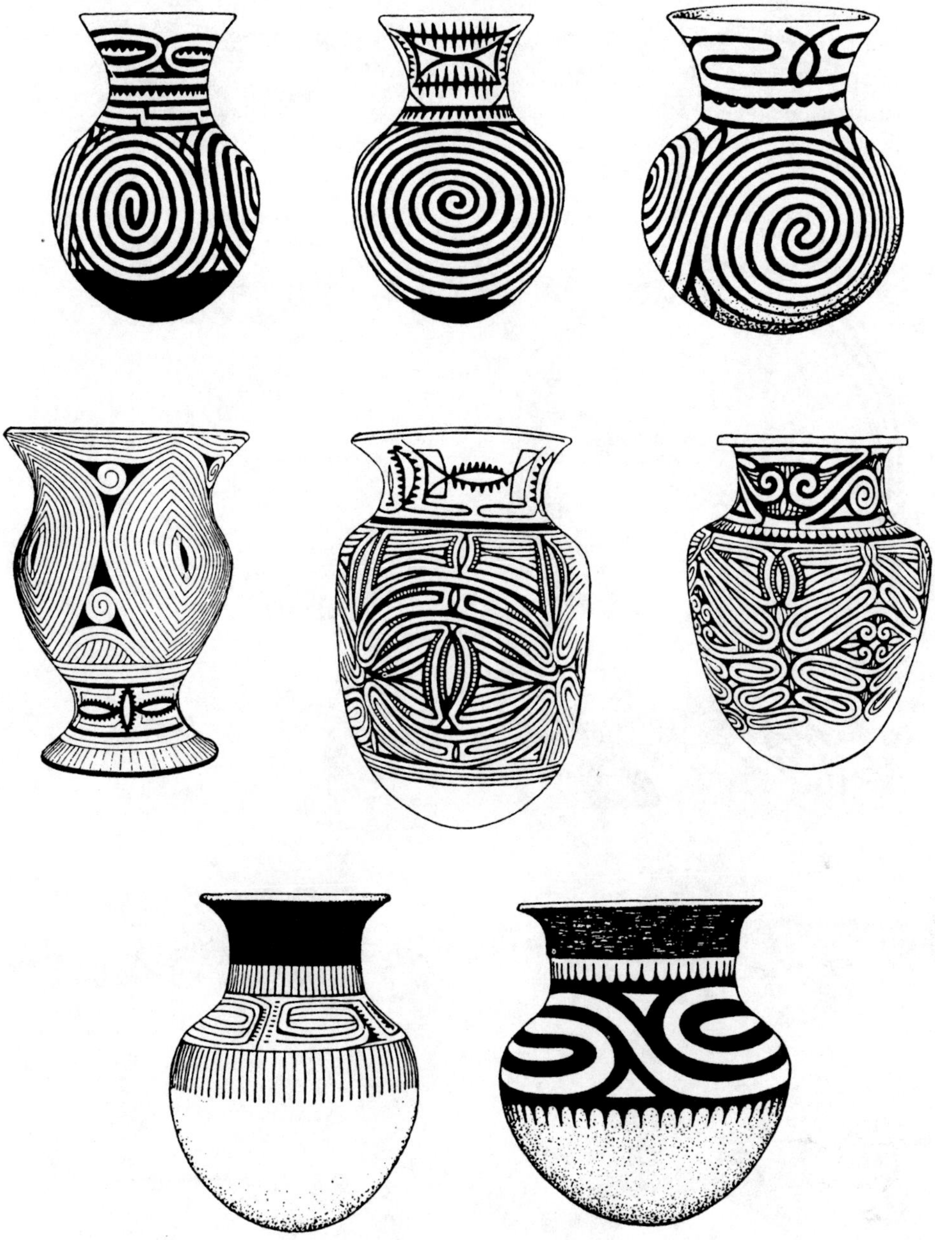

4.25 There is a great variety of decorative motifs in the Late Period painted pottery from Ban Chiang. Height dimensions are top row, l-r: 35 cm, 45 cm, 40 cm; middle row, l-r: 25 cm, 50 cm, 50 cm; and bottom row, l-r: 35 cm and 30 cm. On some occasions, numerous such vessels were placed over human interments and they may well symbolise high rank. (Courtesy P. Van Esterik and *Asian Perspectives*.)

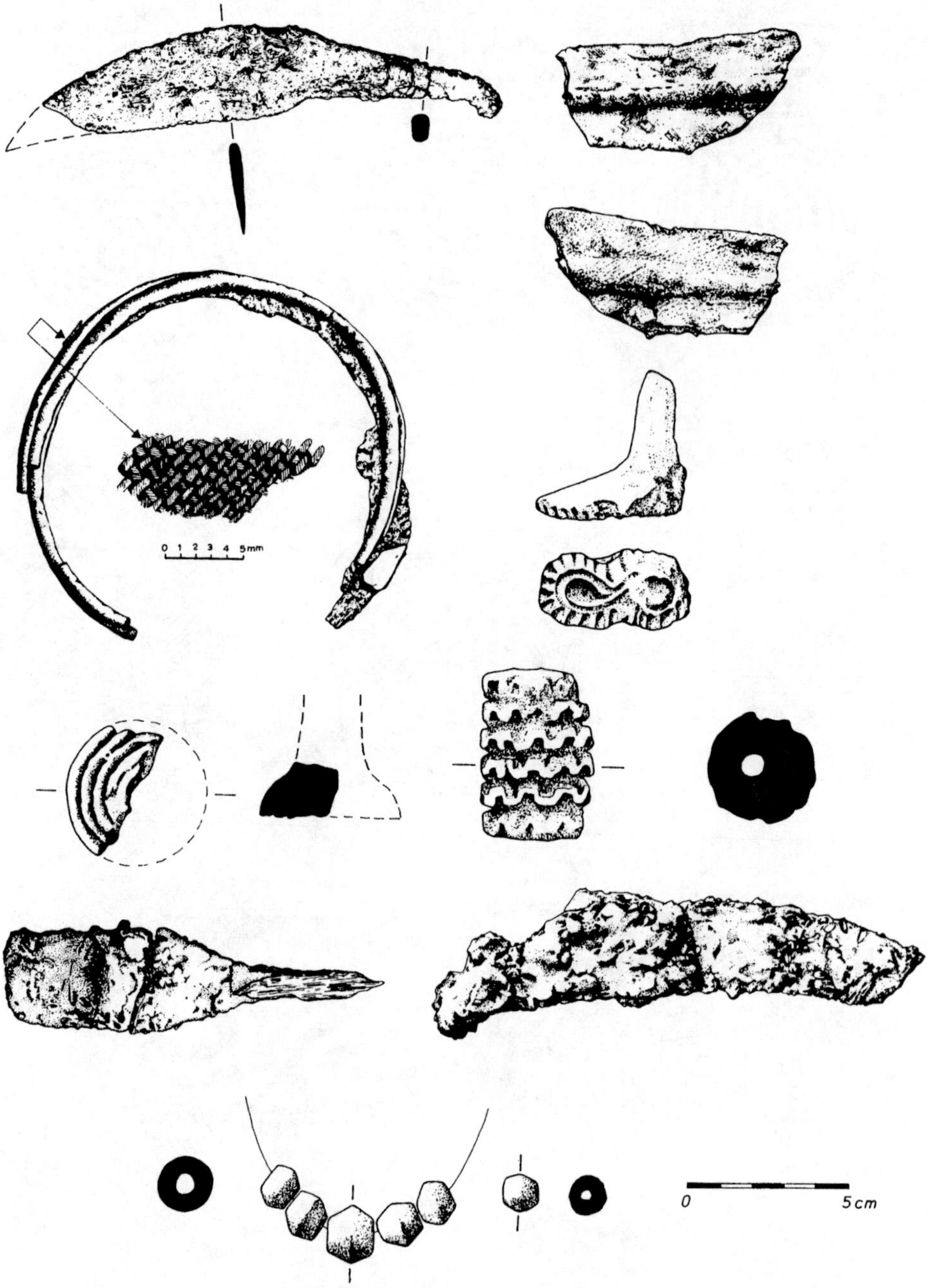

4.26 The material culture from Ban Na Di levels 4–5 shows a marked and pervasive change from earlier contexts. This was heralded by the iron rings, knife and spear-blade seen uppermost, which come from a very late part of the main mortuary phase at the site. Iron then became much more abundant. In this illustration, we can also see clay "seals" and imported glass beads.

of silken cord, suggest suspension. They have been variously interpreted as being rollers to impart patterns onto cloth, as cylinder seals to impress an ownership mark on a plastic medium, such as clay, and as tokens for recording the transfer of goods between centres linked by exchange (Van Esterik and Kress 1978, Folan and Hyde 1980, Higham and Kijngam 1984). Since they have a convex outer surface, and would require fresh inking with every revolution, their use for stamping patterns onto cloth seems unlikely. Their use as a seal or symbol of ownership is also supported by the discovery at Ban Na Di of similarly ornamented seals provided with handles. The Late Period graves also include glass beads, paralleled at Ban Na Di, and the same high tin bronze identified at Ban Don Ta Phet and Ban Na Di was used in the manufacture of a Late Period necklace. This would have demanded high technological skill, and the end product would have been recognisably different from those made of an alloy with less tin (Stech and Maddin 1986). The Ban Chiang burials are still being subjected to laboratory analysis and many questions remain open. Not least is the possibility that the skeletons associated with the Late Period exhibit differences in bone shape consistent with a new population. At present, however, enough is known to support the contention that the Late Period at Ban Chiang is contemporaneous with, and similar, to the major change noted at Ban Na Di, with the transition to level 5.

The next question is whether or not these changes were restricted to the confines of the Kumphawapi survey area. At Don Klang (Fig. 4.4), Schauffler noted that an early horizon of burials was superceded by a level containing painted pottery, glass beads and iron artefacts, some of which were steeled to impart a tough and keen cutting edge (Pigott and Marder 1984). One later pit was filled with several skulls of the water-buffalo. The use of the Non Nok Tha cemetery probably came to a close before iron was generally available in the region, and no burials contain the red-on-buff painted wares recognised at Don Klang, Ban Chiang and Ban Na Di. A broader pattern is also evident from Penny's finding that the initial occupation of a series of sites in the western margins of the Khorat plateau date to the first millennium B.C. Glass beads and iron were identified at one of these sites, known as Ban Phuan Phu (Penny 1982, 1984). These discoveries at individual sites all contribute to a pattern, which cannot be ignored. Some sites in the middle and lower Chi and the Mun valleys grew differentially large. They may well have been provided with moats and walled defences during this period, but as yet there is no evidence for this. The reservoir at Ban Chiang Hian suggests that it was necessary to assure a water supply for a large populace. Iron weapons and tools are found, and glass beads were favoured. There is a consistent thread of evidence in favour of population growth and movement. The same conclusions have resulted from Moore's (1986) consideration of the sites in the Mun valley. She has suggested on typological grounds rather than on the basis of excavated material, that the sites there reflect an expansion of settlement into the surrounding middle-terrace areas. Water

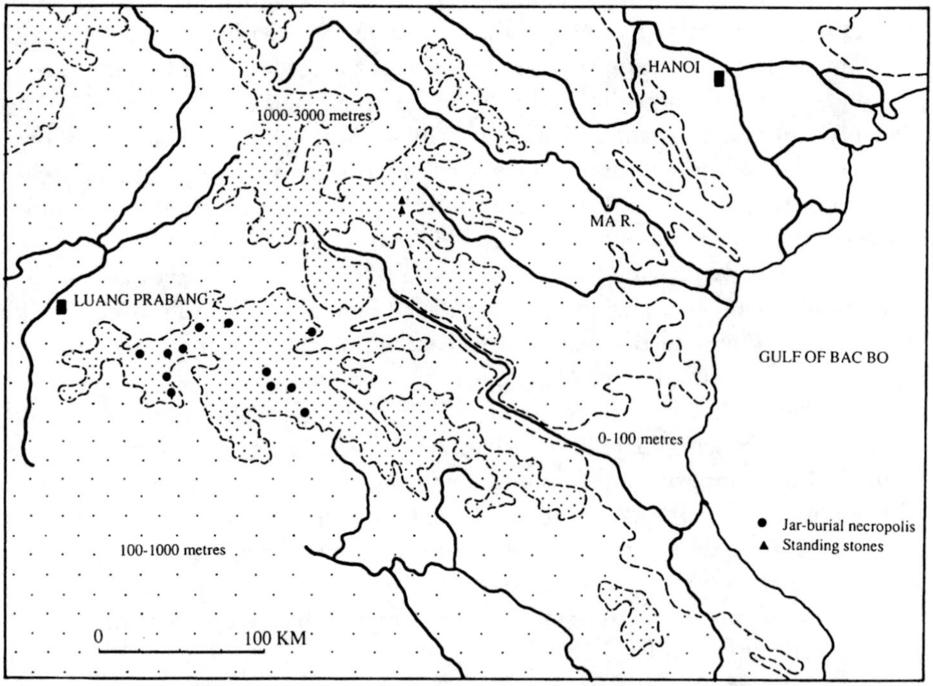

4.27 The distribution of the jar burials in upland Laos was seen by Colani (1935) as reflecting control over exchange routes and commodities, particularly in salt.

conservation measures became more intensive in this new environment, but the benefits included access to iron ore and the necessary reserves of timber for smelting.

The uplands of Laos

Hitherto, our consideration of domestic communities during General Periods A, B and C has been confined to the lowlands. Fifty years ago, however, Colani (1935) undertook fieldwork in the uplands comprising the northern Truong Son cordillera, specifically to enlarge our knowledge of a series of sites there characterised by large stone burial jars and free-standing stone slabs or "menhirs". Only with the recovery of glass and metal artefacts in the Khorat basin sites during the last few years, has it been possible to appreciate the date and cultural affiliations of the upland groups (Fig. 4.27).

The most impressive, and perhaps the most complete of these sites is known as Ban Ang (Figs. 4.28 and 4.29). It is located at an altitude of just over 1000 m, and overlooks an extensive area known as the Plain of Jars. This site is dominated by a central hill within which Colani identified and excavated a prehistoric crema-

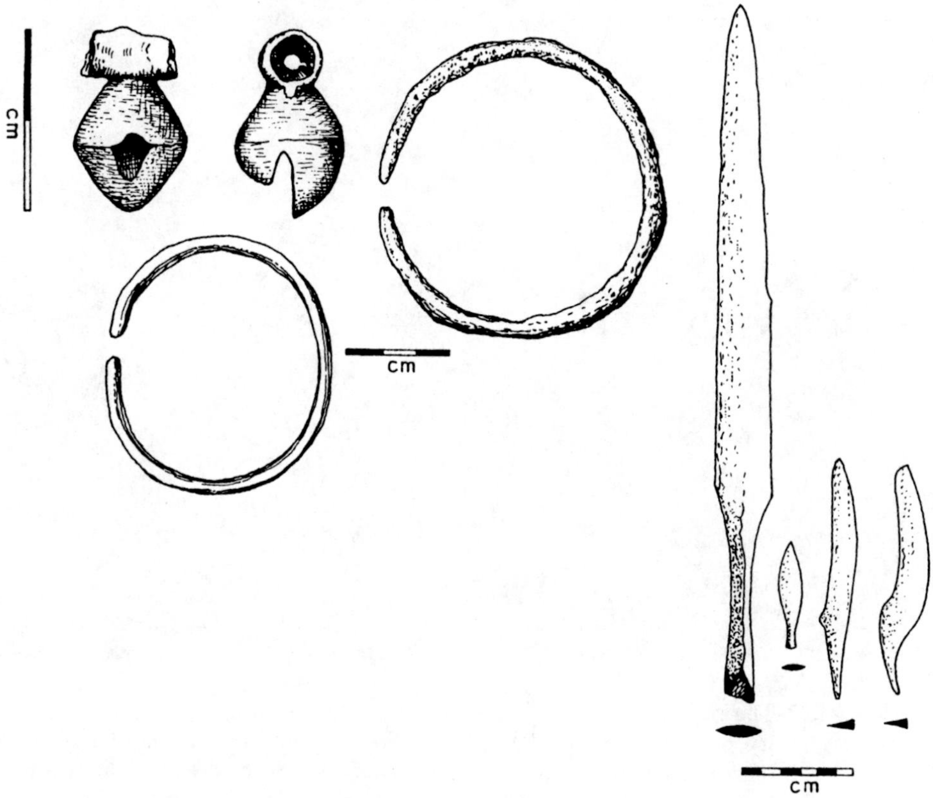

4.28 The material culture from Ban Ang.

torium. There were two groups of burial jars in its vicinity, one on a raised area which Colani ascribed to a ruling group. She found a richer set of grave goods there than in the other rather larger assemblage of jars. The burial offerings found at Ban Ang and, indeed, in the other related sites, include glass and carnelian beads, cowrie shells of coastal origin, bronze helices, bells and bracelets, as well as iron knives, arrowheads and spearheads. The presence of clay mould fragments reveals local bronze-casting, while iron slag is evidence for the local working of iron as well. Of course, some of the metal artefacts could also have been imported.

The parallels with these artefacts (Fig. 4.28) are Period C in the Khorat plateau sites, although one bronze figurine recalls Dong Son traditions of metal-working. A date in the region of 300 B.C. – A.D. 300 is consistent with the material found in and around the stone mortuary jars. Explaining the origins of the people in question, and how they disposed of the manpower to move and shape such impressive stone funerary monuments is not so easy. Colani may well be correct in suggesting that these people were placed to control exchange routes between Southern China, Bac Bo and the burgeoning chiefdoms of the Khorat

4.29 The rolling uplands of Laos were strategically placed to control the salt trade during General Period C. Here, at Ban Ang, is one of the major mortuary complexes centred on the cremation of the dead and interment in large stone jars.

area. She also noted that the uplands in question are, to this day, a major source for salt. Indeed, control of the salt trade may well have provided the resources for the importation of exotic goods from some considerable distance.

The Vietnamese coastal plains

Cremation is an unusual burial technique in prehistoric Southeast Asia, and Colani may be correct in relating the occupants of upland Laos to the so-called Sa Huynh group (Fig. 4.30). The discovery of the relevant sites along the littoral of Central Viet Nam occurred in 1909, when a French customs official, M. Vinet, encountered a collection of urns containing human cremated remains at Thanh Duc, near the village of Sa Huynh. This site was further examined by two amateur archaeologists, and the first professional consideration was given by Henri Parmentier (Parmentier 1918a). By then 120 jars had been unearthed over an area measuring 80 by 50 m, and they were found to be grouped, and to contain cremated human remains in association with a range of grave goods. This Sa Huynh burial practice stands out in Southeast Asia. While it is true that jar burial occurred in Northeast Thailand during General periods A, B and C, it was

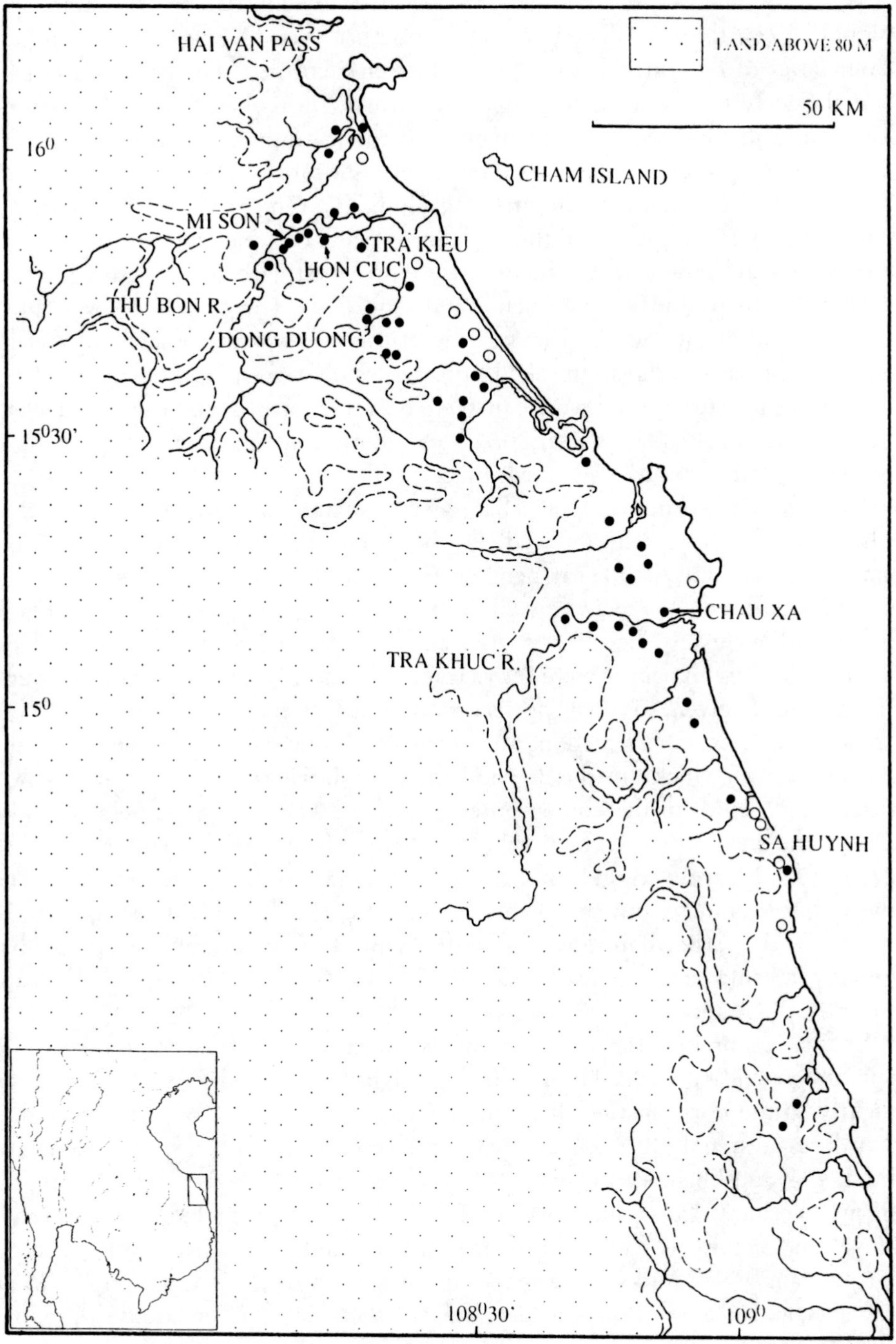

4.30 Map showing the major Sa Huynh sites (hollow circles) in contrast to the later sites of the Cham *maṇḍalas*.

reserved for infants, and the body had never been subjected to cremation. Yet, along the coastal tract almost from the mouth of the Mekong to the southern boundaries of Bac Bo, this burial rite has been identified. The large and elegant burial vessels usually contain a range of offerings. Moreover, the charcoal associated with the cremated human remains and concentrations found in the vicinity of the vessels are unusually good sources of radiocarbon samples. Saurin (1963) has described such an urnfield at Hang Gon. The cemetery covered an area of about 100 by 50 m, the lips of the burial urns being between 0.2 and 1.0 m below the present ground surface. The urns were provided with covers, but contained no bone, perhaps due to locally acidic soil conditions. There was, however, much charcoal and burnt soil. A characteristic of this site was the practice of ritually breaking burial offerings. Smashed pottery vessels were placed inside the large urns. Polished stone adzes were damaged, bowls deformed, and even the sockets of iron axes broken. However, small and durable items of jewellery, such as ear-pendants and beads, remained intact.

Some beads of imported carnelian, agate, olivine and zircon were found at Hang Gon, as well as blue and red glass beads and a solitary bead of gold. There was also a distinctive stone ear-pendant representing a double-headed animal, of a type also found at Sa Huynh itself, in Bac Bo Dong Song contexts, at Ban Don Ta Phet in the lower Chao Phraya area, and on Palawan Island in the Philippines. That the Sa Huynh people were active traders has been long documented through the attention given to their pottery and other artefacts by Solheim (1959). Iron-working is represented in the form of slag as well as implements, the commonest of which are the axe and the sword. There are three radiocarbon dates which confirm the contemporaneity of the Hang Gon urnfield with the Dong Son sites further to the north. One sample from within a jar was dated to 275±150 B.C., and a second from around the same vessel was 403±150 B.C. The third sample comes from an organic residue in a vessel, and is dated to 98±150 B.C. Slightly earlier dates, as well as the same type of double-headed animal ornament, came from the nearby site of Phu Hoa (Fontaine 1972). The dates are 493±140 B.C. and 768±290 B.C.

Vietnamese prehistorians have recently concentrated their efforts on enlarging our understanding of Sa Huynh in the original area of discovery, as well as slightly to the north in the Thu Bon valley. Ha Van Tan (1980) has concluded that the richest and most informative of the recently examined sites is Tam My. Trinh Can and Pham Van Kinh (1977) have recovered large funerary urns there. Again, the burial goods included artefacts made of iron, including spearheads, knives and sickles, as well as bronze spearheads and bells. There is also a stone ear-pendant which looks like a more complex form of those found in Go Mun contexts, and at Khok Phlap in Thailand. In 1980, Ha Van Tan could still report that the origins of this Sa Huynh culture remained an enigma. To a certain extent, this remains true, but Ngo Si Hong has since suggested that the familiar urnfields, with their iron implements and exotic beads, have a long ancestry along the coasts and the hinterland of Central Viet Nam. He cites the excavations at the occupation site of Long Thanh, near Sa Huynh, and Binh Chau. As we have seen, these sites document occupation of what was later to become the focus of Sa Huynh activity and, interestingly, Long Thanh has yielded the remains of burials in oval urns (Ngo Si Hong 1985).

Whether or not the classical Sa Huynh material developed largely from these earlier contexts, or was the result of settlement by Austronesian speakers from island Southeast Asia, remains one of the most fascinating issues in the prehistory of the region.

In any event, the Sa Huynh sites confirm that the second half of the first millennium B.C. saw a string of communities occupying favourable coastal tracts along the shores of Central Viet Nam. By that juncture, there was a widespread use of iron, and an exchange system incorporating exotic glass and stone jewellery. This is precisely the region which, five centuries later, entered history with a Cham-speaking state heavily under the influence of Hinduism. Is it not likely, that the singularity of the urn burial rite and the Cham language reflect the same Austronesian population? There is some supporting evidence for this supposition. When the Chinese described the Cham burial rite, we find that the dead were placed in urns the quality of which varied with the status of the deceased incumbent. The remains were then consigned to the sea.

The transition from autonomy to centrality

There is evidence in each of the lowland tracts covered above, as well as in upland Laos, for major and contemporaneous cultural changes. Before the mid first millennium B.C., settlements covered about the same area, and were, it is argued, autonomous. Thereafter, centres developed which are seen as foci of craft specialisation and more concentrated and intensified production. During the former period, bronze-working was adopted within the small village communities, which had already an established practice of exchange in exotic artefacts. These have been described as primitive valuables, and they underwrote the maintenance of economic, social and political relationships between participating communities. It is argued that the exchange of valuables, and the establishment of affinal ties, promoted alliance. Imbalance, or fluctuations in access to valuables, involved oscillations in rank. Within such a system, much devolves upon the leaders of dominant lineages. They had superior access to prestige valuables, could foster affinal relationships, and play an entrepreneurial role in the transfer of goods.

The distribution of stone, marine shell and metals, the principal surviving materials documenting such exchange, reflects goods crossing the landscape along a variety of routes and in different directions. Further research will surely illuminate the former existence of inter-linked exchange networks with major concentrations in, for example, the Chao Phraya catchment, the Mekong valley and the maritime tracts of Viet Nam. It was, it is held, exactly along such nodes, particularly in the last two networks, that knowledge of bronze travelled. The system was also internally flexible with regard to permanence of rank. It is worth pausing to review such flexibility, as it will sharpen our perception of the transition to centrality.

The sites, during General Period B, were located in small stream valleys and along the margins of the main river floodplains. The technique of rice cultivation probably involved the exploitation of enclaves of land subjected to only a limited degree of flooding following the onset of the monsoon. However, climatic unpredictability involving drought, in some years, and major flooding in others, would doubtless have prejudiced predictable success in the rice harvest. The broad-ranging subsistence activities would, accordingly, have been a valuable buffer against the effects of climatic extremes. At the same time, however, intensifying production to permit participation in a prestige-good exchange system would have come more readily to those commanding the most extensive tracts of cultivable land. Indeed, for many river valleys, good land and communications were their only major resource: there were no local deposits of ore, stone or marine shell. There are, then, conditions under which certain communities might prosper unduly. Among these may be numbered access to a circumscribed resource, be it salt, copper, tin or good land; control over a strategic position such as a mountain pass or river crossing; or a monopoly, through the fortunes of geography, over access to prestige exotic goods such as glass beads, iron or agate jewellery.

The transition to General Period C, with its establishment of highly ranked groups in centres underwritten by intensified production and exchange, represents the growth to prominence of one settlement and its occupants over others within its orbit. In Bac Bo, we can isolate several variables which were intensified, though this area is a special case given its direct contact with Chinese expansion. In terms of agriculture, there was the advent of ploughing and double cropping. As Goody has shown, the application of animal traction to soil preparation greatly magnifies production and thereby makes it more feasible to produce surplus food (Goody 1976). A rice surplus can be employed to attract and maintain followers, thereby concentrating people. It may also be converted, through provisioning specialists, into visible status objects, not least the great ceremonial drums, situlae, body plaques and, in terms of prowess, daggers, swords and axe halberds. On the domestic scene, we can also note the elaborate decoration applied to houses, a decoration matched on the impressive boats (Figs. 4.8 and 4.9). A further and most significant application of a food surplus lies in the provision of feasts. This aspect of ceremonial and ritual behaviour is often overlooked by prehistorians, due, perhaps, to the difficulty of identifying its presence. In the case of the Dong Son material culture, however, it is clear that the large, ornamented, bronze vessels were intended for display. It is a widespread phenomenon, that a means of attaining high rank and prestige lies in providing sumptuous displays of food not so much for eating as for admiring (Wilson, in press). This relationship has been succinctly described by Evans-Pritchard in the context of the Azande:

> The more the wives the more the labour and the more the food; the more the food the greater the hospitality the greater the following; the greater the following the greater the prestige and authority. (Evans-Pritchard 1971:223.)

This sequence of events is no less applicable to the situation in Bac Bo during General Period C, except that it is necessary to substitute water control and the plough in place of women in agricultural production.

There was also a great proliferation of skill on the part of the Dong Son smith, and much more metal was mined, moved and shaped. It is self-evident that the organisation and purpose of all this activity, involving as it did the maintenance of permanent ateliers and control over far-flung ore sources, involved intensification. In this manner, permanent ranking of an elite, craft specialisation and intensified agriculture may well have interacted with each other (Fig. 4.31). Nor must it be forgotten that the Dong Son aristocrats controlled the maritime and riverine routes which exposed Bac Bo first to the importation of Chinese goods, as seen in some of the offerings contained in the Viet Khe boat burial, and then to the admission of Chinese armies.

There is a consistent body of evidence that the use of iron and importation of glass and exotic stone beads took place along the coasts of Central Viet Nam, in the Chao Phraya area, and even on the inland Khorat plateau, during the last few centuries of the first millennium B.C. In this last area, although shielded from Chinese contact by the Truong Son range and remote from immediate, coastal

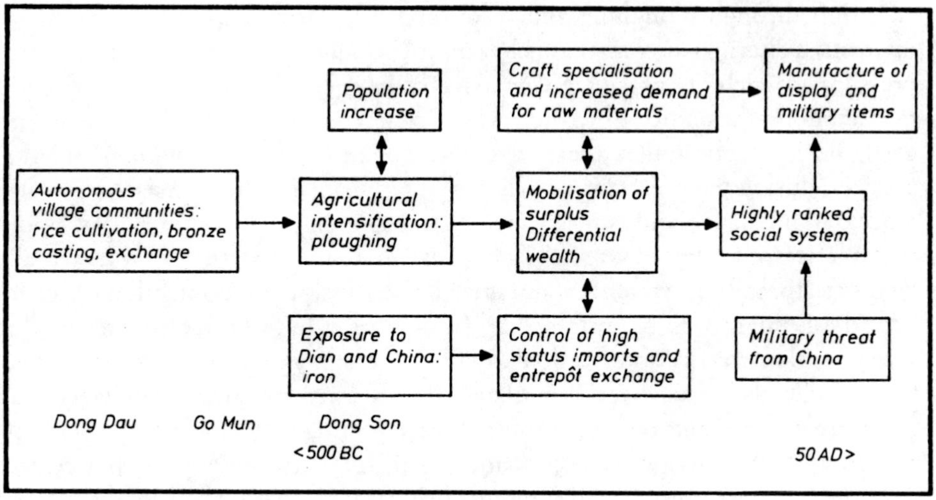

4.31 A scheme linking variables in explaining the origins of complexity during the Dong Son phase.

contact with Indian expansion, Non Chai, on the Khorat plateau, still grew to cover at least 18 ha, and during its occupancy (*c* 400 B.C.–200 A.D.), witnessed the use of iron and importation of exotic glass beads. At Ban Na Di, after the initial presence of a few iron objects in two graves, local iron-smelting was initiated during the build-up of level 5. Higham and Kijngam (1984) have suggested that the major changes noted at Ban Na Di and Ban Chiang, signalled by the advent of red-painted pottery and associated artefacts, reflects the expansion of groups from the fringes of the emergent Chi valley chiefdoms. The same conclusion has been reached by Moore in her consideration of the Mun valley moated sites, where, for the first time, expansion into the higher country away from the low-lying marshes is documented. In this Mun valley context, the moated sites grew considerably larger than the villages of their autonomous predecessors and were, in all likelihood, centres where petty chieftains prospered on the basis of iron-working, the salt trade and increased agricultural production to sustain their followers. The control of water through substantial moats made this move a feasible proposition.

It has been suggested that increased agricultural production was, as in Bac Bo, based upon the buffalo-drawn plough and fixed fields demarcated by bunds (Higham and Kijngam 1979, Higham *et al.* 1981). In more recent publications, the presence of ploughing has been questioned because of the continuing lack of any artefactual evidence corresponding to that available in Bac Bo (Higham and Kijngam 1984). This last publication advocated an agricultural system where the naturally flooded margins of the major rivers were brought into production not necessarily through the medium of ploughing or fixed field creation. Of course, this situation would again alter were actual ploughs to be recovered from General Period C contexts there. In approaching this issue of possible agricultural intensification through ploughing and water control, Welch (1985) has offered the interesting alternative view that it began not so much in response to population pressure in enclaves of suitable marshy terrain, but rather to cope with the marked unpredictability of rainfall which characterises Northeast Thailand. Indeed, he is sceptical that there was ever an initial problem with population pressure during the prehistoric or historic periods in Southeast Asia. Since some aspects of intensified cultivation, such as transplanting, require increased labour at peak seasons of the year, Welch goes on to suggest that it was actually intensification itself which encouraged an expansion of population. Welch's hypothesis might well be sustained by future research, but it is also stressed that agricultural intensification, particularly the increasing importance of rice production, could also have been stimulated by a desire to attract followers, and therefore prestige and power, through lavish feasting behaviour. At present, we can point to various possible contributing factors. It does appear that centres developed, that iron tools and weapons proliferated, that populations grew and expanded and that new sources of prestige goods became available. At the same time, more attention was given to the production of beautiful and prestigious possessions. We are confronted by a complex series of changes, and the reasons are more likely to lie in several interacting shifts in behaviour.

The same phenomena of the growth of certain settlements (such as Ban Tha Kae) and employment of iron and imported jewellery, have been isolated in the Chao Phraya valley. These changes are seen here as consistent with the breakdown of the long-standing affinal alliance and exchange system between independent communities. Occupants of sites such as Non Chai and Phimai for example, had easy access to iron ore, and commanded nodal positions in the upper reaches of the major Khorat plateau rivers (Fig. 4.32). The Sa Huynh sites, likewise, were able to control coastal traffic. Any movement up the Chao Phraya River would involve passage through the territory of such growing centres as Ban Tha Kae. Several interacting variables can therefore be identified. Population growth and agricultural intensification are noted, and were doubtless interactive despite uncertainty over which came first. But the social change was critical in that it involved the growth of centres as foci of population and leadership. There is some archaeological evidence that these centres controlled the large-scale production of salt, exchange of exotic artefacts and the smelting of iron ore. It is proposed that these variables and their interactions reflect the flexibility and opportunism inherent in the system characterising General Period B, wherein those controlling the best tracts of agricultural land and access to a new range of exotic prestige goods enjoyed considerable advantages. In every instance of increased centralisation, there is a recurrent thread of evidence in favour of increasing ritual and display activity. The most impressive are the Dong Son bronze drums, weaponry, boat burials and personal ornamentation. But we also see the same trend in the Ban Don Ta Phet bowls and imported semi-precious

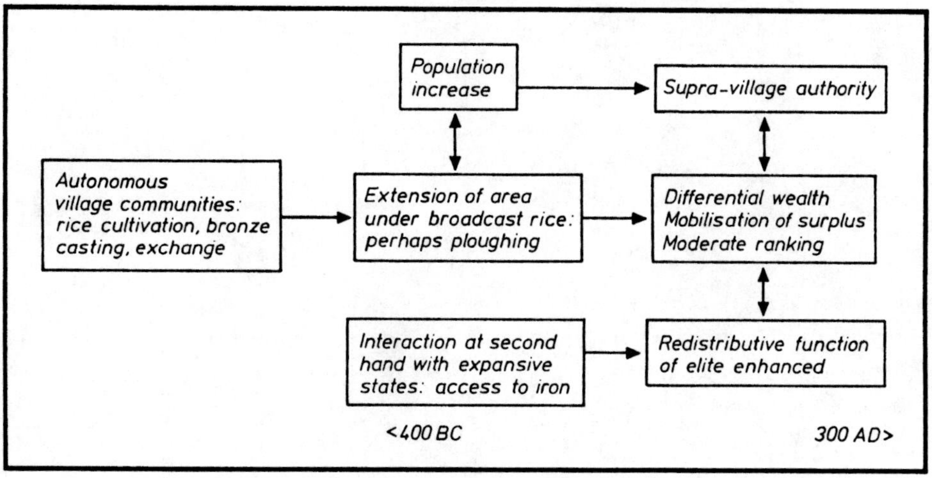

4.32 The relationships between variables in the Khorat plateau which probably influenced the trends towards centralisation characteristic of General Period C.

stone jewellery. In upland Laos, there is clear evidence for particular individuals being given opulent burials in huge stone jars. Along the coast of Viet Nam, jar burials included iron weapons, imported jewellery and beautifully worked burial urns. Even in the remote Songkhram valley, the potters of Ban Chiang made outstandingly beautiful painted vessels for inclusion in human graves. Intertwined in this model is the developing exposure to Indian and Chinese expansive forces. The sequel to this early contact is considered in the chapter below, during which General Period C will be linked not only with what went before it, but also with the subsequent development of considerably more complex centralised polities, which we shall term *maṇḍalas*.

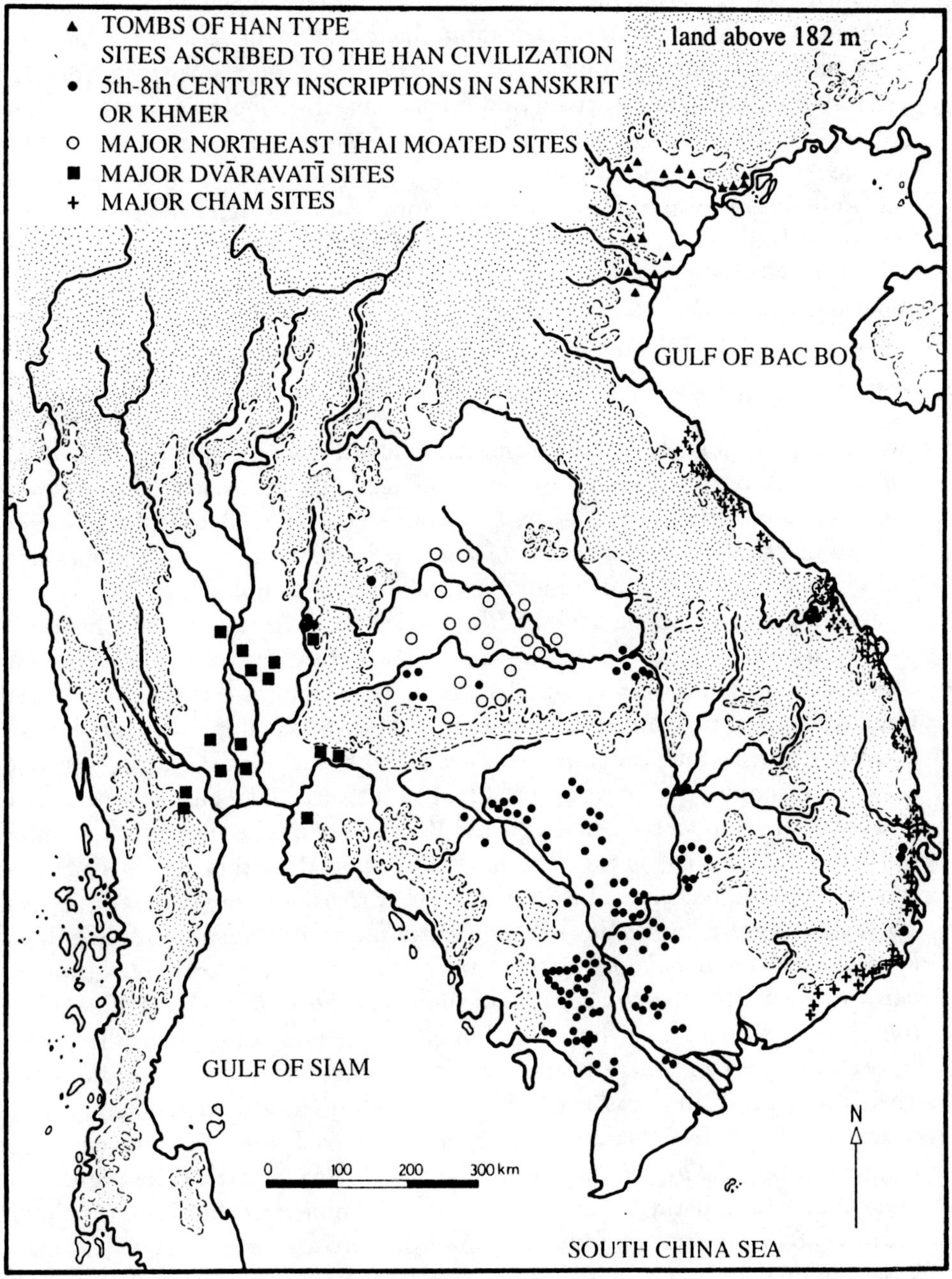

5.1 The distribution of the major *maṇḍalas* in mainland Southeast Asia.

and then seek their interactions? The latter course, which was followed by Renfrew (1972) under the term "the multiplier effect", will be adopted, because it is felt likely that the development of *maṇḍalas* reflects interrelated factors. It is likely that individual magnetism and attainment of divine qualities are factors. Can we, however, divorce our deliberations from the more mundane variables such as strategic location, soils, capacity for intensified production, and the availability of iron, all of which respond more readily to archaeological enquiry? To do so would be unwise, perhaps misleading. Consequently, it is proposed, later in this survey, to consider the interactions between different variables in order to explain the course of events.

India and China

Between approximately 300 B.C. and A.D. 300, the Southeast Asian chiefdoms, particularly those in coastal areas, were increasingly exposed to direct contact with Indian merchants and Chinese emissaries or armies. Before the growth of archaeological research, the origins of states in Southeast Asia was easily ascribed to Indian influence or Chinese invasion. While such simple ideas are no longer tenable, it is still acknowledged that the objectives of the Indian and Chinese are an important issue and need consideration. Historically, the Indian subcontinent during this period witnessed the rise of empires and their subsequent fragmentation into competing kingdoms. The principal participants usually claimed descent from the Indo–Aryans who invaded India during the mid-second millennium B.C., bringing with them the Sanskrit language and a body of oral traditions known collectively as the Vedas. During the ensuing millennium, small polities centred on royal dynasties developed, within which ritual and ceremony lay in the hands of the senior of four social groups (*varṇas* or classes). These priests were known as *brāhmaṇs*, after the word *brāhma*, meaning divine knowledge. The remaining three *varṇas* were known as *kṣatriyas* (nobles), *vaiśyas* (originally a person settled on the land) and *sūdras* (serfs). The critical role of the *brāhmaṇ* regarding kingship lay in his prerogative over the rites of consecration, but they also fulfilled advisory functions and acted as ministers. Their privileged status was marked by exemption from taxes, and by gifts or donations from those seeking merit. Sanskrit evolved into local languages, but was retained by the *brāhmaṇs* as the language of ritual and the sacred texts. The *brāhmaṇs*, who inherited their special status, administered the Hindu religion. There is no one central Hindu deity. Indeed, there are several major and many lesser Hindu gods each of which may manifest itself in several guises. During the first millennium A.D., Śiva and Viṣṇu were the principal deities. According to the Yogasūtra, which presented Yoga as the dominant form of religious expression at the time, devotees may achieve harmony with the god through supreme control of their physical and mental conditions. In a sense, such ascetic control over oneself endowed the worshipper with actual control over divine forces.

Hinduism was not alone in attracting devotees. Buddhism arose from the teachings of Gautama, the Buddha, or enlightened one. There is uncertainty over the dates of his birth and death, but his influence had its origins during the 5th century B.C. He taught in the vernacular Pāli in order to reach the masses to whom Sanskrit was the esoteric liturgical language of the *brāhmaṇ* elite. Neither religion was mutually exclusive, and their co-existence was accepted. It would be wrong to view the *brāhmaṇs* as concerned only with the court and religious ritual. As ministers, they played a central role, and the political theories they espoused and practiced were part of the intellectual heritage of the Indians who visited Southeast Asia. One of the most comprehensive tracts in political theory is reputed to have been set down by Kauṭilya, chief minister to Chandragupta Maurya who established the Mauryan Empire in *c* 325 B.C. His *Arthaśāstra* defined the state under seven heads: the king, his ministers, a territory, a fort, the treasury, an army and allies. The royal office entailed divine sanctions and the king, he argued, possessed a divine nature. His duties were largely paternal: to control crime through the legal system, to protect the people and to foster agriculture, industry and trade. Kauṭilya neatly summarised the very essence of statehood which is still reiterated by anthropologists, namely, the central authority, sustained by taxation and backed by coercion.

The encouragement of agriculture and trade was not an empty precept, since the collection of state revenues turned on their success. Kauṭilya himself advocated central participation in opening up new land to settlement, while both local and international trade were encouraged. The Mauryan Empire, however, was in decline by 150 B.C. and fragmented into regional kingdoms, a situation which prevailed until the emergence of the Kuṣāṇas in North India and the Sātavāhanas in the Deccan (1st century B.C. – 3rd century A.D.). The fall of the Mauryan Empire did not inhibit trade, and it is important that the mechanics of this exchange be appreciated. Indian merchants employed the prevailing winds to travel in both easterly and westerly directions. The latter was concerned with the Iranian and Graeco–Roman worlds, and was stimulated by increasing demands for oriental goods originating with the establishment of peace within the Roman Empire. The conduct of trade was facilitated by the use of currency based on silver and copper coinage, the use of the *Brāhmī* script by specialised merchant guilds in both eastern and western ports, and by the encouragement from merchant bankers who underwrote trading voyages and received interest on their investments. Roman involvement in Indian trade is mentioned in several writings, not least the *Periplus of the Erythraean Sea* (see Wheatley 1961). This compendium of useful information includes itineraries and a list of goods which made up the bulk of the traffic. We find that the Romans were interested in silks, pepper, pearls, ivory and textiles, while for their part the Indians took glass, copper, tin, lead, orpiment, wine, antimony and gold coins. The physical embodiment of this exchange system has been revealed by Wheeler's excavations at Arikameḍu (Wheeler 1955). This Indian site, which was probably the port of

Poduca cited in the *Periplus*, yielded Roman coins, pottery, beads, intaglios, lamps and glass.

If the Indian merchant guilds prospered on the western trade route, why not also in an easterly direction? The seasonal wind pattern across the Bay of Bengal reflects the regular rise and ebb of the monsoon, and maritime technology was well equipped to cope with the necessary distances. Moreover, their boats were large enough to handle at least 200 tons of cargo. The fact is that Indian merchant venturers did sail eastward in growing numbers, and their exploits were incorporated into Hindu epic literature. The fabled land beyond the sunrise is referred to in the Indian literature as *Suvarṇabhūmi*, or *Suvarṇadvīpa*, which meant "land of gold". Gold there was to be found, but the voyages were, according to the *Rāmāyana*, beset by storms and other perils.

While Indian vessels almost certainly reached Southeast Asia before the end of the first millennium B.C., it is probable that interest in the area intensified after the emperor Vespasian, who succeeded in 69 A.D., prohibited the export of gold coinage from the Roman Empire. This edict in itself indicates the drain on the empire's resources to make up for a trade deficit, and it is significant that the majority of Roman coins found in Indian contexts belong to the Julio–Claudian Dynasty. The first Indian merchants who traded with Southeast Asia came from a country with a sophisticated and mature tradition of statehood. They were familiar with the notion of a supreme monarch, and inherited the established role of the *brāhmaṇ* in both ritual and state administration. They visited Southeast Asia to sell, and to fill their holds, with trade goods. The seasonal pattern of the prevailing wind, in which nor'easters dominated between November and May, and southwest winds from May to November, meant that landfall in Southeast Asia lasted for some months. Among their passengers were numbered Hindu *brāhmaṇs* and Buddhist monks.

China also brought to Southeast Asia a mature tradition of statehood, but under quite different circumstances. As in India, China saw a series of centralised dynastic polities, with intervening periods of regional fragmentation and conflict. Between the end of the Zhou, and the unification under the Qin in 221 B.C., China witnessed the period of the Warring States. It was during this time of strife that iron became the predominant metal, with applications in both agriculture and warfare. The brief period of Qin rule, which saw the initial work on the Great Wall, was followed by over four centuries of relative internal peace under the Western and Eastern Han. The central authority set in train wars of territorial conquest in both the northwestern and southern border areas, which involved the incorporation within the empire of formerly independent or quasi-independent territories. This process impinged into Southeast Asia when the Red River delta was seized, and incorporated as a province or "commandery".

The end of the Han Dynasty saw the formation of the Southeast Chinese state of Wu in A.D. 222. This state was cut off from the northern trans-Asian trade route with the west by intervening states, a situation which fostered interest in a southern, maritime route on the part of the Wu and their successors, and the earliest surviving description of mainland Southeast Asia originated in a mission despatched by the Wu emperor. According to Wolters (1967), this visit was designed to gather intelligence on the proposed southern maritime route to India and, ultimately, Rome. Such visits, and reports by embassies to the Chinese court from Southeast Asian *maṇḍalas*, were incorporated into official histories of the succeeding Chinese dynasties. Whereas the Indian accounts of *Suvarṇabhūmi* are couched in vague allusions and romantic fables, the Chinese dynastic annals and geographic tracts belong to a tradition of scrupulous historic scholarship, and provide an invaluable corpus of source material. It must be noted, however, that many texts passed through more than one hand before being set down in their surviving form, and such recensions increased the possibility of errors.

Thus, at about the same juncture, the maritime peoples of Southeast Asia came under the direct influence of an expansive Chinese state and Indian mercantile exchange. We must now consider the impact of this contact.

Geographic regions which sustained *maṇḍalas*

Maṇḍalas waxed and waned, but we can discern regional foci. These were markedly riverine and lowland. Six areas will be considered. First, we will turn to the lower Mekong valley and delta, because it seems that this was among the first to witness *maṇḍala* formation. Although the area in question is now above the actual delta, we will refer to it as the delta region below (Fig. 5.2). Second, we will turn to the middle Mekong valley – that is the area between Phnom Penh and the Dang Raek mountains including the Tonle Sap plains. Third will be a consideration of the Chao Phraya valley. The fourth area comprises the Khorat plateau, with particular reference to the floodplains of the Mun and Chi rivers, and the fifth, is the coastal plain of Central Viet Nam, which witnessed the rise of Cham *maṇḍalas*. Finally, we will turn to Bac Bo, which, for most of the period under review, comprised the southernmost commanderies of the Chinese Empire.

Two sources of information have already been touched upon – the Chinese dynastic annals, and the Indian epic literature. To this we must now add the evidence of the archaeological record, and that obtained from an analysis of inscriptions. The evidence of both archaeology and epigraphy is uneven, and usually either partial or absent.

The lower Mekong and the delta: A.D. *c* 100–550

The lower reaches of the Mekong are flat, low-lying and prone to flooding (Fig. 5.2). Without human modification, the land behind the fringing mangrove belt would probably have been dominated by an open marshland flora, the high water-table and widespread floods inhibiting tree growth. Geographically, however, the area has at least two strategic advantages. In terms of east-west

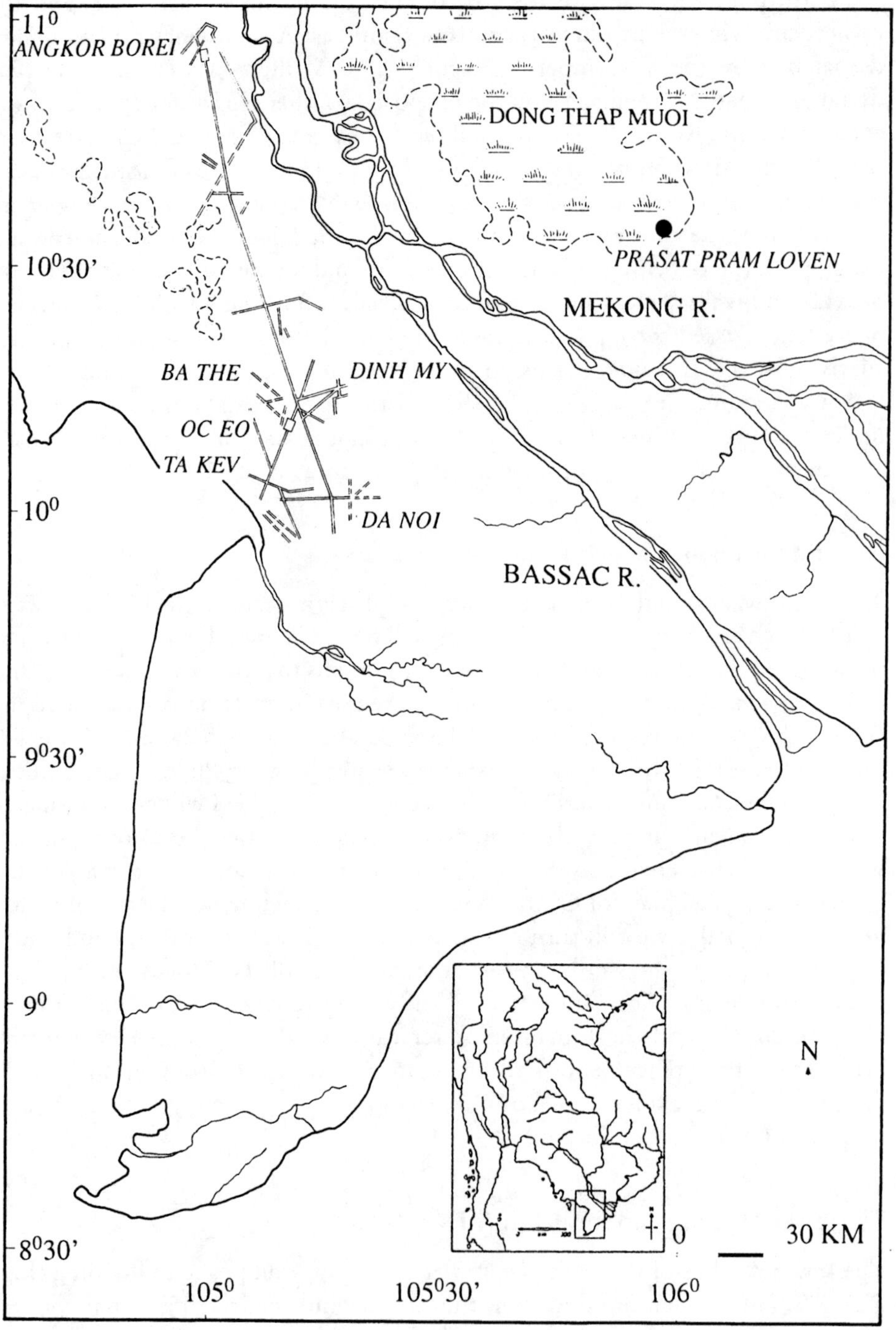

5.2 The principal sites and the canal system of the lower Mekong valley and delta.

exchange, it is a nodal point for transporting goods between the routes over the Malayo–Siamese isthmus and the coastal ports of Viet Nam and Southern China. The marshlands of the delta area are deficient in many of the raw materials which were in demand locally and for exchange, not least metal ores and forest products. The area was, however, able to control the flow of goods which were available via the Mekong valley, from a rich hinterland which extended across the plains of Central Cambodia and up to and beyond the Dang Raek range into the Khorat plateau. This hinterland was both rich in mineral wealth and, according to recent archaeological research, had been studded with agricultural villages whose occupants had used the Mekong valley as a route of exchange for millennia. It is important to appreciate that the impact of flooding from the Mekong is greatly alleviated by the peculiar drainage pattern into the Tonle Sap and, to a lesser extent, the Mun River. Such is the weight of water carried by the Mekong that a proportion flows back into the Tonle Sap. The Mun River also backs up when the Mekong is in spate. Consequently the flat deltaic land to the south is spared intense flooding and, once drained, is able to support the cultivation of rice.

A most important reference to the occupation of this area was contained in the reports of the emissaries Kang Dai and Zhu Ying, who visited the country in about A.D. 250. It was they who were sent by the Wu emperor to gather information about a southern trade route to India. Their accounts have long since been lost, but later writers quoted them at length. We are told that the traditional history of the area refers to a mythical ancestor known as Kauṇḍiṇya, an Indian, who married a local princess. He governed the country, and was succeeded by his male descendants. According to Pelliot (1903), this union must have taken place towards the end of the 1st century A.D. The *Liangshu* (History of the Liang Dynasty), which was compiled in the 7th century, noted that the founder of the local line of rulers gave his son authority over seven dependent settlements. This statement suggests a developing centralised authority structure. It was also put into practice by Hun Panhuang, one of the successive rulers of this early dynasty. Having attacked and conquered chiefs on the periphery of his domain, he installed his sons and grandsons in their place. His son, Pan Pan, had only a brief reign, and was succeeded by a leader of military prowess known to the Chinese as Fan Shiman. He undertook raids against his neighbours, and then mounted a water-borne expedition which subdued over ten chiefs traditionally situated along the shores of the Gulf of Siam. Of course, these vassals could equally have been chiefdoms located in the delta area itself. During the 25 years or so prior to the visit of Kang Dai and Zhu Ying, there was a series of dynastic assassinations by claimants to power, one of which was perpetrated on a son of Fan Shiman by another successful soldier, Fan Xun. This same period saw the first embassy to China, a visit which may have been precipitated by the visit of Kang Dai and Zhu Ying. Whatever the case, the Chinese went beyond allusions to dynastic friction and wars of conquest, and described the people as living in walled settlements which contained a palace. They stressed the importance of agriculture, and noted the local taste for engraving stones with chisels. There was a system of taxation, paid for in gold, silver, perfumes and pearls. The local people were also aware of Indian scripts. Indeed, the two Chinese encountered a representative of the Indian Murunda king on their visit. Clearly, Kang Dai encountered people who had already reacted to the arrival off their coast of exotic Indian traders.

The polity he described was known to the Chinese as Funan. According to the *Liangshu*, the next major stage in the Chinese history of Funan came during the 5th century, when a second Indian, also named Kauṇḍiṇya, was accepted by the Funanese as their ruler. This, again, is little more than the Chinese transcription of a local myth, though the *Liangshu* notes that this *brāhmaṇ* "changed the rules according to the customs of India". Some of these customs can be perceived on the basis of the inscriptions and archaeological evidence, and they set a trend which was maintained even during the classic period of Angkor (A.D. 802–1431). We find, for example, the adoption of the Sanskrit honorific title "– *Varman*". The literal meaning of this word is armour, and it may be translated as "protected by", or "protégé of". The preceding part of the name may refer to a particular Hindu god, or to a particular achievement. Thus, the name Mahendravarman means "protected by, or the protégé of, the great Indra", and Jayavarman means "protégé of victory". With the Sanskritisation of personal names came the Indian calendrical system and, most significantly, the establishment of local cults some of which incorporated such Indian gods as Śiva, Viṣṇu and the Buddha. Śiva was the Hindu god of change and fertility, and he was appropriately represented by a phallic symbol, known as a *liṅga*. The cult of the *liṅga*, whereby the representation of the phallus was perceived as the essence of the *maṇḍala*, engendered the power of shared belief, even on occasions when the ruler professed Buddhism. A less tangible innovation, but of no less importance, was the Indian legal system and science of politics. These are evidenced by allusions on the inscriptions and references to the raising of a statue of a bull, which symbolises Śiva. It is important to appreciate that the overlords were increasingly served by advisers versed in Indian statecraft.

The sequence of overlords following the accession of the second Kauṇḍiṇya, if indeed we are not again confronted with the Chinese version of another founding myth, is not known in detail, but some rulers sent embassies to China and their names have survived. Others are known from their inscriptions. Jayavarman was a major overlord who enjoyed a long reign. He was on the throne in 478 and remained so until at least A.D. 514. It is possible that Jayavarman was father of Guṇavarman, and sent him to the Dong Thap Muoi (Plain of Reeds) to reclaim marshland (see below). Another son, Rudravarman, seems to have usurped the throne through murdering his half brother. This event was followed by a waning in the power of this particular *maṇḍala*, and provided the impetus for a shift in the focus of major *maṇḍalas* to the middle reaches of the Mekong above Phnom Penh.

The practice of raising inscribed stelae began during the latter half of the period under review. This had been a widely adopted practice during the Mauryan Empire in India, and was particularly valued by the third king, Aśoka, as a means of informing his subjects on matters of policy. The few inscriptions which have survived in the delta area provide invaluable information. It is particularly interesting to note that the text often combined Sanskrit and archaic Khmer. One Sanskrit text was found at Prasat Pram Loven on the Dong Thap Muoi. It commemorates the consecration of a footprint of Viṣṇu by the Guṇavarman just referred to as possibly a son of Jayavarman. As is often the case with the inscriptions, it is the incidental information which is most interesting. In this case, we are informed that the prince was sent to reclaim land from the marsh. This was probably achieved by the excavation of drainage canals, which have survived to this day as a dominant feature of the archaeological landscape of the delta region. The inscription ends with a warning that "whoever subverts these gifts to their own use, will suffer with those guilty of the five great crimes". Now these great crimes in the Hindu canon included the murder of a *brāhmaṇ*, adultery with the master's wife, and complicity in the above. They are derived from Hindu law. A second Sanskrit inscription was found at Ta Prohm, as a re-used stone in an encircling wall of a later temple. It describes Rudravarman as a son of Jayavarman, the overlord who appointed the son of a *brāhmaṇ* as inspector of the royal property. Neither inscription carries a date, but on stylistic grounds, Coedès (1931) has assigned them to the early 6th century. They provide invaluable clues for the adoption of Indian inspired religious and legal practices and language. The names of the rulers are in Sanskrit, the reference to Hindu law is clear, and the role of a *brāhmaṇ* in administration is disclosed. Again, the reclamation of marshland recalls the precept of Kauṭilya, that the overlord should participate in land settlement to intensify production.

The documentary sources clearly describe an intensifying trend towards centralisation. It is most fortunate that Malleret undertook archaeological investigations in the very area before the worsening political situation intervened (Malleret 1959–63). For three months in 1944, he excavated at the site of Oc Eo (Fig. 5.3). This extraordinary site comprises a rectangular enceinte measuring 3 by 1.5 km. It lies behind five ramparts and four moats, and covers an area of 450 ha. Viewed from the air, Oc Eo is seen to be bisected by a large canal, off which tributary channels sub-divide the site into segments. Further enquiries undertaken before the second world war by French archaeologists have revealed that the canals of Oc Eo are but part of an extensive series which linked further settlements in this flat terrain into a network (Paris 1931, 1941a). Some canals reach seaward of Oc Eo, intimating that the site was set back from the shoreline but was still linked with it.

The excavations revealed foundations in stone and brick for impressively large structures (Fig. 5.4). Malleret himself has suggested that the building, which was constructed of large granite slabs set on brick foundations and supporting a brick

5.3 Two aerial views of the centre of Oc Eo. The arrows point to the moated perimeter.

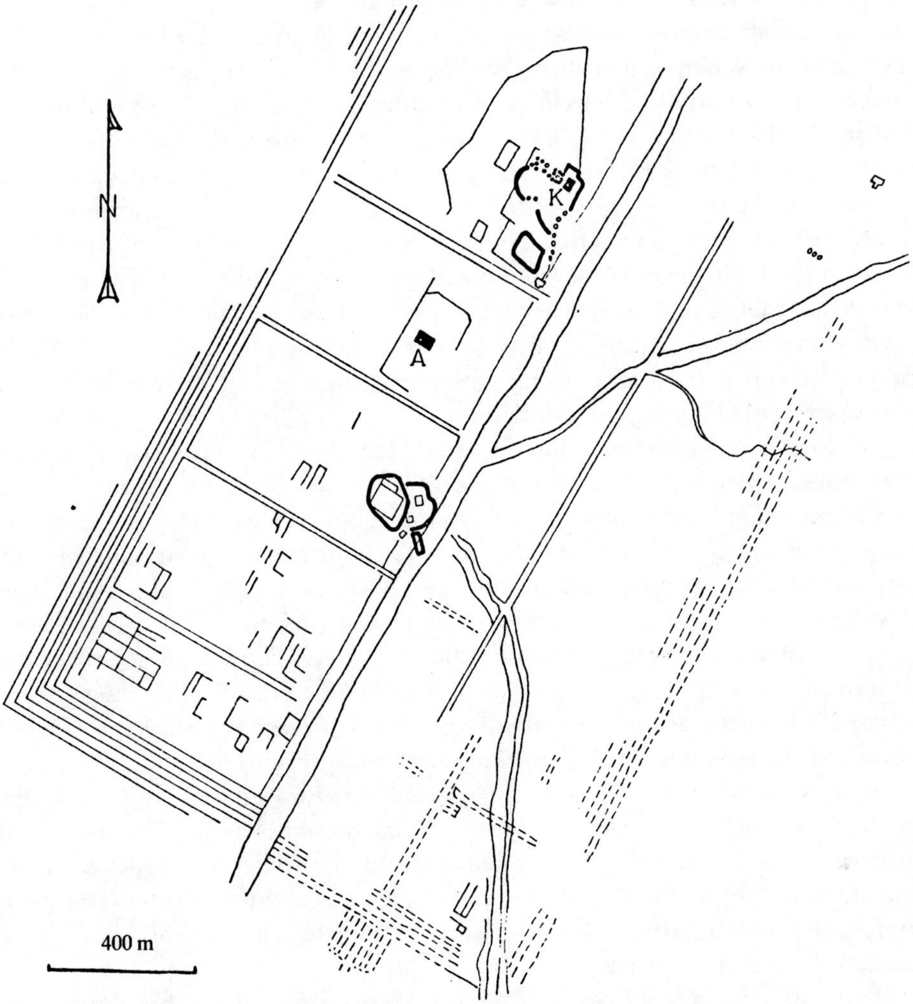

5.4 Plan of Oc Eo prepared by Wheatley (1983) on the basis of air photographs.

superstructure, was a temple. The second building, of which only the brick foundations have survived, was seen by Malleret as possibly being involved in the rites of decarnifying the dead. This entails the consumption by birds of the dead person's flesh prior to burial. These suggestions have not been tested. Malleret had extraordinary difficulties in the field as a result of the activities of looters, but was able to assemble a very large sample of the site's material culture, as well as evidence for the local manufacture of pottery and jewellery (Coedès 1947). We have already seen that two millennia ago, the Indian sub-continent participated in a trading network which incorporated the Roman Empire to the west and the Han to the east. Many of the small artefacts found at Oc Eo confirm that the people of the delta area did, indeed, participate. Thus, Malleret recovered two Roman medallions, one minted during the reign of Antoninus Pius (A.D. 138–161), and the other in that of his successor, Marcus Aurelius (A.D. 161–180). There is also a corpus of jewellery of Mediterranean origin or inspiration. This linkage of the Roman and Chinese Empires at Oc Eo is demonstrated by the discovery of a Chinese mirror which belongs to the same period as the Roman medallions. Along this same route there came Iranian coinage, Indian inspired jewellery and the Indian script. As de Casparis (1979) has shown, the *brāhmī* script at Oc Eo belongs to the late 1st and early 2nd centuries A.D., and is found on small portable objects such as rings and seals. Later Indian writing there takes us down to the 5th century, indicating a period of occupation and trade lasting several centuries and harmonising with the chronology of early *maṇḍalas* deduced from the Chinese historical sources.

The local manufacturing industries attested at Oc Eo are a fascinating blend of introduced articles and local production techniques. The manufacture of glass beads, for example, was introduced from India, but employed clay crucibles with a long local ancestry. The clay anvils used to shape pots were virtually identical with those used for millennia in Southeast Asia. The stone double moulds for casting tin pendants match those found in the Mekong valley, but used in bronze-casting, for the previous two thousand years. Engraving jewellery was indeed practiced, a technique noted by the Chinese visitors. The range of raw materials which were converted into jewellery covers practically the whole gamut of the available metals, precious and semi-precious stones.

As if to confirm the name of *Suvarṇabhūmi*, Oc Eo yielded so much gold that looters, attracted from far and wide, panned the whole site. The list of raw materials used, principally for the manufacture of jewellery, includes diamond, amethyst, jet, amber, malachite, orpiment, sapphires, rubies, corindon, serpentine, feldspar, antigorite, topaz, beryl, zircon, jadeite, garnet, opal, jasper, onyx, agate, carnelian and quartz.

Although alluvial gold can be found in the environs of Oc Eo, most of the precious stones as well as supplies of tin, copper and iron would necessarily have been imported from some distance. The quantity and range of goods which exchanged hands at Oc Eo exceeds by far that evidenced at any other site in Southeast Asia. Clearly, this establishment was not only a port, but also a major manufacturing centre which could dispose of sufficient labour to dig out the moats and erect the girdling walls, as well as manufacture the bricks destined for imposing centrally placed religious monuments. However, the distribution map of the canals shows that Oc Eo was but one node in an extensive settlement network. The canals which radiate from Oc Eo include a channel linking it with Ta Kev, which was probably the actual port. The system links the archaeological sites of Ta Kev and Oc Eo with Da Noi, whence an arterial canal covers nearly 90 km to Angkor Borei which was probably the pre-eminent centre. Indeed, one Chinese report noted that the capital was situated 500 *li* (200 km) from the sea, making it an inland settlement. The canals have not been dated, but the nodal position of Oc Eo leaves little doubt that they belong to the period when the site was occupied (*c* 2nd–6th centuries A.D.). Their function has not been subjected to intensive scrutiny, but it is likely that they fulfilled more than one purpose. One was probably to facilitate drainage of the marshy delta terrain, and thereby improve agricultural prospects. Water volume in the Mekong is markedly seasonal: between May and November the monsoon brings heavy rainfalls at just the time when the headwaters receive the melting snows in the Himalayas. The canals may have been built to expedite drainage just as their modern counterparts do. One canal which proceeds in a southeasterly direction from Angkor Borei terminates in a tributary of the Mekong. The way in which the canals link settlements also makes it likely that they were used to convey goods between the main centres. Modern analogy, too, discloses that the construction of canals in deltaic terrain is a most positive step in encouraging the foundation of new settlements in what was formerly marshy wasteland (Hanks 1972).

Too little, however, is known about the agricultural practices. Food remains from Oc Eo include fish and turtle, and doubtless there was considerable exploitation of aquatic resources. Rice was a staple, and in an enigmatic statement, Kang Dai described their system of cultivation as follows: "The inhabitants of the region engage in farming. They sow in one year and reap for three." Wheatley (1983) has interpreted this passage as implying the practice of ratooning the rapidly growing "floating" variety of rice. Harlan (1977) has described such a variety as a probable native of the deeply flooded delta. The technique is to plant the perennial floating rice and allow it to sprout at the internodes in successive years. One problem with this technique is that yields fall sharply during the second and third seasons, and it might be that the Chinese envoys witnessed only one of several techniques of rice cultivation.

The adoption of the *Śivaliṅga* as an object of veneration in *maṇḍala* religion entailed the provision of a suitable temple to house it. There is abundant archaeological evidence from the late 5th century that the *liṅga* was housed in an impressive brick and stone sanctuary surrounded by a walled precinct. Earlier public buildings, however, were probably wooden, and none has survived. Nor is there a date associated with temple buildings of more durable material, other than the foundations excavated at Oc Eo. Parmentier (1927), however, has suggested that a handful of small brick sanctuaries may belong to this period of early delta *maṇḍalas*. One group identified at Banteay Prei Nokor comprises three sanctuaries. These are smaller and plainer than those characteristic of the later *maṇḍalas* which developed in the region of the Great Lake and middle Mekong south of the Dang Raek range. The best preserved measured only 3.3 by 3.3 m, and rose to a height of about 5 m. It was built of brick, and the walls were sub-divided into undecorated panels by pilasters. There is a low door, and its lintel was undecorated.

Again, no religious statues or representations of deities have been firmly ascribed to these delta *maṇḍalas*, though on stylistic grounds a group of wooden statues of the Buddha from the Delta area may well belong to the part of the period under review (Groslier 1966). This suggestion is supported by five radiocarbon dates from the statues, all of which fall within 2nd to the 8th centuries A.D. (Smith 1979a).

The delta *maṇḍalas*: summary

The lower reaches and delta of the Mekong River was a nodal area for participation in an exchange network which linked Rome and India with China. It is also well placed to act as a gateway for goods traded up and down the Mekong valley. From the 1st century A.D., the delta appears to have sustained *maṇḍalas* which were the foci of intensified centralisation, incorporation of surrounding groups by force and the adoption of some Indian culture traits. The settlement pattern in the core area reveals a series of large centres linked by a network of canals. The indigenous inhabitants incorporated into their culture Indian-inspired ideas of statehood. These included a legal system, calendrics and the establishment of a *maṇḍala*-wide religion. It is possible to discern periods of central power under successive members of the same dynasty. There were also periods of weakness when lords asserted independence. The evidence for the concentration of resources, specialised manufacture, a central court, increased conflict between centres and the despatch of ambassadors, all suggest a level of intensification rather greater than was found with the earlier General Period C chiefdoms. One point of such social groupings is their ephemeral nature. While this area sustained early *maṇḍala* structures, they were not particularly durable and, by the 6th century A.D., the centre of gravity in terms of centralisation passed to the middle Mekong and Tonle Sap plains, leaving the delta region as provincial and politically unimportant.

Maṇḍalas of the middle Mekong and the Tonle Sap plains: A.D. 550–802

This region centres on the junction of the Tonle Sap and Mekong rivers with a lateral branch to include the drainage basin of the Tonle Sap (Figs. 5.4 and 5.5). The lake is fed by numerous smaller rivers, and its level varies greatly between the dry and wet seasons. The Mekong River acts as an arterial route linking the rich lands of Central Cambodia and the Khorat plateau with the sea. From Stung Treng there is also a natural riverine route to the coast of Central Viet Nam, while the gap between the Cardamom and the western edge of the Dang Raek ranges gives access to the Chao Phraya valley. There is good agricultural land along the margins of the Tonle Sap and the tributaries of the Mekong, and the area round Battambang is rich in iron ore. The importance of the Mekong valley in exchange has already been detected on the basis of the early distribution of sandstone moulds for bronze-casting. During the 17th century, this factor was further confirmed when the Dutch merchant Geritt van Wuystoff witnessed the traffic in gold, rhinoceros horn, ivory and salt in the vicinity of Stung Treng (Garnier 1871, Lévy 1970).

During the 1st to the 6th centuries A.D., the period of the delta *maṇḍalas*, this area was probably occupied by chiefdoms shielded from direct contact with Indian and Chinese merchants and visitors by the very presence of overlords in the strategic delta. In discussing this inland area it is more than ever necessary to strip away the heavy overlay of interpretations rooted in Chinese historic accounts and concentrate on the contemporary records, however sparse. The Chinese described the area as Zhenla, a name of unknown meaning but one which has subsequently underpinned the idea that Zhenla was some form of state structured along the centralised and bureaucratic Chinese ideal. Recently, the very name of Zhenla has been called into question by first Jacques (1979) and then Vickery (1986), the latter regarding it as quite useless in any cultural sense. Indeed, Jacques has presented a strong argument in favour of dispensing with the very term Zhenla and substituting, in its place, the actual names of centres derived from inscriptions, such as the *maṇḍala* of Īśānapura. In principle, this step has much merit. The only problem is that until further archaeological research has allowed the reconstruction of more than the present handful of such entities, it is probably wiser to retain the term Zhenla only if it is clearly understood to mean an area, the middle Mekong valley and Tonle Sap plains which, between the middle of the 6th century A.D. and the establishment of the Angkorian *Maṇḍala* in the early 9th century, witnessed the rise and fall of a cloud of ephemeral localised *maṇḍalas*. The possible location of some of the centres involved is seen in Fig. 5.5.

If the Chinese texts and the opinions they impart were our only source of information, and were accepted at face value, we would conclude that Zhenla was originally a vassal to Funan, but that its King, Chitrasena, seized Funan and subdued it. The principal city of Zhenla housed over 20,000 families. In the middle there was a great hall, wherein the overlord gave an audience every third day, wearing a cap covered in gold and precious stones, and reclining on a couch made of different kinds of aromatic wood. He was accompanied by five great officials and many lesser functionaries, and his person and palace were protected by armed guards. His kingdom incorporated 30 other cities, each ruled by a governor (Coedès 1968).

Vickery (1986) has been foremost in replacing these fables with an assessment which has, as its sole foundation, the contemporary epigraphic record. His central theme turns on the title *poñ*, which is found on a series of 7th century inscriptions. It describes a highly ranked individual who served an overlord in the founding of temples and undertaking ritual duties therein. It may well have been the title for an overlord encountered by the Chinese and translated as *fan* or *pan*. The term was also applied to people further down the hierarchy where they were linked with the ownership or administration of *travāṅ*, that is, a man-made

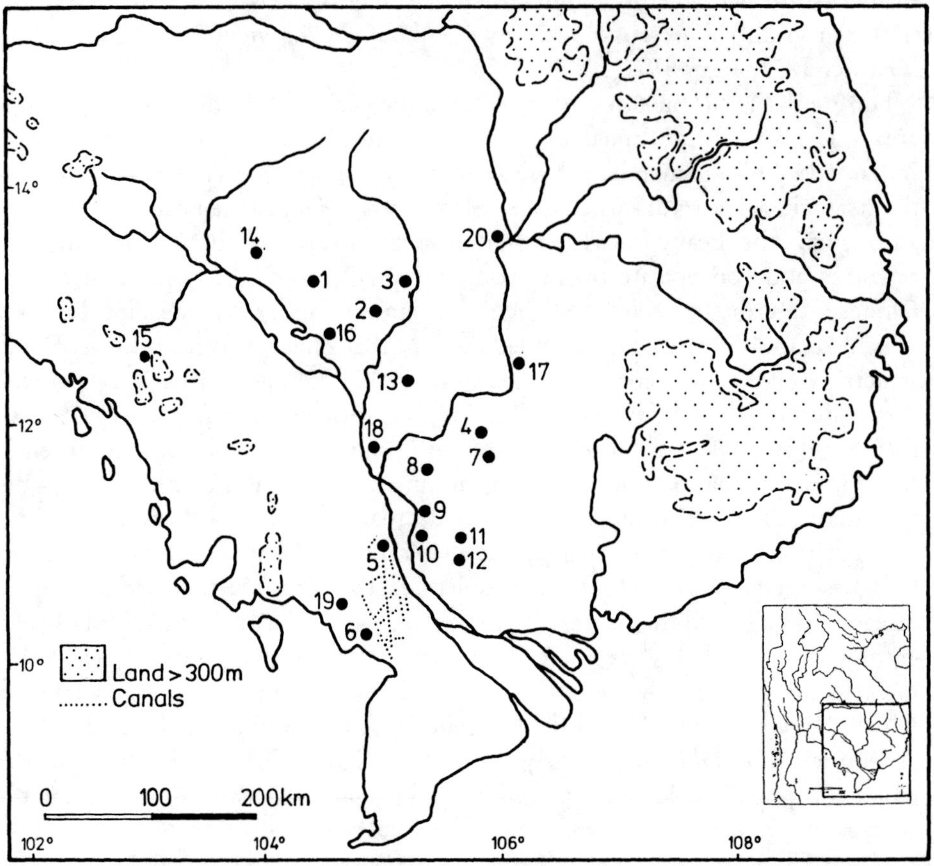

5.5 The principal centres of the middle and lower Mekong valley known from pre-Angkorean inscriptions or archaeological fieldwork. 1. Śreṣṭhapura 2. Bhavapura 3. Īśānapura 4. Indrapura 5. Angkor Borei 6. Oc Eo 7. Vyādhapura 8. Tāmrapura 9. Cakrāṅkapura 10. Āḍhyapura 11. Bhīmapura 12. Amoghapura 13. Ugrapura 14. Puranḍarapura 15. Maleng 16. Svargadvarapura 17. Śambhupura 18. Dharmmapura 19. Dhanvipura 20. Thala Borivat. (Source, M. Vickery. It is particularly emphasised that some locations are provisional.)

pond or reservoir. It is evident that some *travāṅ* were centrally located, and available to more than one *poñ* and his followers, while in others, a *poñ* apparently enjoyed sole rights over a *travāṅ*. The link between inscriptions and archaeology is very close here, for reservoirs have been identified at Chansen in the Chao Phraya valley, numerous sites in the Mun and Chi valleys, and at the great *maṇḍala* centre of Īśānapura (Fig 5.6).The provision and control of water, particularly during the long dry season, is a managerial role which would be critical as the population built up in large centres. Through an examination of the *poñ*, we can begin to grasp how the chiefs of General Period C became the

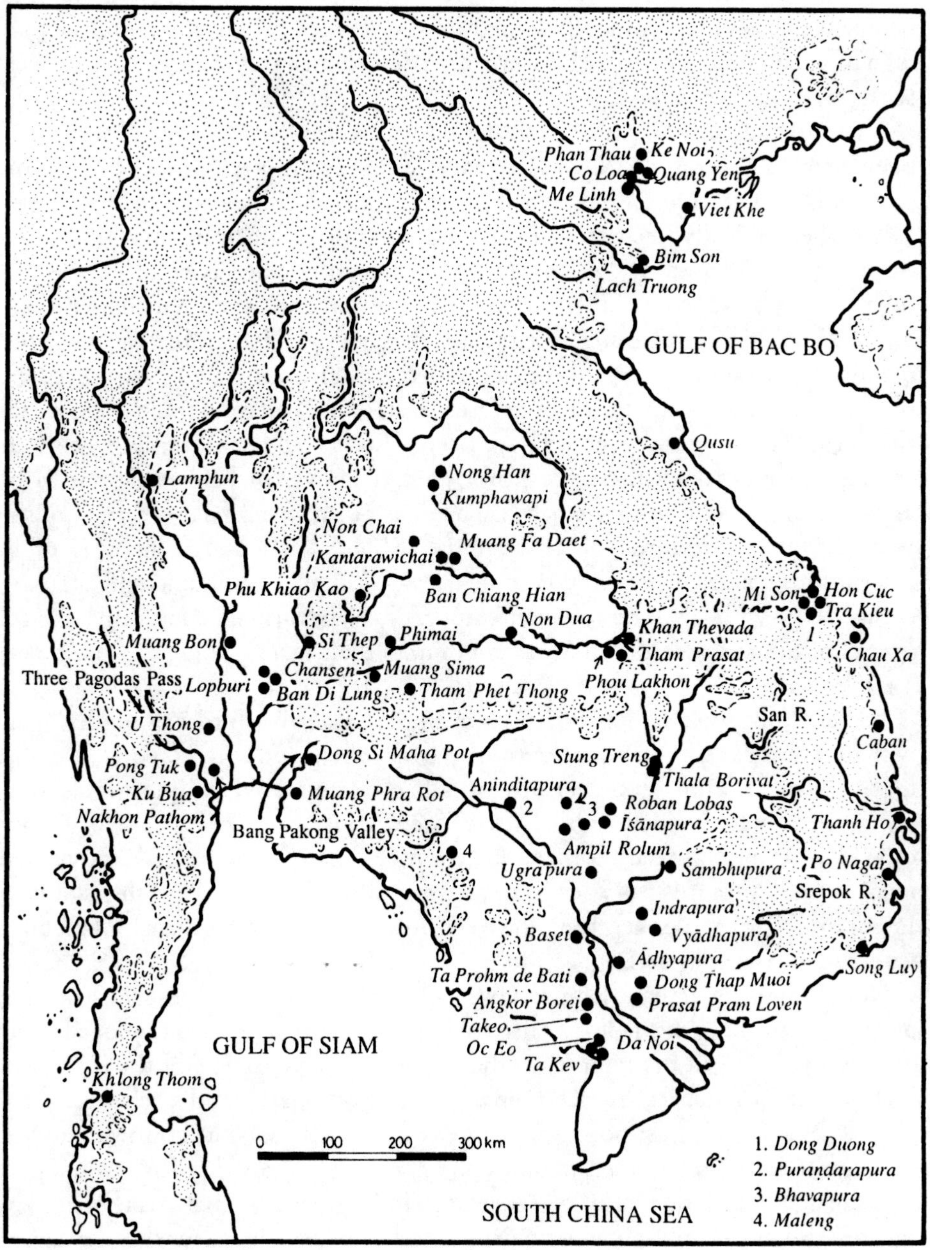

5.6 The distribution of sites mentioned in chapter 5. Stippled area: land above 182 m.

maṇḍala overlords of General Period D. Vickery (1986) has suggested that these people began as chiefs controlling their local reservoirs. With time, some attained high office under overlords who were doubtless themselves descended, in a social sense, from earlier *poñ*.

This title was not durable. By *c* A.D. 650, we find *poñ* being subservient to people with a new rank, known as *mratāñ*. Whereas the *poñ* controlled reservoirs and fields, the *mratāñ* are seldom linked with such facilities and, indeed, appear as a higher rank divorced from local land administration. The changing use of titles is a vehicle used by Vickery (1986) to trace the emergence of increasingly highly ranked overlords. He noted an inscription from Takeo which mentions a *mratāñ kloñ* of Bhavapura. The same area has also yielded an inscription which mentions a *mratāñ kuruṅ* of a place called Vikramapura who had precedence over a *mratāñ kloñ*. Subsequent references to *Raja* Bhavavarman suggest this overlord, Bhavavarman II, could have risen in status from a *mratāñ kloñ* to a *raja* during the first half of the 7th century A.D. The overlord Bhavavarman II has always been difficult to place, because he does not have any defined relationship with the great overlords of an assumed "Zhenla" state. An analysis of his inscriptions makes it evident that he elevated himself in rank and status in competition with his foremost contemporary, Īśānavarman. Naturally, the followers of Īśānavarman did not mention him in their inscriptions, because he was a rival overlord.

Vickery (in progress) has noted an example of an overlord sharing his name with his court centre and giving authority over other centres to his sons. We learn that a Dharmasvāmi was overlord of Dharmmapura, while one of his sons, having already been given authority over Śreṣṭhapura, went on to control a centre called Dhruvapura, while another son governed Dhanvipura. Such acknowledgement of vassal status to a central court is also illustrated by the status of Indrapura, whose ruler accepted the overlordship of Bhavavarman I, Mahendravarman and Īśānavarman.

Nor should the archaic Khmer texts be overlooked for the information they provide on the lives of the less exalted. They provide insight into the social status of those who served the temple, to their duties, and to aspects of the landscape, such as the boundaries of rice-fields, water-tanks, paths and orchards (Jacob 1978, 1979). The clearest point to emerge from her study is the contrast between the dignitaries who founded temples and those they provided for the temple's maintenance. The latter are often referred to in English as "slaves" categorised by age, sex and duties, among which we find herdsmen, rice-field workers, weavers, cooks and guards. We should not be led by a literal use of the word slave into believing that coercion and loss of freedom were involved. Jacques (1984) has persuasively argued that the real meaning is servants, or slaves, of the gods. This gloss gives us a quite different impression, for service in the ancestral temple, a situation widespread throughout much of lowland Southeast Asia today, is quite consistent with willing work in family land holdings.

There were, then, several regionally based ruling families whose names were all given in Sanskrit. Some of the rulers exist as names only, recalled as ancestors in much later genealogies. Hardly anything is known of Śreṣṭhavarman, or his predecessor, Śrutavarman. The former was described in a much later inscription as the founder of a brilliant line of kings, and the supreme overlord of Śreṣṭhapura. We do not know the relationship between these ancestors and the four principal rulers of the land bordering the middle Mekong and Tonle Sap. Contemporary inscriptions, however, have left us much better informed on the careers of the four overlords of *maṇḍalas*: Bhavavarman I, his probable brother Mahendravarman (known as Chitrasena prior to his consecration), the latter's son Īśānavarman, and a later successor, Jayavarman I. This issue of regionality and ephemeral *maṇḍala* structures has also been taken up by Wolters (1974) with particular reference to the political situation in the region lying to the west of Tonle Sap. He began by noting a reference, by Ma Duanlin, to four polities which despatched missions to China but were "subjugated by Zhenla" after A.D. 650. This fragmentation is supported by a further description, this time by Zhui Dangshu in the 8th century, that west of Zhenla were little towns each of which is called a kingdom. The point made by Wolters is that both Bhavavarman I and Mahendravarman campaigned in Northwest Cambodia, leaving inscriptions recording their successes. Nevertheless, the four independent princes asserted their leadership by sending tribute missions to China after the wars of conquest. The date of the mission was A.D. 638. Twenty years later, Jayavarman was again fighting in the northwest. One inscription refers to an autumn campaign, when his enemies' moats were dry. A second inscription from Baset, dated to A.D. 657, describes Jayavarman as "the conqueror of his enemies and living incarnation of victory". In the same year, an inscription from Ba Phnom called Jayavarman "the conqueror of the circle of his enemies", a clear reference to the *maṇḍala* concept.

The latest inscription raised by Jayavarman is dated to A.D. 681. Inscriptions post-dating his overlordship, but prior to the foundation of Angkor, are very rare, and the political situation is described only in retrospective accounts. The latter disclose the possible existence of a minor *maṇḍala* at Śambhupura, a site identified as Sambor on the Mekong River, and another at Aninditapura. Dupont (1943–6) has argued that the period between Jayavarman and the later establishment of the Angkorian *Maṇḍala* in the early 9th century A.D. remained one of marked regionality.

The balance of evidence then, is in favour of the presence of small *maṇḍalas* which oscillated between asserting their independence and accepting vassal status during periods when a particular overlord was powerful enough to mount wars of conquest. It was just such a leader, Īśānavarman, who was described above as giving audiences every three days in his capital. Again, the impact, or perhaps the desire to impress, is seen in the inscriptions of powerful leaders. Bhavavarman I, it is said, "took power with energy". An inscription found at Īśānapura records the qualities of Īśānavarman, and is worth quoting at length as it provides insight into the image the overlord wished his Sanskrit text to project. It notes that the king's successes reflect his personal prestige, wise council and energy. He is like the sun in the sky, radiating an intolerable majesty, the issue of the revered kings of the earth. He was annointed with sacred water, provided blessings and was foremost among the virtuous. The basic point is then reached. He "exceeded the limits of his parents domain." To honour this achievement, he gifted a golden *liṅga* and an image of Śiva to the temple (Coedès 1968).

It is appropriate now to consider how devotion to Hinduism, and, in particular, to Śiva, played a role in cementing the status and authority of such leaders. We have already seen that the contemporary worship in India itself involved the notion of supreme devotion, through the control of mental and physical forces, to Śiva. Both Wolters (1979) and Wheatley (1983) have suggested that such devotion was an integral part of the social setting for the conception of kingship and the granting of royal favour. Śiva was viewed as the omniscient divine creator. His worship required asceticism, humility and absolute devotion. The worship of Śiva was therefore undertaken with undivided asceticism, the supreme exponents of which were known as *Pāśupātas*. These adherents were supposed to have almost equal power to Śiva himself. Wolters has stressed a critical symbiosis in Śiva worship whereby the aspiring ruler obtains proximity to Śiva by supreme ascetic effort and, in return, absorbs Śiva's *śakti*, or physical and spiritual power. The *Pāśupātas*, therefore, became important advisors to the ruler in his quest for *śakti*, which, once obtained, conferred on the ruler the aura of divinity. One inscription, for example, refers to Jayavarman as "an incarnate portion of the god".

Symbiosis likewise characterised the worship of Śiva by royal servants and other members of the elite seeking the warmth of royal preferment. Devotion to Śiva, the foundation of temples, and their endowment with land and servants, were rewarded by royal favours such as administrative duties, honorific emblems and status symbols. The devotion to Śiva was not, therefore, a simple acceptance of a novel, alien religion, but rather a mechanism which provided a divine charter to the exercise of kingship and a religious focus for the overlord's advisers and followers. The particular inscription referred to above described the consecration of Īśānavarman, a necessary rite in the accession to kingship undertaken by a *brāhmaṇ*. The corpus of Zhenla inscriptions provides further, albeit scattered and oblique, references to kingship and political organisation. There is, in effect, a consistent thread of evidence in favour of a deeply embedded layer of Indian political philosophy. Thus, an inscription of A.D. 668 refers to two ministers educated in the *Dhamaśāstra* and *Arthaśāstra*. These are *brāhmaṇic* treatises on law and politics, respectively. In the same century, a school of study for the *Dhamaśāstra* was founded in Īśānapura. It is relevant to appreciate that the *Dhamaśāstra* was concerned with the duties of the overlord and the legal system. Indeed, this same inscription goes on to refer to the seven elements which make up the state, that is, the same foundations for statehood advanced in India a millennium earlier in the *Arthaśāstra* of Kauṭilya.

The existence of great and wealthy families is indicated by an inscription dating to the reign of Jayavarman. It describes four generations of functionaries spanning the transition of the centre of power of *maṇḍalas* from the delta to the middle Mekong region. Brahmadaṭṭa and Brahmasiṃha were doctors under Rudravarman. Their nephews, Dhamadeva and Siṃhadeva, were ministers to Bhavavarman I and Mahendravarman, and, in turn, the former minister's son Siṃhavira became a poet and minister to Īśānavarman. Siṃhavira's son then became a doctor under Jayavarman, who appointed him governor of Āḍhyapura. Such regional governors were accorded symbols of their authority and status. Under Bhavavarman II, the governor of Ugrapura was provided with a parasol surmounted by a golden globe, a gold-ornamented chariot and a suite of horses and elephants. The white parasol is still a symbol of rank in Thailand. Jayavarman's governor of Śreṣṭhapura was honoured with a white parasol. These hereditary nobles, with their Sanskrit names, were called upon to advise and serve the court. We find, for example, that the same Siṃhadeva, minister to Mahendravarman, was sent as a royal emissary to the court of a Cham *maṇḍala*.

We have seen that the accumulation of wealth was necessary to sustain the essential services in administration, defence and the law. The Zhenla inscriptions throw little light on this important issue, although even from the earliest Chinese descriptions of "Funan", the imposition of a tax on trade goods is described (Sahai 1970). The customs revenue was also an important source of state wealth in India, but the tax on land was the mainstay of the Indian exchequer. The same is true of Cambodia under the overlords of Angkor, but for the preceding Zhenla period there is little information available from inscriptions. An example dating to the period of Jayavarman I refers to a *brāhmaṇ* who was royal treasurer. We also know of an impost on salt, because a particular religious foundation was exempt. During periods of warfare, booty was taken, and in one recorded instance Bhavavarman I presented war booty to a religious foundation. Apart from providing the overlord with disposable goods used in feasting and gifting, offerings made to him, and booty seized, sustained armed retainers. The *Suishu* (History of the Sui) describes Īśānavarman's palaces as bristling with armed guards, while there is epigraphic evidence for the governor of Dhanvipura maintaining a thousand soldiers.

The foundation and maintenance of temples to the cult of Śiva represents the deep penetration of Indian ideas, and the dedicatory inscriptions have proved an invaluable source of information on the political instruments of government. They also contain lists of people and land donated to the upkeep of the temples, and these are usually inscribed in archaic Khmer. Such gifts to religious foundations are a recurrent theme in the inscriptions of Zhenla, and it is important to understand why they were made. Hagesteijn (1984) has clearly pointed out that the foundation and endowment of temples was closely related to the donor's position in the social hierarchy. High power and status followed outstanding and visually impressive foundations. Gift-giving and feasting were, in effect, ways for measuring the status and pull of competing or aspiring overlords. Indeed, Kulke (1982), in his consideration of early Javanese states, notes how central overlords *lessened* the wealth of potential rivals by encouraging them to give feasts which gravely sapped their resources.

Hitherto, the culture of Zhenla has been described on the basis of the inscriptions, along with a few fragments in the literary record, which portray the land and people through Chinese eyes. We know of a royal capital under Īśānavarman and the presence of 30 fortified centres, and of Jayavarman campaigning in autumn when his enemies' moats were dry. There are dedications to temples and references to fields and water storage in tanks. But what is known of the archaeological landscape, and to what extent does it add to the textual information? Sadly, there has not yet been any intensive fieldwork of the type undertaken recently in Thailand, in order to evaluate the settlement patterns of a specified area. Such programmes are aimed not only to discover the major centres, but also to isolate the small villages which produced the surplus agricultural resources; the industrial locations such as quarries, mines, iron and salt-workings; and the remains of the dams and reservoirs which evidence the control of water for agricultural and residential purposes.

During an earlier stage of archaeological fieldwork, most energy was devoted to the discovery and recording of the major monuments (Aymonier 1900–1903, Parmentier 1927). This has resulted in an invaluable corpus of information on the religious monuments of Zhenla, and more detailed studies of their architectural decoration have revealed pervasive Indian inspiration (Bénisti 1970). The distribution of the religious monuments known to Parmentier matches very closely that for inscriptions seen in Fig. 5.1. It is seen that the delta area is virtually devoid of structures, and it is important in considering this gap to recall that, in India itself, the construction of Hindu temples in stone and/or brick was not underway until the Gupta period (A.D. 320–540). These Indian temples had a central chamber to house a statue of the god or the *liṅga.* These temples, which were rock-cut rather than free standing, attracted endowments of land and became centres for the study of law and government. The absence of temples built of permanent materials in the delta area – other than a few small and probably late examples – possibly reflects construction in wood. The changes in building technique in favour of permanent materials began in the Gupta period and was soon adopted in the middle Mekong valley.

The architectural style of the buildings in the Mekong valley, and particularly the decoration on wall surfaces and door lintels, are rich sources of information on the religious practices and their inspiration. Bénisti (1970) has considered the range of motifs and figures employed in the sanctuaries, and reviewed their parallels in Indian temple contexts. Take, for example, the *makara*, a fantastic marine monster commonly depicted on the lintels. Similar depictions are represented in India by 300 B.C. A frieze of geese is another popular motif in the middle Mekong valley which has an Indian origin. The decorative motif incorporating foliage employed at Īśānapura, has its parallels in India at Ajantā and Ellorā Cave XIV (*c* A.D. 550). Even such simple geometric motifs as the chequerboard are represented in both areas. A form of embellishment to the outer walls of temples, the depiction of a storied building revealing personages within, is found at Īśānapura. A similar building adorns the wall of Ajantā Cave XIX in India. The *kūdu* motif, which comprises a niche or circlet often containing a human head, is common in Zhenla art, and there is even a ceramic representation at Oc Eo. This motif had a long currency in India from Amarāvati to Pallava art. Bénisti's detailed review has established that the closest parallels with the art of Zhenla lie in the Indian styles seen at Ajantā, Ellorā and Māmallapuram, and dated to the period *c* A.D. 500–650. Above all else, however, we must note the monumentality and magnificence of these temple structures and the size of the surrounding precincts, for it is in the marshalling of labour and construction of awe-inspiring buildings that we can recognise the power of the central overlords.

The fieldwork initiated by Aymonier (1900–1903) and Parmentier (1927) laid the foundations for an appreciation of the nature of the major settlements of Zhenla, but the concentration on brick sanctuaries at the expense of the total configurations of the settlements means that, to this day, we have no settlement plans. All we know is that, like Oc Eo, the surrounding moats were square or rectangular. We have already referred to life in the capital of Īśānavarman as described by the Chinese. The very site of that royal centre of Īśānapura has been identified, on the basis of epigraphic evidence, as Sambor Prei Kuk. This great site is located in the valley of the Stung Sen, which flows on a parallel course with the Mekong and empties into the Tonle Sap River. The design of the sanctuaries there recall the simple structures from Banteay Prei Nokor, and are paralleled by many other Zhenla buildings. They are usually raised on a platform, and comprise a single-chambered shrine room surrounded by thick walls which rise to a considerable height (Figs. 5.7 and 5.8). The central sanctuary of the southern group at Īśānapura, for example, measured 17 by 13 m at the base, and rose to a height of at least 16 m. The object of the sanctuary was to house the statue of the deity, or the sacred *liṅga*, for which purpose a pedestal was set up in the sanctuary chamber. Since the rituals involved the use of lustral water, a small drain and exterior gargoyle were often provided. There was usually just one door into the shrine room, but the remaining three walls were provided with false doors. These temples were decorated, but not to the same extent as the later temples of the Angkorian period. The lintel over the doorway, which was made of carved stone in contrast to the brick structure itself, was embellished with carvings. The sanctuary walls likewise bore ornamental carvings and mouldings, but only in a limited area. Many surfaces were left plain. The Zhenla architects were not familiar with the structure of the true arch and they used the corbelled roof to vault ceilings. This imposed a restriction on enclosed space in brick or

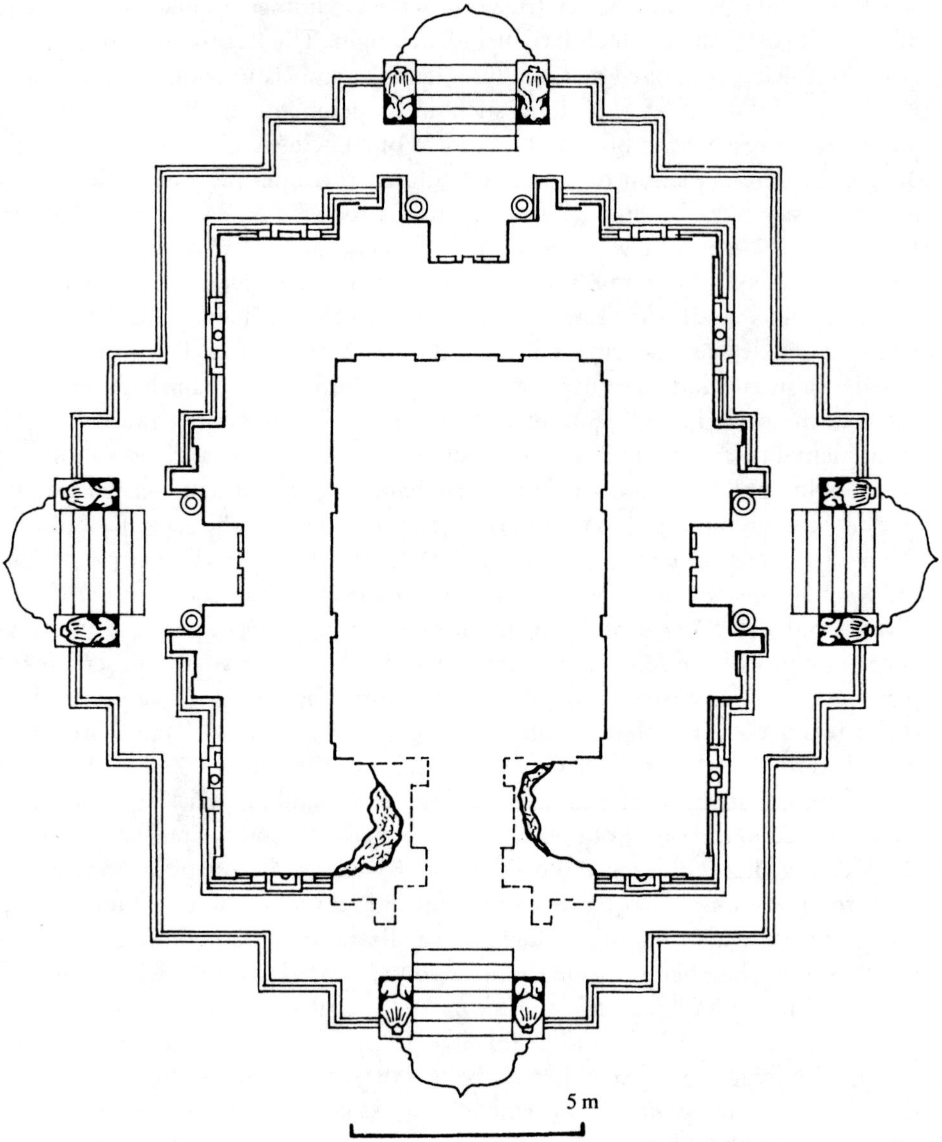

5.7 Plan of temple C1 at Īśānapura. It is, like most Zhenla temples, single-chambered (see also Fig. 6.13.)

stone which persisted throughout the Angkor period, and which involved the continued use of wood for secular buildings. Perhaps because of the necessarily small area within the central sanctuary, this structure was surrounded by one or two walled precincts. These sacred precincts themselves housed subsidiary sanctuaries, and both the walls and the gateways into the enclosure were vehicles for decoration.

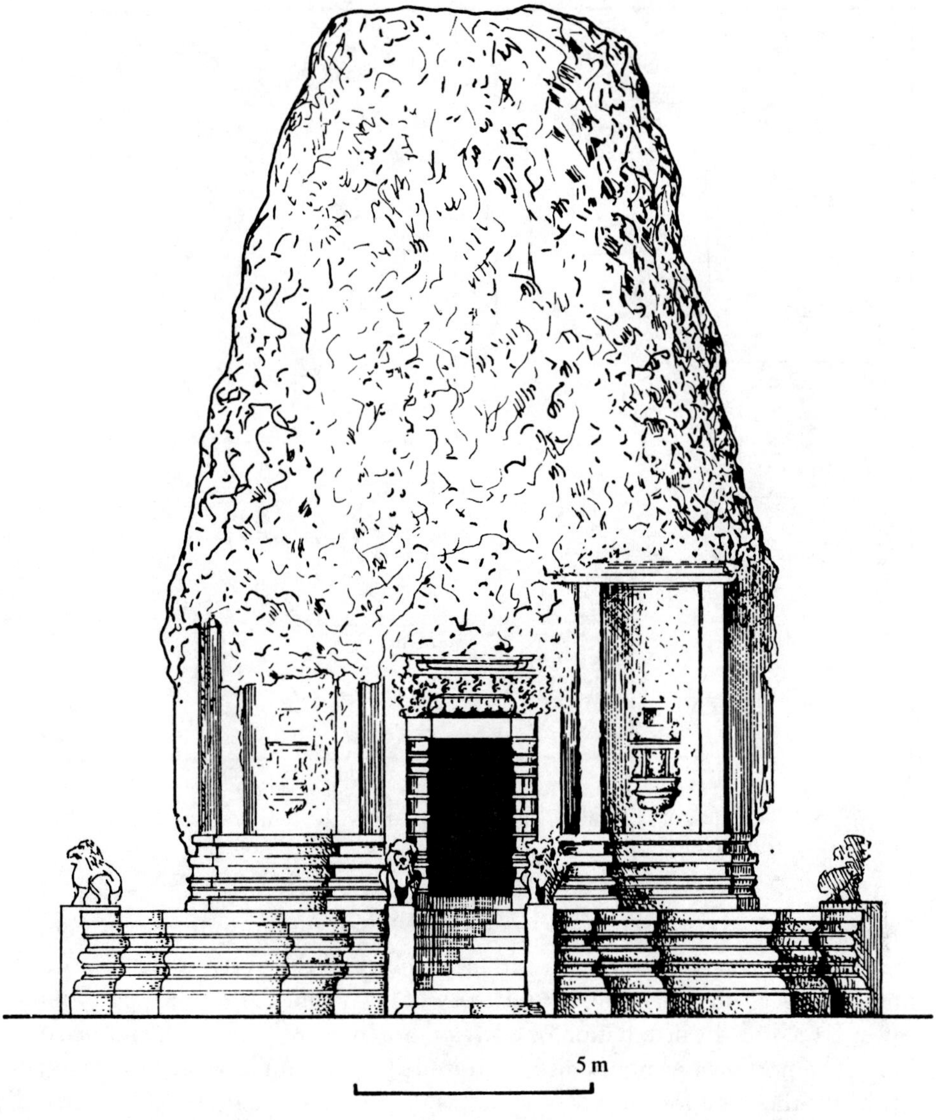

5.8 Elevation of temple C1 at Īśānapura. Indian influence is evident both from the worship of Śiva and the decorative elements on such temples.

These are general features. Let us now look in more detail at the religious monuments of Īśānapura. Figure 5.9 reveals the presence of three separate walled precincts, each dominated by a large central sanctuary. These are designated the central, southern and northern groups by Parmentier (1927). The southern group comprises one principal and five lesser sanctuaries, set within an inner wall which was, in turn, enclosed by an outer enceinte, measuring 300 by 270 m. Four inscriptions are associated with this complex, and they make it clear that it was a

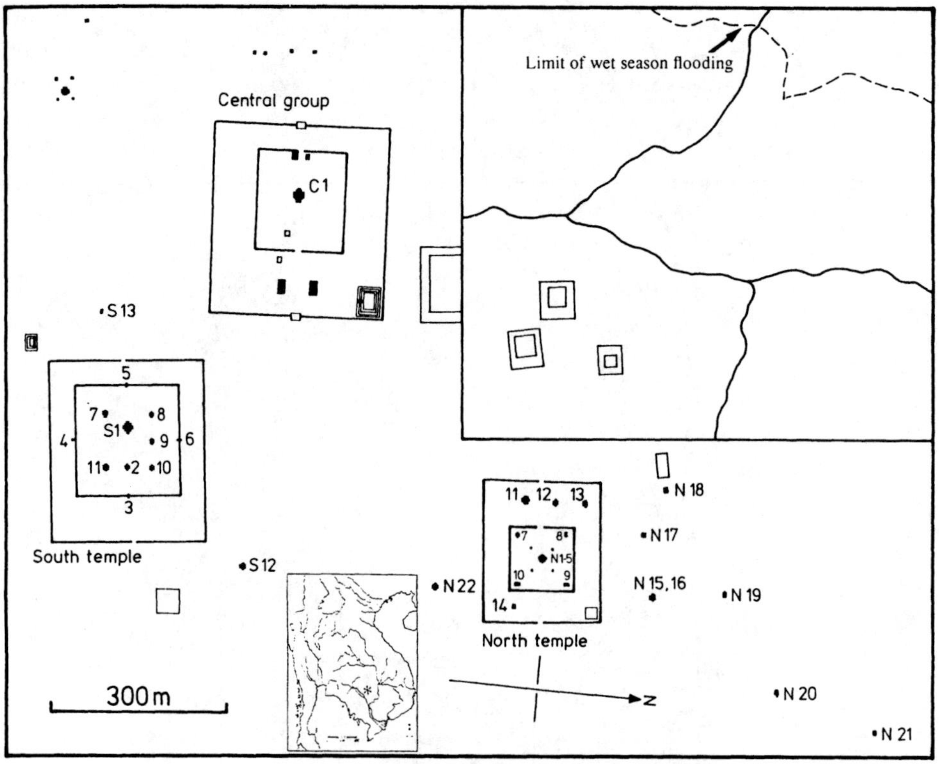

5.9 The plan of central Īśānapura. Note how the temples are enclosed by walls to provide large sacred precincts.

foundation of Īśānavarman himself. An inscription found on the eastern door of the exterior wall refers to the power and majesty of the overlord and records his military success in expanding the territory of his parents. An inscription found in tower F records the installation of a *liṅga* there by a *brāhmaṇ* in the service of the king. The northern group is also surrounded by a double wall, but, unlike the southern, there are four lesser sanctuaries set between the inner and outer walls. Outside the eastern gate on the outer wall, an avenue leads to a large reservoir demarcated by earthern banks.

Unfortunately, there are no inscriptions found with the central group. Like the other two, it has a principal sanctuary which was raised on a platform reached by a flight of steps. Carved lions guard access to the immediate surrounds of the temple terrace, the sanctuary of which measures 14 by 14 m, with walls 2.8 m thick. An aerial reconnaissance of Īśānapura has revealed that the sanctuaries are set within a double walled enclosure measuring 2 by 2 km and, therefore, enclosing an area of 400 ha. The reservoir was found outside the centre's walls. If the Chinese sources can be relied upon, the enclosed area would have incorporated dwellings and a palace, in addition to the large central ceremonial precincts just described. These royal temple foundations, together with the means to sustain them, represent gifts from the overlord. Their size and impressive embellishments inform us, just as they informed his contemporaries, that Īśānavarman was a very great overlord indeed.

Van Liere (1980) has considered the hydraulic system of Īśānapura. One of the problems is that the site was occupied for many centuries following the end of Īśānavarman's reign. Indeed, it was a centre of culture and learning during the period of the classic Angkorian *Maṇḍala* (Osborne 1966), when it was linked to the great road system laid down by Jayavarman VII. However, it is quite feasible that some of the reservoirs and the moated enceinte of Īśānapura were constructed during the Zhenla period. These were probably designed more for supplying the moats, religious foundations and urban populace, than for irrigating rice-fields.

Īśānapura contains the largest and most impressive religious monuments from the Zhenla period, but several other sites have also revealed a nucleus of brick sanctuaries. Ampil Rolum, 35 km southwest of Īśānapura, incorporates three largely ruinous sanctuaries some of which have yielded inscriptions. One refers to a Buddhist foundation, and lists the slaves provided for its maintenance. The second, which was set up during the reign of Jayavarman IV (A.D. 928–942), refers to "this town of Bhavapura". This ascription has lead to the suggestion that Ampil Rolum was the capital of Bhavavarman I, but it could equally have been founded by Bhavavarman II. The archaeological remains of Thala Borivat, in the vicinity of Stung Treng on the Mekong River, are large and impressive. This site commands a major trade route, where the valleys of the San and Srepok rivers give access to the territory of the Chams. Bénisti's (1968) analysis of the decoration of the Thala Borivat lintels has led her to date them earlier than those of Īśānapura, and it is on such chronological evidence that Lévy (1970) has suggested that the site was a major centre.

Reference has been made to the existence of a local dynasty based on Śambhupura during the 8th century and this site has been identified as Sambor, also on the banks of the Mekong River. Āḍhyapura is identified with the area of the hill of Ba Phnom. Vickery (in progress), basing his conclusions on the location of 7th and 8th century inscriptions mentioning centres, has suggested that Vyādhapura was located at or near Banteay Prei Nokor, while three other centres, Cakrāṅkapura, Bhīmapura and Amoghapura, were probably located south of the junction of the Tonle Sap and Mekong rivers. He has also suggested that Śreṣṭhapura was situated in the region north of the Great Lake. However, it is not always possible to relate centres described on inscriptions with those identified on the basis of archaeological evidence. At Roban Lobas, for example, which is only a few kilometres northwest of Īśānapura, there is an impressive sanctuary with the unusual feature of a vestibule. An inscription there describes Narasiṃhagupta as the hereditary overlord of Indrapura. The location of Indrapura has not been identified with certainty. Coedès (1943–6) has suggested that it was in the region of Thbon Khmum, but Vickery (in progress) has advanced compelling arguments for placing it in modern Kompong Thom Province, and probably close to Īśānapura.

Zhenla *maṇḍalas*: summary

The earliest development of General Period D *maṇḍalas* occurred in the flat floodplains of the lower Bassac and Mekong rivers where there was ready access to the sea. The *maṇḍalas* which developed there lasted from the 2nd to the 6th centuries A.D. During the 6th century, they gave way to competing *maṇḍalas* located in the middle reaches of the Mekong valley and Tonle Sap plains between the Dang Raek range and the vicinity of Phnom Penh. The archaeological evidence reveals very clearly that the principal settlements were extensive (*c* 400 ha), defended, and dominated by central religious buildings erected and decorated according to Indian traditions of temple architecture. The inscriptions indicate that the rulers were aided by *brāhmaṇs* versed in Indian political and legal doctrines, who played a central role in the consecration of overlords according to Hindu ritual. Sanskrit was the language employed in such rituals, but archaic Khmer was the vernacular language. When considering the surviving inscriptions and Chinese records of visiting embassies, it is evident that there was not one centralised state, but several competing regional *maṇḍalas*. We know the names of several overlords who expanded their domains. During such periods, minor lords acknowledged the supremacy of the *maṇḍala*. Any weakening of the central authority, such as the death of a powerful and charismatic ruler, fostered regional independence and political fragmentation.

The evidence available from archaeology and inscriptions is unanimous in supporting the conclusion that between *c* A.D. 100 and the end of the 8th century, the middle and lower Mekong area sustained a number of *maṇḍalas* organised along the principles of the centralising attainment of wealth and power by an overlord. One key point about this situation is that it was fluid. The fact that a system capable of conceiving the canal network of the delta plains was not durable should occasion no surprise, for the overlord had rivals. This is the essence of the *maṇḍala*. The social mechanics may well have been similar to that described by Leach (1954) for the Kachin of upland Burma where centralisation and high status were unstable and oscillated even within the span of a human lifetime. Some centuries after the florescence of the delta *maṇḍalas*, we can still perceive an ambitious man, Bhavavarman II, seeking to haul himself above his peers and establish his overlordship. Some possible factors which help us understand this course of events will be considered below.

The Dvāravatī *maṇḍalas* of the Chao Phraya plains and their antecedants: A.D. 200–950

The Chao Phraya is the principal river which debouches into the Gulf of Siam. There are three other main rivers: to the west there are the Mae Khlong and Ta Chin and, to the east, the Bang Pakong. The Chao Phraya has numerous tributaries, that which concerns us most being the Pa Sak, which originates in the Phetchabun mountains. This area is one of the major rice-producing regions of Southeast Asia, a situation which results from the construction of flood and water-control systems during the past century (Judd 1973). The floodplains of these four rivers and their tributaries, however, would have provided in their "back swamps" a suitable milieu for the extensive cultivation of rice. During the late prehistoric and early historic periods (*c* 500 B.C. – A.D. 900), the sea level was probably rather higher than at present, and the extensive build-up of the Chao Phraya delta was at an earlier stage. Archaeological sites now set back from the coast, therefore, were likely to have had direct access to the sea (Supajanya and Vanasin 1979).

While the low-lying riverine floodplains provided suitable conditions for rice cultivation, they were lacking in tin, copper, iron and lead ores. However, this deficiency was compensated for by routes of communication to both the Cambodian plain and the headwaters of the Mun River, and so on to the Khorat plateau. Like the lower Mekong area it was positioned so as to control a major communication route to India by means of the Three Pagodas pass, and commanded a rich hinterland.

The documentary sources for protohistoric and early historic societies in this area are poorer than are those for the lower Mekong valley and Tonle Sap plain. Early Chinese sources are all based on hearsay, rather than direct observation, while Indian references are of a general and illusory character. The earliest possible reference to the Chao Phraya plains is contained in the *Qian Hanshu* (History of the Early Han). It records a journey which originated on the South Chinese coast, and ended at a place called Huangzhi. It was a very long journey which lasted about one year and, most interestingly, involved a ten-day sector which was undertaken on foot. Wheatley (1961:9) has suggested that the ultimate destination was the eastern shores of India, and that the overland sector involved, perhaps, the Three Pagodas pass.

The itinerary will only be generally known, however two points particularly stand out. Firstly, the events described took place about 100 B.C. Secondly, as the historian Pan Gu states:

> From the barriers of Rinan (southern Bac Bo). It is about nine and a half months journey to Shenli (possibly the Chao Phraya valley). It is rather more than ten days' journey on foot to the country of Fugandulu whence it is something over two months' voyage to the country of Huangzhi (probably India).....(officials and volunteers) put out to sea to buy lustrous pearls, glass, rare stones and strange products in exchange for gold and various

silks. It is a profitable business for the barbarians, who also loot and kill. (Tr. Wheatley 1961:8.)

The possible route of this most important passage may well, according to Wheatley, have included the Three Pagodas pass. If true, it would confirm the early exchange of Indian objects of which glass and rare stones are archaeologically recoverable.

The next relevant text is the *Liangshu*, which was written in the early 7th century A.D. and drew on earlier documentary sources. We read of a maritime expedition by Fan Man, ruler of "Funan" in the early 3rd century A.D. Apparently he

Used troops to attack and subdue the neighbouring kingdoms, which all acknowledged themselves his vassals. He himself adopted the style of Great King of Funan. Then he ordered the construction of great ships and crossing right over the Gulf of Siam, attacked more than ten states. (Ibid.:15.)

The location of these entities is not easily resolved, but it is possible that they were situated on the shores of the Gulf of Siam. Dunsun is the best known, because it receives further mention in the *Liangshu*. It was clearly a centre of intensive long-distance exchange in exotic goods. The author states:

More than 3,000 li from the southern frontier of Funan is the kingdom of Dunsun which is situated on an ocean stepping stone. The land is 1,000 li in extent; the city is 10 li from the sea. There are five kings who all acknowledge themselves vassals of Funan. The eastern frontier of Dunsun is in communication with (Bac Bo), the western with India. All the countries beyond the frontier come and go in pursuit of trade... At this mart East and West meet together so that daily there are innumerable people there. Precious goods and rare merchandise, there is nothing which is not there. (Ibid.:16.)

The location of Dunsun is not known. Recent excavations conducted at Khlong Thom in Krabi Province (Fig. 5.6), however, have revealed the sort of site which corresponds to the written record. Veeraprasert, in describing the material found there in 1983, has drawn our attention to a range of artefacts matching many found by Malleret at Oc Eo. These include glass and carnelian beads in various stages of manufacture, inscribed stone seals and stone moulds for casting jewellery (Veeraprasert 1985). Such exotic materials stress the role of a strategic location in the exchange of goods between India and both Southeast Asia and China. The point was not lost on Fan Man who, if we accept the Chinese accounts, resolved to bring it and other maritime entities into his *maṇḍala*.

Very few inscriptions are known from the Chao Phraya valley. There is little doubt that the erection of stelae was not undertaken to anything like the same extent as in the middle Mekong area. Nor are there many allusions to the Chao Phraya area in later Chinese texts. A Chinese pilgrim named Xuan Dang, however, described a state called Duoluobodi as existing west of Īśānapura. The existence of a *maṇḍala* in this area receives confirmation from a Sanskrit inscription on a copper plate found at U Thong. It states that:

Śrī Harṣavarman, grandson of Īśānavarman, having expanded the sphere of his glory, obtained the Lion Throne through regular succession.

The next two stanzas record gifts: a jewelled litter, a parasol and musical instruments to the *liṅga* Āmrātakeśvara, a situation suggesting that the overlord followed Śaivism. There is no date on the inscription, but Coedès (1958) has suggested a mid-7th century context on the basis of the style of lettering. This is a most intriguing document for several reasons. It indicates, if it originated in the area of U Thong (Fig. 3.39), the establishment of a kingdom by those who adopted the honorific style of - *Varman*. The religion favoured identity with Śiva, but most challenging is the identity of Īśānavarman. Is this ruler the same overlord (*c* A.D. 611–636) whose capital was located at Īśānapura? Or is he a different person and dynasty? If the former is the case, then we have a possible situation wherein a royal scion was given authority over a peripheral area as a vassal to a Mekong valley *maṇḍala*. That overlords there had an interest in the Chao Phraya valley is demonstrated beyond reasonable doubt by an inscription from Si Thep in the Pasak valley (Coedès 1958). It records the establishment of images of Śiva by Bhavavarman on the occasion of his accession. The Sanskrit text has been dated stylistically to the 6th or 7th centuries.

Such a Khmer presence in the Chao Phraya valley was neither influential nor enduring. Lopburi, and the area around it, was a centre of considerable importance from the late prehistoric to the present, and has yielded two inscriptions in Mōn, a language related to Khmer which was spoken in the Chao Phraya valley before being superceded by Thai. One inscription, a single line, is dated to the 7th century, and the longer one, which records offerings of slaves and a cart to a Buddhist monastery, was set up probably in the 8th to the 9th centuries.

Until recently, the name of a *maṇḍala* lying west of Īśānapura was known only from the monk Hsuandang and the tribute missions of A.D. 638 and 649 which came from "Duoheluo to China" (Smith 1979b). Two silver medallions, however, have now provided the local name for this *maṇḍala*. They were found beneath a sanctuary at Nakhon Pathom and proclaim that it was "the meritorious work of the King of Śrī Dvāravatī." The script is in South Indian characters of the 7th century. If it were necessary to rely on documentary and epigraphic evidence alone, we would know that the Chao Phraya valley was one of several strategic points in the development of exchange relationships with India, and that, by the 7th century, a *maṇḍala* existed, whose kings were familiar with Sanskrit. Mōn was the indigenous language, but Sanskrit names were accorded the overlords. Religion incorporated Vaisnism and Buddhism. Archaeological research, however, has expanded our appreciation of the Dvāravatī *maṇḍalas* and their origins. It is important to recall the growing body of evidence that there was a vigorous local population in the Chao Phraya valley when Indian contact began. Several sites are now known which reveal the presence of late prehistoric communities long adapted to the environments on the margins of the Gulf of Siam. We have already seen that the cemeteries at Ban Don Ta Phet included glass, agate and carnelian beads of Indian origin (Glover *et al.* 1984). Excavations at Ban Tha Kae have revealed three occupation phases in a stratigraphic sequence 2.5 m thick. This site was a centre for the manufacture of shell jewellery and pottery vessels, as well as bronze-casting: iron-working was added in the middle layers, and some of the beads were made of blue and orange glass and agate. By the late prehistoric period, the local population used several artefacts with parallels at Oc Eo. There is a gold bead, querns and stamp seals. The point is that the occupation reveals continuity from the late prehistoric period, through a middle period which incorporates Indian trade objects, to a late period with a clear relationship, in terms of material culture, with Oc Eo. The archaeological remains from Ban Tha Kae cover a roughly oval area 1 km long and 700 m wide, giving an area of over 40 ha (Natapintu 1985).

A recent site survey in the lower Bang Pakong valley has revealed several sites yielding glass, agate and carnelian of Indian origin (Bannanurag 1984). There is, then, no shortage of late prehistoric sites in the Chao Phraya plains occupied by those who were initially exposed to exotic Indian artefacts. The most completely published site is Chansen (Bronson and Dales 1973, Bronson 1979). Unlike Ban Tha Kae and Ban Don Ta Phet, it is surrounded by a moat and ramparts and has an associated reservoir. Excavations revealed a 6-phase cultural sequence. The first two are prehistoric and date to between *c* 800 B.C. and A.D. 200/250. Unfortunately, no burials were identified so no range of grave goods, including possible Indian imports, is available. The phase 2 level, however, has yielded an ivory comb decorated with a goose, two horses and Buddhist symbols, in association with two radiocarbon dates suggesting a 1st to 2nd century A.D. context, or possibly a little later (Fig. 5.10). Phases 3–4 are dated between A.D. 200/250–600/650. These levels have yielded tin amulets, pottery stamps, decorative bronze bells and stone bivalve moulds for casting jewellery. All are paralleled at Oc Eo. Bronson has also described eight bowls in a "metallic" black ware with parallels in Śrī Lanka. He has suggested that they may be imported exotic pottery.

Thus far, the sequence of events is very similar to that outlined at Ban Tha Kae, but from phase 5, the situation differed in that a roughly circular moat was excavated, with an internal diameter of *c* 640 m, associated with an external, rectangular reservoir. Judging from the increased quantities of pottery recovered from this settlement area, there was a sharp increase in population at least during the last two phases. The pottery now belonged to a style found in the Dvāravatī sites of the Chao Phraya valley rather than the local forms which preceded them. The excavation of Chansen reveals continuity of occupation from the late prehistoric through to the 7th century, by which time many other large moated sites had been constructed. These have many features in common, and may well have belonged to a Dvāravatī *maṇḍala*.

Most commentators have concentrated on the major moated sites, and these

5.10 The ivory comb from Chansen is one of a growing number of archaeologically recovered artefacts which evidence exchange links between the inhabitants of the Chao Phraya plains and India.

have provided the clearest evidence for the acceptance of Buddhism and centralised political authority. There are about a dozen such sites in the Chao Phraya valley, and their location, configuration and the importance of architectural remains, should not be underestimated. What has been lacking prior to the excavation of Ban Tha Kae is archaeological data bearing on life outside the large moated centres. Moreover, we still have few data on settlement patterns and can only speculate on the presence or otherwise of different levels in the settlement hierarchy.

The major centres have in common a moat and bank, the outline of which differs markedly from the rectangular geometry of the Zhenla centres. Usually they are oval or sub-rectangular in plan, and situated so that a stream filled the moats. Where excavation has taken place, the foundations and remains of the superstructure of religious buildings have been recovered, laterite and brick being the dominant materials used. The buildings include *stūpas* and *caityas.* A *stūpa* is a circular structure built to house relics of the Buddha or his disciples, or to commemorate a place or event in his life. Often the focus of pilgrimages, the *stūpa* has the form of a cupola on a raised platform. A *caitya* is also a Buddhist architectural form, and was a building or temple which housed a sacred object, such as an image of the Buddha. Such structures for the practise of Buddhism were found both within and outside the moated perimeters of the major Dvāravatī centres. The brick superstructure was used as a vehicle for stucco decoration, and the wall niches provided space for the images of the Buddha and animal figures. Quaritch-Wales (1969) has divided the major Dvāravatī centres of the Chao Phraya valley into three regional groups which he has labelled Western, Central and Eastern. There is no reason to suppose that these were political units.

The major sites in the Western group are strategically located on the floodplains of the Mae Khlong and Chao Phraya rivers. Pong Tuk, the first to be identified and excavated, is a major site yielding the remains of Buddhist structures, but it is not moated. When Coedès (1928) visited it, he was shown a bronze Roman lamp of a style current during the 1st to 2nd centuries A.D., a freak discovery when it is considered that a group of entertainers from the Roman Empire traversed Southeast Asia in 120 A.D. on their way to the Chinese court. The early dating of this Roman lamp seemed confirmed by evidence for the equally early date for an unprovenanced bronze statue of the Buddha proposed by Coedès. A subsequent analysis by Dupont (1959), however, has placed this Buddha image as post-Gupta (i.e., later than A.D. 540). Excavations at Pong Tuk revealed the laterite foundations of a series of Buddhist religious structures. A circular building is thought to have been a *stūpa* variety, and a square building may have been a *caitya*, or shrine. A third comprises a rectangular structure to which access was gained by a flight of steps. Bases for columns were noted and it is probable that it represents the remains of a *vihara* or meeting hall. The discoveries at Pong Tuk were the first clear archaeological evidence in the Chao

Phraya area for a society which had adopted Buddhism and had the capacity to raise large religious structures of stone and brick.

U Thong was occupied for many centuries prior to the advent of Dvāravatī *maṇḍalas*, and the impressive artefactual remains have many parallels with Oc Eo. The site is ringed by an oval moat which encloses an area of 1690 × 840 m. This moat is linked with a small stream. It was here that the copper inscription was recovered, recording the accession of Harṣavarman to the lion throne. Although it is clear that there was room for Śaivism in the religious practices at U Thong, the great majority of structures are of Buddhist inspiration. As is often the case, the *stūpa* foundations are distributed inside and outside the moats. Excavations by Boisselier (1968) revealed the foundation for a Buddhist assembly hall about 200 m east of the moats, as well as the foundations for three octagonal brick *stūpas*. These excavations also furnished the fragmented remains of the stucco which covered the brick superstructure. They reveal a wide range of motifs including plant ornaments, mythical *garuḍas, makaras* and *nāgas*, as well as lions. To guage from the description of the lion throne in the U Thong copper tablet, and the number of terracotta models of lions discovered, this animal may have had some special significance to the occupants of this site. Indeed, most writers have referred to it as at one stage a Dvāravatī *maṇḍala* centre (Quaritch-Wales 1969, Diskul 1979:90). If that was the case, then it may well have been in competition with Nakhon Pathom. This is the largest Dvāravatī settlement, having an approximately rectangular plan measuring 3700 × 2000 m. The two silver medallions bearing the inscription "the meritorious work of the King of Dvāravatī" were found beneath a sanctuary within the moated area. Coedès has dated the foundation on the basis of the script to the 7th century A.D., and the sanctuary in question may have been associated with the Phra Pathom *caitya*, a large and impressive structure which is located in the centre of Nakhon Pathom. This building was clearly of considerable importance: it was altered on three occasions during the Dvāravatī occupation of the city (Dupont 1959). It was designed as a rectangular building, access being by flights of steps at each end. The basement pediment has exterior panels decorated with alternating *garuḍas* and elephants. Each flight of steps is flanked by carved lions. The exterior walls of the *caitya* itself bore five inset niches each containing a stucco statue of the Buddha. Several artefacts were found *in situ* under the central tower: they included a bronze chandelier, bells, cymbals, and a representation of the Buddha which Quaritch-Wales ascribes to an early phase in the art of Dvāravatī.

There are many smaller artefacts from Nakhon Pathom which date from the period of Dvāravatī *maṇḍalas*, including statues of the Buddha, and stucco or mouldings used in the decoration of the religious buildings. Perhaps the most important for those concerned with identifying the presence of social stratification are two terracotta "toilet trays" (Boeles 1964). The complete specimen measures 350 × 250 mm, and was used to hold the cosmetics of a very high-status

5.11 The Nakhon Pathom toilet tray was almost certainly used by an overlord of a Dvāravatī *maṇḍala*. It measures 350 × 250 mm. (Courtesy, Elizabeth Lyons.)

individual (Fig. 5.11). The surface is decorated with symbols of royalty: there are fly-whisks, parasols, conch shells, two turtles, thunderbolts and elephant goads, from which Quaritch-Wales (1969:45) has noted survivals in the Thai royal regalia to this day. In the centre, and at each corner, are depressions to contain cosmetic preparations. Lyons (1979) has suggested that this artefact may have been used in the investiture of a ruler. Ku Bua (Fig. 5.6) reflects all the essential characteristics of Dvāravatī centres: a roughly rectangular moated enclosure linked with a stream, and with Buddhist foundations within and outside the moats. This site is smaller than Nakhon Pathom, measuring 2000 by 800 m. Just as at Nakhon Pathom, however, there is a raised and rectangular central *caitya*, measuring 45 by 22.5 m, and abundant evidence for the application of stucco decoration to the religious monuments. Some of those found at Ku Bua are particularly interesting in that they very probably illuminate the activities of classes of individuals who lived at, or visited, the settlement. One depicts a seated royal personage, and another, a group of musicians playing stringed instruments and cymbals. There is a graphic portrayal of prisoners with their hands bound,

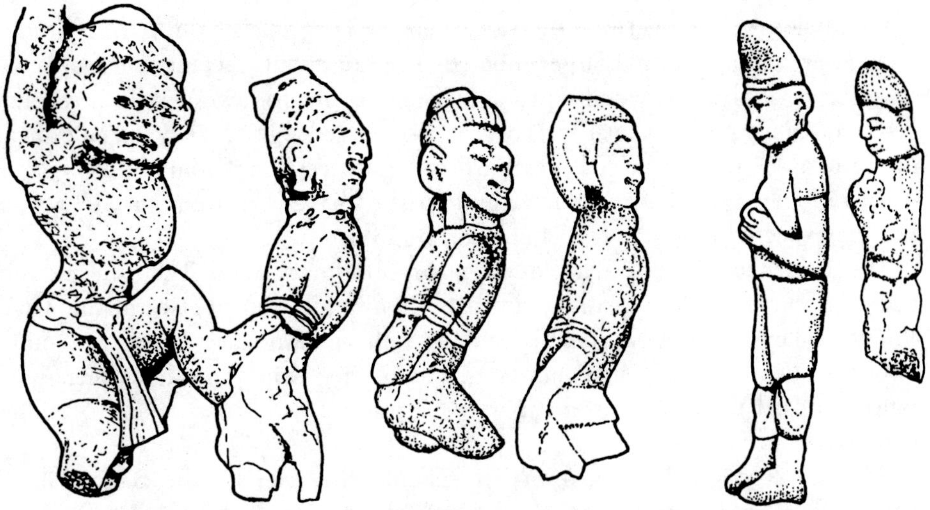

5.12 The stucco figures from Ku Bua reveal many aspects of life in a Dvāravatī centre. Here we see prisoners and visiting Semitic merchants.

the last in line being kicked by their guard (Fig. 5.12). A delightful scene shows a high-status female, perhaps a princess, and her attendants. Then, too, there are servants carrying goods, soldiers, and perhaps most intriguing of all, a group of individuals whom Lyons (1965) has described as Semitic traders (Fig. 5.12). While Quaritch-Wales has warned that these figures may represent fictitious characters from Buddhist *jātaka* stories, their personal jewellery, for example the disc earrings, are characteristically Dvāravatī. It is hard not to associate these lively figures with the realities of social structure characteristic of Ku Bua and the other centres of the Mae Khlong valley.

We have seen that the Lopburi region was rich in late prehistoric settlement. The presence there of a major Dvāravatī centre is known from the discovery of Buddhist images, one bearing two lines of Sanskrit text dated to the 8th century. A stone rendition of the *Thammachakra*, the "wheel of the law", has been found at Lopburi, inscribed this time not in Sanskrit, but Pāli. The wheel of the law was set in motion by the Buddha during a sermon delivered in a Benares deer park, and several such wheels have been found in Dvāravatī contexts. Pāli is the liturgical language of Theravāda Bhuddism. Mōn is also the language used in an inscription recording the gift of slaves and cattle to a monastery dated stylistically to the mid 8th century A.D. (Coedès 1958). Lopburi was subsequently occupied by the Khmer, and indeed remains a thriving regional centre to this day. Hence, nothing is known of the layout and size of the settlement during the Dvāravatī period. Lopburi is located so as to command the junction of the Chao Phraya and Pa Sak rivers. About 100 km up the valley of the latter river, one finds the large moated site of Si Thep. It was near here that a stela was raised to commemorate the accession of the overlord Bhavavarman. Si Thep itself comprises a circular moated area linked with a larger moated enceinte of sub-rectangular shape. We have seen that Śiva was worshipped at Si Thep, for the followers of Bhavavarman consecrated Śiva images nearby. There is also evidence for Mahāyāna Buddhism in the form of figures carved on the rocks of a cavern in Thomarat hill near Si Thep itself. Images of Viṣṇu, Sūrya and Krishṇa have been found at Si Thep, as has the expected evidence for Theravāda Buddhism.

The presence of so much evidence for Hinduism at Si Thep should not occasion surprise. Its position controls communications between the Chao Phraya valley and the Khorat plateau. As will be seen, the plateau was under strong influence from Zhenla *maṇḍalas*, and Si Thep would thus have been much more exposed than the western margins of the Chao Phraya valley to Khmer contact.

The same geographic proximity to Zhenla characterises the Bang Pakong valley. The three large moated settlements there control the passage from the Gulf of Siam up the river valley and so towards Tonle Sap. The site closest to the sea is known as Muang Phra Rot. It is sub-rectangular, and its moated enceinte encloses an area of 1350 by 700 m. Quaritch-Wales has suggested that the feet of a statue there belong to an image of Viṣṇu, and he has also reported a stone relief of the Buddha in association with Brahmā and Indra. Quaritch-Wales (1969) excavated further, and expanded the edge of an area dug as an irrigation tank into a test square which revealed a thin layer of Dvāravatī-style sherds. This site was included in an area subjected to intensive survey for archaeological remains in 1984 (Bannanurag 1984). The pottery found on the surface of Muang Phra Rot was matched at several small, unmoated settlements within the surveyed area. This suggests that the moated city was contemporary with dependant agricultural villages in its hinterland. Furthermore, the presence of marine shells at Muang Phra Rot suggests that it was located much closer to the sea than it is at present (*c* 26 km). It is also interesting to note that a stone mould for casting tin amulets, identical to those from Oc Eo, has been found there, indicating an earlier occupation of the site than has been accepted hitherto.

Dong Si Maha Pot is very similar in size and shape to Muang Phra Rot. It measures 1500 by 800 m and has a rectangular reservoir which covers 2 ha at the northeast corner. Hinduism is evidenced by two *liṅgas* and several statues of Viṣṇu. Casual finds include statues of the Buddha, usually in stone, but in one case, made of gold. There are many laterite foundations for religious edifices inside and outside the moats. A bronze mirror frame from the foundations of a Khmer building has been found. An inscription of A.D. 1187 refers to the town as Watsapura, a name which may have originated when the Chao Phraya valley was incorporated into the Angkorian *Maṇḍala* in the early 11th century.

Past studies of the Dvāravatī material have concentrated heavily on art history. This situation has been redressed by an important analysis of the evidence for iron-working undertaken by Suchitta (1983). His excavations at Ban Di Lung, about 40 km northeast of Lopburi, have revealed evidence for local specialisation in iron-smelting and forging. He recovered much slag, as well as surviving fragments of tuyeres, nozzles, iron ore and clay furnaces. His radiocarbon determinations fall within the 6th and 7th centuries A.D., and reflect the presence of a specialised iron-working village. The interior of many of the moated sites in the Chao Phraya valley likewise reveal concentrations of iron slag, which indicates a widespread practice of iron-working by the direct method of smelting and forging.

In most syntheses of Dvāravatī sites it is assumed that they comprise constituent parts of a kingdom, with a capital first at U Thong and later at Nakhon Pathom. Quaritch-Wales has gone further, and suggested that this Dvāravatī state expanded into the Mun and Chi valleys in Northeast Thailand. But the existence of a state encompassing the entire region of the Chao Phraya, Bang Pakong and Mae Khlong valleys, while feasible, is not yet based on any firm evidence. Indeed, our knowledge of Dvāravatī is still at a very preliminary stage. We know that the area is strategically placed to take advantage of long-distance trade originating in India, and that there were long-established prehistoric communities there when such trading links were forged. There are some finds from Chansen, Ban Tha Kae and Muang Phra Rot which indicate similarities with the material culture of Oc Eo. From the mid 7th century, there were at least ten large moated settlements which were foci for the construction of monumental Buddhist structures in laterite and brick. Buddhism was not exclusive by any means, and the sites in the Pa Sak and Bang Pakong valleys evidence adherence to Hinduism as well. There is evidence from U Thong, Nakhon Pathom and Ku Bua for the presence of a ruling class, of conflict, an army and the taking of prisoners. Indeed the very presence of moats and ramparts at the main sites reflect a need for defence. At present, there is no evidence in favour of one large *maṇḍala* as against a series of small ones each vying for ascendancy. Some evidence in support of the latter comes from the *Songshu* (History of the Sung Dynasty), which refers to Lavo rather than Dvāravatī in the year 1001 A.D. (Pelliot 1904:233). The truth may fall between the two extremes as in Zhenla, where periods of unity under rulers of vigour were punctuated by episodes of fragmentation and regional autonomy. This last possibility is relevant when we turn to the consideration of events in Northeast Thailand, with particular reference to the Mun and Chi valleys.

The Mun and Chi valleys in Northeast Thailand

Northeast Thailand was shielded from early and direct contact from either Indian traders or the expansion of the Han. The Phetchabun range lies between these two river valleys and the Chao Phraya plains, and the Dang Raek range lies between them and the lowlands bordering Tonle Sap and the middle Mekong.

There is, however, an artery of communication via the Mekong valley, and access to the Chao Phraya system is effected via the Pa Sak valley or further to the south via Nakhon Ratchasima. As has been shown, the Mun, Chi and Songkhram valleys were settled two or three millennia before the first glass and agate beads reveal exchange, albeit at second hand, with Indian merchants. Indeed, it has been argued that the period between *c* 500 B.C. – A.D. 500 witnessed the local development of centralised chiefdoms which concentrated along the broader backswamp rice-lands of the Mun and Chi river systems.

There are several sources of information which illuminate the development of such chiefdoms into *maṇḍalas*. There is a corpus of inscriptions, and a few Chinese records which may be relevant. There has been some archaeological research in the area, and surface finds can be analysed from the point of view of art history. Finally, the analysis of folklore has added some interesting information.

It will be recalled that Bhavavarman and Mahendravarman were the overlords responsible for the development of a major *maṇḍala* in the middle reaches of the Mekong. This occurred between *c* A.D. 550–610. There is a corpus of inscriptions which record military activity in the Mun valley during the same period. The earliest was erected at Tham Phet Thong, between the Mun and the Dang Raek mountains, during the reign of Bhavavarman, and commemorates a victory. There is a very fragmentary inscription from as far north as Kumphawapi which also mentions Bhavavarman. It is hard to imagine this overlord being active in a military sense so far from his base in Cambodia (Coedès 1958). The remaining three relevant inscriptions were set up closer to home, in the strategic area where the Mun joins the Mekong. The one from Phou Lakhon records that Mahendravarman was the son of Vīravarman, and younger brother of Bhavavarman. The inscription from Khan Thevada repeats the ancestry and records the raising of a *liṅga* there to commemorate his victory. The cave of Tham Prasat is located one km from the confluence, and Seidenfaden (1922) described a sealing wall, the base for a statue and a Sanskrit inscription recording that a stone statue of a bull, symbolising Śiva, was erected there. The duration of political influence over the settlements in the Mun valley is not known, but is unlikely to have been long. It is also only possible to speculate on the impact upon the occupants of the valley of an expedition under the great overlord Mahendravarman. There can, however, be little doubt that the ruler seized the booty and "slaves" which were one objective of such wars.

The brevity of his dominion is demonstrated by a slightly later group of inscriptions which concentrate in the upper reaches of the Mun valley. A 7th century inscription from Muang Sima, for example, records in Sanskrit and Khmer the donation of buffalo, cattle and slaves of both sexes to a Buddhist community by the overlord of Śrī Canāśa. Another Sanskrit inscription found at Phu Khiao Kao, 50 km northwest of Chaiyaphum, is dated stylistically to the 7th–8th centuries, and mentions an overlord Jaya Siṃhavarman. Again, at Hin

Khon 35 km south of Nakhon Ratchasima, an overlord Nṛipendradhipativarman erected four *sema* stones (for marking Buddhist sacred enclosures) and founded a Buddhist temple during the 8th century. He gifted rice-fields, 10 pairs of cattle, gold and silver utensils, an elephant and a plantation of 20 areca (betel nut) trees. Finally, an inscription, doubtless relocated, found in Ayutthaya and erected in A.D. 937 by a ruler called Mangalavarman, records that his ancestral line of kings ruled over Śrī Canāśa. This inscription is also in Sanskrit and Khmer, rather than the Mōn language which was used in most inscriptions of the Chao Phraya valley, and therefore supports the finding that a *maṇḍala* persisted in the upper Mun valley over several generations.

Between A.D. 798–805, a Chinese official called Jia Dan described an overland route from the coast of Viet Nam over the Truong Son mountains to the "small sea" which is probably the Gulf of Siam. Such a route could hardly have avoided the Khorat plateau. The itinerary describes how it took 16 days to reach the inner capital of a state called Wendan (Pelliot 1904, Smith 1979b). This same state of Wendan is recorded as having sent tribute missions to China in A.D. 753–4, 771 and 779. It is not possible to correlate Wendan with Śrī Canāśa, or any other part of the Mun–Chi area. Nevertheless, the Chinese accounts do provide grounds for suspecting that Northeast Thailand sustained polities able to send ambassadors and recognise capital centres by the period of Śrī Canāśa.

The presence on the Khorat plateau of large settlements behind moats and ramparts has been known at least since the early years of this century (Lunet de Lajonquière 1902), though it was the publication of the results of an air survey by Williams-Hunt (1950) which revealed the extraordinary number of these moated sites, and the great variation in their size. Most scholarly study has been concerned with a limited amount of excavation and the analysis of the art style of objects recovered from excavation and surface recovery. Quaritch-Wales's early excavations within the moats at Muang Phet and Thamen Chai revealed relatively shallow cultural deposits with iron present in the basal levels, and pottery styles which reminded the excavator of Dvāravatī specimens from the Chao Phraya valley. At a time when iron in Southeast Asia was synonymous with Indian influence, these findings led Quaritch-Wales (1957) to conclude that the sites resulted from a movement of people from the Dvāravatī sites of the Chao Phraya onto the Khorat plateau. His description at Thamen Chai of *sema* stones and a bronze Buddha image in Dvāravatī style supported his proposal.

Subsequent excavations at two other large moated sites have provided an alternative view. Both at Ban Chiang Hian and Non Dua, there were lengthy periods of occupation (Higham 1977, Chantaratiyakarn 1984). The initial settlement of the former stretches back in a stratigraphic sequence 6 m thick to the mid-second millennium B.C. At Non Dua, initial occupation took place in the first millennium B.C. As has been shown above, the outstanding unanswered question in all these moated sites is the date when the defences and reservoirs were constructed. At present, the only evidence available is based on reasoned guesswork and, as we shall see, local folklore. Nevertheless, the development of substantial sites which acted as foci for Buddhism is beyond doubt. There are, moreover, two sites which stand out on account of their area and richness of religious structures, one is in the Mun valley and the other in the region of the middle Chi. To judge from their plans, these sites were progressively enlarged. Muang Fa Daet, in the Chi valley, ultimately covered an area of 171 ha, and Muang Sima, in the Mun, grew to rival it in size. The former is situated strategically near the confluence of the Pao and Chi rivers, in an area favourable to the extensive cultivation of rice on backswamps (Fig. 5.13). Its position provides control of the route north via the Pao valley to the Sakon Nakhon basin, and it is likewise axially situated to take advantage of traffic up and down the Chi valley. It was initially reported by a local revenue official who disclosed to Seidenfaden (1954) that there were over two thousand *sema* stones there. That figure might be an exaggeration, but there is no doubting that the site was the focus of an extraordinarily intensive use of these sacred boundary markers. The location of the actual precincts is now lost due to the relocation of the stones to the principal modern village within the enceinte. They still, however, provide

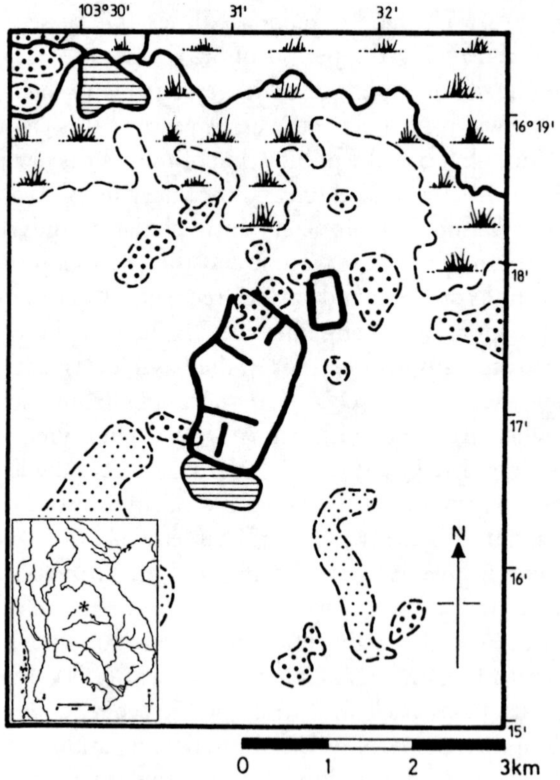

5.13 The location of Muang Fa Daet. The site commands good rice-land (white) rather than land unsuited to rice (stippled).

much information because they are carved to depict Buddhist scenes. One, for example, shows the Buddha in association with Indra and Brahmā. A second shows him with his wife and son following his enlightenment. It is particularly interesting because it shows him seated in front of a wooden hall, or *sālā*, which provides a glimpse of the nature of secular architecture at that period. A town wall and gateway defended by soldiers at the base of this *sema* stone give an idea of what once lay above the barely perceptable ramparts which still demarcate this ancient settlement (Figs. 5.14 and 5.15). Muang Fa Daet was also provided with a substantial rectangular reservoir which covered an area of 15 ha, and recalls similar structures at Chansen and Dong Si Maha Pot in the Bang Pakong valley, and Īśānapura in the valley of the Stung Sen. Further parallels with the former area are seen in the number of brick bases to support *stūpas*, characteristically ringed by the remains of stucco ornamentation. Much energy was required to excavate the moats and ramparts at Muang Fa Daet. Even if we discount completely the construction of a city wall, like that depicted on one of the *sema* stones, and suppose that the moats were only a metre deep, at least 370,000 m^3 of soil would have been relocated in order to complete the outer moat and reservoir at this site. A conservative estimate is that this would have involved well over a million man hours.

Kantarawichai is a smaller moated site situated 20 km west of Muang Fa Daet (Fig. 5.16). Excavations there in 1972 revealed the foundations of an *ubosoth*, or

5.14 The moats of Muang Fa Daet, now scarcely perceptable among the dry season rice stubble, were formerly flanked by the city walls.

5.15 Scene of a town wall and gate with defending soldiers from one of the Muang Fa Daet *sema* stones.

Buddhist ordination hall, built of brick over a laterite base measuring 37 by 10.5 m. A foundation deposit was found in this laterite sub-structure comprising a bowl containing 66 silver plaques (Fig. 5.17, Diskul 1979). These are of exceptional interest because they parallel, in many respects, the motifs and characteristics of the Buddhist buildings of which only the foundations remain. Diskul has identified one figure probably representing a deity-attendant of the Buddha. He has a halo and wears a crown, earrings and an elaborate necklace. A second figure is a royal personage who likewise wears ear ornaments and a necklace. The parallels with these plaques lie in Muang Fa Daet and to the southwest and in the Dvāravatī sites of the Chao Phraya valley.

The region of Nakhon Ratchasima is nodal in any regular contact between the Mun and the Chao Phraya valleys. Indeed, the name means the royal frontier city. Its predecessor, and possibly the main centre of Śrī Canāśa, was the moated site of Muang Sima (Fig. 5.6). Like Muang Fa Daet, it was probably enlarged on two occasions, and the presence there of brick structures and stone representations paralleling those from Dvāravatī indicate a large centre similar in date to Muang Fa Daet. As was the case for the Dvāravatī sites, we remain largely unaware of the relationships between sites and the presence or otherwise of *maṇḍalas* on the Khorat plateau. In purely geographic terms, hegemony from such outstandingly large centres as Muang Fa Daet and Muang Sima over their surrounding territory seems likely. In the case of Muang Sima, there is some epigraphic evidence for this in the references to the polity of Śrī Canāśa. It should

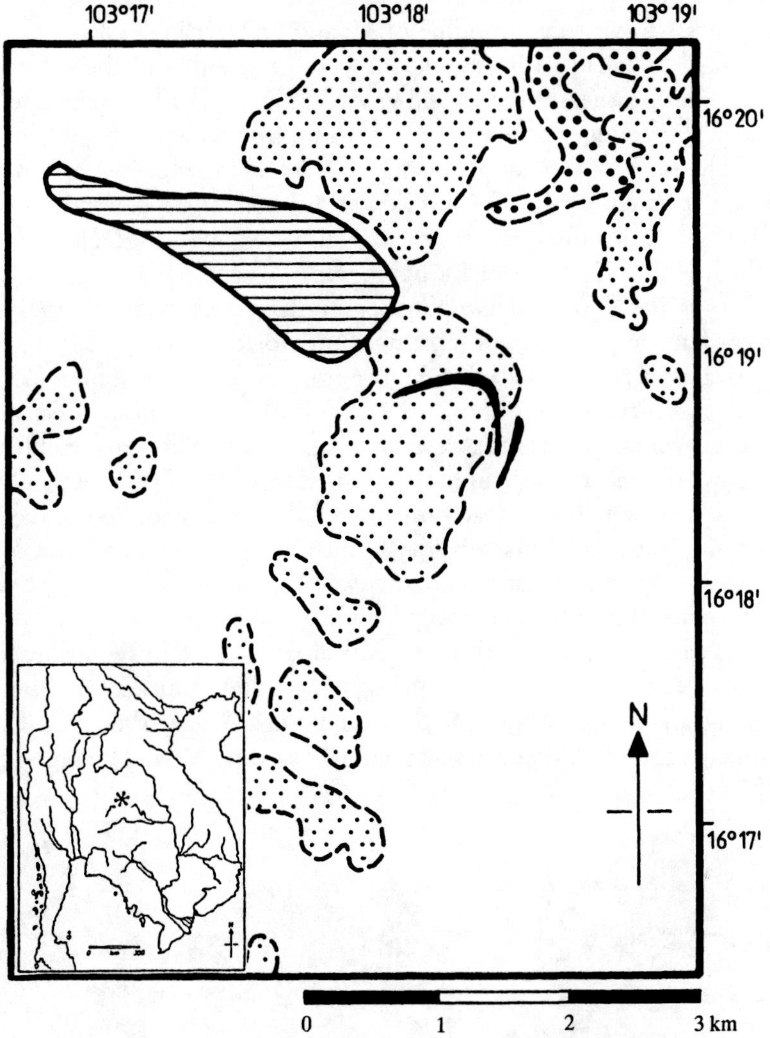

5.16 The location of Kantarawichai. This large moated site is located so as to have access to good rice soils, depicted above as white areas in contrast to the stippled areas which are generally unsuited to wet rice agriculture.

not be forgotten, however, that contemporary events in the middle Mekong, where inscriptions are much more numerous, reveal a fluid political situation where centrality reflected the vigour of individual rulers and was constantly prone to fragmentation. Certainly the widespread presence of moats and reservoirs recalls the association between *poñ* and *travāñ* further down the Mekong valley.

There are some intriguing hints that such a situation also existed on the Khorat plateau. These come from the consideration of local folklore, and have been commented on by Seidenfaden (1954) and Keyes (1974). The former recorded a mythical story of the founding of Muang Fa Daet in A.D. 621. It was evidently founded by Chao Fa Ra-ngum, the younger brother of the ruler of Nong Han. The older brother, as the legend goes, was jealous of Ra-ngum and sent him into exile. The younger prince travelled south, following the course of the Pao River until he reached the site of Muang Fa Daet and established his own principality. Apart from some outposts, his power did not extend beyond his city walls. His daughter was subsequently wooed by a neighbouring ruler, and war ensued which led to the death of Ra-ngum and his neighbour.

Keyes has described two further myths which relate to the same area and record actual place names. One accounts for the origins of Bang Fai, an annual festival which takes place just before the arrival of monsoon rains. It is clearly a festival which owes nothing to Hinduism or Buddhism, but which has very ancient roots. At present, several villages participate in a competition for the biggest and most powerful rocket, which takes the form of a phallus. The idea is that the rocket should reach the clouds, fertilize them and induce rain. It is an occasion for uninhibited ribaldry, which brings together several communities to a central location (Bayard and Uthaiwee 1985). The local legend of Bang Fai, and its origins, recounts a genealogy beginning with Phaya Khom, the ruler of Nong Han, whose marriage with Nang Pathumat resulted in two sons, and a daughter called Nang Ai. The oldest son ruled over Ban Chiang Hian and Ban Iat, the younger son over Muang Si Saeo and Phak Waen. One grandson controlled Muang Hong and Muang Thong, and the second, Muang Phang. Keyes has noted

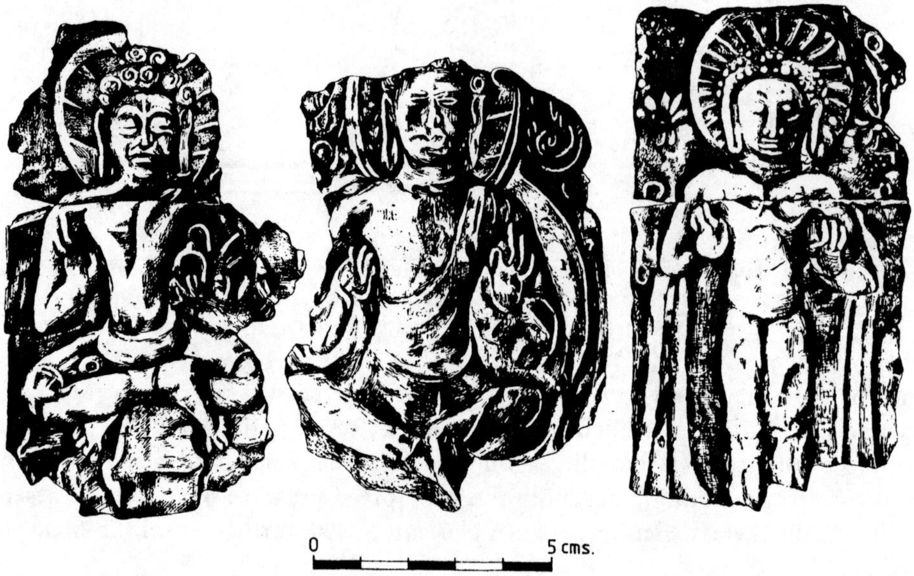

5.17 Excavations at Kantarawichai recovered a number of silver plaques which add to our knowledge of the spread of Buddhism in Northeast Thailand.

that some of the personal names have a Sanskrit derivation, and that place names are paired, for example, Ban Chiang Hian with Ban Iat, and Muang Hong with Muang Thong. Apart from Nong Han, all these sites are situated in the middle and lower valley of the Chi River. It is interesting to note that the sons of a given noble or royal line boasting Sanskrit names ruled over individual centres, with at least one named subsidiary settlement. This structure recalls that described for the initial stages in the formation of Mekong delta *maṇḍalas*, where the overlord placed his sons in charge of settlements within his domain, and is a small thread of evidence for the existence of a *maṇḍala* with dependant vassals. If the folklore reflects some sort of proto-historic reality, and Bayard (1980) has warned that they could be of much more recent date, then these princelings engaged in rivalries expressed not only in a rocket tournament, but also in genuine warfare. As was the case for Chao Phraya Dvāravatī settlements, however, these little *maṇḍalas* bowed to the strength of the Khmer and joined the Angkorian *Maṇḍala* during its period of expansion which began in the 9th–10th centuries.

The Han: three border commanderies

The Red River valley and delta not only comprises one of the most extensive tracts of flat agricultural land in Southeast Asia, but it also occupies a nodal position for exchange between the coasts of the Gulf of Bac Bo and the hinterland of Yunnan. It was the area which sustained a long-term occupation of agriculturalists beginning with the Phung Nguyen phase and culminating with the culture of Dong Son. South of Ninh Binh, the flat, agriculturally rich coastal belt narrows from the broad expanse of the delta and gives way to the valleys of first the Ma, and then the Ca, rivers. The delta, therefore, stands out as an oasis of flat terrain, ringed by uplands, and facing the Gulf of Bac Bo. The archaeological and Chinese documentary sources, as well as surviving fragments of indigenous folklore, are unanimous in confirming the local development of one or more chiefdoms in the area during the period 500–1 B.C.

Bac Bo

As the Dong Son chiefdoms were developing, major events were occurring in China which were to have a profound impact, not only on the occupants of the Red River area, but also the people who lived along the coastal fringes of Central Viet Nam. During the appropriately named "Warring States" period, (*c* 453–221 B.C.), a power struggle between the royal Zhou Dynasty and the states of Qin, Wei, Han, Zhao, Chu, Yan and Qi, preoccupied political events and precipitated profound social, technological and bureaucratic changes (Creel 1964). These events occurred in the basin of the Yellow River about 1800 km north of Bac Bo. The interior valleys and coastal areas south of the Qin and Han Empires were, at that juncture, occupied by numerous regional chiefdoms uniformly regarded by the Chinese as southern barbarians, the Nan Yue. Three trends can be detected during the period of Warring States which ultimately affected the southern barbarians, including the Dong Son chiefs of Bac Bo. Firstly, military techniques and weapons underwent a transformation. The Warring States maintained large armies, and they were equipped with technologically radical weapons. The crossbow was developed, together with the increasing application of iron to armaments and improved tactical skills in the construction, defence and investment of walled cities. At the beginning of the Warring States period, Chinese polities were still organised along lines recalling the European feudal system. New lands were enfeoffed to noble families and accorded limited sovereignty. Regional loyalty, under these circumstances, was directed to the great landed families rather than the central ruler, and the result was potential instability and insurrection. Shen Buhai, who died in *c* 337 B.C., was the author of an influential text which had a lasting influence (Creel 1964). He recognised the impermanent nature of the system and advocated the appointment of bureaucrats from the central authority. No one minister, he said, should be too powerful, but rather ministers should move in harmony, like the spokes of a wheel. The end of the period of Warring States came with the supremacy of the state of Qin in 221 B.C. The victories of Shi Huangdi, the first emperor of China, were facilitated not only by economic efficiency and army discipline, but also by a system of choosing bureaucrats on the basis of merit. The Qin Dynasty was hardly to outlive the life of its founder, and the struggle for power which took place between 209–202 B.C. resulted in victory for the first emperor of the Han Dynasty. It was under the Han (202 B.C.–A.D. 220) that the Chinese exercised an increasingly direct influence over the course of events in Bac Bo.

An appreciation of this impact turns on understanding the new organisational structure imposed in conquered territories. Han rulers maintained the Qin system of a centralised bureaucracy in which the empire was divided into commanderies, each of which was sub-divided into *xian*. At the centre of each, and synonymous with, the *xian*, was a walled settlement. Indeed, the Chinese ideograph for city wall and city are identical. Under Shi Huangdi, all 36 of his commanderies had a centrally appointed civilian and military governor, and a superintendant. The Han formalised this system by appointing officials through an entrance examination, and training them, from 124 B.C. in a university centre for administration. By A.D. 1, there were 130,285 centrally appointed officials in charge of the day-to-day functions of the state.

The weight of the Han military machine, and the imposition of the commandery and *xian* structure, were powerful tools for centralisation. With the Han, expansion into what was described as barbarian territory became state policy. The territorial extent of the Han Empire can be measured by the establishment of *xian* walled centres (Creel 1964). These were essentially foci for Chinese administrative control and the collection and deployment of taxation.

As is so often the case, documentary and legendary sources for historic events must be treated with the greatest caution. O'Harrow (1979) has reminded us of this in his circumspect analysis of such records as they apply to Han expansion in the direction of Bac Bo. It must be recalled that the Nan Yue to the north of Bac Bo provided a buffer against direct Han contact for a critical couple of centuries, though this did not rule out exchange contact or even the payment, when felt prudent, of tribute.

According to documentary and legendary sources, the earliest impact of Chinese expansion to be felt in Bac Bo was an indirect result of the conflict between the Warring States and the occupants of Nan Yue. In 333 B.C., the Chu state subjugated Nan Yue, and, slightly later, Qin conquered Shu. Taylor (1983) has proposed a most plausible hypothesis, that the bulk of the conquered population remained in their native villages but the rulers with armed retainers moved away from the source of attack in a southerly direction. The establishment of new principalities led to the Chinese referring to the area as "the hundred Yue". It is quite possible that a Nan Yue aristocrat, known in historic sources as An Duong, was one such displaced leader. He is said to have moved into Bac Bo and replaced the indigenous Hung kings in 258 B.C. establishing the kingdom of Au Lac. His capital was, according to tradition, located at Co Loa. This date marks the inception of a period when the Red, Ma and Ca river valleys came progressively within the orbit of China. During the brief period of Qin rule, the first emperor despatched several armies totalling a reputed half million men to Nan Yue to expand the imperial frontier. Among other things, the emperor was said to be interested in the ivory, rhinoceros horn, kingfisher feathers and pearls supplied by the southern barbarians.

The step to incorporation within the Chinese Empire came closer following the downfall of the Qin Dynasty. During the ensuing struggle for power, which resulted in the establishment of the former Han Dynasty, Zhao Tuo, a Chinese administrator in the Guangdong region, siezed power and proclaimed himself king of Nan Yue. The power in his southern kingdom was acknowledged by the Han emperor in 196 B.C., while 11 years later, the Han empress issued an edict which forbade the export of strategic goods to Nan Yue. The list is interesting: it includes gold, iron, weapons, cattle and horses. Zhao Tuo was also interested in expanding his new kingdom and his attention turned south to the Red River polity of Van Lang. By 208 B.C., Van Lang had been conquered and replaced by two new commanderies: Jiaozhi in the Red River valley and Jiuzhen in the Ma valley. These owed allegiance not to the Han Dynasty, but to the sinicised rulers of the kingdom of Nan Yue. The relationship probably involved the extraction of tribute from chiefdoms whose structure seems to have remained intact. Indeed, a century was to elapse before the Han rulers finally resolved to replace Nan Yue with their own centrally administered system of commanderies. They moved in 111 B.C., and in the reorganisation which followed the arrival of the successful Chinese armies, Nan Yue was subdivided into seven commanderies, of which three concern us. Jiaozhi and Jiuzhen remained, the former with 10 districts and the latter with seven. A third, Rinan, was founded, and comprised five districts. It is at this juncture that we are again provided with a glimpse of the social organisation in Bac Bo. Evidently the local chiefdoms maintained their hold on land and their status as regional leaders. The "Lac" lords, a name given in Chinese sources to the local leaders, were familiar with the rise of the river levels during high tides, and introduced water into their rice-fields to intensify production. Their leadership role in local affairs, where the Chinese presence must have been concentrated in commandery seats, was recognised by their appointment as sub-prefects within the Han administration (Taylor 1983, Wheatley 1983).

There was, nevertheless, an inherent tension in a system where traditional leadership roles were subservient to local bureaucrats answerable to a distant court. Moreover, the pace of change accelerated. We read of the local people being "instructed in justice and ritual", required to accept Chinese marriage rituals and to wear hats and sandals (Taylor 1983). This change in marriage ritual is, as O'Harrow (1979) has stressed, of considerable importance, because if his thesis that the Dong Son pattern of inheritence was organised along matrilineal lines is correct, then Han men marrying local women would, according to local lore, have been unable to inherit land. In any event, the brief interregnum between former and later Han (A.D. 9–23) was also an occasion when numerous Chinese sought refuge from danger in this remote southern corner of the empire.

The official biography of the governor of Jiuzhen from A.D. 25 also provides insight into Chinese aims and, by inference, local conditions and changes. Ren Yan found that his commandery relied upon rice imported from its northern neighbour due to local concentration on fishing and hunting, and an insufficiency of land under agriculture. He therefore encouraged the production of iron implements and an increase in the area under cultivation. One effect of this would have been an enlarged tax revenue, and easier control over the more sedentary farmers. This increased Chinese influence on affairs in this remote corner of their empire was evidently irksome to the Lac chiefs and, in A.D. 40, a major rebellion broke out led by an aristocratic woman called Trung Trac, assisted by her sister. She hailed from Me Linh, for generations the heartland of Bac Bo, and the revolt rapidly spread to the southerly commanderies. Evidently 60 strongholds were overrun, and the Chinese administration swept aside. For two years she was recognised as paramount over the Lac lords, who briefly found themselves freed from the tribute required of them from their foreign masters.

The course of events following the rebellion is well-documented in the Chinese annals. In A.D. 42, the Chinese general Ma Yuan marched into Bac Bo. He defeated the Trung sisters and their followers in battle, and then proceeded further south to the Ma valley, where he subjugated the rebellious chiefs and their supporters. Hitherto, the Lac lords had, through several generations, retained their land rights and status as local leaders. After his military successes, Ma Yuan introduced structural changes, which brought the leadership role of the surviving Lac lords to an end. Ma Yuan formalised and intensified the establishment of *xian* cities, and expanded agriculture by the excavation of irrigation facilities. Taylor (1983) sees the latter as implying the imposition of Chinese ownership and control over productive land and the replacement of the Lac chiefs. Ma Yuan also specified clearly the legal obligations within the Chinese system of provincial administration. The aftermath was the establishment of the so-called Han–Viet period. This saw the replacement of the former attempt to integrate indigenous chiefdoms with a loosely imposed Han tribute system by the imposition of a full Chinese administration.

It is easy to be diverted by the course of historic events from the underlying developments and changes in the economic basis of life in the Red River area. We do know that the impact of Chinese contacts involved more intensive agriculture, and it is not coincidental that the Dong Son ploughshares are not only of Han-type, but also restricted to the areas of Southeast Asia which fell under Han control. We know that the Qin and Han rulers were interested in exotic southern products such as ivory and rhinoceros horn, plumage and pearls. Iron was sent in the opposite direction, while salt and slaves were important in the exchange activities. However, it should not be overlooked that the Red River delta occupied a nodal position in the developing maritime trade with the coastal communities of Southeast Asia, India and beyond, even to the eastern provinces of the Roman Empire. Wang (1958) has traced the history of the so-called Nanhai (southern sea) trade. Essentially, the great expansion of the Han Empire brought a new order of demands for goods. Particularly during periods of relative peace, this exposed the indigenous societies of coastal Southeast Asia to a concept of extraction and trade radically distinct from that described above for the autonomous, ranked communities or even developing chiefdoms.

Even if no documentary sources had survived, the major changes described above would have been evident from the archaeological record. Any further increase in our appreciation of the period of Chinese expansion is far more likely to come from archaeology rather than from documentary sources. We have seen that the expansion of the Han Empire had a growing impact on the Dong Son chiefdoms of the Red and Ma river valleys. There is clear evidence for such contact in the later graves of the Dong Son cultural phase, in the form of Chinese artefacts. Janse (1958), for example, found in the "Indonesian" (i.e., prehistoric Dong Son) grave number 2, both metal coins and beads made of glass and carnelian. The jewellery is probably of Indian origin, but the coins come from China. So, too, does the iron sword found in this grave. His tomb number 1 contained a bronze vase with tripod feet and ringed handles which is clearly of Chinese inspiration. The great boat-coffin from Viet Khe, near Haiphong, was richly endowed with bronze vessels and arms of Chinese origin or inspiration, while the Red and Ma valleys have yielded numerous Han-type ploughshares, crossbow bolts and trigger mechanisms and axe-halberds. Iron implements were very much rarer in late Dong Son contexts. Both the documentary and the archaeological evidence point to a Chinese origin for iron artefacts during the last few centuries of the first millennium B.C.

The Dong Son burial rite centred on inhumation, sometimes in a coffin, in association with pottery vessels, bronze artefacts and jewellery, which was often exotic, such as glass and carnelian. Some graves were particularly rich, and surely house the Lac aristocrats themselves. This ritual changed markedly, and the available chronological evidence points to a date later than the punitive campaign of Ma Yuan. The new burial rite involved the construction of a brick chambered tomb and the raising of an earth mound over it: these are found grouped together so as to form a necropolis. The first such chambered tomb was investigated in 1896 (Parmentier 1917) at Ke Noi, just outside Hanoi. It comprised five chambers, but it had been looted in antiquity and little remained inside. The scattered finds were nevertheless interesting – they included a bronze spearhead and part of a clay house model. The provision of such models is a characteristic of Han tombs in China. Further tombs were reported in the vicinity of Quang Yen, northeast of Haiphong, while another from Phan Thau was found intact. It was a far simpler structure than the example from Ke Noi, comprising but two chambers. Grave goods included Chinese coins, a Han-style bronze bowl and several pottery vessels. The example from Nghi Ve is particularly impressive, having a whole series of underground chambers and niches (Fig. 5.18). The most complete survey of Han Dynasty tombs was undertaken by Janse (1947), in the years preceding the second world war. In all, he identified 13 groups, and excavated numerous individual burials. Although no structure rivalled that from Ke Noi in complexity of design, it is clear from the rich burial offerings in the few intact tombs, that the Han–Viet were prepared to invest much energy and wealth in burying the dead. The tumuli average 20 by 17.5 m, and some still stand to a height of 2–3 m. The chambers were constructed of bricks which were locally made and often decorated. No complete skeletons have survived, but fragments of wood in some graves suggest the use of wooden coffins. It may be that the acidic soil has destroyed human remains, but it is also possible that bodies were ultimately removed to China for interment.

Most of the grave structures comprised two chambers, one for the burial, and the smaller one for placing the grave goods. The most impressive necropolis was found in the vicinity of Lach Truong. This site is located east of Thanh Hoa, and the river estuary there is still a haven for coastal shipping. Janse (1947) has suggested that it was formerly a Han port, a situation which might explain the variety and richness of the grave furniture which includes a great variety of pottery vessels, some of which are glazed. Glazing was not practiced in prehistoric Southeast Asia, and the technology of closed kiln firing to sustain a high temperature over a lengthy period of time was one of the technological innovations introduced by the Han. Jars, cups and tripod-based bowls were used in cooking and eating, but pottery lamps and incense burners also represent a

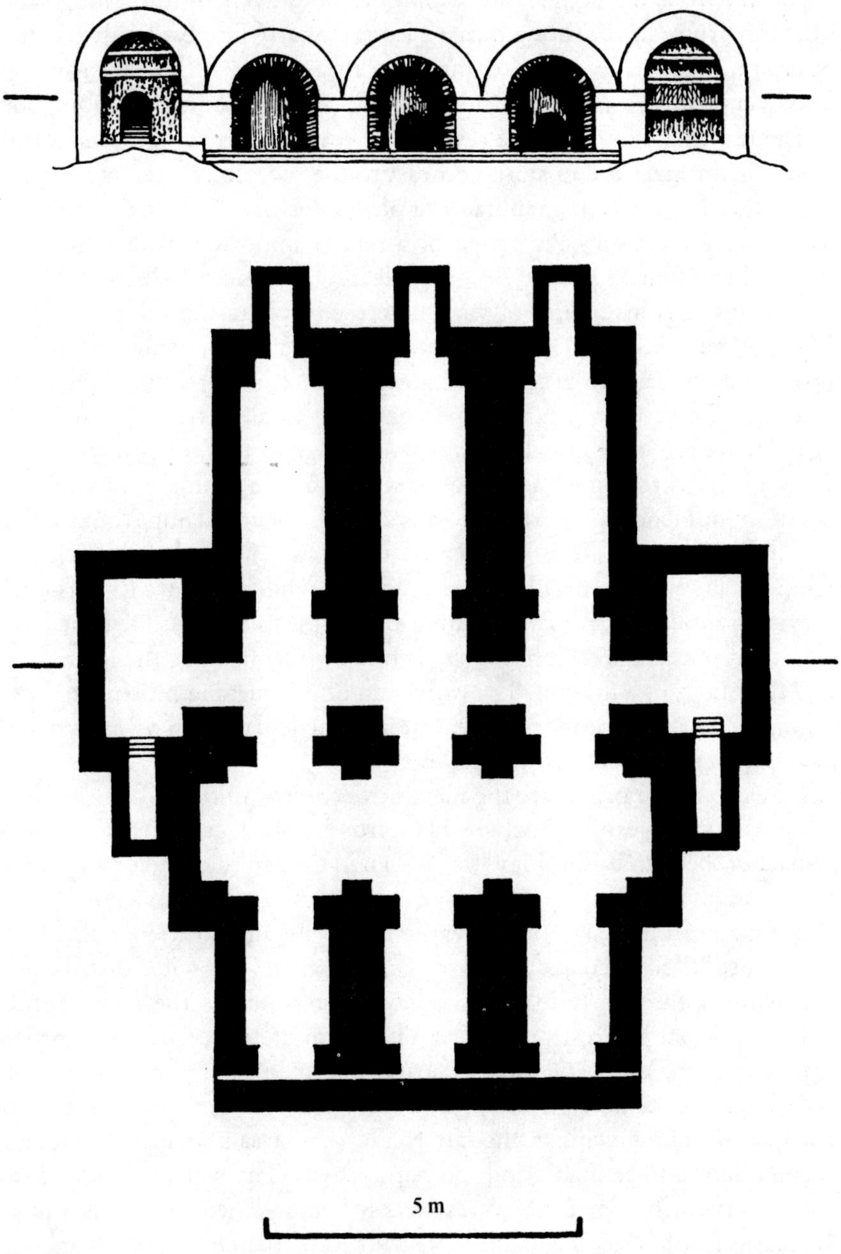

5.18 The Han Chinese introduced their own style of burial into Bac Bo, which involved subterranean brick chambers complete with the objects owned by the dead. This particularly impressive example comes from Nghi Ve.

departure from the styles and techniques employed by the Dong Son potters. One tray from Lach Truong burial 1 is particularly interesting. Its central motif is of clear Chinese inspiration, comprising three fishes with heads touching. Yet it also bears a design of circles linked by tangents, a traditional Dong Son motif.

The few intact burials have revealed a wealth of bronze objects, but very little iron. The bronzes are in stark contrast to the repertoire characteristic of the late Dong Son burials. The manufacture of the decorated drums and situlae ceased. These were replaced by a range of artefacts imported from China, or at least inspired by Chinese prototypes. The clearest evidence of Chinese inspiration are the strings of coins, many of which were minted during the rule of the usurper Mang Wang (A.D. 9–23). These coins must be earlier than the burials, but by how much is hard to ascertain. Indeed, such coins are still used as good-luck charms. The bronze tripods, vases and kettles all reveal Han inspiration but, again, there are some novel bronzes which suggest that the heirs to the Dong Son bronze-smiths remained active and subject to non-Chinese, possibly ultimately Western, influence. Of particular interest is the bronze lamp from tomb 3 at Lach Truong (Fig. 5.19). It is dominated by a human figure which is clearly not Chinese. He wears a necklace and bracelets, while there are dwarfs on his knees playing musical instruments. Three branches are also embellished with small figures of musicians each holding a lamp. Two lamps take the form of a chicken, and the other, of a dragon. The provision of oil-burning mortuary lamps in Han China was a widespread practice, but this particular lamp owes as much to local and Indian inspiration as to Chinese.

Of clearer Han origin are the metallic decorated mirrors, bells and belt-hooks, while the rare weapons include Han crossbow triggers and axe-halberds. The impact of the Han technology is also seen in the rare survival of lacquerwork, and the wrapping of some grave goods in silk cloth. Personal jewellery included beads made from glass, amber, carnelian, agate and rock-crystal. Occasionally, too, Janse discovered jade split rings, which have a wide distribution in late prehistoric contexts. Indeed, some have been found in the Dong Son burials.

Of particular interest are the clay house models, because they provide some insight into the domestic architecture of the Han–Viet period. It is evident that security was considered necessary, because the domestic quarters were ringed by a single or double wall. In the latter cases, the area between the walls provided accomodation for animals and, perhaps, slaves. The walls provided foundations for a house of one or two stories, access being gained by a removable wooden staircase. Roofs were probably constructed of thatch or split bamboo, kept in place by wooden ridge-poles. The walled enclosures also contained miniature ovens with cooking pots in place, together with a well. One example from Tho Dai contained a miniature conical granary. The design of such house compounds contrasts markedly with the pile dwellings depicted on the earlier Dong Son drums.

Lach Truong is one of the most impressive of the Han–Viet cemeteries in

Jiuzhen commandery. It comprises approximately 30 tumuli, located on a plain of the Linh Truong Giang River, about 5 km from the present coast. Janse excavated 27 tombs, the mounds of which varied in length between 10–35 m. Only tombs 3 and 4 were found intact, so the information which the tomb group once contained has been largely lost. The two undisturbed examples reveal considerable grave wealth. Number 3 comprised three compartments under a 35 m long mound. The bronze lamp already described was found in the archway leading from the "chapel" into the mortuary chamber proper. The chapel also housed several other bronze receptacles including a jar, and a basin containing a bowl. One bronze bottle was still partially covered by silk material. Unfortunately, the coffin and human remains have not survived, but the mortuary chamber did contain an iron sword, some carnelian beads, three bronze cymbals, and the remains of red lacquer. The third chamber also housed two bronze kettles, and a number of pottery containers including a steamer for cooking. The excavator suggested that these vessels had formerly been placed on wooden shelves, and fell when the wood decayed.

5.19 The lamp holder from tomb 3 at Lach Truong is probably a locally made item. Janse (1962) has detected ultimately Western influence in the central figure. Janse (1962) did not supply a scale. (Courtesy, W.G. Solheim and *Asian Perspectives.*)

The mound of burial 4 measured 25 by 17 m, and was probably terraced into two tiers. Again, the brick structure had three chambers on a brick pavement, and was found intact. The central mortuary chamber did not contain a coffin, but burial 8 did reveal one, made from a tree trunk and measuring 2.75 by 0.60 m. The burial 4 mortuary chamber contained an iron cauldron, two bronze bowls, two sets of Han coins, a disc-shaped mirror and a bronze cane with a bird-headed handle. The bird in question is probably a pigeon, symbol of longevity. One ante-chamber contained 36 complete pots, and the other revealed an iron lamp, and more ceramic jars and vases.

A second major necropolis was found at Bim Son. It comprised 15 mounds, of which one tomb was undisturbed. In this case, two human tibiae indicated that the human remains had not been disturbed or removed in antiquity. The funerary remains were rich, and Janse has suggested that they were the possessions of a military mandarin. A prominant item among the grave goods was an iron sword, with a blade 1.25 m long, in an iron scabbard. This was associated with an iron dagger, as if they comprised a set. The scabbard was embellished with an applied jade ornament. Bronzes included bowls, a belt-hook and mirror, and a bronze tripod-bowl with handles and a decorated lid.

The distribution of these Han–Viet tumuli reveals a preference for lowland tracts of good agricultural land near waterways. It is unfortunate that so little archaeological attention has been paid to the settlements which presumably existed in the vicinity of the burial grounds. The potential of settlement archaeology is only too obviously shown by the recent excavations at Co Loa. These revealed, as should be expected for a 3rd century B.C. foundation, Dong Son-style pottery under the middle rampart. Within this enceinte, excavations also uncovered a magnificent Dong Son drum which contained over one hundred bronze ploughshares, while outside the ramparts, was a cache of Han-style triple-barbed arrowheads. Of equal interest is the discovery of the very kilns which were used to fire the tiles, bricks, glazed pottery and house models which were used in the construction and embellishment of the tombs. A mound 37 by 34 m in extent covered a brick kiln at Tam Tho Phu. It was among the vast quantity of wasters from this enclosed kiln that Janse (1951) identified parts of miniature houses as well as glazed ceramics, and even spindle whorls and net weights. Some of the roof tiles bore imprints of the Chinese characters for "long life" and "joy".

The real turning point in the Chinese contacts with their three southern commanderies of Jiaozhi, Jiuzhen and Rinan came with the campaigns of Ma Yuan. The imposition of Han admininstration changed the basis of land tenure, and the emasculation of the power of Lac aristocrats, described in the surviving literature and Vietnamese folklore, is confirmed by archaeological investigations. Henceforth, events in Bac Bo were greatly influenced by political events in the Han Empire. The imposition of the Han commanderies on indigenous chiefdoms cannot have failed to have an impact on the inhabitants of adjacent territory.

The *maṇḍalas* of Champa

The late prehistoric settlement in the coastal tracts of central coastal Viet Nam involved cremation. The ritual involved the interment of the human ashes in a large pottery urn, often in association with grave goods made of iron and exotic stone jewellery. This group is called after the site of Sa Huynh. Cremation was a most unusual burial practice in mainland Southeast Asia during the prehistoric period, but became widespread with increased Indian influence. As we shall see, the Sa Huynh culture was located in an area where later inscriptions reveal Cham as the vernacular tongue. Cham is an Austronesian language, quite distinct from the Vietnamese and Mōn–Khmer languages spoken two millennia ago in mainland Southeast Asia outside the terrain occupied by the Chams. Speakers of Cham seem to have occupied a narrow coastal strip, where flat land was at a premium. The rivers are short and prone to sharp flooding when rains are heavy on the Truong Son cordillera to the west. The enclaves of flat land are cut where mountain spurs reach out to the coast. The spurs fragment the coastal strip into several distinct valley systems, and blur any semblance of territorial continuity. In this respect, the area lacks the unifying characteristics of the major river valleys. As was the case for Dvāravatī, it is highly likely that only in exceptional circumstances, if ever, was there just one large Cham *Maṇḍala*. The existence of several *maṇḍalas* is supported by the regional names used by the Chams themselves (see below and Jacques 1984). Given such geographic fragmentation, and the constrained nature of the coastal plain, communication and exchange along this coast was most easily undertaken by sea. To the west lay the Truong Son range, which provided a major obstacle to communication with the Mekong valley, save for three passes. This long coastline was nevertheless strategically placed, particularly as the pace of maritime commerce, the Nanhai trade, accelerated with Chinese interest in a southern route to India and the Roman Empire. Not only were the Cham speakers who controlled this coast able to supply goods sought for the China trade, they also collected dues from ships which passed by or through their harbours. Parmentier (1909, 1918b) has recognised five major subdivisions in this coastal strip, divisions which are geographically validated and were recognised politically by the Chams themselves. The first need hardly detain us. It lies between Ham Tan and Cape Nay, an inhospitable stretch of coastline with little rainfall and thin, sandy soils: it was a refuge for the Chams, when on the point of annihilation by the expanding Viets, and is the only part of the coastal tract which retains significant numbers of Cham speakers (Fig. 1.2). There are very few Cham monuments there. Between Cape Dinh and Cape Nay, however, there are three well-watered valleys separated by low passes. There are some surviving vestiges of evidence for irrigation systems, and several Cham sites. The area was known to the Chams as Pāṇḍuraṅga.

North of Cape Dinh, the coastal strip broadens into a plain *c* 70 by 70 km in extent. There are many sites on this plain, known to the Chams as Kauṭhāra, with its centre at Po Nagar. Further north again, we come to another focus of settlement and ritual activity known as Vijaya. The region of Amarāvati, however, which lies between the Hai Van pass and Quy Nhon, was nearly always the dominant area of Cham political centrality (Fig 5.20). It has a reasonable area of land available for agriculture, and several well-sheltered harbours. The last area lies north of the Hai Van pass, with most archaeological sites being concentrated in the vicinity of Quang Tri.

Being located on the doorstep of China's most southern commandery, it is hardly surprising to find that most of the documentary evidence for the Chams is found in Chinese sources. There is a consistency in these descriptions from which several important points emerge. The first is that there were episodes of warfare and raiding on the southern frontier of Rinan which provoked either punitive expeditions or diplomatic negotiations. At times of a relatively weak administration, when central authorities were engaged in internal friction, the "barbarians" beyond the frontier had less to fear from reprisals, and were able to make territorial gains. The second point is that such periods of open conflict were punctuated by the restoration of diplomatic relations which involved tribute missions being sent to the Chinese court. The Chinese histories recorded such missions as coming from the "state" of Linyi. They inform us of the civil centres of Linyi, and the names of their overlords up to the early 6th century. From that period local inscriptions provide the names of some rulers in Sansksrit (Maspero 1928).

The dynastic history of Linyi

Already by 1928, Maspero (1928) was arguing that it would be premature to regard Linyi as a state when it was first described in the Chinese histories. Rather, he saw it as a series of regional chiefdoms linked, no doubt, by a common language, and further bonded by the presence of a common adversary in the form of the Han Chinese. This suggestion is supported by the *Jinshu* (History of the Jin) which, towards the end of the 3rd century A.D., noted that Linyi comprised numerous tribes which provided mutual assistance and refused submission to China. Given this situation, it is not surprising that the initial references in documentary sources recorded a raid into southern Rinan commandery, during which the local sub-prefect was killed. In the *Houhanshu* (History of the later Han), the thousand or so belligerents were referred to as the Zhu Lian, and this raid is dated to A.D. 137. In A.D. 192, there was further border unrest and, on this occasion, the Chinese refer to the leader of the uprising as Zhu Lian, who seized part of southern Rinan and proclaimed himself king. This event set in train the first dynasty of Linyi. Between A.D. 220–230, the Linyi sent their initial tribute mission to the governor of the southern commanderies. We do not know the name of Zhu Lian's successor, only that the middle years of the 3rd century saw continued raiding. During one such campaign, the dominant border strong-

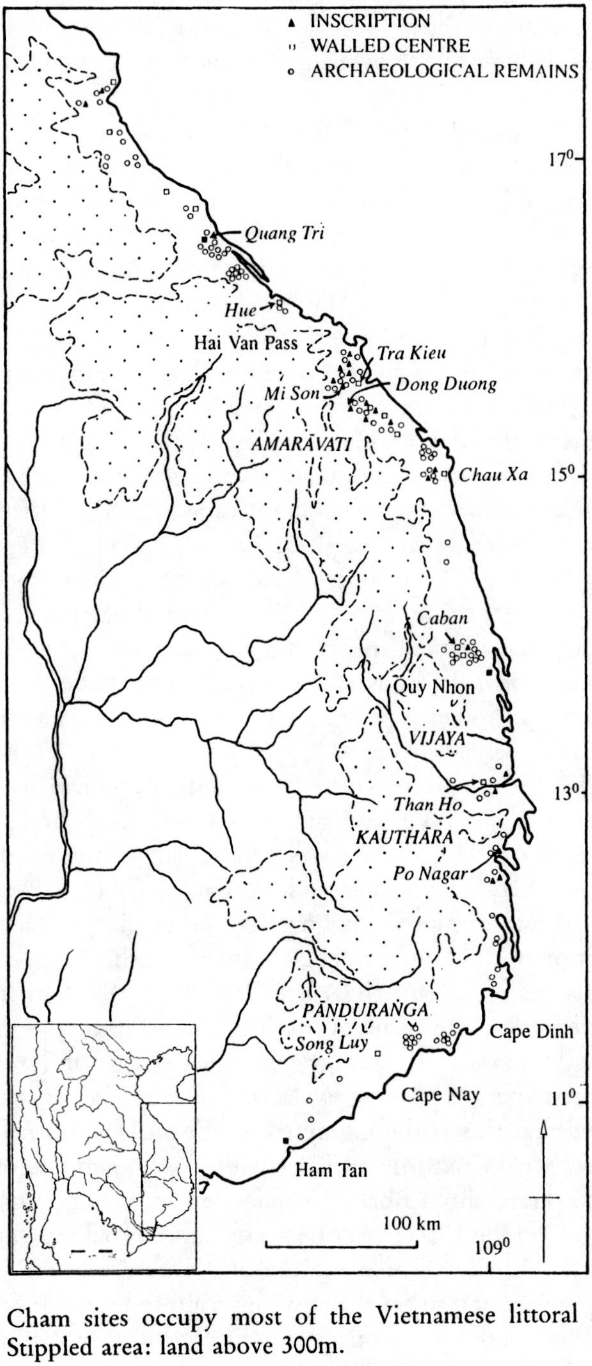

5.20 Cham sites occupy most of the Vietnamese littoral south of Bac Bo. Stippled area: land above 300m.

point of Qusu was taken by Linyi. This centre was strategically placed on a mountain spur adjacent to the river Giang. It controlled the southern defences to Rinan and one of the few routes over the Truong Son mountains to the Mekong valley.

In *c* A.D. 270, we are informed of the first overlord of Linyi, after the initial reference to the founder of the dynasty, Zhu Lian. He was evidently the grandson of the founder, and he was recorded under the name Fan Xiong. His son was called Fan Yi who, in A.D. 284, despatched the first official embassy to the Chinese court rather than to the governor of Jiaozhi. An interesting insight into the impact of China on the Linyi at this juncture is provided by the activities of Fan Yi's principal adviser, a man known as Wen. The latter was of Chinese origin who, through his travels, was well informed on Chinese military architecture and tactics. He brought his experience to bear by advising the ruler on the construction of walled and moated defences and the design and manufacture of up-to-date weapons. His experience was also influential in civil architecture, for apparently he advised the overlord on the construction of a colonnaded hall. Fan Yi died only a decade after entering the king's service, and his legitimate descendants were apparently poisoned. Wen, now titled Fan Wen, accordingly took power upon himself and, in A.D. 336, founded the second dynasty of Linyi. Fan Wen was clearly concerned with the expansion of his territory. He evidently imposed his authority on previously independent tribes and, while sending a tribute mission to China, continued a policy of border conflict. His embassy took a letter from him written in a "barbarian", presumably Indian, script. It should not be overlooked that the expansion of trade to Southern China from the Mekong delta area occurred at this time, and that Indian merchants and religious functionaries were regular callers at the ports which Fan Wen controlled.

Fan Wen was succeeded by his descendants Fan Fo (A.D. 349–) and Fan Hua (A.D. 399–413). It was during the reign of the latter that the Sanskritisation of names and adoption of the Hindu religion were established. The evidence comes from inscriptions instigated by the ruler Bhadravarman. Christie (1970) has considered the derivation of this name, noting that, according to the 6th century Chinese document known as the *Shuijingzhu*, the east gate of the capital of Linyi led to a winding road beside which was placed a stela bearing the name of Hu Da. He has suggested that this is the Chinese rendition of the Cham word *hudah*, meaning brilliant. Sanskritisation could provide the known epigraphic name of Bhadra. We know more about Bhadravarman from surviving inscriptions (Finot 1902). That from Cho Dinh was inscribed on a natural rockface, and describes a sacrifice to Śiva by Bhadravarman or one of his descendants. The Hon Cuc inscription is a short recital to Śiva, and an inscription from Mi Son records the gift of land to sustain a temple dedicated to Śiva founded by Bhadravarman. Mi Son is a small valley screened by hills. It houses several groups of outstanding Cham temple complexes. The earliest temple there, which was later destroyed by fire, was a foundation of Bhadravarman (Finot 1902, 1904). The establishment, in his temple, of a *liṅga* called Bhadreśvara, confirms the development of the cult of the named *liṅga* which, as has been seen, provided a unifying force in the *maṇḍalas* of the middle Mekong valley. Among the most important of Bhadravarman's inscriptions is that from Dong Yen Chau, which contains a text written in Cham. This confirms that the Linyi were Cham speakers by the end of the 4th century A.D. Clearly, the Hindu religion was becoming effectively established in court circles because Bhadravarman's successor, Gaṅgārāja, abdicated in order to undertake a pilgrimage to India, a remarkable if not unique event in the dynastic history of any Southeast Asian *maṇḍala*. His departure occasioned civil war over a disputed succession.

With the third dynasty, established in A.D. 421, we return to king lists available only through Chinese sources. The founder was Fan Yangmai, a name which Christie (1970) sees as a Chinese transcription of the Cham Yang-mah or "golden prince". We know little about him, but his son of the same name followed in a long tradition of Linyi rulers by supporting sea-borne raiding along the coast of Rinan. This troublesome and persistent piracy goaded the Chinese to act, and the punitive expedition in A.D. 446 led to first the sack of Qusu and then the pillaging of the Linyi capital. The vengeance was terrible in terms of loss of life and booty seized. At Qusu, all inhabitants over the age of 15 were put to the sword, and gold, silver and other valuable were seized. The taking of the Cham capital, following a major military defeat at the hands of the Chinese armies, led to the destruction of temples, and melting down of gold statues into ingots. The recorded removal of *c* 48,000 kg of gold is, even allowing for exaggeration, some indication of the wealth which the rulers of Linyi had amassed. Apart from the resumption of tribute missions following this catastrophe, we know little of the remaining rulers of the dynasty founded by Fan Yangmai.

The succeeding dynasty was founded in *c* 529 and lasted until A.D 757. The first ruler took the name of Rudravarman, and claimed descent from Gaṅgārāja, the overlord of the previous line who had abdicated. This new overlord continued the policy of border raiding interspersed with the despatch of tribute missions to China, but his successor, Śambhuvarman (meaning the protégé of Śiva) was the victim of a further Chinese punitive expedition under the general Liu Fang. In the spring of A.D. 605, having marched past the copper columns set up to mark his southern frontier by Ma Yuan, the Chinese arrived once more at the Cham capital. There, the general seized enormous booty, including golden tablets on which were recorded the names of the preceding 18 overlords of Linyi. Liu Fang went further, and divided the conquered Cham territory into four new commanderies. Illness among his men, however, as well as difficulties in surveying the new lands and transport problems, ruled out a permanent arrangement, and Śambhuvarman was able to re-occupy the capital and commence reconstruction. Wisely, he sent regular tribute missions thereafter. It was this same Cham overlord to whom Mahendravarman of Zhenla sent his ambassador, Siṃhadeva. Doubtless, he would have found himself at home at a court practising the same Hindu religion and adhering to the same system of government as his own. Indeed, Śambhuvarman is recorded as having set in train the reconstruction of Bhadravarman's burnt temple at Mi Son. An inscription from Mi Son tells us that "Śambhuvarman's glory rose like the autumn moon".

The next two reigns followed peaceful courses, but the second ruler, Bhasadarma, was murdered by one of his ministers and the crown passed to his nephew, Bhadreśvaravarman. A dynastic struggle ensued, which resulted in the coronation of Vikrāntavarman I. This ruler was descended, on the paternal side, from Rudravarman, and his maternal side, from Īśānavarman, thus linking two leading families of Zhenla and Champa. It was reasonable, therefore, for Vikrāntavarman, on one of his stelae at Mi Son, to stress the purity of his royal blood. Indeed, his reign appears to have been relatively peaceful, and was marked by the construction of brick sanctuaries at Mi Son, together with a munificent series of donations. These, as in contemporary Zhenla, included rice-fields, slaves, dancers and singers, musicians, and domestic stock including elephants, cattle and water-buffalo. The foundation grants, the inscriptions stress, were to provide for perpetual sacrifices, and those who failed to honour this edict would suffer the same infinite punishment as those who murder a *brāhmaṇ*. Again, the same importance of asceticism in obtaining divine power which characterised Zhenla at this juncture was observed in a further inscription which Finot has ascribed to Vikrāntavarman I. The same concern with issuing regular tribute-missions and founding religious establishments continued under his successors Vikrāntavarman II and Rudravarman II, with whom the dynasty ended in A.D. 758 (Maspero 1928).

The archaeological remains of Linyi: the Cham *maṇḍalas*

When we turn to the archaeology of the Cham *maṇḍalas*, we are confronted by one of the least known but potentially most interesting topics in the archaeology of Southeast Asia. Since independence, however, there has been little concern for this subject. Indeed, Davidson (1979) has noted that:

> our knowledge of Champa remains so fragmentary, vague and inaccurate that the whole subject must be reworked. (Davidson 1979:215-6.)

The Chinese records have bequeathed some intriguing descriptions of Cham centres, and we know that Fan Wen introduced much knowledge gained at first hand of the Chinese system of city defence. From the *Shuijingzhu*, we know that Qusu was defended by walls and towers and that its defences enclosed a densely occupied area 6 *li* (2.4 km) in perimeter. However, it is to archaeology that we must turn for primary sources of Cham domestic, military and religious architecture. The principal Cham sites are set out in Fig. 5.20. As may be seen, they concentrate in riverine plains, though it must be stressed that the distribution map includes all sites known, and is not confined to those dating up to the death of Rudravarman II in A.D. 758. Indeed, the majority of sites probably date to the later dynasties. Nevertheless, the trends of religious architecture were established by the 7th century, when Vikrāntavarman I initiated a major building programme at Mi Son. According to Parmentier (1904, 1918b), he was responsible for sanctuary F1 (Fig. 5.21). This has in common with later temples there, and, indeed, with those ascribed to the Zhenla *maṇḍalas*, the provision of an exterior enclosing wall within which was set a single chambered sanctuary. The building medium was again brick, and the exterior surfaces bore strip pilasters, false doors and window niches. The complete plan of Mi Son represents an extraordinary concentration of effort, and continuity of construction, over a period which began with Bhadravarman, and continued at least to the reign of Jayaindravarman towards the end of the 11th century. This ceremonial centre was one of several which have been identified in Champa (Fig 5.21). In the southernmost *maṇḍala* of Kauṭhāra, there is the centre of Po Nagar. The six sanctuaries there also cover a lengthy timespan, beginning before the 7th century A.D. with a wooden structure burnt down in A.D. 774. The northwest tower dates to A.D. 813 and further sanctuaries were added at intervals to A.D. 1256. At the end of the fourth dynasty in A.D. 757, the southern *maṇḍalas* assumed prominence, and the early inscriptions of Po Nagar reveal that the onset of sanctuary construction there commenced in earnest under Satyavarman, second overlord of the fifth or southern dynasty.

A third major religious centre is located at Dong Duong, but like Po Nagar,

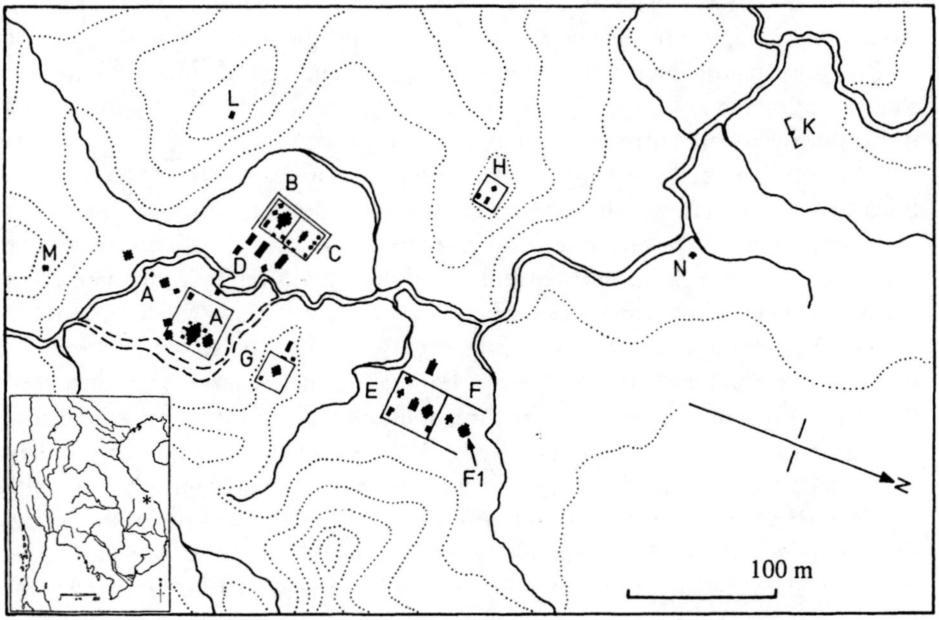

5.21 Mi Son was one of the great ritual centres of a Cham *maṇḍala*.

the sanctuaries all belong to later stages of Cham history – the earliest inscription from Dong Duong is as late as *c* A.D. 875. Less is known of the dating of the major Cham defended centres, although it is known from Chinese documents that defences at Qusu, for example, were in place by the 4th century A.D. The archaeological traces of Cham centres of occupation reveal a number of features in common with those of Zhenla, Northeast Thailand and Dvāravatī, but also some local variations. They share the same provision of ramparts with a single moat, but both documentary and archaeological evidence indicate that the earthen ramparts were revetted with brick or stone. They are located back from the coast itself, and, as a rule, on or near a river which supplied moats with water. While usually orientated according to the cardinal points, they lacked the severe geometric layout of Zhenla, and, later, Angkorian plans. They often have a bailey, or perhaps a later city annexe, built on. The citadel of Song Luy is the most southerly, being located on the coast south of Cape Dinh. It has a rampart which still stood 6–8 m high a century ago, and the river Luy bisects the site, beyond which is a small annexe.

Thanh Ho is located on the northern bank of the Da Rang River, and is particularly well preserved. The main enceinte is square, and encloses an area of 49 ha. There is a smaller annexe on the western side. The brick-built walls still stood 3-5 m high when Parmentier visited the site in the early years of this century, and the foundations of towers were seen at regular intervals along the walls and at the corners (Fig. 5.22). A 30 m wide moat lay in front of the walls. The citadel at Caban is much bigger, the walls measuring 1400 by 1100 m, and enclosing an area of 155 ha. It, too, was orientated to the cardinal points, and two streams have their confluence within the enceinte before they enter the river which flows parallel with the eastern rampart. The foundations of perimeter towers and gateways survive, as does a large central sanctuary. This site was probably the court centre of the *maṇḍala* of Vijaya.

A smaller defended site has been identified at Chau Xa, enclosing 25 ha. It has brick or brick-revetted walls, berm and moat. It follows the preceding two sites in having a rectangular enceinte, and traces of an extension are visible extending south from the west wall. Further remains of defended sites are known near Hue and at Tra Kieu. The former was located between two streams which flowed into a bend of the Hue River. Its brick walls enclose an area of *c* 25 ha. Tra Kieu was probably the Siṁhapura of the Chams. Excavation there in the 1920s uncovered the foundations of a sanctuary structure, adding to the information gained from the surviving vestiges of the walls (Claeys 1927, 1931). Two lengths of wall have been traced, but it is not possible to assess the enclosed area. Typically, the centre was located at the junction of two rivers. Only excavation will reveal the history of each defended site. It is very likely that the visible remains described above date to a relatively late phase in Cham history, but the probability that they were built on earlier foundations is very real.

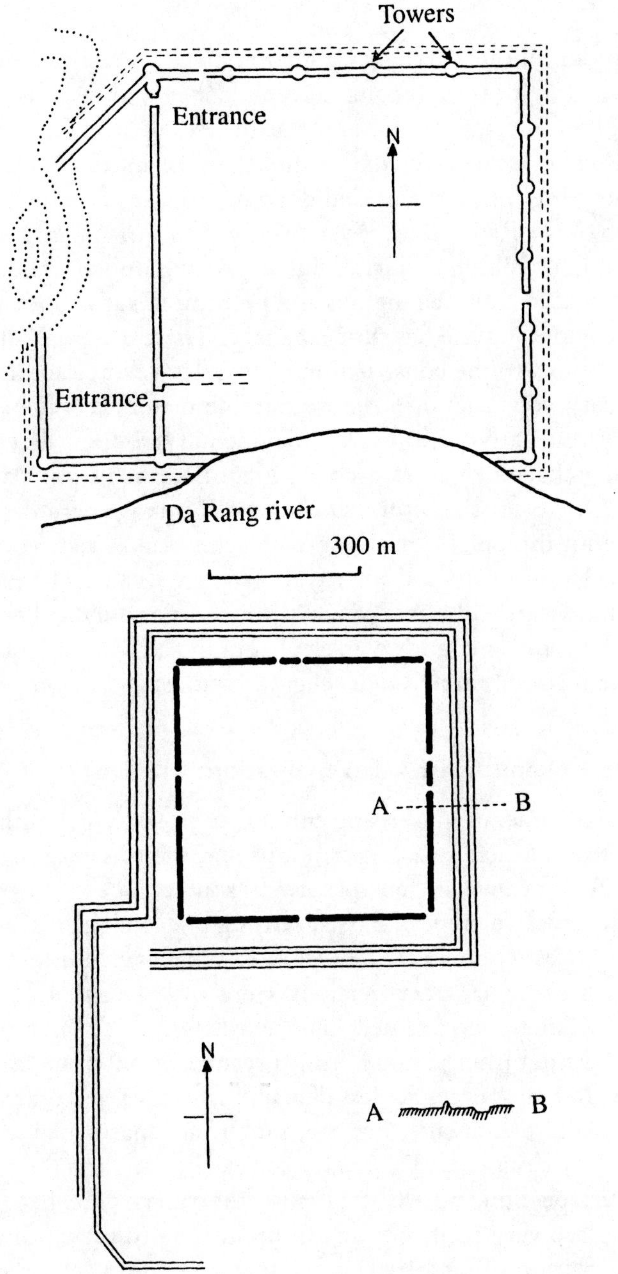

5.22 The plans of the Cham centres of Thanh Ho (upper) and Chau Xa.

Champa: summary

The present description of the Linyi, or Cham *maṇḍalas*, is restricted in time to the period corresponding to the Mekong delta and Zhenla *maṇḍalas* up to the foundation of Angkor. We are still ignorant of the extent to which the coastal enclaves sustained one or several *maṇḍalas*, and the possibility of there being a fluid situation is very high. Epigraphic and documentary sources reveal that the coastal plains south of the Red and Ma rivers were the foci of similar centralising tendencies as noted in Cambodia which, while involving military and tributary relations with China, accepted the religious and political forms of India, expressed in the Hindu religion and the Sanskrit language. There are brief allusions in the surviving inscriptions to the construction of temples devoted to the worship of Śiva, but sanctuary construction in more durable materials was begun only towards the end of this early period. The documentary sources describe large walled centres, and archaeological research has identified such sites. Dating their development, however, is for the future. During the formative period, the Cham overlords entered into diplomatic relations with China and Zhenla and, in the case of the latter, engaged in at least one royal marriage alliance. To judge from the records of Chinese wars and booty taken, the rulers not only had substantial, well-equipped armies which included war-elephants and a fleet, but also amassed much wealth in the form of embellished religious statues and *liṅga*.

The formative stages of Southeast Asian civilisation: a review

Our sources for the consideration of rising cultural complexity in Southeast Asia comprise Chinese texts, Indian tales, inscriptions and the evidence of archaeology. The Chinese documents are an important source, but must be treated judiciously because most references passed through several hands before the surviving manuscript was set down. Moreover, while they were initially reported by visitors to Southeast Asia, later versions were often written by Chinese scholars residing in China, who imbued their words with their own prejudices and expectations. Distinguishing reality from preconception is not easy under such circumstances. Indian sources are less demanding in the sense that they were not intended as historic documents, but are, rather, an unashamed mixture of legends and tales. Inscriptions are a major source but, again, they must be handled with circumspection, not least because the rulers who had them inscribed and set in place very probably had in mind the projection of an image rather than the description of historic fact. Thus, the conquest of a region by a potent overlord may in reality have been no more than a face-saving raid. If we are ever to come close to appreciating the processes involved in state formation in Southeast Asia, the only way open is greatly to expand our knowledge gained from archaeology. Sadly, archaeological information is uneven in areal coverage, contextual control and quality of publication. This situation has caused Wheatley

(1983) to adopt the pessimistic stance that the data to hand prejudice a proper consideration of state formation in our area. This is a valid standpoint, but it should also be stressed that archaeological information is steadily accumulating, while theoretical approaches are now more sophisticated than when Coedès (1968) assembled his comprehensive analysis of what he termed the Indianised states of Southeast Asia.

Among the most critical advances has been a clearer understanding of the cultures of Southeast Asia prior to Indian and Chinese contact. The traditional view arose in the context of a pessimistic and patronising view of indigenous culture, firmly rooted in a paucity of information. This view held that Indian expansion encountered a stone-age society of little complexity. Within this framework, such innovations as metallurgy were late and derivative, or worse, the acceptance of Indian religious and political ideas was passive and inevitable, just as blotting paper absorbs water. A contribution of recent archaeological research has been to establish, beyond reasonable doubt, the existence of village communities in the major river valleys whose subsistence included rice cultivation. Between at least 2000 to 500–200 B.C., and probably for a millennium earlier too, these village communities participated in an exchange network which saw exotic goods change hands many hundreds of kilometres from their sources. It has already been suggested that this exchange of exotic goods reflects flexible lineage ranking within autonomous village communities. These people had been familiar with bronze-working for at least 1500 years before the first Indian contact. The settlement data support the hypothesis that there was a trend towards centralisation during the period 500–1 B.C., which involved certain centres expanding significantly in area relative to others. Non Chai was one such centre in which iron was found in addition to glass beads. The degree to which iron-working antedated Indian contact, or resulted from it, is far from resolved, but the formation of centralised chiefdoms and attainment of sophistication in metal-working when Indian expansion reached mainland Southeast Asia is a serious possibility.

These chiefdoms were, to various degrees, exposed to the impact of Indian and Chinese expansion. In the case of the former, the initial contact was, in the main, restricted to maritime areas, while in Bac Bo, Chinese influence was felt both down the Red River corridor and by sea. This maritime aspect makes it necessary to review the characteristics of those areas most exposed to Indian contact. Clearly, the west and east coasts of the peninsula would have been in the vanguard, but any exchange, direct or indirect, down the Three Pagodas pass, would have had an impact on the communities of the Chao Phraya valley. The expansion of the Indian trade to incorporate China would have opened the lands of the lower Mekong and coastal Viet Nam to direct contact. These areas of extensive, flat, and deeply flooded deltaic or river valleys were those most susceptible to agricultural intensification given adequate technology and labour supplies. Those occupying the interior plains of the middle Mekong and Khorat plateau were necessarily precluded from initial contact with maritime expansion, but still occupied tracts of land which could bear agricultural intensification.

It has been shown that Indian religions, political theories, scripts and the Sanskrit and Pāli languages, were incorporated into the indigenous cultures. It occurred among Mōn speakers in the Chao Phraya valley, Khmer speakers of the middle and lower Mekong, and the speakers of Cham in central coastal Viet Nam. Moreover, the earliest phases of this phenomenon have been identified in areas which controlled the coastline, with later manifestations in the plains of the middle Mekong and river valleys of the Khorat plateau. The abundant evidence for Indian influence on the *maṇḍalas* of Angkorian Cambodia and classical Champa, allied to the notion of a passively receptive Neolithic populace, made the process of state formation so obvious as to discount the need for explanation. The Indian colonialist and Indianisation models are no longer tenable. A more sophisticated and scrupulously documented model has recently been advanced by Wheatley (1983). He stressed the acceptance of Hinduism by the later prehistoric elite as an important factor in the intensification and reinforcement of centralisation. He sees this move to a self-identification with Śiva of the emergent ruler as an expedient which enhanced his own sanctity and thereby affirmed his grip on power. Early evidence for this comes from the inscriptions of Bhadravarman of Champa. Again, a major early centre was Vyādhapura, the city of the hunter. The hunter in question was Śiva. Wheatley does not discount other inputs. In his own words, it is not improbable "that the settlements of *kṣatriyan* adventurers and their followers and the trading factories of merchant corporations played a part in this transformation" (Wheatley 1983:296). But he clearly favours a primary role for Śaivism, and, in stressing the term *Nāgara*, the Sanskrit term for holy city, in the very title of his book, sees the emergent city as a symbolic and ritual centre above all else.

This view has not won universal acceptance (Bronson 1985). That adopted here differs from Wheatley's interpretation in viewing the critical period between 500 B.C. and A.D. 800 as a continuum, with the Indian presence as but one of several interacting variables. This approach is influenced by the results of recent examples of growing cultural complexity under conditions which resemble those inferred for Southeast Asia. Let us consider three of these. The first occurred during the 19th century in the Malagasy Republic, and has been described by Bloch (1977). It is a particularly relevant example, because it is concerned with people of Austronesian origin who grew rice. The principal points are these. The Merina occupied a terrain characterised by hills, restricted valleys and marshland. Rice cultivation in valleys entailed the diversion of water into small-scale terraced fields. Land was owned by descent groups or "*demes*". These were endogamous, and concerned to retain their hold on land. Valley-wide decisions were taken by a consensus of elders. These cultivators were subjected to predatory and opportunistic bands of brigands who occupied defended hilltops and exacted tribute in the form of rice. Bloch calls these "pre take-off states". The ruler was not involved in agriculture other than as a predator. In contrast, "take-off states" were those wherein the military brigand took an active role in rice agriculture, a step leading to major social changes. The process began with marsh drainage, a task requiring a major input of labour for the excavation of dykes. The result was greatly increased output, and a move from the fortified hilltops to the plains adjacent to the reclaimed marsh. Increased production went directly to the king, who was able to sustain his followers. Labour was supplied as corvée (four days labour per week is the quoted figure), or by taking slaves. The latter required predatory wars and, therefore, a well-supplied army. Such take-off states engendered rivalry and war. They tended to be transient. That of King Andrianimpoinimerina, however, involved durability and a massive expansion of territory, because the king had preferred access to European trade goods and, not least, to firearms with which to equip his army. Therefore the cycle of slave-wars leading to marsh irrigation to provide food for the maintenance of the army was secured. Growth was very rapid, but the variables were interdependent, and contact with an expanding, but on this occasion, European state, was one of several critical elements.

Ekholm has considered the effect of exotic prestige goods in a second African context. She prefaced her review by stressing that "In Central Africa, power relations are established, consolidated and maintained through the control of prestige articles" (Ekholm 1977:119). These are, she asserts "absolutely indispensable for the maintenance of social relations" (ibid.:119). This situation reflects the use of rare prestige valuables in various rites of passage, for example in the payment of bride price and appropriate recognition of status in mortuary practices. A chief who exercises control over the source of prestige goods, which in Central Africa included copper, salt and shells, also controls a source of power. Such goods can be invested in people as retainers and followers at the expense of peripheral groups, thereby attracting more people and increasing demands on food production. The arrival of a new source of prestige goods can have a double effect. If their acquisition and disposal is restricted to the existing chief, then his prestige is enhanced. Moreover, the exchange of local products for the prestige goods places a further call on intensified production, be it for agricultural products, raw materials, manufactured goods or slaves. Indeed, the slave trade exercised a considerable impact on the development of complex society by emphasising the distributional role of strategically placed chiefs. A corollary to the new supply is that peripheral chiefs may develop their own source, and thereby out-flank and rival their former superiors. This possibility encourages the expansion of the area ruled by the senior line by coercion.

The third instance of growing cultural complexity has been reported by Alpers (1969) for the Yao. This group occupies an inland tract of East Africa in modern Malawi. Traditionally, life centred on the village led by the headman. Kinship was matrilineal, and the core of each village was a set of sisters whose oldest brother was the headman. The power of each headman was determined by the size of his village, but set against his ambition to increase numbers was a selection for fission, as younger brothers or maternal nephews to the headman moved off to found their own villages. Therefore, villages rarely exceeded 10–15 huts sheltering 50 or 60 people.

However, this mould could be broken by attracting followers other than matrilineal kinsmen. Yet how were followers lured to one leader and not another? One way was to display outstanding leadership as a hunter. Another was to control trade, and particularly the trading caravans to the coast. The export commodities began with ivory and soon incorporated slaves. The Swahili and Arab traders on the coast supplied, in return, beads, cloth and salt. This trade was controlled by the headman-chief. He had the usufruct of one tusk from each elephant killed in his territory, and the duty to bless the departing caravan in the name of the ancestors. On the caravan's return, he had the prerogative to distribute the cloth, brass wire and beads to his followers. With the accumulated goods at his disposal the chief was able to purchase slaves, with a preference for females whom he could marry and thus increase his followers. The point about slave wives was that the children remained his own and were not able to depart to found a new village under a younger leader. It is recorded that the great chief Mataka I Nyambi (*c* 1800– between 1876 and 9) accumulated 600 slaves in this manner.

The career of this king is worth recounting. Frustrated by life in a village controlled by his grandmother, he set out to found his own. There, he and his followers wove baskets, which they exchanged for iron hoes. These were, in turn, exchanged for slaves. When he had sufficient warriors, he began raiding to augment the number of slaves. His prowess attracted numerous followers to his capital at Mwembe. When he died, he was buried with 30 youths and 30 girls, along with their guns and large quantities of beads, cloth and salt. By that time, Mwembe had grown to incorporate at least 1000 houses. Such a concentration required increased production of food and, in the 1860s, Livingstone described spring-fed irrigation channels feeding terraced fields, and cassava even being cultivated on narrow ridges on the town's thoroughfares. It had been traditional practice to level a house and move on the occupant's death. At Mwembe, a new house was built nearby and the levelled ground laid down to crops.

Mataka did not maintain a standing army because all men were warriors. He did, however, appoint administrators for his trade caravans, and disposed of power by the ownership of guns obtained by coastal trade. As head of the lineage he attracted deference through his proximity to the ancestors, but this only applied to his own relatives. Therefore, we find his successor, Mataka II Nyenje (*c* 1876 to 1885), appointing his heirs and cousins to rule over dependent villages within his chiefdom. This ruler employed Arabs as scribes, and was converted to Islam. On his death, he was interred under the verandah of the mosque at Mwembe. Mataka I and II were not the only great territorial chiefs who rose to prominence with their growing control over coastal trade. Makanjila was another, and he followed his military and trading success by adopting Arab ways. Livingstone noted that his followers planted coconuts round a lake to imitate the vegetation of the coast, and built *dhows* after the Arab fashion. An English visitor to the capital, in 1877, was able to converse with Makanjila in Swahili, and noted that lessons were being given on the Koran. The chief's residence copied the coastal architectural style. Fourteen years later a raid on his house yielded several boxes containing letters in Swahili and Arabic. Like Mataka, Makanjila was converted to Islam. A third chief, Monjesa, adopted Islam in about 1880, and changed his name to the Arabic Zuraf.

The importance of these three examples, drawn from the period of European–Arabic expansion along the African coast, is that it allows us to grasp the interplay between several aspects of behaviour over time. The variables which stand out as significant can be listed. They begin with the tension between expansive and fissioning tendencies in autonomous village communities. Men with special qualities break the impasse by building up a group of followers. This was achieved through success in war and trade. Trade goods gave emergent chiefs added scope to attract retainers, and the larger settlements which followed required agricultural intensification. Territorial chiefs increased their standing by adopting the styles and customs of the Swahili and Arab coastal traders. They adopted writing, Islam and its religious architecture.

The pre-colonial African experience has been lucidly summarised by Goody (1971). Centralisation of power and authority are, in his view, related to several variables. Foremost is unilateral control of the means of destruction, which in turn provides for the maintenance of peaceful conditions necessary for long-term trade to prosper. Such trade is a source for the extraction of taxes for the central authority. Within this context, control of the source of weapons, or of iron and iron-workers, or the horse, are seen as crucial. The control over sea-borne foreign traders operating through entrepôts is very much easier to achieve than the more diffuse continental exchange with fewer fixed nodes. Indeed, the Ashanti and Dahomey refused to countenance the passage of guns across their territory, since to do so would have allowed possession of force to pass into the hands of their neighbours. These rulers were therefore able to centralise and concentrate power by establishing a fort with a magazine of guns and paid marksmen. Such a state of affairs bears profound implications when we turn to Southeast Asia.

In Eastern and Central Africa, and in Malagasy, the incorporation of novel goods into an existing system was an important variable in the generation of new social forms. What is needed is a general model for such growing complexity as an exploratory framework for reviewing the Southeast Asian data. Such a general framework has been formulated and applied to the development of complex society in the Aegean area by Renfrew (1972). His scheme followed a general systems approach, involving the characteristics of the component parts of cultural and environmental systems, and mapping their interactions through time.

This identified as crucial the multiplier effect, that is, the way in which change in one aspect of behaviour promotes and is, in turn, affected by change in another.

The rise of the Merina state, for example, involved intensified agriculture, exchange with Europeans, slave raids, appropriation of surpluses and personal ambition. It would be absurd to promote one as any more or less significant than another, but the significance of various factors can be expected to vary from one case to another. In his application of the multiplier effect, Renfrew (1984) isolated a specific example and considered it within the general model. We shall now do the same for Southeast Asia.

The initial or starting conditions for the change to complex *maṇḍalas* are not clearly defined. Indeed, the period 500–1 B.C. is one of the most important but least-known periods of Southeast Asian prehistory. There may well have been a trend in some river valleys towards centralisation in place of autonomy. Non Chai, which covered at least 18 ha at some time between 400 B.C. – A.D. 200, was larger than any known General Period B site. If it is the case that this and other contemporary sites harboured a population measured in thousands rather than hundreds, then some form of centralisation was probably in being. There is a faint possibility that agriculture was intensified in the Non Chai area by the use of the plough, but the evidence is indirect and circumstantial. We are on firmer ground when turning to the use of iron, which was present at Non Chai, and at other sites over a wide area, during the later part of the first millenium B.C. Bronze-working was displaying hints of craft specialisation both in extraction, distribution and casting. New exotic goods such as glass beads were travelling along the exchange networks. They are found at Non Chai, Ban Chiang, Ban Chiang Hian and Ban Na Di, but not in profusion. The old exchange networks, then, were admitting new goods, and doubtless undergoing major change. Iron ore, so much more widespread than those of either copper or tin, was opening new dimensions in terms of dominance strategies and impact on the environment.

The fact of the matter is that we do not know whether exotic Indian influence, either direct or through intermediaries, was one variable in an assumed centralising trend. Only archaeology will dissolve our uncertainty. From about A.D. 1–200, however, we know that iron-working was well established, and coastal regions were developing exchange relations with exotic offshore traders. If it is the case that for at least two millennia, and probably much longer, status was signified by the ownership and disposal of exotic goods, then the impact of a new source must become an important variable in our attempt at an explanation. This takes several forms. Firstly, the source was unequal in availability and gave a major advantage to communities most able to attract and control the purveyers of new rarities. Those occupying trans-peninsula or coastal-estuarine situations would have been particularly favoured. Secondly, the new commercial contacts involved bi-directional exchange. Indians sought local products and, through their demands, initiated intensified aquisition of goods such as gold, spices or bronze bowls, which were often not immediately available in the coastal areas. We might, therefore, expect the impact of coastal exchange to have a ripple effect deep into the interior. Again, Indians brought not only exotic goods made of glass, agate and carnelian, but also exotic ideas on kingship and religion.

One particularly favoured area was the floodplain of the lower Mekong. In terms of environment the land is flat and regularly flooded, but, with appropriate drainage, rice cultivation is possible. It is well placed to control the flow of goods into the Mekong valley, but is itself devoid of iron, many of the precious or semi-precious stones and spices, which are strong candidates as items increasingly in demand.

No preference is given to a particular variable in accounting for the change which witnessed the development of the delta *maṇḍalas*. Rather, different aspects of behaviour are reviewed in conjunction. With reference to socio-political change, it is argued that the advent of a new range of exotic goods provided local leaders with a new means of controlling access to status. Their chance to control the concentration and export of slaves, food, spices and gold, provided a gateway to attracting and sustaining followers. A further means of augmenting control over status goods was to manufacture them locally, an activity clearly documented at Oc Eo. This entailed the sustenance of specialist craftsmen. The concentration of followers had its impact on the food supply. Intensification of production was necessary, and this was effected by, *inter alia*, the excavation of drainage canals. To judge from Kang Dai's account of his visit to Funan, by the 3rd century the overlord Fan Shiman was engaged in sea-borne raids to enlarge his domain. This is to be expected, and may well have been in part, at least, an attempt to secure a monopoly over the supply of novel prestige goods which were now reaching Southeast Asia in growing quantities. It is interesting to note that his ambitions were directed towards coastal areas like his own, rather than inland. Again, we owe a debt to the Chinese sources for confirming a further prediction, that the ruler's sons were despatched to rule over the new dependencies. The clearest evidence for assembling corvée or slave labour in the interests of the *maṇḍala* is to be seen in the extensive network of canals which criss-crossed the flat delta landscape. These certainly linked major settlements, but were also probably excavated to facilitate drainage, thereby intensifiying rice production. Nor should one overlook the extent of the moats and defences of Oc Eo, and the large brick structure which was built in its central area. Such an investment in agricultural and defensive works recalls the concern for augmenting production which characterises the rise of the Merina state in 19th century. It is also illuminating to find that one of the few available inscriptions, albeit rather late in the period, describes how Guṇavarman, probably the son of the king, was responsible for the reclamation of land from the marshes which comprise the Dong Thap Muoi.

It is noted that, thus far, the role played by Indians themselves is restricted to the supply of prestige valuables to the local overlords. The immediate impact on local societies may well have been as a catalyst, but the Indian presence would have played a more direct and positive role with time. Among the principal adoptions are numbered the writing system, political philosophy and, perhaps most significantly, the Hindu religion. It is here argued that the development of complexity witnessed archaeologically in the delta centres and canals is most logically conceived of as a process in a particularly favoured area, within a local cultural matrix to which the development of exchange relations with India contributed.

The early role played by the adoption of kingship manifested through Hindu court ritual is hard to define. Wheatley (1983) elevates it to a position of central, almost paramount, importance, while Bronson (1985) argues in favour of a long interlude before it had a major impact. It is not denied that it played a positive role in the projection of elevated status and in binding aristocrats to the centre through shared devotion to Śiva. Such a trend could only have been reinforced if, through supreme ascetic effort, a ruler actually acquired divinity. In the case of the delta communities, however, it is necessary to stress the territorial expansion, the intensification of craft and agricultural production, and exposure to prestige goods which occurred in the wake of Indian contact. This was described by Kang Dai in about A.D. 245, and his account was recorded in the 7th century *Jinshu*. Indeed, it may be profitable to conceive of the Indian court rituals, not least the *brāhmaṇic* role in consecration, as an intangible but highly potent form of prestige good in its own right.

Here, however, it is necessary to ring a cautionary bell. Equally compatible with the data is the possibility that the archaeological landscape in the delta region depicts one or a series of *maṇḍalas* with the concertina working. At times one may have encompassed a larger area, at times a smaller. The famous canals may have been built at times of concertina expansion, or they could reflect co-operation between interlocking *maṇḍalas* in a manner resembling the control of water in 19th century Bali, so fastidiously described by Geertz (1980). At present, the alternatives are equally viable. We must defer to future research for the means of discriminating between them.

Nor should we be deluded by Chinese references to a state of "Zhenla". No states in the Western sense existed in Southeast Asia until the 19th century. Dupont (1943–6), Wolters (1979) and Vickery (1986) have shown, convincingly, that hegemony over other centres was transient at best. The inscriptions rather favour the presence of competing regional *maṇḍalas*, at times asserting independence and, at others, prepared or required to accept a tributary relationship. We can discern glimmerings through the inscriptions of the existance of *maṇḍalas*, of shifting alliances and occasional interludes of an expanded concertina. There is some evidence for private land ownership too, but the wealth which resulted was measured not only in material possessions, but also in terms of temple foundations and merit-making.

The events which have survived in Chinese accounts and local inscriptions must be weighed within a geographic framework. The delta *maṇḍalas* were coastal, and favourably situated to receive the initial Indian impact. Provided the social conditions at impact were sufficiently complex, the shift to centralisation could have been very rapid. In the Malagasy context, the process took only a generation or two. The effect on the chiefdoms which occupied the interior, that is, the margins of the Mekong above Phnom Penh, must have been considerable. They were cut off from the source of supply of prestige goods, became reliant on the expanded production established in the delta area, and were exposed to pressures to display subservience to *maṇḍalas* there. At the same time, the demand for goods to supply the requirements of delta overlords would have opened up opportunities for those who commanded the strategic routes, particularly the Mekong River itself. Classically, the elites in this interior area should have sought out their own sources to counter the delta stranglehold. There are basically three options. One is to control the western route via Aranyaprathet to the Chantaburi coast at the head of the Gulf of Siam. A second is to enter into exchange relations with the Cham *maṇḍalas* of Vijaya and Kauṭhāra by means of the Tonle Srepok valley. The last was to dominate over the delta *maṇḍalas* themselves (Fig. 5.23). There is evidence that all three paths were taken. Those occupying the Stung Treng area entered into exchange relations with coastal Viet Nam. The early Khmer structures in Chantaburi also show expansion to the coast in a westerly direction. An inscription from Chantaburi also records the foundations of a temple by Īśānavarman (Coedès 1924).

Although initially barred from direct Indian contact, the area has considerable potential not only in controlling the Mekong route, but also in terms of productive agricultural land and iron ore deposits. The demise of the delta *maṇḍalas* occurred when ambitious men established themselves as overlords. There are reasonable grounds for supposing that the delta area was, for three or four centuries, a focus of *maṇḍalas*. Archaeologically, the extensive canal system, the large defended centres of Oc Eo and Angkor Borei, and intensive production, sustain such a conclusion. In terms of Chinese documents, we learn of taxation and ambassadors. This pattern was later repeated to the north. Clearly, it was a period of militarism, punctuated with bids for overlordship. Centres such as Īśānapura housed monumental religious structures and a royal palace with *brāhmaṇs*, aristocrats and armed retainers. The rulers wore rare and prestigious goods, and were personally identified with the cult of Śiva. Their followers received honours and emblems of status. But Īśānapura was not a durable capital of the state of Zhenla. Īśānavarman may have achieved hegemony over other centres, but the pattern perceived from inscriptions was of competition and warfare between the regions. Within such a framework, possessing Śiva's favour became a positive advantage. It is significant that much energy was expended in the construction of temples in permanent materials to advertise the rulers' identification with Śiva, and that further resources were allocated to embellish and endow the foundations with land, livestock and slaves. Being the favoured

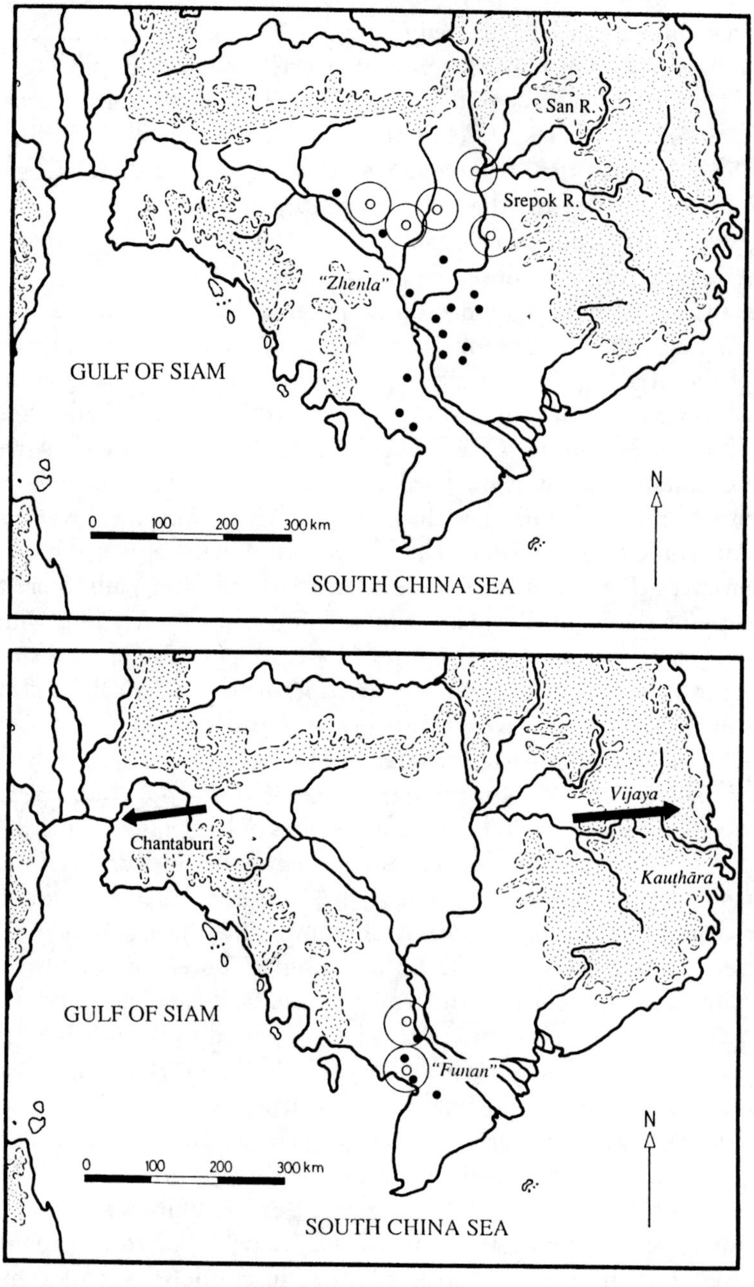

5.23 The lower map stresses the dominating strategic position of the *maṇḍalas* in the Mekong delta in controlling early maritime trade. The large circles ring major centres. In the upper map, we find that the centre of political gravity during the 7th and 8th centuries A.D. moved to the middle Mekong valley. The main centres are ringed and lesser ones shown as filled circles. The stippled area shows land above 182 m.

protégé of the god, as well as being the object of *brāhmaṇic* consecration, doubtless greatly enhanced a ruler's hold on loyalty. When we review the actual size and magnificence of the buildings in the court centres, their rich decoration and placement within walled precincts, it is necessary to recall the energy expended in their design and construction. In a real, almost tangible, sense, the buildings were statements of the overlord's power. This was critical when it is recalled that regional rivalries fed on competition, and its fabric comprised many strands: there was competition for land, strategic dominance, religious sanctity, for labour and raw materials.

Naturally, the Zhenla of Chinese accounts exhibits its own specific properties, not least, the incorporation of the Hindu religion as an element in dominance strategies. The extensive documentary and epigraphic evidence for this adoption of Indian religious and political systems has laid a false scent: it has, in some respects, made it seem necessary only to account for why the natives became "Indianised" in order to understand the origin of Southeast Asian statehood. It is argued here that the shift of major centres from the lower to the middle Mekong valley involved the interplay of several variables, but the central issue was competition between regional groups in the middle Mekong River under an initial condition of exclusion from sources of prestige expressed in terms of goods and religious sanctity. Further probing of the issue relies, in the main, on archaeology. We need to trace (a), the changing settlement patterns; (b), the extent, and intensity, of exchange in prestige goods between centres and peripheries; (c), excavate within centres to illuminate the spacial layout of structures; and (d); determine the duration of the occupation of these central places. The techniques for recovering the economic, social and technological data are available. Most of all, it is crucial to view the cultural changes in the middle-lower Mekong as part of a continuum rooted in the prehistoric past. "Indianisation", the adoption of the Hindu religion, was not forced on the local inhabitants, it was one of several variables with adaptive potential for change in the local system. The changes which occurred, underwritten as they were by the expansion of rice cultivation, were directed towards intensification and competition.

One of the most interesting aspects of Southeast Asia during the first millennium A.D. is that intensification, akin to that considered in the middle and lower Mekong, occurred in the Chao Phraya valley and coastal plains of Viet Nam among people with different languages. We have seen that the vernacular language of Zhenla was Khmer. In the Chao Phraya, it was Mōn, and in the coastal tract of Viet Nam, Cham. Despite such discontinuity in language and culture, there is evidence that similar variables were involved in the pattern of growing cultural complexity. In the Chao Phraya valley, the dominant settlements and largest monumental structures are found round the margins of the Gulf of Siam. We lack the epigraphic evidence to ascertain whether the defended sites were at any stage foci of small, separate *maṇḍalas*, but the logic of attaining regional hegemony was great, as it would have provided the paramount with control over the resources of the entire area and concentrate wealth derived from exchange. As yet, however, we lack the textual, epigraphic and archaeological information necessary to consider in more detail how the variables interacted.

The Cham area of coastal Viet Nam presents some interesting contrasts with developments in the lower Mekong. The northern Chams were exposed to direct military threat from China, and indeed suffered a series of major punitive campaigns. Again, the long narrow coastal strip meant that no lowland area was precluded from early contact with the coastal traffic in prestige goods of distant origin. We are not yet equipped to consider events there in any detailed way. However, urban architecture and military techniques were early influenced by Chinese practices, and the identification of local rulers with Śiva, as in the case of Bhadravarman, occurred surprisingly early. A local variation of some importance was probably speed of communication by ship. Supremacy in naval warfare, and the rapid transport of armed retainers by sea, may well have been instrumental in securing control over the long coastline. Naturally, monopoly over dues imposed on the merchants plying the route from the delta to South China would have concentrated considerable wealth in the overlord's hands. To judge from the weight of booty alleged to have been taken by the Chinese, a proportion of such wealth was employed, as in Zhenla, to project the king as an embodiment of Śiva.

A fourth major language, Vietnamese, was already spoken in Bac Bo when Han expansion reached south. The incorporation of the Dong Son culture into the Han Empire represents a quite different course towards complexity than the more internally generated developments to the south and southwest. The archaeological record for the last three or four centuries B.C. reveals an aristocratic chiefdom in which the Lac lords held preferential land rights and may already have engaged in intensified agriculture by utilising flood waters generated by tidal flows. These aristocrats were incorporated into the Han bureaucratic machine, but tribute payments were now diverted towards the Chinese state or to local functionaries. Agricultural intensification under the Han certainly involved the introduction of the plough. The Han had by then also developed the inundation technique of wet rice cultivation, and this, together with transplanting rice from seed beds, may have been introduced as well. This most productive technique for expanding the area under agriculture and maximising returns is now employed across lowland Southeast Asia. After the campaign of Ma Yuan, in response to the Trung sisters' insurrection, Han administration became markedly more rigorous and extractive.

Summary

The data which are relevant and available for a consideration of rising cultural complexity have been considered against recent ethnographic examples and within an approach which seeks the interplay of many cultural and environmental variables. It is possible to discern a patterned interaction between certain variables. The point of departure is the existence in the early first millennium B.C. of independent village communities engaged in the exchange of prestige goods, and within which there was lineage ranking. There followed the development of differentially large centres which represent chiefdoms. At this juncture, the last few centuries B.C., Indian trade goods became increasingly available, but only to strategically placed coastal chiefdoms. They included glass, agate and carnelian beads, and there is a possibility that the knowledge of iron-forging may also have been introduced through this channel. The initiation and growth of Indian trade, together with Chinese expansion in the period A.D. 1–500, were most keenly felt in strategic coastal tracts which provided the opportunity for agricultural intensification and control over riverine routes to the interior plains or mountain passes. The coastal chiefs of the lower Mekong were particularly well placed to take advantage of the India trade. They were able to accumulate and distribute a new range of prestige goods and intensify local manufacture. Evidence for three variables can be recognised: concentration of population in large centres; agricultural intensification by draining marshland; and warfare for territorial expansion and the accumulation of slaves. Conquered land was placed under the relatives of the leader of this expanding *maṇḍala*. The overlords also adopted Indian scripts, titles and the Hindu religion. Their *maṇḍalas* were known as Funan by the Chinese. We can detect similar changes in Champa and the Chao Phraya area.

We need much more information before being able to present any conclusions with confidence, but at present it seems likely that the interior chiefdoms of the middle Mekong had restricted or secondhand access to the coastal trade and associated religious and political changes. Caught up in a situation of increasing rivalry and emulation, they developed alternative routes via Chantaburi, and across the Truong Son passes, to Champa. Those to whom iron was readily available, who controlled tracts of good rice-land and trade routes, not least the Mekong valley itself, were, if ambitious and energetic, able to attract followers. It is also highly likely that the formation of alliances for defence against larger predatory *maṇḍalas* was highly advantageous. The surviving inscriptions certainly indicate that friction ensued, and, in due course, the status of the delta *maṇḍalas* waned.

Power then passed into the hands of competing local overlords, some of whom were able to establish transient hegemony over their rivals. Identity with Śiva was a selective advantage in this process of domination, and temple-sanctuaries were constructed in the ruler's base to emphasise his close affinity with the gods as well as to demonstrate his power and status. On the one hand, overlords sought hegemony through the establishment of the *liṅga* cult, but on the other, competing grandees were always prone to overshadow rivals and attract followers.

While we can discern the hazy existence of a constellation of *maṇḍalas*, each with a particular centre, there is no doubting the energy expended in the construction of buildings. Whether we consider Mi Son, Īśānapura or Nakhon Pathom, we find an essentially similar pattern. There was a central temple set within an enclosed sacred precinct. Overlords were increasingly taking on the role and status of gods, and the performance of appropriate rites took place in the temple. In areas where Śaivism was preferred, the essence of the ruler and his *maṇḍala* was symbolised by the decorated phallus or *liṅga*, the focus of ritual activity. In all these affairs, we can perceive a central marshalling of the populace in the construction of religious monuments and subsequent obeisance to the overlord. It is argued that there are local precedents for these displays of ceremony and ritual which were, in essence, fuelled by contact with Indians and their ideas.

At the same time, *maṇḍalas* were not durable, and much depended on the energies and status of the overlord. It would be wrong to consider General Period C as being restricted to chiefdoms, and General Period D to *maṇḍalas*, for the distinction between the two is not absolute. As perceived here, a chief expected deference from the dependent communities in his territory, but the overlord of a *maṇḍala* had wider horizons and used force, the magnetism of the gods and of himself, to attract followers and workers from a wider orbit. The less able son or brother of a great overlord could well have found himself acknowledging the supremacy of a rival.

As may be expected, in such a competitive environment, it was a period of chronic warfare resolved, albeit with only limited success, by the establishment of the great *maṇḍala* of Angkor over much of mainland Southeast Asia.

CHAPTER 6

THE ANGKORIAN *MAṆḌALA*: A.D. 802-1431

The establishment of a grand and long-lasting *maṇḍala* centred on the northern littoral of the Tonle Sap does not represent a major dislocation with the preceding *maṇḍalas* of the middle Mekong and Tonle Sap plains, but rather the fulfilment of the aims of the overlords whose inscriptions spoke of political supremacy over wide areas. All the characteristics of the *maṇḍala* of Angkor were previously represented, but they were magnified and given stability through the centralising manipulation of power exercised by members of an elite lineage imbued with unusual charisma and prowess. We know of the principal historic events on the basis of the Sanskrit and Khmer inscriptions, accounts written by foreign visitors and the evidence of archaeology. Indeed, the École Française concentrated more of its research upon the epigraphy and archaeology of the monuments of Angkor than on any other particular topic.

The name Angkor is derived from the Sanskrit word *Nāgara*, meaning holy city. It is the modern name for the complex of monuments, reservoirs and walls which served as the centre of political influence over much of mainland Southeast Asia during the period under review. There were several other major *maṇḍalas* but none, apart from brief episodes of civil war between rival claimants for power, rivalled Angkor. Its original name derives from King Yaśovarman (A.D. 889– *c* 910), who founded the first capital (Fig. 6.1). The proper name for the centre is, therefore, Yaśodharapura. This chapter will use the term Angkorian to describe the *maṇḍala* centred there.

The six centuries of this period of centrality, the Angkorian *Maṇḍala*, are given coherence by the establishment of a court in the Angkor region. The buildings at Angkor were far larger than those of the preceding *maṇḍalas*. They include temple-mausolea, palaces and reservoirs which reflect a well-developed capacity to organise labour. Angkor was conceived as a centre for the performance of ritual and cult activities which advertised to all the power of the overlord. The founder of this *maṇḍala* was Jayavarman II. It was he who instituted the central royal cult of the *kamrateṅ jagat ta rāja*, meaning, in Jacques's translation, "The god who is king" (Jacques 1985:286). This aura of divinity projected from the central court was a stimulus to the construction of appropriate buildings in which to undertake the necessary rituals, not least among which was the interment of the remains of the dead and deified overlord. Again, the essence of the overlord and, in a sense, his *maṇḍala*, was represented in the *liṅga* which bore his name linked with that of Śiva. Hence, the *liṅga* of Jayavarman was called

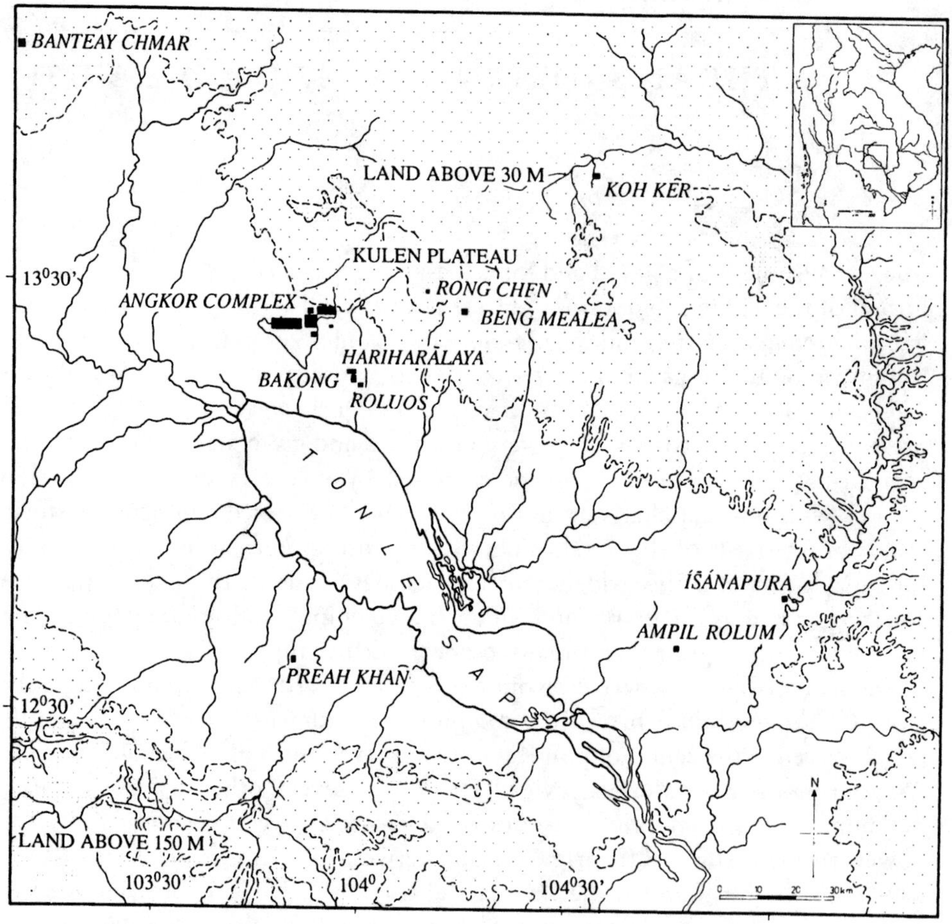

6.1 Map of the major sites in the Tonle Sap region.

Jayeśvara. It was housed in the temple-mausoleum for the ruler after his death. There is no instance of a ruler employing his predecessor's monument: each provided his own.

This great site witnessed numerous phases of rebuilding and additions by successive overlords. As may be seen in Table 6.1, there was a remarkable continuity of rulers within successive dynasties. What were the guiding principles to the succession? Vickery (1986) has recently reassessed the genealogical claims and relationships of the early Ankorian overlords, particularly Indravarman I, Yaśovarman I and Rājendravarman. One of his most important points is that their genealogies, set out in a series of inscriptions, were not designed as received historic facts, but rather as claims to genealogical position, and therefore, status relative to the ancestors. This situation must also be considered with the lack of any sure path to the overlordship even within the dynasty. While

Table 6.1 *The overlords of the Angkorian Maṇḍala.*

No.	Overlord	Relationship with predecessor	Date of accession
1	Jayavarman II	–	802
2	Jayavarman III	son of 1	834
3	Indravarman I	cousin of 2	877
4	Yaśovarman I	son of 3	889
5	Harṣavarman I	son of 4	910
6	Īśānavarman II	brother of 5	922
7	Jayavarman IV	grandson of 3	928
8	Harṣavarman II	son of 7	942
9	Rājendravarman	cousin of 8	944
10	Jayavarman V	son of 9	968
11	Udayādityavarman I	maternal nephew of 10	1001
12	Jayavīravarman I	?	1002
13	Sūryavarman I	claimed descent from 3	1002
14	Udayādityavarman II	probably son of 13	1050
15	Harṣavarman III	brother of 14	1066
16	Jayavarman VI	usurper	1080
17	Dharaṇīndravarman I	brother of 16	1107
18	Sūryavarman II	maternal grand-nephew of 17	1113
19	Dharaṇīndravarman II	cousin of 18	1150
20	Yaśovarman II	son of 19	1160
21	Tribhuvanādityavarman	usurper	1166
22	Jayavarman VII	son of 19	1181
23	Indravarman II	son of 22	1219
24	Jayavarman VIII	grandson of 23	1243
25	Indravarman III	family of 24	1296

Source: After Sahai 1970. There is uncertainty over some of the relationships.

seniority was important, so too was ability and support from relatives. Vickery has noted a recurrent thread in the inscriptions of these three overlords in that they claimed the highest possible position in lineal descent from the senior line of the ancestors. Thus Indravarman I virtually ignored Jayavarman II in claiming the senior line and earlier ancestors. Rājendravarman traced his senior claim right back to Kambu, the mythical founding father. This situation is seen by Vickery as compatible with the presence of a "conical clan" whereby status is defined by the seniority of descent from the earliest ancestors. The overlordship in this framework could, and often did, pass laterally between brothers rather than downward to the next generation, a situation plagued by problems over the succession, and therefore, a possible cause of friction. It seems probable that the line of Indravarman I was senior to that of Jayavarman II, but the overlords and grandees alike at the apex of the Angkorian hierarchy were members of the aristocratic lineage of Aninditapura which included Jayavarman II.

The further unifying force underlying the Angkorian *Maṇḍala* was a shared religious adherence. This included Śaivism, but there were strong undercurrents of Buddhism as well as instances of syncretism between Śiva and Viṣṇu. A seriously overlooked subject of enquiry is the degree to which local ancestral gods with prehistoric origins continued in popular religious experiences. The bonding effect of the religion based on the temples, the sustaining communities and the functionaries, is hard to over emphasise. Its physical manifestation is seen, not only in the great temple-mausolea, but also in the symbolism of the *nāgara*. Angkor was, in effect, the representation on earth of Mount Meru, the home of the gods. Anyone entering it equipped with the code for the symbolism around him would appreciate that he was leaving earth and entering heaven.

The dynastic history and main historic events

Jayavarman II, who realised the religious and political ideals of the divine overlord in a ramifying *maṇḍala*, was a member of the leading aristocratic family in the region of Śambhupura. He came of age at a particularly difficult period towards the end of the 8th century, when competing centres vied for ascendancy in Zhenla, and the prince of one of them was taken by the ruler of "Java" in battle and killed. It seems that the young Jayavarman spent some time in "Java", where he encountered the established presence of a god-like ruler in possession of a sacred court centre.

According to Jacques's (1972) recent reassessment of the relevant inscriptions, Jayavarman returned to the mainland, probably about A.D. 770, and established his first capital at Indrapura. This was probably at or near Banteay Prei Nokor (Fig. 5.6). Politically, his first task was to eliminate competing regional overlords, and this was undertaken by armies under his principal adherents. We find, for example, that between A.D. 770–780, he overcame the *maṇḍala* of Śambhupura, followed by Aninditapura and Bhavapura (Fig. 5.5). The land south of Tonle Sap was subdued by his follower Prithivīnarendra. It is instructive to note that the conquered people were required to furnish tribute, and that generals were given land grants. In terms of religion and ritual, Jayavarman underwent a ceremony on Mount Kulen which was so meaningful that it was described 250 years later in the Sdok Kak Thom inscription (Chandler 1983).

Wolters (1973) has commented on the nature of Jayavarman's political and military affairs. Later inscriptions leave us in little doubt that much of his early success turned on military force. Some small *maṇḍalas*, such as that in Maleng southwest of Tonle Sap, succumbed to his generals. Others recognised a man of considerable magnetism, and rallied to his banner. They were rewarded with land grants in conquered territory, and honorific appointments in his entourage. We can also detect the practise of regional aristocratic families providing the overlord with wives, and thereby acquiring both social proximity to him and influence in the centre of affairs.

When pacification was largely accomplished, Jayavarman moved his capital to the northern shores of Tonle Sap. This had been a major regional centre during the preceding centuries, and had the advantage of easy river and lacustrine communication by boat, a broad band of regularly flooded land along the lake margin suited to receding flood farming, considerable resources of fish from the lake, and several perennial streams issuing from the Kulen plateau to the north. The political and religious innovations of Jayavarman were then set in place.

The king's quest for a suitable location for his new court was not straightforward. His first court was probably located at Indrapura. From there, he moved to Hariharālaya, and probably set in train the construction of new, or the embellishment of older, temples. He then moved first to Amarendrapura and then up to the Kulen plateau, where he founded an entirely new complex known as Mahendraparvata. His temple-pyramid, designed to house the royal *liṅga*, is known as Rong Chen (Briggs 1951). The time was now considered opportune for his own consecration and, in a series of *brāhmaṇic* rituals, the promulagation of the cult of the *kamrateṅ jagat ta rāja*, the god who is king. This took place in A.D. 802. In the final move of his reign, he returned to the northern floodplain of the Great Lake at Hariharālaya.

Compared with previous overlords, Jayavarman established a *maṇḍala* of considerable durability. He was succeeded by five kings over the next century, and their achievements in terms of unification and centralisation built on the strong foundations he set in place up to his death in A.D. 850. Two of his descendants particularly stand out. Indravarman I (A.D. 877–889) was probably a nephew of Jayavarman II. He set in train at Hariharālaya a pattern of building activity leading to a settlement form followed by successive kings until the reign of Jayavarman VII almost four centuries later. This involved first the construction of a reservoir, then a raised temple-pyramid housing images of deified royal ancestors and, finally, a temple-mausoleum for the overlord himself which was normally associated with the *liṅga* which bore his name linked with that of his preferred god. While the water in the great reservoirs may well have been used for irrigation, and doubtless also to furnish residential requirements, it must also be remembered that the mythical home of the Hindu gods was Mount Meru, located north of the Himalayas. Traditionally, the mountain was surrounded by lakes, and the representation of Mount Meru as the royal mausoleum naturally required the provision of the lakes in the form of reservoirs. Previous centres, such as Īśānapura, had been provided with moats and small reservoirs, but the Indratātaka, Indravarman's baray (reservoir) at Hariharālaya, represents a major advance in hydraulics, both in size and conception (Fig. 6.2). It covers an area of 3.3 by 0.7 km. The Bakong, Indravarman's temple-pyramid, was also gigantic compared with its predecessors (Fig. 6.3). Its outer limits are demarcated by a moat with exterior dimensions of 650 by 800 m. It contained several small sanctuaries dedicated to the royal ancestors, and a central raised shrine dedicated, in A.D. 881, to Indreśvara, the royal *liṅga*. A measure of Indravarman's achievement is that his reservoir was 150 times the area of that of any of his predecessors,

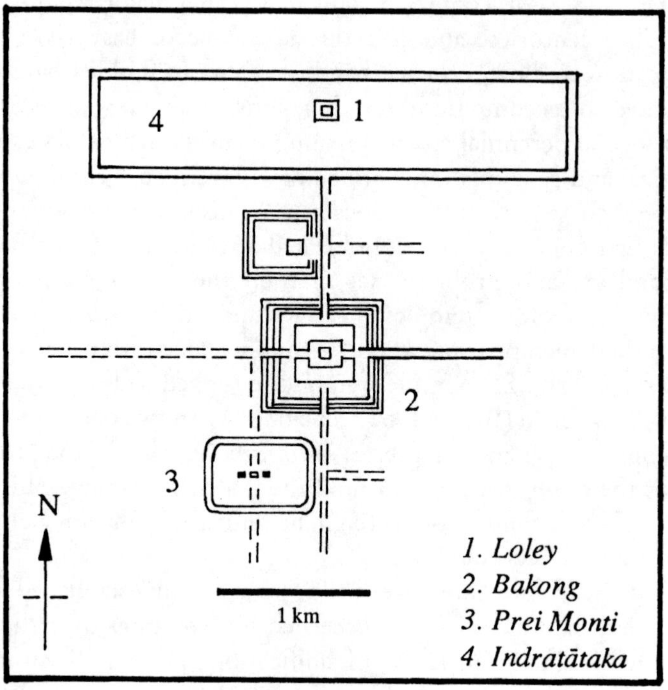

6.2 The layout of Hariharālaya, Indravarman's first capital.

containing 10 million m^3 of water, and the Bakong, built of stone rather than brick, incorporated a volume of building materials 100 times greater than any earlier temple.

Hariharālaya was not to remain the political centre for long. Indravarman's son and successor, Yaśovarman founded a new capital just to the west, where a low hill known as the Bakheng (meaning Mount Mighty Ancestor) rises 65 m above the surrounding countryside (Chandler 1983). The symbolism of the hill as Mount Meru, home of the gods, was enhanced by the construction of Yaśovarman's temple-pyramid on its summit to house Yaśodhareśvara. The Bakheng was located centrally within an enormous rectangular enclosure whose walls of earth were associated with a moat 200 m wide. This was one of the largest Angkorian walled enclosures, covering an area of 1600 ha. The Bakheng was, to the initiated, a vehicle of deep religious symbolism. Spaced around the central temple tower were a further 108 smaller towers. Filliozat (1954) has pointed out that the perfect symmetry of the plan (Fig. 6.4) means that, from a central position opposite any side of the monument, only 33 of the towers are visible, a number corresponding to the gods in Indra's heaven. The 7 levels of the monument represent the 7 heavens. The monument also has cosmic imagery. The 108 towers divided by 4 provide a figure of 27, each set representing the phases of the lunar

6.3 This aerial view of the Bakong (late 9th century), the temple-mausoleum of Indravarman at Hariharālaya, represents a major development in Khmer religious and funerary architecture.

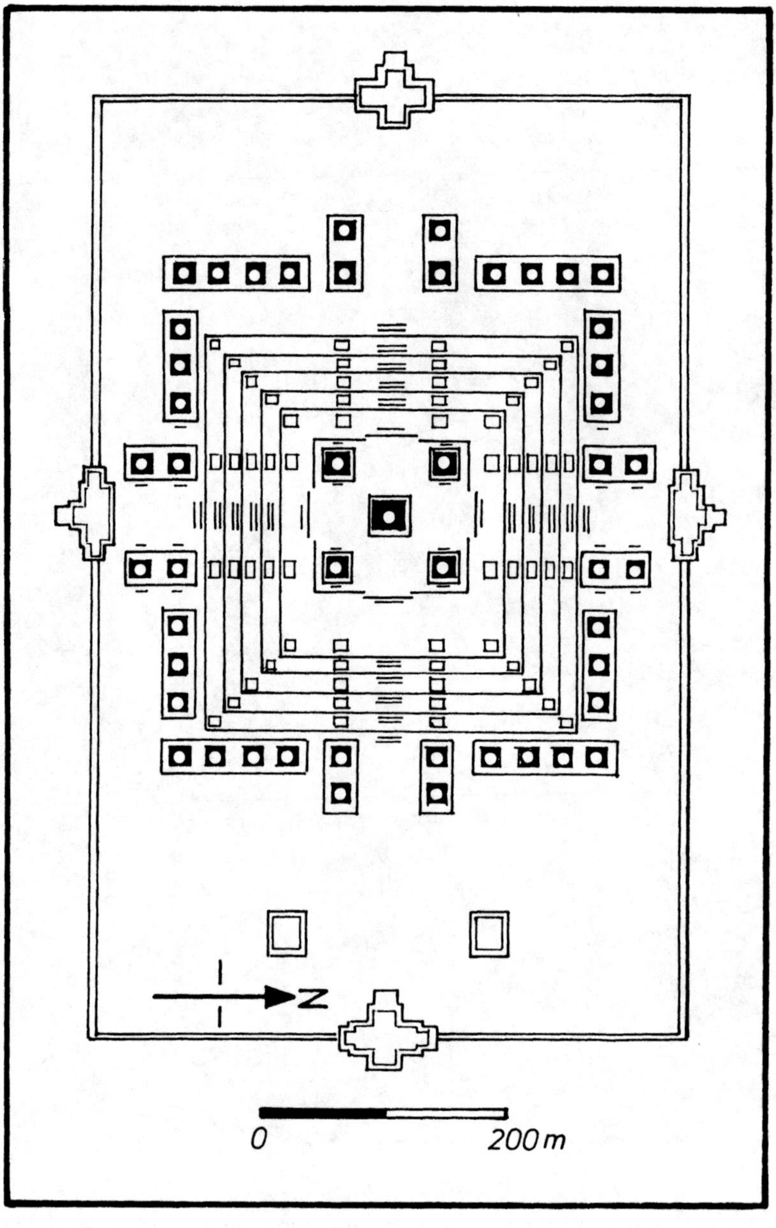

6.4 The Bakheng is one of the great temple-mausolea of the Angkorian *Maṇḍala*. It was constructed for Yaśovarman, the overlord who founded Yaśodharapura, now known as Angkor.

cycle. Finally, each terrace contains 12 towers. Wheatley (1971) has noted that each terrace represents the 12-year cycle of Jupiter

> which, in multiples of five, was used as a dating era from early in the 5th century A.D. ... Thus, while in elevation, the Bakheng was a plastic representation of Mount Meru, the axis of the universe, the kingdom, and the capital, in plan it constituted an astronomical calendar in stone, depicting from each of the four cardinal directions the positions and paths of the planets in the great Indian conception of cyclic time (Wheatley, 1971:437).

Without excavations in the enclosed area of Angkor, it is not possible to be sure whether there was an appreciable urban populace, or on the contrary, that the enclosure was reserved for members of the retinue whose presence near the overlord was considered necessary. According to Briggs (1951) the interior incorporates up to 800 smaller reservoirs, perhaps for domestic use, which were excavated along the margins of the axial avenues which radiated from the Bakheng out to the site's entrances. There is some evidence from surface finds of pottery that there was, indeed, a residential component to Angkor. Just outside, and to the northeast of the city moat, the king set in train the excavation of the Yaśodharataṭāka. This reservoir, the so-called Eastern Baray, covers an area of 7120 by 1700 m, and held up to 60 million m^3 of water. It was fed by the Siem Reap River, which was diverted round its northeast corner to feed both the reservoir and the moats of the new city.

Yaśovarman's two sons, Harṣavarman I and Īśānavarman II, experienced difficult political conditions due to the superior claims of the earlier generation in the person of Jayavarman IV. For about seven years, until A.D. 928, they occupied Angkor while Jayavarman IV founded a new capital at Koh Ker (Fig. 6.1). The size of Koh Ker reveals that Jayavarman IV was able to attract a considerable number of followers, while the importance of legitimacy through religion is seen in the consecration at Koh Ker of a *kamrateṅ jagat ta rāja* to rival that in Angkor. Perhaps to signal his prominence and claim to the overlordship, he indulged in the construction of a temple-mausoleum known as Prasat Thom, which ranks only behind the much later Angkor Wat in terms of size (Fig. 6.5). Jayavarman also built the obligatory reservoir, which covers 1200 by 560 m. It is also possible that two stone structures there represent secular buildings, perhaps palaces.

With the accession of Rājendravarman in A.D. 944, the interlude at Koh Ker came to an end, and Angkor was again the unrivalled centre of the *maṇḍala*. Rājendravarman was related of both Yaśovarman I and Jayavarman IV and so had direct descent from the founder of the dynasty. He did not extend the water storage capacity at Angkor, but restored older buildings and built several new ones. These included his temple-pyramid which was, in all probability, the Eastern Mebon, located on an island in the centre of the Eastern Baray. This housed Rajendreśvara, while four subsidiary temples were dedicated to the deified ancestors of the king and a further eight, to manifestations of Śiva. A

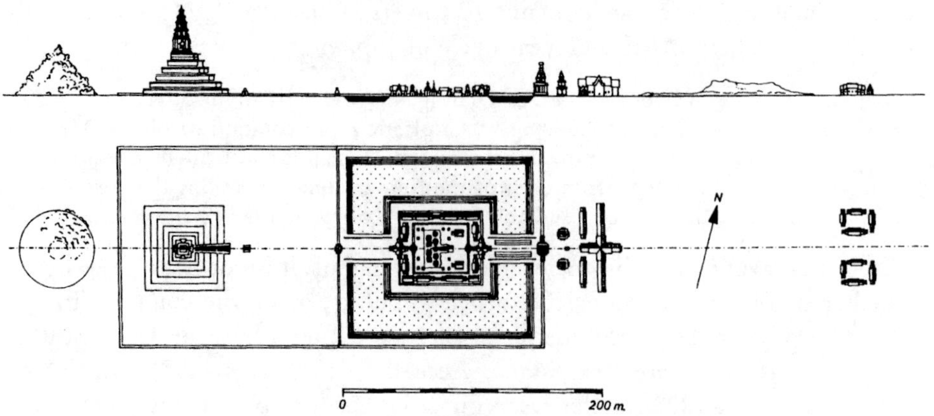

6.5 The Prasat Thom, temple-mausoleum of Jayavarman IV at Koh Ker, is second only to Angkor Wat in size. It was built by an overlord whose centre was located away from Angkor and who displayed his status and worth by a magnificent and dominating structure for himself.

second major temple-pyramid, known as Pre Rup, was constructed due south of the reservoir. It linked the king with Bhadreśvara, the old national deity, and with the *liṅga* called Rājendrabhadreśvara. The other temples were devoted to royal relatives. The available inscriptions suggest that he set in train the firm policy which diminished the power of the great regional families, converting their home bases into provinces and increasingly drawing them into the centre, where they were provided with honorific emblems and status positions.

Sūryavarman, the "sun king", claimed Indravarman among his ancestors (Vickery 1986). It is likely that, during his years of conflict with Jayavīravarman, which occurred during the early 11th century, he followed precedent by building his own cult centre at Preah Khan of Kompong Svai (Fig. 6.6). This is the largest enclosed centre of the Angkorian *Maṇḍala*, the outer moats being about 5 km long. A baray cuts through the walls on the eastern side. At present, it is unclear how much of this conception can be credited to Sūryavarman's reign. He was, however, clearly a man of vision. Chandler (1983) has noted how his accession to power closely followed the course of Jayavarman II in that he sought alliances with great families and conquered those who resisted him one by one. When he finally took Angkor and had himself consecrated overlord, he required the nobles to take an oath of allegiance, and had both their names and works carved in stone. They promised, for example, to offer their lives to the king, never to revere another, nor be accomplices to an enemy. In war, they promised to fight and pledge their lives, and in peace, to undertake their tasks with devotion and loyalty. Those loyal to him were rewarded with land grants and temples (Coedès 1913).

During a reign which lasted until 1050, Sūryavarman greatly expanded

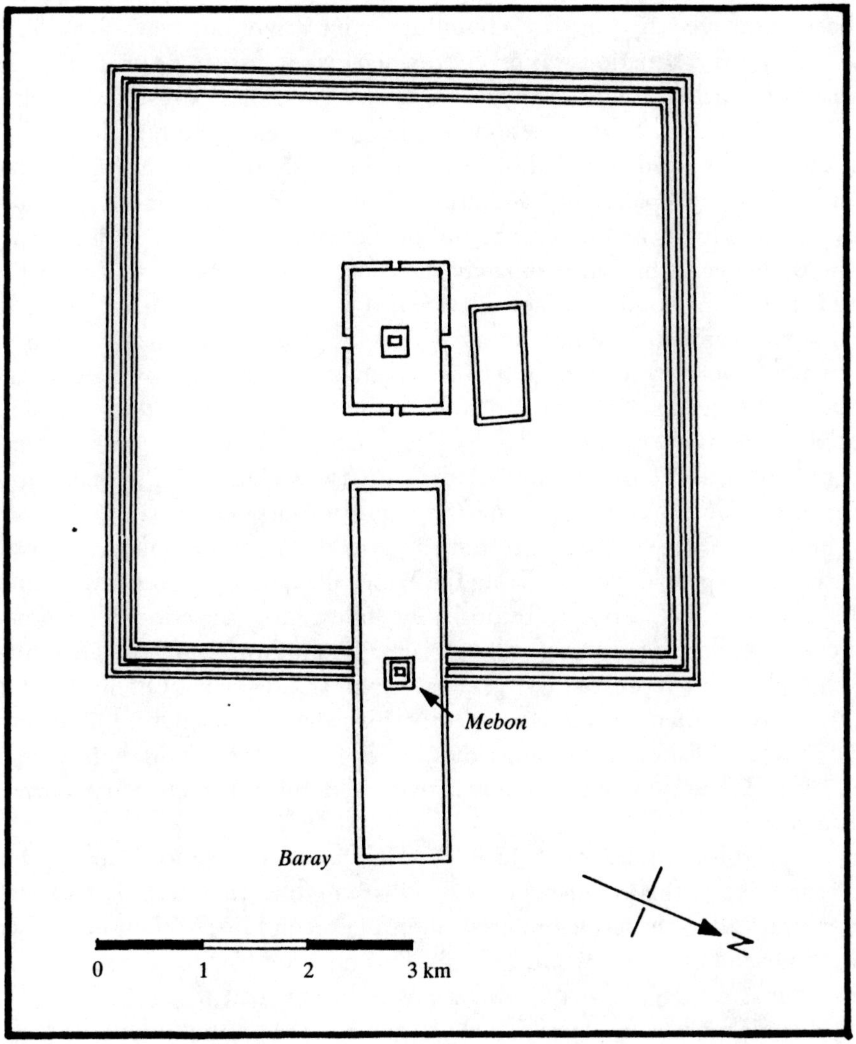

6.6 Phreah Khan of Kompong Svai is the largest of the Angkorian enclosed centres. It was probably the work of Sūryavarman I before he took Angkor from his rivals.

Angkor. The central part covered a slightly smaller area than the enceinte of Yaśovarman, and was located just to the north of it. The new moats were fed by a diversion of the Siem Reap River. It is also beyond reasonable doubt that Sūryavarman had the Western Baray excavated. This is the largest reservoir in the Angkor complex, covering an area of 8 by 2.1 km and able to store up to 70 million m^3 of water. It was meshed into the existing system by a canal. Sūryavarman professed Buddhism, but tolerated other religions, not least the long established adherence to Śiva. No temple-mausoleum to him is known, but it may well have been destroyed by the later building activity within Jayavarman VII's Angkor Thom. This situation was reversed when his successor, the precise family relationship is unclear, came to power. Udayādityavarman II restored Śaivism and proceeded with the construction of the largest temple-pyramid yet conceived, the Baphuon. Surrounded by a wall 125 by 425 m in extent, it is located just south of the royal palace of Yaśovarman. The entrance walls of the second of the three stages are decorated with highly proficient bas-reliefs depicting scenes from the Indian epics but unfortunately the central tower, which was probably rendered in gilded wood, has not survived. Two revolts late in the reign of Udayādityavarman II record interesting aspects of the organisation and climax of the campaigns. Both were internal rebellions, and each was put down under the direction of the general Saṅgrama. The booty taken was due to the king, who requested Saṅgrama to retain it. The general then persuaded the king to allow him to present it to the golden *liṅga* Udayādityeśvara, housed in the Baphuon. These insurrections continued during the reign of Harṣavarman III, who succeeded his brother in 1066 and ruled until a vassal prince, who to judge from his early inscriptions probably hailed from the Mun valley, took the title Jayavarman VI. His claims to the throne were probably followed by a period of factional strife between followers of this northern claimant and those who remained loyal to the legitimate line represented by Harṣavarman and his heirs. On his death in A.D. 1107, Jayavarman VI was succeeded by his elder brother, Dharaṇīndravarman I. This established a new and durable dynasty, that of Mahīdharapura (Briggs 1951). It had two outstandingly active and dominant rulers, Sūryavarman II and Jayavarman VII.

The former ruled from A.D. 1113–1150. He was, according to an inscription from Preah Vihear, the grand-nephew of Dharaṇīndravarman and Jayavarman VI. Four years after his accession, according to a second inscription, he "raised corvée labour and dug towers and basins". This may not be a direct reference to his greatest masterpiece, known as Angkor Wat, but the construction of this, the largest religious monument known, must have taken the greater part of his reign, and it was probably completed after his death (Fig. 6.7). Sūryavarman II was probably a Viṣṇuite rather than an adherant of Śaivism, and his temple-pyramid was placed outside the confines of the central enceinte of the Angkor complex (Fig. 6.10). The scale of the monument represents a quantum change on the temple-mausolea which preceded it. The outer moat encloses an area of 195 ha. The moat itself was 200 m wide, large enough to make a significant addition to the area of irrigated rice-land (Groslier 1979). The monument within links open spaces, walls and courtyards, which culminate in the centre with five sandstone towers designed in the form of lotus buds. The sense of space and grandeur is accentuated by immense vistas and the dramatic rise in height of the central lotus tower. Thus a raised avenue 350 m long links the outer and second walled enclosure, which itself encloses an inner area 340 by 270 m in extent. Hitherto, the visitor would have crossed a moat and two distinct open areas, the inner one being slightly elevated. The causeway now gave access to a raised terrace surrounded by a roofed gallery. This terrace measures 215 by 187 m. It in turn gives way to a second, about half the size of the former, finally giving access to the uppermost third terrace which is in the form of a square with sides 75 m long. This square was surmounted by five towers, the central one rising 65 m above the natural level of the surrounding terrain. It is hard to conceive the amount of labour necessary to raise such a monument, given the fact that the stone quarries were located *c* 30 km away. But the size of the monument is not all, for its construction was followed by the chiselling of bas-reliefs on the stone walls. These are the greatest known linear arrangement of stone carving. The walls of the outermost terrace are covered in reliefs over a distance of more than 800 m and to a height of 2 m. Scenes are drawn from the Indian epic literature, and include depictions of Sūryavarman himself, known in death by his posthumus name, Paramaviṣṇuloka (meaning "one who has gone to the supreme world of Viṣṇu"). He is seen reviewing his armies and giving an audience. We have glimpses of Khmer warfare, one scene showing Jayasiṃhavarman, general of the troops of Lopburi, seated on the back of a great war elephant (Fig. 6.8). This monument, which stands out from all others at Angkor, fulfilled the role of temple to the god-king and as a mausoleum after his death.

The intimate relationship between structures and symbols at Angkor has already been noted in the construction of the Bakheng. A similar symbolism has been detected in the design of Angkor Wat by Stencel, Gifford and Morón

6.7 Angkor Wat is the supreme achievement of the Angkorian *maṇḍala.* It was built as the temple-mausoleum of Sūryavarman II.

6.8 The Angkor Wat bas-reliefs are a rich source of information on life in the Khmer *maṇḍala.* This scene shows General Prince Śrī Jayasiṃhavarman with Khmer troops and Thai mercenaries to the right.

(1976). Having taken the lowest common denominator of the major dimensions of the buildings, they calculated that the unit of measurement employed (known as the *hat*) was 0.435 m. They then found that the length and the breadth of the central structure adds up to 365.37 *hat*. Further calculations reveal that the four major axial distances associated with the long causeway – which links the main entrance to the complex with the central towers – correspond with the four great eras in the Hindu conception of time. Again, the building was laid out in such a way that it could be used to make astronomical observations of the passage of the moon and sun, and thereby predict eclipses. Thus, if one stands in front of the western entrance on the day of the spring equinox, the sun rises directly over the central lotus tower. As the sun progresses on its annual round, so it illuminates the great continuous series of bas-reliefs which cover the inner wall of the third gallery. In Hindu astronomy, the beginning of the sun's annual round is the spring equinox. Stencel, Gifford and Morón have noted a most intriguing relationship between the passage of the sun and the content of the bas-reliefs. In the earliest part of the year, it illuminates the creation. On the side of the setting sun, the autumn equinox, the reliefs depict the terrible battle of Kurukshetra. During the dry season, the north wall of the gallery loses the sun. The reliefs on the south wall, lit up by the sun, take as their theme the kingdom of the king of death. As at the Bakheng and, as we shall see, the Bayon, cosmic and religious symbolism penetrate the buildings to the core. Given the harmony between Angkor Wat and the sun, it is hardly surprising that Sūryavarman's name means protégé of, or protected by, the sun.

The four decades following the death of Sūryavarman saw a return to friction over the succession. The weakness of the central authority was associated with a major military setback when the Chams brought their navy up the Mekong, across the Tonle Sap to the very gates of Angkor. In 1177, they sacked the city. It was Sūryavarman's second cousin, Jayavarman VII, who restored the lineage of Mahīdharapura in 1181. He was a Buddhist, soldier, and of all Khmer kings, the most active builder of monuments (Fig. 6.9). Indeed, it was during his reign that Angkor reached its final form. One of his initial projects was to construct a temporary capital, known as Preah Khan, just outside the centre of the city. This alone covered an area of 640 by 820 m (Fig. 6.10). It preceded the construction of the stone walls which enclose Angkor Thom. These were set behind a 100 m wide moat. The walls were about 8 m high, and within them all aspects of the city were on a massive scale and indicating to the world, through its symbolism, that it was the home of gods. The outer walls and moat represent the mountain range and ocean which bound the cosmos. Outside each of the main gates, one encounters a battle between heavenly and underworld gods over a serpent, the whole represented in stone. The line of the serpent, when extended back, reaches the central temple mountain of the Bayon so that, in Wheatley's words,

> the whole is in fact a representation of the myth in which the gods and demons churned the ocean to extract the liquor of immortality, using the cosmic serpent Vāsuki as a rope and Mount Meru as a churning stick (Wheatley 1971:438).

The centre of Angkor Thom contained the Bayon, a most remarkable monument inspired by the king's devotion to mystical Buddhism (Fig. 6.11). Its towers bear images of the Buddha which, Wheatley feels, might represent the miracle of the Buddha ascending and multiplying himself to confuse his adversaries. Mus (1936) has suggested that each of the 50 towers of the Bayon represents a province of the *maṇḍala*, and Jayavarman, seen as the apotheosis of Buddha, faces in benefaction in all four directions from each. Meanwhile, the fact that the

6.9 This sandstone statue from Angkor Thom probably represents Jayavarman VII. It stands 1.13 m high.

Bayon was the home of the gods is represented by the fish carved round the exterior, which point to the nether world below the oceans. The supreme artistry of the Khmer stone worker is best seen in less grandiose works photographed before extensive restoration. The Thommanom, situated within the Angkor Thom complex and photographed over 70 years ago (Fig. 6.12), is a fine example

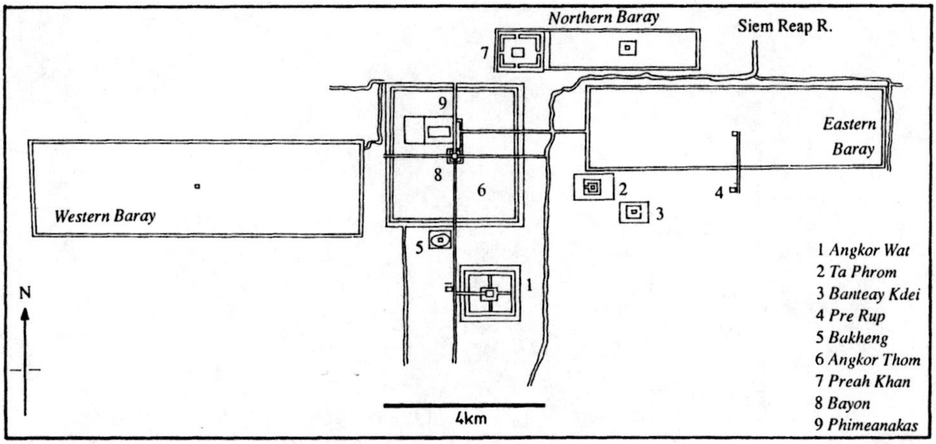

6.10 The present plan of Angkor dates to the reign of Jayavarman VII.

of proportion and attention to the detail of stone carving. Jayavarman also addressed himself to the question of hydraulics. He built the third and smallest of the Angkor barays, known as Jayatatāka. It increased the storage capacity of the system and permitted more land to be irrigated. Many construction projects proceeded outside the capital too. Preah Khan of Kompong Svai probably reached its final form, covering 2500 ha and being provided with a large baray. Northwest of the capital, he built the huge site of Banteay Chmar. The central temple there, which rivals Angkor Wat in size, was built as the temple-mausoleum for Jayavarman's deified crown prince, Śrīndrakumāra. This richly ornamented structure was surrounded by the customary walled enclosure incorporating a reservoir. The erection of huge temple-mausolea to close relatives is also seen at the Rājavihāra, now known as Ta Prohm. It was dedicated to the king's mother in the guise of the mother of Buddha. The temple of Preah Khan of Angkor was devoted to Jayavarman's deified father, Dharaṇīndravarman II. The Rājavihāra is an indication that the king projected himself as none other than the Buddha himself. An inscription from the temple refers to the erection of 23 statues of Jayabuddhamahānātha, meaning, according to Coedès (1941), the great saviour Jayavarman the Buddha.

As Buddha, guardian and saviour of his people, Jayavarman's building programmes extended beyond temples to include hospitals and guest houses. The latter were spaced about 15 km apart along highways, one of which linked Angkor with Phimai via Banteay Chmar, 225 km distant (Fig. 6.13). Where necessary, bridges spanned the intervening rivers. These roads doubtless assisted in the transport of goods appropriated in the service of the temples, inns and hospitals. The amount consumed was very great. The foundation stela of the temple of Ta Prohm records that 79,365 people occupying 3140 villages were

6.11 The Bayon is the temple-mausoleum of Jayavarman VII, last of the great Khmer overlords.

6.12 The stone carving of Thommanom, Angkor Thom, reveals the skill ot the Khmer craftsmen.

assigned to its upkeep. The 102 hospitals founded by Jayavarman were supplied with 11,370 tonnes of rice provided by 81,640 people residing in 838 villages. In other words, villages with an average population of about 100 people had to supply 13.5 tonnes of rice each in taxation. That represents a need to produce nearly double their own requirements.

Such figures provide a clear insight into the way in which excess production, as well as corvée labour, was channeled towards the requirements of a religion which had at its apex, the overlord himself. No ruler, before or after Jayavarman VII, galvanized so much energy in the pursuit of monumentality and display. While Angkor continued as the centre of the *maṇḍala* for a further 150 years after his death, there was no further major rebuilding, and the ruins of Angkor today reflect the plan of the city as he left it.

Some insight into life at the capital between August 1296 and July 1297, however, has survived in a report by Zhou Daguan, who visited Angkor with a Chinese embassy (Pelliot 1902). He travelled by boat up the Mekong and across the "fresh water sea" (Tonle Sap) to the porterage at Angkor. It is clear that the principal temple-mausolea dominated the great centre. He described the central tower of gold (the Bayon), the tower of copper (the Baphuon) and the royal palace surmounted by another golden tower (the Phimeanakas). Outside the city confines, was the tomb of Lu Ban (Angkor Wat). Perhaps the most arresting

6.13 Phimai was one of the major Khmer regional centres. It is located in the upper valley of the Mun River.

insight, however, is provided by the description of life there. He noted, for example, that there were at least 1–2000 servants who lived "all over the capital". Their houses were smaller than those of the aristocrats and bureaucrats, and made of poorer materials. He further noted the presence of numerous slaves, some people owning over 100. They could be bought and sold.

To sustain such a concentrated populace, Zhou Daguan noted the cultivation of three to four rice crops a year, using soil enriched by the annual flooding of the lake. Curiously, he did not discuss the irrigation system, though, by the time of his visit, silting may already have restricted its use. He also mentioned the importance of the lake as a source of fish, turtle and crocodile. Infrastructure for transport entailed large oar-propelled boats, and the use of carts, elephants and horses. For a good location in the market, merchants had to pay a tax to the administration. The list of imports for sale included silks, ceramics, iron and copper receptacles, gold and silver. Outside the capital, Zhou Daguan referred to over 90 provinces, each with a governor and defended centre, as well as villages, each dominated by a temple. Perhaps the most significant observation made, however, is the attention paid to royal ritual and display. In Zhou Daguan's own words, translated by Chandler (1983), we learn that:

> When the king goes out, troops are at the head of the escort; then come flags, banners, and music. Palace women, numbering from three to five hundred, wearing flowered cloth, with flowers in their hair, hold candles in their hands, and form a troupe. Even in broad daylight, the candles are lighted. Then come other palace women, carrying lances and shields, the king's private guards.... carts drawn by goats and horses, all in gold, come next. Ministers and princes are mounted on elephants, and in front of them one can see, from afar, their innumerable red umbrellas. After them come the wives and concubines of the king, in palanquins, carriages, on horseback and on elephants. They have more than a hundred parasols, flecked with gold. Behind them comes the sovereign, standing on an elephant, holding his sacred sword in his hand. The elephant's tusks are encased in gold. (Chandler 1983:75.)

Life at Angkor, even during a reign not noted for building activity, was thus concerned with grandiose royal display. By this juncture, however, we are nearing the contraction of the Ankorian *Maṇḍala* and, although Zhou Daguan's words suggest prosperity and stability, events were to prove otherwise. We have seen that the *maṇḍala* of Angkor involved a central royal dynasty and adherence to a state religion administered by followers steeped in statecraft of Indian origin and expressed in the Sanskrit language. The deeds of kings and great officers of state were recorded on stelae carved in Sanskrit. Much wealth was appropriated to maintain the centralised apparatus, not least the means of destruction, the religious rites and the economic infrastructure. This system came to an end at Angkor by the mid 15th century A.D., though many of its forms survived into the 1970s, and were incorporated, and continue, in the court rituals of the Thai monarchy.

Mabbett (1978) has offered a persuasive analysis of the *maṇḍala* apparatus which lies behind the hyperbole of the Khmer inscriptions. He visualises the king as being absolutely pivotal in managing the affairs of state, but not absolutely powerful. He had to be versed in the law, religion, tradition and military matters, and was the ultimate source of authority in land tenure. His hold on the reins of power was enhanced by his control of patronage. He made land grants, bestowed honorific and administrative posts involving visible status symbols, and conferred rights to establish religious foundations. Mabbett, however, points out that the system was maintained not by established appointments and bureaucratic procedures, but rather by favour, influence, cliques and sponsorship. It was more effective to retain a hold on the provinces by attracting the devotion of regional landowners and spiritual leaders than by coercion. Alienation of supporters was not good government. The king was everyman. He mediated with heaven for the provision of rains, he was available for mediation between individuals over disputes. Metaphorically, he consumed the land for goods, and redistributed them among his retainers and servants. He despatched his officials to all parts of his *maṇḍala* to gather information and undertake his requirements. He patronised the great aristocratic families and, in return, anticipated their loyalty. The notion of the *maṇḍala* was abroad. The universal ruler occupied the centre of the circle, and its perimeter was represented by the ebb and flow of shades of influence. Obeisance, not border posts, defined boundaries. As if to legitimise his position, the overlord followed precedent by founding and sustaining temples. What we see in the Angkorian *Maṇḍala* is a progressive increase in scale. Perhaps this is best illustrated by comparing the size of the central precinct at Īśānapura with Angkor Wat, the temple-mausoleum of Sūryavarman II (Fig. 6.14). Indeed, during the history of the Angkorian *Maṇḍala*, the legitimization of power by display, feasting and the bestowal of patronage increased in steps until the apogee was reached under Jayavarman VII.

One of the basic points about the Angkorian *Maṇḍala* was its durability. This is thrown into sharp relief when it is considered that, of the overlords of middle Mekong *maṇḍalas* prior to Jayavarman II, only three were probably related, Bhavavarman, Mahendravarman and Īśānavarman. Again, each overlord known to us through the inscriptions seems to have had his own centre. Kulke (1984) has highlighted a major operational difference with the advent of Jayavarman II, which essentially involved the replacement of vassal *maṇḍalas* by provinces, known as *viṣaya* or *pramān*. When ambitious aristocrats sought to usurp authority, rather than set themselves up as overlords in their own territory, they attempted to take over the centre, Angkor itself. This pull of the sacred centre was strong, but even so, centuries after the changes imposed by the early overlords of Angkor, there was still a strong element of provincialism and fissioning as occurred in the aftermath of the sacking of Angkor by the Chams in 1177 (Kulke 1984).

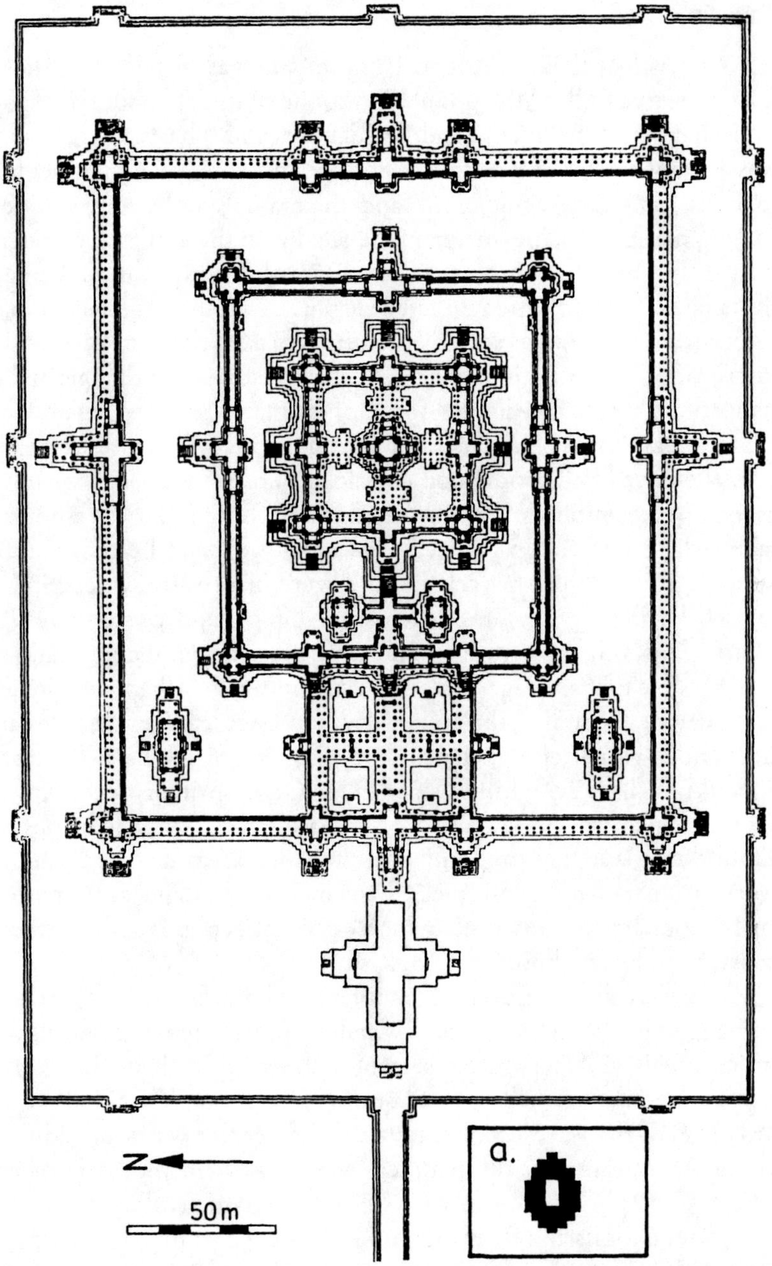

6.14 While the religious foundations of both Zhenla and Angkor were projections of an overlord's power and status, there was a massive increase in scale, as can be seen by comparing the size of Īśānavarman I's temple C1 (inset a, see Figs. 5.8 and 5.9) at Īśānapura with the temple-mausoleum of Sūryavarman II.

Taxation

It is self-evident that the Angkorian *Maṇḍala* was sustained by the flow of goods from the large bulk of the population to the centre. The source of such goods was overwhelmingly from land and, as Ricklefs (1967) has shown, ownership of land was a major source of wealth and power. The generation of agricultural surpluses to meet *maṇḍala* obligations and maintain temple communities resulted in gaining merit and achieving prominence. From the earliest campaigns of Jayavarman II, his important followers were rewarded with land. Our understanding of the taxation system which directed surpluses – in the absence of money – towards the centres and upper social echelon, is based on a small sample of Sanskrit inscriptions. The Khmer had no monetary system of exchange, and consequently obligations were met in the form of primary produce, manufactured goods, labour and merit. The payment of a proportion of agricultural yields entailed not only the intensified production over local subsistence needs, but also a system of assessing due amounts. This required special functionaries responsible for maintaining land ownership registers, the quality of land holdings and the resultant tax obligations. Some parcels of land were in private ownership, with the king himself having large estates. The ownership of land was also vested in religious foundations, but the nature of land tenure among rural communities is less clear. It is possible that a village was assessed for tax rather than its individual members. One way of expanding the tax base was to establish new temples and communities, under which circumstances the payment of goods was deferred until the agricultural base was fully established. Other primary products taken by the *maṇḍala* included honey and wax, sugar, spices, salt, medicines and livestock. From the upland and predominantly wooded areas it took feathers, rhino horn, ivory, aromatic wood and spices. Each major category was overseen by a particular functionary and his staff, which operated centrally, and without needing to consult the local administration.

There were also imposts on manufactured goods, such as cloth, and on goods exchanged in the market place. War-booty, tribute from vassals, fines imposed on criminals and personal assets of a deceased with no heir, also augmented treasury receipts. It is clear from several inscriptions that civil works such as the provision of roads, reservoirs, canals and defensive walls, in addition to the most visible of all remains, the temples, were raised on the basis of corvée labour, whereby people worked in part fulfilment of their obligations. Although religious foundations and their functionaries were exempt from the payment of a tax determined in goods, they yielded to the king a proportion of the merit they earned through their devotions.

The physical assets and corvée labour due to the king were administered by officials in order to fulfil the functions necessary for the maintenance of the *maṇḍala*. The strands of political, economic and religious behaviour of the Angkorian *maṇḍala* were interwoven into one fabric. The king, and to a certain extent, his close relations, were living gods. The temple symbolised the home of the gods. This crucial concept was the motivating force which set goals for the economy and justified the functionaries required to fulfil them. There was, then, an unusually sharp distinction between the court at the centre of the web of activities, and the provinces which sustained it. The former required both ritual and secular administrators. The fundamental change in the organisation of the *maṇḍala* issuing from the policy of Jayavarman II saw the establishment of the cult of the *kamrateṅ jagat ta rāja* which countenanced, in theory, only one supreme centre. The regional aristocratic families of the Zhenla *maṇḍalas* were therefore increasingly drawn into the centre to fulfil the roles of ceremonial and ritual, and their territories became provinces, known as *pramān* or *viṣaya*, ruled by the overlord's appointees. This procedure was energetically pursued under Rājendravarman (Kulke 1984). In practice, weak central administration was associated, from time to time, with regional unrest and fissioning of the *maṇḍala*.

The king was served by aristocratic grandees who were often his relatives, whose positions were inherited and set up in an hierarchy designated by emblems instigated by royal patronage. The crown prince, or *yuvarāja*, was second to the king in order of precedence, followed by the other royal princes. The highest officers of state were accorded a palanquin with gold stretchers and four parasols with gold handles. The lowest in the hierarchy were granted the privilege of a parasol with a silver handle. In the 10th century Kambu, an agent of the king, was provided with a grant of land, a gold palanquin, gold cup, a white parasol, another with peacock feathers and a spitoon. The *purohita*, or chief priest, was one of the greatest and most influential positions. Śivakaivalya was *purohita* to Jayavarman II, he and his descendants being given the exclusive right to consecrate a new overlord. The succession of *purohitas* was through the female line, so Śivakaivalya was followed by his sister's son, Sūkshmavindu. This master stroke enabled Jayavarman and his successors, at least in theory, to exclude would be usurpers from the means of consecration by confining the office and controlling access to the necessary rituals. In the event, Śivakaivalya's descendants exercised the right until A.D. 1050 but, of course, it was perfectly possible for claimants to establish their own means of consecration.

The post of *hotar*, or royal chaplain, was not exclusive, and indeed more than one could serve contemporaneously. The officers were again chosen from the great aristocratic families, and initial access conferred hereditary rights. The position of *vraḥ guru*, spiritual adviser to the king, drew upon aristocrats of learning and administrative skill. When Jayavarman VI usurped the throne in A.D. 1080, he appointed Divākarapaṇḍita as his *vraḥ guru*. This functionary had previously served Udayādityavarman II and Harṣavarman III, and was responsible for the consecration of Jayavarman and his two successors. The role of the *vraḥ guru* also extended to more temporal matters, not least in the discharge of orders for the donation and demarcation of land. The ministers of state in charge of civil and religious affairs were known as *mantrin*, with the greatest adviser to the overlord being called the *rājakulamahāmantrin* (Sahai 1970).

These were the great offices over which the overlord exercised patronage. Below them was a host of other appointments. The *sañjak* was a guard who protected the king's person. The *anak sañjak* protected religious foundations. There was the royal archivist, who maintained the genealogical records and exploits of the king's ancestors. There were the hereditary carriers of the royal fly whisk and fan, pages and doctors. Further from the royal entourage was the *pratyaya glāṇ*, adminstrator of the kings warehouses and the chief artisan. Again, below the *mantrin* were subordinate officials known as *śreṣṭhin*, whose status attracted a silver-handled parasol. The *vyāpāra's* role included the fixing of land boundary markers. The *pratyaya* was an official concerned with setting in train the delineation of land for tax purposes.

It is evident that the overlord and his followers were most concerned with the registration of land ownership and the fixing of tribute. Directives and policy were centrally promulgated and reached out, through the hierarchy, into the provincial administrative structure. It seems that provinces, each administered by a *khlon viṣaya*, were units for tax and judicial purposes. *Tamvrāc* were those who articulated local provincial affairs with the centre. The individual unit within each *viṣaya* was the village, or *sruk*. There may have been administrative units comprising groups of villages, but this is unclear. The headman, or *khlon sruk*, apart from parochial affairs, was ultimately responsible for the payment of goods and services where a community was bonded to the maintenance of a particular temple. We have seen how, under the reign of Jayavarman VII, for example, many settlements were enfeoffed to the support of specific temples. In this manner, there was a direct link between the greatest sanctuaries in the land and the broad spectrum of sustaining village communities.

The means of destruction

Controlling the means of destruction is a factor isolated by Goody (1971) as central to the maintenance and success of the upper echelon of society. In the Angkorian *Maṇḍala*, warfare had three principal manifestations. Firstly, there was friction between rivals for central power. It is clear that Jayavarman II subjugated rival princes before establishing the cult of the *kamrateṅ jagat ta rāja* on Mount Mahendraparvata. Subsequent episodes of civil war saw conflict between Sūryavarman I and Jayavīravarman I and between the followers of Dharaṇīndravarman I and Sūryavarman II. Rājendravarman was particularly involved in subduing regional unrest following his policy of centralisation, and, according to one of his inscriptions, he "cut off the heads of a crowd of kings".

Secondly, it was necessary to subdue vassals and appropriate tribute. The *maṇḍala* had no boundaries, but rather a waxing and waning of spheres of influence. At its edges were small polities which found it expedient to acknowledge vassal status. At times of a strong central authority this became an imperative, but a weak and divided administration provided the opportunity to set aside the payment of tribute and to assert a degree of independence. The last and most intensive form involved neighbouring *maṇḍalas*. There are several instances, for example, when the Khmer either attacked its neighbours or were, in turn, the object of attack. Such instances rarely resulted in a long-term occupation of alien territory. The major powers of mainland Southeast Asia between A.D. 802–1431 were the Khmer of Angkor, the Chams, the Vietnamese and, by degrees, the Thais of Sukhothai and Ayutthaya.

The means of waging war during those six centuries are unlikely to have been static. To judge from battle scenes depicted on the bas-reliefs from Angkor Wat, the Bayon and Banteay Chmar, the most impressive and significant means of maintaining power on land were the war elephants. The Angkor Wat bas-reliefs show them in action as bearers of spear-wielding soldiers. The rather later reliefs from Banteay Chmar and the Bayon show ballistae mounted on the backs of elephants. One man guided the elephant, and it took two to arm and fire the ballista. This technique was probably an innovation of the reign of Jayavarman VII and was, according to Mus (1929), derived from China through Cham intermediaries. One of the Bayon reliefs actually shows Cham merceneries operating their ballista. The elephant was the animal par excellence for dealing with the terrain over which fighting occurred, for providing added height when confronting enemy walls, and the capacity to cross defensive moats. The ruler who controlled war elephants was powerful indeed (Fig. 6.8). Horses, by contrast, do not appear to have been so significant, and were probably used by officers in charge of infantry, rather than in massed engagements.

Little is known of methods of recruitment or training, nor for how long people served. There were permanently appointed generals rewarded by land grants, status symbols and booty. Much of the rank and file may well have been raised during periods of need, particularly in the dry season, when military activity was favoured and agricultural tasks were minimal. They appear to have been granted tax exemption, provided with food and, where possible, with a share of booty. Under conditions of extreme danger to the state, as when the Chams sacked Angkor, even temple servants were pressed into service.

It is recalled that naval warfare was an important consideration, even as far inland as Angkor, since the Mekong was navigable up to the Tonle Sap by ocean-going vessels. Again, the late bas-reliefs of Angkor Wat, the Bayon and Banteay Chmar reveal aspects of naval warfare during the 12th and 13th centuries. The scene from Banteay Chmar reveals a naval engagement between the Khmer, who wore loincloths, and an enemy whose flowered head dresses indicate that they were Chams (Paris 1941b). They seem to have used boats as floating fortresses, from which they fought with spears (Fig. 6.15).

6.15 This scene from the Banteay Chmar murals records a naval engagement between Chams and Khmer.

Agriculture

The concentration of people at Angkor and the other cult centres, such as Beng Mealea and Banteay Chmar, as well as the need to sustain followers and retainers, made it necessary to intensify food production well above the level of subsistence. The Angkor complex and other centres located between Tonle Sap and the Kulen plateau were favourably placed because the rivers originating in the latter area flow perennially. To a certain extent, this factor made it possible to counter the fact that the area lies in a rain shadow, and the onset and duration of the rains are unpredictable (Fig. 6.16). It is not unusual to experience a little dry season during the critical growing period of late July and August, and during the dry season proper, the long sunny days increase the rate of evaporation. Alleviating these problems was the presence of Tonle Sap, one of the great inland fisheries of the world.

Rice and fish were the staples. The monsoonal conditions do not make the cultivation of rice outside its natural marshy habitat straightforward, because the

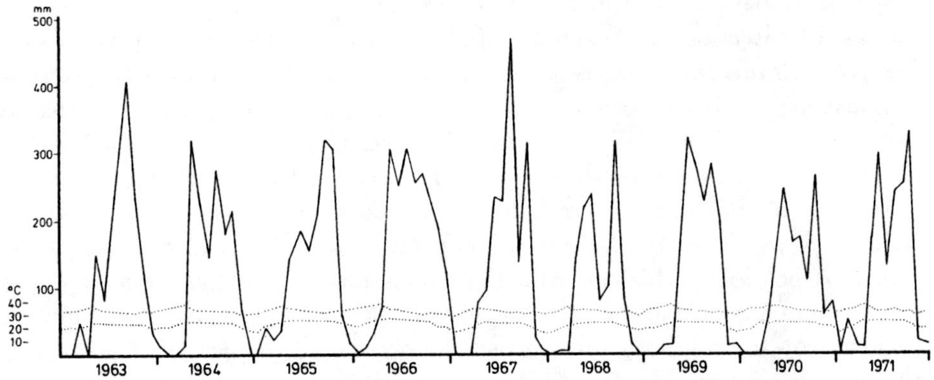

6.16 Rainfall at Siem Reap, near Angkor, is unpredictable in duration and amount. There is often a lull in rainfall in July or August. The great reservoirs were used to compensate for such unpredictability.

annual quantity of rainfall is variable. It has been suggested that the General Period C on the Khorat plateau and later rice cultivation in the Mekong delta took advantage of naturally flooded riverine land. In Bac Bo, the Han Chinese system of plough cultivation was adopted. The Han had, by that juncture, developed the technique, now universal across the lowlands of Southeast Asia, of creating swampland suited to rice by bunding. Essentially, this technique involves sculpturing the landscape by creating almost flat rice-fields demarcated by raised earthern banks. The characteristics of natural swampland are mimicked by adjusting the flow of retained rainwater through successive fields and so, ultimately, to the natural stream or river. This technique is currently imposed on slightly elevated land above natural flood level, so it is usually too dry to risk broadcasting seed in the early weeks of the wet season. Consequently, rice plants are raised in seed beds and transplanted when the fields are prepared. A second major Han innovation was the application of the tractive power of water-buffalo or cattle to drawing a plough. It is much more efficient to plough the soil than to break it with a hoe. One man can bring more land into cultivation than is necessary to support his immediate dependants, thus opening the door to the generation of disposable surpluses. When ploughing, which aerates the soil and controls weeds, is allied with harrowing to break down the clods of soil and provide a creamy soil to receive the transplanted rice, a predictably greater yield is achieved (Hanks 1972).

The existence of a plough-based cultivation system in the Chinese provinces of Bac Bo at least eight centuries before the establishment of the Angkorian *Maṇḍala* makes it very probable that, under appropriate conditions, the technology could be adopted and, along with it, the control of water flows into bunded field systems.

One of the essential features of the lands bordering the northern margins of

Tonle Sap is that the rivers issuing from the Kulen plateau are perennial, and flow southward, bisecting the terrain like spokes of a wheel. During the rainy season, the lake itself fills and expands greatly. This leads to the deposition of a thin layer of lacustrine silt, but according to Delvert (1961), this is not highly regarded by rice farmers at present. The slope of the land is much more gradual on the southern shore than it is on the northern. Hence, rising floodwaters travel 29 km to reach 14 m above sea level on the former, but only 4 km on the latter. Several techniques are currently used for rice cultivation in the area surrounding Tonle Sap. It is possible to harvest wild rice grains into receptacles strapped to the gunwhale of a boat. Floating rice, with stalks up to 7 m long is grown, and it is preferred on the southern edge of the lake because of the gentler flood regime. On the northern margin, floodwaters rise more sharply and, if the rate exceeds about 10 cm per day, the plants cannot keep pace and die. There is some shifting agriculture in fields cut from the degraded deciduous forests, but yields are very low. The most widespread technique involves the bunding of fields, use of animal traction and transplanting. There remains one system peculiar to the margins of the lake, whereby receding floodwaters are trapped behind barrages or "*tnub*". These loci are then cultivated in the early part of the dry season.

It is important to realise that the Angkorian *Maṇḍala* was underwritten by the production of rice to feed the elite, the bureaucrats, specialists and the corvée labour force. The number of references to cadastral surveys, assessments of land capability and fixing of tribute in kind, indicate a central concern for this crucial matter. Royal, and that is synonymous with divine, intervention to counter unpredictable rainfall was one of the hallmarks of Angkor. It is true that Īśāna-varman and his predecessors constructed moated enclosures which assured some dry-season water supplies for a concentrated populace, but the innovations of Indravarman I were critical. Like his successors, his temple centre was set back above the maximum rise of the flood waters. At Hariharālaya, he had constructed the Indratātaka, a reservoir with a capacity of 10 million m^3 of water. The river Roluos flowed into the northeastern, and left at the southwestern corner of the baray, whence it was directed through the temple moat of Preah Ko, then on through the double moats of the Bakong, past the Preah Monti, and so to what was probably the main distribution canal to reticulate water into the rice-fields. We do not know for sure, but it seems highly likely that the further distribution of water was regulated by the creation of bunds along the Han model (Groslier 1979).

Angkor itself is located between the valleys of the Stung Roluos and Stung Puok. Its foundation involved the same reworking of the landscape and imposition of water control as was pioneered at Hariharālaya. The source of water for the Eastern Baray, or Yaśodharatatāka, was the Siem Reap River. At some point in the development of the Angkorian complex, this river's flow was augmented by the diversion of the Stung Puok along a 4 km long canal. This system established by Yaśovarman was greatly expanded by his successors, and Groslier

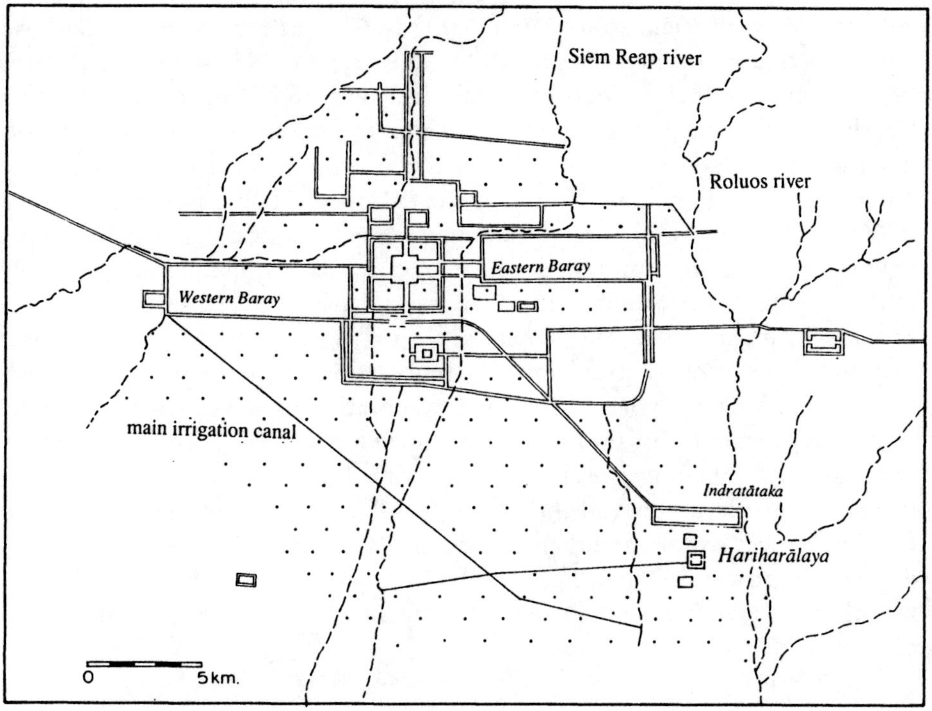

6.17 This plan of the completed Angkor irrigation system shows the maximum likely area under irrigation (stippled area) in the reign of Jayavarman VII (after Groslier 1979).

has proposed four major phases. Angkor II was the creation of Sūryavarman I, who excavated the Western Baray and linked it by means of a feeder canal with the Yaśodharatatāka. Angkor III was the work of Sūryavarman II, whose temple-mausoleum, Angkor Wat, was provided with moats capable of storing 5 million m^3. While a relatively small amount of water, Groslier has suggested that it filled an important gap in the irrigated area downstream. The final addition came with the new baray of Jayavarman VII, which added a futher 10 million m^3 to the capacity, and further increased the irrigated area (Fig. 6.17). While this system was the most extensive, it was one of many within the *Maṇḍala*.

The interpretation of the impact of the Angkor system is controversial. Van Liere (1980) has adopted a pessimistic stance, arguing that the water retained at such expense in the barays and moats never reached the rice-fields, and therefore had no impact in terms of food production. His argument centres on the lack of any physical evidence for a system of distributaries issuing from the barays. Both Groslier (1979) and Bronson (1978) agree that the water was ultimately used for field irrigation, but they differ in their conclusions regarding its efficacy. On the one hand, Bronson feels that the impact in terms of area irrigated and increased yields has been exaggerated. The total amount of stored water, he claims, would not have been sufficient to irrigate more than 6700 ha for one four month rice crop. At a figure of 1.46 tonnes of rice/ha, this area would have produced almost 10,000 tonnes, sufficient food to sustain just over 50,000 people for one year. Groslier, on the other hand, has made the important point that the water retained in the barays would have been used to maintain a continuity of supply, with most water coming from rainfall. If this is accepted, then the system could have kept 86,000 ha under production. Using the same production and consumption figures, that is, 1.46 tonnes of rice/ha and an annual requirement of 1.1 tonnes for 5.25 people, the system could, at its height, have produced 126,000 tonnes of rice and maintained 600,000 people. Such raw figures should be viewed with caution. There were the problems of sedimentation in the reservoirs and canals, of laterization of the irrigated soils and evaporation of stored water. Again, no account is given to the quantum of food supplied to the centre from non-irrigated areas, nor from floating rice. Perhaps the critical point about the barays is that they could artificially extend the continuity of supply beyond the natural confines of the wet season, and therefore compensate for inconsistent precipitation during the growing season. The fact that the system was inspired by the gods underlines their importance in modifying this most basic variable – the human environment.

The pursuit of perfection

In many respects, the objectives of the Angkorian *Maṇḍala* represent the fulfilment of those described for the *maṇḍalas* of Zhenla. It has been argued that the overlords of Zhenla sought power, and its maintenance, through divinity. This was achieved, to a remarkable degree, at Angkor. Angkor was essentially the centre of a court society involved in the pursuit of perfection. The successive temple-mausolea constructed there represented heaven in stone, and they were built to house the immortal essence of successive overlords. They were also centres for ritual performances, reviews and displays of wealth and munificence which advertised the overlord's god-like status. It is argued that such buildings and attendant rituals were a means to exhibit and maintain the central hold on power. Certainly, at times of dynastic change, the usurper was quick to build his own equivalent centre, complete with temples, enclosed spaces and reservoirs. Reservoirs are an especially important element in this theatre, for control of water involves the god most intimately in the affairs of man by providing water at times of agricultural stress. By achieving this, the overlord overcame the single most important limiting factor to Southeast Asian rice agriculture.

The court system of great overlords and the many office-holders in their orbit were literally established in heaven, and it is in Angkor, at its subsidiary centres, that we can witness the perfection of their power. It is represented in their great buildings, their reservoirs, and manifest ability to organise a host of devotees to the essence of the *maṇḍala*, the golden *liṅga* and the *kamrateṅ jagat ta rāja*. It was thus influence and display, rather than border walls and remote armies, which secured the *maṇḍala's* well-being, and it would last as long as its basic beliefs were held by its membership.

Summary and conclusions

The principal achievement of Jayavarman II was the establishment of a centralised *maṇḍala* which ruled out rivals: there could only be one overlord. In practice, rivals were not deterred. Consecration of the ruler was the preserve of one dynasty, thus, in theory, excluding usurpers. The *kamrateṅ jagat ta rāja* promoted widespread loyalties. Former *maṇḍalas* were drawn into the orbit of Angkor, and became known as *viṣaya*. It is hard to define this term adequately in English, but private land ownership was possible, and the principal families saw themselves as obliged to the overlord at Angkor. Their religious foundations provided them with merit, and their surplus production went to sustain the central court. The divine qualities of the overlord were symbolised both in the *kamrateṅ jagat ta rāja* and the golden *liṅga*, which was given a name combining that of the sovereign with Śiva. Śiva was not the only deity. Sūryavarman II preferred Viṣṇu, and Jayavarman VII, the Buddha.

The main thrust of Angkorian production was the provision of surpluses for the overlord to exhibit and distribute to his supporters, to fulfill appropriate rituals, and sustain functionaries in the service of the gods. Surpluses of food and labour were also necessary in the construction of temples, walls, roads, and water-distribution systems. Some communities were ascribed to specific temple foundations and required to produce goods surplus to requirements. Great aristocrats were gifted estates for services rendered to the crown and they, too, met their obligations to the *maṇḍala*.

The intensification of rice production involved a major reworking of the landscape. This took the form of the diversion of rivers, storage of water and distribution into rice plots, when it was necessary to compensate for a natural shortfall. Again, symbolism was clear – the centre of the great barays at Angkor contained temples devoted to the god-king and, indeed, the layout of Angkor represented Mount Meru, the home of the gods.

Although a ceremonial religious centre, Angkor must also have housed a central, secular populace. There were the noble families, their retainers and slaves, artisans who made the palanquins and parasols, the functionaries of the temples, keepers of royal warehouses, toilers in the rice-fields, fishermen, porters, boat-builders, soldiers, musicians and lapidaries, and those who maintained the war elephants. Angkor thus combined the spiritual and the secular.

The overlord brooked no rival, but his commands carried the sanction of the law and power of destruction only as long as he attracted the loyalty of his followers. When in possession of this critical element, central control to the

Angkorian Khmer involved armies spearheaded by elephant divisions. Friction with rival *maṇḍalas*, particularly Champa and Ayutthaya, also entailed war on land and sea. Ultimately, survival turned on the deployment of force. This, in turn, involved the provision of iron, horses, elephants, boats, men and food. Śiva, personified in the king, was invoked before battle and received oblations after victory.

The end of the classic Angkorian civilization involved a change in religion and of belief in the *kamrateṅ jagat ta rāja*, which coincided with a shrinking of territory as the Thai *Maṇḍala* based first at Sukhothai, and from 1350 at Ayutthaya, began to expand. In the place of Hinduism and mystical high Buddhism, came the more democratic and universally popular Hināyāna Buddhism, whose direct appeal to the common man obviated the need for a sacerdotal apparatus and monumentality in religious expression. After the building activities of Jayavarman VII, no major new works were undertaken. Again, the practice of erecting Sanskrit stelae was discontinued long before the abandonment of Angkor. If the need for corvée labour to construct and maintain the religious centres declined, so too did the supply of workers. The expansionary Thai *Maṇḍala* absorbed allegiances on the Khorat plateau and the Chao Phraya valley, areas hitherto under vassalage to Angkor. This cut off a substantial resource of land and people. At Angkor itself, the sophisticated system of irrigation fell into desuetude as the canals and reservoirs silted up (Groslier 1973, 1974).

The abandonment of Angkor, Banteay Chmar, Banteay Srei and Phimai has some intriguing parallels in the collapse of the Peten Maya civilization, in the 9th century A.D., when Tikal, Quirigua and similar centres failed and were abandoned. There are no documentary sources to assist in isolating causes for the Maya collapse, but numerous reasons have been advanced. Foremost, was the inability of the sustaining villages to cope with the demands made on them for surplus production. Indeed, human skeletal remains reveal poor physical condition. Renfrew (1979) has modelled the collapse of the central administration among the Maya within the framework of catastrophe theory, and specifically by employing what he describes as two "control variables". These relate the degree to which a community attracts or imposes adherence to the central authority in terms of the successive conditions of two variables. One is investment in charismatic authority, the other is net rural marginality. Both are related, and involve interaction between rulers and functionaries on one hand, and the sustaining rural population on the other. The system is stable as long as the food producers countenance the provision of surpluses by way of taxation. They might, for example, believe in the existence of a god-king and rely on his intercession for the success of their endeavours. The provision of water through sacred reservoirs is a physical manifestation of reciprocal benefits. Net rural marginality involves the degree to which it is possible to sustain surplus production within the taxation system. As demands rise, marginality increases. It becomes more stressful, in other words, to provide for the gods. Within the framework of the general model, the collapse of the system is always a danger, and can occur quite rapidly (Renfrew 1979).

It would be tempting to see if the information available allows the end of the Angkorian *Maṇḍalà* to be viewed within this same framework. It is not impossible, for example, that investment in charismatic authority fell and rural marginality rose sharply under the building programmes and increased demand for goods imposed by the policy of Jayavarman VII. It has been said that more stone was moved and shaped under his reign than that under all his predecessors combined. Indeed, the decline of the hierarchic Angkorian *Maṇḍala* may have involved the same interplay of variables as have been advanced by Renfrew in considering the demise of the Mayan and Mycenaean states. Under these circumstances, inroads of the Thai *Maṇḍala*, centred at Ayutthaya, from the north and west, and the expansion of Champa from the east, were just as much symptoms as causes of the end of the Angkorian *Maṇḍala*. Hagesteijn (1984) has followed this line of reasoning in advancing possible causes for the end of the Angkorian *Maṇḍala*. She noted that, with time, increasing amounts of land passed into the hands of grandee families, which opened up the possibility of pursuing power through religious munificence in competition with the central overlord. This, in turn, required the overlord to out perform them, an objective clearly achieved by Jayavarman VII, but not so obviously by his successors. Secondly, the spread of Buddhism had the important effect of altering the ultimate destination of gifts made to religious foundations, for whereas those made to a Śaivite establishment were made in the name of the overlord and were part of the *maṇḍala* system for appropriating goods, those made to a Buddhist monastery were for personal merit-making and locally retained to sustain monks (Hagesteijn 1984). The loss of income to the overlord thus had the same effect as an increase in rural marginality. The labour and goods available for him to distribute decreased. This situation brings us again to the heart of the *maṇḍala* system. Just as it expanded under Jayavarman II by attracting adherents and cowing into vassal status a cloud of lesser centres, so it could contract as local leaders sought protection under an alternative overlord and its members adopted new beliefs. As the Sukhothai and Ayutthaya *maṇḍalas* waxed and absorbed a web of affiliations, so the Angkorian waned at its margins. Shades of influence changed, tribute began to move in different directions. In this sense, the Angkorian *Maṇḍala* did not so much collapse as shift ground as it moved its centre from Angkor to the area round the junction of the Tonle Sap and Mekong rivers. It contracted, changed, rode out the storm and modified its horizons.

CHAPTER 7

CONCLUDING REMARKS: THE STRUCTURE OF THE PAST IN SOUTHEAST ASIA

This book began by stressing the diversity of Southeast Asia, in geography, climate, languages and political systems. Although archaeology has much still to do, it is held that there is now sufficient information to argue that there is a unity in the area's prehistory and early history.

In this study, I have tried to identify images, to seek explanations, and to focus on possibilities. I have not sought answers, but rather to pose questions and propose explanatory structures. Southeast Asia's past has attracted several other attempts at synthesis, and all tell us more about the authors and their prejudices than the matter at hand. Colani brought with her images of Upper Palaeolithic French art, and had in mind the expertise of the prehistoric stone workers when she spoke of the Hoabinhian people in Viet Nam as poor savages. Coedès, too, had little empathy for the prehistoric people when composing his monumental study on the Indianised States of Southeast Asia. As a reaction to this pessimism, some more recent workers have claimed remarkably early dates for agriculture, bronze and iron-working. Further research has now set these in perspective. A few years ago, some Western-trained scholars working in Southeast Asia would probably have recognised and followed some familiar signposts based on the three age system. This would have involved a Mesolithic prelude – the Hoabinhian – followed by the expansion of Neolithic societies, the development of the Bronze and Iron Ages, followed by civilization.

Parallels with developments elsewhere would have been noted and, perhaps, similar explanations offered. There would have been numerous migrations. Solheim (1972) wisely suggested an alternative structure, which he based on important variables in the Southeast Asian environment. My own attempt has also tried to set prehistoric and early historic data within its local matrix, while at the same time calling on a general theoretical approach. I have identified several themes and offered tentative explanations. One is the nature of the hunter-gatherer groups now known to us, some of which appear to have been conservative, others complex and prone to change. Much emphasis has been given to the major loss of land which accompanied the post-Pleistocene rise in sea level. Settlements situated on raised fossil beaches, formed when the sea stabilised at a level rather higher than at present, are now revealing the richness of a distinctive maritime way of life. The adoption of rice cultivation has been described, rightly, as a basic question in Southeast Asian prehistory. Some light has been cast on this issue, and pertinent questions have been formulated. One of the most encouraging aspects of recent approaches to this area, is that historians have discovered relevance in the prehistoric period, and we prehistorians are continuing our interest into the timespan covered by written records. Unwittingly, errors will be made, but the dialogue of common concerns can only be fruitful.

Within this wider frame, I have tried to define a system involving the exchange of exotic goods as emblems between status-conscious people living in independent villages. Their world changed when iron became readily available and a new range of valuables and novel ideas penetrated first the coasts, and then the interior valleys, of Southeast Asia. This process encompassed the millennium which starts before the first Indian impact, and finishes at a point where overlords claimed divine qualities and vied with each other for status and followers.

I will now touch on these themes in a little more detail, to spotlight areas which merit further research. One is undoubtedly the role of rice cultivation. Such is the potential for intensifying returns from this plant that the visitor to Southeast Asia, viewing the manufactured landscape in favour of rice production, could easily be led to believe that rice was of primary importance in the lives of expanding agricultural societies. This may well be an illusion. The richest prehistoric site in terms of the survival of rice remains is Khok Phanom Di. It was occupied by a coastal community, probably between about 2000 and 1400 B.C. The habitat included an estuary, mangrove-lined tidal flats and freshwater ponds. The people had a rich marine diet, were masters in the art of pottery making and used polished stone adzes. They were sedentary, and their settlement covers 5 ha. To judge from the superbly decorated pottery, wealth of burial goods and presence of a raised mortuary structure, the people were concerned with ritual and display. Yet it is quite possible that they obtained their food without reliance on agriculture or the domestication of animals for most of their occupancy there. This site is so large, and its later burials so rich, that it is viewed as a ranked social system, at least during Zone B, sustained, in purely subsistence terms, by the wealth of its coastal food resources. I have argued that a key issue in understanding this coastal adaptation is domestication. Here, I refer to changes in human behaviour resulting from permanent occupation of one settlement, rather than in the way animals and plants were exploited. There is no doubt, in terms of archaeological remains, that the occupants of Khok Phanom Di entered into a social world of status and display quite different from anything bequeathed us by the mobile bands of foragers documented in the evergreen forest habitat of the interior. It is quite conceivable that, when major excavations in the huge coastal sites of Viet Nam are undertaken, similar findings will be made there. We are left to speculate on the nature of the coastal communities antedating Khok Phanom Di, which have been covered by the rising waters of the Gulf of Siam.

Guided by Johnson's (1982) and Forge's (1972) findings that when domestic communities reach a certain size threshold there is a tendency to split, I have suggested that sites such as Khok Phanom Di were foci of population growth within a limited series of optimal enclaves, and that from them, sections of the population fissioned and ultimately set in train the expansion of domestic settlements into the interior. Once away from the coast, the impact of the long dry season is encountered, and it may be in such inland "marginal" zones that rice grown in modified riverine habitats played a role in determining where people chose to live. Between, say, 3000 and 500 B.C., however, there is no evidence that rice was a critical or major resource. Indeed, all the available evidence indicates a catholic diet involving domestic livestock, hunting large mammals, trapping, fishing, shellfish collection and doubtless, too, the collection of a wide range of wild plants. The human remains indicate a well fed and robust population.

Far from reflecting an expansionary quest for agricultural land, the explanation may be more subtle and archaeologically less tangible. One factor I have put forward for consideration is that settlements fissioned at stressful social thresholds far below the carrying capacity of their respective territories. Food, under this explanation, was not an issue.

Whatever the causes, we are now able to expand upon Wolter's (1982) conception of prehistoric settlements as being isolated from each other. Scratch the surface of any of the sites, and you find exotic goods. Those which have survived are ceramics, shell, stone, tin, silk and copper. Doubtless a host of other items which do not survive the rigours of time could be added. Salt, for example, and foodstuffs, basketry, feathers, spices and cloth come to mind without too much reflection. Where goods change hands, ideas flow. The presence of exotic goods – primitive valuables as Dalton calls them – is seen as indicative of different levels of prestige and status within essentially autonomous village communities. Along the linked networks which are now being recognised on the coast of Viet Nam, up the Red River, in the Mekong catchment and across the inland plain of Cambodia, there moved the knowledge and practice of another prestige valuable, bronze. Metal ornaments and weaponry were, it seems, locally cast from imported ingots, following the same techniques over a wide area. I am not alone in being unable as yet to identify the origins of bronze-working, but do argue that it represents a particularly Southeast Asian technological tradition quite distinct from that centred to the north in China. This, again, is a strong argument for a coherence and unity to our area during prehistory. These bronze objects were only found in a few burials. The mortuary evidence currently available suggests that bronze ornaments and implements, as well as exotic stone and shell jewellery, registered status through display.

All interested parties are agreed that prehistoric societies became more complex in terms of social organisation between 500–1 B.C. There was a trend towards dominance over previously autonomous communities by the occupants of relatively large central places. Iron-working was one of several important variables in the rising tide of complexity. Particularly when hardened through carburisation, iron was undoubtedly a most significant new resource. It was made into agricultural implements, weapons and ornaments. Most important too, was its wide availability as an ore. While iron did not replace bronze in the manufacture of jewellery, it became the medium for more abundant and efficient tools and weapons.

It remains possible that trends towards centralisation were underway before the initial trickle of Indian contact turned into a flood, but it is felt that Indian coastal traders fuelled the process at least in the more favoured coastal tracts. I cannot help but be influenced in this by my reading of the events following Arab and European expansionary contact along the coasts of Africa or, for that matter, with my discussions on the same subject with Peter Wilson, Henry Wright and Jack Goody. An approach seeking the interplay between several variables is but one way of assessing the development of complexity. When I read Friedman's and Rowlands's (1977) ideas on the development of societal complexity, I was struck by the apparent fit with some of our information from Southeast Asia. In an early draft of chapter 6, I attempted to weigh the evidence for a rising tide of cultural complexity within their epigenetic model. Some of the variables fitted quite well. For the sake of a uniform approach to successive issues, however, I decided to retain a more general framework. In either case, the same variables come to the fore. Is it, for example, the case that *maṇḍalas* developed earliest at the interface between local coastal communities and Indian traders? Again, did the intensification of production both of food and artefacts occur in the tracts under the sway of an overlord? The canals of the Mekong delta region, and intensity of manufacturing at Oc Eo, suggest so. Did overlords augment their standing by self-identification with Śiva? The answer again seems positive, according at least to the inscriptions. Thus, we can identify the continuity of centralisation whereby a local chief became an overlord of a *maṇḍala*.

Is this just a change of name to describe the same phenomenon? The reality of the situation is probably that some chiefs, by degrees, extended their sphere of influence and strengthened their position through increased identity with gods, more building activity and investment in ritual. It is strongly argued that access to exotic Indian or Chinese goods placed coastal chiefs in a particularly favoured position.

Factors identified with states elsewhere are manifest within archaeological and literary sources as the first millennium progressed. We find evidence for large, defended settlements and temple construction requiring corvée labour, as well as the appropriation of surpluses for the display of wealth and status, feasting and the sustenance of the central people. Land increasingly passed into private hands, and large estates were accumulated and maintained over several generations. The overlord controlled the means of destruction. If we base our interpretations largely on archaeological remains, and paint our conclusions with broad strokes, the origins and development of Southeast Asian states presents many similarities with developments elsewhere.

The sources, however, are as much documentary and epigraphic as archaeological, and the former allow a more detailed portrait to be painted if used with circumspection. In this, I am influenced by the sensitive and revealing portrayal of the 19th century Balinese state by Geertz (1980). We perceive, through the concept of the *maṇḍala*, entities which, while subscribing to centrality in appropriating goods and requiring loyalty, were politically fluid. The overlord was powerful, but his power was checked and balanced by his capacity to attract and retain vassals and landed grandees. Some *maṇḍalas* were doubtless small and ephemeral. Where there was an appropriate mix of environmental largesse and energetic overlords, *maṇḍalas* could expand greatly and reveal durability over several centuries. Retraction in the sphere of one *maṇḍala* was taken up by the expansion of another. Is it, then, appropriate to talk of the collapse of the classic Khmer, or are we, in fact, dealing with shifts and changes as their *maṇḍala* declined at the expense of Ayutthaya? Whichever the case, we are again operating in a particular Southeast Asian context within which to set human behaviour against the pervading variability in the personality of Southeast Asia. Just as that Angkorian *Maṇḍala* was at its maximum extent, hunter-gatherers at Banyan Valley Cave were fashioning stone tools and harvesting wild rice. The visitor who is today caught up in a traffic jam in Bangkok could reflect on the fact that, while he is in the centre of a great royal overlord, he is also only an hour's flying time from present hunter-gatherers.

I have, despite such contrasts, tried to isolate a common thread of continuity which runs though a complex and variable fabric of cultural development. This thread involves the attainment of status through the attraction of followers, advertised through ritual acts, monumental buildings and the display of rare or highly crafted artefacts. It may, of course, be a coincidence, but the raised platform structure at Khok Phanom Di, built perhaps 3500 years ago, was laid out on the same orientation as the much later sacred precincts of Īśānapura. We are on firmer ground, however, when emphasising the importance attached to the attainment of domesticity, the permanent occupation of a particular place. This, especially in maritime contexts, was associated with the establishment of a long-term cemetery at Khok Phanom Di, the manufacture of works of art in ceramics and shell, and of their interment with the dead. We encounter an exchange network which involved a variety of stone adzes and ceramics, and the growth of a settlement to cover about 5 ha. These aspects of behaviour, it is argued, were based on sedentism and domesticity. An examination of the mounded settlements of the riverine valleys in the interior discloses a similar, if not as rich, series of establishments. Again, rarities changed hands, beginning with stone and shell, and later incorporating copper, tin, lead and iron. It is very likely that the occupation of most, if not all, tracts of suitable marshland in the interior had taken place by the mid first millennium B.C., and that increased competition and emulation in pursuit of status was a factor in the establishment of centrally based chiefdoms. This process, it is argued, was fuelled by the increasing Indian and Chinese arrivals along the coasts of Southeast Asia. The situation up to, and indeed beyond the first Indian contact, is strongly reminiscent of Leach's conclusion following his consideration of the Kachin of highland

Northern Burma (Leach 1954), a situation already noted by Kennedy (1977). So similar is my conception of the situation in prehistory to that described by Leach, that it is perhaps better to employ his words:

> What we have found is roughly this. The population of the Kachin Hills Area is not culturally uniform; one would not expect it to be for the ecology varies. But if we neglect that very large part of culture which is concerned with practical economic action, ...we are still left with something, that something which in this book I have dealt with under the heading of ritual action. And as concerns these ritual aspects of culture the population of the Kachin Hills Area is relatively uniform. The people may speak different languages, wear different kinds of clothes, live in different kinds of houses, but they understand one another's ritual. Ritual acts are ways of "saying things" about social status, and the "language" in which these things are said is common to the whole Kachin Hills Area. (Leach 1954:279).

One of the most important results of research over the last two decades has been this appreciation that the Indian traders encountered sophisticated societies engaged in widespread and competitive ritual expressions of status. Indian contact within this context provided a new range of exotic goods to a long-established system, and furnished political ideas which local leaders could tap. Concern with the control of water and the construction of ritual centres and attraction thereto of adherents was, it is argued, a continuation of practices with a long local ancestry.

Surely, the successive shifts in the direction of complexity which have been identified reflect, in large measure, social actions within a myriad of lowland communities. The demands for display valuables saw rarities change hands through a whole series of networks. In its turn, the control over sources, or manufacturing processes such as the smelting or casting of bronze, doubtless conferred advantages, although this was fickle if tastes changed or more novel goods became available. There are some grounds for supposing that economic and technological changes were stimulated by the social demands placed on them. Feasting and display are integral to this system, and they, in turn, placed demands on a particularly elastic subsistence activity, rice production. On a grander scale, the control of water under the Angkorian *Maṇḍala* fundamentally altered the greatest limiting factor in the Southeast Asian environment, the unpredictability of the monsoon.

There are signs, then, of a coherent pattern of cultural development to these river valleys rooted deep in the prehistoric past. It is one where the central focus is increasing complexity, intensity and richness in human culture achieved through competition, emulation, ritual, display and, in its final lap, the creation of gods and their heaven on earth. In stages which had their principal focus in lowland coastal or riverine contexts, those communities, through increased technological prowess, relaxed the environmental limitations they confronted. On the one hand, we can recognise immense regional diversity. On the other, there is a distinct communality of experience. Both contribute to the individuality of mainland Southeast Asia, but simultaneously provide the basis for a cultural development with marked parallels in other regions. If this study has helped establish and portray the area as one which fully illustrates the human capacity for adaptation, innovation and change, it will have achieved its main purpose.

REFERENCES

Abbreviations

AIB-L	Académie des Inscriptions et Belles-Lettres.
AP	*Asian Perspectives.*
APAO	*Archaeology and Physical Anthropology in Oceania.*
BEFEO	*Bulletin de l' École Française d'Extrême Orient.*
BIPPA	*Bulletin of the Indo-Pacific Prehistory Association.*
BSGI	*Bulletin de la Service Géologique d'Indochine.*
BSOAC	*Bulletin of the School of Oriental and African Studies.*
CA	*Current Anthropology.*
EFEO	École Française d'Extrême Orient.
JA	*Journal Asiatique.*
JAH	*Journal of African History.*
JAS	*Journal of Archaeological Science.*
JMBRAS	*Journal of the Malay (Malaysian) Branch of the Royal Asiatic Society.*
JRAS	*Journal of the Royal Asiatic Society.*
JSS	*Journal of the Siam Society.*
KCH	*Khao Co Hoc*
MEFEO	*Mémoires de l'École Française d'Extrême Orient.*
MQRISA	*Modern Quaternary Research in Southeast Asia.*
MSGI	*Mémoires du Service Géologique de l'Indochine.*
OUSPA	*Otago University Studies in Prehistoric Anthropology.*
PEFEO	*Publications de l'École Française d'Extrême Orient.*

Alpers, E.A. 1969, Trade, state and society among the Yao in the nineteenth century. *JAH* 93:405-520.

Aymonier, E. 1900-1903, *La Cambodge II: Les Provinces Siamoises.* Paris, Ernest Leroux.

Bannanurag, R. 1984, *Report of the first season's site survey in the Bang Pakong Valley, Chonburi Province* (in Thai). Report to the Fine Arts Department, Bangkok.

Barnard, N. 1986, Bronze casting technology in the peripheral "Barbarian Regions". Paper prepared for the symposium *Early metallurgy in Japan and the surrounding area*, Metals Museum, The Japan Institute of Metals, Sendai.

Barth, A. 1885, *Inscriptions Sanscrites du Cambodge.* Notices et extraits des mss. de la Bib. Nat., t. XXVII, le partie, fasc. 1, Paris.

Basham, A.L. 1954, *The Wonder that was India.* Macmillan, London.

Bayard, D.T. 1971, Non Nok Tha. The 1968 excavation: procedure, stratigraphy and a summary of the evidence. *OUSPA* 4:77 pp.

1972a, Excavations at Non Nok Tha, Northeastern Thailand 1968: an interim report. *AP* 13:109-43.

1972b, Early Thai bronze: analysis and new dates. *Science* 176:1411-12.
1977, Phu Wiang pottery and the prehistory of Northeast Thailand. *MQRISA* 3:57-102.
1979, Comment on the linguistic history of mainland Southeast Asia by H.L. Shorto. R.B. Smith and W. Watson (eds.) *Early South East Asia* pp 278-80. Oxford University Press, Oxford.
1980, The Pa Mong archaeological survey programme, 1973-5. *OUSPA* 13:175 pp.
1984a, Rank and wealth at Non Nok Tha: the mortuary evidence. *Southeast Asian Archaeology at the XV Pacific Science Congress. OUSPA* 16:87-128.
1984b, A tentative regional phase chronology for Northeast Thailand. *Southeast Asian Archaeology at the XV Pacific Science Congress. OUSPA* 16:161-8.
1984c, A checklist of Vietnamese radiocarbon dates. *Southeast Asian Archaeology at the XV Pacific Science Congress. OUSPA* 16:305-22.
Bayard, D.T., Charoenwongsa, P. and Rutnin, S. 1986, Excavations at Non Chai, Northeastern Thailand. *AP* 25(1): 13-62.
Bayard, D.T. and Parker, R.H. 1976, Interpretation of Sai Yok and Ban Kao sites, Central Thailand. *AP* 19(2):289-92.
Bayard, D.T. and Uthaiwee, T. 1985, Time, false noses and skyrockets: the "Skyrocket Song" of Northeast Thailand in its cultural context. *Mankind* 15(1):18-25.
Bellwood, P. 1985, *Prehistory of the Indo-Malyasian Archipelago*. Academic Press, New York.
Bénisti, M. 1968, Recherches sur le premier art Khmèr 1. Les Linteaux dits de Thala Borivat. *Arts Asiatiques* XVIII:85-102.
1970, Rapports entre le premier art Khmèr et d'art Indien. *MEFEO* V.
Bennett, A. 1982, *Metallurgical Analysis of Iron Artifacts from Ban Don Ta Phet, Thailand.* M.A. dissertation, University of London.
1986, Prehistoric copper smelting in Central Thailand. Paper delivered to the Association of Southeast Asian Archaeologists in Europe Conference, London, September 1986.
Bergaigne, A. 1893, *Inscriptions Sanscrites de Campa et du Cambodge.* Notices et extraits des mss. de la Bib. Nat., t. XXVII, le partie, fasc. 2, Paris.
Binford, L.R. 1968, Post-Pleistocene adaptations. S.R. Binford and L.R. Binford (eds.) *New Perspectives in Archaeology* pp.313-41. Aldine, Chicago.
1971, Mortuary practices: their study and their potential. J.A. Brown (ed.) Approaches to the social dimensions of mortuary practices. *Mem. Soc. Amer. Arch.* 25:6-29.
Bloch, M. 1977, The disconnection between power and rank as a process: an outline of the development of kingdoms in central Madagascar. J. Friedman and M.J. Rowlands (eds.) *The Evolution of Social Systems* pp.303-40. Duckworth, London.
Boeles, J.J. 1964, The King of Dvāravatī and his regalia. *JSS*:LII(1):99-114.
Boisselier, J. 1968, *Nouvèlles Connaissances Archéologiques de la Ville d' U T'ong.* Bangkok.
Boonsong, L. and McNeely, J.A. 1977, *Mammals of Thailand.* Sahakarnbhat, Bangkok.
Bourke, W.W. 1905, Some archaeological notes on Monton Phuket. *JSS* II:49-62.
Bray, F. 1984, *Science and Civilisation in China; vol.6, Biology and Biological Technology. Part II: Agriculture.* Cambridge University Press, Cambridge.
Briggs, L.P. 1951, The Ancient Khmer Empire. *Trans. Am. Phil. Soc.* 4(1).
Bronson, B. 1978, Angkor, Anuradhapura, Prambanan and Tikal: Maya subsistence in an Asian perspective. P.D. Harrison and B.L. Turner (eds.) *Pre-Hispanic Maya Agriculture* pp.255-300. University of New Mexico Press, Albuquerque.

1979, The late prehistory and early history of Central Thailand with special reference to Chansen. R.B. Smith and W. Watson (eds.) *Early South East Asia* pp. 315-36. Oxford University Press, Oxford.

1985, Nāgara and Commandery. A review of *Nāgara and Commandery: Origins of the Southeast Asian Urban Traditions* by Paul Wheatley. *South-East Asian Studies Newsletter* 20:1-4.

1986, Notes on the history of iron in Thailand. *JSS*, in press.

Bronson, B. and Dales, G.F. 1973, Excavations at Chansen, Thailand, 1968, 1969: a preliminary report. *AP* 15(1):15-46.

Buchan, R.A. 1973, *The Three-dimensional Jig-saw Puzzle: a Ceramic Sequence from NE Thailand.* M.A. dissertation, University of Otago.

Calder, A.M. 1972, *Cracked Pots and Rubbish Tips: an Ethnoarchaeological Study of Thai-Lao village*. M. A. dissertation, University of Otago.

Carbonnel, J.P. and Delibrias, G., 1968, Premières datations absolues de trois gisements néolithiques Cambodgiens. *Comptes-rendues Acad. Sciences Paris* 267:1432-4.

Cartailhac, É. 1890, Les bronzes préhistoriques et les recherches de M. Ludovic Jammes. *L'Anthropologie* 6(1):41-50.

Chandler, D. 1983, *A History of Cambodia.* Westview Press, Boulder, Colorado.

Chang, T.T. 1976, The rice cultures. *Phil. Trans. Royal Society of London B. series* 275:143-57.

Chang, T.T. and Loresto, E. 1984, The rice remains. C.F.W. Higham and A. Kijngam (eds.) *Prehistoric Investigations in Northeast Thailand*. British Archaeological Reports (International Series) 231(2):384-5. Oxford.

Chantaratiyakan, P. 1983, *The Prehistory of the Middle Chi Valley: a Pioneer Study.* M.A. dissertation, University of Otago.

1984, The Middle Chi research programme. C.F.W. Higham and A. Kijngam (eds.) *Prehistoric Investigations in Northeast Thailand.* British Archaeological Reports (International Series) 231(2):565-643. Oxford.

Chappel, J. and Thom, B.G. 1977, Sea levels and coasts. J.Allen, J. Golson and R. Jones (eds.) *Sunda and Sahul* pp.275-91. Academic Press, New York.

Charoenwongsa, P., Khemnak, P. and Kwanyuen, S. 1985, *An Inventory of Rock Art Sites in Northeast Thailand.* Semeo Projects in Archaeology and Fine Arts, Bangkok.

Christie, A. 1970, The provenence and chronology of early Indian cultural influence in Southeast Asia. H.B. Sarkar (ed.) *R.C. Majumdar Felicitation Volume* pp.1-14. Mukjopadhyay, Calcutta.

Claeys, J.Y 1927, Configuration du site de Tra-Kieu. *BEFEO* 27:469-82.

1931, Simhapura, la grande capitale Chame (VI-VIIIe S.A.D.). *Revue des Arts Asiatiques* VII:93-104.

Coedès, G. 1913, Le serment des fonctionnaires de Sūryavarman I. *BEFEO* 13:11-17.

1924, Études cambodgiennes XVIII. L'extension de Cambodge vers le sud-ouest au VIIe siècle (nouvelles inscriptions de Chantaboun). *BEFEO* 24:352-8.

1928, The excavations of Pong Tuk and their importance for the ancient history of Siam. *JSS* XXI(3):195-209.

1931, Deux inscriptions Sanskrites de Fou-nan. *BEFEO* 31:1-23.

1937-1954, *Inscriptions du Cambodge*. (6 vols.) Hanoi: 1937, 1942. Paris: 1951, 1952, 1953, 1954: EFEO.

1943-6, Études Cambodgiennes. Quelques précisions sur la fin de Fou-nan. *BEFEO* 43:1-11.

1947, Fouilles en Cochinchine. Le site de Go Oc Eo, ancien port du Royaume Fou-nan. *Artibus Asiae* X:193-99.
1958, Nouvelles donnees épigraphiques sur l'histoire de l'Indochine Centrale. *JA* 246:125-42.
1968, *The Indianised States of Southeast Asia*. East-West Centre Press, Honolulu.
Colani, M. 1927, L'âge de la pierre dans la province de Hoa Binh. *MSGI* XIII:1.
1930, Recherches sur le préhistorique Indochinoise. *BEFEO* 30:299-422.
1935, Mégalithes du Haut-Laos. (2 vols.) *PEFEO* 25-6.
Condominas, G. 1977, *We Have Eaten the Forest*. Hill and Wang, New York.
Corre, A. 1879, Rapport sur les objets de l'âge de la pierre polie et du bronze recueillis à Som-Ron-Sen (Cambodge) et note annexe sur des instruments en pierre polie et en bronze trouvés aux environs de Saigon. *Excursions et Reconnaissances* (Saigon) 1:71-91.
Creel, H.G. 1964, The beginnings of bureaucracy in China: the origin of the *Hsien*. *JRAS* XXIII(2): 155-83.
Daeng-iet, S. 1978, Khok Phlap: a newly discovered prehistoric site (in Thai). *Muang Boran* 4(4):17-26.
1980, *A preliminary report on the Ban Waeng excavation* (in Thai). Fine Arts Department, Bangkok.
Dalton, G. 1977, Aboriginal economics in stateless societies. T.K. Earle and J.E. Ericson (eds.) *Exchange Systems in Prehistory* pp.191-212. Academic Press, London.
Dao The Tuan, 1982, Some remarks on rice specimens excavated at Xom Trai cave in 1982. Paper read to the Conference on the Hoabinhian, Ha Noi.
Davidson, J.H.C.S. 1979, Archaeology in Southern Viet-Nam since 1954. R.B. Smith and W. Watson (eds.) *Early South East Asia* pp.215-22. Oxford University Press, Oxford.
de Casparis, J.G. 1979, Palaeography as an auxilliary discipline in research on early Southeast Asia. R.B. Smith and W. Watson (eds.) *Early South East Asia* pp.380-94. Oxford University Press, Oxford.
Delaporte, L. 1880, *Voyage au Cambodge. L'architecture Khmère*. Paris.
Delvert, J. 1961, Le Paysan Cambodgien. *Le Monde d'Outre Mer Passé et Présent*. Premiére Série No.10. École Practique des Hautes Études, Sorbonne.
Diskul, M.C. Subhadradis 1979, The development of Dvāravatī sculpture and a recent find from Northeast Thailand. R.B. Smith and W. Watson (eds.) *Early South East Asia* pp.360-70. Oxford University Press, Oxford.
Dobby, E.H.G. 1967, *Southeast Asia*. University of London Press, London.
Dufour, H. and Carpeaux, G. 1910, *Le Bayon d'Angkor Thom* . E. Leroux, Paris.
Dupont, P. 1943-6, Études sur L'Indochine ancienne: II la dislocation du Tchenla et la formation du Cambodge Angkorien. *BEFEO* 42:17-55.
1959, *L'Archéologie Mône de Dvāravatī*. *EFEO*, Paris.
Doudart de Lagrée, E. de G. 1883, *Explorations et missions*. A.B. de Villemereuil, Paris.
Ekholm, K. 1977, External exchange and the transformation of central African social systems. J. Friedman and M.J. Rowlands (eds.) *The Evolution of Social Systems* pp.115-36. Duckworth, London.
Evans-Pritchard, E.E. 1971, *The Azande: History and Political Institutions*. Oxford University Press, Oxford.
Filliozat, J. 1954, Le symbolisme du monument du Phnom Bakheng. *BEFEO* 44:527-54.
Finot, M.L. 1902, Deux nouvelles inscriptions de Bhadravarman 1, roi de Champa. *BEFEO* 2:185-91.
1904, Les inscriptions de Mi-son. *BEFEO* 4:897-977.

Folan, W.J. and Hyde, B.H. 1980, The significance of clay rollers of the Ban Chiang Culture, Thailand. *AP* 23(2):153-63.
Fontaine, H. 1972, Deuxieme note sur le "Néolithique" du bassin inferieur du Dong-Nai. *Archives géologiques du Viet-Nam* 15:123-9.
Forge, A. 1972, Normative factors in the settlement size of Neolithic cultivators (New Guinea). P.J. Ucko, R. Tringham and G.W. Dimbleby (eds.) *Man, Settlement and Urbanism* pp.363-76. Duckworth, London.
Friedman, J. and Rowlands, M.J. 1977, Notes towards an epigenetic model of the evolution of civilization. J. Friedman and M.J. Rowlands (eds.) *The Evolution of Social Systems* pp.201-76. Duckworth, London.
Garnier, F. 1871, Voyage des Hollandais en Cambodge et Laos en 1644. *Bulletin de la Soc. de Géographie* II-19:251-89.
1873, *Voyage d'Exploration en Indochine, Effectué Pendant les Années 1866 et 1868.* Paris.
Geertz, C. 1980, *Negara: the Theatre State in Nineteenth-century Bali.* Princeton University Press, Princeton.
Geyh, M.A., Kudrass, H.R. and Streif, H. 1979, Sea level changes during the late Pleistocene and Holocene in the straits of Malacca. *Nature* 278:441-3.
Glover, I.C. 1980, Ban Don Ta Phet and its relevence to problems in the pre- and protohistory of Thailand. *BIPPA* 2:16-30.
1983, Excavations at Ban Don Ta Phet, Kanchanaburi Province, Thailand, 1980-1. *South-East Asian Studies Newsletter* 10:1-4.
Glover, I.C., Charoenwongsa, P., Alvey, B. and Kamnounket, N. 1984, The cemetery of Ban Don Ta Phet, Thailand: results from the 1980-1 season. B. Allchin and M. Sidell (eds.) *South Asian Archaeology 1981* pp.319-30. Cambridge University Press, Cambridge.
Goody, J. 1971, *Technology, Tradition and the State in Africa.* Hutchinson, London.
1976, *Production and Reproduction.* Cambridge University Press, Cambridge.
Gorman, C.F. 1971, The Hoabinhian and after: subsistence patterns in Southeast Asia during the late Pleistocene and early Recent periods. *World Archaeology* 2(3):300-20.
1972, Excavations at Spirit Cave, North Thailand: some interim impressions. *AP* 13:79-107.
1977, *A priori* models and Thai prehistory: a reconsideration of the beginnings of agriculture in Southeast Asia. C.A. Reed (ed.) *Origins of Agriculture* pp.322-55. Mouton, The Hague.
Gorman, C.F. and Charoenwongsa, P. 1976, Ban Chiang: A mosaic of impressions from the first two years. *Expedition* 8(4):14-26.
Gourou, P. 1955, *The Peasants of the Tonkin Delta.* Human Relations Area Files, New Haven.
Groslier, B.P. 1966, *Indochina.* Miller, London.
1973, Pour une géographie historique du Cambodge. *Les Cahiers d'Outre-Mer* 26:337-9.
1974, Agriculture et religion dans l'Empire Angkorien. *Études Rurales* 53-56:95-117.
1979, La cité hydraulique Angkorienne. Exploitation ou surexploitation du sol? *BEFEO* 66:161-202.
Hanks, L.M. 1972, *Rice and Man. Agricultural Ecology in Southeast Asia.* Aldine, Chicago and New York.
Hagesteijn, R. 1984, Continuiteit en verandering in vroeg Zuid-Aziatisch politiek

leiderschap. H.J.M. Claessen (ed.) *Macht en Majesteit, Idee en Werkelijkheid Rond Het Koningschap* pp. 103-12. Diemen: De Bataafsche Leeuw.

Harlan, J. 1977, The origins of cereal agriculture in the old world. C.A. Reed (ed.) *The Origins of Agriculture* pp.357-84. Mouton, the Hague.

Ha Van Phung, 1979, In search of relations between Go Mun and Dong Son cultures (in Vietnamese). *KCH* 29:43-61.

Ha Van Phung and Nguyen Duy Ty 1982, *Di Chi Khao Co Hoc Go Mun* (in Vietnamese). Nha Xuat Ban Khoa Hoc Xa Hoi, Ha Noi.

Ha Van Tan, 1976, The Hoabinhian in the context of Viet Nam. *Vietnamese Studies* 46:127-97.

1977, Excavations at Phoi Phoi. *Nhung phat hien moi ve khao co hoc nam* (New archaeological discoveries in Viet Nam in 1976). Ha Noi.

1980, Nouvelles recherches préhistoriques et protohistoriques au Viet Nam. *BEFEO* 68:113-54.

Heine-Geldern, R. 1932, Urheimat und fruheste Wanderungen der Austronesier. *Anthropos* 27:543-619.

1951, Das Tocharer problem und die Pontische Wanderung. *Sauculum* 11/2:225-55.

Higham, C.F.W. 1975a, Non Nok Tha, the faunal remains. *OUSPA* 7:187 pp.

1975b, Aspects of economy and ritual in prehistoric Northeast Thailand. *JAS* 2(4):245-88.

1977, The prehistory of the Southern Khorat Plateau, with particular reference to Roi Et Province. *MQRISA* 3:103-42.

1983, The Ban Chiang culture in wider perspective. *Proc. Brit. Acad.* LXIX:229-61.

Higham, C.F.W., R. Bannanurag, B.K. Maloney and B.A. Vincent 1987, Khok Phanom Di: the results of the 1984-5 excavation. *BIPPA* 7:148-78.

Higham, C.F.W. and Kijngam, A. 1979, Ban Chiang and Northeast Thailand; the palaeoenvironment and economy. *JAS* 6(3):211-34.

1982, Prehistoric man and his environment: evidence from the Ban Chiang faunal remains. *Expedition* 24(4):17-24.

1984, *Prehistoric investigations in Northeast Thailand.* British Archaeological Reports (International Series) 231(1-3). 923 pp. Oxford.

Higham, C.F.W., Kijngam, A. and Manly, B.F.J. 1980, An analysis of prehistoric canid remains from Thailand. *JAS* 7(2):149-66.

Higham, C.F.W. and Parker, R.H. 1970, *Prehistoric Investigations in Northeast Thailand 1969-70: preliminary report.* University of Otago, Anthropology Department.

Ho, C.M. 1984, *The pottery of Kok Charoen and its farther context.* Ph.D. dissertation, University of London.

Hoang Xuan Chinh, 1984, The Hoabinhian culture and the birth of botanical domestication in Viet Nam. D.T. Bayard (ed.) *Southeast Asian Archaeology at the XV Pacific Science Congress. OUSPA* 16:169-72.

Hoang Xuan Chinh and Nguyen Khac Su, 1977, The late Neolithic site of Cau Sat (Dong Nai). (in Vietnamese) *KCH* 24:12-18.

Hoang Xuan Chinh and Nguyen Ngoc Bich, 1978, *Di Chi Khao Co Hoc Phung Nguyen.* Nha Xuat Ban Khoa Hoc Xa Hoi. Ha Noi.

Holdridge, L.R. 1967, *Life Zone Ecology.* (rev. edn.) Tropical Science Centre, San Jose, Costa Rica.

Houghton, P. and Wiriyaromp, W. 1984, The people of Ban Na Di. C.F.W. Higham and A. Kijngam (eds.) *Prehistoric Investigations in Northeast Thailand.* British Archaeological Reports (International Series) 231(2):391-412. Oxford.

Hutchinson, E.W. 1940, *Adventurers in Siam in the Seventeenth Century*. The Royal Asiatic Society, London.

Izikowitz, K.G. 1951, Lamet: hill peasants in French Indochina. *Etnologiska Studier* no. 17.

Jacob, J.M. 1978, The ecology of Angkor: evidence from the inscriptions. P.A. Stott (ed.) *Nature and Man in South East Asia*. School of Oriental and African Studies, London.

1979, Pre-Angkor Cambodia: evidence from the inscriptions concerning the common people and their environment. R.B. Smith and W. Watson (eds.) *Early South East Asia*. pp.406-26. Oxford University Press, Oxford.

Jacques, C. 1972, Études d'Épigraphie Cambodgienne VIII: la carrière de Jayavarman II. *BEFEO* 59:205-20.

1979, "Funan", "Zhenla". The reality concealed by these Chinese views of Indochina. R.B. Smith and W. Watson (eds.) *Early South East Asia* pp. 371-9. Oxford University Press, Oxford.

1984, Sources on economic activity in Khmer and Cham lands. Paper read at the Symposium on Southeast Asia in the 9th-14th Centuries, Australian National University, 9th-14th May 1984.

1985, The *Kamrateṅ Jagat* in Ancient Cambodia. Noburu Karashima (ed.) *Indus Valley to Mekong Delta* pp. 269-86. New Era Publications, Madras.

Jamieson, N. 1981, A perspective on Vietnamese prehistory based upon the relationship between geological and archaeological data: summary of an earlier article by Nguyen Duc Tam. *AP* 24:187-92.

Janse, J.M. 1947, *Archaeological Research in Indo-China. Volume I, The District of Chiu-Chen During the Han Dynasty*. Harvard-Yenching Institute Monograph Series, Vol.VII. Harvard University Press, Cambridge, Mass.

1951, *Archaeological Research in Indo-China. Volume II, The District of Chiu-Chen During the Han Dynasty. Distribution and comparative study of the finds.* Harvard-Yenching Institute Monograph Series, Vol.X. Harvard University Press, Cambridge, Mass.

1958, *Archaeological research in Indo-China. Volume III, The Ancient Dwelling Site of Dong-S'on (Thanh-Hoa, Annam)*. Harvard University Press, Cambridge, Mass.

1962, On the origins of traditional Vietnamese music. *AP* 6(1-2):145-62.

Johnson, G.A. 1982, Organisational structure and scalar stress. A.C. Renfrew, M.J. Rowlands and B.A. Segraves (eds.) *Theory and Explanation in Archaeology* pp.389-421. Academic Press, New York.

Judd, P. 1973, Irrigated agriculture in the Central Plain of Thailand. R. Ho and E.C. Chapman (eds.) *Studies in Contemporary Thailand*. Dept. Human Geography Pub. HG/8:137-72. Australian National University, Canberra.

Kennedy, J. 1977, From stage to development in prehistoric Thailand: an exploration of the origins of growth, exchange and variability in Southeast Asia. *Michigan Papers on Southeast Asian Studies* 13:23-38.

Kethutat, P. 1976, Preliminary report on the test excavation at Ban That, Tambon Ban Ya, Amphoe Nong Han (in Thai). *Journal of Anthropology*, Thamasat University, Bangkok, 1976:27-38.

Keyes, C.F. 1974, A note on the ancient towns and cities of Northeast Thailand. *Tonan Ajia Kenkyu* 11(4):497-506.

Kiernan, K., Dunkley, J. and Spies, J. 1987, Prehistoric occupation and burial sites in the mountains of the Nam Khong basin, Northwestern Thailand. Paper in preparation.

Kijngam, A. 1979, The faunal spectrum from Non Chai (in Thai). *Silpakon* 23(5):102-9.
1981, Report on the excavation of Ban Kok, Khon Kaen Province (in Thai). Fine Arts Department, Bangkok.
Klein, J., Lerman, J.C., Damon, P.E. and Ralph, E.K. 1981, Calibration of radiocarbon dates. *Radiocarbon* 24(2):103-50.
Kuchler, A.W. and Sawyer, J.O. 1967, A study of vegetation near Chiang Mai, Thailand. *Transactions Kansas Academy of Sciences* 70:3.
Kulke, H. 1982, *State Formation and Legitimization in Early Java.* Working paper, University of Beilefeld.
1984, Structural changes in larger states in Southeast Asia. Paper read at the Symposium on Southeast Asia in the 9th-14th Centuries, Australian National University, 9th-14th May 1984.
Leach, E.R. 1954, *Political Systems of Highland Burma.* Harvard University Press, Cambridge, Mass.
Lebar, F., Hickey, G. and Musgrave J. 1964, *Ethnic Groups of Mainland Southeast Asia.* Human Relations Area Files, New Haven.
Le Van Thieu, 1979, The wild pig and the domestic swine from the site of Hoa Loc (Thanh Hoa) (in Vietnamese). *KCH* 29:37-42.
Lévy, P. 1943, Recherches préhistoriques dans la region de Mlu Prei. *PEFEO* 30.
1970, Thala Borivat ou Stung Treng: sites de la capitale du souverein Khmèr Bhavavarman 1er. *JA* 257:113-29.
Le Xuan Diem, 1977, Ancient moulds for casting bronze artefacts from the Dong Nai basin (in Vietnamese). *KCH* 24:44-8.
Li Chung 1986, The development of iron and steel technology in ancient China. Paper read to the Conference on the origins of metals and alloys under the auspices of the Beijing University of Iron and Steel Technology, Zhengzhou, China, 21st–27th October, 1986.
Loofs-Wissowa, H.H.E. 1970, A brief account of the Thai-British archaeological expedition, 1965-1970. *APAO* 5:177-84.
Loubère, S. de la, 1693, *A New Historical Relation of the Kingdom of Siam.* Tho. Horne, London.
Lunet de Lajonquière, E. 1902, Inventaire Descriptif des Monuments du Cambodge. *PEFEO* 4.
1907, *Inventaire Descriptif des Monuments du Cambodge, Vol.2.* Inventaire Archéologique de l'Indo-Chine, Vol.8, No.1. Paris, Leroux.
Luu Tran Tieu, 1977, *Khu Mo Co Chau Can.* Ha Noi.
Lyons, E. 1965, The traders of Ku Bua. *Archives of the Chinese Art Society of America* XIX:52-6.
1979, Dvāravatī; a consideration of its formative period. R.B. Smith and W. Watson (eds.) *Early South East Asia* pp.352-9. Oxford University Press, Oxford.
Mabbett, I.W. 1978, Kingship at Angkor. *JSS* LXVI(2):1-58.
MacDonald, W.G. 1978, The Bang site, Thailand. An alternative analysis. *AP* 21(1):30-51.
McGovern, P.E., Vernon, W.W. and White, J.C. 1985, Ceramic technology at prehistoric Ban Chiang, Thailand: physiochemical analyses. *Masca Journal* 3(4):104-13.
Maddin, R. and Weng, Y.Q. 1984, The analysis of bronze "wire". C.F.W. Higham and A. Kijngam (eds.) *Prehistoric Investigations in Northeast Thailand.* British Archaeological Reports (International Series) 231(1):112-16. Oxford.
Malleret, L. 1959-63, *L'Archéologie du Delta du Mekong* (4 vols.) *EFEO*, Paris.
1969, Histoire abrégée de l'archéologie Indochinoise jusqu'à 1950. *AP* 12:43-68.
Maloney, B.K. 1987, Report on the pollen remains from Khok Phanom Di. C.F.W.

Higham, B.A. Vincent, R. Bannanurag and B.K. Maloney, Khok Phanom Di: the results of the 1984-5 season. *BIPPA* 7:148-78.

Mansuy, H. 1902, *Stations préhistoriques de Samrong-Seng et de Longprao (Cambodge).* F.H. Scheider, Hanoi.

1923, Contribution a l'étude de la préhistoire de l'Indochine. Résultats de nouvelles recherches effectuées dans le gisement préhistorique de Samrong Sen (Cambodge). *MSGI* XI(1):5-24.

1924, Stations préhistoriques dans les cavernes du massif calcaire de Bac-Son (Tonkin). *BSGI* 11.2.

Marshall, J. 1951, *Taxila.* Cambridge University Press, Cambridge.

Maspero, M.G. 1928, *Le Royaume de Champa.* Librairie Nationale d'Art et d'Histoire. Paris and Bruxelles.

Moore, E. 1986, *The Moated Mu'ang of the Mun River Basin.* Ph.D. dissertation, University of London.

Moorman, F.R., Montrakun, S. and Panichapong, S. 1964, Soils of Northeastern Thailand: a key to their identification and survey. Soil Survey Division, Land Development Dept., Bangkok.

Mouhot, H. 1864, *Travels in the Central Parts of Indo-China (Siam), Cambodia and Laos.* (2 vols.) J. Murray, London.

Mourer, C. and Mourer R. 1970, The prehistoric industry of Laang Spean, Province Battambang, Cambodia. *APAO* 5:128-46.

Mourer, R. 1977, Laang Spean and the prehistory of Cambodia. *MQRISA* 3:29-56.

Murowchick, R.E. 1986, The development of early bronze metallurgy in Vietnam and Kampuchea: a reexamination of recent work. Paper read to the Conference on the origins of metals and alloys under the auspices of the Beijing University of Iron and Steel Technology, Zhengzhou, China, 21st–27th October, 1986.

Mus, P. 1929, Les Ballistes du Bayon. *BEFEO* 29:331-41.

1936, Sybolism à Angkor Thom. Le "grand miracle" du Bayon. *AIB-L* 57-68.

Natapintu, S. 1984, Ancient settlement at Ban Tha Khae in Lopburi. *Muang Boran* 10(4).

1985, *Prehistoric investigations in the lower Chao Phraya Valley 1983-5* (in Thai). Fine Arts Department, Bangkok.

Ngo Si Hong, 1980, Binh Chau (Nghia Binh). A newly discovered Bronze Age site on the central Vietnamese coast (in Vietnamese). *KCH* 33:68-74.

1985, *Sa Huynh culture, recent excavations* (in Vietnamese). Institute of Archaeology, Viet Nam.

Nguyen Ba Khoach, 1980, Phung Nguyen. *AP* 23(1):23-54.

Nguyen Duc Tam, 1969, Some historical periods related to Quaternary activity and archaeological characteristics and rules in Vietnam and Southeast Asia. *Nghien Cuu Lich Su* 122:28-47.

Nguyen Duc Tung and Pham Van Hai, 1979, The various pollen complexes in the Quaternary sediments of the Bac Bo plains (in Vietnamese). *KCH* 32:34-8.

Nguyen Duy Hinh, 1983, The birth of the first state in Vietnam. Paper prepared for the XV Pacific Science Congress, Dunedin, February 1983. Viet Nam Social Sciences Commission, Archaeology Institute, Hanoi.

Nguyen Van Hao, 1979, The Neolithic in the northeastern region of Viet-nam (in Vietnamese). *KCH* 29:29-36.

Nguyen Viet, 1983, The Dong Son civilisation and the foundation of a developed rice planting. Paper prepared for the XV Pacific Science Congress, Dunedin, February 1983. Viet Nam Social Sciences Commission, Archaeology Institute, Hanoi.

Nguyen Xuan Hien, 1980, The vestiges of burned rice in Viet Nam (in Vietnamese). *KCH* 35:28-34.

Noksakul, D. 1983, *Khok Phanom Di* (in Thai). M.A. dissertation, Silpakon University, Bangkok.

Noulet, J.B. 1877, L'âge de la pierre dans L'Indo-Chine. *Matériaux pour L'Histoire Primitive et Naturelle de l'Homme,* Series 2(8).

1879, L'âge de la pierre polie et du bronze au Cambodge d'après les découvertes de M.J. Moura. *Arch. Mus. Hist. Nat. de Toulouse* 1.

O'Harrow, S. 1979, From Co-loa to the Trung sisters' revolt: Viet-Nam as the Chinese found it. *AP* 22(2):140-64.

Oka, H.I. and Morishima, H. 1971, The dynamics of plant domestication: cultivation experiments with *Oryza perennis* and its hybrid *Oryza sativa. Evolution* 25(2):365-74.

Osborne, M. 1966, Notes on early Cambodian provincial history. Īśānapura and Śambhupura. *France Asie* 186:433-49.

1975, *River Road to China. The Mekong river expedition, 1866-1873.* Liveright, New York.

Paris, P. 1931, Anciens Canaux reconnus sur photographies aériennes dans les provinces de Ta-Kev et de Chau-Doc. *BEFEO* 31:221-4.

1941a, Notes et melanges: anciens canaux reconnus sur photographies aériennes dans les provinces de Ta-Keo, Chau-Doc, Long-Xuyen et Rach-Gia. *BEFEO* 41:365-70.

1941b, Les bateaux des bas-reliefs Khmèrs. *BEFEO* 41:335-61.

Parker, R.H. 1968, Review Article: Review of *Archaeological Excavations in Thailand Vol. 2, Ban Kao, Part 1.* by P. Sørensen and T. Hatting. *Journal of the Polynesian Society* 77(3):307-13.

Parmentier, M.H. 1904, Les monuments du cirque de Mi-son. *BEFEO* 4:805-96.

1909, *Inventaire Descriptif de Monuments Cams de L'Annam.* Ernest Leroux, Paris.

1917, Anciens tombeaux au Tonkin. *BEFEO* 17:1-32.

1918a, Dépots de jarres à Sa-Huynh. *BEFEO* 24:325-43.

1918b, *Inventaire Descriptif de Monuments Cams de L'Annam.* Ernest Leroux, Paris.

1927, L'Art Khmèr Primitif. *PEFEO* XXI-XXII.

Patte, E. 1924, Le kjökkenmödding néolithque de Bau Tao près de Dong Hoi (Annam). *BEFEO* 24:521-61.

1925, Le kjökkenmödding néolithique de Bau Tro a Tam Tao pres de Dong Hoi (Annam). *BSGI* 14(1).

1932, Le kjökkenmödding néolithique de Da-but et ses sépultures. *BSGI* 19(3).

Peebles, C.S. and Kus, S.M. 1977, Some archaeological correlates of ranked societies. *American Antiquity* 42(3):421-48.

Pelliot, P. 1902, Mémoires sur les coutumes du Cambodge, par Tcheou Ta-kouan. *BEFEO* 2:123-77.

1903, Le Fou-Nan. *BEFEO* 2:248-333.

1904, Deux itinéraires de Chine en Inde à la fin du VIIIe siècle. *BEFEO* 4:131-413.

Penny, J.S. 1982, Petchabun piedmont survey. *Expedition* 24(4):65-72.

1984, Fish in the water and rice in the paddy: contributions to the study of the Southeast Asian Iron Age. D.T. Bayard (ed.) *Southeast Asian Archaeology at the XV Pacific Science Congress. OUSPA* 16:152-60.

Pham Huy Thong 1980, Con Moong Cave, a noteworthy archaeological discovery in Vietnam. *AP* 23(1):17-22.

Pham Minh Huyen 1984, Various phases of the development of primitive metallurgy in Viet Nam. D.T. Bayard (ed.) *Southeast Asian Archaeology at the XV Pacific Science Congress. OUSPA* 16:173-82.

Pham Quang Son, 1978, The first tentative links between the late neolithic and early metal using cultures in the basin of the Dong Nai (in Vietnamese). *KCH* 25:35-40.

Pham Van Kinh, 1977, Excavations at Ben Do (Ho Chih Minh City) (in Vietnamese). *KCH* 24:19-21.

Pietrusewsky, M. 1974, The palaeodemography of a prehistoric Thai population: Non Nok Tha. *AP* 27(2):125-40.

1982, The ancient inhabitants of Ban Chiang: the evidence from the human skeletal and dental remains. *Expedition* 24(4):42-50.

1984, Pioneers on the Khorat Plateau: the prehistoric inhabitants of Ban Chiang. *Journal of the Hong Kong Archaeological Society* X:90-106.

Pigott, V.C. 1984, The Thailand archaeometallurgy project 1984: survey of base metal resource exploitation in Loei province, Northeastern Thailand. *South-East Asian Studies Newsletter* 17:1-5.

1986, Pre-industrial mineral exploitation and metal production in Thailand. *Masca Journal* 3(5):170-4.

Pigott, V.C. and Marder, A.R. 1984, Prehistoric iron in Southeast Asia: new evidence from Northeast Thailand. D.T. Bayard (ed.) *Southeast Asian Archaeology at the XV Pacific Science Congress. OUSPA* 16:278-308.

Pilditch, J. 1984, Sections in the material culture of Ban Na Di. C.F.W. Higham and A. Kijngam (eds.) *Prehistoric investigations in Northeast Thailand*. British Archaeological Reports (International Series) 231(1):57-222. Oxford.

Pookajorn, S. 1981, *The Hoabinhian of Mainland Southeast Asia: New data from the Recent Thai Excavation in the Ban Kao Area*. M.Sc. dissertation, University of Pennsylvania.

Preecha, K. and Pookajorn, S. 1976, Preliminary report on test excavations at Ban Om Kaeo, Tambon Ban Chiang, Amphoe Non Han, Changwat Udorn. *Journal of Anthropology,* Thamasat University, Bangkok, 1976:17-26.

Price, T.D. and Brown, J.A. (eds.) 1985, *Prehistoric Hunter-Gatherers: the Emergence of Cultural Complexity*. Academic Press, New York.

Quaritch-Wales, H.G. 1957, An early Buddhist civilisation in Eastern Siam. *JSS* XLV(1):42-60.

1969, *Dvāravatī: The Earliest Kingdom of Siam*. Bernard Quaritch, London.

Rajpitak, W. and Seeley, N.J. 1979, The bronze bowls from Ban Don Ta Phet: an enigma of prehistoric metallurgy. *World Archaeology* 11(1):26-31.

1984, The bronze metallurgy. C.F.W. Higham and A. Kijngam (eds.) *Prehistoric investigations in Northeast Thailand*. British Archaeological Reports (International Series) 231(1):102-12. Oxford.

Renfrew, A.C. 1972, *The Emergence of Civilisation*. Methuen, London.

1979, Systems collapse as social transformation; catastrophe and anastrophe in early state societies. A.C. Renfrew and K.L. Cooke (eds.) *Transformations. Mathematical Approaches to Culture Change*. pp. 481-506. Academic Press, London.

1984, *Approaches to Social Archaeology*. Edinburgh University Press, Edinburgh.

Ricklefs, M. 1967, Land and law in the epigraphy of tenth-century Cambodia. *JRAS* XXVI(93):411-20.

Robinson, G.H. and Steel, F. 1972, *Classification and Evaluation of Soils for Wetland Rice.* Soil Survey Division, Land Development Dept., Bangkok.

Rutnin, S. 1979, *A pottery sequence from Non Chai, Northeast Thailand.* M.A. dissertation, University of Otago.

Sahai, S. 1970, Les Institutions politiques et l'organisation administrative du Cambodge ancien (VI-XIII siècles). *PEFEO* 75.

Sahlins, M. 1972, *Stone Age Economics*. Aldine-Atherton, Chicago and New York.

Sanders, W.T., Parsons J.R. and Santley, R.S. 1979, *The Basin of Mexico*. Academic Press, New York.

Saurin, E. 1963, Station préhistorique à Hang-Gon près Xuan Loc. *BEFEO* 51:433-52.

1969, Les recherches préhistoriques au Cambodge, Laos, et Viet Nam (1877-1966). *AP* 12:27-41.

Saxe, A.A. 1971, Social dimensions of mortuary practices in a Mesolithic population from Wadi Halfa, Sudan. J.A. Brown (ed.) Approaches to the Social Dimensions of Mortuary Practices pp.39-57. *Mem. Soc. Am. Arch.* No.25.

Schauffler, W. 1976, Archaeological survey and excavation of Ban Chiang culture sites in Northeast Thailand. *Expedition* 18:27-37.

1978, An archaeological perspective on prehistoric rice cultivation in N.E. Thailand. Paper presented to CSAS symposium on Agriculture, 1978.

Seidenfaden, E. 1922, Complément à l'inventaire descriptif de monuments du Cambodge. *BEFEO* 22:58-99.

1954, Kanok Nakhon, an ancient Mōn settlement in Northeast Siam and its treasures of art. *BEFEO* 44(2):643-7.

Shorto, H.L. 1979, The linguistic protohistory of mainland South East Asia. R.B. Smith and W. Watson (eds.) *Early South East Asia* pp.273-80. Oxford University Press, Oxford.

Siripanith, S, 1985, *An analytical study on pottery from the excavation at Ban Thakae, Muang District, Lopburi Province.* M.A. dissertation, Silpakon University, Bangkok.

Smith, C.S. 1973, Bronze technology in the east; a metallurgical study of bronzes, with some speculations on the cultural transmissions of technology. M. Teich and R. Young (eds.) *Changing Perspectives in the History of Science: Essays Presented to Joseph Needham* pp.21-32. Heineman, London.

Smith, R.B. 1979a, A comment on the Non Nok Tha dates. R.B. Smith and W. Watson (eds.) *Early South East Asia* pp 39-41. Oxford University Press, Oxford.

1979b, A check-list of published carbon-14 datings from South East Asia. R.B. Smith and W. Watson (eds.) *Early South East Asia* pp. 493-507. Oxford University Press, Oxford.

1979c, Mainland South East Asia in the seventh and eighth centuries. R.B. Smith and W. Watson (eds.) *Early South East Asia* pp. 443-56. Oxford University Press, Oxford.

Solheim, W.G. II 1959, Sa-Huynh related pottery in Southeast Asia. *AP* 3:177-88.

1968, Early bronze in Northeastern Thailand. *Current Anthropology* 9(1):59-62.

1969, Review of *Archaeological Excavations in Thailand Vol. 2, Ban Kao, Part 1.* by P. Sørensen and T. Hatting. *AP* 12:127-30.

1970, Northern Thailand, Southeast Asia, and World prehistory. *AP* 13:145-62.

1972, An earlier agricultural revolution. *Scientific American* CCVI(4):34-41.

Solheim W.G. II and Gorman, C.F. 1966, Archaeological salvage program: Northeastern Thailand, first season. *JSS* LIV:111-81.

Sørensen, P. 1973, Prehistoric iron implements from Thailand. *AP* 16(2):134-73.

1979, The Ongbah cave and its fifth drum. R.B. Smith and W. Watson (eds.) *Early South East Asia* pp.78-97. Oxford University Press, Oxford.

Sørensen, P. and Hatting, T. 1967, *Archaeological Investigations in Thailand. Vol.II, Ban Kao, Part 1: The Archaeological Materials from the Burials.* Munksgard, Copenhagen.

Stech, T.S. and Maddin, R. 1976, The techniques of the early Thai metalsmith. *Expedition* 18(4):38-47.

1986, Reflections on early metallurgy in Southeast Asia. *Proceedings of the Symposium on Early Metallurgy in Japan and the Surrounding Area, October 1986. Special Issue no. 11, Bulletin of Metals Museum* pp 43-56.

Stencel, R., Gifford, F. and Morón, E. 1976, Astronomy and cosmology at Angkor Wat. *Science* 193:281-7.

Suchitta, P. 1983, *The Development of Iron Technology in Thailand.* Ph.D. dissertation, Brown University.

1985, Early iron smelting technology in Thailand and its implications. *Research conference on early Southeast Asia* pp. 25-40. Silpakon University, Bangkok.

Supajanya, T. and Vanasin, P. 1979, *Ancient cities on the former shoreline in the Central Plain of Thailand: the study of sites and geographical correlation* (in Thai). Chulalongkorn University Press: Bangkok, Research Report No. 1.

Suthiragsa, N. 1979, The Ban Chieng culture. R.B. Smith and W. Watson (eds.) *Early South East Asia* pp.42-52. Oxford University Press, Oxford.

Tainter, J. 1978, Mortuary practices and the study of prehistoric social systems. M.B. Schiffer (ed.) *Advances in Archaeological Method and Theory* No.1:105-41. Academic Press, New York.

Takaya, Y. 1969, Topographical analysis of the southern basin of the Central Plain, Thailand. *Tonan Ajia Kenkyu* VII(3):293-300.

Taylor, K.W. 1983, *The Birth of Viet Nam.* University of California, Berkeley.

Thongmitr, W. and Karakovida, B. 1979, Prehistoric rock paintings in Uthai Thani. *Muang Boran* 5(5):13-14.

Tjia, H.D. 1980, The Sunda Shelf, Southeast Asia. *Zeitschrift f. Geomorphologie* NF 24.4:408-27.

Trinh Can and Pham Van Kinh, 1977, Excavations of the urnfield of Tam My (in Vietnamese). *KCH* 24:49-57.

Trinh Sinh, 1977, From the stone ring to the bronze ring (in Vietnamese). *KCH* 23:51-6.

Trinh Sinh and Na Nguyen Diem, 1977, The shape of pottery vessels from Phung Nguyen to Dong Son (in Vietnamese). *KCH* 22:50-67.

United Nations, 1968, *Atlas of Physical, Economic and Social Resources of the Lower Mekong Basin.* United States Agency for International Development, Bureau for East Asia. Washington D.C.

Vallibhotama, S. 1982, *Archaeological Study of the Lower Mun-Chi Basin* (in Thai). NEDECO, Bangkok.

1984, The relevence of moated settlements to the formation of states in Thailand. D.T. Bayard (ed.) *Southeast Asian Archaeology at the XV Pacific Science Congress. OUSPA* 16:123-8.

van der Kelvie, W. 1971, Acid sulphate soils in Central Thailand. FAO/UNDP regional seminar on soil survey and soil fertility research, New Delhi.

van Esterik, P. and Kress, N. 1978, An interpretation of Ban Chiang rollers: experiment and speculation. *AP* 21:52-7.

van Heekeren, H.R. and Knuth, E. 1967, *Archaeological Excavations in Thailand, volume 1: Sai Yok.* Munksgaard, Copenhagen.

van Liere, W.J. 1980, Traditional water management in the lower Mekong Basin. *World Archaeology* 11(3):265-80.

Veerapan, M. 1979, The excavation at Sab Champa. R.B. Smith and W. Watson (eds.) *Early South East Asia* pp.337-41. Oxford University Press, Oxford.

Veeraprasert, M. 1985, Khlong Thom: an ancient bead-manufacturing location and an ancient entrepôt. *Research conference on early Southeast Asia* pp. 168-9. Silpakon University, Bangkok.

Vickery, M. 1986, Some remarks on early state formation in Cambodia. D.G. Marr and A.C. Milner (eds.) *Southeast Asia in the 9th to 14th Centuries* pp. 95-115. Research

School of Pacific Studies, Australian National University, Canberra, and Institute of Southeast Asian Studies, Singapore.

in progress, *Locations of certain -pura.* Pre-Angkor Cambodia, Research in Progress.

Vincent, B.A. 1984, The analysis of prehistoric pottery from Ban Na Di, Northeast Thailand. D.T. Bayard (ed.) *Southeast Asian Archaeology at the XV Pacific Science Congress. OUSPA* 16:50-9.

1987, The ceramics, in C.F.W. Higham, B. Maloney, R. Bannanurag and B.A. Vincent. Khok Phanom Di: the results of the 1984-5 season. *BIPPA* 7:148-78.

Vishnu-Mittre 1975, The early domestication of plants in South and South East Asia: a critical review. *The Palaeobotanist* 22:83-8.

Voorhies, B. 1973, Possible social factors in the exchange system of the prehispanic Maya. *American Antiquity* 38(3):486-9.

Vu The Long, 1977, The faunal remains from Hang Con Moong (in Vietnamese). *KCH* 22:19-23.

Vu Thi Ngoc Thu and Nguyen Duy Ty, 1978, A tool set for casting bronze from Lang Ca (Vinh Phu) (in Vietnamese). *KCH* 26:36-9.

Wang, Gungwu, 1958, The Nanhai Trade. *JMBRAS* XXXI(2):1-135.

Watson, W. 1979, Kok Charoen and the early metal age of Central Thailand. R.B. Smith and W. Watson (eds). *Early South East Asia* pp.53-62. Oxford University Press, Oxford.

1983, Pre-Han communication from West China to Thailand. Paper prepared for CISHAAN, Tokyo, September 1983.

Watson, W. and Loofs-Wissowa, H.H.E. 1967, The Thai-British archaeological expedition: a preliminary report on the work of the first season, 1965-66. *JSS* 55(2): 237-62.

Webb, M.C. 1975, The flag follows trade: an essay on the necessary interaction of military and commercial factors in state formation. J.A. Sabloff and C.C. Lamberg-Karlovsky (eds.) *Ancient Civilization and Trade* pp.155-209. University of New Mexico Press, Albuquerque.

Welch, D. 1984, Settlement pattern as an indicator of sociopolitical complexity in the Phimai region, Thailand. D.T. Bayard (ed.) *Southeast Asian Archaeology at the XV Pacific Science Congress. OUSPA* 16:129-51.

1985, *Adaptation to Environmental Unpredictability: Intensive Agriculture and Regional Exchange at Late Prehistoric Centers in the Phimai Region, Thailand.* Ph.D. dissertation, University of Hawaii.

Wheatley, P. 1961, *The Golden Khersonese: studies in the historical geography of the Malay peninsula to A.D. 1500.* University of Malaya, Kuala Lumpur.

1971, *The Pivot of the Four Quarters.* Aldine, Chicago.

1983, *Nāgara and Commandery.* University of Chicago Department of Geography Research Paper Nos. 207-8.

Wheeler, R.E.M. 1955, *Rome Beyond the Imperial Frontiers.* Bell, London.

White, J.C. 1982a, Prehistoric environment and subsistence in Northeast Thailand. *Southeast Asian Studies Newsletter* 9:1-3.

1982b, *Ban Chiang. The Discovery of a Lost Bronze Age.* University of Pennsylvania Press, Philadelphia.

1982c, Natural history investigations at Ban Chiang. *Expedition* 24(4): 25-32.

1986, *A revision of the chronology of Ban Chiang and its implications for the prehistory of Northeast Thailand.* Ph.D dissertation, University of Pennsylvania.

White, J.C. and Gorman, C.F. 1979, Patterns in "amorphous" industries: the Hoabinhian viewed through a lithic reduction sequence. Paper presented at the 44th annual meeting of the Society for American Archaeology, Vancouver.

Wichakana, M. 1984, *The Rimsherds from Ban Na Di and their Implications for the Prehistory of the Sakon Nakhon Basin*. M.A. dissertation, University of Otago.

Wilen, R. 1987, Excavation and site survey in the Huay Sai Khao basin, northeastern Thailand. *BIPPA* 7:94-117.

Williams-Hunt, P.D.R. 1950, Irregular earthworks in Eastern Siam: an air survey. *Antiquity* 24:30-7.

Wilson, P.J. 1988. *The Domestication of the Human Species. Yale* University Press, New Haven.

Wiriyaromp, W. 1983, *The Human Skeletal Remains from Ban Na Di*. M.A. dissertation, University of Otago.

Wittfogel, K.A. 1957, *Oriental Despotism, a Study of Absolute Power*. Yale University Press, New Haven.

Wolters, O.W. 1967, *Early Indonesian Commerce: A Study of the Origins of Srivijaya*. Cornell University Press, Ithaca.

1973, Jayavarman's military power: the territorial foundation of the Angkor empire. *JRAS* 1:21-30.

1974, North-Western Cambodia in the seventh Century. *BSOAS* XXXVII(2):355-84.

1979, Khmer hinduism in the seventh century. R.B. Smith and W. Watson (eds.) *Early South East Asia* pp.427-42. Oxford University Press, Oxford.

1982, *History, Culture and Region in Southeast Asian Perspectives*. Institute of Southeast Asian Studies, Singapore.

Worman, E.C. 1949, Somrong Sen and the reconstruction of prehistory in Indo-China. *Southwestern Journal of Anthropology* 5:318-29.

Wu Kunyi, Sun Shuyun, Zhang Shiquan and Wang Dadao, 1986. Bronze drum making in ancient Southwestern China. Paper read to the Conference on the origins of metals and alloys under the auspices of the Beijing University of Iron and Steel Technology, Zhengzhou, China, 21st–27th October, 1986.

Yen, D.E. 1977, Hoabinhian horticulture: the evidence and the questions from Northwest Thailand. J. Allen, J. Golson and R. Jones (eds.) *Sunda and Sahul* pp.567-99. Academic Press, New York and London.

1982, Ban Chiang pottery and rice. *Expedition* 24(1):51-64.

Yesner, D.R. 1980, Maritime hunter-gatherers. Ecology and prehistory. *CA* 21:727-50.

You-di, C. 1975, *Ban Chiang Prehistoric Cultures*. Fine Arts Department, Bangkok.

1978, Nothing is new. *Muang Boran* 4(4): 15-16.

INDEX

Principal references are in **bold** type.

Printed in the United Kingdom
by Lightning Source UK Ltd.
252